OXFORD

UNIVERSITY PRESS

Oxford University Press is a department of the
University of Oxford. It furthers the University's objective
of excellence in research, scholarship, and education
by publishing worldwide.

Oxford   New York
Auckland   Cape Town   Dar es Salaam   Hong Kong   Karachi
Kuala Lumpur   Madrid   Melbourne   Mexico City   Nairobi
New Delhi   Shanghai   Taipei   Toronto

With offices in
Argentina   Austria   Brazil   Chile   Czech Republic   France   Greece
Guatemala   Hungary   Italy   Japan   Poland   Portugal   Singapore
South Korea   Switzerland   Thailand   Turkey   Ukraine   Vietnam

Oxford is a registered trade mark of Oxford University Press in the
UK and certain other countries.

Published in the United States of America by
Oxford University Press
198 Madison Avenue, New York, NY 10016

© Oxford University Press 2014

Library of Congress Cataloging-in-Publication Data
The social scientific study of Jewry :
sources, approaches, debates / edited by Uzi Rebhun.
pages   cm.—(Studies in contemporary Jewry, an annual,
ISSN 0740-8625 ; 27)
"The Avraham Harman Institute of Contemporary Jewry,
The Hebrew University of Jerusalem."
ISBN 978-0-19-936349-0 (alk. paper)
1. Jews—Social conditions—Research.   2. Jews—Social conditions—History.
3. Jews—United States—Social conditions—History.   4. United States—Ethnic relations.
I. Rebhun, Uzi, editor of compilation.   II. Waxman, Chaim I., 1941– author.
The professional dilemma of Jewish social scientists: the case of the ASSJ
III. Makhon le-Yahadut zemanenu 'a. sh. Avraham Harman.
DS102.95.S594   2014
305.892'4—dc23   2013047261

1 3 5 7 9 8 6 4 2
Printed in the United States of America
on acid-free paper

THE AVRAHAM HARMAN INSTITUTE OF
CONTEMPORARY JEWRY
THE HEBREW UNIVERSITY OF JERUSALEM

THE SOCIAL SCIENTIFIC STUDY OF JEWRY: SOURCES, APPROACHES, DEBATES

STUDIES IN CONTEMPORARY JEWRY AN ANNUAL XXVII

2014

Edited by Uzi Rebhun

Published for the Institute by
OXFORD
UNIVERSITY PRESS

STUDIES IN CONTEMPORARY JEWRY

The publication of
Studies in Contemporary Jewry
has been made possible through the generous assistance
of the Samuel and Althea Stroum Philanthropic Fund,
Seattle, Washington

STUDIES IN CONTEMPORARY JEWRY

Preface

The social sciences (in particular, demography, sociology, economics, psychology, and political science) are central for the understanding of contemporary Jewish life. Each of these fields deals with data that provide insights into characteristics of the Jewish population. Yet the data are far from being all of a kind: they are of differing levels of accuracy depending on time and place, and their interpretation varies widely. In consequence, there is no clear agreement with regard to the evolving trajectory of world Jewry. Differences of opinion often stem from disagreements on the boundaries of the Jewish people; the use of different measures of demographic and social patterns; different approaches to data analysis; and different assumptions regarding the future direction and pace of socio-demographic and identificational components. Another source of inconsistent findings is the use of different sets of data, namely nationwide versus local data collected on behalf of a specific Jewish community. Still other differences are tied to more substantive issues: for instance, appropriate expressions of Jewish identification, whether religious, ethnic, or cultural.

To a large extent, the multitude of approaches toward Jewish social science research reflects the nature of population studies in general, and that of religious and ethnic groups in particular. At the same time, the variation in methodology, definitions, and measures of demographic, socioeconomic, and cultural patterns is perhaps more salient in the study of Jews, for several reasons. For one thing, different data sets have different definitions for what is "Jewish" or "who is a Jew." Second, Jews as a whole are characterized by high rates of migration—including repeated migration—which makes it difficult to track any given Jewish population. And third, the question of identification is especially complicated with regard to Jews. In most places, especially outside of Israel, it is not clear whether "being Jewish" is primarily a religious or an ethnic matter (or both, or neither). Some individuals are fearful of publicly identifying themselves as Jewish. Still others are ambivalent or indifferent.

The symposium of Volume XXVII of *Studies in Contemporary Jewry* comprises 11 essays that examine sources, approaches, social categories, measures, and interpretations in the research of Jewish social sciences. These essays cover different aspects of social scientific research as well as various areas of Jewish life. Accordingly, the authors include demographers, sociologists, geographers, social psychologists, and methodologists.

After this volume went to press, the Pew Research Center released its survey report on the U.S. Jewish population in 2013. The report provided updated estimates on the number of Jews in the United States according to different definitions (for instance, people who identify solely as Jewish as opposed to those who identify as partly Jewish) as well as findings pertaining to numerous other socio-demographic issues, among them the extent of interfaith marriages and the levels of fertility among different Jewish denominations. The essays in the symposium are based on the most current information available to the authors at the time of writing; in many instances, findings from the Pew report corroborate or even strengthen their arguments.

The opening article, by Sergio DellaPergola, begins with an overview of the discipline of world Jewish demography, the boundaries of the Jewish collective, the quality of demographic data, and those scholars who have been involved in the field of Jewish population study in the modern era. This is followed by an analysis of demographic processes in the two largest Jewish populations in the world today, those of the United States and Israel.

Five essays focus on the United States. In the first, Leonard Saxe, Elizabeth Tighe, and Matthew Boxer postulate that socio-demographic studies designed to estimate the size and characteristics of the Jewish population have become increasingly costly and difficult to conduct. It is particularly problematic to rely on individual studies that make use of random-digit-dialed telephone samples. Accordingly, the authors propose the application of meta-analytic techniques, namely, greater reliance on meta-analyses that synthesize data about religious and ethnic identification across multiple samplings and studies of the U.S. population. The results of such syntheses can be used in conjunction with other data and surveys to enhance the validity of estimates of the Jewish population, their attitudes, and their behaviors. A somewhat different approach is presented by David Dutwin, Eran Ben-Porath and Ron Miller. After outlining a number of major concerns of Jewish population research, they offer several solutions for problems connected with communal (as opposed to national) studies and a number of alternative approaches to Jewish community and population research.

Harriet Hartman tackles the issue of Jewish identity and continuity by means of three axes of differentiation: survival, authenticity, and boundaries. Such competing perspectives, she shows, are not confined to studies of American Jewish identity but rather are applicable to research on diaspora Jews throughout the world. She discusses how competing perspectives play out on a number of different levels of Jewish space, from the intra-personal to the Jewish collective (*klal yisrael*), and the collective vis-à-vis the broader society. Although research on U.S. Jewish identity focuses on multiple levels of Jewish "space," there tends to be more emphasis on individual Jewish identity rather than that of the collective, in contrast to studies of Jewish identity in areas such as Europe or Latin America. Hartman examines how these perspectives are related to considerations of Jewish continuity, and concludes with a number of ideas aimed at furthering intersectional analysis of Jewish identity in a cross-cultural manner.

Esther Wilder outlines a variety of approaches that have been employed to measure and evaluate the socioeconomic position of the Jews. She describes the data sources used in various countries, both in the past and in the present, assessing the strengths and weaknesses of such sources as well as the challenges associated with research on Jewish socioeconomic status. In addition, Wilder looks at the ways in which scholars have explained the Jews' socioeconomic distinctiveness and evaluates the implications of such distinctiveness.

Chaim Waxman directs our attention to the history and underlying goals of the major professional organization of Jewish social scientists, the Association for the Social Scientific Study of Jewry (ASSJ), both in the context of American social science as a whole and the Jewish "guild" of social scientists in particular. Among the factors that contributed to the emergence of the ASSJ were increased ethnic and religious consciousness at the end of the 1960s, alongside a growing number of connections between Jewish communal agencies and scholars engaged in Jewish social research projects.

David Graham's contribution shifts the focus to Europe as he makes use of two case studies—one political, the other legal—to demonstrate how contradictory definitions of "Jewish" can exist in the same system. As he shows, there is an unavoidable need for subgroups to be defined, both for practical and for functional reasons. Britain's political framework (in which the national census operates) constructs a faith-based definition of Jewish, whereas its legal system (mandated to protect minority groups) relies on a broader, ethnicity-based definition. Neither construction is more accurate or more correct than the other—each is appropriate in its own context. The challenge of demographers, according to Graham, is to embrace such realities, lest their work becomes disassociated from the "real world."

Mark Tolts shows how the demographic study of Jews in the former Soviet Union has a long and well-established tradition based on a wealth of data derived, in the main, from census results coupled with vital and migration statistics. His essay begins with an overview of tsarist and Soviet statistical legacies and then moves to a discussion of developments of the last quarter century. Tolts explores both the role of the Soviet internal passport (which, with its listing of ethnicity, was the basis for Jewish statistics) and the consequences of the elimination of compulsory ethnic identification in the post-Soviet Slavic countries.

From a Latin American perspective, Judit Bokser Liwerant, argues that Jewish social studies and research have attained a high level of specialization and make use of increasingly sophisticated investigatory tools and techniques. In a wide-ranging discussion referring to general theoretical traditions as well as ongoing debates, she demonstrates how the field is characterized by growing levels of conceptual and institutional complexity—affected by socio-cultural transformations in Jewish life and that of Latin America more generally.

Rounding out the symposium are two Israel-centered essays. In an overview and analysis of studies dealing with Israeli ethnicity, Aziza Khazzoom suggests moving away from the binary classification of "Mizrahi" Jews (originating in Muslim countries) and "Ashkenazi" Jews from Christian countries toward a split approach based on countries of origin. Such an approach is better equipped to reveal distinct patterns of discrimination, identity, and the distribution of government resources, as well as links between ethnic inequality and other cleavages. Khazzoom describes two additional frameworks of research—pan-ethnicity and Orientalism—that were applied to studies dealing with mass immigration to Israel in the first years of statehood. Although some of the insights deriving from this research continue to be useful, new categories have come to play an important role in studies dealing with subgroups in present-day Israeli society—among them, third-generation Israelis, foreign workers, and immigrants from Ethiopia and the former Soviet Union.

Finally, Arnon Soffer draws attention to crucial demographic debates regarding issues of majority versus minority populations in Israel. According to Soffer, demography is a major factor underlying the very existence of a sovereign state and hence has existential security implications. This is especially the case with regard to discussions concerning the possibility of annexing areas of "greater Israel," where the (fiercely debated) outcome may be a Jewish minority within the Jewish state.

Following the symposium, Volume XXVII presents an essay authored by Avi Picard on efforts to persuade American Jewry to contribute funds to projects connected with the immigration to and absorption in Israel of North African Jews. More specifically, in the years 1954–1956, Israel adopted a new policy of immigration absorption known as "Ship to Village," in which new immigrants were sent directly to settlements located on Israel's geographical periphery. Picard analyzes the reasons why the fundraising campaign had only limited success, pointing, among other things, to sensitivity surrounding public discussion of the precarious situation of North African Jews who were still under French colonial rule; the attitude among some American Jews that local Jewish communities should be loyal to their own country; and negative stereotypes with regard to North African Jews.

The book review section of the volume begins with four review essays, three of which center on the immediate post-Holocaust period. Judith Tydor Baumel-Schwartz and Gabriel Finder survey books dealing with Holocaust survivors and their resettlement in the aftermath of the war, whereas Laura Jockusch reviews five works about Nazi war trials in postwar Germany. A fourth review essay, by Olga Litvak, critiques three biographical works on Jewish historians and historiography. Reviews of some two dozen recent books with contemporary Jewish themes conclude the volume.

Over the years, numerous essays published in *Studies in Contemporary Jewry* have explored social aspects of contemporary Jewish life. These have formed part of symposia dealing with broad and varied themes—among them, Jews and ethnicity; the Jewish family; Israeli state and society; and American Jewry. The present volume is unique in that the entire symposium is devoted to the social sciences of Jews. The focus, as noted, is on methodological issues, terminology, and measures of the various social behaviors, with empirical data presented only marginally and indirectly. As such, this volume contributes to the multidisciplinary nature of the annual and pays tribute to its academic home, the Institute of Contemporary Jewry at the Hebrew University of Jerusalem.

This volume is the first to appear under my editorship. For their crucial assistance and useful insights, I would like to thank my colleagues, Richard I. Cohen, Anat Helman, and Eli Lederhendler. I am grateful to Laurie Fialkoff and Hannah Levinsky-Koevary, both for their diligent and professional editing and for their arranging all stages of preparing the manuscript for press. The publication of this volume has been facilitated by generous resources from the Samuel and Althea Stroum Fund and the Lucius N. Littauer Foundation, as well as funds donated by the Nachum Ben-Eli Honig Fund, for which we are most appreciative.

U.R.

Contents

Review Essays

The Postwar Era: Repatriation, Resettlement, and Justice

Book Reviews

Antisemitism, Holocaust, and Genocide

Contents

Cultural Studies, Literature, and Thought

Contents

Symposium

The Social Scientific Study of Jewry: Sources, Approaches, Debates

Jewish Demography:
Fundamentals of the Research Field

Sergio DellaPergola
(THE HEBREW UNIVERSITY)

Demography is the statistical study of human population.[1] With its inductive-deductive, theory-informed, and fact-dependent approach, it is centrally positioned in the sphere of the social sciences, constituting a natural bridge between disciplines in the humanities and those in the natural sciences. Jewish demography—the specialized study of Jewish population characteristics and trends—operates within the distinctive parameters of demography and applies a somewhat expanded investigative scope to a more narrowly focused research subject.[2]

Over time, Jewish demography has received a significant amount of scholarly attention as well as provoking public debate. What is often at issue are specific and limited aspects of global or local Jewish population trends, but debate can also focus on the gamut of past, present, and future connections between an unfolding Jewish *population* and the underlying existence of a Jewish *peoplehood*. The concept of a population refers to an aggregate of individuals falling under a single definition but not necessarily linked by meaningful mutual relations. In contrast, that of peoplehood implies a deeper layer of voluntary interconnectedness among the relevant individuals. A number of linkages between an amorphous aggregate of individual Jews and a socially meaningful representation of the collective have been solidly grounded in scientific research, whereas others have tended to be expressed merely as ideational propensities and states of mind, or else fall somewhere between the two poles.

Among the quandaries faced by researchers in the field are how best to define Jewish population studies and what are the boundaries of the Jewish collective at the global and local level. Other issues relate to the quality of data, the background and ideological stance of Jewish demographers, and the main interpretative directions and implications of their research. This essay will first address these matters in some detail, and will then turn to an overview of the two sets of Jewish demographic trends most frequently at the center of debate: those concerning Jews in the United States, on the one hand, and Jews in Israel, on the other.

3

The Discipline of Jewish Demography

The core issues of Jewish demography—counting Jews, describing their characteristics, analyzing their transformations, and even projecting their future—are as old as the Bible.[3] In the modern era, starting with Leopold Zunz in the 1820s and later with Abraham Moses Luncz in the last quarter of the 19th century, the main activity consisted of compiling statistical data about the number of Jews in different places. It is only later that Jewish demography began to make use of more sophisticated methodological and substantive research, while continuing to reflect the widely differing intellectual backgrounds of its practitioners.[4] Under the broad umbrella of demography, a variety of topics came under the scrutiny not only of scholars but also of publicists, community activists, planners, and policymakers. Such topics included estimating the number of Jews; assessing their rate of growth versus that of other populations; determining the anthropological ("racial") similarity or dissimilarity between Jews and others; analyzing health and behavioral patterns among Jews (in the context of the debate regarding the merits of mutable environment versus inherited character); and examining the role of the Jews in the wider society and economy. Research findings often pointed to clear and persisting differences between Jews and non-Jews in terms of marriage, fertility, and mortality levels; composition by age and marital status; geographical and socioeconomic mobility; and social structure and occupational skills. There were also unique patterns of Jewish population growth or decline, and concentration and dispersion among the broader population.[5] These findings formed the basis for idealistic analyses of the "Jewish condition" and concrete programs designed to improve the Jews' position in society.[6]

Against the backdrop of widespread anti-Jewish prejudice and in contrast to the determinist explanations of earlier researchers in the biological and social sciences,[7] Jewish demographers of the late 19th and 20th centuries sought to provide a rational and systematic explanation for the apparently unique characteristics of the Jews.[8] Another major preoccupation was to sustain Jewish continuity in the face of perceived threats, both external (for instance, the threat of physical violence) or internal (a loss of cultural identity or community cohesion).[9] Although early studies of Jewish demography were often tied to physical anthropology, later research more frequently focused on the relationship between population characteristics and cultural identity. In the past few decades, the growing volatility of certain issues in Jewish demography gave rise to more eclectic modes of research that emphasized specific content and policy implications rather than broader conceptualization of issues; moreover, there were few if any commonly agreed upon procedural guidelines.

Such analytical diffusion is an outgrowth of the somewhat unbounded contour of demography. As with any discipline, population studies constitute an ever-expanding body of accumulated knowledge, theories, and hypotheses; analytic tools and techniques; empirical observations (usually synthesized in the form of quantitative data); and emerging policy options and directions. More specifically, it looks at variables that reflect (and affect) the internal fabric of relations within a given society or community, as well as mutual relations between societies or communities. It deals with basic aspects of the life cycle, among them birth, death, marriage, residence in a certain place at a certain time, and movement from place to place. When focusing on a specific group, it also examines issues connected with group identification—for instance, what aspects of group identity are most commonly shared, or how individuals shift from one particular group identification to another.

Whereas demography, as noted, is situated at the crossroads of the social sciences and the humanities in terms of its subject matter, it relies on methods and hypotheses originally developed for the natural sciences, with important input from mathematical statistics. Clearly multidisciplinary in nature, demography is most often taught in the framework of a broader program, usually in sociology or statistics.[10] Jewish demography has never gained the status of an independent field (unlike Jewish history or Jewish philosophy) but instead has evolved at the borderline between the social sciences and Jewish studies.

Serious discussion of Jewish demographic trends is contingent on an understanding of the broader processes that generally determine the development of any given population. To begin with, although "population" is a collective, macro-social concept, its changes reflect events that mostly occur at the individual, micro-social level. Thus, changes in world population size are the consequence of shifts in the balance between births (reflecting fertility levels and a population's age composition) and deaths (reflecting life expectancy and age composition). When a given population is considered within a definite geographical area in which in- and out-migration is possible, this geographical mobility must also be factored in. And when a population is further defined by culturally determined characteristics such as religion, ethnicity, language, or other divisions, a somewhat more complex *balancing equation* becomes necessary to express population change over time. The important underlying principle is the continuity of a human population that is not created from a vacuum (apart from quite rare cases of ethnogenesis, the initial act of a new group coming into existence)[11] but is rather constantly evolving over a long period of time.

With this in mind, Jewish demography can serve, and indeed has served, as a paradigm for the more general case of subpopulations whose existence and development over time is determined not only by demographic-biological factors, but also by cultural-ideational factors.

As shown in Fig. 1.1, four main measures, or dependent variables, whether alone or (preferably) in combination, allow for an evaluation of Jewish population trends: 1) Jewish population *size*; 2) Jewish population *composition*; 3) Jewish *share* of total population; and 4) the *intensity and quality* of Jewish identification and interactions. At any given point in time, changes in the status of these variables are the outcome of intervening shifts in operational variables over the span of time considered. There are three pairs of operational variables: *immigration* and *emigration*;[12] *birth rate* and *death rate* (affected by changes, respectively, in marriage and fertility levels and in overall health and longevity);[13] and *accessions* to and *secessions* from Judaism, which often appear under the heading of conversions.[14] An additional factor, related to corporate rather than personal transformation, is changes in *territorial definitions* (boundaries). Several examples of this last factor are the partition of Poland, the creation of the Pale of Settlement in the late 18th century, and the definition and re-definition of boundaries of the state of Israel (in particular, in the wake of the Six-Day War of 1967) relative to the total territory of Palestine that was under British Mandate jurisdiction until 1948.

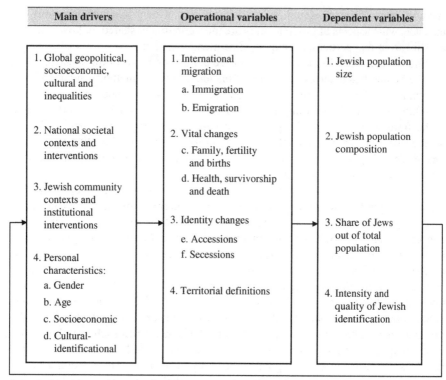

Figure 1.1. Main determinants of Jewish demographic and identificational change

   The impact of any of these factors can be of varying magnitude at different stages of a population's history. In the case of world Jewry, the frequencies of birthrates, death rates, migrations into and out of an area, and conversions to and from Judaism have undergone drastic variations in the course of history. Demographic events—such as a birth, a death, a marriage, moving to another location—occur at times because of individual choices and at other times result from circumstances beyond an individual's control. In similar fashion, changes in Jewish population may reflect the scope and balance of external factors that forcibly affected Jews as well as internal factors operating within the community.

   Each component of demographic change influences the various age cohorts in a population in different and specific ways. In turn, age itself functions as a powerful intermediary referent, synthesizing past demographic change and significantly affecting the likelihood of future demographic events and overall population change. For instance, an older population will have a lower birth rate and a higher death rate than a population with a relatively larger share of younger individuals. As this example indicates, it is important to disaggregate the demographic process into its various component parts—vital events, geographical mobility, identity shifts—as much as possible, in order to reach a deeper understanding of the mode of operating and effects of each separate component. Population characteristics and the components of population change stand in tight mutual relationships, and analyses that ignore these basic relationships have the cumulative effect of "inventing" a population disconnected from its continuously evolving context.

Definitions

Prior to investigating socio-demographic characteristics and trends among Jews, it is necessary to have some conceptual grounding concerning the very nature of "Jews," the main variable of reference. That is, before addressing the better-known "who is a Jew" issue, we need to consider *what* are the Jews. "Jews" are posited here as one subset within a broader class of groups defined by *religious, ethnic, geographic, cultural* or, more broadly, *civilizational identities*, often abridged in the research literature under the rubric of *ethnicity*. From here, matters become more complicated. Demographers and other observers (in this case, those engaged in Jewish demography) generally adopt one of four main approaches in investigating the basic nature and societal role of Jews. The *maximizing* approach looks at Jewish populations as a conglomerate—the largest possible conglomerate of all populations that can be defined through one or more criteria possessing any pertinence or affinity with a Jewish category of any sort.[15] The *consolidationist* approach, in contrast, views Jewish populations as discrete objects for conceptual definition and empirical measurement, based on coherent and comparable criteria.[16] Conceptually different is the *situational* approach, which regards Jewish populations as groups that can be recognized and studied at a given point in time but not really quantifiable in the longer term, given ever-changing exogenous and endogenous circumstances and attitudes.[17] Finally, there is the *manipulative* approach, whose practitioners view Jewish collectives as lacking historical continuity and as essentially generated by the calculated interventions of elites or special interest groups, hence without any serious claim to empirical reality or even legitimacy.[18]

This essay utilizes a basically consolidationist point of view (though paying due attention to the situational claim) in its argument that Jewish communities, both in the diaspora and in Israel and whether in the past or present, *do* constitute a target for empirical investigation. Jewish populations, in our view, are composed of people who can be identified by specified, multiple criteria of inclusion and exclusion, and who display individual perceptions of group boundaries and collective identities as well as unique and recognizable patterns of social and demographic composition and mobility.

This said, the paradigmatic issue of "who is a Jew" continues to bedevil researchers. What, exactly, are the boundaries of the Jewish collective? The literature on this matter is characterized by a lack of both coherence and uniformity.[19] Thus, Jewish population estimates may rely on either *normative* or on *operational* definitions. One example of the former is provided by traditional Jewish law (halakhah), according to which Jewishness rests on the concept of matrilineal descent and on codified rules for cooptation better known as *conversion*.[20] An alternative normative definition adopted by the Reform Jewish movement in the United States in 1983 embraces patrilineal descent as well. In many cases, however, it is simply too costly or time-consuming to undertake the stringent controls involved in ascertaining each individual's Jewish identity according to either set of criteria. Therefore, Jewish populations are usually identified in censuses or surveys through operational criteria—that is, by means of more or less accurate proxies such as responses to questions regarding religion or ethnic origin or (more indirectly) regarding countries of origin or languages.[21]

Here, however, there is an additional complication: self-identification. The increasing frequency of intermarriage (out-marriage) has generated a growing number of individuals whose Jewish identification is one among several possible or shared ancestries. Many of them, even if Jewish from a normative point of view, do not know whether, when, or how to identify as Jewish and may therefore refrain from doing so. Others do not deem their Jewishness to be mutually exclusive with other religious or ethnic identities (in contrast with the normative assumption that Jewish identity is incompatible with other religious identities). Many more do not care either way—a situation that holds true as well for many descendants of endogamous Jewish marriages.

Thus, research findings reflect, with varying degrees of sophistication, only that which it is possible to uncover. That which cannot be uncovered directly can sometimes be indirectly estimated through various imperfect techniques. One such technique, designed to provide solid comparative foundations for the study of Jewish demography, makes use of the concept of *core* versus *enlarged* Jewish populations (Fig. 1.2).[22]

In diaspora countries, a core Jewish population may be defined as one that includes all socio-demographic survey respondents who identify themselves as Jews; who are

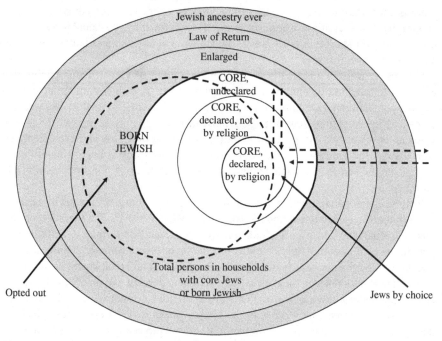

Figure 1.2. Defining contemporary Jewish populations

identified as Jews by a respondent in the same household; or who have Jewish parentage and, while agnostic or indifferent to Judaism, do not formally identify with another monotheistic religion.[23] This definition, which reflects subjective perceptions, broadly overlaps but does not necessarily coincide with halakhah or other normatively binding definitions of Jewishness. Moreover, inclusion does not depend on any measure of a person's Jewish commitment or behavior in terms of religiosity, beliefs, knowledge, or communal affiliation. To be sure, the primary component of a core Jewish population consists of individuals who define themselves as Jews by religion. Judaism, however, cannot be reduced to solely religious concepts, as evidenced by the fact that there is a second component of the core population: Jews who define themselves as such by ethnicity, nationality, or culture.

These two components form the more visible, or *declared* part of the core. In addition, there are people who, when asked, would not immediately declare their Jewish identity, although they are the descendants of Jewish parents and do not possess an alternative identity. These *undeclared core* individuals can be detected by means of inquiring in greater detail about parental background and childhood. It is important to note that, reflecting the increasingly fluid character of contemporary identities, many individuals move back and forth between the declared and undeclared segments of the core population, "feeling Jewish" one day and not the next.[24]

The question whether core Jewish identification can or should be mutually exclusive vis-à-vis other religious and/or ethnic identities is a major bone of contention. With regard to U.S. Jewry, the issue emerged on a significant scale in the course of developing and analyzing the National Jewish Population Survey of 2000–2001 (2000 NJPS). The solution preferred by the National Technical Advisory Committee (NTAC)—after much debate—was to allow for Jews with multiple religious identities to be included under certain circumstances in the core Jewish population definition. This resulted in a multilayered definition of the United States Jewish population.[25] In addition, a category titled "Persons of Jewish Background" (PJBs), consisting of interviewees who did not declare being Jewish but who reported some Jewish family background, was introduced in the 2000 NJPS. Some PJBs were included in the core Jewish population count and others were not, based on a thorough evaluation of each individual ancestry and childhood. Following the same logic, persons with multiple ethnic identities, including a Jewish identity, have been included in Jewish population counts for Canada. The adoption of such extended criteria by the research community tends to stretch Jewish population definitions beyond usual practices of the past, and certainly beyond the limits of the typical core definition. These procedures may respond to local needs and sensitivities but tend to limit the comparability of the same Jewish population over time and of different Jewish populations at one given time.

Conceptually stemming from the core Jewish population is the *enlarged Jewish population*,[26] representing the sum of (a) the core Jewish population; (b) all other persons of Jewish parentage who—by core Jewish population criteria—are *not* Jewish at the time of investigation (non-Jews with Jewish background); and (c) all other non-Jewish members (spouses, children, etc.) in mixed religious households. Non-Jews with Jewish background, insofar as they can be ascertained, include persons who have adopted another religion or otherwise opted out (although, with the caveat just mentioned for recent United States and Canadian data, they may claim to be Jewish as well, on the grounds of ethnicity or culture) and individuals whose parents were born Jewish, but who later opted out. Clearly, most PJBs who are not part of the core Jewish population will belong under the enlarged definition.

It is customary in socio-demographic surveys to consider the religio-ethnic identification of parents, although some censuses also ask about more distant ancestry. For both conceptual and practical reasons, the enlarged definition usually does not include non-Jewish relatives who may have a Jewish background and who live in exclusively non-Jewish households. Historians might wish to engage in the study of the number of Jews who *ever* lived and how many persons today are the descendants of those Jews—for example, *conversos* who lived in the Iberian Peninsula during the Middle Ages, of whom numerous descendants may be found in Mediterranean and in Central and South American countries. The ancient Jewish backgrounds of a few other currently non-Jewish population groups have been uncovered in recent studies of population genetics.[27] These long-term Jewish roots have attracted growing interest as a topic for analysis and speculation, and have also been investigated by some Jewish organizations that are active in bringing what they call the "Lost Tribes" back to Judaism.[28]

As noted, the definition of core Jewish population is applicable in diaspora countries. In Israel, the situation is different: an individual's personal status as a Jew is determined by the Ministry of the Interior, which relies on criteria established by rabbinic authorities and by the Israeli supreme court, namely, matrilineal Jewish origin or conversion to Judaism, and not holding another religion. At the same time, there are much broader criteria for being eligible to attain Israeli citizenship (as well as various economic benefits) under the framework of the Law of Return. This law extends its provisions to all current Jews, their children, and grandchildren, as well as to their respective Jewish or non-Jewish spouses.[29] As a result of its three-generation and lateral extension, the law of return applies to an "aliyah-eligible" population whose scope is significantly wider than the core and enlarged Jewish populations defined for diaspora populations—in fact, it is difficult to estimate its possible total size.

The collection of Jewish population data is a complex and often policy-sensitive matter. Several major Jewish organizations in Israel and the United States, among them the quasi-governmental Jewish Agency for Israel, the global and social service-oriented American Jewish Joint Distribution Committee (JDC), and the Jewish Federations of North America (formerly, the Council of Jewish Federations and later, United Jewish Communities) have sponsored data collection. To some extent, they have influenced the rules of research, as their mandate is to serve their perceived constituencies rather than promote pure scientific research. More specifically, the understandable interest of Jewish organizations in functioning and in securing budgetary resources increasingly influences them toward defining Jewish target populations in terms that are closer to the enlarged and Law of Return definitions rather than the core definition. It appears that some socio-demographic surveys, by investigating people who "were born" or were "raised" or who are "currently" Jewish, may be envisaging a population that *ever* was Jewish, regardless of its present identification.

Although the core definition is the necessary starting point for any discussion about Jewish population collection data, it is also true that distinctions between (declared and undeclared) core Jews and others who share their daily lives in the same households have become ever more elastic. Accordingly, a great amount of latitude characterizes the definitional solutions adopted in socio-demographic research, with obvious consequences for the ensuing population counts and their policy implications. Unfortunately, these various definitional concepts are often confused, which renders it difficult to make accurate comparisons or to analyze trends. In the ensuing debate about Jewish population trends, it is important to realize that a given *enlarged* Jewish population may be growing at the same time that the respective *core* Jewish population is declining.

In sum, we remain with a significant and growing amount of ambivalence in the definition of the Jewish collective. It is legitimate to posit that these difficulties of definition pinpoint the challenges inherent in the effort to conceptually synthesize the notion of Jewish peoplehood. The empirical Jewish population equivalent of *klal yisrael*—the normative Jewish collective—implies not only a given aggregate of people, no matter how well technically defined, but also the bonds of mutual responsibility that provide it with contemporary meaning and long-term resilience. The best research strategy may be to create a set of alternative definitions and to provide the empirical evidence that will allow investigations appropriate for each of those definitions. If individual investigators take on the responsibility of explaining their decision to use any given definition, the possibility of meaningful comparisons will be preserved.

Data

Data on population size and characteristics are a primary tool in the evaluation of Jewish demographic trends and consequently of community needs and prospects at the local, national, and international levels. In modern historical experience, the database for the study of Jewish populations has been a mixed and complementary pool of state-sponsored data collections—mainly obtained through national and local censuses and vital statistics records—and independent data collection initiatives sponsored by a large variety of public and private Jewish organizations, often in collaboration with scholarly bodies.

From the Jewish side, there were successful efforts to create stable institutional bases for research and a systematic output of studies. Two important examples in the late 1920s were the Bureau fuer Juedische Statistik in Berlin (and its publication, *Zeitschrift fuer Demografie und Statistik der Juden*) and YIVO (*Bleter far yidishe demografye, statistik un ekonomik*). At this time, much of European Jewry lived in countries with an established tradition of documenting the religious and ethnic origins of their populations. But with the outbreak of the Second World War and the destruction of Jewish communities, a tremendous amount of documentation was lost. At war's end, the flow of Jewish migration led to the strengthening of communities in countries such as the United States and France where, because of the separation between church and state, no such documentation was legally allowed.

Following the Second World War, Israel's Central Bureau of Statistics (CBS) and the Hebrew University of Jerusalem played a central role in promoting the study of Jewish population. From its inception, the CBS (headed for many years by Roberto Bachi, who built it on the foundations of the British Mandate's Palestine Department of Statistics) has served as the state's central authority for data collection and processing; although part of the government, it is independent and not subject to political pressure. As the Israeli component of world Jewry has increased dramatically, there has been a correspondent growth in the number of Jews covered by sound demographic documentation. Moreover, Israeli data has provided important insights on the characteristics of Jews who previously had lived in other countries. The division of Jewish demography and statistics at the Institute of Contemporary Jewry at the Hebrew University (established by Bachi with the help of Oscar Schmelz in 1959) was also instrumental in creating a rigorously professional central database and library.[30] The division also publishes a highly regarded series, *Jewish Population Studies,* and sponsors Jewish demography sessions at the quadrennial World Congress of Jewish Studies.

Some other important institution-building efforts in Jewish population research occurred in the United States. The *American Jewish Year Book*, sponsored for many decades by the American Jewish Committee (and for part of the period by the Jewish Publication Society), offered a podium for systematic documentation of Jewish life in the United States—publishing, among other things, the findings of the Bureau of Jewish Statistics (long headed by Harry Linfield). The cessation of the yearbook in 2008 was one of the sadder milestones in the rapidly changing Jewish institutional landscape both in the United States and internationally.[31] However, systematic updates on Jewish population spread and change across the United States were provided by the research division of the Jewish Federations of North America. The North American Jewish Data Bank (NAJDB), established at the initiative of Mandell Berman (of the Jewish Federations) with the scientific sponsorship of Brandeis University and the Hebrew University's Institute of Contemporary Jewry, later moved from New York to Brandeis, and finally found a permanent seat at the University of Connecticut at Storrs. Brandeis also founded the Steinhardt Social Research Institute (SSRI) at the Maurice and Marilyn Cohen Center for Jewish Studies, which in terms of budget and manpower is probably the largest academic institution specializing in Jewish social scientific research. Finally, there is the Association for the Social Scientific Study of Jewry (ASSJ), which brings together many of the mostly American experts and practitioners in the field (at annual conferences sponsored by the Association of Jewish Studies), publishes the journal *Contemporary Jewry*, and awards the coveted Marshall Sklare prize for career achievement.

Over the past decades, efforts to clarify the worldwide Jewish demographic picture have expanded significantly, often as the result of collaborative work undertaken by scholars and institutions across a range of countries.[32] Particularly worthy of mention are the efforts initiated by the Jewish Agency through its Demographic Initiative at the beginning of the 2000s[33] and the subsequent foundation and activity of the Jewish People Policy Institute.[34] It should be emphasized, however, that the elaboration of truly comparable estimates for the Jewish populations of various countries is beset with difficulties and uncertainties.[35] The problem of data consistency is particularly acute given the very different legal systems and organizational provisions governing Jewish communities in different countries. Thus, the basic typology must refer to whether a given country conducts a national population census that includes a category for *Jewish* (or something similar) as one of the census variables,[36] maintains a central national population register with such a category, and/or has a central Jewish community organization (or a set of smaller communities somewhat coordinated by a central Jewish body) whose membership covers the vast majority of existing Jews. Today the situation is highly variable: for instance, two of the largest Jewish populations in the world are located in countries (the United States and France) in which there is neither a relevant census category for Jews, a central population register with this category, or a centralized or umbrella organization to which most Jews belong. In spite of keen efforts to create a unified analytic framework for Jewish population studies, users of Jewish population estimates should be aware of these inherent limitations, alongside the paradox of the permanently provisional character of Jewish population estimates.[37]

While the quantity and quality of documentation on Jewish population size and characteristics remain far from satisfactory, the past 20 years have nonetheless witnessed the emergence of important new data and estimates for several countries, both through official population censuses and Jewish-sponsored socio-demographic surveys. During the first decade of the 21st century, national censuses conducted in a number of countries with large Jewish populations—among them, Israel, Canada, the United Kingdom, the Russian Republic, Australia, Brazil, Ukraine, South Africa, Hungary, and Mexico—provided updated data on Jews. In the United States, population censuses do not provide information on religion but do furnish relevant data on countries of birth, spoken languages, and ancestry. Permanent national population registers, including information on Jews as one of several documented religious, ethnic, or national groups, exist in Israel as well as in several European countries with admittedly small Jewish populations.[38]

In addition, privately sponsored socio-demographic studies have provided valuable information on Jewish demography and socioeconomic stratification, as well as on Jewish identification. In the United States, important new insights were provided by several large national surveys: not only the 2000 NJPS but also the American Jewish Identity Survey (AJIS 2001), and the American Religious Identification Survey (ARIS 2008), both sponsored by Felix Posen; the Heritage, Ancestry, and Religious Identity Survey (HARI 2001–2002), sponsored by the Institute for Jewish and Community Research; and the Pew Forum on Religion and Public Life (2008), sponsored by the Pew Research Center. Smaller Jewish samples are routinely obtained from the General Social Survey and similar national studies (see below). Moreover, numerous localized Jewish population studies have been conducted in major cities in the United States[39] and in several other countries, including France, the United Kingdom, Argentina, Australia, Hungary, Mexico, and the Netherlands.[40] Since 2000, a national census with data on Jews, a specially focused population survey, or a Jewish community population register has been available in every country with a Jewish population of 15,000 and above, with the exception of Belgium. A number of synoptic studies of several Jewish communities in different countries have also been undertaken.[41]

Additional evidence on Jewish population trends may come from the systematic monitoring of membership registers, vital statistics, and migration records available from Jewish communities and other Jewish organizations in many countries or cities.[42] As noted, the detailed data on Jewish immigration that is routinely collected in Israel can be used to assess Jewish population changes in other countries. The cross-matching of more than one type of source about the same Jewish population, although not frequently feasible, can provide mutual reinforcement of the available data, or important critical insights.

National boundaries have constituted a powerful defining constraint for Jewish population studies—perhaps underlying the more powerful issue of the characterization of Jewish identity as a derivative of national identities or as a transnational construct.[43] A very large segment of available information, both historical and current, reflects the data collection initiatives undertaken by public or private bodies whose mandate corresponded with given national boundaries. Geopolitical changes such as the disaggregation of countries into smaller independent states (as in the case of the Soviet Union, Yugoslavia, or Czechoslovakia), or the reverse process of the merging of individual countries into broader socio-political conglomerates (as in the case of West and East Germany and, at a looser level of aggregation, the European Union) have influenced only to a limited extent the nature of demographic research of the respective Jewish populations. Availability of data has mostly continued along the preexisting patterns, introducing, if anything, greater variation in definitions.[44] Although the desirability of coordinating data collection and analysis at the broader, super-national level has been perceived and discussed, the lack of adequate community institutions and resources has not enabled the task to be carried out in any systematic way.[45]

Investigators

Although ideological biases need to be taken into account in reading the literature on Jewish demography that was produced in the 19th century and up to the mid-20th century, the output, taken as a whole, represents a remarkably high level of scholarly work. Early researchers, principally grounded in Europe, included Zionists of various stripes, among them Alfred Nossig, Arthur Ruppin, and Jacob Lestschinsky; diasporists such as Liebmann Hersch (a Bundist) and Joseph Jacobs (a more traditional encyclopaedist); and non-Jewish scholars, among them Corrado Gini and Livio Livi.[46] Later works reflected the dominance of Jewish investigators in the United States (for instance, Nathan Goldberg, Salo Baron, Simon Kuznets, and, more recently, Sidney Goldstein)[47] and in Israel (Arieh Tartakower, Roberto Bachi, Oscar [Uziel] Schmelz).[48] These researchers were primarily concerned with the compilation of data from various available sources and the application of sophisticated (or at least feasible) techniques of population analysis to the data. A number of American scholars in a variety of academic centers also played a leading role in developing social theory that was especially oriented toward a better understanding of the large U.S. Jewish community. All in all, the challenge of investigating a relatively small and somewhat elusive subpopulation seems to have stimulated the development of innovative research methods and analytic approaches.

In the past, those engaged in demographic research generally made use of data stemming from governmental or other public bodies. Today, however, the progressive privatization of research initiatives entails a growing direct involvement of investigators in the creation and processing of a database. Hence, data quality increasingly reflects the characteristics of the investigators (most often termed "demographers," although their academic qualifications vary widely) and their analytic assumptions and hypotheses. No less important is the question of who commissions demographic research. In a situation in which researchers are dependent on resources provided by sponsoring organizations, a certain loss of independence may result. There is a clear difference between, on the one hand, academic research carried out by tenured scholars who work as employees of public universities or research institutes (similar to civil servants, and part of an epistemic community regulated by academic rules), and, on the other hand, investigators who work in the framework of projects or institutions supported by renewable budgetary resources (known as "soft money"). In the latter instance, the rules for quality control and personal advancement may be similar to those in academic institutions. However, especially when funding comes from private sources, the need to provide results that are more or less compatible with the expectations of the commissioning person or body may create some constraints on academic freedom. Still more problematic is a situation in which demographic research is carried out by entrepreneurs in the private sector whose income depends on contracts in a competitive market. Whenever there is an agenda focused on specific research needs, there is a greater risk that findings will be biased, not because the data are inaccurate or underresearched, but rather because certain relevant issues may not have come under scrutiny.[49] Ideally, research should be undertaken by independent, high-quality professional bodies isolated from organizational agendas and, as far as possible, budgetary pressures. Needless to say, this ideal is not easily attainable.

Interpretations

As has been noted, Jewish social research was never the mere exercise of human curiosity or analytical skill. Rather, it was often a means of advancing specific theses regarding the nature of the Jews vis-à-vis world society; their unique character; their just claim to respect, equality, individual, and corporate rights; and the legitimacy of their quest for cultural resilience or assimilation into surrounding societies—or even, as an ultimate goal, political sovereignty.

In the 19th century, descriptive and interpretative efforts were imbued with the emancipatory ethos of Wissenschaft des Judentums. Remarkably, some ideas that were originally developed in the particularistic framework of Jewish demography—for instance, Ruppin's ideas regarding models of assimilation—anticipated similar approaches developed more than two decades later by Robert Park and his fellows of the Chicago school of sociology.[50] Likewise, Shmuel Eisenstadt's models of immigrants' absorption in the specific context of early Israeli statehood largely anticipated more general models such as Milton Gordon's assessments of assimilation in American society.[51] Jewish social scientists produced a critical mass of studies that was larger and more articulated than that available for most other religious, ethnic, or cultural groups, although the main scope of the debate remained within a Jewish context. As a result, such studies did not usually find a place in the mainstream of general scholarship.

In the 20th century, Jewish demographic efforts often drew from the ferments of Zionism, and specifically the engagement of nation-building in Palestine/Israel, though they also reflected non-Zionist aspirations of Jewish autonomism in different times and places. Over time, as noted, the initial concern with race and physical anthropology gave way to more qualitative insights concerning the mutual relationships between demographic patterns and Jewish identification. Social scientific studies regarding the effects of assimilation were ultimately an inquiry into collective Jewish identity (both historical and contemporary), the changing boundaries of the collective, and the question of Jewish corporate survival in the longer term. Thus, Ruppin's early 20th-century discussion of the central issue of survival of the Jewish diaspora in the post-emancipation era formed the basis for later research that assessed the demographic, socioeconomic, and cultural role of the Jewish community in Palestine (and later, Israel), for global Jewish continuity.[52] Other important research strands included analysis of the determinants and consequences of an early Jewish demographic transition (to reduced mortality and reduced fertility) in most European and Middle Eastern countries vis-à-vis the majority populations of the same countries, and the direct and indirect consequences of the Shoah for Jewish demography.[53] Eventually, assessing the socio-demographic and identificational trends of American Jewry became the central fixture in the field.[54]

By the turn of the 21st century, analytic efforts in the field of demography increasingly reflected post-modern relativism (discussed below in greater detail). The discipline also continues to be distinguished by two competing approaches to Jewish population studies: global-comparative versus local. To some extent, the distinction between the two approaches reflects immediate research needs and available data resources, but it also stems from contrasting ideational views: the first regarding Jewish peoplehood as one overarching global entity, and the second focusing on a constellation of largely unrelated local and national experiences.[55]

Quite a few observers have been tempted to provide mono-causal and narrowly geographical explanations of the trend they are investigating. At one end of the continuum is an inside-oriented view, grounded in Jewish mysticism, of a Jewish world that continues to evolve, regardless of outside intervention. Put somewhat differently, while Jewish communities may experience temporary ups and downs, their existence reflects an *eternal Israel*.[56] An alternative approach focuses on the more active component of the identifiable collective, reaching the conclusion that there always exists some kind of lively Jewish community, regardless of size or characteristics.[57] At the opposite end of the continuum is historical materialism, which posits that everything is determined by social class and political power conflicts, leaving no apparent role to any specifically "Jewish" culture. In this view, Jewish communities are destined to disappear as human society moves inexorably toward a new order.[58]

As against these deterministic points of view, a more balanced and pragmatic interpretative strategy may outline the expected causality chain for socio-demographic events among a minority or sub-population, and undertake quantitative analyses based on inference about a limited set of variables that operationally represent the selected hypotheses. In this perspective, it is imperative to note that the goal of statistical "explanation" of human behaviors is very imperfect and never should ignore the presence of a substantial, often dominant, unexplained residual. Human behaviors fortunately are more complex than any sophisticated model can unveil.

Social and demographic trends of any subpopulation, and in this case, Jews, depend on three major types of explanatory factors: (1) the complex of *distinctive* religious imperatives, ethic values, social norms, ancestral traditions, popular beliefs, local customs, and community institutions peculiar to the given group; (2) legal and other *interactive* modes between that group and the rest or the majority of society; and (3) circumstances *shared* by the specific group and the majority concerning the general character of society, its patterns of modernization, economic resources, modes of production, social structures and stratification, political institutions, level of technology, climatic and other environmental conditions.[59] The main drivers of demographic change operate at different levels of societal aggregation: (1) the *world societal system*, namely geopolitical, socioeconomic, and cultural changes across the world's different regions, and extant inequalities among countries; (2) the respective contexts of *national societies* in which Jewish communities are located, including relationships between the majority of society and the Jewish minority, and policy interventions by national governments and other authorities; (3) the specific internal contexts of *Jewish communities*, including interventions enacted by Jewish institutions internationally and locally; (4) the *personal* characteristics of individual Jews, and in particular their gender, age, socioeconomic status, and cultural-identificational patterns.[60] Global patterns mostly escape influences by specific individuals, community groups, or even countries, but they do reflect influences occasionally stemming from large and powerful nations, or from widespread communities—such as global religions. In turn, national experiences may be powerfully influenced by changes at the global level.

Religio-ethnic communities, including Jews, are affected by the overall context of national societies of which they are a part, but also reflect transnational processes and influences somewhat indifferent to space and time. Such communities may significantly influence national population trends in order to advance their own corporate interests—for example, by advocating particular policy interventions. While demographic events always concern one specific individual, as a rule individuals are subject to significant influences on the part of their communities of belonging. The intensity and quality of group identification—in this case, Jewish identification—is not only a matter of cultural style and tastes of a community, but also a fundamental mechanism of population growth or decline. A major constant throughout Jewish history is the exposure to contextual circumstances simultaneously perceived in different national-territorial areas. Population studies predominantly cover national societies, and this is largely true of the investigation of Jewish communities as well. But the latter have often been affected by sweeping trends of broad global importance. Geographical dispersion through large-scale migration and the progressive expanding of globalization and transnational networks and identification patterns across Jewish communities call for addressing world-system structure and change as a prerequisite to understanding the position of Jewish communities internationally and locally.[61]

Five variables that operate at the (Jewish) community level in particular determine the preferred strategies that may or may not lead toward a given demographic event: (1) the group's unique *traditional culture and organization*, with special reference to religious and social norms relevant to the given demographic event, as well as community frameworks and institutions established to implement those norms; (2) the group's legal status or—more relevant to the contemporary situation—subjective perceptions of its own *dominance/dependence* versus the majority of society or other minorities within it; (3) the group's *social class stratification*, implying significant inter- and intra-group differences in perceived interests and access to resources relevant to the demographic event; (4) the group's available *knowledge* with respect to the given socio-demographic process, whether acquired through formal education or other channels, and the consequent behavior relative to the given demographic event; and (5) the group's specific *biological constraints* namely in relation to genetically inherited properties that may enhance or hinder exposure to certain diseases, thus affecting survivorship chances. Population composition by a variety of personal characteristics such as age, marital status, years of residence in a given country, or income, is a crucial mediating factor in the chain of demographic events. Individual characteristics directly or indirectly reflect the influence of the abovementioned broader determinants that simultaneously shape the lives of many members of the group, thus determining the aggregate profile of a population.[62]

As noted, the ultimate dependent variable is whether or not a given single demographic event occurs. Most socio-demographic processes functionally depend and can be statistically explained by an appropriate set of proximate determinants or intermediate variables. One classic example is viewing birthrates as the joint product of couple formation frequencies, natural fertility levels, and fertility control.[63] Each of these proximate determinants evidently is by itself the dependent variable of a more complex explanatory chain. Demographic events finally reflect the combined power of three factors operating at the individual or household level: (1) the event's cultural *desirability*, that is, its compatibility with the prevailing social norms within a given population; (2) its economic *feasibility*, that is, the presence of material resources needed for the event to happen; and (3) the *availability* of event-specific tools and conditions instrumental for the event to occur.[64] Explanation and interpretation particularly focus on the frequency of events, their distribution over the life cycle, particularly in relation to age at event, and their distribution over calendar time measured in months and years. In inter-group comparisons, no less important than events' frequencies are the roles played by a community as a forerunner or a late joiner in the occurrence and diffusion of a given phenomenon,[65] and sometimes in being the unique actor and carrier of the given circumstance and process of demographic interest. This is in no way a deterministic view, because no relations are expected to occur necessarily, hence affecting a final result known in advance. Rather, the range of possible occurrences should be circumscribed, suggesting what the actual occurrences might likely be.

In the past, the conventional wisdom was that policymaking and implementation were derived from the interpretation of various ascertained facts. Lately, however, a more complex and reciprocal interplay of facts, interpretations, and policies has emerged. The reading of basic findings with regard to Jewish populations is increasingly influenced by preexisting interpretative assumptions, with positive or negative interpretations of the trends often preceding in-depth analyses. If one were to offer a sweeping view of the more recent research efforts, it would focus not on the fact that the quality of available data is sometimes far from ideal, but rather that knowledge acquired is underutilized, such that substantive debates too often rest on a shallow analytic basis. In turn, policies—in particular, choices made by different large Jewish organizations in order to determine and service their target constituencies—tend to directly affect not only interpretations but also the very nature of the underlying data: if reality needs to be perceived in a certain way, data pointing in a different direction risk being dismissed as irrelevant.

Indeed, in recent interpretative debates on Jewish demography, various critiques were expressed on the role of data, namely, that

- data are not important for revealing or assessing the given process;
- they are important, yet those needed to assess the given process are not available;
- they are available, but not reliable enough;
- they are reliable, but have been misused;
- they have been used appropriately, but are not sufficiently conclusive;
- although they do adjudicate the given issue, the issue itself is unimportant in light of broader conceptual considerations and normative goals.

Some of the critics have pointed to connections between allegedly biased data and the personal background of researchers making use of the data. For example, a number of Israel-based researchers who analyzed downward population trends among U.S. Jewry have been labeled "Zionist intellectuals," holders of a worldview denying legitimacy to the Jewish diaspora.[66] (Ironically, as will be seen, some of these same researchers sparked an outcry and were labeled "anti-Zionist" in the wake of their analysis of the diminishing Jewish share of total population in the area covering Israel, the West Bank, and Gaza.)

The most extreme position holds that the very existence of (problematic) data is inherently responsible for creating social and political issues that would not otherwise exist. In this perspective, data are seen as instrumental in the misrepresentation, manipulation, and domination of society.[67] Criticism focuses on the allegedly exploitative concept of group relations. For instance, the categorization of new immigrants to Israel in the early years of the state as coming from "Europe," "America," "Asia," or "Africa" is blamed for fostering ethnic and subethnic divisions and gaps. The common thread of these and similar arguments is that authors' preconceptions and hidden agendas percolate into the data and thus affect interpretations and, quite possibly, the ensuing debates about possible policy interventions. What is left unexplored is the fact that the critics themselves may have their own agendas.

So far, this essay has focused mainly on the Jewish collective from a global perspective. In the concluding sections, we will consider two specific cases, U.S. Jewry and Israeli Jewry, each of which requires somewhat different, if not contrasting, sets of analytic tools. Outside of Israel, Jewry operates as a set of *minorities* of different absolute sizes, each of which constitutes a miniscule to small share of the total national population. Israeli Jews, in contrast, are the *majority* population in their sovereign state. As will be seen, the demographic expectations for these two typological components of world Jewry are not the same. Nonetheless, there are a number of commonalities of patterns and outcomes in the two largest world Jewish communities; these may point to commonalities among world Jewry as a whole. As with other issues discussed above, this matter requires validation by means of comparable, coherent, and complementary description and theory.

U.S. Jewry: A Shrinking Core?

The demography of Jews in the United States has been the subject of a rich and diverse literature.[68] Within the operational limits of social scientific research in the United States, definitions of who is a Jew have tended to evolve. In the beginning was the straightforward question, "What is his religion?" asked with regard to the "head of household" query in the Current Population Survey of 1957—the only occasion on which religious affiliation was explicitly addressed in an official U.S. population source.[69] Following this were several definitional labels devised for the 1970 NJPS[70] and the 1990 NJPS. As has been seen, the definition of "Jewish" became increasingly nuanced in the 2000 NJPS, being neither normative nor mutually exclusive of other group identifications. This move toward greater inclusiveness in the definition of Jewishness was made at the request of the United Jewish Communities (UJC), the institution sponsoring the survey, in accordance with its policy of serving the broadest possible target population; consequently, the operational definitions of the survey primarily reflected the guidelines of UJC service provisions rather than research-oriented commitments.[71]

In 2001, the NJPS estimated 5.2 million *core* Jews in the United States, based on detailed tabulations for the equivalent of slightly more than 5 million Jewish individuals, plus an allocation of about 200,000 additional people (mostly to cover for older Jews residing in institutions). A competing study done in 2001, the American Jewish Identity Survey (AJIS), estimated the Jewish population at 5.3 million.[72] Both figures were lower than the estimate of 5.5 million Jews in the 1990 NJPS. The possibility—actually, plausibility—of such a decline had long been predicted, given the increasing rate of out-marriage, low Jewish fertility rates, diminishing Jewish immigration to the United States, and declining rates of participation in the organized Jewish community.[73] Another national study conducted at about this time, the Heritage and Religious Identification Survey (HARI), yielded an estimate of 6 million "persons of Jewish origin," which would presumably yield a significantly lower core Jewish population similar in number to those found in the other two surveys.[74]

In 2008, the American Religious Identity Survey (ARIS)[75] found evidence of Jewish population stagnation or decline in the framework of spreading secularism in the United States—a finding that was highly compatible with those of the NJPS and AJIS. The 2007 Pew Survey of the American Religious Landscape found 1.67 percent of Jewish adults by religion out of the total U.S. adult population.[76] Factoring in the lower percentage of children among Jews, the lack of Jewish socialization among a substantial share of the children of mixed marriages, and a share of Jewish persons not reporting religion that was similar to that of the total U.S. population, a national estimate of 5.49 million Jews could be obtained. A similar estimate was found by an initial compilation of Jewish sub-samples in a large number of general national surveys under the general heading of the meta-analysis undertaken by the SSRI at Brandeis.[77] Each of these national surveys included small samples of Jews identified by religion, which were complemented by assumptions about the share of Jews who did not declare a religion.[78] Perhaps the most influential of these sources, the General Social Survey (GSS) undertaken by the National Opinion Research Center (NORC) for the period of 1972–2008, reported a small but statistically significant decline in "percent Jewish" in the United States, averaging just under 2 percent of adults in recent years,[79] and pointing to a lower share once children were included.

Although the body of evidence reviewed above was quite consistent, it was the 2000 NJPS that was singled out for controversy, in part because of its unprecedented scale, cost, and media coverage, but also because the findings, if true, would raise significant questions about the current structure and future growth of the American Jewish population.[80] Criticism focused on a number of technical mistakes made in the course of the survey, in particular the so-called "lost data."[81] There were also some doubts expressed with regard to the thoroughness of the fieldwork, which was mostly conducted via telephone conversations at a time when systematic canvassing of cellular phones was not feasible. Later research sought to verify or disprove the results of the 2000 NJPS by means of projections based on the estimates presented in the previous NJPS of 1990 (which were widely regarded as reliable). Utilizing external data concerning the volume of international migration, as well as built-in data taken from the 1990 and 2000 surveys on age composition, fertility, intermarriage, and the percentage of children raised as Jewish, along with solidly based assumptions concerning life expectancy among U.S. Jews, our study came up with a projected 2001 U.S. Jewish population profile that in most respects was quite consistent with that of the 2000 NJPS.[82] The one prominent exception was the projection for the age cohort born in 1950–1970, which appeared to have been underestimated by 286,000 in the 2000 NJPS. This group was largely composed of the so-called "baby-boomers," noted for their large cohort size, high social mobility, and cultural volatility.[83] The underestimate could be explained either by undercoverage resulting from ineptitude of the surveyors, or by the propensity of these individuals to distance themselves from any sense of significant Jewish identification. Until further and updated information is collected, it will be difficult to finally adjudicate this controversy. Overall, our new projection findings pointed to an upward correction of 200,000 above the original NJPS estimate, bringing it from 5.2 to 5.4 million in 2001. Extending the projection a few years ahead, it appeared as though the U.S. Jewish population would total approximately 5,425,000 in 2010. These findings fall well within the range of the other nationwide surveys mentioned above.

All of these figures relate to a concept of core Jewish population that falls somewhere between the more restrictive and more inclusive definitional criteria outlined above. An identificational stratification of U.S. Jewry—as unveiled by NJPS, after our upward correction—is presented in Table 1.1. While the evidence of a deficit of Jewishly identified births versus Jewish deaths suggests that the *core* Jewish population is past its peak, at least another 1.5 million people of Jewish parentage—children of intermarriage or Jews who have opted out—live in the United States, bringing the expanded total of those currently Jewish or of Jewish ancestry to 6.8 million. In addition, about the same number of persons of non-Jewish origin live in mixed

Table 1.1. Number and Percent of U.S. Jews, by Different Identification Criteria, 2010

Jewish population definition	Jewish population	
	Millions[a]	Percent of total U.S. population[b]
Identify by denomination as Orthodox	± 0.7	0.2
Devote time to Jewish community	± 1.5	0.5
Affiliated with Jewish organization/s	± 3.0	1.0
Jewish by self-declaration	± 4.6	1.4
Core Jewish population	± 5.4	1.7
Have Jewish parent/s	± 6.8	2.2
Total in households with Jews or persons of Jewish ancestry	± 8.0	2.6
Law of Return eligible	± 12.0	4.0
Have ancestors who ever were Jewish	??	??

[a] Source: Sergio DellaPergola, "How Many Jews in the United States? The Demographic Perspective," *Contemporary Jewry* 33, nos. 1–2 (2013), 15–42.
[b] Based on a 2010 estimate of 310 million; see Population Reference Bureau, *2010 World Population Data Sheet* (Washington, D.C.: 2010).

Jewish households, thus creating an *enlarged* population of about 8 million in households with Jews or persons of Jewish ancestry. The population theoretically eligible for Israel's Law of Return, which would include non-Jewish children and grandchildren and their spouses, would be considerably larger—more than 10 million and possibly closer to 12 million. Overall, however, one detects a shrinking Jewish core and expanding peripheral belts.

A number of critics have expressed disagreement with various aspects of the population estimates outlined above. Higher core Jewish population estimates of 6.0–6.5 million Jews have been suggested on the basis of compilations of Jewish population surveys and other sources from local Jewish communities.[84] An even higher estimate, up to 6.5–7.5 million Jews, relies on data obtained from a selection of surveys included in the SSRI meta-analysis.[85] On the basis of such evidence, it has been submitted that American Jewry has actually been growing—at a rate that would be significantly higher than that of the total U.S. white population and similar to that of the Jewish population in Israel.[86] This is truly implausible, given all available data on Jewish population composition and movements.

Critics might counter that many general national surveys and local Jewish surveys have better response rates than the large national Jewish population surveys. Yet such an argument overlooks the many problems associated with the use of non-comparable data collected by means of various and not always random methods, reporting to different commissioning agencies (each with its own agenda), relying on different definitions of who is a Jew, and not comparable in their topical contents, sometimes not even with respect to the same variable. Given the tremendous variation of Jewish behavioral and ideational patterns across states and cities in the United States,[87] any single local community source is inadequate to portray the whole profile of American

Jewry. Moreover, in a country characterized by a high level of geographical mobility,[88] local research efforts share the critical weakness of not being based on simultaneous data collection efforts as in national censuses; of not relying on consistent and identical population definitions; and of not covering representative samples of the whole national territory or of the whole gamut of age groups (most surveys included in the SSRI meta-analysis cover adult respondents only). The higher Jewish population estimates produced by some of these research efforts are credible only as they reflect broader definitions of the Jewish collective. Finally, it should be noted that most American social surveys oversample Jews: in such instances, the proper weighting factors must be applied in order to correctly adjust the figure downward.[89] The doubt persists that such corrections may not have been sufficient and that some of the bias remains in the data.

Population size is a synthetic indicator of a whole array of demographic, socioeconomic, and socio-cultural trends: the numbers are important because they can reveal the basic dynamics of growth, resilience, or decline among a given group investigated in historical perspective. Therefore, whereas the number of Jews living in the United States may not be the most important statistic to emerge from population studies, its importance cannot be underestimated. In the current debate, the main points of contention are that the assimilatory erosion of the U.S. Jewish population has been greatly exaggerated,[90] and that the size of American Jewry has been greatly underestimated.[91] Should this be the case, the United States, not Israel as suggested by recent research,[92] would continue to have the largest Jewish population in the world.[93] Which country has the largest Jewish population may have scarce relevance in a technically delimited analysis, but may stimulate intriguing confrontations between "egos" in the respective Jewish communities and among their leadership in particular.

To be sure, there are other participants in the Jewish population debate who advance a more radical position, advocating a de-emphasis on spatial-temporal continuity (inherently related to genealogy) in favor of greater attention to changes in the U.S. intellectual and institutional milieu. In this vein, relativist or post-modernist arguments have questioned the relevance of real or imaginary roots of corporate ethnic identities,[94] focusing instead on a group's ability to shape, invent, or reinvent its own sense of personal and collective belonging and solidarity regardless of fixed normative constraints. When applied to the study of Jewish community identities, this approach calls for constantly redefining basic terms of reference such as the "boundaries" and "contents" of Jewishness.[95] In place of the traditional notion of Jewish identification being necessarily related to a given set of beliefs and behaviors, a post-modern Jewish identification can be expressed through such means as "connecting," "traveling," "journeying," "surfing," or "zapping"—all of which imply eclectic, selective, and subjective reconstruction of the subject matter and its meaning.[96] The notion of historical continuity tends to lose relevance amid the pressure of new needs and norms in contemporary culture and society. In such a fluid conceptual context, one may question the very relevance of demography as a useful tool in the appraisal of the U.S. Jewish population.

A related question is whether identificational trends among American Jewry should be interpreted primarily in the framework of American society, or rather as part of a global configuration of Jewish communities. While the obvious answer is *both*, the conclusions that are drawn with regard to the same socio-demographic and socio-cultural patterns can be quite different. For instance, what may appear, from the internal perspective, to be significant assimilation and erosion may be regarded (from a viewpoint outside the community) as distinctiveness and resilience.[97] Another question is whether the criteria used to define the U.S. Jewish population should be the same or different from criteria used to define Jews in other countries. Some exceptionalism provided by the American societal context can be expected in the analysis of Jewish social patterns at the substantive level. However, if the *definitional criteria* themselves take into account American exceptionalism, the implication is that *Jewishness* has become a subsidiary attribute of *Americanness*, and hence American Jewry cannot be compared across Jewish populations and communities worldwide.[98]

A systematic reconsideration of these issues is necessary, along with careful reading of factual results. Following the decision of the Jewish Federations not to sponsor a new national survey in 2010, it appeared as though the 2000 NJPS offered the last opportunity for the scholarly profession, for the U.S. Jewish community leadership, and for the public at large to benefit from a systematic, large-scale national tool for assessment, analysis, and policy planning. (The Pew Research Center conducted a national survey of the U.S. Jewish population in 2013.) Studies concerning the impact of programs such as Birthright may not suffice in providing an overall assessment of the demography of American Jewry. Beyond the continuing discussion about the merits and flaws of the 2000 NJPS, it is important to consider the possibility that long-term demographic trends challenge the assumption of continuing population growth or stability among U.S. Jewry.[99]

Israeli Jewry: A Shrinking Majority?

Israel's population has been thoroughly documented,[100] studied, and debated by several generations of scholars.[101] Currently, one of the issues arousing the most controversy is that regarding the demographic balance between Israel and the Palestinians. A number of studies have pointed to an ongoing decline in the Jewish share in Israel's population vis-à-vis the Palestinian and other population groups.[102] This position has been countered by those who think such an outlook is an artifact of analytic error and political manipulation.[103]

At the beginning of 2011, the demographic composition of the population in Israel (including East Jerusalem and the Golan Heights) and the Palestinian territory (defined here as the West Bank, including its Israeli citizens, and Gaza), consisted of the following: 5,802,000 Jews, plus 320,000 other members of Jewish households; and 1,573,000 Arabs, including Muslims, Christians, Druze, and other very tiny minorities—for a total of 7,695,000.[104] These figures include 304,000 Jews and 7,000 non-Jewish family members in the West Bank; 189,000 and 6,000, respectively, in East Jerusalem;[105] and 18,000 and 1,000, respectively, in the Golan Heights. In the Palestinian territory, there were 2,240,000 Palestinians in the West Bank (excluding East Jerusalem, already accounted for in Israel's data), and 1,510,000 in Gaza, for a total of 3,750,000. These last estimates for 2011 are based on our critical reading of the census undertaken by the Palestinian Central Bureau of Statistics (PCBS) four years earlier, and are clearly lower than the PCBS figures. In November 2007, the PCBS reported a population of 3,760,000, including East Jerusalem—higher by 870,000 than in the previous census of 1997, when the population had been assessed at 2,890,000, but lower by at least 350,000 than what the PCBS' own population projections had anticipated (assuming, among other things, a positive international migration balance that did not materialize).[106] The annual population growth of Palestinians in the intercensal period, excluding East Jerusalem, was close to 2.9 percent—the same as among Israel's Muslims.[107] In other words, while the official Palestinian data must be critically de-inflated, discounting for immigration that never occurred, the rate of current natural increase (births minus deaths) is plausible by regional standards.

In 2011, the estimated total population in Israel and the Palestinian territory was thus 11,445,000, of which the core Jewish population accounted for 50.7 percent and the enlarged Jewish population (including non-Jewish members of Jewish households) 53.5 percent. Adding in at least 240,000 foreign workers, refugees, and displaced persons in Israel, the grand total rises to 11,685,000 and the core Jewish and enlarged Jewish populations fall to 49.8 percent and 52.6 percent, respectively.

Table 1.2 reports (for 2010) the percentage of Jews, according to the *core* and *enlarged* definitions, out of the total population of an area from which we gradually and cumulatively deduct the Arab or otherwise non-Jewish population of designated areas, while keeping constant the (core or enlarged) Jewish population. The result of this exercise is a gradually growing Jewish share of the total population according to the different territorial configurations considered. This allows a better evaluation of the current share of Jewish population out of the total population under alternative assumptions.[108] In 2010, the core Jewish population accounted for 49.8 percent of the total population present between the Mediterranean Sea and the Jordan River. Excluding the foreign workers, refugees, and the Palestinian population of Gaza, the

Table 1.2. Percent of *Core* and *Enlarged* Jewish Population out of Total Population in Israel and Palestinian Territory, according to Different Territorial Definitions, 2010

Area	Percent of Jews,[a] by definition	
	Core	Enlarged
Grand total of Israel and Palestinian territory	49.8	52.6
After deducting foreign workers and refugees	50.8	53.6
After deducting Gaza	58.5	61.7
After deducting West Bank	75.5	79.7
After deducting Golan Heights	75.7	79.9
After deducting East Jerusalem	78.6	82.9
After deducting the "Triangle" area	81.5	85.9

[a] Based on constant total Jewish population of Israel, including East Jerusalem, West Bank, and Golan Heights.

Source: Sergio DellaPergola, *World Jewish Population 2010* (Storrs, Conn.: 2010).

core Jewish population constituted 58.5 percent of the total, and the enlarged Jewish population, 61.7 percent. Excluding as well the West Bank (but including East Jerusalem), the core Jewish population constituted 75.5 percent and the enlarged Jewish population, 79.7 percent. When the Golan Heights and East Jerusalem's Arab population are also excluded, the Jewish percentages rise to 78.6 percent and 82.9 percent, respectively. If the "Triangle area"—a territorial strip containing a predominantly Israeli Arab population, located in the center of Israel adjacent to the West Bank—is also excluded (which is submitted here for the sake of exercise), the core Jewish population would constitute 81.5 percent of the total, and the enlarged Jewish population, 85.9 percent.

Clearly, there is a tremendous gap between the figures of 49.8 percent "core" Jews among the total population present over the whole territory, and 85.9 percent of "enlarged" Jews over a much reduced territory designed to enhance the Jewish majority. The gap illustrates the enormous impact of possible policy decisions that may affect the future nature of the state of Israel.

Critics of these findings have focused both on the data sources and on underlying assumptions concerning Palestinian fertility rates and levels of emigration (of Palestinians) and immigration (of Jews). It is argued, for instance, that the Israeli "demographic establishment" faithfully accepted data put forward by the PCBS in Ramallah despite the fact that the data may well have been tainted by political bias. Moreover, it is claimed, the Arab population in East Jerusalem was double-counted (both in the Israeli and Palestinian data), and both the 1997 and 2007 censuses of the Palestinian population were inflated by the inclusion of several hundred thousand people who lived permanently abroad. In addition, according to the critics, the data concerning Palestinian fertility contradicts trends predicted by the "Swedish model," which would point to a significant decline in the Palestinian birthrate; does not take into account the significant amount of Palestinian emigration in recent years; and overlooks the possibility of an increase in Jewish immigration. Therefore, according to the critics, the estimated Palestinian population in the West Bank and Gaza should be reduced by one to one and a half million, and there is thus no urgency for Israel to address demographic trends in Israel and the territories.[109]

Most of these contentions are easily rejected. Without dwelling on the issue at length,[110] it may be noted that Palestinian fertility levels, while indeed on the decline, remain significantly higher than among Jews in Israel and are sociologically very distant from the givens assumed by the "Swedish model." Moreover, because of its young age composition, the Palestinian population has a relatively low death rate; the youthfulness of the population also acts as a multiplier of natural growth (the technical term for this, "momentum," has been both misunderstood and misused by the critics). It is also the case that, in the current global and world Jewish demographic situation, levels of Jewish immigration are not likely to approach those following the collapse of the Soviet Union, when more than a million Jews (according to the enlarged definition) emigrated to Israel.

What has been missed in this debate is the fundamental issue at stake: not the specific percentage point of the extant Jewish majority, or the specific date when Jews will (or will not) lose their current majority over the entire territory between the Mediterranean Sea and the Jordan River, or what will be the exact percent of a continuing Jewish majority within the "green line" (pre-1967 borders), or even the geo-strategic and international implications of a possible majority-minority shift. What is rather at stake is the political, historical, sociological, cultural, and symbolic nature of the state of Israel—which, while ensuring the security of its inhabitants, also strives to consolidate its historical and civil identity. Israel stands at the bifurcation of being a national or a bi-national state, and it cannot escape the issue of how much corporate autonomy a majority in a democratic state can afford to yield to an already substantial, and, from our projections, growing minority.[111] Demography stands at the heart of these unresolved questions; the fact that an increasing share of the world Jewish population lives in Israel adds salience to the role of Jewish demography within the broader assessment of global Jewish peoplehood.[112]

Conclusion

What is the future of Jewish demographic studies? Much depends on how—or even whether—Jews are designated as an *identifiable* or *non-identifiable* sub-population; and to what extent the discipline maintains its current scholarly status or, (in the best-case scenario) acquires the status of an independent sub-discipline, or (in the worst case scenario) becomes marginalized in an increasingly ideological public discourse. All of this, in turn, revolves around different and competing conceptions of Jewish peoplehood, the diverse relationships these entail between cultural, social, and biological processes, and the most appropriate methodologies for the study of such a complex cluster of issues. Demographic research, as such, is not responsible for the field's inherent quandaries of definition and focus. However, it needs to address these matters at both the empirical and interpretative level if it is to preserve a sustained level of scientific integrity and public relevance.

At the same time, Jewish demography is characterized by a delicate relationship between the research-oriented and public-applied domains. Community leaders and policymakers need a sound basis for their programs and policies. To obtain this, it is necessary to commit resources to the ongoing and objective study of population characteristics, trends, and longer-term implications on the local community and global levels. Equally important is the need to be aware of possible gaps between the results of systematic research and existing conceptions, hopes, and fears.

Notes

1. See, for instance, Paul Demeny and Geoffrey McNicoll (eds.), *The Encyclopedia of Population* (New York: 2003). Some of the materials in this essay draw from Sergio DellaPergola, "Demography," in *The Oxford Handbook of Jewish Studies*, ed. Martin Goodman (Oxford: 2002), 797–823; idem, "World Jewish Population 2010," in the North American Jewish Data Bank (NAJDB) publication *Current Jewish Population Reports* 2 (Storrs: 2010); idem, *Jewish Demographic Policies: Population Trends and Options in Israel and the Diaspora* (Jerusalem: 2011).

2. The terms *demography* and *population studies* are used here as synonyms, although sometimes a distinction is suggested between demography as more formal and population studies as more descriptive. See Geoffrey McNicoll, "The Agenda of Population Studies: A Commentary and Complaint," *Population and Development Review* 18, no. 3 (1992), 399–420; Hendrik P. van Dalen, and Kène Henkens, "What is on a Demographer's Mind? A World-Wide Survey," *Demographic Research* 26 (2012), 363–408.

3. "Take ye sum of all the congregation of the children of Israel, by their families, by their fathers' houses, according to the number of names" (Num. 1:2).

4. Leopold Zunz, "Grundlinien zu einer künftigen Statistik der Juden," *Zeitschrift für die Wissenschaft des Judentums* (1823), 1: 523–532; Abraham Moses Luncz, *Jerusalem, Jahrbuch zur Beförderung einer wissenschaftlich genauen Kenntnis des jetzigen und des alten Palästina*, 6 vols. (Jerusalem: 1881–1903).

5. See one early example in G. Lagneau, *Remarques à propos du dénombrement de la population sur quelques différences démographiques présentées par les catholiques, les protestants, les israélites* (Paris: 1882).

6. Mitchell B. Hart, *Social Science and the Politics of Modern Jewish Identity* (Stanford: 2000).

7. See, for instance, Jean Christian Boudin, *Traité de géographie et de statistique médicales*, vol. 2 (Paris: 1856); Maurice Fishberg, *The Jews: A Study in Race and Environment* (New York: 1911). For a broader overview, see Léon Poliakov, *Le mythe aryen* (Paris: 1973).

8. See, for instance, Roberto Bachi, *Population Trends of World Jewry* (Jerusalem: 1976); DellaPergola, *Jewish Demographic Policies*.

9. See, for instance, Felix A. Theilhaber, *Der Untergans der deutschen Juden* (Munich: 1911).

10. At the Hebrew University, for example, demography is currently taught in the department of sociology. It was initially taught in the department of statistics, and for several years it constituted a separate department. Demography of the Jews was taught primarily in the department of contemporary Jewry, until its recent merger with the department of Jewish history.

11. The typical case of ethnogenesis occurs when an individual founder departs from prevailing social norms and networks and establishes a new and resilient societal division—such as with Abraham and the Israelites, or Martin Luther with the Reformed Church, or Joseph Smith Jr. with Mormonism. Alternatively, a new societal category can emerge from the fusion of pre-existing categories, as was the case of the "coloureds" under the South African apartheid regime. The coloureds were persons of mixed white and/or black and/or Asian ancestry and were counted as a separate population group. As such, they were also allocated some political representation status. See Gideon Shimoni, *Community and Conscience: Jews in Apartheid South Africa* (Waltham: 2003).

12. Moshe Sicron, *Immigration to Israel 1948–1953* (special publication of the Central Bureau of Statistics) (Jerusalem: 1957); Sergio DellaPergola, "The Global Context of Migration to Israel" in *Immigration to Israel: Sociological Perspectives*, ed. Elazar Leshem and Judith T. Shuval (New Brunswick: 1998), 51–92; idem, "International Migration of Jews," in *Transnationalism: Diasporas and the Advent of a New (Dis)order*, ed. Eliezer Ben-Rafael and Yitzhak Sternberg (Leiden: 2009), 213–236; Uzi Rebhun and Lilach Lev Ari, *American Israelis: Migration, Transnationalism, and Diasporic Identity* (Leiden: 2010).

13. On fertility, see Paul Ritterband (ed.), *Modern Jewish Fertility* (Leiden: 1981); Eric Peritz and Mario Baras (eds.), *Studies in the Fertility of Israel* (Jerusalem: 1992); Sergio DellaPergola, *Fertility Prospects in Israel: Ever Below Replacement Level?* (New York: 2011), 1–36. On childhood mortality, see U.O. Schmelz, *Infant and Early Childhood Mortality among the Jews in the Diaspora* (Jerusalem: 1971).

14. See DellaPergola, *Jewish Demographic Policies*, ch. 7; Sylvia Barack Fishman, *Double or Nothing? Jewish Families and Mixed Marriage* (Hanover: 2004); Shulamit Reinharz and Sergio DellaPergola (eds.), *Jewish Intermarriage around the World* (New Brunswick: 2009).

15. Abraham Moles, "Sur l'aspect théorique du decompte de populations mal definies," in Centre national des hautes études juives–Bruxelles, Institute of Contemporary Jewry of the Hebrew University of Jerusalem, *La vie juive dans l'Europe contemporaine* (Brussels: 1965), 81–87.

16. Sergio DellaPergola, *World Jewry beyond 2000: The Demographic Prospects* (Oxford: 2000).

17. Dominique Schnapper, "Israélites and Juifs: New Jewish Identities in France," in *Jewish Identities in the New Europe*, ed. Jonathan Webber (London: 1994).

18. Baruch Kimmerling, "Be'ayot konseptualiyot behistoriografiyah shel eretz uvah shnei 'amim" in *One Land, Two Peoples*, ed. Danny Jacoby (Jerusalem: 1999), 11–22; Shlomo Sand, *The Invention of the Jewish People* (New York: 2009).

19. Interesting surveys of alternative definitions of the target Jewish population are reported in Yiddish Scientific Institute—YIVO, *The Classification of Jewish Immigrants and Its Implications: A Survey of Opinions* (New York: 1945); Sidney B. Hoenig (ed.), Baruch Litvin (comp.), *Jewish Identity: Modern Responsa and Opinions on the Registration of Children of Mixed Marriages—David Ben-Gurion's Query to Leaders of World Jewry—A Documentary Compilation* (Jerusalem: 1970).

20. This has long been the case, though not always. See Shaye Cohen, *The Beginnings of Jewishness: Boundaries, Varieties, Uncertainties* (Berkeley: 1999).

21. Eric Rosenthal, "The Equivalence of United States Census Data for Persons of Russian Stock or Descent with American Jews: An Evaluation," *Demography* 12 (1975), 275–290; DellaPergola, "World Jewish Population," 8–13.

22. The term *core Jewish population* was initially suggested in Barry A. Kosmin, Sidney Goldstein, Joseph Waksberg, Nava Lerer, Ariela Keysar, and Jeffrey Scheckner, *Highlights of the CJF 1990 National Jewish Population Survey* (New York: 1991), 4.

23. The issue of making a distinction between monotheistic and non-monotheistic religions was raised by members of the National Technical Advisory Committee (NTAC), which was charged with planning the 2000–2001 National Jewish Population Survey on behalf of the United Jewish Communities. On that occasion, it was argued that there was no incompatibility between Judaism and some Asian traditions, such as Buddhism. A recent case was quoted of a prominent Buddhist leader in California, himself born Jewish, who was sending his children to a Jewish educational facility. David Ben-Gurion's declared interest in Asian religions alongside his intense study of Jewish sources was also offered as relevant evidence of compatibility.

In Israel, the issue of incompatibility between a Jewish and a Christian identity was addressed by a 1962 landmark decision of the Israeli supreme court in the case of Oswald (Brother Daniel) Rufeisen. Rufeisen, born a Jew and converted to Catholicism, had asked to be recognized a Jew for the purpose of the Law of Return, which grants eligibility and citizenship rights to Jewish immigrants to Israel. The court ruled that Rufeisen had opted out of Judaism and thus had forfeited his eligibility to become a citizen under the Law of Return (see n. 29). At the same time, he was free to immigrate to Israel through its general immigration law, which he did.

24. Barry A. Kosmin, personal communication, 1990. Kosmin was the scientific director of the 1990 NJPS and personally supervised the telephone interviewing, overhearing the answers given by respondents.

25. In the 2000 NJPS version initially processed and circulated by the United Jewish Communities, a Jew is defined as "a person whose religion is Judaism, OR whose religion is Jewish and something else, OR who has no religion and has at least one Jewish parent or a Jewish upbringing, OR who has a non-monotheistic religion and has at least one Jewish parent or a Jewish upbringing." See United Jewish Communities, *The National Jewish Population Survey 2000–01: Strength, Challenge, and Diversity in the American Jewish Population* (New York: 2003), 2. A special issue of *Contemporary Jewry* (25), edited by Samuel Heilman (2005), is devoted to critical essays and analyses of NJPS methods and findings.

26. The term *enlarged Jewish population* was initially suggested by Sergio DellaPergola, "The Italian Jewish Population Study: Demographic Characteristics and Trends," in

Studies in Jewish Demography: Survey for 1969–1971, ed. U.O. Schmelz, Paul Glikson, and S.J. Gould (Jerusalem: 1975), 60–97.

27. See Michael Hammer et al., "Jewish and Middle Eastern Non-Jewish Populations Share a Common Pool of Y-chromosome Biallelic Haplotypes," *Proceedings of the National Academy of Sciences* 97, no. 12 (6 June 2000), 6769–6774; Doron M. Behar et al., "MtDNA Evidence for a Genetic Bottleneck in the Early History of the Ashkenazi Jewish Population," *European Journal of Human Genetics* (2004), 1–10; idem et al., "The Genome-wide Structure of the Jewish People," *Nature* (9 June 2010), 238–242, online at www.nature.com/dofinder/10.1038/nature09103 (accessed 4 April 2012).

28. Tudor Parfitt, *The Lost Tribes: The History of a Myth* (London: 2002).

29. By ruling of Israel's supreme court, conversion from Judaism, as in the case of some ethnic Jews who currently identify with another religion, entails loss of eligibility for Law of Return purposes. Thus, the Falash Mura—a group of Ethiopian non-Jews of Jewish ancestry—must undergo conversion to be eligible for the Law of Return, though such conversions sometimes take place after they have actually immigrated to Israel. For a concise review of the rules of attribution of Jewish personal status in rabbinic and Israeli law, including reference to Jewish sects, isolated communities, and apostates, see Michael Corinaldi, "Jewish Identity," in his *Jewish Identity: The Case of Ethiopian Jewry* (Jerusalem: 1998). On the Law of Return, see Ruth Gavison, *Shishim shanah leḥok hashevut: historiyah, idiologiyah, hatzdakah* (Jerusalem: 2009).

30. U.O. Schmelz (ed.), *Demography and Statistics of Diaspora Jewry 1920–1970; Bibliography*, vol. 1 (Jerusalem: 1976); Roberto Bachi, "Personal Recollections in the History of Research in Jewish Demography," in *Papers in Jewish Demography 1993 in Memory of U.O. Schmelz*, ed. Sergio DellaPergola and Judith Even (Jerusalem: 1997), 33–37.

31. In 2012, at the initiative of an independent team of researchers with the support of the North American Jewish Data Bank and a commercial publisher (Springer), the *American Jewish Year Book* resumed publication.

32. Many of these global activities have been promoted, executed, or coordinated by the division of Jewish demography and statistics at the Avraham Harman Institute of Contemporary Jewry (ICJ), at the Hebrew University.

33. Two major projects sponsored in this framework were an (as yet unpublished) survey of the Jewish population in Buenos Aires by Yaacov Rubel ("La población judía de la ciudad de Buenos Aires, perfil socio-demográfico") and a survey conducted in Israel in 2004–2005 by Sergio DellaPergola, Mina Tzemach, Rimona Viesel, and Moran Neuman, "Fertility Levels in Israel: Jewish Population Performances and Attitudes" (paper presented at World Congress of Jewish Studies, Jerusalem, August 2005).

34. See the Institute's annual reports, and DellaPergola, *Jewish Demographic Policies*.

35. For overviews of subject matter and technical issues, see Paul Ritterband, Barry A. Kosmin, and Jeffrey Scheckner, "Counting Jewish Populations: Methods and Problems," *American Jewish Year Book* 88 (1988), 204–221; DellaPergola, "Demography"; idem, "World Jewish Population 2010."

36. From this point of view, Jews in the former Soviet Union—whose quantitative assessment has often been deemed to rely on weak grounding—have constituted one of the best documented sections of world Jewry. See Mordechai Altshuler, *Soviet Jewry since the Second World War: Population and Social Structure* (Westport: 1987); Mark Tolts, "Jewish Demography of the Former Soviet Union," in DellaPergola and Even (eds.) *Papers in Jewish Demography 1997,* 109–139. See also Mark Tolts' essay in this volume.

37. DellaPergola, "World Jewish Population."

38. For a more detailed review, see ibid.

39. See a synopsis of the main findings in Ira M. Sheskin, *How Jewish Communities Differ: Variations in the Findings of Local Jewish Demographic Studies* (New York: 2001).

40. DellaPergola, "World Jewish Population."

41. András Kovács and Ildiko Barna, *Identity à la carte: Research on Jewish Identities, Participation and Affiliation in Five European Countries. Analysis of Survey Data* (Budapest: 2010).

42. Notably in Buenos Aires at the Centro de Investigaciones Sociales, in the United Kingdom at the Community Research Unit of the Board of Deputies of British Jews, in Germany at the Zentralwohlfhartstelle, in Italy at the Unione delle Comunità Ebraiche Italiane, and in São Paulo at the FISESP.

43. See the essays in Ben Rafael and Sternberg (eds.), *Transnationalism: Diasporas and the Advent of a New (Dis)order.*

44. Mark Tolts, "Demography of the Contemporary Russian-Speaking Jewish Diaspora" (paper presented at the conference on the contemporary Russian-speaking Jewish diaspora, Harvard University, November 2011).

45. On the more problematic aspects of the interrelation between data and interpretations, see below.

46. For the Zionists, see Alfred Nossig, *Materialien zur Statistik des jüdischen Stammes* (Vienna: 1887); Arthur Ruppin, *Die Juden der Gegenwart* (Berlin: 1904); idem, *Soziologie der Juden* (Berlin: 1930); idem, *The Jewish Fate and Future* (London: 1940)—see also Sergio DellaPergola, "Arthur Ruppin Revisited: The Jews of Today, 1904–1994," in *National Variations in Modern Jewish Identity: Implications for Jewish Education,* ed. Steven M. Cohen and Gabriel Horenczyk (Albany: 1999), 53–84; Jacob Lestschinsky, "Probleme der Bevölkerungs-Bewegung bei den Juden," *Metron,* 6, no. 2 (1926), 1–157; idem, "Die Umsiedlung und Umschichtung des jüdischen Volkes im Laufe des letzten Jahrhunderts," a two-part article appearing in *Weltwirtschaftliches Archiv* 30 (1929), 123–156, and ibid. 32, (1930), 563–599; idem, *Crisis, Catastrophe and Survival* (New York: 1948). See also Paul Glikson, "Jacob Lestschinsky: A Bibliographical Survey," *The Jewish Journal of Sociology* 9, no. 1 (1967), 48–57. For diasporists, see Liebmann Hersch, "International Migration of the Jews," in *International Migration,* vol. 2, ed. Walter F. Willcox (New York: 1931), 471–520; idem, *Le Juif delinquant: étude comparative sur la criminalité de la population juive et non-juive de la République Polonaise* (Paris: 1938); Joseph Jacobs, *Studies in Jewish Statistics* (London: 1891). Among non-Jewish scholars, Corrado Gini, the developer of the index of income inequality, was interested both in Italian Jewry and in the Karaite communities in Eastern Europe. See "Alcune ricerche demografiche sugli Israeliti in Padova," *Atti della R. Accademia di Scienze, Lettere e Arti* 32, no. 4 (Padua: 1916), 467–485. For a representative work on Livi, see *Gli ebrei alla luce della statistica* (Florence: 1918–1920, rpt. 1978).

47. Nathan Goldberg, "Occupational Patterns of American Jews," *Jewish Review* 3, no. 4 (1946), 280–290; Salo W. Baron, "Population," *Encyclopaedia Judaica* (Jerusalem: 1971), 13: 866–903 (a large amount of demographic material is also interspersed in Baron's monumental work, *A Social and Religious History of the Jews,* 18 vols. [New York: 1952–1983]); Simon Kuznets, "Economic Structure and Life of the Jews," in *The Jews: Their History, Culture and Religion,* 2nd ed., ed. Louis Finkelstein (New York: 1960), 1597–1666; idem, *Economic Structure of U.S. Jewry: Recent Trends* (Jerusalem: 1972); idem, "Immigration of Russian Jews to the United States: Background and Structure," *Perspectives in American History* 9 (1975), 35–124; Sidney Goldstein and Calvin Goldscheider, *Jewish Americans: Three Generations in a Jewish Community* (Englewood Cliffs: 1968); Sidney Goldstein, "Profile of American Jewry: Insights from the 1990 National Jewish Population Survey," *American Jewish Year Book* 92 (1992), 77–173; idem and Alice Goldstein, *Jews on the Move: Implications for Jewish Identity* (Albany: 1996).

48. Arieh Tartakower, *In Search of Home and Freedom* (London: 1958); Bachi, "Personal Recollections in the History of Research in Jewish Demography"; idem and Sergio DellaPergola, "Did Characteristics of Pre-Emancipation Italian Jewry Deviate from a General Demographic Paradigm for Jewish Traditional Communities?" in *Contemporary Jewry, Studies in Honor of Moshe Davis,* ed. Geoffrey Wigoder (Jerusalem: 1984), 159–189; U.O. Schmelz, "A Guide to Jewish Population Studies," in *Jewish Population Studies 1961–1968,* ed. U.O.

Schmelz and P. Glikson (Jerusalem: 1970), 11–94; idem, "Jewish Survival: The Demographic Factors," *American Jewish Year Book* 81 (1981), 61–117; idem, *World Jewish Population: Regional Estimates and Projections* (Jerusalem: 1981).

49. An example of an incomplete or biased analytic perspective would be a hypothetical study of Jewish education exclusively focusing on—and drawing policy insights from—pupils in Jewish educational systems, without paying attention to Jewish children who do not receive any Jewish education.

50. Ruppin, *Die Juden der Gegenwart*; Robert Park, R.D. McKenzie, and Ernest Burgess, *The City: Suggestions for the Study of Human Nature in the Urban Environment* (Chicago: 1925); Louis Wirth, *The Ghetto* (Chicago: 1928).

51. Shmuel Noah Eisenstadt, *The Absorption of Immigrants* (London: 1954); Milton M. Gordon, *Assimilation in American Life: The Role of Race, Religion and National Origins* (New York: 1964).

52. Ruppin, *The Jewish Fate and Future*; U.O. Schmelz, *World Jewish Population: Regional Estimates and Projections* (Jerusalem: 1981).

53. Sergio Della Pergola, *La trasformazione demografica della diaspora ebraica*, (Turin: 1983); idem, "Major Demographic Trends of World Jewry: The Last Hundred Years," in *Genetic Diversity among the Jews*, ed. Batsheva Bonné-Tamir and Avinoam Adam (New York: 1992), 3–30; idem, "Some Fundamentals of Jewish Demographic History," in DellaPergola and Even (eds.) *Papers in Jewish Demography 1997*, 11–33; idem, "Between Science and Fiction: Notes on the Demography of the Holocaust," *Holocaust and Genocide Studies* 10, no. 1 (1996), 34–51. See also Hayim Shalom Halevi, *Hashpa'at milḥemet ha'olam hasheniyah 'al hatekhunot hademografiyot shel 'am yisrael* (Jerusalem: 1963).

54. See the several volumes devoted to the topic by the journal *Contemporary Jewry*, sponsored by the Association for the Social Scientific Study of Jewry.

55. Compare the local- and national-oriented approaches in Jeffrey Lesser and Raanan Rein, *Rethinking Jewish Latin-Americans* (Albuquerque: 2008) versus the comparative-transnational approaches in Judit Bokser Liwerant, Sergio DellaPergola, Haim Avni, Margalit Bejarano, and Leonardo Senkman, "Cuarenta años de cambios: transiciones y paradigmas," in *Pertenencia y alteridad: Judíos en/de America Latina: cuarenta años de cambio*, ed. Haim Avni, Judit Bokser Liwerant, Sergio DellaPergola, Margalit Bejarano, and Leonardo Senkman (Madrid: 2011), 13–83.

56. "The eternal glory of Israel shall not fail" (I Samuel, 15:29).

57. See, for instance, Calvin Goldscheider, *The American Jewish Community: Social Science Research and Policy Implications* (Atlanta: 1986); Steven M. Cohen, *American Assimilation or Jewish Revival?* (Bloomington: 1988).

58. This view is classically reflected in Karl Marx, "Zur Judenfrage," *Deutsch Franzosische Jahrbücher* (1844), but it also appears—in the totally different context of the revival of an autonomous Jewish society in Palestine—in the writings of Arthur Ruppin. See his *Memoirs, Diaries, Letters*, ed. Alex Bein (London: 1971).

59. DellaPergola, *Jewish Demographic Policies*. For a reflection on which might be the most appropriate interpretive framework, see Marshall Sklare, "On the Preparation of a Sociology of American Jewry," in *Understanding American Jewry*, ed. Marshall Sklare (New Brunswick: 1982), 261–271.

60. Sergio DellaPergola, "Jewish Women in Transition: A Comparative Sociodemographic Perspective," in *Studies in Contemporary Jewry*, vol. 16, *Jews and Gender: The Challenge to Hierarchy*, ed. Jonathan Frankel (New York: 2000), 209–242; Harriet Hartman and Moshe Hartman, *Gender and American Jews: Patterns in Work, Education, and Family in Contemporary Life* (Hanover: 2009).

61. Sergio DellaPergola, Uzi Rebhun, and Mark Tolts, " Contemporary Jewish Diaspora in Global Context: Human Development Correlates of Population Trends," *Israel Studies* 11, no. 1 (2005), 61–95.

62. For interpretations of Jewish demographic and socioeconomic patterns focusing on minority-majority interaction, see Kuznets, "Economic Structure and Life of the Jews"; idem, *Economic Structure of U.S. Jewry: Recent Trends* (Jerusalem: 1972); Calvin Goldscheider,

Population, Modernization and Social Structure (Boston: 1971), ch. 10. See also Barry Chiswick, "The Occupational Attainment and Earnings of American Jewry, 1890–1990," *Contemporary Jewry* 20 (1999), 68–98; idem, *The Earnings of American Jewish Men: Human Capital, Denomination and Religiosity*, IZA [Institute for the Study of Labor] discussion paper no. 2301 (Bonn: 2006).

63. See, for instance, Kingsley Davis and Judith Blake, "Social Structure and Fertility, an Analytic Framework," *Economic Development and Cultural Change*, 4 (1956), 211–223.

64. See, for instance, Ruth Dixon, "Explaining Cross-Cultural Variations in Age at Marriage and Proportions Never Marrying," *Population Studies* 25, no. 2 (1971), 215–233.

65. Massimo Livi Bacci, "Social-group Forerunners of Fertility Control in Europe," in *The Decline of Fertility in Europe*, ed. Ansley Coale and Susan Cotts Watkins (Princeton: 1986) 182–200.

66. See the critique in Charles E. Silberman, *A Certain People: American Jews and Their Lives Today* (New York: 1985).

67. Anat Leibler, "Statistician's Ambition: Governmentality, Modernity and National Legibility," *Israel Studies* 9, no. 2 (2004), 121–149.

68. See, for instance, Sophie M. Robison with Joshua Starr, *Jewish Population Studies* (New York: 1943); Goldstein and Goldscheider, *Jewish Americans*; Goldstein, "Profile of American Jewry," 77–173; Roberta Rosenberg Farber and Chaim I. Waxman, *Jews in America: A Contemporary Reader* (Hanover: 1999); Uzi Rebhun, *Hagirah, kehilah, hizdahut: yehudei aratzot habrit beshalhei hameah ha'esrim* (Jerusalem: 2001); Sergio DellaPergola, "Was It the Demography? A Reassessment of U.S. Jewish Population Estimates, 1945–2001," *Contemporary Jewry* 25 (2005), 85–131.

69. Unlike censuses, whose mandate is typically to cover the entire existing population, surveys are based on sampling from the total population. Because they directly question only a tiny minority out of the total population, their findings must be interpreted in the light of sampling errors and other biases that can be predicted on the basis of statistical theory. See U.S. Bureau of the Census, "Religion Reported by the Civilian Population in the United States, March 1957," *Current Population Reports, Population Characteristics*, Series P-20, No. 79 (Washington, D.C.: 1958); idem, *Tabulations of Data on the Social and Economic Characteristics of Major Religious Groups, March 1957* (Washington, D.C.: 1968). The lack of gender-related political correctness appeared in the original questionnaire.

70. Fred Massarik, "National Jewish Population Study: A New United States Estimate," *American Jewish Year Book* 75 (1974), 296–304; idem, "The Boundary of Jewishness: Some Measures of Jewish Identity in the United States," in *Papers in Jewish Demography* 1973, ed. U.O. Schmelz and Sergio DellaPergola (Jerusalem: 1977), 117–139; Bernard Lazerwitz, "An Estimate of a Rare Population Group—The U.S. Jewish Population," *Demography* 15, no. 3 (1978), 389–394; Ira Rosenwaike, "A Synthetic Estimate of American Jewish Population Movement over the Last Three Decades," in *Papers in Jewish Demography* 1977, ed. U.O. Schmelz and Sergio DellaPergola (Jerusalem: 1980), 83–102.

71. For an example of past Jewish communities' commitment to research, see Jerry A. Winter and Lester I. Levin (eds.), *Advancing the State of the Art: Colloquium on Jewish Population Studies,* 2 vols. (New York: 1984).

72. Egon Mayer, Barry Kosmin, and Ariela Keysar, *American Jewish Identity Survey 2001: An Exploration in the Demography and Outlook of a People* (New York: 2002).

73. U.O. Schmelz, *World Jewish Population: Regional Estimates and Projections* (Jerusalem: 1981); U.O. Schmelz and Sergio DellaPergola, "The Demographic Consequences of U.S. Jewish Population Trends," *American Jewish Year Book* 83 (1983), 141–187; idem, *Basic Trends in American Jewish Demography* (New York: 1988); Vivian Klaff, "Broken Down by Sex and Age: Projecting the American Jewish Population," *Contemporary Jewry* 19 (1998), 1–37.

74. Gary Tobin and Sid Groenman, *Surveying the Jewish Population in the United States*, Part 1: *Population Estimate*; Part 2: *Methodological Issues and Challenges* (San Francisco: 2003).

75. Barry A. Kosmin and Ariela Keysar, *American Religious Identification Survey (ARIS 2008) Summary Report* (Hartford: 2009).

76. Pew Forum on Religion and Public Life, *U.S. Religious Landscape Survey, Religious Affiliation: Diverse and Dynamic* (Washington, D.C.: 2008).

77. Elizabeth Tighe, Leonard Saxe, Darren Brown, Jennifer Dillinger, Aron Klein, and Ashley Hill, *Research Synthesis of National Survey Estimates of the U.S. Jewish Population: Project Summary, Method and Analysis Plan* (Waltham: 2005).

78. Leonard Saxe, Elizabeth Tighe, and Benjamin Phillips, with Ariel Libhaber, Daniel Parmer, Jessica Simon, and Graham Wright, *Understanding Contemporary American Jewry* (Waltham: 2006).

79. Tom Smith, personal communication, January 2011. See also Tom W. Smith, *Religious Switching among American Jews* (New York: 2009).

80. J.J. Goldberg, "A Jewish Recount," *New York Times* (17 September 2003), 27.

81. There actually were no "lost data." What was lost was some important technical information about data collection that would later be missed at the stage of evaluating the survey's exact response rates and sampling errors—hence the range of variation of population estimates. Mark Schulman, one of the leading statistical consultants in the United States, was asked by UJC to independently review and assess the NJPS methodology. His main conclusion was that, while the NJPS suffered from a number of mishandlings and should be given comparatively low marks, it was usable and in any case within the range of acceptable professional standards. See Mark Schulman, "National Jewish Population Survey 2000–2001: Study Review Memo" (unpublished report, New York: 2003).

82. DellaPergola, *Jewish Demographic Policies*.

83. Chaim Waxman, *Jewish Baby Boomers: A Communal Perspective* (Albany: 2001).

84. Ira M. Sheskin and Arnold Dashefsky, *Jewish Population in the United States, 2009–10* (North American Jewish Data Bank, Current Jewish Population Reports 1) (Storrs, Conn.: 2010).

85. Elizabeth Tighe, Leonard Saxe, and Charles Kadushin, with assistance from Raquel Magidin dee Kramer, Begli Nursahedov, Janet Aronson, and Lynn Cherny, *Estimating the Jewish Population of the United States: 2000–2010* (Waltham: 2011) (draft).

86. See United States Census Bureau, *Statistical Abstract of the United States* (Washington, D.C.: 2012).

87. Sidney Goldstein, "American Jewish Demography: Inconsistencies that Challenge," in *Papers in Jewish Demography* 1985, ed. U.O. Schmelz and Sergio DellaPergola (Jerusalem: 1989), 23–42; Sheskin, *How Jewish Communities Differ*.

88. Uzi Rebhun and Sidney Goldstein, "Changes in the Geographical Dispersion and Mobility of American Jews, 1990–2001," *Jewish Journal of Sociology* 48, no. 1 (2006), 5–33.

89. For the original detailed data, see Tighe et al., *Estimating the Jewish Population of the United States*.

90. Calvin Goldscheider, *Studying the Jewish Future* (Seattle: 2004).

91. Joe Berkofsky, "Experts Find Holes in Survey, But Say NJPS Remains Useful," Jewish Telegraphic Agency (JTA) (29 October 2003).

92. DellaPergola, *World Jewish Population*.

93. Sheskin and Dashefsky, *Jewish Population in the United States*; Tighe et al., *Estimating the Jewish Population of the United States*.

94. Benedict Anderson, *Imagined Communities: Reflections on the Origin and Spread of Nationalism* (London: 1991).

95. Zvi Gitelman, "The Decline of the Diaspora Jewish Nation: Boundaries, Content and Jewish Identity," *Jewish Social Studies* (n.s.) 4 (1998), 112–132; Steven Cohen, *De-constructing the Outreach-Inreach Debate* (Jerusalem: 1996).

96. Bruce A. Phillips, *Re-examining Intermarriage: Trends, Textures, Strategies* (New York: 1997); Steven M. Cohen and Arnold M. Eisen, *The Jew Within: Self, Family, and Community in America* (Bloomington: 2000); Lasse Dencik, "'Homo Zappiens': A European-Jewish Way of Life in the Era of Globalisation," *Paideia* (2002), 1–34; Bethamie Horowitz, *Connections and Journeys: Assessing Critical Opportunities for Enhancing Jewish Identity*

(New York: 2003); Chaim I. Waxman, "Jewish Identity and Identification of America's Young Jews," in *Facing Tomorrow: Background Policy Documents*, ed. Rami Tal and Barry Geltman (Jerusalem: 2008), 173–178; Sergio DellaPergola, Shlomit Levy, Uzi Rebhun, and Dalia Sagi, "Patterns of Jewish Identification in the United States, 2001," in *Theory Construction and Multivariate Analysis: Applications of Facet Approach*, ed. Dov Elizur and Eyal Yaniv (Tel Aviv: 2009), 305–318.

97. Goldscheider, *Studying the Jewish Future*.

98. Bethamie Horowitz, "Reframing the Study of Contemporary American Jewish Identity," *Contemporary Jewry* 23 (2002), 14–34.

99. Theodore Sasson, Charles Kadushin, and Leonard Saxe, "Trends in American Jewish Attachment to Israel: An Assessment of the 'Distancing' Hypothesis," *Contemporary Jewry* 30, nos. 2–3 (2010), 297–319, and 149–153 (the latter a rebuttal); Leonard Saxe, Benjamin Phillips, Theodore Sasson, Shahar Hecht, Michelle Shain, Graham Wright, and Charles Kadushin, "Intermarriage: The Impact and Lessons of Taglit-Birthright Israel," *Contemporary Jewry* 31, no. 2 (2011), 151–172; DellaPergola, "Was it the Demography?"

100. Israel Central Bureau of Statistics, *Statistical Abstract of Israel* (Jerusalem: yearly).

101. See, among others, Roberto Bachi, *The Population of Israel* (Jerusalem: 1977); Dov Friedlander and Calvin Goldscheider, *The Population of Israel* (New York: 1979); U.O. Schmelz, Sergio DellaPergola, and Uri Avner, *Ethnic Differences among Israeli Jews: A New Look* (Jerusalem: 1991); Calvin Goldscheider (ed.), *Population and Social Change in Israel* (Boulder: 1992); Sergio DellaPergola, "Demographic Changes in Israel in the Early 1990s," in *Israel Social Services 1992–93*, ed. Yaacov Kop (Jerusalem: 1993), 57–115; Calvin Goldscheider, *Israel's Changing Society: Population, Ethnicity, and Development* (Boulder: 1996); Uzi Rebhun and Chaim I. Waxman (eds.), *Jews in Israel: Contemporary Social and Cultural Patterns* (Hanover: 2004).

102. Sergio DellaPergola, "Demographic Trends in Israel and Palestine: Prospects and Policy Implications," *American Jewish Year Book* 103 (2003), 3–68.

103. Bennett Zimmerman, Roberta Seid, and Michael L. Wise, "Battle of Numbers: What Demographic Time Bomb?" *Jerusalem Post* (17 May 2005).

104. DellaPergola, "World Jewish Population 2010."

105. East Jerusalem is here defined as all territory incorporated within the Jerusalem municipality soon after the June 1967 war. It includes the urban parts of the city of Jerusalem that were incorporated in the Hashemite Kingdom of Jordan after the 1948 war, and larger suburban areas, of which parts were inhabited by Arabs in 1967 and parts were not built up. On some of the latter areas, several new Jewish neighborhoods were built, which in 2011 housed just over 40 percent of Jerusalem's total Jewish population. See U.O. Schmelz, *Modern Jerusalem's Demographic Evolution* (Jerusalem: 1987); Sergio DellaPergola, "Jerusalem's Population, 1995–2020: Demography, Multiculturalism and Urban Policies," *European Journal of Population* 17, no. 2 (2001), 165–199.

106. Palestine National Authority, Palestinian Central Bureau of Statistics, *Population, Housing and Establishment Census 1997, Final Census Results* (Ramallah: 1998); Palestinian National Authority, Palestinian Central Bureau of Statistics, *Population, Housing and Establishment Census 2007. Census Final Results—Population Report—Palestinian Territory* (Ramallah: 2012); also see website at www.pcbs.gov.ps.

107. Israel Central Bureau of Statistics, *Statistical Abstract of Israel* 62 (Jerusalem: 2011), table 3.1. For the Israel Central Bureau of Statistics website, see www.cbs.gov.il.

108. DellaPergola, "Demographic Trends in Israel and Palestine"; idem, "Correspondence," *Azure* 27 (2007), 3–33; idem, "Israel's Existential Predicament: Population, Territory and Identity," *Current History* 109 (December 2010), 383–389; Evgenia Bystrov and Arnon Soffer, *Israel: Demography and Density 2007–2020* (Haifa: 2008).

109. Bennett Zimmerman, Roberta Seid, and Michael L. Wise, "Voodoo Demographics," *Azure* 25 (2006).

110. A more detailed rebuttal appears in Sergio DellaPergola, "Population Trends and Scenarios in Israel and Palestine," in *Population Resettlement in International Conflicts: A*

Comparative Study, ed. Arie M. Kacowicz and Pavel Lutomski (Lanham: 2007), 183–207; idem, *Jewish Demographic Politics*.

111. DellaPergola, "Jerusalem's Population, 1995–2020: Demography, Multiculturalism and Urban Policies"; idem, "Demographic Trends in Israel and Palestine."

112. Sergio DellaPergola, Uzi Rebhun, and Mark Tolts, "Prospecting the Jewish Future: Population Projections, 2000–2080," *American Jewish Year Book* 100 (2000), 103–146.

Measuring the Size and Characteristics of American Jewry: A New Paradigm to Understand an Ancient People

Leonard Saxe, Elizabeth Tighe, and Matthew Boxer
(BRANDEIS UNIVERSITY)

In the last several decades, the Jewish community in the United States has invested more resources in socio-demographic studies of the Jewish population than in any other type of systematic research.[1] National studies of the size and characteristics of American Jewry were conducted by the Council of Jewish Federations in 1970 and in 1990, and also in 2000 (by which time the organization had been renamed the United Jewish Communities). In addition, many large and moderately sized Jewish federations conduct decennial studies of their populations.[2] Although recent socio-demographic work on the U.S. Jewish population is too fresh to evaluate comprehensively, the research has stimulated contentious debate about the trajectory of contemporary Jewish life. Discourse has focused on different, deeply held narratives of the Jewish future; underlying the discussion are a set of disagreements about the reliability and validity of the research. The intensity of these methodologically fueled debates has increased in recent years, reflecting both the difficulties of identifying a Jewish population that is highly integrated in American society and the increased complexity and sophistication of social research.

This essay focuses on the state of methodology with regard to counting and assessing the characteristics of U.S. Jewry. There is already an extensive methodological literature on past efforts to measure this population.[3] We seek first to provide a contemporary update and will then outline a new paradigm for counting and describing American Jews. We also consider the role of socio-demographic studies in providing scholarly understanding of U.S. Jewish life and the development of communal policy.

Conceptual Considerations

Contemporary problems of counting U.S. Jewry are challenging. The U.S. census, the only full population count of the country, has never asked Americans to identify themselves by religion,[4] in part because of concern on the part of members of religious minorities (including the Jewish community) that such identification would lead to discrimination. In the absence of a census, scholars of the American Jewish community have relied in recent decades on two strategies to produce estimates: (a) the systematic combination of local population estimates; and (b) national, community-sponsored population surveys.[5]

Unfortunately, neither local nor national surveys provide fully adequate estimates. In the case of local surveys, although it is estimated that 80 percent or more of the U.S. Jewish population live in a few dozen metropolitan areas,[6] many of these communities do not conduct demographic studies at regular intervals, and some do not conduct them at all. Smaller communities outside of these few dozen areas typically lack the resources to commission demographic studies; consequently, information is lacking for about 20 percent of the American Jewish population. Perhaps more problematic, there is little standardization across studies, and their sampling designs yield difficult-to-interpret findings. Lack of standardization is due, in large part, to the fact that such studies are developed for the benefit of sponsoring communities rather than the national polity and are typically overseen by groups of laypeople. Thus, they often reflect parochial interests and, because of limited resources and poor understanding of survey techniques, fail to use cutting-edge methodologies.

A common methodological flaw of local community studies is that they rely on list-based methods, such as synagogue or Federation lists, that tend to overestimate affiliated Jews and to undercount those who are less active or visible in the Jewish community. Furthermore, because there is little synchronization among studies and the Jewish population is highly mobile, a household that moves from one community to another may end up counted in one community, in neither, or in both. Similarly, seasonal residents who spend part of the year in each of two or more communities may be included or excluded depending on the time of year in which the survey is conducted.[7] In addition, there are a host of issues with regard to ensuring representative samples of subgroups of American Jews, among them young adults and immigrant populations; in particular, those from the former Soviet Union and Israel.

For national surveys of the Jews, the underlying issue is that American Jewry is a "rare population," accounting for approximately 2 percent of the total number of individuals in the United States. This means that any probability-based sample, whether address-based or based on random-digit-dialing (RDD), will reach far more non-Jews than Jews, making such samples extremely expensive. Figure 2.1 illustrates this problem, showing the number of screener interviews required to achieve a sample of 1,000 respondents of a rare population by incidence of the population. The bend of the curve reveals that the number of interviews required (and, thus, the cost of identifying the population) increases significantly at an incidence of 4–5 percent and may be unfeasible below 2 percent of the population.

This sampling problem has been exacerbated over the last two decades because of changes in the telephone system and the profusion of surveys that flood Americans' telephones, email, and mail. The introduction and proliferation of technologies such as caller ID, call blocking, privacy managers, answering machines, and voicemail make it easier to avoid survey researchers and have led to a steep decline in response rates.[8] Additionally, more than one-third of U.S. households lack landline telephones,[9] a fact that creates several problems for use of RDD sampling frames. The

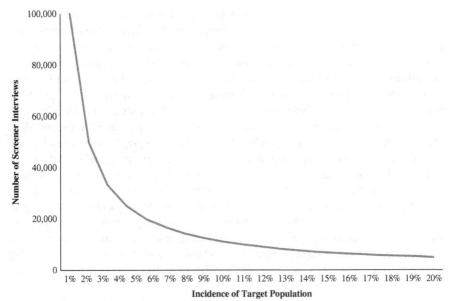

Figure 2.1. Screener interviews required for a sample of n = 1,000

federal Telemarketing Consumer Protection Act of 1991 (47 U.S.C. 227) prohibits use of auto-dialers to contact wireless telephones without the user's prior expressed consent. Moreover, the ethical guidelines of the American Association for Public Opinion Research (AAPOR), the leading association of public opinion and survey researchers in the United States, note that soliciting survey respondents on their wireless phones potentially exposes them to greater risk of physical harm than if they were contacted on landlines, particularly if they are "operating a motor vehicle or any type of potentially harmful machinery...during a research interview."[10] Further, because wireless phone users sometimes have to pay for the time they spend on the phone even when someone else has called them, they may be less willing to cooperate.

The widespread growth of survey research also threatens response rates. Both customer satisfaction surveys and political polls have become nearly ubiquitous.[11] There is longstanding concern that the growth of survey research and subsequent increase in number of contacts per person will depress response rates.[12] Indeed, a wide array of surveys—across topics and using different methodologies—has been marked by declining response rates.[13] Surveys of U.S. Jews are clearly affected by this problem, which has sometimes led to controversial sampling techniques with attendant statistical adjustments. In addition, there is the question of how best to address the complexity of contemporary Jewish identity within the format of population surveys.[14]

The increasing expense and difficulty of relying on RDD sampling frames in national studies of the Jewish community is illustrated by two of the National Jewish Population Surveys (NJPS), those of 1990 and 2000–2001.[15] The 1990 NJPS, comprising an amalgam of data collected as part of omnibus market research surveys, was relatively inexpensive. Its successor was more costly, with an initial budget of $2.5 million that eventually ballooned to a reported $6 million.[16] The overruns were attributed to a series of methodological difficulties, including low response rates.[17]

The sampling issues are made complex by the difficulty of applying uniform definitions of Jewish identity. Intermarriage and secularization, in particular, have created a host of problems in terms of framing questions about who is Jewish. "Who is a Jew" is no longer a binary categorization, but rather a social classification with vague boundaries that depends variously on Jewish law (halakhah), religious identity, ethnicity, culture, language, and/or descent. Accordingly, "who is a Jew" to one person may not be considered Jewish by another. Further, individual survey respondents may identify themselves inconsistently across surveys, perhaps depending on the context and question wording.[18] Thus, studies of the American Jewish population are socio-psychological assessments, less concerned with the precise location of boundaries between Jewish and non-Jewish than with the ways in which those boundaries are socially constructed and reconstructed in different contexts. In general, a survey respondent's claim of Jewish identity is accepted at face value. Theological perspectives are not determinative, although they can influence individuals' views of their identity.

Definitional concerns notwithstanding, for most purposes of understanding American Jewry, the exact size of the population is not a central concern. Although changes in the size of the population can reflect the extent to which Jewish identity is valued, knowing the size of the American Jewish community does not, in itself, yield useful information about the lived behavior or attitudes of individual Jews. At the same time, reliable and valid estimates that can be compared over time do provide some useful information and are the basis for other, more substantive descriptions of the state of the community.

Further complicating the interpretation of socio-demographic studies of the U.S. Jewish population is the fact that most national population surveys rely on complex sample designs, with some areas oversampled and with statistical adjustments applied, post hoc, to improve estimates. Such design and post-stratification weights account for the complexity of the design, as well as factors that could bias the estimates. Biases result from survey non-response and over- or underrepresentation of particular groups. Decisions about which factors to include in calculating weights can greatly influence the resultant estimates. The greater the bias in the sample, the larger the effect such weighting decisions have on final estimates.[19]

The need for adjustments to account for a particular sub-sample that participates in a survey is common. Typically, however, adjustments to account for disproportionate sampling are based on externally valid data about the population. This presents particular challenges to Jewish population surveys because, unlike demographic characteristics such as age and sex that can be compared against the U.S. census, there is no valid source of data on the distribution of the Jewish population in the United States. The expense of conducting a national population survey, combined with low response rates and the potential bias introduced by sampling error and weighting, point to a need for a new method to estimate the American Jewish population—one that is cost-effective as well as sensitive to and able to account for the variation in estimates that are introduced by different study and sampling designs.

A New Paradigm

In the wake of the challenges inherent in the use of general population surveys to study American Jews, we have been developing a new approach to estimation of the size and characteristics of the population.[20] The methodology is based on the premise that no single study (or survey) is without error. Our methodology improves estimation by drawing on repeated independent sampling of the entire U.S. population and synthesizing data across these repeated observations. The methods go beyond simple averaging of all the estimates. Instead, the raw individual-level data across studies are combined by means of statistical techniques that take into account the different variance distributions, thereby enabling not only overall estimates across surveys, but also distributions by age, sex, education, and geographic areas. These distributions can then be used to evaluate and adjust for bias in targeted surveys.[21]

Combining multiple data sources to increase the reliability of estimates is the basic premise of traditional meta-analytic methods,[22] and more recently of methods of small area estimation (SAE).[23] The Jewish population estimation project goes beyond the traditional meta-analytic approach by synthesizing original data rather than relying on summary statistics from each data source. Furthermore, the approach extends SAE methods. Rather than relying on the assumption that repeated independent samples from the surveys can be combined, each survey sample is treated as unique; thus, the specific properties of each survey, in particular survey variances, are taken into account when the data are combined. This method also affords the ability to be able to explore other potential sources of bias in sample surveys, such as response rates, survey purpose, survey sponsorship, and question wording. A key feature of this approach is that all available and relevant sources of data are reviewed. The systematic review of a representative sample of studies or surveys allows one to assess the reliability of estimates from individual studies. This is particularly important in estimating the size of a small population group. As Jon Rao explains: "In making estimates for small areas with adequate level of precision, it is often necessary to use 'indirect' estimators that 'borrow strength' by using values of the variable of interest, *y*, from related areas and/or time periods and thus increase the 'effective' sample size."[24]

In the present case, we "borrow strength" from the vast extant data on religious/ethnic identification for our variable of interest—whether a person is Jewish—along with related factors such as geographic dispersion and demographic composition. These data were not originally collected for the purpose of population estimation, and certainly not for estimating the Jewish population in particular. All of the surveys, however, are designed to provide representative samples of the U.S. population and include assessment of religious or ethnic identification. They are thus well-suited for purposes of population estimation. In addition, the surveys are fielded with sufficient frequency as to generate a substantial amount of data on the subgroup of the U.S. population that self-identifies as Jewish. Typically, the data emerge from a question about current religious identity or affiliation. A smaller number of surveys include assessment of religious upbringing or parents' religious/ethnic identification, or non-religious Jewish identification (for instance, "Do you consider yourself Jewish?") in addition to current religious affiliation. Data from this subset of surveys can be used both as part of the full sample of surveys used to estimate the proportion of the U.S.

population that identifies as Jewish by religion and, as well, for supplemental analyses of the subset of the population that identifies as Jewish in other ways.

Although any single survey might contain too few respondents who identify as Jewish to serve as a reliable source of data on its own, systematically combining data from repeated, independent samples of the U.S. population provides a highly reliable source of data. It allows one to describe the basic demographic composition of the U.S. Jewish population. Such data syntheses have become common throughout the social sciences and biomedical and physical sciences[25] but have yet to be utilized in the study of the Jewish population.

The results described here focus on data related to the estimation of the adult Jewish population as identified through responses to questions about religious identity. With estimates of the adult population who self-identify by religion as a base, additional sources of data that assess other forms of Jewish identification, such as lineage or ethnicity, or that assess subgroups (children/youth) can be used to supplement or adjust population estimates. Self-identification by religion accounts for a substantial proportion of the population and is the group that is most commonly assessed across the many general population surveys conducted in the United States. Often the question is asked as "What is your religion? Is it Protestant, Roman Catholic, Jewish, something else, or no religion?" With increased attention to the variety of religious groups in the United States, and depending on the purpose of the survey, the discrete options that are provided may vary. For example, the series of surveys on religion and public life conducted jointly by the Pew Research Center for the People and the Press and the Pew Forum on Religion asks, "What is your religious preference, do you consider yourself Christian, Jewish, Muslim, other non-Christian such as Buddhist or Hindu, atheist, agnostic, something else, or don't you have a religious preference?" Nearly all include Jewish as one of the discrete options. A few surveys, such as the American Jewish Identity Survey (AJIS) and NJPS, provide no discrete options. Instead they ask simply, "What is your religion, if any?" and record all self-generated responses to the question. Whether the way the question is asked or worded influences Jewish population estimates can be examined directly and taken into account as necessary.

The breadth of available data is displayed in Figure 2.2, which shows the estimated percentage of the U.S. population that self-identifies as Jewish (by religion) across a subsample of 128 surveys of the U.S. population conducted between 2000 and 2008 that are part of our database.[26] The bars around each estimate indicate the confidence interval, or the range that is expected to include the "true population" proportion that identify as Jewish based on the particular sample of people included in each survey. Factors such as how many people were surveyed and what kinds of weighting and adjustments were employed affect this range. The lowest estimate was observed in a survey conducted by International Communications Research (ICR) for a group at Georgetown University in 2006, which estimated that less than 1 percent of U.S. adults identified as Jewish by religion. The highest was 3.2 percent, observed in one of Gallup's 2008 "mood of the nation" polls.

Although many of the surveys yield estimates that are substantially higher than previous Jewish population-focused surveys, some surveys yield estimates of 1.3 percent and 1.4 percent, on par with that observed in the 2000 NJPS and the 2000

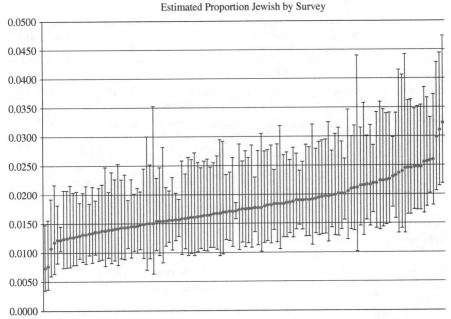

Figure 2.2. Estimated proportion Jewish by survey, 2000 to 2008

AJIS. These include a CBS news poll conducted in 2007, a Gallup survey in 2004, an ABC poll in 2005, and two of the Pew surveys on religion and public life. The religion and public life survey conducted in April 2001 indicated that 1.2 percent of the population was Jewish by religious identification. The same survey, administered just two years later in 2003, indicated that 1.8 percent self-identified as Jewish. And, in 2006 and 2007, respectively, the estimates from this survey were 2.2 percent and 1.8 percent. In 2007, Pew sponsored the U.S. Religious Landscape Survey, which was a large-scale survey of more than 35,000 people. This survey estimated 1.7 percent of the population as Jewish, with a confidence interval that ranged from 1.6 percent to 1.9 percent.[27] Other surveys, such as the Baylor Religion Survey, estimate more than 2 percent of the population as Jewish.[28]

Any single sample of the same underlying population yields a somewhat different estimate of that population. The advantage of the current approach is that, rather than relying exclusively on one source and ignoring all others, we examine the range in estimates. The goal is to determine how best to derive meaning from these multiple snapshots of the U.S. population. Any number of factors could affect an estimate observed in a single sample, such as the purpose of the survey, the identity of the person conducting or sponsoring the survey, or even methodological idiosyncrasies affecting the makeup of the sample. The benefit of our approach is that the variability in these estimates and possible explanations can be analyzed directly.

To identify surveys to include in our analyses, major data repositories were searched for any studies conducted since the year 2000 that assessed religious identification or affiliation.[29] The archives included the Inter-University Consortium for Political and

Table 2.1. Characteristics of the Surveys

	Number of Surveys	Percent of Surveys		Number of Surveys	Percent of Surveys
Primary Purpose			*Survey Organization*		
Religion	26	19	Princeton Survey Research Assoc.	42	30
Politics	63	45	University-affiliated	16	11
Social life	14	10	SRBI	14	10
Other	37	26	TNS Research	24	17
			Major poll/news poll	33	24
Survey Sponsor			Other private survey group	11	8
Pew	48	34			
News and other polls	56	40	*Respondent Selection*		
University	30	21	Kish selection method	17	12
Other	6	4	Last birthday		
			youngest male/ youngest female	42	30
Question Wording			youngest male/ oldest female	24	17
Open-ended	34	24	youngest male/ youngest female (proportional selection)	23	16
Closed-ended	106	76	last birthday, unspecified	12	9
			"Random" adult	8	6
			Other	7	5
			Unspecified	7	5
Response Rates[a]			*Sample Sizes*		
Greater than 40%	14	10	< 3,000	124	88
			3,000–5,000	11	8
Valid Response to Religion			> 5,000	5	4
Average across all surveys		97			

[a] Response rates calculated using Response Rate 3 of the American Association for Public Opinion Research standard definitions; see http://www.aapor.org/AM/Template.cfm?Section=Standard_Definitions2&Template=/CM/ContentDisplay.cfm&ContentID=3156. Average response rate across all surveys was 31%, with a standard deviation of 14%. The average across all surveys for response rates to the religious identification question was 97%, with a standard deviation of +/1–1%.

Social Research (ICPSR) and the American Religion Data Archive (ARDA), as well as collections such as the Institute for Quantitative Social Sciences Dataverse Network at Harvard. In addition, poll archives at the Odum Institute, the Roper Center, Gallup, and Pew Research were searched. Keywords used for each of the databases were: religion; relig*; Protestant; Catholic; Jewish; denom*; religious preference; and religious id*. Searches of the social science and religious studies literature were also conducted. Criteria for inclusion were: (1) a nationally representative sample of the U.S. adult population;[30] (2) information to classify respondents by current religious identity; and (3) baseline demographic information (sex, race, education, and age). The search strategy yielded 301 surveys conducted since the year 2000.

Although the goal was to include all available sources, constraints on time and resources caused priority to be given to surveys with the greatest sample sizes (at least 1,000 respondents or more), and, within any given year, to a representative sample of surveys from different sources. The analyses reported below are based on a set of 140 independent samples of the U.S. adult population collected between 2000 and 2008, with a total of 390,728 respondents. About 20 percent of the surveys specifically addressed topics of religion (see Table 2.1). The rest were on more general topics such as politics, social life, health care issues, and combinations thereof. The average response rate across the surveys was 31 percent, with a high of 73 percent. Average response to the religious identity question across the surveys was 97 percent, and more than 75 percent of the surveys obtained a valid response rate of more than 98 percent to this particular question.

Combining Data across Surveys

In traditional design-based survey analysis, weights are used to account for the factors associated with the sample design, including adjustments such as post-stratification and non-response. Most surveys have unique methods of sampling and weighting. In many cases, the sample sizes are designed for estimation of the U.S. population as a whole rather than specific subgroups. This limits adjustments that can be made based on geographic and demographic distributions of respondents. For example, although there is tremendous variation in the Jewish population across U.S. states and across metropolitan areas, many surveys have only a sufficient number of cases to adjust for broad geographic regions. Weighting procedures that do not take into account the particular factors associated with Jewish population estimation will be biased; that is, they will either over- or underestimate the population depending on how the sample that was obtained compared to the Jewish population as a whole.

Thus, rather than relying solely on design-based analysis weights provided by the original researchers—which were developed for purposes other than Jewish population estimation—the present approach is model-based,[31] meaning that sampling variables and their effect, if any, on Jewish population estimates are examined directly. Due to the substantial variability within geographic regions—the Jewish population tends to cluster in metropolitan areas—and the lack of surveys with sufficient number of respondents for reliable estimates of smaller geographic areas down to the state level, we employ a method (hierarchical Bayesian analysis) that is better suited to estimation of small cell sizes such as this.[32] Results from this analysis are then used to obtain estimates post-stratified to the U.S. population totals for sampling variables such as age, education, state, and metropolitan status, which are included in the model.[33]

For the set of surveys from 2000 to 2008, once variables associated with sampling are included, there is very little variability associated with the surveys themselves. Survey variance is .01, which corresponds to an intra-class correlation of .003 and a Median Odds Ratio (MOR) of 1.1. The MOR is a way to quantify the variation between surveys in terms of odds ratios, in this case the likelihood (or odds) that any given individual identifies as Jewish. An MOR of 1.1 indicates that, given two persons with the same covariates, randomly chosen from two different surveys, the odds that the person identifies as Jewish in the survey with the lowest estimated proportion of Jews are nearly equal (1.1 times) to the odds that a person identifies as Jewish in the survey with the highest estimated proportion of Jews. Thus, although surveys may have varied in the specifics of how the particular question used to assess Jewish identity was asked, or the purpose for which the survey was conducted, or the type of organization that collected the data, once one takes into account the composition of the survey samples—that is, the distributions of age, race, education, and geographic composition (by state and metropolitan area) across the many independent samples—the surveys yield highly similar estimates.

Results from the model are used to calculate the proportion of the U.S. adult population that identifies as Jewish for the demographic groups represented in the model. These estimates are then post-stratified to the U.S. adult population totals for the corresponding groups. To obtain estimates for single years, models were fit separately, pooling across multiple years around the target year and post-stratified to the March supplement of the Current Population Survey for that year. Fitting multiple years of data improves estimation of some smaller groups. For example, for the year 2004, estimates are based on data from 2002 to 2006. In the future, estimates for single years could be improved and yearly change estimated by including more surveys within each year, which would both improve estimation for some of the low-frequency states and facilitate the testing of possible interactions of changes in state-level demographics with Jewish population estimation. Based on the current sample of surveys, however, once distributions by age, race, education, state, and metropolitan status are accounted for across the entire sample of surveys, estimates converge on an estimated proportion of the U.S. adult population that identifies by religion as Jewish as close to 1.9 percent (see Table 2.2).

Distributions by state and metropolitan area based on 2008 data are displayed in Figure 2.3. As expected, the Jewish population is more highly concentrated in metropolitan areas and in areas in the Northeast, in particular New York, New Jersey, Connecticut, Maryland, and Massachusetts. In New York State, 5.6 percent of the metropolitan population self-identifies as Jewish when asked about religious identity.[34]

The development of population models is an ongoing process.[35] Nevertheless, the estimates—when one adjusts for distributions by state, metropolitan area, race, age, education, and the interaction of age and education—appear to have remained consistent over the past two decades. As with any approach to the study of the Jewish population in the United States, it is based on survey estimates, not actual census data. There will continue to be developments and advancements in how best to esti-

Table 2.2. Estimated Percent and Number of U.S. Adults Who Identify by Religion as Jewish, 2000, 2004, 2008.

Year	Percent	Number
	(95% CI)[a]	(95% CI)
2000	1.89	3,780,000
	(1.7–2.1)	(3,416,378–4,216,721)
2004	1.89	3,964,000
	(1.77–1.95)	(3,779,851–4,154,069)
2008	1.86	4,153,000
	(1.68–2.04)	(3,760,689–4,563,542)

[a] CI = credible interval, which for Bayesian analysis is similar to "confidence intervals" (both measure the degree of certainty associated with a given estimate). See E.T. Jaynes, "Confidence Intervals vs. Bayesian Intervals," in *Foundations of Probability Theory, Statistical Inference, and Statistical Theories of Science*, ed. W.L. Harper and C.A. Hooker (Dordrecht: 1976), 175–257.

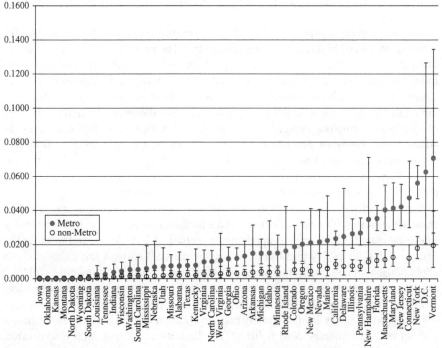

Figure 2.3. Estimated Jewish population by state and metropolitan status: 2008

mate and describe the population at the national level. In the present "information age," drawing on as much data as is available, and making use of the analytical methods and tools for synthesizing large amounts of data, greatly improves our ability to examine basic questions concerning the demographic composition of the U.S. Jewish population.

Using Estimates

The application of these cross-survey synthesis methods yields a consistent annual growth rate in the U.S. adult Jewish population (approximately 1 percent) between 1990 and 2000. This translates to a 2010 estimate of 4.2 million adult American Jews by religion, a significantly higher estimate than that provided by the NJPS, which estimated 3.4 million adult Jews in 1990 and 3.1 million in 2000. As discussed earlier,[36] we believe that the 2000 NJPS estimate is incorrect (a function of the unique methodology of the study, in which religion, for example, was framed as an open-ended question). In contrast, the 1990 NJPS estimate is consistent with our findings from the cross-survey analysis. There are several plausible explanations for our findings. First, there was substantial immigration during this period.[37] Second, the Reform movement's decision in 1983 "to consider as Jewish anyone born of a Jewish mother *or* father" changed liberal Jewish attitudes concerning Jewish identity.[38] Finally, there may have been a substantial increase in the proportion of intermarried families who raise Jewish children.[39] Understanding the factors contributing to changes in the population is a goal of future research and will be facilitated by the availability of estimates that can be updated on an annual basis.

The new paradigm represented by the cross-survey analysis is based on the synthesis of dozens of high-quality national surveys. The presumption is that the quantity and quality of the pooled information, which far exceeds that available from any individual survey (in particular, those conducted or sponsored by Jewish communal organizations), yields more reliable estimates than those of a single study. Over time, the synthesis and comparison of multiple surveys also allows one to identify the type of questions, sampling designs, and response rates that yield different rates. In addition, the synthesis procedure permits the comparison of rates over time and formal trend analysis. This approach substitutes for census data and, given the unlikely change in policy with respect to the U.S. census and the collection of data about religion, represents the best alternative to a national census.

Synthesis of national surveys that include questions about religion and ethnicity does, nevertheless, involve limitations. Three problems, in particular, limit our ability to use the data to develop a comprehensive portrait of U.S. Jewry and to make the data available for policy purposes. First, many national surveys fail to collect data about household composition, making it difficult to estimate the number of children. Second, the standard questions about religion may not capture those Jews who identify culturally or ethnically. Finally, and perhaps most important, using extant surveys not designed to assess Jewish identity and engagement does not allow one to draw a portrait of contemporary Jewish life. These limitations are potentially resolvable, however, as we outline below.

Counting Children

As noted, the surveys used in the synthesis procedure do not typically ask about children in a respondent's household; thus, the estimates derived from the meta-analysis do not directly translate to an estimate of the total Jewish population. There are two potential means of resolving this problem. One, which we have used as an interim step, is to track the trajectory of population growth, focusing in particular on those aged 18–25. Of course, if the population under age 18 is growing at a faster rate than the group aged 18–25, this method will result in an underestimation of the child population. In other words, it does not account for dramatic changes in birthrates. Notwithstanding, over time, the trajectory tracking should provide relatively good estimates of the child population. The second method, which will be increasingly possible as the database expands, is to use the subset of surveys that include household counts and/or specifically ask about respondents' children.

Inclusion of Culturally/Ethnically Identified Jews

Some studies, among them local and national socio-demographic studies that include non-probabilistic samples (for instance, list samples), often report both the proportion of respondents who consider their religion to be Judaism and those who consider themselves Jewish for other reasons. Estimates of the total population that identifies as Jewish—but not by religion—are as high as 30 percent. Thus, for example, the 1990 NJPS found that 20 percent of all adult Jews did not identify in terms of religion. The finding from the 2000 NJPS was even higher, 22 percent, and the figure from AJIS 2000 was 28 percent. These examples indicate that any estimate based solely on responses to a question about religion will underestimate the population. Two approaches can be used to improve the cross-survey estimate based on religious identification. One is to try to integrate these data to estimate the increase. The other (described below in more detail) is to conduct a non-probabilistic national survey that is weighted by the meta-analytic findings. The advantage of this approach is that it allows one to ask the cultural/ethnic identity question in a variety of ways, thus enabling more direct comparison with the results of the synthesis.

Jewish-specific Attitudes and Behavior

As noted, the key limitation associated with using a synthesis of secular studies of the U.S. population is the lack of data on Jewish-specific behavior and attitudes. At the same time, results of the cross-survey meta-analysis can be used to weight focused surveys of Jewish respondents, including local studies and surveys based on opt-in panels. Because the synthesis yields detailed information about the geographic, educational, and socioeconomic status of the Jewish population, it is possible to use this information to correct biases in a targeted survey and to generalize the findings to the Jewish population as a whole. Essentially, the results of the cross-survey analysis can serve as a proxy for census information. In addition, for some attitudes and behaviors of interest, for example, religious service attendance or political attitudes, there is a sufficient number of surveys that include measures of these along with Jewish religious identification. Thus, their prevalence or how they are distributed across the Jewish population (for instance, by geographic region or socioeconomic status) can be estimated directly through the cross-survey analysis approach. These data, in turn, could be used to analyze the "representativeness" of any sample obtained in a targeted survey of the population.

Understanding Jewish Life

In theory, any survey of American Jews can be weighted by the results of the cross-survey synthesis. Doing so effectively, however, is dependent on the survey having adequate demographic information (for instance, that pertaining to geographic region, educational background, or socioeconomic status) and, to some extent, on the quality of the sample. Weighting can correct some, but not all, of the problems associated with having a non-representative sample. Thus, an important strategy for understanding the socio-demography of U.S. Jewry is to use the weights in conjunction with a targeted survey of the population.

A cost-effective strategy for developing such a "reasonably representative" Jewish-focused sample is to use an existing panel. In parallel with conducting cross-survey syntheses, we have been experimenting with using phone- and web-based panels that are created for other purposes, but which also allow for identification of Jews, both by religion and by other criteria. One such panel has been developed by Knowledge Networks, a national opinion research firm. The sampling frame for its largest panel includes 50,000 U.S. households, of which nearly 1,500 have some Jewish connection. The Knowledge Networks panel was recruited using traditional, high-quality methods: random-digit-dialing supplemented with a cell phone frame and address-based sampling. According to a review conducted by a panel of the American Association of Public Opinion Research,[40] the methods used by Knowledge Networks are the most effective of available techniques in reducing bias. It is not a perfect sample, since those willing to participate in an ongoing panel may be different from the population at large, particularly in terms of socioeconomic status.

We have used this panel in several recent studies,[41] including the American Jewish Survey (AJS) of 2010.[42] For the AJS, members of the Jewish sub-sample of the Knowledge Networks panel were asked a full battery of questions about their Jewish backgrounds and identity. The questions paralleled items used on multiple national and local population studies. Jewish respondents were identified by a question about whether they considered themselves Jewish by religion; in addition, they were asked whether they considered themselves Jewish for any reason and whether they had a Jewish mother or father. In total, 1,400 panelists were identified as Jewish by religion or some other criterion.

Preliminary weights were applied to the AJS 2010 dataset to enable generalization of the Knowledge Networks Panel data regarding Jewish attitudes and behavior to the population as a whole. Weighting was done in three stages. The first stage consisted of a sampling weight provided by Knowledge Networks. A non-response adjustment was then applied, based on comparison of Jewish panel members who participated in the AJS and the few panel members (18 percent) who did not. This adjustment included factors of age, geographic region, and household size. The last stage of weighting consisted of a post-stratification adjustment. Because the sample is exclusively Jewish, post-stratification was based on the distribution of the Jewish population estimated via the cross-survey analysis for factors of age, race, geographic region, and education.

Using the youngest adults as the basis for estimating the size of the under-18 population, along with a similarly conservative estimate of "Jewish" by criteria other than religion, and combining this with our cross-survey estimates, translates to a

2010 total Jewish population estimate in the United States of 6.5 million. This number is significantly higher than suggested by NJPS and other Jewish-focused studies, but is likely an underestimate of the number of Americans who regard themselves as Jewish. This proportion translates to the U.S. Jewish population being slightly more than 2 percent of the total population. The proportion has remained steady, even as the overall U.S. population has grown.

Future Prospects

The theme of the present discussion of methods to measure the U.S. Jewish population—our proposed "new paradigm"—is that we need to shift our focus from RDD-type population studies that seek to identify Jews to synthesizing the large quantity of survey data that includes data about Jews, along with focused studies of Jewish populations. The tradition of one-off national decennial studies is no longer a practical approach. The measurement and sampling problems inherent in surveying the contemporary U.S. Jewish community are too complex to be resolved by single studies, and we do not, as yet, know enough about how sensitive survey results are to factors such as question types and sampling strategies. What we know is that the synthesis of multiple studies, along with allowing greater statistical precision, also enables comparison of findings over time, which is critical in answering key questions about the state of the American Jewish community.

Comparisons across studies will also help resolve a host of methodological issues. It will make it possible to answer questions about the impact of different sampling strategies, the effect of low and high response rates, and the use of different types of questions about Jewish identity. The availability of data over time will also allow one to conduct systematic trend analyses and to track the growth and decline of populations and subgroups. This essay has summarized some of our recent findings, focusing on the last decade. However, the methodology also makes it possible to assess older data (in particular, 1990–2000). Doing so would, potentially, enable one to untangle the reasons for population change and growth.

To be sure, in order to take full advantage of data synthesis, it is necessary to combine data from different types of studies. Thus, while secular studies that include questions about religion can be used to develop a demographic portrait of American Jewry, these need to be combined (through the use of weighting techniques) with Jewish-focused surveys. The process is undoubtedly complex, but the problem of measuring a rare population such as the American Jews is inherently difficult. Viewing the project as an ongoing process, rather than a cross-sectional event, is essential.

Judaic scholar Simon Rawidowicz famously coined the term "the ever-dying people" to describe the Jewish people.[43] In every generation, he noted, there are concerns about Jewish survival. Yet this very concern about survivability was what helped to ensure that the community would continue to live and thrive. The ability of social scientists to count American Jews, to understand their attitudes and behavior and be able to track the evolution of the people, is perhaps the modern expression of this concern. "Counting"

American Jewry with greater accuracy and fidelity contributes both to our understanding of an ever more complex world and to the survival of Jewish culture.

Notes

1. We are not aware of any systematic data regarding the investment in social research on the part of the Jewish community, but the costs of demographic studies (for instance, the estimated $6 million spent on the 2000 NJPS—see Benjamin Phillips, "Numbering the Jews: Evaluating and Improving American Jewish Population Studies" [Ph.D. diss., Brandeis University, 2007]) are on an order of magnitude greater than any other study we know of in the Jewish world.

2. The North American Jewish Data Bank maintains a collection of such studies. Over the past few decades, communities such as Atlanta, Baltimore, Boston, Cleveland, Denver, Hartford, Las Vegas, Miami, Nashville, New York, Philadelphia, Pittsburgh, and Washington, D.C. have conducted studies roughly every ten years.

3. Jack J. Diamond, "A Reader in the Demography of American Jews," in *American Jewish Year Book* 77 (1977), 251–319; Sidney Goldstein, "Jews in the United States: Perspectives from Demography," in *American Jewish Year Book* 81 (1981), 3–59; Sidney Goldstein, Sidney Groeneman, Frank and Susan Mott, and Joseph Waksberg, *Towards a National Survey in 1990* (New York: 1988); Barry A. Kosmin, Paul Ritterband, and Jeffrey Scheckner, "Jewish Population in the United States, 1987," in *American Jewish Year Book* 88 (1988), 222–243; Fred Massarik, "Knowledge About U.S. Jewish Populations: Retrospect and Prospect 1970–2001," *Journal of Jewish Communal Service* 68, no. 4 (1992), 299–305; Phillips, "Numbering the Jews"; Uziel Schmelz, "Evaluation of Jewish Population Estimates," in *American Jewish Year Book* 70 (1969), 273–288; Ben B. Seligman, "The American Jew: Some Demographic Features," in *American Jewish Year Book* 51 (1950), 3–52.

4. Dorothy Good, "Questions on Religion in the United States Census," *Population Index* 25, no. 1 (1959), 3–16.

5. Sergio DellaPergola, "Was It the Demography?: A Reassessment of U.S. Jewish Population Estimates, 1945–2001," *Contemporary Jewry* 25, no. 1 (2005), 85–131; Barry A. Kosmin, Egon Mayer, and Ariela Keysar, *American Religious Identification Survey* (New York: 2001).

6. See, for instance, Ira M. Sheskin and Arnold Dashefsky, *Jewish Population in the United States, 2011* (Storrs: 2011).

7. Two examples of efforts to address the problem of seasonal residents are Daniel Parmer, Benjamin Phillips, and Leonard Saxe, *The 2008 Berkshire Community Study: For the Jewish Federation of the Berkshires* (Waltham: 2009); and Matthew Boxer and Benjamin Phillips, *The 2010 Western North Carolina Jewish Demographic Study* (Waltham: 2011). Both studies focused on communities that include large proportions of seasonal residents.

8. Richard Curtin, Stanley Presser, and Eleanor Singer, "Changes in Telephone Survey Nonresponse over the Past Quarter Century," *Public Opinion Quarterly* 69, no. 1 (2005), 87–98.

9. Stephen J. Blumberg and Julian V. Luke, "Wireless Substitution: Early Release of Estimates from the National Health Interview Survey, July–December, 2011," *National Center for Health Statistics* (2012), online at www.cdc.gov/nchs/data/nhis/earlyrelease/wireless201206.pdf (accessed 17 February 2013).

10. AAPOR Cell Phone Task Force, "New Considerations for Survey Researchers When Planning and Conducting RDD Telephone Surveys in the U.S. with Respondents Reached via Cell Numbers" (2010), online at www.aapor.org/AM/Template.cfm?Section = Cell_Phone_Task_Force_Report&Template=/CM/ContentDisplay.cfm&ContentID=3189 (accessed 15 October 2012).

11. Robert M. Groves, Floyd J. Fowler, Jr., Mick P. Couper, James M. Lepkower, Eleanor Singer, and Roger Tourangeau, *Survey Methodology* (Hoboken: 2009).

12. See, for instance, Robert M. Groves, Robert B. Cialdini, and Mick P. Couper, "Understanding the Decision to Participate in a Survey," *Public Opinion Quarterly* 56, no. 4 (1992), 475–495.

13. Sandro Galea and Melissa Tracy, "Participation Rates in Epidemiologic Studies," *Annals of Epidemiology* 17 (2007), 643–653.

14. Charles Kadushin, Benjamin Phillips, and Leonard Saxe, "National Jewish Population Survey 2000–01: A Guide for the Perplexed," *Contemporary Jewry* 25, no. 1 (2005), 1–32; Phillips, "Numbering the Jews."

15. Marketing Systems Group, *1990 Survey of American Jews* (Philadelphia: 1991); United Jewish Communities, *National Jewish Population Survey/National Survey of Religion and Ethnicity 2000–2001: Study Documentation* (New York: 2003); hereafter: 1990 NJPS and 2000 NJPS.

16. Debra Nussbaum Cohen, "NJPS Credibility Questioned: $6 Million Study Delayed," *New York Jewish Week* (22 November 2002), online at www.thejewishweek.com/features/njps_credibility_questioned (accessed 17 February 2013).

17. Response rates were especially low for households identified in the screener as religiously mixed. For a full discussion of this and other potential sources of bias, see Phillips, "Numbering the Jews."

18. Gary A. Tobin and Sydney Groeneman, *Surveying the Jewish Population in the United States* (San Francisco: 2003); Roger Tourangeau and Ting Yan, "Sensitive Questions in Surveys," *Psychological Bulletin*, no. 133, no. 5 (2007), 859–883. In his post-hoc review of the methodology of the 2000 NJPS, Mark Schulman speculated that beginning the survey with the religious identification question may have unnecessarily prompted refusals to complete the survey (Mark A. Schulman, *National Jewish Population Survey 2000–2001: Study Review Memo* [New York: 2003], 5).

19 For a discussion of weighting in the 2000 NJPS, see Kadushin, Phillips, and Saxe, "National Jewish Population Survey 2000–01."

20. See Leonard Saxe, Elizabeth Tighe, Benjamin Phillips, and Charles Kadushin, *Reconsidering the Size and Characteristics of the American Jewish Population: New Estimates of a Larger and More Diverse Community* (Waltham: 2007); Elizabeth Tighe, David Livert, Melissa Barnett, and Leonard Saxe, "Cross-Survey Analysis to Estimate Low-Incidence Religious Groups," *Sociological Methods & Research*, 39, no. 1 (2010), 56–82.

21. Elizabeth Tighe et al., *Estimating the Jewish Population of the United States: 2000–2010* (Waltham: 2011), online at www.brandeis.edu/ssri/pdfs/EstimatingJewishPopUS.1.pdf (accessed 18 February 2013); Leonard Saxe and Elizabeth Tighe, "Estimating and Understanding the Jewish Population in the United States: A Program of Research," *Contemporary Jewry* (forthcoming); Matthew Boxer, Janet Krasner Aronson, and Leonard Saxe, "Using Consumer Panels to Understand the Characteristics of U.S. Jewry," *Contemporary Jewry* (forthcoming).

22. See, for instance, Larry V. Hedges, "Meta-Analysis," *Journal of Educational and Behavioral Statistics* 17, no. 4 (1992), 279–296.

23. Sharon Lohr and Narasimha Prasad, "Small Area Estimation with Auxiliary Survey Data," *Canadian Journal of Statistics* 31 (2003), 383–396; Danny Pfeffermann, "Small Area Estimation: New Developments and Directions," *International Statistical Review* 70, no. 1 (2002), 125–143; Jon N.K. Rao, *Small Area Estimation* (Hoboken: 2003).

24. Rao, *Small Area Estimation*, 2.

25. See, for instance, Gary King, "Ensuring the Data-Rich Future of the Social Sciences," *Science* 331 (2011), 719–721.

26. The 128 surveys are a subset of the full sample, which includes a set of final survey weights for secondary analysis. More information regarding the surveys is found in a technical appendix to this essay, online at www.brandeis.edu/cmjs/pdfs/MeasuringSizeAmJewry-Appendix.pdf (accessed 15 October 2012).

27. Pew Forum on Religion and Public Life, *U.S. Religious Landscape Survey. Religious Affiliation: Diverse and Dynamic* (Washington, DC: 2008).

28. Baylor Institute for Studies of Religion, *American Piety in the 21st Century: New Insights to the Depth and Complexity of Religion in the U.S.* (Waco: 2006).

29. In addition, some surveys that were conducted in 1997, 1998, and 1999 were included for 2000, and a subset of surveys conducted around the year 1990 was included for purposes of comparison with the 1990 NJPS. For present purposes, the results reported here focus only on those surveys conducted since 2000.

30. National samples are of the continental United States, including Washington, D.C. Some surveys include Alaska and Hawaii. Only the continental United States portion of their samples is included here. Surveys of specific populations, such as specific age groups or geographic areas such as New York State or the New York City metropolitan area, were also identified. In the long run, data from these sources can be incorporated to contribute to estimation of those specific subgroups.

31. See, for instance, David A. Binder and Georgia Roberts, "Design- and Model-Based Inference for Model Parameters," in *Handbook of Statistics, 29b: Sample Surveys: Design, Methods and Applications*, ed. Danny Pfeffermann and C.R. Rao (Amsterdam: 2009), 33–54; Jean D. Opsomer, "Introduction to Part 4," in ibid., 3–9; Richard Valliant, "Model-Based Prediction of Finite Population Totals," in ibid., 11–31.

32. See, for instance, Andrew Gelman and Jennifer Hill, *Data Analysis Using Regression and Multilevel/Hierarchical Models* (New York: 2007); Rao and Yu, *Small Area Estimation*; Jon N.K. Rao and Mingyu Yu, "Small-Area Estimation by Combining Time-Series and Cross-Sectional Data," *Canadian Journal of Statistics* 22, no. 4 (December 1994), 511–528.

33. David K. Park, Andrew Gelman, and Joseph Bafumi, "Bayesian Multilevel Estimation with Poststratification: State-Level Estimates from National Polls," *Political Analysis* 12, no. 4 (2004), 375–385; Tighe et al., "Cross-Survey Analysis to Estimate Low-Incidence Religious Groups," *Sociological Methods & Research*, 39, no. 1 (2010), 56–82.

34. See technical appendix to this essay (n. 26); cf. Sheskin and Dashefsky, "Jewish Population in the United States, 2011." The former includes Jews by religion only, whereas Sheskin and Dashefsky's estimates include cultural/secular Jews.

35. See citations in n. 21.

36. See also Saxe, Tighe, Phillips and Kadushin, *Reconsidering the Size and Characteristics of the American Jewish Population* (Waltham: 2007).

37. On the particularly large immigration from the former Soviet Union, see Larissa Remennick, *Russian Jews on Three Continents: Identity, Integration and Conflict* (New Brunswick: 2007).

38. See Alexander M. Schindler, "Not by Birth Alone: The Case for a Missionary Judaism," in *Contemporary Debates in American Reform Judaism: Conflicting Visions*, ed. Dana E. Kaplan (New York: 2001).

39. Fern Chertok, Benjamin Phillips, and Leonard Saxe, *"It's Not Just Who Stands under the Chuppah": Intermarriage and Engagement* (Waltham: 2008); Leonard Saxe, Benjamin Phillips, Charles Kadushin, Graham Wright, and Daniel Parmer, *The 2005 Boston Community Survey: Preliminary Findings* (Waltham: 2006).

40. See Reg Baker et al., "Research Synthesis: AAPOR Report on Online Panels," *Public Opinion Quarterly* 74, no. 4 (2010), 311–381.

41. See, in particular, Theodore Sasson, Benjamin Phillips, Charles Kadushin, and Leonard Saxe, *Still Connected: American Jewish Attitudes about Israel* (Waltham: 2010); idem, *Technical Appendices-Still Connected: American Jewish Attitudes about Israel* (Waltham: 2010).

42. Leonard Saxe, "U.S. Jewry 2010: Estimates of the Size and Characteristics of the Population" (Powerpoint presentation at the Association for Jewish Studies, Boston [December 2010]); Saxe and Tighe, "Estimating and Understanding the Jewish Population in the United States."

43. Simon Rawidowicz, *State of Israel, Diaspora, and Jewish Continuity: Essays on the "Ever-Dying People,"* ed. Benjamin Ravid (Hanover: 1988).

U.S. Jewish Population Studies: Opportunities and Challenges

David Dutwin, Eran Ben-Porath and Ron Miller
(JEWISH POLICY AND ACTION RESEARCH)

Jewish population surveys are an important tool both for researchers interested in understanding population trends, social dynamics, and the societal needs of local and national Jewish communities, and for Jewish communities seeking to plan for future communal needs. In the United States, which is the main focus of this essay, these surveys have also informed the research community about American Jews' attitudes, beliefs, and sense of identity.[1] Over the past 50 years, more than 70 Jewish communities in the United States have conducted wide-scale population surveys, generally under the sponsorship of the local Jewish Federation.[2] Major metropolitan areas strive to conduct a survey every ten years, and there have also been several national, decadal studies, the most recent being the National Jewish Population Survey (NJPS) conducted in 2000–2001 (hereafter: 2000 NJPS).[3]

Unfortunately for Jewish research scholars and the Jewish community at large, the 2000 NJPS generated nearly as much controversy as it did data. One representative critique maintained that, whereas the survey held the potential for fruitful studies of interrelated variables, "the population estimates are problematic and continued emphasis on them ultimately will distract from the study's utility."[4] Several problems were unique to the 2000 NJPS—in particular, the loss of data concerning a portion of the non-responding population.[5] On a more generalized and substantive level, however, the criticisms directed at the survey and its administrators point to more far-ranging difficulties with regard to Jewish population research. Indeed, although a number of valuable studies based on the survey were subsequently published,[6] the problems connected with the 2000 NJPS led several scholars to question whether national Jewish population surveys were feasible in a manner that was methodologically sound and cost-effective; some argued that, in their present form, such surveys should not be undertaken.[7]

We believe that mistakes of the past can serve as a learning tool for designing future Jewish community surveys. In what follows, we first identify the main concerns facing Jewish population research and then detail a set of solutions, focusing in particular on community (as opposed to national) studies. A number of alternative approaches to Jewish community and population research will also be presented and critiqued.[8]

Jewish Population Studies and Their Problems

Jewish communal groups in the United States, including Jewish Federations, foundations, local health and welfare organizations, congregations, and schools, raise several billion dollars each year. Given the enormous competition in the field of fundraising, these organizations increasingly rely on data concerning actual and potential clients, consumers, and donors. Although the U.S. census might appear to be the obvious resource for learning about the Jewish population, it does not include questions about religious affiliation (this, in contrast to other countries such as Canada and Great Britain).[9] Thus, in the absence of census data, local Jewish population studies have been utilized to describe basic Jewish population demographics: age, gender, household structure, marital status, mobility patterns, and various socioeconomic characteristics. While often called demographic studies, these studies are, in effect, Jewish community population studies, since the data collected on Jewish households and people living in those households are not restricted to purely demographic-population issues but also provide information about Jewish identity, Jewish household and individual connections (or lack of connections) to the organized Jewish community, philanthropic patterns of Jewish households, Jewish individuals' attitudes toward Israel and being Jewish, and a variety of other topics appearing under religious studies or social dynamics.[10]

The data in such studies can be classified in two broad categories. The first contains basic information with regard to demography and Jewish characteristics. Included in this category are Jewish household and population estimates, both for the entire area under study and for each county within the region (and sometimes for major Jewish neighborhoods within each county); data on the age and gender structure of the Jewish community; statistics concerning Jewish household size and structure; and respondents' socioeconomic attainment, marital status (including data on in-marriage and intermarriage), education (secular and Jewish), and employment status. In addition, there may be data concerning such matters as the number of years respondents have been living in the area, their previous place of residence, and their region or country of birth.

The second category of data, used mainly for planning and policy-making, is based on survey material tailored to the needs of the community under study. Topics may include Jewish (and Israel-related) connections and respondents' familiarity with various Jewish programs and services offered in the community. There may also be statistics relating to such matters as respondents' social service and health care needs; their levels of philanthropy and voluntarism for both Jewish and non-Jewish organizations; the amount and frequency of visits to Israel; and their level of support for Israel.

Jewish community studies have evolved as researchers have learned from past mistakes and become more sophisticated in their methodology.[11] Early studies varied greatly in their methods, the most common sources of data being surveys using a basic random-digit-dialing (RDD) model; surveys of households that had a published phone number and a recognizable Jewish last name (known as "distinctive Jewish name" [DJN] surveys); and informal lists of Jewish households that were compiled by various local Jewish organizations. Each of these methods had serious drawbacks. RDD was inordinately expensive, given the low incidence of Jews in the United States. DJN surveys were less expensive, but it soon became apparent that, in most areas, fewer than one out of six Jewish households had a distinctively Jewish surname and a published telephone number—moreover, such households were by no means representative of the Jewish population as a whole. Similar, if not more acute, issues in coverage and bias also characterized "list-only" surveys of Jewish populations.

A second major issue in Jewish population research, as in any high-quality population research, is "non-response bias," a situation in which the accuracy of survey data is compromised because of insufficient response (whether on the part of the total population being surveyed or among subgroups within the total population).[12] Recent developments have exacerbated the problems connected with attaining sufficiently high levels of survey respondents. For instance, people have become increasingly wary of unsolicited telephone calls, especially from telemarketers; in consequence, many potential respondents make use of technologies such as voicemail and caller identification in order to prescreen their calls.[13] Thus, whereas the 2000 NJPS was marked by an overall low response rate (28 percent)—and an even lower rate of individuals who completed the full questionnaire rather than merely the initial Jewish identity screener—it is currently not uncommon to encounter response rates for telephone surveys that hover in the lower 20-percent range.[14] Such figures are 10 or even 15 percentage points lower than was typical a decade ago; several researchers have expressed their concern that low response rates may call into question the validity of the data in these surveys.

Low response rates increase the chance of non-response bias. This said, it is important to note that so far there is little evidence suggesting that low response rates necessarily create non-response biases in surveys.[15] Penny Visser, Jon Krosnick, Jesse Marquette, and Michael Curtin, for example, found that surveys with response rates of 20 percent and lower often attain measurements comparable to surveys with higher response rates.[16] Richard Curtin, Stanley Presser, and Eleanor Singer looked at the Index of Consumer Sentiment (ICS), comparing the data of the full sample with a smaller sample showing only those respondents who did not initially refuse to be interviewed, as well as a somewhat larger sample that excluded respondents who required more than five calls to complete the interview. They found no meaningful difference between the full sample and their reduced, "easier to complete" samples from one month to the next, although an aggregated sample of all ICS respondents across an entire year did show a very modest difference.[17] In a third study, Allyson Holbrook, Jon Krosnick, and Alison Pfent examined 81 national surveys whose response rates ranged from 5 to 54 percent; they found that surveys that had a lower response rate were only slightly less accurate.[18] And finally, Scott Keeter, Carolyn Miller, Andrew Kohut, Robert Groves, and Stanley Presser compared the results of the Pew Research Center's usual 5-day survey fielding (response rate: 36.0 percent) with results from the same survey conducted over an eight-week period (response rate: 60.6 percent), finding only very slight differences between the two.[19] Overall, research on the impact of response rates finds that differences in response rates have little to no effect on most survey estimates.

Nevertheless, in the case of Jewish surveys, there is some concern that low response rates may increase non-response bias. It has been shown, for example, that people in urban areas are more likely to refuse surveys than those in rural areas,[20] and this phenomenon may lead to an underestimation of the U.S. Jewish population, which tends to live in and around major cities.[21] Another concern is that Jews of varying denominations may be differentially more or less likely to respond to surveys. Simply attaining a higher rate of response may be insufficient to overcome the problem of non-response if, for example, Conservative and Reform Jews respond more willingly to surveys than do Orthodox Jews or non-denominational Jews.[22]

A well-conceived weighting plan can mitigate problems associated with non-response bias. One of the flaws of the 2000 NJPS weighting scheme was its assumption that non-response patterns between Jews and non-Jews were identical,[23] which disregarded evidence that Jews were more likely to refuse these types of surveys.[24] Certainly, weighting Jewish population studies is particularly challenging, given that there are no preexisting parameters (such as census counts by religion) by which the survey data can be corrected. However, as will be seen, sophisticated weighting designs can correct for biases in the likelihood of selection as well as in differing patterns of non-response.

As noted, another central issue in Jewish population research pertains to coverage. To some extent, new research methods have overcome the coverage problems inherent in older surveys (for example, those that utilized DJN lists). At the same time, other challenges have emerged, among them the growing prevalence of cell phone use. In 2010, the National Health Interview Survey found that just over a quarter of all households were "cell phone only" (CPO)—that is, there were no landlines in these households. The percentage rose above 50 percent for households consisting of young adults between the ages of 24 and 29.[25] Clearly, landline-only studies are insufficient to cover large swaths of just about any target population surveyed, and especially an audience containing representative numbers of young persons. Some critics of the 2000 NJPS have suggested that several of the survey's surprising findings concerning Jewish young adults—for instance, that a relatively large percentage were Orthodox, and that a high percentage were living with their parents—may be inaccurate, given that the landline-only survey may have missed many young adults who were living away from their parents and relying exclusively on cell phones.[26]

Solutions for the Research of Rare Populations and American Jews

In tackling the specific challenges posed by Jewish population surveys, it is useful to consider Jews as a "low incidence" or "rare population" group—that is, as a relatively small group within the larger population.[27] In general, surveys of rare populations (which also include such groups as Native Americans, military families, Asian Americans, households whose incomes fall below the Federal Poverty Level, the disabled, and the uninsured) are more susceptible to problems connected with non-response or insufficient coverage. The solutions that we detail below are a product of years of specialized experience acquired in the subfield of rare populations, which will now be applied more specifically to the issue of Jewish population surveys.

Survey Quality Best Practices

High-quality surveys are those following what is known in the field as "best practices"—procedures that, on the one hand, add to the cost of the survey, while at the same time ensuring a high level of accuracy. Of all the best practices, a high rate of response continues to be considered the single most important measure of a given survey's quality. Yet we have seen already that response rates tend to be a poor measure of the accuracy of survey estimates. As well, there are a number of problems in using response rate measurements as the "gold standard" for survey quality. For one thing, researchers have not always employed the same means to calculate response rates, despite the publication of standard guidelines for such calculations by the American Association for Public Opinion Research (AAPOR).[28] Second, response rates vary greatly in accordance with a number of factors. For example, Behavioral Risk Factor Surveillance Surveys (BRFSS) conducted for the Centers for Disease Control and Prevention attain response rates in the teens and the low 20s in some of the northeastern states, in contrast to rates of 50 percent or more in portions of the Midwest.[29] With this in mind, it may make more sense to focus on yardsticks other than response rate that are more consistent from survey to survey. Such yardsticks include the number of calls placed to each potential respondent, the extent to which attempts are made to convince those who initially refuse to take part in a survey to reconsider ("refusal conversions"), and the degree to which other best practice procedures, such as long field periods, are enacted.[30]

Surveys vary greatly in the effort put forth to interview a given population. On one end of the spectrum are omnibus surveys or fast-turnaround public opinion polls, which are typically conduced over a period of five days or less. This short time frame places many constraints on the level of effort—callbacks and refusal conversion attempts are severely limited, as are the number of initial call attempts (such studies generally average two or three call attempts). At the other end are high-quality policy research studies such as the health interview surveys conducted by most states. In such studies, the field period can last six months, and firms that conduct the surveys are typically contracted to make a minimum of 12 to 20 call attempts. In addition, callbacks are made to persons who initially refuse to be interviewed; these are optimally placed at least six days to two weeks after the initial refusal.[31] At times, a second refusal conversion attempt may be made at least a month after the first. Other callback procedures include the following:

- Numbers are called at varying times of the day and week.
- Messages are left on answering machines urging people to call back or to pick up the phone the next time they see the survey caller ID.
- Caller IDs are customized in order to display the actual study name—equally important, they show a local telephone exchange number rather than a generic 1–800 number.

- Extensive and continuous training of interviewers is carried out: interviewers with the lowest cooperation rates are removed from the project.
- Calls are made by means of manual speed dialing rather than by computers utilizing a "predictive dialing" program.[32]

This set of procedures maximizes the cooperation of the target population and is thought to lead to significantly less concern with regard to non-response and low response.

It is critical that best practice procedures be followed in every Jewish population study. When we examined recent Jewish community surveys conducted in Chicago, Cleveland, Philadelphia, New York, and Baltimore, we found a significant relationship between the number of call attempts and Jewish incidence. Specifically, we conducted an advanced statistical analysis (logistic regression) on being Jewish, where the explanatory variables included the total number of calls made to each respondent who eventually completed a screening survey and an indication as to whether each individual respondent had at any point refused to complete the interview; we also looked at callbacks. To control for extraneous factors, we added sample type (that is, whether the sample was provided by the local Jewish Federation as opposed to being a DJN sample or a basic RDD); the hour of completion; the day of completion; and the county of completion (Fig. 3.1).

On average across all five cities, the odds of reaching a Jewish individual were 1.28 times greater for every call attempt made. As shown in Fig. 3.2, this has a measurable impact on the cumulative estimate of Jewish households in each city. In short, the more call attempts one makes, the greater the incidence of Jewish households that are reached (though since fewer and fewer interviews are successfully completed in each call attempt, the increase tends to flatten out over the course of the survey).

We also explored the impact of refusal conversions and callback attempts. As might be expected, we found that, on average, the incidence of being Jewish among converted refusal respondents and those responding to a callback was much higher than in interviews that were not attained by such procedures. This makes sense, since interviewers are not likely to make recalls to households known (or suspected) not to have Jewish members.

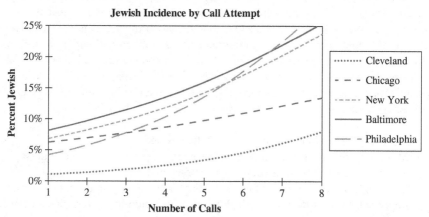

Figure 3.1. Number of call attempts on Jewish incidence

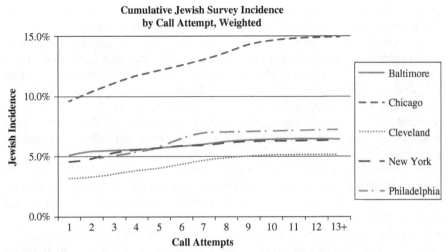

Figure 3.2. Cumulative Jewish incidence by call attempt

Interestingly, we did not find a relationship between denomination and the level of response in the two cities we analyzed. No differences were detected between those who defined themselves as Orthodox and those who did not with respect to the number of respondents who required repeated callbacks or refusal conversion attempts. Similarly, there were no differences characterizing those who identified themselves as secular as opposed to those who did not. These results run counter to the hypothesis that Jews of varying denominations may be differentially more or less inclined to respond to surveys.

Modified Random-Digit-Dialing (RDD) Designs

In order to be conducted in the first place, low-incidence population studies must be adequately funded. In most instances, budgets are limited in a way that does not allow for a full-scale RDD survey; in Jewish population studies, for example, screening typically accounts for about half the total budget. Accordingly, there is a need to make use of sophisticated sampling techniques that maintain the basic RDD framework at a greatly reduced cost.

RDD is the best telephone survey sampling methodology because everyone with a landline telephone has an equal chance of being called. In a modified RDD design, certain households in a given survey area are accorded a greater probability than others of being contacted, with this disproportionality then corrected by means of weighting procedures involving the use of a small-scale RDD survey. Because of the smaller sample size, costs are reduced considerably, though to some extent, as will be seen, this leads to a greater margin of error in the final results.

The most common alternative to the RDD design is the List-Assisted Disproportionate Stratified (LADS) design, which was first utilized in a Jewish population study conducted in Philadelphia in 1996.[33] This design first generates an RDD-based random sample of the target population in which all potential land-line telephone numbers are in the initial sampling frame. Next, telephone numbers from a known list of Jews (provided by the local Jewish Federation and other Jewish organization databases) are eliminated from the total RDD pool. As a result, there are two major sampling frames: the "Jewish list" frame and a residual RDD frame. The residual RDD frame is then further stratified into three sub-strata: (a) numbers published in telephone directories that are listed under a distinctively Jewish name (DJN); (b) published numbers of telephone subscribers who do not have distinctively Jewish names; and (c) unpublished ("unlisted") telephone numbers.

In a typical LADS study, we expect 20–50 percent of the households in the DJN frame to be Jewish (the number would be higher were it not for the fact that distinctively Jewish names appearing on the "Jewish list" have already been eliminated from the RDD frame). In the second and third sub-frames, consisting of published and unpublished numbers of subscribers without a distinctive Jewish name, anywhere between 2 and 6 percent of the subscribers may be Jewish; in areas with a more concentrated Jewish population, the figure may be as high as 15 percent. By segregating the "Jewish list" from the larger RRD sample, the LADS design reaches a disproportionate number of Jewish households relative to the total surveyed population. Put somewhat differently, the "Jewish list" is over-sampled, with this sampling disproportionality later adjusted during the estimation and weighting phase. The outcome is a survey based on a RDD model that is much more efficient—hence, cost-effective—in locating its target population.

Jewish community lists are not the only means by which a population survey sample can be stratified. Both the 2000 NJPS and the Jewish Community Survey of New York (2002) disproportionally stratified telephone exchanges that were thought to have a higher incidence of Jewish households. This practice, in fact, is an industry standard that is frequently utilized in studies of Hispanics, Asians, the uninsured, and other populations of interest. With regard to Jews, however, the LADS design is preferable because it is more efficient: a stratum of telephone exchanges that are relatively high in Jewish incidence may yield only 10 percent Jewish households, as opposed to up to 80 percent in a Federation ("Jewish") list sample and between 20–50 percent in a DJN sample.

A key feature of the LADS design is its ability to obtain more interviews (vis-à-vis the survey as a whole) in strata of high Jewish incidence. Consider the example given in Table 3.1, in which 30 percent of all Jewish households in the survey area appear on a Federation ("Jewish") database of telephone numbers, whereas 62 percent of completed interviews are obtained from this group. As a result, the survey-interviewing incidence rises from 7.1 percent to 14 percent.[34] Such a survey design requires only half the screens of an RDD design, and saves as much as 40 percent of survey fielding costs in the process.

In addition to its lower costs, a LADS survey results in more accurate estimates of the target population. A simple RDD design bases its estimate of Jewish incidence on the incidence of Jews identified during the fielding of the survey. Although such data may be weighted by certain parameters such as age and gender, it is essentially an uncontrolled design. In contrast, the LADS design for a large metropolitan study will

Table 3.1. Example of LADS Design

Strata	Total households	Jewish households	Jewish incidence	Percent of all Jewish households	Completed interviews	Percent of all completed interviews
Federation list	35,973	31,182	86.6%	30%	740	62%
DJN	15,762	5,726	36.3%	5%	100	8%
Residual RDD	1,418,070	68,795	4.8%	65%	360	30%
TOTAL	**1,469,805**	**105,702**	**7.1%**	**100%**	**1,200**	**14% incidence**

typically break down the residual RDD strata into published and unpublished telephone numbers, and will further develop counts at the county level. In the case of an area with, say, five counties, this results in a five (county) by four (strata) design (the strata being the Jewish community list, plus the three sub-strata of the RDD design).

In the example given above, Jewish incidence in a LADS survey is measured separately for each of 20 units defined by county and sampling stratum. In this manner, a number of critical factors are controlled at the county/stratum level that would not be controlled in a pure RDD design. First and most important is the cooperation rate of Jews. Experience has shown that Jews whose telephone numbers appear on a "Jewish list" or within a DJN frame are far more likely to participate in a Jewish population survey than are Jews who are located in a residual RDD frame. This makes sense, as Federation-list Jews are by definition formally connected to Jewish life in some fashion. In contrast, Jews who are located in the unpublished residual frame are apt to be less connected to their religion/culture. Moreover, their having an unpublished number is an indication of a desire for privacy, which often goes along with a disinclination to participate in surveys: indeed, study after study confirms that response rates are lower within unpublished telephone frames as compared with published telephone frames. In addition, individuals located in the published and unpublished frames, whether Jewish or not, are also less likely to disclose whether they are Jewish or not. Thus, not only the response rate but also the identification rate of households in the residual RDD frames is lower than in the other frames.

In a pure RDD design—one lacking the controls built into the county-level LADS design—disproportionalities in the identification rate and the cooperation rate will consistently lead to findings showing the Jewish population to be larger and more affiliated than is truly the case. The following example from the 2007 Metropolitan Denver/Boulder Jewish community survey illustrates the limitations inherent in a pure RDD design as opposed to the benefits provided by the LADS design (Table 3.2).

The first five rows of Table 3.2 show, by sampling frame and for the combined total, (1) the total number of households in the study area; (2) the LADS design estimate of the number of Jewish households within the total; (3) the estimated percentage of Jewish households ("Jewish incidence") within each sampling frame; (4) the cooperation rate, that is, the percentage of Jewish respondents who agree to be

Table 3.2. Bias Comparison of LADS and Simple RDD Designs (Metropolitan Denver/Boulder, 2007)

	TOTAL	Fed. List	DJN	RDD published	RDD unpublished
Households	1,009,603	22,511	7,609	537,175	442,308
Jewish household estimate (LADS)	47,531	14,375	1,070	12,963	19,123
Jewish incidence		63.86%	14.06%	2.41%	4.32%
Cooperation rate of Jewish respondents		82.30%	68.00%	51.10%	56.30%
Identification rate of respondents		69.80%	54.40%	50.90%	45.70%
Percent of total households		2.23%	0.75%	53.21%	43.81%
RDD design sample	92,895	2,071	700	49,426	40,697
Religious identity determined	45,583	1,446	381	25,158	18,599
Identified as Jews	2,388	923	54	607	804
Jews in dataset interviews	1,559	760	36	310	453
Weighted Jews in dataset (LADS)[a]		30%	2%	27%	40%
Jews in dataset (RDD)		49%	2%	20%	29%
Jewish household estimate for total households (RDD)	52,891	25,774	1,235	10,524	15,357

[a] Percentages derived from Jewish household estimates (LADS) line—each cell is divided by the total estimated number of Jewish households (n = 47,531).

interviewed; and (5) the identification rate, that is, the percent of households reached that were willing to provide information as to whether or not they were Jewish.

Subsequent lines show the anticipated estimates in a simple RDD design (shown broken down by stratum). The first column on the first line shows the total sample (92,895) that would be taken in a survey area of this size. This number is then broken down in accordance with the percentage of total households for each stratum that appears on the previous line. Thus, the figure of 2,071 Jewish households that appears under the Federation list column represents 2.23 percent of the total number of households in the Denver metropolitan area. Given an identification rate of 69.80 percent, we estimate that overall, out of the 2,071 households on the Federation list, 1,446 households would have been identified as either Jewish or not Jewish ("religious identity determined"). Of that number, 63.86 percent, or 923 households, would be identified as Jewish and, given a cooperation rate of 82.30 percent, representatives of 760 Jewish households would agree to be interviewed. In a simple RDD design, the source of these 760 interviews would remain unknown. That is, there would be no way to distinguish between respondents whose names appear on a Federation list as opposed to appearing in a DJN frame or in an RDD unpublished telephone number frame. All that would be known is that 2,388 Jewish households would have been identified out of 45,583 households that were known to be either Jewish or not Jewish, amounting to a Jewish incidence of 5.2 percent.

The problem with this is apparent in the subsequent rows of the table. Because of a much higher cooperation rate among Federation list households and subsequently a higher identification rate, the percentage of Jewish interviews in a simple RDD design would have been biased toward Federation list members—there is no specific method by which to correct for this bias in an RDD design. Whereas we found, using a LADS design, that 33 percent of all Jewish households in the Denver metropolitan area were households that were on the Federation list, a simple RDD design would have yielded a comparable figure of 49 percent. This, in turn (not shown in the table), would have resulted in a higher estimate of Jewish households—5.2 percent, compared with 4.7 percent that was found in the LAD/S design. The simple RDD design would have yielded a Jewish household overestimate of more than 5,000—compare the figure of 47,531 in the "Jewish household estimate (LADS)" in the upper part of the table with that of 52,891 at the bottom of the table. Even worse, the simple RDD estimate would have estimated that 25,917 of those households were Federation list households, compared to 14,375 in the LADS design. In short, not only would there be an overestimate of the number of Jews, but the Jewish community would appear to be far more connected to Jewish life than it actually is (as reflected in the LADS design). This discrepancy has serious implications with regard to critical policy and planning decisions by the local Jewish Federation.

Alongside the benefits of the LADS design is one drawback: a higher margin of error as compared with a pure RDD design. The margins of error in the LADS design are inflated because of increased variance in the weights needed to correct for the disproportionate design. Simply put, the larger the variance in the weights, the larger the margin of error associated with a population estimate based on data employing those weights. In Denver, 1,405 interviews were completed with Jews, and approximately 45,000 screener interviews were conducted with Jews and non-Jews overall. Based on the standard calculation for margin of error, these numbers of interviews produce a margin of error for the incidence of Jews of 2.57 percent, and a margin of error in estimates of the incidence of Jews of 0.1 percent. However, because of the variance in the weights needed to correct for the disproportionality of the LADS design, the margin of error with regard to the incidence of Jews is actually 3.98 percent, whereas the margin of error in the estimates of Jewish incidence is still essentially 0.1 percent.

Undeniably, the margin of error increases in such a design. But there are two important qualifications. First is the consideration of cost. Consider, for example, a study that determines that 50 percent of all Jews in a given survey community—say, 2,500 individuals—are intermarried. Both a simple RDD and a LADS design come up with the same number—the difference is that, in the case of the RDD survey, the estimate is more *reliable*, as the margin of error is 2.5 percent, compared with a margin of error of 4 percent for the LADS design. At the same time, there is a significant difference in cost for the two designs: the RDD design, which necessitates a much larger survey sample, costs $250,000, compared with $150,000 for the LADS design. Most Jewish organizations and Federations will not hesitate to accept a somewhat higher margin of error in return for substantially lowered costs.

Beyond this, however, is the fact that, in a number of significant ways, the LADS survey is more accurate—that is, more *valid*—than a pure RDD-based survey. As we have seen in the Metropolitan Denver/Boulder survey, a simple RDD design ends up biasing the findings toward Federation list interviews. Since intermarriage rates are consistently lower among Federation-listed Jews as compared with other Jewish sub-groups, there is a greater likelihood that the RDD design will result in a lower esti-mate of intermarriage—for instance, 40–45 percent (plus or minus 2.5 percent), as compared with the LADS estimate of 50 percent (plus or minus 4 percent). Although the margin of error may be higher in the LADS survey, the numbers themselves are more likely to be accurate, as the figures are broken down in accordance with the various sub-strata providing the overall data.

Cell Phone Interviewing

As noted earlier in the discussion, a new challenge has emerged in the field of popu-lation surveys: the widening use of cell phones. In the past decade, the maximal cov-erage rate of landline-based U.S. telephone surveys has declined from 98 percent to—at best—60 percent.[35] Consequently, survey research in the past few years has undergone a metamorphosis. Today, nearly all high-quality surveys dial both landline telephones and cell phones. The primary issue with regard to dialing cell phones is cost. Typically, cell phone interviewing costs about twice as much as landline interviewing. For one thing, a large number of cell phone owners are under the age of 18 and are thus disqualified from participating in many surveys. In addition, cell phone owners refuse calls more frequently than those using landline telephones. Finally, the "telephone frame" is itself less efficient—at any given time, there are more non-working and "no answer" numbers among cell phones.

To be sure, a properly conducted study of the Jewish population requires cell phone interviewing in order to cover the Jewish population. There is no prohibition against dialing cell phones (insofar as one abides by FCC regulations and refrains from using automated dialers). We recently conducted community studies in Baltimore, Chicago, Cleveland, and New York City, designing them with a cell phone frame in addition to the landline frame. Specifically, we have dialed cell phone num-bers obtained by means of lists provided by local Federations as well as incorporat-ing an RDD component of cell phones. Overall, the steps required to incorporate cell phones into Jewish studies are becoming standardized and, while complex, are rela-tively straightforward. The results have been quite positive, and the LADS design has fared well with the inclusion of cell phones.

Weighting

Weighting procedures in Jewish surveys range from the complex to the very com-plex. The goal in weighting is always twofold: to correct for every known systematic bias associated with the survey design, and to correct, after data collection, for any biases inherent to response and non-response patterns. An additional consideration is the desire to avoid an overly large variance in the weights, lest this variance increase margins of error beyond tolerable levels.

High-quality research, such as state-level health interview surveys, typically involves a number of weighting adjustments. These include corrections for the number of telephones in a household, the number of adults or persons in a household, the percent of interviews that are cell phone versus landline, corrections for any disproportionality in the sampling, non-response adjustments, and several post-stratification adjustments intended to match the survey findings to the target population based on known parameters such as age, gender, home ownership, region, education, and race/ethnicity. This last set of adjustments corrects for many systematic patterns of non-response.

Most often, Jewish research has not made all of these corrections; in many instances, studies have justly been criticized for not sufficiently guarding against biased data. More recently, however, Jewish population studies have incorporated each of these corrections. The LADS design naturally lends itself to non-response correction, since one has both county and strata to use as controls. In addition, it has become a standard procedure to administer demographic questions to a random sample of non-Jews, so that one can adjust the entire Jewish/non-Jewish sample by a host of measures, including age, gender, educational attainment, and race/ethnicity. Of course, corrections for the disproportionality of the LADS design are always a prerequisite, as are adjustments for numbers of persons and phones in each household. The inclusion of cell phones has complicated the method, requiring accurate estimates of the number of households in the target area that are cell phone only. These can be attained by modeling National Health Interview Survey data to the specific geographic area in question. "Dual users," that is, households that have both landlines and cell phones, must also be taken into account; unfortunately the survey industry has yet to settle on a unified method for doing so. That said, for Jewish population studies, we have developed a unique method to obtain the telephone numbers within each household and to "segregate" dual users, post-hoc, into whichever stratum their household resides (for instance, if an individual reached via a cell phone number has a landline number appearing on a Federation list, the sample record would be moved to the Federation list strata), in this way enabling us to match the sample to household estimates derived from census and other data. In the end, this procedure ensures that no sample records suffer from any overlap in selection.

Discussion and Conclusion

Jewish population surveys have warranted concern with regard to their reliability and feasibility. We maintain, however, that the conclusion stemming from these concerns is not to give up on the notion of Jewish community surveys, but rather to meet the challenges they pose. To be sure, local Jewish population/community studies must be conducted with the utmost care and consideration; yet when carefully designed and executed, such studies yield highly accurate estimates of Jews.

Obviously, there is more than one solution to each of the problems outlined in this essay, and there is room for debate about possible ways to improve data collection and analysis. It is nonetheless disconcerting to encounter sweeping rejections of high-quality methods, which were voiced particularly in the wake of the 2000 NJPS (whose problems, as noted, went far beyond those connected with non-response and insufficient coverage). The argument against Jewish community surveys has several components. First, it has been argued that, "knowing the number of Jews in the U.S. and in local communities is far less interesting and important than understanding their character."[36] Although this argument addresses an issue beyond the scope of this essay, we may note that "counting" is only one of a host of research goals of a Jewish population study, and by no means the most important one. Among other things, Jewish community leaders are interested in learning where their members live and whether they are in need of more Jewish education and Jewish social services (or better access to existing services); whether their community is relatively devout or secular; and how they can better connect with their constituents. It is true that all Jewish population surveys ask one "counting" question (namely, "is anyone in your household Jewish?"). This question, however, appears alongside about 100 other questions focused on the community; consequently, about 99 percent of the data produced by such studies is in fact directed at "understanding the character" of a given community.

A second criticism (more directly addressed in this essay) is that good studies of the Jewish community simply do not exist, yet nonetheless "are treated as if they are censuses that yield actual counts."[37] This argument overlooks the fact that hundreds of demographic studies unconnected to the census are carried out in the United States every year. Five decades of scientific method and survey sampling theory—backed by data—provide ample evidence that one need not conduct a census in order to produce reasonably accurate estimates of a population.

Finally, the argument has been made that Jewish research needs to be able to look backwards in order to see how Jewish identity and engagement have evolved, something that a single population survey does not do. As noted, however, most major Jewish communities have been conducting population studies every ten years—some are now on their sixth such survey. These surveys are designed to be coupled with others. As such, and especially when carried out on a regular basis, they serve to indicate trends both stemming in the past and pointing toward the future.

Among the proposed alternatives to Jewish population surveys are meta-analyses of preexisting surveys conducted for the purposes of other research[38] and "recontact" studies in which individuals who have previously responded to a certain survey are asked to participate in a different survey. Both alternatives have a number of serious problems. Meta-analyses are generally based on mass surveys that are not geared specifically, or certainly not primarily, to the Jewish community. At most they give us a count of Jews, and a poor count at best. This is understandable, given that such polls are not about Jews per se but rather about such matters as the upcoming election and the name recognition of various candidates; or whether the respondent feels the country is headed in the right or wrong direction. Even when such surveys are broken down by religious and/or ethnic group, and even when a number of surveys are compiled and utilized, there is not enough specific data available for analysis.

In addition, meta-analysis forgoes quality control. The typical news poll may field for a few days; more exacting opinion research will field for about 10 days and make six call attempts. If a survey is conducted over the course of a weekend, no adjustments will be made to counter the fact that Orthodox Jews do not answer telephone calls on the Sabbath. Weighting procedures in these surveys are not uniformly rigorous. And the fact that meta-analysis makes use of a number of surveys can itself be problematic: one does not get more accurate results merely by combining data from different surveys with varying levels of response.

Further, secondhand polls do not allow for framing the important questions that Jewish communal leaders in every community ask: whether or not a household contains a person who self-identifies as Jewish (even if the household/respondent professes not to have a religion), whether the household behaves Jewishly, whether it is intermarried, and whether intermarried households are raising their children as Jewish. Most general surveys ask about religious identification, yet it is generally thought that only about 80 percent of Jews identify themselves as Jewish based on a question about their religion; others are Jewish by identity and/or by culture and ethnicity. How does one "find" this missing 20 percent of Jews? The solution is to use some kind of statistical model. Yet it is hard to see how this is superior to Jewish population surveys that ask more numerous (and nuanced) questions, and that directly interview those who respond.

In contrast to meta-analysis, which is based on wide-scale surveys conducted among the general U.S. population, "recontact" surveys revisit individuals who have already been identified. It has been proposed that national studies of the Jewish population can be constructed by means of recontacting religiously identified Jews who have participated in an online panel survey such as the one conducted by Knowledge Networks. Considered the best of the online surveying companies, Knowledge Networks makes use of sophisticated random-based methods; in the past, it used RRD telephone designs, but today makes use of address-based sampling (ABS) designs. A host of researchers have fruitfully utilized Knowledge Networks panels for insightful attitudinal research. Nonetheless, it is questionable whether such panel surveys can produce highly accurate and valid counts of the national Jewish population. For one thing, Knowledge Networks surveys to date have asked about religious identification rather than Jewish identity. This question, as seen, inevitably results in an undercount that must be modeled into the final data. A second concern relates to response rate. Address-based designs ordinarily attempt to match up addresses to telephone numbers and at best are successful for about half the population; for the other half, telephone numbers are not successfully matched and therefore potential respondents can be obtained only through the U.S. mail. Even given high incentivization (that is, participants are paid to complete a survey), multiple mailings, and a professionally designed and attractive survey format, an unlisted ABS sample will attain AAPOR response rates that range from 4 to 25 percent.[39]

It is important to keep in mind that Knowledge Networks surveys are based on recruiting surveys: that is, respondents are first recruited to a panel and then, at a later date, are asked to participate in a custom survey. The recent use of the Knowledge Panel for a national survey of Jews claimed a response rate in excess of 80 percent. While it may be true that 80 percent of Jews invited to take part in this survey in fact participated, this is built upon a much lower recruiting response rate. (Knowledge Networks provides explicit instructions on its website as to how to calculate a response rate using its panel—in its example, the response rate is calculated to be 13.5 percent.) It is also important to recall our analysis of the way in which a simple RDD (or in this case, ABS) design overestimates affiliated Jews and tends to overcount the Jewish population significantly. Barring post hoc adjustments, the same situation will occur in a panel survey of this sort.

In sum, the alternative methods outlined here do not offer greater quality control, on a range of quality criteria. These methods are less precise in their measurement of the Jewish population, and just as important, fail in respect to the very criteria—lack of coverage and low response rate—that originally framed critical arguments against direct Jewish community research.

Jewish research scholars are absolutely justified in demanding high-quality research, and specifically research that approaches near universal coverage, low non-response, and context and insight into the Jewish community. Many of these concerns are shared by survey researchers in dozens of other fields. Nevertheless, they have a unique applicability to Jewish research. This essay demonstrates the ways in which survey researchers can meet the challenge by being careful in their design of surveys, their fielding of surveys, and their weighting of survey data. It is our belief that the science of survey research offers a set of tools enabling us to confront a range of methodological difficulties, and thus allowing us to continue the centuries-long tradition of the *mifkad*, the Jewish population count.

Notes

The authors would like to thank Steven Cohen, Jack Ukeles, Robyn Rapoport, and Melissa Herrmann for their review of and commentary on earlier drafts of this paper.

1. Laurence Kotler-Berkowitz, "Ethnic Cohesion and Division among American Jews: The Role of Mass-level and Organizational Politics," *Ethnic and Racial Studies* 20, no. 4 (1997), 797–829; Harriet Hartman and Moshe Hartman, "Denominational Differences in the Attachment to Israel of American Jews," *Review of Religious Research* 41, no. 3 (2000), 394–417; Uzi Rebhun, "Jewish Identification in Intermarriage: Does a Spouse's Religion (Catholic vs. Protestant) Matter?" *Sociology of Religion* 60, no. 1 (1999), 71–88; Robert P. Amyot and Lee Sigelman, "Jews without Judaism? Assimilation and Jewish Identity in the United States," *Social Science Quarterly* 77, no. 1 (1996), 177–189; Alan S. Miller, "The Influence of Religious Affiliation on the Clustering of Social Attitudes," *Review of Religious Research* 37, no. 3 (1996), 219–232.

2. Most of these surveys are available at the North American Jewish Data Bank, online at www.jewishdatabank.org. The authors of this essay make up the core methods team of Jewish Policy and Action Research (JPAR), a collaborative research partnership of Social Science Research Solutions (SSRS, formerly ICR/International Communications Research) and Ukeles Associates, Inc. (UAI). JPAR has conducted Jewish community surveys in New York, Chicago, Philadelphia, Baltimore, Cincinnati, Cleveland, San Diego, Pittsburgh, Phoenix, Denver, and Atlanta.

3. See United Jewish Communities, *The National Jewish Population Survey 2000–01: Strength, Challenge, and Diversity in the American Jewish Population* (New York: 2003).

4. Charles Kadushin, Benjamin T. Phillips, and Leonard Saxe, "National Jewish Population Survey 2000–1: A Guide for the Perplexed," *Contemporary Jewry* 25 (December 2005), 2. To be sure, the 2000 NJPS survey also had proponents. See, for instance, Sergio DellaPergola, "Was it the Demography? A Reassessment of U.S. Jewish Population Estimates, 1945–2001," ibid., 85–131.

5. Mark A. Schulman, *National Jewish Population Survey 2000–2001: Study Review Memo* (New York: 2003), 12; Charles Kadushin, Benjamin Phillips, Leonard Saxe, and Elizabeth Tighe, *Reconsidering the Size and Characteristics of the American Jewish Population: New Estimates* (Waltham: 2007).

6. See, for instance, the following articles, all of which appear in *Sociology of Religion* 67, no. 4 (Winter 2006): Nancy Ammerman, "Religious Identities in Contemporary American Life: Lessons from the NJPS," 359–364; Charles Kadushin and Laurence Kotler-Berkowitz, "Informal Social Organizational Membership among American Jews: Findings from the National Jewish Population Survey 2000–01, 465–485; Laurence Kotler-Berkowitz, "An Introduction to the National Jewish Population Survey 2000–01," 387–390.

7. Leonard Saxe, "Counting American Jewry," *Sh'ma: A Journal of Jewish Responsibility 41* (October 2010), 14–15.

8. Ibid.

9. In 1957, a special census study of 35,000 households did ask about religion.

10. See, for instance, the following (on religious studies): Roberta G. Sands, Steven C. Marcus, and Rivka A. Danzig, "The Direction of Denominational Switching in Judaism," *Journal for the Scientific Study of Religion* 45, no. 3 (2006), 437–447; (on social dynamics): Kadushin and Kotler-Berkowitz, "Informal Social Organizational Membership among American Jews"; Uzi Rebhun, "Jewish Identities in America: Structural Analysis of Attitudes and Behavior," *Review of Religious Research* 46, no. 10 (2004), 43–63; (on the attitudes, beliefs, and identity of Jewish Americans): Kotler-Berkowitz, "Ethnic Cohesion and Division among American Jews"; Moshe Hartman and Harriet Hartman, "Gender and Jewish Identity," *Journal of Contemporary Religion* 18, no. 1 (2004), 37–61; Rebhun, "Jewish Identification in Intermarriage"; Robert P. Amyot and Lee Siegelman, "Jews without Judaism? Assimilation and Jewish Identity in the United States," *Social Science Quarterly* 77 (March 1996), 177–189.

11. A history of such studies is well documented in Kadushin, Phillips, Saxe, and Tighe, *Reconsidering the Size and Characteristics of the American Jewish Population*.

12. Robert M. Groves, "Nonresponse Rates and Nonresponse Bias in Household Surveys," *Public Opinion Quarterly* 70, no. 5 (2006), 646–675.

13. Robert W. Oldendick, and Michael W. Link, "The Answering Machine Generation: Who are They and What Problem Do They Pose for Survey Research?" *Public Opinion Quarterly* 58, no. 2 (1994), 264–273; Don A. Dillman, *Mail and Internet Surveys* (New York: 2007).

14. Kadushin, Phillips, and Saxe, "National Jewish Population Survey 2000–1," 1–32; Schulman, *National Jewish Population Survey 2000–2001*, 1–24.

15. Michael W. Traugott and Paul J. Lavrakas, *The Voter's Guide to Election Polls*, 47th ed. (Lanham: 2008), 78.

16. Penny Visser, Jon A. Krosnick, Jesse A. Marquette, and Michael Curtin, "Mail Surveys for Election Forecasting? An Evaluation of the *Columbus Dispatch* Poll," *Public Opinion Quarterly* 60, no. 2 (1996), 181–227.

17. Richard Curtin, Stanley Presser, and Eleanor Singer, "The Effects of Response Rate Changes on the Index of Consumer Sentiment," *Public Opinion Quarterly* 64, no. 4 (2000), 413–428.

18. Allyson Holbrook, Jon Krosnick, and Alison Pfent, "Response Rates in Surveys by the News Media and Government Contractor Survey Research Firms," in *Advances in Telephone Survey Methodology*, ed. James M. Lepkowski et al. (New York: 2007), 499–528.

19. Scott Keeter, Carolyn Miller, Andrew Kohut, Robert M. Groves, and Stanley Presser, "Consequences of Reducing Nonresponse in a National Telephone Survey," *Public Opinion Quarterly* 64, no. 2 (2000), 125–148.

20. Peter Tuckel and Harry O'Neill, "The Vanishing Respondent in Telephone Surveys" (paper presented at the annual meeting of the American Association for Public Opinion Research, Montreal, 17–20 May 2001).

21. Kadushin, Phillips, and Saxe, "National Jewish Population Survey 2000–1," 1–32.

22. Yet another concern relates to the reliability of measures of response rates. In an analysis conducted by Kadushin, Phillips, Saxe, and Tighe (*Reconsidering the Size and Characteristics of the American Jewish Population*), a positive relationship was found between the level of response to population surveys and the estimated number of Jews in the area being surveyed. However, some of the response rates in this study are subject to question. In 22 percent of the surveys, the reported rates were 60 percent or higher—a level that is considered to be virtually

unobtainable (even the most rigorous surveys, such as those conducted by the Behaviorial Risk Factor Surveillance System for the Centers for Disease Control and Prevention, rarely attain rates above the upper 40 percent range). There is also the possibility that some response rates may have been misreported. The 1990 NJPS, for example, was derived from an omnibus survey that has regularly reported response rates in the single digits to low teens. Notwithstanding, the overall response rate of the 1990 NJPS was said to be 36 percent.

23. Kadushin, Phillips, and Saxe, "National Jewish Population Survey 2000–1," 1–32; Schulman, *National Jewish Population Survey 2000–2001*, 1–24.

24. Gary Tobin and Sid Groeneman, *Surveying the Jewish Population in the United States* (San Francisco: 2003).

25. Stephen Blumberg and Julian V. Luke, "Wireless Substitution: Early Release of Estimates from the National Health Interview Survey, January–June 2010," National Center for Health Statistics (December 2010), online at www.cdc.gov/nchs/data/nhis/earlyrelease/wireless201012.htm (accessed 12 February 2012).

26. Kadushin, Phillips, Saxe, and Tighe, *Reconsidering the Size and Characteristics of the American Jewish Population*. A different explanation for this finding is that the screening for the previous NJPS survey (1990) was based on an omnibus study unrelated to Jewish population research. In this study, screening was conducted without regard to the Sabbath or to Jewish holidays; in consequence, Orthodox households may have been underrepresented. In contrast, the 2000 NJPS applied the schedule used in the majority of Jewish population studies, in which no calls are made on Friday nights, Saturdays, and Jewish holidays. This may have resulted in a (perceived) overrepresentation of Orthodox households.

27. Bernard Lazerwitz, "An Estimate of a Rare Population Group: The U.S. Jewish Population," *Demography* 15, no. 3 (August 1978), 389–394.

28. "Standard Definitions: Final Dispositions of Case Codes and Outcome Rates for Surveys," *American Association for Public Opinion Research* (2009), online at www.aapor.org/AM/Template.cfm?Section=Standard_Definitions1&Template=/CM/ContentDisplay.cfm&ContentID=1814 (accessed 12 February 2012).

29. "BRFSS Annual Survey Data: 2005 Summary Data Quality Report," *Behavioral Risk Factor Surveillance System*, 2005, online at www.cdc.gov/brfss/technical_infodata/2005qUALITYreport.htm (accessed 12 February 2012).

30. Christopher McCarty, Mark House, Jeffrey Harman and Scott Richards, "Effort in Phone Survey Response Rates: The Effects of Vendor and Client-Controlled Factors," *Field Methods* 18, no. 2 (2006), 172–188.

31. Timothy Triplett, Julie Scheib, and Johnny Blair, "How Long Should You Wait before Attempting to Convert a Telephone Refusal?" (proceedings of the annual meeting of the American Statistical Association, 5–9 August 2001), online at www.amstat.org/sections/srms/proceedings/y2001/Proceed/00288.pdf (accessed 12 February 2012).

32. In predictive dialing, a computer dials more numbers than there are available interviewers, since some percent of the numbers will be non-working, busy, or otherwise unresponsive. In this manner it "predicts" when presently busy interviewers will be available for a live call, significantly increasing the productivity of the interviewers. However, the practice also leads to "nuisance calls," a situation in which a potential respondent picks up the phone and does not hear anything on the other end for about 5 seconds, since the predictive dialer misjudged when a potential respondent would in fact be available to talk. Such nuisance calls typically result in the respondent hanging up, hence a refused interview.

33. The LADS design was first utilized in Jewish population research in the 1996 Philadelphia community study conducted by Ron Miller and Jack Ukeles of Ukeles Associates, Inc. (UAI), the late Dale Kulp of Marketing Systems Group (MSG), and the social science research team at International Communications Research (now Social Science Research Solutions, SSRS).

34. Survey incidence refers to the percentage of people who qualify to participate in a survey, based on an initial screening question. When the screening is for Jewish status, an RDD sample shows a survey incidence roughly equal (not always exactly equal, since there may be a range of sampling error) to the population incidence. The LADS design, by targeting

Jewish population more precisely, attains a survey incidence significantly higher than the Jewish population incidence.

35. This essay does not deal with the phenomenon of "zero-bank households"—those falling within a 1,000-block series of telephone numbers (for instance, 999-999-1000 through 999-999-1999) in which none of the numbers is a "white pages" listed telephone number. Such numbers are excluded from RDD sampling. On the impact of zero-bank households, see John Boyle, Michael Bucuvalas, Linda Piekarski, and Andy Weiss, "Zero Banks: Coverage Error and Bias in RDD Samples Based on Hundred [sic] Banks with Listed Numbers," *Public Opinion Quarterly* 73, no. 4 (2009), 729–750.

36. Leonard Saxe, "What Numbers Tell Us about Jewish Community," *New Jersey Jewish News* (6 October 2010).

37. Ibid.

38. Ibid.

39. This range is based on studies conducted by David Dutwin, who taught courses on ABS at the American Association for Public Opinion Research in 2010 and 2011 and at the Pacific chapter in 2009. Dutwin also conducted a number of major health interview surveys utilizing ABS methods and an ABS-based weekly omnibus for SSRS.

Studies of Jewish Identity and Continuity: Competing, Complementary, and Comparative Perspectives

Harriet Hartman
(ROWAN UNIVERSITY)

Nearly a decade ago, Steven M. Cohen wrote an essay reflecting on Jewish identity research in the United States, in which he noted a shift in focus from "integrationism" to "survivalism."[1]After 1967, he wrote, American Jews no longer were marginalized in terms of the broader society, but seemed instead to be threatened from within: at risk was the exceptionalism with which Jews had come to be regarded from both outside and inside. Cohen offered competing explanations on the part of "assimilationists," "transformationists," and those discerning polarization or bimodality as to whether and how the Jewish community would survive.

In the following, I will elaborate on Cohen's analysis of the various perspectives regarding the quality of Jewish survival and will propose two additional dimensions (authenticity and boundaries) relevant to the study of Jewish identity. I will also show that competing perspectives are not confined to studies of American Jewish identity but can rather be used to clarify the challenges faced by diaspora Jews throughout the world. The research on U.S. Jewish identity focuses on different levels of Jewish "space,"[2] but also tends to put more emphasis on individual Jewish identity rather than that of the collective, in contrast to studies of Jewish identity in areas such as Europe or Latin America. Following a discussion on how competing perspectives on survival, authenticity, and boundaries play out on a number of different levels of Jewish space, I will examine how these perspectives are related to those on Jewish continuity and will offer some ideas for furthering intersectional analysis[3] of Jewish identity in a cross-cultural manner.

Competing Perspectives

Survival

A major differentiation in perspectives on North American Jewish identity concerns the quality of "survival." Many assimilationists pessimistically foresee a "vanishing

74

American Jew" as a consequence of assimilation, high rates of intermarriage, low levels of ritual observance, and a weak commitment to Jewish communal institutions.[4] (Vanishing, in this sense, refers to the disappearance of the exceptionality of American Jews vis-à-vis other ethnic or religious groups, as distinctive Jewish ways of life are abandoned in the interest of blending in with the broader society.) Writing about Europe, Bernard Wasserstein echoes this pessimism, predicting a gradual demise of European Jewry due to increased secularization as well as the factors mentioned above.[5] A more sanguine view is voiced (for the U.S. context) by Jonathan Sarna, who notes that, whereas dire predictions have been a constant companion to studies of American Jews, with roots early in U.S. history, American Jewry nonetheless persists.[6]

A second school of thought, that of the "transformationists," sees Jewish identity persisting but under different terms than in the past. Calvin Goldscheider was an early and consistent proponent of this approach, suggesting that despite waning traditional religious practices, Jewish ethnic identification would remain strong because of the social, economic, and structural ties promoting American Jewish solidarity.[7] Tom Smith has documented many ways in which the distinctiveness of American Jews has been preserved, though his analysis makes little reference to religious practices.[8] David Graham typologizes European Jewish identity on a continuum ranging from "no tradition" and "abandonment of tradition" to "reverting to tradition" and "preserving traditions" (in the middle are "secularising" and "tradition as a symbol"). One trend, he notes, is that "the meanings attached to the celebration of Jewish holidays have changed from an expression of religious commitment to an expression of 'a bond with Jewish tradition'"—echoing a theme put forth by the transformationist perspectives on American Jewry.[9]

In *Shylock's Children* (2001), Derek Penslar chronicles the development of the perception of Jewish socioeconomic exceptionalism in Europe, concluding, however, that such "associational" Judaism has declined as the "privatization of Jewish identity" has increased. Arnold Dashefsky, Bernard Lazerwitz, and Ephraim Tabory differentiate between the "straight" and "roundabout" journeys of Jewish identity. The former refers to the traditional journey by which Jewish identity develops (Jewish parentage, formal Jewish education, intra-marriage, Jewish identity and communal participation, and transmission of Jewish identity to the next generation), as embodied in Jewish religious law (halakhah), with greater emphasis on communal responsibility rather than individual rights.[10] A traditional journey also includes the creation of an ethnic identity, which has been marked by such behaviors as social networking and mate selection, participation in ethnic festivals and in non-synagogue Jewish communal organizations, the acquisition of language skills, visits to Israel, and the reading of Jewish periodicals.[11] "Roundabout" journeys, in contrast, represent a transformation of Jewish identity by means of individual choices; Bethamie Horowitz provides a number of examples of such "roundabout paths" in her *Journeys and Connections*, as have Debra Kaufmann, Steven Cohen and Arnold Eisen, and Shaul Kelner.[12]

A third school of thought attempts to synthesize these two approaches, positing increasing polarization or "bi-polarity," with growth among both the most identified and least identified segments of the Jewish community. This view was first proposed by Harold Himmelfarb and Michael Loar and also appears in work authored by Jack Wertheimer, Steven Cohen, and Jonathan Sarna.[13] Cohen suggests a research strategy of "segmenting the market" by means of marriage patterns, looking for separate and differentiated patterns among the in-married, the intermarried, and the unmarried.[14] Bruce Phillips' research on Jewish secularism supports this approach; he shows that Jews who espouse no religion also have weaker ethnic identification as Jews, which can be explained by the much greater likelihood of such Jews having parents of mixed ancestry.[15] Jacob Ukeles, Ron Miller, and Pearl Beck have advocated including the Orthodox as a distinctive fourth major segment, different from all non-Orthodox.[16] Wertheimer, similarly, suggests that the key divide in American Jewish life today is between the Orthodox and everyone else.[17]

The polarization thesis has been challenged by a number of empirical findings. In a structural analysis of Jewish identity attitudes and behaviors, Uzi Rebhun found that subpopulations of American Jews share a coherent analytical structure of Jewish identity.[18] Further, Jewish identity in the United States and Israel is characterized by similar components of normative ritual behaviors; educational and learning behaviors; philanthropy and participation in organizations; family and life cycle events; and a commitment to the Jewish peoplehood as central. (To be sure, American and Israeli Jews differ in terms of how they relate to Israel—as a source primarily of personal fulfillment or, alternatively, as a source of personal responsibility. In addition, Israeli identity has a core, "civic society" component, which corresponds to the more general "culture and politics" component of U.S. Jewish identity.)[19] Elihu Katz cites research showing that, even in the largely secularized Israeli society, religious identity falls on a continuum as opposed to being polarized between the observant and nonobservant.[20] These findings, as we shall see, argue against the polarization thesis, as do more comprehensive views regarding the persistence of a sense of Jewish collective (*klal yisrael*).

Judit Liwerant and Eliezer Ben-Rafael suggest that, globally, Jewish identities and Jewish life are split along two major dimensions: a transnational dimension, related to the content of Judaism, and a spatial dimension, related to geography and culture. Notwithstanding, Jewish identity draws on the same "trove of customs and narratives," and this preserves a sense of global Jewish identity.[21] In his recent survey of Jewish identity research, Erik Cohen situates the study of Jewish identity in the context of broader trends in contemporary identity research, as well as global trends in the study of Jewish identity.[22] For example, the transition from an emphasis on assimilation—or "integrationism," as he terms it—to that of greater focus given to the quality of a group's identity parallels the shift from early research on minorities in western cultures (which assumed their gradual assimilation) to later research dealing with the question of how cultural identity is formed and transformed in pluralistic societies.[23]

Gabriel Sheffer sketches the varying positions of pessimists and optimists in the study of European Jewry, starting with Wasserstein's *Vanishing Diaspora* and ending with Diana Pinto's optimism regarding the cultural revival of European Jewry. Indeed, Pinto suggests that European Jewry, with its renewed and expanded Jewish educational networks and large and thriving organizations, can represent a third pillar of global Jewry.[24]

Authenticity

A second axis of differentiation in approaches to Jewish identity is that of authenticity. On one side are "essentialists," who claim that there is a minimum component of content requisite for an identity to be Jewish (even if the actual components may be in dispute).[25] The most primordial essentialism involves biological parentage or genetics. Traditionally, Jews have been defined as those born to a Jewish mother (or to any Jewish parent, according to the Reform and Reconstructionists), but more recently some Jews have also expressed their Jewishness as a perceived genetic or biological essentialism.[26] While it might be expected that such ascriptive definitions of Jewish identity would have disappeared by the 21st century, Susan Kahn suggests that new genetic technologies have reformulated questions about the biological essentialism of Jewishness in the varied fields of population genetics, medical genetics, and rabbinic discourse on reproductive technologies.[27] Similarly, Shelly Tenenbaum and Lynn Davidman find that some Jews have chosen to appropriate the genetic or biological definition of Jewishness, as this minimizes the effort that must be expended to establish Jewish identity. A different approach is taken by Gad Barzilai, who demonstrates the complexities of applying essentialist definitions of "who is a Jew" both within and outside of Israel.[28]

Liwerant and Ben-Rafael express a different essentialist position when they state: "Jewish identities elaborate on the codes of traditional Judaism which has implied a triple commitment—to the Jewish People, to the singularity perceived as embodied in the Torah, and to the Land of Israel."[29] Jewish peoplehood implies an ethnic bond, Torah a religious bond, and the land of Israel primarily a historical and geographical bond. Yet the extent to which Jewish identity is based on religion and/or ethnicity has also generated controversy. Herbert Gans, among others, has noted the strongly intertwined religious and ethnic identities among Jews.[30] However, Stephen Sharot argues that the process of secularization made it possible for Jews to identify in purely religious terms or else to identify with the Jewish people without concern for a religious dimension. He also provides numerous examples of Jews with religious *and/or* ethnic identity, including Jewish Christians (who maintain their Jewish ethnicity) and converts to Judaism (who maintain a non-Jewish ethnicity).[31] Caryn Aviv and David Shneer, as well as Denise Roman, similarly document either/or identifications.[32] S. Daniel Breslauer develops the idea of Judaism without religion even further, expanding the "covenant" of Jewishness to encompass many more facets of Jewish life that give meaning at any given time/place to a community and its adherents.[33] In this, he is supported by findings of the Posen Foundation's American Jewish Identity Survey (2001), in which about a third of American Jews (defined by ancestry) professed "no religion." This is the highest proportion of any religious subgroup in the United States, according to the parallel American Religious Identity Survey (2001) conducted by Barry Kosmin and Ariela Keysar at the Trinity College Center for the Study of Religion in Public Life. These "nones" mostly defined themselves as "secular" or "somewhat secular," although nearly a fourth defined themselves as "religious" or "somewhat religious."[34]

Further complicating the understanding of Jewish identity is Gans' insight into symbolic ethnicity and religiosity: the former, relating to consumption of ethnic symbols of Jewish identity (for instance, foods, books, household items with Jewish themes or symbols) without participation in an existing ethnic organization or an on-going ethnic culture, is symbolic, whereas symbolic religiosity is the consumption of religious symbols that are decontextualized from traditional, comprehensive religious culture.[35] Sharot, following Gans, suggests that the ethnicity of contemporary American Jews is expressed through religious symbolism (for instance, traditional foods, candlesticks, and even occasional synagogue attendance), and that Gans' observations of "symbolic religiosity" reflect the ethnic function of religious practice and identification in the United States. Sharot reframes Gans' concepts in terms of ethnic acculturation and religious acculturation (as, for example, introducing English into traditionally Hebrew religious services), which fits the "survival" dimension noted above. Yet he also notes that there has been a "deacculturation" in Reform Judaism (more Hebrew, more reference to Zion, use of head covering and tallit in synagogue). This "re-appropriation of traditional forms does not make the religious behavior…less symbolic…in the sense of providing symbols for ethnic feelings" but rather goes to show that both ethnic and religious identity have undergone a "bumpy-line process" of acculturation, characterized especially by the bi-polar tendencies mentioned above.[36] Sharot, therefore, does not agree with the "ethnic de-cline" perspective espoused by Steven Cohen or Dashefsky, Lawerwitz, and Tabory.[37] Instead, he regards the re-adoption of traditional religious practices as a process of strengthening ethnic re-identification.

In contrast to the essentialists are those who question the legitimacy of essen-tialism, challenging particular elements of identity or the very notion of a fixed con-tent as essential. They tend to focus on (in Bethamie Horowitz's words): "how Jews are Jewish" rather than "how Jewish" they are.[38] Their emphasis is on what self-identifying Jews do, and they question the legitimacy of a standard against which anyone's Jewishness can be measured and labeled as more or less authentic. Debra Kaufman, for instance, asks whose experiences constitute shared culture and whose authority authenticates a tradition.[39] A major contribution from the direction of feminism is the heightened awareness that the experience of Jewishness, and its expression in terms of Jewish identity, varies by gender, age, and life cycle stage.[40] For example, because of different traditional obligations in terms of performing religious commandments, even Orthodox women and men observe ritual in different fre-quency and constancy; because of men's traditionally greater investment in careers, communal participation may be more advantageous to them; and because of the pre-dominance of widows (rather than widowers), communal Jewish activities are more meaningful for older women than for men.[41] Further, the gendering of Jewish life actually reflects identity struggles that Jews experience with regard to class and culture.[42]

Samuel Heilman notes that American Jewish identity may be determined from at least four perspectives: ethnicity, culture, religion, and personal choice, and that these are not mutually exclusive (some Jews express only one type of identity, while others express all four).[43] Pinto adds that "one can be Jewish in a religious, cultural, intellectual, ethnic, and political sense," and one type of identity does not necessarily imply any other.[44] Werner Sollors has suggested that ethnic identity can be considered in terms of "descent" (ascribed status) or "consent" (achieved status); Karen Brodkin extends this idea into that of a continuum.[45] In our analysis of intermarriage, Moshe Hartman and I have suggested that conversion for the purpose of marriage often assumes a meaning of achieved ethnicity rather than achieved religion, although achieved ethnicity may not be completely accepted by others.[46]

Vincent Brook offers yet another way of thinking about ethnicity: "dissent," in which lines of descent and consent are both rejected in favor of a "post-ethnic" adoption (and, perhaps, rejection) of Jewish identity almost at will, suggesting that this conceptualization represents a postmodern version of Gans' "symbolic" Judaism.[47] According to Michelle Byers, the concept of "dissent" reflects the "deep ambivalence, fluidity, contradiction of ethnicity"—ethnicity "destabilized."[48] David Hollinger uses the term "post-ethnicity" to imply "a strong legacy from the past, but a refinement of that legacy in relation to new opportunities and constraints."[49] Shmuel Magid, for his part, suggests that Hollinger's notion of post-ethnicity relates not only to voluntary identities reclaimed from various available options, but also *invented* identities, moving away from the idea that "descent is destiny." This shift may make it possible for those whose "descent" is less traditional (for example, not through kinship) to identify with the idea of "Jewish peoplehood."[50]

Such post-traditional outlooks raise new questions about the structure of Jewish identity—and also call for new answers. Liwerant and Ben-Rafael trace this development to "radical modernity and globalization processes," which have both challenged shared values and "deconstructed certainties and reconstructed belongingness."[51] Indeed, they suggest that Jewish identity

> has never been homogeneous, a statement all the more true today. Internal differentiations, divergent symbols of identification and differences in the meanings ascribed to them, as well as enduring dialogues and debates, have unfolded within the changing perimeters of the Jewish world in various spatial, geopolitical, and socio-cultural contexts. The present recovers and reshapes old and new historical conditions: religion coexists with secularization processes; peoplehood develops hand in hand with national existence; ethnicity and civic commonalities reaffirm one another, and collective belongingness interacts with assimilation trends, while new forms of cohesiveness find their way into the private and public realms of a diversified Jewish existence.[52]

Aviv and Shneer's *New Jews: The End of the Jewish Diaspora*, an excellent example of this approach, deconstructs Jewish identity away from the land of Israel as central and even away from a sense of Jewish peoplehood. In an epilogue, the authors argue that "the only thing that Jews have in common is the fact that they self-identify as Jews." The autonomous self becomes the center of identity, a perspective echoed in Cohen and Eisen's *The Jew Within*.

Liwerant and Ben-Rafael suggest that globalization processes have reordered territorial and even communal spaces, resulting in both elective sources of identity as well as a revival of primordial identities. "Old and new identities thus oscillate in a tense fluctuation between the moment of the unique and the universal, the moment of the common and the particular."[53] This oscillation, perhaps, should be seen as a synthesis of the previous positions. It is a point made also by Daniel and Jonathan Boyarin when they claim that what consistently characterizes Jewish identity—and what Jewishness most valuably contributes to the world—is the tension between its different components: "Jewishness disrupts the very categories of identity because it is not national, not genealogical, not religious, but *all of these in dialectical tension with one another.*"[54]

Boundaries

Scholars also differ in the ways they draw the boundaries of Jewish identity and how they evaluate the challenges to them.[55] There is, indeed, a recent book of this title that brings many of the issues to the forefront.[56] Similarly, Riv-Ellen Prell notes the centrality of boundaries (along with belief and belonging) as central tenets of Jewish identity and its scholarship.[57] This can be seen, for instance, in analyses of the National Jewish Population Surveys, where distinctions were drawn between a variety of Jewish subpopulations, among them "core" Jews, who reported Judaism as their present religion; ethnic Jews (or "just Jewish"), who defined themselves as Jews but declared no religious preference; persons of Jewish background, who did not self-identify as Jews; and Jews by choice, who either formally converted to Judaism or are Jewish only by personal self-definition.[58] Sometimes non-Jews living in close quarters with Jews (that is, married to a Jewish spouse, or a child of intermarriage who is not being raised as Jewish) are included in studies of American Jews, at least as members of Jewish households. In their analyses, scholars draw the boundaries of their samples in different places, as Kotler-Berkowitz points out.[59] As we shall see, Theodore Sasson, Leonard Saxe, and Charles Kadushin, in their analysis of the attitudes and attachment toward Israel of American Jews, rely on the American Jewish Community surveys, which are restricted to those who self-define as "Jews-by-religion." Yet part of the debate over the validity of their conclusions is the willingness to accept their boundaries of exclusivity.[60]

In their analysis of Jewish identity, Europeans tend to disregard the issue of boundaries. Indeed, a recent study found that East European Jews in Bulgaria, Hungary, Latvia, Poland, and Romania were quite comfortable with the permeable boundaries of their Jewish communities: most agree that it is not important whether someone is Jewish or not with regard to marriage, and only a minority think it would be better if there were fewer mixed marriages.[61] Empirical research is needed to determine whether this is increasingly true of American Jews as well.

Complementary Levels of Focus

Research on Jewish identity typically focuses on one or two levels. First, we can distinguish between individual and collective Jewish identity. Second, when we speak of an individual's Jewish identity, we can distinguish between the identity expressed in private or intimate settings and that voiced in public settings.[62] This individual identity, in turn, is related to, and influenced by, collective Jewish identity, which characterizes a (Jewish) community. Third, collective Jewish identity can pertain to the local community, the broader Jewish community—often referred to as *klal yisrael*—and the broader society, either vis-à-vis the immediate broader context or in a more universalistic context. As mentioned above, Pinto presents these parameters of Jewish life as a set of distinct Jewish "boxes" forming the "Jewish space," each expandable or contractible according to circumstances.[63]

Figure 4.1 presents these levels of "Jewish space" as concentric circles, which indeed may contract or expand in different circumstances. Individual identity can be expressed in each of the collective levels; hence, a person may manifest his or her individual Jewish identity when engaging in activities in the name of *tikun 'olam* (repairing/bettering the world) or *klal yisrael* (or both). But these collective levels are also characterized by an identity of their own, beyond the individual, which may influence the individual while at the same time interacting with the broader society. Figure 4.1 also shows how the competing perspectives mentioned above (survival, authenticity, and boundaries) cross-cut each of these levels of identity.

Rebhun suggests that Jewish identity varies by time, space, and sub-identity: time situates the identity historically and generationally as well as by age and life cycle stage; space situates the identity in a cultural, ideological, and social context as well as in a particular immigrant and demographic situation; sub-identity refers to the extent to which an identity is distinguishable from other identities that may co-exist within the individual or collectivity.[64] Rebhun recognizes that each of these dimensions is multilayered, expressing itself at individual, institutional, national, and even international levels. He adds to the distinctions mentioned above the variation in individual Jewish identity in terms of whether it is attitudinal or behavioral in nature, publicly or privately expressed, religious or ethnic, and persistent or intermittent. He suggests that the type of Jewish identity a given individual holds is determined by a constant interaction both between primordial or ascribed affinities and the time, space, and exclusivity dimensions. The current attempt to understand Jewish identity uses some of these same axes of differentiation: our axes of boundaries relates to Rebhun's exclusivity dimension, whereas the survival orientation relates to his time orientation. Instead of the space dimension, however, we consider how these axes affect the different levels of "Jewish space," and we add the axis of authenticity to the picture.

Interestingly, the region being studied appears to influence which level of Jewish identity is emphasized. In line with the strong value on individualism in contemporary American society and a less pronounced focus on organizational and communal arenas,[65] the most prominent studies of Jewish identity in the United States deal with the intrapersonal level of the self, and the self in relation to these other levels. Research on Jewish identity in Israel has also focused on an individual's Jewish identity.[66] In Israel, however, the study of Israeli institutions is itself a study of Jewish communal organizing and, to some extent, the Jewish community's relations with its non-Jewish counterparts in Israel and neighboring countries. This level of focus is more common in Israel than in the United States. Fewer studies of individual Jewish identity have been done in Europe or Latin America.[67] Graham has summarized the European research (up to 2004); only recently has a ground-breaking study of individuals' Jewish identity in five East European countries been undertaken.[68]

While less has been done on collective Jewish identity in the United States, community studies are a primary source for current data collection, each of which addresses the collective Jewish identity of the community (even if not labeled explicitly as such), at least with regard to relationships among Jews and with Jewish institu-

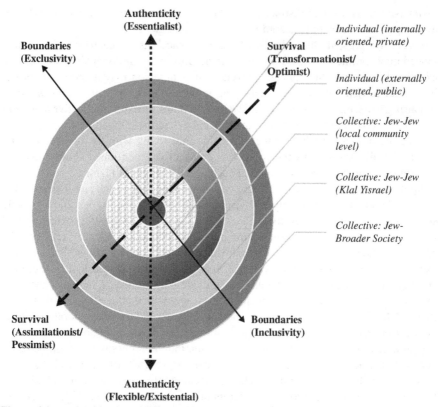

Figure 4.1. Jewish identity at different levels of "Jewish space"

tions in the community.[69] In a recent article, Paul Burstein begins to update our knowledge of Jewish communal organizations, but acknowledges that his is but a first step in understanding American collective Jewish identity through its organizations.[70] In contrast, studies of Jewish identity in Latin America have concentrated almost exclusively on the Jewish communal level as well as its relation to the broader society.[71] European studies have focused primarily on the relationship between the wider society and the Jewish community with regard to such issues as responses to the Holocaust, how to deal with new immigrants who pose antisemitic challenges to the society; and the possible role of Jews in creating a new social order in the broader European Union.[72]

Shmuel Trigano suggests that in Europe, the Holocaust ended the Emancipation era in which Jews were recognized as individuals and as unidentified, anonymous citizens. In postwar Europe, Jews were assigned a collective, non-voluntary identity—a phenomenon that American Jews experienced to a much lesser extent. Moreover, European Jewish life was reconstituted on the basis of communal (collective) identities, whereas the broader society, in institutionalizing the memory of the Holocaust, found a way to legitimize Jewish existence by identifying Jews as victims and martyrs. The challenge, as Trigano and Pinto (and others) see it, is to transform the conceptualization of European Jews, in the eyes of both European Jews and non-Jews, from a "dead and celebrated people" to a "living and legitimate people."[73]

Individual Jewish Identity

Survival

Most of the research on American Jewish identity focuses on the individual's sense of Jewish identity, which is carried through an extensive set of particularistic group beliefs, values, commandments, behavior patterns, and attitudes.[74] As noted, Hartman and Hartman, and later Rebhun, distinguish between private, more internally oriented religious and ethnic identity, on the one hand, and public, collective, or externally oriented religious and ethnic identity, on the other.[75] Charles Liebman differentiates between social/behavioral and personalized/privatized ethnicity. In his view, privatized ethnicity entails less commitment than outwardly oriented social and behavioral ethnicity.[76]

The Hartman and Hartman study, in contrast to that of Liebman, indicates that the private dimension of identity includes a personal commitment to rituals that are carried out either as an individual or in intimate and often daily settings. Hence, it involves more intensive commitment than the less frequent rituals performed in more communal settings. Liebman's concept of personalized, privatized ethnicity has more in common with Gans' notion of symbolic ethnic and religious identity, which delineates an individual's "consumption and other use" of ethnicity or religious identification without any actual participation in the religious or ethnic community or practices. The controversy over Gans' symbolic ethnicity centers on whether it truly reflects a "mental ethnicity" rather than a more committing, social/behavioral ethnicity; or perhaps simply a nontraditional identity, which may be as compelling as the traditional.[77] Mary Waters, for her part, suggests that (symbolic) ethnicity fulfills the need among many Americans to be connected to community without sacrificing individuality.[78]

The understanding of individual Jewish identity is also intricately related to methodology. Up until the 1990s, data were most commonly gathered in quantitative studies, which were often not focused explicitly on the issue of Jewish identity. The repeated repertoire of indicators—including childhood family religious and ethnic background and religious education; religious participation; family involvement in Jewishness during childhood; and children's socialization[79]—allows for comparability between studies and populations, but has been critiqued for its bias toward the "essentialist" position of the "necessary ingredients" of traditional Jewish identity, as well as for the way it has been used to characterize "more" as opposed to "less" Jewishness.[80] In the late 1990s, a number of researchers, among them Bethamie Horowitz in her *Connections and Journeys* and Steven Cohen and Arnold Eisen, in *The Jew Within*, broke tradition by introducing qualitative studies of individual Jewish identity.[81] In both cases, new understandings of contemporary Jewish identities were revealed, giving more detailed content to the "roundabout paths" to

Jewish identity that Dashefsky, Lazerwitz, and Tabory described in the following manner:

> As American Jewry has become transformed by a postmodern, individualistic, multicultural society, so Jewish identity and its measurement have been altered from relying on more external, objective measures (corresponding to the "straight way") to more subjective ones (related to the "roundabout path"). This shift has led to even less consensus as to what Jewish identity means to American Jews and has complicated its measurement by researchers as well. ...
>
> Such a change ... led Charles Liebman ... to suggest that American Jews have become less Jewishly identified in the past half century, but modern scholarship, he argued, has reformulated Jewish identity as "multivalenced" without a central core of mandated obligations, thereby muting this decline in identity. Thus, American Jewish identity becomes a mere personal experience rather than a communal attachment, leading to a diminution of Jewishness (as ethnicity) and accentuation of Judaism (as religion) but without normative standards.[82]

In this fashion, perspectives on how Jews self-identify and the content of this identity are intricately tied to the cross-cutting dimensions of survival and authenticity. That is, to the extent that researchers are open to understanding nontraditional self-definitions of Jews, they are more likely to perceive nontraditional forms of Jewish identity as transformations, as producing "new Jews" or even as being "post-Jewish," in the sense of "post being Jewish as it has thus far been imagined, represented, and circumscribed" (rather than in the sense of its being "over and done with").[83] In contrast, those who fear assimilation as a result of changes in Jewish identity are more likely to see some types of individual Jewish identity as "deficient" or "defective" in terms of their lasting value, or the extent to which they result in lessened commitment and continuity.

Authenticity

Quite a bit of controversy has been generated over the issue of "authenticity" of individual Jewish identity, and in particular, whether it is inner and/or externally directed. Erik Cohen showed that Jewish identity can be typologized in relation to values that arrange themselves along two dimensions or axes: authority/autonomy; and altruism/egoism.[84] Clearly the first axis is related to authenticity: whether there is an external authority, an external criterion, against which we measure how authentic Jewishness is, or whether Jewishness is subjective and determined autonomously. The second dimension, of altruism versus egoism, is related to the levels or foci of Jewish identity, ranging from the most completely self-directed to the most universally directed (we will later return to this point). Obviously, a completely self-directed identity has little use for external authority.

Stuart Charmé presents Sartre's discussion of "existential authenticity" in *Anti-Semite and Jew:*

> From this [that is, Sartre's] point of view, a person's understanding of his or her identity is inauthentic when the person either denies the historical, cultural, and political contexts of that identity or denies the variety of possible ways of assuming it on an individual level....An authentic identity, therefore, is never an entity or substance that we possess but rather a project situated in time and space.[85]

The result is that "there are multiple authentic Judaisms"[86]—a decentered, deconstructed, pluralistic view of authenticity. Moreover,

> authenticity is not about finding one's "true self" or the "real tradition" but about maintaining an honest view of the process by which we construct the identities and traditions we need to survive.... [A] position can be authentically Jewish only by realizing its own potential inauthenticity: that it is historical, and becomes fixed or congealed only at the price of bad faith.[87]

Alain Finkielkraut also discusses Sartre. In *The Imaginary Jew* (1997), he links the question of authenticity to assimilation, suggesting that the guiding assimilationist principle in the past was for the Jew to be "a man in the street and a Jew at home."[88] Sartre, in contrast, exhorted the Jews to stop pretending—whether to be something they were not, or not to be something they were. Finkielkraut, for his part, is concerned that contemporary Jews keep quiet about the fact that at home, they are like everyone else, whereas externally, they promote a role as Jew so as to hide the "insubstantiality of their identities."[89] (He ties this to the mass production of identities in postindustrial society.)

Another scholar, Zygmunt Bauman, refers to the "post-war market stall of selves" of European Jews and laments that "'identity' has become for all intents and purposes, an 'identainment': it has moved from the realm of physical and spiritual survival to that of recreational amusement...it has undergone a fast and thorough process of *commercialization*."[90] Riv-Ellen Prell advocates creating spaces and institutions that will resist the allure of the market as a source of identity by shaping and transmitting alternative forms of culture based on memory, values, and social collectivity.[91] Steven Cohen suggests that American Jewish identities have become transformed from normative constructions to "aesthetic" understandings of Jewishness as being a matter of beauty and culture rather than a set of ethical or moral imperatives.[92] Finally, Nathan Glazer, in *American Judaism,* predicted that Jews were on the road to becoming "custodians of a museum."[93] It is this kind of inauthenticity that Gans was trying to capture with his concepts of symbolic ethnicity and symbolic religiosity.

Boundaries

The diversity of Jewish identities that has been opened up with the post-modernist (or "post-Jewish") perspective naturally pushes the boundaries of who is considered a Jew and of what challenges arise when individuals confront their Jewish identities. For example, Debra Kaufman and I, following the research of Nadia Kim, examined the identities of a growing population of Asian-American Jews in the United States, including mixed-race individuals born to Asian and non-Asian Jewish parents, Asians adopted by non-Asian Jewish parents, Asian converts to Judaism, and Asian-American Jews born to Asian-American Jewish parents. There are difficulties in locating Asian-Americans in the dominant black-white binary of race in the United States; similarly, it is difficult to "place" a Jewish identity as white (rather than ethnic) or as not white (but also not black). How, then, does one deal with a dual difficult-to-place identity?[94] What about the "transnational" Middle Eastern Jewish immigrant to the United States who comes via Western Europe? Which identity is dominant—that of Middle Eastern Jew, transnational Jew, or new immigrant in

American society?[95] Or the grandchild of Holocaust survivors who converted to Catholicism during the war and never revealed their Jewish ancestry to their children?[96] As these examples show, new identities are improvised under the pressure of shifting historical circumstances, and Jewish identity intersects with other layers of identity and circumstance.[97] When confronting the realities of Jewish identity construction in the various circumstances of history and culture, one understands that the traditional definitions of Jewry are challenged to accommodate new realities.

Both Erica Lehrer and Ruth Ellen Gruber discuss the issues arising from the heavy involvement of non-Jewish Poles in commemorating and revitalizing Jewish culture in Poland.[98] As Lehrer notes: "The sense of ethnic boundaries—of memory, of representation, of identity—is a central challenge.... Who owns the Jewish past, Jewish culture, the right to mourn Jewishness lost, the right to act Jewish, to feel Jewish, to define Jewish, to 'be' Jewish?"[99] Is there such a phenomenon as (unintentional) "false witness" (fabricated memory, as Lehrer describes)? Is "Jewish like an adjective" (as in "feeling Jewish") different from actually being a Jew, as Lehrer's subjects suggest? Is "vicarious identity" a roundabout path into "authentic" identity? And if so, who is the gatekeeper?

Collective Jewish Identity

The nature of collective Jewish identity seems even more elusive than that of individual Jewish identity. Liwerant and Ben-Rafael suggest that "the normative core on which consensus and family resemblance [between Jewish identities] have been constructed seems to have narrowed, posing the question about the nature(s), scope, and frontiers of the collective... extending from support to critical distance, and from solidarity with to abandonment of the real or imagined Jewish community."[100] Rebhun points to the complexity and confusion in defining collective boundaries and group belonging in situations in which formal provisions do not regulate group identity, as is the case in the United States.[101] Sarna suggests that the individual gratification promoted by the broader American society has led to toleration of communal diversity.[102] Indeed, understanding collective Jewish identity in the United States, especially in comparative perspective, is challenging precisely because of its diversity. While Liebman argues that the privatization of Judaism weakened the basic Jewish notions of peoplehood, community, and solidarity, it may be the case that weakened individual Jewish identity and intermarriage increase the need for formal Jewish institutions for socialization to Jewish culture and tradition.[103] Indeed, the attention given to communal Jewish institutions in the United States often focuses on their contribution to individual Jewish identity.[104]

In the following section, studies of collective Jewish identity will be examined at three levels: the (local) Jewish community, the broader notion of Jewish peoplehood, or *klal yisrael,* and the interface of the collective Jewish identity with the broader society.

The Jewish Community

Survival. Suggesting that the emphasis on individual gratification poses a major challenge to the American Jewish community, Mark Pearlman asks: "Can beginning with the 'I' effectively lead to the 'we'?"[105] Concern about the eclipse of the Jewish community has led to a new "Jewish Peoplehood" movement that aims to understand current conceptions of the Jewish community (both local and beyond, including virtual community), and to strategize and reinforce ways to strengthen commitment to the Jewish collectivity. To study how the "we" is developed, Steven Cohen developed a "peoplehood index" that includes Jewish association (informal networks), affiliation (ties to institutions), socialization (organic process of value inculcation), and education.[106] (Note that this index relates particularly to involvement in the local Jewish community.) David Mittelberg suggests that "Jewish peoplehood education" promotes connectivity between different types of Jews, including transnational populations, by promoting commonalities and mutual respect.[107]

Authenticity. We have seen that a distinction may be drawn between "essential" and "existential" authenticity—that is, the acceptance of some authority's (external) standards versus the autonomous functioning of the individual. Cohen and Eisen found that their sample of "moderate affiliated" American Jews was committed to the idea of the "sovereign self" rather than acceptance of some authority telling them what to observe, how to observe, and how much to observe.[108] As Cohen and Eisen note, the implications for Jewish communal institutions are certainly challenging: "Historically, the absence of any central religious authority helps to explain the oft-noted contentiousness of American Jewish life. No ultimate authority in American Judaism—no rabbi, no court, no lay body—makes religious decisions that are ever broadly accepted as final."[109]

Perhaps because of the lack of one authority, there is a good deal of innovative transformation going on at the communal level. In a different study, Steven Cohen and Ari Kelman note innovative communal organization in congregational life, social justice activism, philanthropy, music, filmmaking, and other cultural endeavors, especially among people under the age of 35.[110] Adding to the list, Wertheimer cites grassroots *minyanim* (prayer groups), salons, environmental organizations, and other volunteer efforts.[111]

Hence, at the community level, American Jewish institutions are reflecting the diversity of individual interests in the community, allowing for multiple "roundabout" paths to individual identification with the broader community. Acknowledging pluralism rather than fighting against it allows the community to flourish, though there is a certain fear that institutions are promoting greater diversity at the expense of a sense of broader Jewish peoplehood.[112]

As discussed by Liwerant, Jewish community-building in Latin America (as in the United States) proceeded without national legitimation or monetary support. Communal institutions sought to address material, spiritual, and cultural needs and in so doing became a source of collective identity—overshadowing the domain of individual Jewish identity. Moreover, regions and countries of origins were the defining criteria of organization, so that many parallel institutions developed in the Latin American "community of communities." Historically, ethnic components of identity were dominant, but the more recent "de-privatization" of religion in the public sphere has led to a renaissance of religious organizations and programming. Jewish values of group solidarity, mutual cohesion, and support have become legitimate role models for the developing civil society, much as Pinto envisions the role of

European Jewry for Europe. As Liwerant notes: "The current space of Latin American Jewish identities…shows a permanent pluralization of identification, and of interactions with the surrounding world and amidst the Jewish world itself."[113]

Boundaries. The issue of boundaries encompasses who is to be included in the Jewish community, in the sense of both demarking Jews versus non-Jews, and distinguishing between denominations (or else transcending denominations, in a post-denominational world).[114] As Wertheimer notes, the question of "Who is a Jew" is as unresolved in the United States as it is in Israel:

> There is no agreement among American Jews on patrilineality… on what ought to be expected of potential converts to Judaism…on what is required to obtain a religious divorce…on the status of children born to Jewish parents who did not obtain a Jewish bill of divorce, a *get*, from a previous marriage.…Significantly, in Israel, where various groups are forced to confront one another within a single polity, religious leaders continue to propose new and creative ways of addressing questions of personal status.…American Jews, by contrast, have concluded with great self-satisfaction that the magic bullet is "pluralism," a fine ideal that simply avoids confronting differences by celebrating them.[115]

Wertheimer fears that such openness will strip Judaism of its authenticity and meaning: "As 'nonjudgmentalism' has seeped into the way American Judaism is taught and marketed, promoters of Judaism emphasize the personal benefits to be derived from religion, but refrain from speaking a language of religious responsibilities."[116]

Commenting on the Peoplehood Project, Lisa Grant sums up the complexities of developing Jewish community in the United States, and in so doing presents at least one way in which the boundaries of collective Jewish identity are challenged:

> If Peoplehood consciousness is to take root among contemporary American Jews, it needs to be an inclusive idea that actively welcomes Jews from diverse backgrounds and experiences. But, its very inclusivity may challenge its acceptance as a unifying idea. From the perspective of denominational and ideological educators, it may be perceived as a force competing against their desire to induct learners into a particular Jewish worldview and way of living. And the Universalists may not be able to distinguish sufficiently between an open, flexible, inclusive view of the Jewish collective and a basic appreciation for all of humanity. In other words, Jewish Peoplehood as a core value may simply be perceived as unnecessary or irrelevant to living a meaningful life, Jewish or otherwise.[117]

Samuel Heilman notes the problem of determining the place that non-Jews can play within the American Jewish community: "Does their presence require downplaying sectarian, distinctive, and particularistic aspects of Jewish communal life in favor of shared and universalistic ones that blur the boundaries between Jews and others?"[118] Interestingly, and as mentioned above, American Jews seem to be much more troubled by this issue than the European Jewish community.[119] Estimates of intermarriage among European Jews tend to be higher than in the United States,[120] and the penetration of non-Jews into "Jewish space" seems likewise to be higher (for instance, many European Jewish cultural events are often run by non-Jews).[121]

Leonard Saxe and colleagues differentiate between two different approaches taken by the U.S. Jewish community with regard to intermarried couples. The "inreach" approach, focusing on the threats posed by intermarriage to Jewish demographic vitality and the Jewish identity of children and grandchildren of intermarriage, advocates in-marriage or conversion by non-Jewish partners, alongside increasing investment in Jewish education. In contrast, the "outreach" perspective accepts intermarriage as inevitable and advocates Jewish continuity by welcoming all, celebrating diversity, and minimizing boundaries of the Jewish community.[122] Interestingly, a recent study concerning the impact of Taglit-Birthright (a program providing free, 10-day trips to Israel for young Jewish adults) on its participants raises questions about both approaches.[123] On the one hand, the persuasive influence of the Birthright experience on raising children as Jewish—even in instances of intermarriage—indicates that intermarriage does not inevitably lead to the "loss" of Jewish children. At the same time, the impact of Birthright suggests that the rate of intermarriage can itself be influenced. Saxe and his co-authors conclude that the two approaches can work in tandem.

In *All Quiet on the Religious Front?* Jack Wertheimer recalls an essay written by Irving (Yitz) Greenberg in the 1980s that warned against the prospect of intensifying religious polarization and even schism as a result of very real differences in religious policies, especially over matters of personal status such as conversion, divorce, *mamzerut*,[124] and the Jewishness of children whose mother was not Jewish. Exacerbating the situation, in Greenberg's opinion, was the trend toward a hardening of positions within the various denominations, which resulted in unilateral decision-making that showed no regard for how such actions would affect other groups of Jews.[125] By the end of the following decade, Samuel Freedman had documented several instances of harsh, "Jew versus Jew" divisiveness.[126] Wertheimer, however, takes a more optimistic view. He argues that schism has in fact been averted, as evidenced by numerous instances of cooperation ranging from the Partnership for Excellence in Jewish Education (which establishes and maintains day schools, summer camping, and preschool education) to Taglit-Birthright, the Wexner leadership programs, Limmud conferences, and a plethora of Jewish outreach programs (often sponsored by Orthodox groups and aimed at the non-Orthodox community). According to Wertheimer, the various Jewish denominations

> are all facing a common challenge: How to respond to the argument of post-denominationalists who regard all the religious movements as passé; who claim the trouble is caused by out-of-touch, elite denominational leaders who insist on drawing boundaries between Jews when *amcha* [the general Jewish population] is not interested in such boundaries; and who cast the denominations as selfishly absorbed with their own institutional survival to the detriment of the true interests of *clal yisrael*.[127]

Along similar lines, Gershon Winkler, a Jewish renewal rabbi, promotes a conception of Judaism he calls "flexidoxy," because he believes that many American Jews are "turned off by the rigidity of established 'standards' found in every Jewish denomination."[128]

Klal Yisrael

Survival. Central to the research on *klal yisrael*, or Jewish peoplehood, is the role of Israel in the Jewish identity of global Jewry. Uzi Rebhun found that attention to Israel was the most significant common denominator of Jewish identification for various subpopulations of American Jews,[129] a finding that echoed an earlier conclusion by Jonathan Woocher.[130] In the last several years, however, debate has focused on the "distancing hypothesis," according to which American Jews are becoming increasingly estranged from Israel.

On one side of the debate are Steven Cohen and Ari Kelman, who argue that younger, non-Orthodox Jews are becoming less supportive and less engaged with Israel. In addition, this trend is likely to continue because of a broader detachment of Americans in general from "fixed identities of all sorts"; weakening ethnic cohesion among American Jews; higher rates of intermarriage; lower rates of in-group friendship; the weakening centrality of formal Jewish organizations for American Jewish life; and more personalized forms of religion and spirituality.[131] Peter Beinart agrees that there has been a distancing, particularly among non-Orthodox young adults, but puts the blame on the Jewish establishment's unwavering support for Israeli government policies.[132] In contrast, Theodore Sasson, Leonard Saxe, and Charles Kadushin claim that the alienation of the young is related to their life cycle stage and is likely to attenuate over time; moreover, they argue, longitudinal data suggests that "distancing" from Israel has not increased significantly.[133] Further, Irving Horowitz, Morton Weinfeld, and Ronald Zweig point out in their commentaries on the debate that American Jewish attitudes and attachment to Israel, far from being predictable, are strongly influenced by political events (such as the 1967 war, the Lebanon war, the two Palestinian uprisings [intifadas], and 9/11).[134]

To be sure, the relationship between Israel and the diaspora goes beyond the relationship between U.S. Jews and Israel. Another important issue of current debate is whether Israel is the center of global Jewry, or whether there are multiple centers— and if the latter, what they are, and what are their respective roles for *klal yisrael*. The Kinneret Agreement, authored in 2002 by the Israeli Committee for National Responsibility (a group of several dozen Israeli intellectuals and communal leaders), restates the social contract among the Jewish people that establishes Israel as the "national homeland of the Jewish people, positing a democratic and Jewish Israel, and calling upon all parties to maintain a social contract as legal citizens of a Jewish state, while recognizing that different groups and individuals have widely varying definitions as to what terms like democracy, Jewish state, and peoplehood actually connote."[135] Arnold Eisen suggests that this contract was prompted by a "sense that the Zionist revolution has transformed the very notion of Jewish national responsibility. We, the Jewish people, are now responsible for a state ... for the welfare of all the citizens of that state, Jewish or not," but he recognizes that "many American Jews remain uncomfortable with any robust sense of Jewish peoplehood, and even deny obligations to fellow Jews that go beyond obligations to fellow citizens or fellow human beings as such."[136]

Originally positioning itself as the center of Jewry, Zionism mobilized diaspora support for the nascent state of Israel and at the same time called for widespread aliyah. The inherent contradiction of needing the diaspora for material, political, and moral support while undermining its legitimacy in calling for Jews to resettle in Israel led to tension, especially in Latin America (and also, to some extent, in the United States and Europe). Eventually the de-legitimizing of the diaspora was muted, though Israel continued to "organize" the diaspora in terms of uniting disparate partners (as we have seen above) by means of a common allegiance and focus of communal activity. In 2010, the Jewish Agency, once the center of Zionism and a chief promoter of aliyah, declared that its traditional mission had outlived its usefulness; hence its new focus on Jewish identity, especially among the young, as a means to promote Jewish "peoplehood."[137] This fits in well with Shaul Kelner's analysis of Birthright, in which he concludes that the Israel "experience" is primarily intended to bolster (diaspora) Jewish identity.[138] As Eran Lerman notes, the Israel-diaspora relationship has become one of equals, the two groupings roughly the same in number, and each dependent on the other.[139] Israel's central role has become less salient to American Jews as they become more comfortable in American society and as gaps between Israeli and American Jews grow.[140] The symbiotic relationship is thus in the process of transformation, and for some, is becoming irrelevant or even a distraction from the more central role of diaspora.[141] A similar transformation is occurring in Latin America and in Europe.

Authenticity and boundaries. Despite the fact that Jews in different geo-political circumstances have different conceptions with regard to what being Jewish means, there is general consensus that Israel is essential to *klal yisrael*. Indeed, those who deny this connection are often perceived to be alienated from the Jewish collective. When John Jay College of the City University of New York decided to award an honorary doctorate in 2011 to the playwright Tony Kushner—an outspoken critic of Israel—protests were spearheaded by prominent Jews affiliated with CUNY, who charged that Kushner was a "Jewish antisemite." The incident brought to the forefront of public Jewish discourse the question whether at least tacit support of Israel is an *essential* ingredient of American Jewish identity, and whether criticism of Israeli policies is legitimate, especially for Jews speaking in the public sphere. Yet there is also some evidence of an opposite phenomenon—a tendency in some circles to consider *support* for Israel to be politically incorrect.[142] Jewish Federations of North America, for instance, do not bring up the subject of Israel in their fundraising campaigns directed at Jews under the age of 40.[143] In Europe, meanwhile, some Jews adopt what Liwerant and Ben-Rafael refer to as the "good Jew" syndrome, admitting to Jewish origins while expressing highly critical opinions with regard to Israel.[144]

Concerning the contemporary status of *klal yisrael*, Liwerant and Ben-Rafael conclude:

> In today's Jewish world, the abandonment of historical criteria of belongingness coexists with the revitalization of Jewish life. On the one hand are declining rates of ethno-religious marriages and of predominantly Jewish social networks, and declining percentages of Jews in the total population. On the other hand is a sustained ongoing effort to promote what the organized Jewish community calls "continuity" and "renaissance." It is indeed undeniable that, at least so far, *Klal Yisrael* has held together. Many Jews throughout the world do attach importance to their Jewishness and, despite the many variations, inhabit a wide shared space of identity.[145]

As we have noted, research indicates that the structure of Jewish identity is shared globally. In an overview of this research, DellaPergola concludes:

> The demonstrable existence of overarching and shared global patterns of Jewish identification is no minor finding. It provides powerful empirical evidence for the proposition of

resilience of transnational coherence in contemporary Jewish symbolic and institutional perceptions over the opposite of a Jewish identification that essentially stems from the variable circumstances of the different local national contexts.[146]

Jews vis-à-vis Broader Society

Survival. Attitudes of the broader society to Jews as individuals and to the Jewish collectivity often frame the context of Jewish identity, whether through "a-semitism" (according to which Jews are not considered to be in any way "other"); acceptance (whereby Jews are regarded as one of many "other" groups); philo-semitism (which sets Jews apart as "other," but in a favorable sense); or, lastly, antisemitism.[147] It has often been noted that the necessity of confronting antisemitism binds Jews together and strengthens their feelings of "we-ness" and tribalism. Steven Cohen cites as one of American Jews' collective achievements the defeat of antisemitic discrimination in housing, resorts, education, and business during the 1970s.[148] Sartre predicted that, without antisemitism, Jews would cease to exist as a distinct group;[149] in contrast, Shmuel Trigano and Léon Askénazi argue that Jews must be understood as "self-normative, internally formulated and consistent, not merely a response to external pressures."[150] It is also the case that, whereas antisemitism may once have influenced the collective and individual Jewish identities of American Jews, it appears to have much less impact on contemporary American Jews.

In an analysis of 36 local community studies, Ira Sheskin and Arnold Dashefsky have found that while the experience and perception of antisemitism have not disappeared, both have decreased in recent years. However, no relationship was found between these variables and levels of Jewish connectivity such as denominational affiliation, synagogue membership, or membership in other Jewish organizations. Combating antisemitism, it should be noted, is a strong motivation for American Jews to donate to Jewish organizations, and numerous Jewish organizations, such as the Anti-Defamation League, the American Jewish Committee, and the Jewish Community Relations Councils of the Jewish Federations devote considerable re-sources to this cause.[151] In the European context, what is referred to as the "new antisemitism" takes the form of anti-"Zionist" (but really anti-Israel), pro-Palestin-ian violence or threats and abuse against Jews. This phenomenon is clearly linked to the presence of a large number of Muslim immigrants from North Africa and the Middle East. Among American Jews, the impact of the "new" antisemitism is con-fined in the main to a minority of writers and intellectuals who promote the "good Jew" phenomenon of attempting to be "politically correct" by means of distancing oneself from Israel.

Attitudes toward Jews in the United States are far more likely to fall under the rubric of a-semitism or acceptance, both of which have liberated Jews to partake fully in the broader society. The danger here is that American Jewish distinctiveness may thereby be compromised. Compared to the American mainstream and other minorities, American Jewry has long been distinguished by its older age, lower fer-tility, later ages of marriage, high socioeconomic achievement in terms of education, occupational prestige, and class identification, concentration in large metropolitan centers, strong individualism, and an unusual extent of endogamy among married couples. To a great extent, this situation prevails despite rising levels of intermarriage.[152] At the same time, as Zygmunt Bauman reminds us, contemporary media have made Jews and their success ever more visible and accessible to public scrutiny. As a result, he maintains, the distinctiveness of American Jews resists erosion.[153] A different approach is taken by Diana Pinto, who argues that indifference to the Jew as "other," and the fact that Jews are no longer perceived as the only "diasporic" people, or as the most significant "other" in the society, relieves Jews of burden but at the same time deprives them of privilege—especially in post-Holocaust Europe, where Jewish communities and commemorative projects often benefit from government funding.[154]

Interactions between Jews and the broader society are often a function of multiculturalism. In Canada, and also in many European countries, multiculturalism is a matter of national self-definition (designating, among other things, linguistic rights), whereas in the United States, it is more an aspiration for equal rights, regardless of ethnic or religious subgroup.[155] According to Liwerant and Ben-Rafael:

> While the Jews' transnational connections with Israel and with the Jewish world have gained new visibility and legitimacy, a new discourse fits the oxymoronic logic of "assimilated ethnicity."[156]... Jews take an interest in democratic political culture and in becoming full citizens in order to participate in the public sphere, but maintain their ethnic difference. This interest does not imply belief in the global desirability of individual assimilation, but concern with the civic commonality.[157]

One implication of multiculturalism is that Jews form at least part of their identities in spaces of interaction with the broader society. With this in mind, Adam Gaynor suggests that efforts be made to strengthen Jewish identity not only in exclusively Jewish places, but also in multicultural spaces such as schools and colleges/universities.[158]

Authenticity. In the view of Jonathan Sarna, the meshing of values of the broader society with more specific Jewish values is one of the major challenges facing the contemporary American Jewish community.[159] Chaim Waxman provides examples of attempts to mesh Jewish and more universalistic values, among them Arthur Waskow's Alliance for Jewish Renewal and its alternative hagadah (*The Freedom Seder*, 1969), and Zalman Schacter-Shalomi's concept of eco-kosher.[160] As we have seen, another concern is that individuals are concerned only with their own Jewish identity without commitment to the broader community or continuity of the Jewish people or, alternatively, embrace commitment to the wider society without concern for the broader Jewish peoplehood.[161] Reinforcing the latter concern is a recent study sponsored by Repair the World (a non-profit organization devoted to enabling service activities "rooted in Jewish values").[162] The study found that, while most young American Jews engage in volunteer activities, few volunteer for Jewish causes or through Jewish organizations, either because of lack of knowledge of relevant activities, inaccessibility, or because causes embraced by Jewish organizations do not seem as meaningful as other, more universalistic, causes.[163]

Boundaries. The greatest effect of the blurring of boundaries between Jew and non-Jew in the United States may be on where Jews live, and on who is included in the Jewish community. Jews have become increasingly mobile and dispersed across the country, with Jewish institutions becoming more accessible (more recently, they have also become somewhat accessible through virtual space).[164] As a result, and reinforced by the privatization of religious practice, individual Jewish identity appears to be less related to where Jews live than it once may have been. In a study co-authored by me and Ira Sheskin, a mega-file consisting of data on 22 Jewish communities was analyzed; we found minimal impact of the broader communal context and Jewish infrastructure on most expressions of individual Jewish identity (though measures of the broader society were limited).[165]

Notwithstanding, the boundaries of the American Jewish community are stretched by increasing levels both of intermarriage and of adoption, by waves of immigrants from areas such as the former Soviet Union and Iran, and by claims of marginal Jews living outside the mainstreams of Jewish life to be recognized as Jews. Among the issues explored in *Boundaries of Jewish Identity* are the contemporary challenges of Conversos, Marranos, and Crypto-Latinos to Jewish boundaries in the American Southwest, and the ramifications of Holocaust experiences on survivors' children and grandchildren in Poland.

The Relationship of Jewish Identity to Jewish Continuity

The threat of assimilation through a-semitism and intermarriage has made Jewish continuity an issue of primary concern. As Erik Cohen and Rachel Werczberger show in an exploratory study of alumni of an Israeli leadership institute for youth counselors from abroad, this concern bridges all religious and ideological streams and therefore appears at the core of the structure of attitudes regarding Jewish norms.[166] It is therefore fitting to conclude this discussion with some reflections on the relationship of Jewish identity to Jewish continuity.

Survival

There is an implicit assumption that strong Jewish identity translates into Jewish continuity. Stuart Charmé calls this the "drink-your-milk" approach—with proper nourishment, a strong Jewish identity will develop, which in turn implies strong commitment to the Jewish community and, de facto, Jewish continuity.[167] This is the "straight" path that Dashefsky and colleagues describe. It is also the perception reinforced by the Cohen-Werczberger study, which examined three traditional cornerstones of Jewish identity: Israel-related norms, Jewish people-related norms, and Jewish religion-related norms. In mapping the responses, Cohen and Werczberger graphically created a structure that showed the difference in importance allocated to norms in each of these three areas, conforming to the traditional "essentialist" elements discussed above; in addition, the responses also differentiated a fourth, "universal" domain, corresponding to the broader values we have discussed in the previous section. At the center of all of these norms was the importance placed on ensuring that one's children are Jewish.[168]

Shaul Kelner, however, argues that efforts to strengthen Jewish identity rarely have direct, straightforward outcomes. Through his ethnographic study of the Birthright program, he shows that both those who are encouraging strong Jewish identity and those who are being "manipulated" (however willingly) have their own complex agendas, which result in a far more dynamic and unpredictable flow of events.[169] It does not take much to extrapolate this finding to other scenarios charged with inculcating Jewish identity.

Jewish identity is related to Jewish continuity (and survival) in a more directly demographic way: fertility. Deborah Skolnick Einhorn, and especially Sylvia Barack Fishman, discuss the relationship between Jewish identity, commitment to the Jewish people, and fertility.[170] Fishman notes the reluctance to engage in a frank, public discourse on the issue, despite what seems to her to be a clear relationship. Fishman's challengers might be those described by Einhorn—the "neutral-natalists" (who favor women's personal agendas over the communal need for reproduction) and the "non-natalists" (who oppose the Jewish communal agenda's orientation toward increased fertility), along with others who put the liberal causes of the broader society before the needs of the Jewish people.

Authenticity

The risk of transforming Jewish identity into a matter of choice and selectivity is that when Jewish identity becomes a matter of personal authenticity, it is much more difficult to pass it on to the next generation.[171] As Steven Cohen and Jack Wertheimer note: "Those of us who wish to build a strong and authentic Jewish life dare not communicate to our children that everything is up for grabs, that their Jewish descent is nonbinding, and that Jewish living is merely one option among a broad array of lifestyle choices."[172] When flexible authenticity becomes the model, Tsvi Blanchard suggests, no one group of experts or authorities is recognized as legitimate gatekeeper to Jewish institutions; ethnic and religious identity formation are not essentially linked to particular institutions (the roundabout path); and Jewish identity becomes more fluid and linked to life-context, shape-shifting identities. He suggests that identities might be treated as "branded" commodities, so that even if the content changes, the label remains. Jewish continuity, he concludes, will be perpetuated by passing on to our children a sense of how important and vital it is for them to "choose Jewish," even if how (and whether) they do so is left up to them.[173]

Boundaries

The accepted boundaries of Jewish identity have implications for whether individuals of various circumstances feel comfortable identifying as Jews and perpetuating that identity among others, including their children. Thus, we have the "inreach" and "outreach" approaches discussed above. Marlene De Vries, discussing Dutch Jewry, argues that if Dutch Jewish organizations continue to apply strict halakhic criteria vis-à-vis who is considered to be Jewish, non-halakhic Jews will remain outsiders in many respects, however strong their feelings toward Judaism may be.[174] Sergio DellaPergola relates the example of Scottish Jewry, for which detailed census data are available with regard to those who left and those who joined the Jewish population in 2001. The data show significant movement in both directions. This instability may result in weakened interest to be part of, or at least to explicitly state that one belongs to the less clearly defined Jewish section of the total society. DellaPergola suggests that the ultimate challenge is "the ability to preserve not a mere *community of presence*—driven by and dependent on favorable market forces, but a *community of creativity*—able to nurture and transmit its own demographic momentum and cultural identity."[175]

Conclusion

Seeking to understand contemporary American Jewish identity is a complex undertaking. Not only are there multiple levels and layers of Jewish identity, but these are fluid and fluctuating, related to transnational and global as well as historical patterns. We must be attentive to the different levels of expression, their interrelationships, and their respective roles in Jewish continuity. In particular, more systematic attention should be given to collective Jewish identity in the U.S. setting and the ways in which it influences and is influenced by individual Jewish identity.

The challenges of survival, authenticity, and boundaries of Jewish identity cut across each level, as summarized in Table 4.1. Pessimists with regard to the survival of American Jewry fear assimilation, inauthenticity, and the individualization of Jewish identity; they emphasize the negative implications for a cohesive Jewish community transcending particularistic concerns, the diminishment of attachment to Israel and its implications for a sense of Jewish peoplehood, rising intermarriage, and a loss of distinctiveness vis-à-vis the broader society. Optimists see transformation of the bases of individual Jewish identity not as a threat but as an opportunity, pointing to innovative developments in trans-denominational organizing and programming, and a new positive role for Jews as models for a pluralist multiculturalism. Essentialists stress the persistence both of ascriptive and traditional elements of individual Jewish identity and of external authorities uniting diverse Jews; those perceiving existential and flexible authenticity stress the new configurations wrought by multiple identities and the dynamic processes of identity building—all of which call for new types of organizations, bridging, and programming to establish a viable collective Jewish identity. The traditional boundaries both of individual and collective Jewish identity are challenged by postmodern circumstances at each level of "Jewish space." Perhaps because of the greater level of transnationalism that is made possible both by easier mobility and communication, or the more general globalized culture characteristic of our times (not unique to Jews), many of these issues are addressed in studies of Jewish identity in different parts of the world.

The variety of perspectives leads me to comment, finally, on the methods by which we arrive at our understandings of Jewish identity. In recent research, Steven Cohen and Ari Kelman argue: "For Jewish social thinkers and public intellectuals, the roles that both we and our colleagues occupy in Jewish life, ultimately, it's not about the data. It's about the ideas and the people whose lives are impacted by them."[176] This perspective is important when it comes to applying the research: it is worthwhile noting how many social scientists of American Jewry are funded by communal or other organizations with varying agendas. In *Speaking of Jews,* Lisa Berman shows

Table 4.1. Issues of Jewish Identity at Different Levels of Jewish Space and with Cross-cutting (Competing) Perspectives

Cross-cutting Perspectives	Value	Individual Jewish Identity	Collective Jewish Identity	Klal Yisrael	Broader Society
		Self	*(Local) Jewish Community*	*Yisrael*	*Society*
Survival	Pessimists	Assimilation; concern about symbolic ("inauthentic") identity and non-shared self-definitions of Jewishness	Fragmentation; sees each part of the community inward-looking; individualism	Distancing from Israel; labeling of good/bad Jews	New antisemitism; dwelling on history (for instance, on the Holocaust) rather than on "living Jews"; loss of distinctiveness; intermarriage
	Optimists	Transformation; new ways of expressing, developing, and maintaining Jewishness	Peoplehood Project; local renaissances; new institutions and umbrella organizations, many of them trans-denominational; perception of structural cohesion (not necessarily religious or Jewish)	Continuing importance (perhaps centrality) of Israel; religion, peoplehood, and collective memory; bridging religious-secular, Ashkenazi-Sephardi denominational divides	Jews as model for minorities in pluralism; feeling comfortable within broader society; distinctiveness within a-semitic society, intermarriage as reservoir of new Jews
Authenticity	Essential	Genetic, biological definitions of Jewishness; three essential ingredients of Jewishness: peoplehood, Torah, Israel	Acceptance of unifying, external authority	Essentialism of religion, peoplehood, and support of Israel; *tikun 'am yisrael* (focus on Jewish people)	Jews as self-normative and internally formulated, not merely responding to external pressures

(*continued*)

Table 4.1. Continued

Cross-cutting Perspectives	Value	Individual Jewish Identity *Self*	Collective (Local) Jewish Community	*Klal Yisrael*	*Broader Society*
Boundaries	Exclusive	Traditional criteria for inclusion (parentage, conversion)	Narrow definition; "inreach" to reduce intermarriage	Strict adherence to halakhic definitions of "who is a Jew"	Strict adherence to halakhic conversion; only Jews "own" Jewish memory, space
	Inclusive	Hyphenated Jews; non-Jews feeling Jewish identity; trans-national identities, flexible boundaries	Broader and fluid definition; outreach to include intermarried	Bridging religious-secular, ethnic, denominational, intermarried-intramarried divides	Inclusion of intermarried, adopted, and non-Jews in "Jewish" endeavors, including collective memory-making and "Jewish space"

the influence social scientists have had both in formulating the nature of the Jewish community for communal leaders and for offering solutions to the problems faced by American Jewry. It is also critical to recognize the influence of ideas, motivations, and agendas in fashioning the research. In true "Jewish" fashion, even the same researcher may reach different configurations of the parameters of individual Jewish identity by using different data sets. Varying results concerning Jewish identity may be less related to differences in various subpopulations than to the fact that different questions are formulated for every study; there may well be different research objectives as well. Discussing the 1990 National Jewish Population Survey, Blanchard noted that assimilation and acculturation models led to a certain way of inquiring about Jewish identity (focusing primarily on traditional religious and ethnic practices) rather than being open to new ways of expressing and experiencing Jewish identity.[177]

With this in mind, Steven Cohen now includes different measures of Jewish identity—maintaining "legacy measures" but also including questions on "Jewish talk," Jewish friends, and Shabbat meals.[178] As both David Graham and Erik Cohen show, the various constructs for the content of individual Jewish identity are amazingly diverse. Graham suggests that "a useful analogy" for the variety of research approaches "is perhaps the Tower of Babel: with so many different 'languages' spoken, it becomes almost impossible to draw up useful comparative conclusions."[179] He therefore calls for a standardization of measures of Jewish identity (what he calls the "proverbial 'Jewish kilo'"). Put somewhat differently, the ideas drive (or should drive) the data, but the data also validates or undermines the ideas. It cannot be one *or* the other, and we must not lose sight of this.

A second methodological issue is what kind of research design will shed light on the complexity of the issues of Jewish identity we have discussed above. Much of the insight into the cross-cutting dimensions, as well as the different levels of "Jewish space" in which identity is expressed, is gleaned from qualitative studies and interpretation rather than from quantitative survey research. On the individual level, we need more in-depth study of how Jews are conceiving of Jewry and Jewishness today. Although we know that there are new activities and behavioral outlets for expressing Jewish identity, the "meaning-making" that Jews undergo as they construct identities is changing and variable over the life course, birth cohorts, and space. These insights need to be incorporated in survey research, even at the community level, to provide a comparative database from which to learn more about how Jews are Jewish today. There needs to be a continual dialogue between qualitative and quantitative approaches, something that is often foregone in order to meet time or budgetary constraints, or a funder's underlying agenda. On the community level, we need systematic institutional analysis, especially of a kind that can be combined with individual analyses. Community studies sometimes provide this kind of information: we need to analyze it, as well as to obtain more data on the innovative community activities and efforts discussed above. In terms of *klal yisrael*, we need more rigorous comparative studies across countries and transnational populations. The incorporation of many findings in this essay from international sources shows how many of the concerns are shared across the Jewish population, but without a consciousness of the commonalities (or the variations). Action research (designed as systematic intervention addressing a social problem) as conceived, for example, by the Peoplehood Project, has begun to address such concerns. But comparative focus is needed at the level of basic research as well as applied intervention, and basic research may result in important (and, at a later stage, applicable) insights.

Indeed, it would behoove us to regain a sense of *klal yisrael* in our studies of Jewish identity, which necessitates an effort to standardize measurement at least to some extent, while allowing for necessary flexibility in the face of different spatial, historical, and cultural contexts. In this way, the data are essential, and can provide insight into the variability that exists beyond research design and agenda. Yet without an ongoing dialogue between qualitative and quantitative research and researchers, there can be no real insight with regard to either the multiple layers and levels in which Jewish identity manifests itself, or the cross-cutting axes of perspective. Embracing both approaches as necessary and complementary will best allow us to understand the many variations and constant changes in the conceptualization of Jewish identity, within the United States, across the globe, and transnationally.

Notes

1. Steven M. Cohen, "Jewish Identity Research in the United States: Ruminations on Concepts and Findings," in *Continuity, Commitment and Survival: Jewish Communities in the Diaspora,* ed. Sol Encel and Leslie Stein (Westport: 2003), 1–22.

2. I borrow from Diana Pinto the idea of "Jewish space" (from "Asemitism or a Society without Antisemitism or Philosemitism: Dream or Nightmare?"—unpublished ms., February 2010). Pinto presents the "spaces" as boxes that expand and contract according to circumstance, and she does not include the individual level of Jewish identity, as I do. I have not made use here of Pinto's distinctions between Jewish-friendly neutral space, non-Jewish public space, and universal space ("the 'world out there'"), although I think fruitful distinctions can be made about how Jewish identity intersects with these various parts of the broader society.

3. Intersectional analysis studies "the relationships among multiple dimensions and modalities of social relationships and subject formations" (Leslie McCall, "The Complexity of Intersectionality," *Signs: Journal of Women in Culture and Society* 30, no. 3 [2005], 1771–1800), recognizing that abstracting independent effects of each of the dimensions results in a partial loss of understanding with regard to how social phenomena actually occur and the effects that they have. Thus, it is necessary to understand Jewish identity in its particular socio-cultural environment, without oversimplifying comparisons.

4. Alan Dershowitz, *The Vanishing American Jew: In Search of Jewish Identity for the Next Century* (New York: 1997). See also Cohen, "Jewish Identity Research in the United States"; Arnold Dashefsky, Bernard Lazerwitz, and Ephraim Tabory, "A Journey of the 'Straightway' or the 'Roundabout Path': Jewish Identity in the United States and Israel," in *Handbook of the Sociology of Religion,* ed. Michelle Dillon (Cambridge: 2003), 240–260; Charles Liebman, *The Ambivalent American Jew* (Philadelphia: 1973); Stephen Sharot, *Comparative Perspectives on Judaisms and Jewish Identities* (Detroit: 2011).

5. Bernard Wasserstein, *Vanishing Diaspora: The Jews in Europe since 1945* (Cambridge: 1996).

6. Jonathan Sarna, *American Judaism: A History* (New Haven: 2004).

7. See, for example, Calvin Goldscheider, *Jewish Continuity and Change: Emerging Patterns in America* (Bloomington: 1986); Charles Silberman, *A Certain People: American Jews and Their Lives Today* (New York: 1985).

8. Tom Smith, *Jewish Distinctiveness in America: A Statistical Portrait* (New York: 2005).

9. David Graham, *European Jewish Identity at the Dawn of the 21st Century: A Working Paper* (Budapest: 2004), 8.

10. Dashefsky, Lazerwitz, and Tabory, "A Journey of the 'Straightway' or the 'Roundabout Path.'"

11. Uzi Rebhun, "Jewish Identity in America: Structural Analysis of Attitudes and Behaviors," *Review of Religious Research* 46, no. 1 (2004), 43–63.

12. Bethamie Horowitz, *Connections and Journeys: Assessing Critical Opportunities for Enhancing Jewish Identity*, revised ed. (New York: 2003); Debra R. Kaufman, "Embedded Categories: Identity among Jewish Young Adults in the United States," *Race, Gender & Class: American Jewish Perspectives* 6, no. 4 (1999), 76–87; Steven M. Cohen and Arnold Eisen, *The Jew Within: Self, Family, and Community in America* (Bloomington: 2000); Shaul Kelner, *Tours that Bind: Diaspora, Pilgrimage and Israeli Birthright Tourism* (New York: 2010). Kelner's book is reviewed in this volume, 357–361.

13. Harold Himmelfarb and R. Michael Loar, "National Trends in Jewish Ethnicity: A Test of the Polarization Hypothesis," *Journal of the Scientific Study of Religion* 23, no. 2 (1984), 140–154; Jack Wertheimer, *A People Divided: Judaism in Contemporary America* (New York: 1993); Steven M. Cohen, "A Tale of Two Jewries: The 'Inconvenient Truth' for American Jews" (2006), online at www.jewishlife.org/pdf/steven_cohen_paper.pdf (accessed 2 July 2012); Jonathan Sarna, *American Judaism*.

14. Steven M. Cohen, "Engaging the Next Generation of American Jews: Distinguishing the In-married, Inter-married, and Non-married," *Journal of Jewish Communal Service* (2005), 43–52.

15. Bruce Phillips, "Accounting for Jewish Secularism: Is a New Cultural Identity Emerging?" *Contemporary Jewry* 30, no. 1 (2010), 63–85.

16. Jacob B. Ukeles, Ron Miller, and Pearl Beck, *Young Jewish Adults in the United States Today* (New York: 2006), 4–5.

17. Jack Wertheimer, *All Quiet on the Religious Front? Jewish Unity, Denominationalism, and Postdenominationalism in the United States* (New York: 2005), online at www.bjpa.org/Publications/details.cfm?PublicationID=142 (accessed 2 July 2012).

18. Rebhun, "Jewish Identity in America."

19. Sergio DellaPergola, "Distancing, Yet One," *Contemporary Jewry* 30, nos. 2–3 (2010), 188–189; idem, Shlomit Levy, Uzi Rebhun, and Dalia Sagi, "Patterns of Jewish Identification in the United States, 2001," in *Theory Construction and Multivariate Analysis: Applications of Facet Approach*, ed. Dov Elizur and Eyal Yaniv (Tel Aviv: 2009), 305–318; Shlomit Levy, Hannah Levinsohn, and Elihu Katz, *A Portrait of Israeli Jewry: Beliefs, Observances and Values among Israeli Jews 2000* (Jerusalem: 2002); Shlomit Levy, "Smallest Space Analysis of Jewish Identification Indicators in Israel 2000," quoted in DellaPergola, "Distancing, Yet One," 189.

20. Elihu Katz, "Two Dilemmas of Religious Identity and Practice among Israeli Jews: The Marshall Sklare Lecture," *Contemporary Jewry* 27, no. 1 (2007), 157–169.

21. Judit Bokser Liwerant and Eliezer Ben-Rafael, "Klal Yisrael Today: Unity and Diversity. Reflections on Europe and Latin America in a Globalized World," in *A Road to Nowhere? Jewish Experiences in the Unifying Europe*, ed. Julius H. Schoeps and Olaf Glöckner (Leiden: 2011), 299, 329.

22. Erik H. Cohen, "Jewish Identity Research: A State of the Art," *International Journal of Jewish Education Research* 1, no. 1 (2010), 7–48.

23. See, for example, Martha E. Bernal, *Ethnic Identity: Formation and Transmission among Hispanics and Other Minorities* (Albany: 1993); J.W. Berry, "Cultural Relations in Plural Societies: Alternatives to Segregation and Their Socio-psychological Implications," in *Groups in Contact: The Psychology of Desegregation*, ed. Norman Miller and Marilynn Brewer (New York: 1984), 11–27; idem, "Psychology of Acculturation: Understanding Individuals Moving between Cultures," in *Applied Cross-Cultural Psychology*, ed. Richard W. Brislin (Thousand Oaks, Calif.: 1990), 232–253.

24. Diana Pinto, "Towards an European Jewish Identity" (2010), online at www.hagalil. com/bet-debora/golem/europa.htm (accessed 2 July 2012); Gabriel Sheffer, "The European Jewish Diaspora: The Third Pillar of World Jewry?" in Schoeps and Glöckner (eds.), *A Road to Nowhere?*, 35–44.

25. Eliezer Ben-Rafael, "Contemporary Dilemmas of Identity: Israel and the Diaspora," in *Jewry between Tradition and Secularism: Europe and Israel Compared*, ed. Eliezer Ben-Rafael, Thomas Gergely, and Yosef Gorny (Leiden: 2006), 279–288; Steven M. Cohen and Jack Wertheimer, "Whatever Happened to the Jewish People?" *Commentary* 121, no. 6 (June 2006), 33–37; Liebman, *The Ambivalent American Jew*.

26. Shelly Tenenbaum and Lynn Davidman, "It's in My Genes: Biological Discourse and Essentialist Views of Identity among Contemporary American Jews," *The Sociological Quarterly* 48 (2007), 435–450.

27. Susan Martha Kahn, "Are Genes Jewish? Conceptual Ambiguities in the New Genetic Age," in *Boundaries of Jewish Identity*, ed. Susan A. Glenn and Naomi B. Sokoloff (Seattle: 2010), 12–26.

28. Gad Barzilai, "Who is a Jew? Categories, Boundaries, Communities, and Citizenship Law in Israel," in Glenn and Sokoloff (eds.), *Boundaries of Jewish Identity*, 27–42. Yonatan Touval points out an interesting caveat regarding this complexity in a *New York Times* op-ed piece concerning demands that the Palestinians recognize Israel as a "Jewish" state—see "Israel's Identity Crisis" (30 July 2011), online at www.nytimes.com/2011/07/30/opinion/30iht-edtouval30.html?r=1 (accessed 2 July 2012).

29. Liwerant and Ben-Rafael, "Klal Yisrael Today," 301.

30. Herbert Gans, "Symbolic Ethnicity: The Future of Ethnic Groups and Cultures in America," *Ethnic and Racial Studies* 2 (1979), 1–20.

31. Stephen Sharot, "A Critical Comment on Gans' 'Symbolic Ethnicity and Symbolic Religiosity' and Other Formulations of Ethnicity and Religion Regarding American Jews," *Contemporary Jewry* 18, no. 1 (1997), 90.

32. Caryn Aviv and David Shneer, *New Jews: The End of the Jewish Diaspora* (New York: 2005); Denise Roman, *Fragmented Identities: Popular Culture, Sex, and Everyday Life in Postcommunist Romania* (Lanham: 2003).

33. S. Daniel Breslauer, *Creating a Judaism without Religion: A Postmodern Jewish Possibility* (Lanham: 2001).

34. Ariela Keysar, "Secular Americans and Secular Jewish Americans: Similarities and Differences," *Contemporary Jewry* 30, no. 1 (2010), 29–44. As noted above, Phillips shows that a high proportion of the "nones" are intermarried or the offspring of intermarriage (see "Accounting for Jewish Secularism," 73, 77).

35. Herbert Gans, "Symbolic Ethnicity and Symbolic Religiosity: Towards a Comparison of Ethnic and Religious Acculturation," *Ethnic and Racial Studies* 17, no. 4 (1994), 577–592.

36. Sharot, *Comparative Perspectives on Judaisms*, 159.

37. Steven M. Cohen, "Jewish Identity Research in the United States"; Dashefsky, Lazerwitz, and Tabory, "A Journey of the 'Straightway' or the 'Roundabout Path.'"

38. Bethamie Horowitz, "Reframing the Study of Contemporary American Jewish Identity," *Contemporary Jewry* 23, no. 1 (2002), 14–34. Note a parallel question surfacing with relation to Jewish history, in Moshe Rosman's *How Jewish is Jewish History?* (Oxford: 2008).

39. Debra Kaufman, "Post-Holocaust Memory: Some Gendered Reflections," in *Gender, Place, and Memory in the Modern Jewish Experience: Re-placing Ourselves,* ed. Judith Tydor Baumel and Tova Cohen (London: 2003), 187–196.

40. Kaufman, "Post-Holocaust Memory"; Susan Sered, *Women as Ritual Experts: The Religious Lives of Elderly Jewish Women in Jerusalem* (New York: 1996); Harriet Hartman and Moshe Hartman, *Gender and American Jews: Patterns in Work, Education, and Family in Contemporary Life* (Waltham: 2009); Sylvia Barack Fishman, *A Breath of Life: Feminism in the American Jewish Community* (Waltham: 1995).

41. Moshe Hartman and Harriet Hartman, *Gender Equality and American Jews* (Albany: 1996), 212.

42. Riv-Ellen Prell, *Fighting to Become Americans: Assimilation and the Trouble between Jewish Women and Jewish Men* (Boston: 1999).

43. Samuel Heilman, "American Jews and Community: A Spectrum of Possibilities," *Contemporary Jewry* 24, no. 1 (2003), 51–69.

44. Diana Pinto, *A New Jewish Identity for Post-1989 Europe* (London: 1996), online at www.jpr.org.uk/Reports/CS_Reports/PP_no_1_1996/index.htm (accessed 30 October 2012). It is noteworthy that intellectual and political perspectives are added for the European context, reflecting the different roles of Jews in Europe and the United States.

45. Werner Sollors, *Beyond Ethnicity: Consent and Descent in American Culture* (New York: 1986); see also Karen Brodkin, *How Jews Became White Folks: And What That Says About Race in America* (New Brunswick: 1998).

46. Moshe Hartman and Harriet Hartman, "Jewish Attitudes toward Intermarriage," *Journal of Contemporary Religion* 16, no. 1 (2000), 45–69.

47. Vincent Brook, *Something Ain't Kosher Here: The Rise of the "Jewish" Sitcom* (Piscataway: 2003).

48. Michelle Byers, "Post-Jewish? Theorizing the Emergence of Jewishness in Canadian Television," *Contemporary Jewry* 31, no. 3 (2011), 249.

49. David Hollinger, "Communalist and Dispersionist Approaches to American Jewish History in an Increasingly Post-Jewish Era," *American Jewish History* 95, no. 1 (2009), 23.

50. Shmuel Magid, "Be the Jew You Make: Jews, Judaism, and Jewishness in Post-Ethnic America," *Sh'ma* (March 2011), 3–4; see also Steven M. Cohen and Jack Wertheimer, "What is So Great about 'Post-Ethnic Judaism'?" (ibid., 5–6) and Noam Pianko, "Post-Ethnic but not Post-Peoplehood" (ibid., 7–8).

51. Liwerant and Ben-Rafael, "Klal Yisrael Today," 302.

52. Ibid., 299.

53. Ibid., 305.

54. Daniel Boyarin and Jonathan Boyarin, "Diaspora: Generation and the Ground of Jewish Identity," *Critical Inquiry* 19 (1993), 721 (emphasis added).

55. See, for instance, Glenn and Sokoloff (eds.), *Boundaries of Jewish Identity*; Riv-Ellen Prell, "Boundaries, Margins, and Norms: The Intellectual Stakes in the Study of American Jewish Culture(s)," *Contemporary Jewry* 32, no. 2 (2012), 189–204.

56. Glenn and Sokoloff, *Boundaries of Jewish Identity*.

57. Riv-Ellen Prell, "Boundaries, Margins, and Norms."

58. For discussions of these different subpopulations, see Laurence Kotler-Berkowitz, "An Introduction to the National Jewish Population Survey 2000–01," *Sociology of Religion* 67, no. 4 (2006), 387–390; Frank Mott and Diane B. Patel, "The Implications of Potential Boundaries and Definitions for Understanding American Jewry: Can One Size Fit All?" *Contemporary Jewry* 28, no. 1 (2008), 21–57; Rebhun, "Jewish Identity in America."

59. Laurence Kotler-Berkowitz, "An Introduction to the National Jewish Population Survey 2000–01," *Sociology of Religion* 67, no. 4 (2006), 387–390.

60. Theodore Sasson, Leonard Saxe, and Charles Kadushin, "Trends in American Jewish Attachment to Israel: An Assessment of the 'Distancing' Hypothesis," *Contemporary Jewry* 30, nos. 2–3 (2010), 297–319. The bulk of the issue is devoted to commentary on their article and on Steven M. Cohen and Ari Kelman's lead article (see n. 131).

61. Andras Kovacs, Ildiko Barna, Sergio DellaPergola, and Barry Kosmin, *Identity à la Carte: Research on Jewish Identities, Participation and Affiliation in Five Eastern European Countries* (Oxford: 2011), online at bjpa.org/Publications/downloadPublication.cfm?PublicationID=11736 (accessed 3 July 2012).

62. Harriet Hartman and Moshe Hartman, "Dimensions of Jewish Identity among American Jews," in *Papers in Jewish Demography, 1997*, ed. Sergio DellaPergola and Judith Even (Jerusalem: 2001); Hartman and Hartman, *Gender and American Jews*.

63. Pinto, "Asemitism or a Society without Antisemitism or Philosemitism." Pinto's notion of "boxes" does not necessarily suggest one embedded in the other. The flexibility of each level is also proposed by Stuart Charmé in an article co-authored by himself and Bethamie Horowitz, Tali Hyman and Jeffrey S. Kress, "Jewish Identities in Action: An Exploration of

Models, Metaphors, and Methods," *Journal of Jewish Education* 74, no. 2 (2008), 115–143. Charmé presents a spiral of the individual Jewish "skeleton," or "brain," as it interfaces with Jewish and non-Jewish space. Like Pinto, he suggests that the spiral is expandable and contractible according to individual, social, and cultural circumstances.

64. Uzi Rebhun, "Jews and the Ethnic Scene: A Multidimensional Theory," in *Studies in Contemporary Jewry*, vol. 25, *Ethnicity and Beyond: Theories and Dilemmas of Jewish Group Demarcation*, ed. Eli Lederhendler (New York: 2011), 91–101.

65. In his *Bowling Alone: The Collapse and Revival of American Community* (New York: 2000), Robert D. Putnam presents a widely accepted thesis, namely, that Americans have become increasingly disconnected from one another and much less likely to participate in groups or organizations for informal or formal purposes.

66. See, for example, Uzi Rebhun and Shlomit Levy, "Unity and Diversity: Jewish Identification in America and Israel 1990–2000," *Sociology of Religion* 67, no. 4 (2006), 391–414.

67. Erik Cohen, "Particularistic Education, Endogamy, and Educational Tourism to Homeland: An Exploratory Multi-dimensional Analysis of Jewish Diaspora Social Indicators," *Contemporary Jewry* 29, no. 2 (2009), 169–189. For a review of existing studies on Jewish Latin Americans, see Judith Laikin Elkin, "Rethinking Latin American Jewish Studies," *Latin American Research Review* 45, no. 2 (2010), 253–265.

68. Graham, *European Jewish Identity*; Kovacs, Ildiko, DellaPergola, and Kosmin, *Identity à la Carte*.

69. See the website of the North American Jewish Data Bank, www.jewishdatabank.org.

70. Paul Burstein, "Jewish Nonprofit Organizations in the U.S.: A Preliminary Survey," *Contemporary Jewry* 31, no. 2 (2011), 129–148.

71. Judit Bokser Liwerant, "Latin American Jewish Identities: Past and Present Challenges. The Mexican Case in a Comparative Perspective," in *Identities in an Era of Globalization and Multiculturalism: Latin America in the Jewish World*, ed. Judit Bokser Liwerant, Eliezer Ben-Rafael, Yossi Gorny, and Raanan Rein (Leiden: 2008), 81–108.

72. Diana Pinto, "Are There Jewish Answers to Europe's Questions?" *European Judaism* 39, no. 2 (2006), 47–57.

73. Shmuel Trigano, "The Future of European Jewry—A Changing Condition in a Changing Context?" in Schoeps and Glöckner (eds.), *A Road to Nowhere?* 298.

74. In *The Wandering Jew* (New York: 2011), Uzi Rebhun sums up foundational work on individual Jewish identity. See also Cohen, "Jewish Identity Research in the United States" and Cohen, "Jewish Identity Research: A State of the Art."

75. Hartman and Hartman, "Dimensions of Jewish Identity"; idem, *Gender and American Jews;* idem, *Gender Equality and American Jews*; Rebhun, "Jews and the Ethnic Scene."

76. Charles Liebman, "Jewish Identity in the United States and Israel," in *New Jewish Identities: Contemporary Europe and Beyond*, ed. Zvi Gitelman, Barry Kosmin, and András Kovács (New York: 2003), ch. 14.

77. Debra Kaufman, "The Place of Judaism in American Jewish Identity," in *The Cambridge Companion to American Judaism*, ed. Dana Evan Kaplan (Cambridge: 2005), 171–172; Harriet Hartman and Debra Kaufman, "Decentering the Study of Jewish Identity: Opening the Dialogue with Other Religious Groups," *Sociology of Religion* 67, no. 4 (2006), 365–387.

78. Mary Waters, *Ethnic Options: Choosing Identities in America* (Berkeley: 1990).

79. Summarized in Dashefsky, Lazerwitz, and Tabory, "A Journey of the 'Straightway' or the 'Roundabout Path.' "

80. Harriet Hartman and Debra Kaufman, "Decentering the Study of Jewish Identity"; Moshe Hartman and Harriet Hartman, "How Survey Research Shapes the Understanding of Jewish Identity," paper presented at the Association for Jewish Studies annual meeting, Boston (December 2003).

81. Bethamie Horowitz, *Connections and Journeys*; Cohen and Eisen, *The Jew Within*.

82. Dashefsky, Lazerwitz, and Tabory, "A Journey of the 'Straightway' or the 'Roundabout Path,' " 246–247.

83. Byers, "Post-Jewish?" 252. See also Aviv and Shneer, *New Jews*.

84. Erik H. Cohen, *The Jews of France at the Turn of the Third Millennium: A Sociological and Cultural Analysis* (Jerusalem: 2009).

85. Stuart Charmé, "Varieties of Authenticity in Contemporary Jewish Identity," *Jewish Social Studies* 6, no. 2 (2000), 143.

86. Jonathan Webber, "Modern Jewish Identities," in *Jewish Identities in the New Europe*, ed. Jonathan Webber (London: 1994), 82.

87. Charmé, "Varieties of Authenticity," 150–151.

88. The phrase itself was coined by Yehuda Leib Gordon in the 19th century; see Lisa Grant, "The Front Porch," *Sh'ma* (June 2009), 2.

89. Alain Finkielkraut, *The Imaginary Jew*, trans. Kevin O'Neill and David Suchoff (Omaha: 1997), 114.

90. Zygmunt Bauman, "Jews and Other Europeans, Old and New," *European Judaism* 42, no. 1 (2009), 121–133.

91. Riv-Ellen Prell, *Memory vs. Markets: The Future of Jewish Identity* (New York: 2002).

92. Steven M. Cohen and Manfred Gerstenfeld, "Changes in American Jewish Identities: From the Collective to the Personal, from Norms to Aesthetics: An Interview with Steven M. Cohen," in *American Jewry's Comfort Level: Present and Future*, ed. Steven Bayme and Manfred Gerstenfeld (New York: 2010), 123–132, online at www.bjpa.org/Publications/details.cfm?PublicationID=8253 (accessed 3 July 2012).

93. Nathan Glazer, *American Judaism* (Chicago: 1972), 142.

94. Hartman and Kaufman, "Decentering the Study of Jewish Identity"; see also Nadia Kim, "Guests in Someone Else's House? Korean Immigrants in Los Angeles Negotiate American 'Race,' Nationhood and Identity" (Ph.D. diss., University of Michigan, 2003); Helen Kim and Noah Leavitt, "The Newest Jews? Understanding Jewish American and Asian American Marriages," *Contemporary Jewry* 32, no. 2 (2012), 135–166.

95. Calvin Goldscheider, "Boundary Maintenance and Jewish Identity: Comparative and Historical Perspectives," in Glenn and Sokoloff (eds.), *Boundaries of Jewish Identity*, 110–131.

96. See, for example, Madeline Albright, *Prague Winter: A Personal Story of Remembrance and War, 1937–1948* (New York: 2012).

97. Laada Bilaniuk, "The Contested Logics of Jewish Identity," in Glenn and Sokoloff (eds.), *Boundaries of Jewish Identity*, 203–215.

98. Ruth Ellen Gruber, "Beyond Virtually Jewish: New Authenticities and Real Imaginary Spaces in Europe," *The Jewish Quarterly Review* 99, no. 4 (2009), 487–504; Erica Lehrer, "'Jewish Like an Adjective,'" in Glenn and Sokoloff (eds.), *Boundaries of Jewish Identity*, 161–187.

99. Lehrer, "'Jewish Like an Adjective,'" 166.

100. Liwerant and Ben-Rafael, "Klal Yisrael Today," 304.

101. Rebhun, "Jewish Identity in America," 43–44.

102. Sarna, *American Judaism*.

103. Charles S. Liebman, "Post-War American Jewry: From Ethnic to Privatized Judaism," in *Secularism, Spirituality, and the Future of American Jewry*, ed. Elliot Abrams and David G. Dalin (Washington, D.C: 1999), 7–18; Chaim Waxman, "*Religion, Spirituality and the Future of American Judaism,*" in *Jewish Spirituality and Divine Law*, ed. Adam Mintz and Lawrence Schiffman (New York: 2005), 489–515, online at www.bjpa.org/Publications/details.cfm?PublicationID=4025 (accessed 3 July 2012).

104. Arnold Dashefsky and Howard Shapiro, *Ethnic Identification among American Jews: Socialization and Social Structure* (Lexington, Mass.: 1974). Dashefsky and Shapiro found that while family and peers had stronger effects on Jewish identity, Jewish education had a significant independent effect. A number of subsequent studies corroborated this finding.

105. Mark B. Pearlman, "'I' to 'We': Personalized Judaism Inspires Collective Jewish Action and Peoplehood," *Sh'ma* 37 (October 2006), 10.

106. Steven M. Cohen, Misha Galperin, and Yoav Shoham, *The Power of Peoplehood: How Commitment to the Jewish People Undergirds Tzedakah for Jewish Causes* (Washington D.C.: 2009), 22; online at www.bjpa.org/Publications/details.cfm?PublicationID=5900 (accessed 3 July 2012).

107. David Mittelberg, "Jewish Peoplehood Education," in *The International Handbook of Jewish Education*, ed. Helena Miller, Lisa D. Grant, and Alex Pomson (Dordrecht: 2010), 515–539.

108. Cohen and Eisen, *The Jew Within.*

109. Sarna, *American Judaism,* 368.

110. Steven Cohen, and Ari Y. Kelman, *The Continuity of Discontinuity: How Young Jews Are Connecting, Creating, and Organizing Their Own Jewish Lives* (New York: 2001), online at www.bjpa.org/Publications/details.cfm?PublicationID=327 (accessed 3 July 2012).

111. Wertheimer, *All Quiet on the Religious Front?* 3–5.

112. Jack Wertheimer, *Linking the Silos: How to Accelerate the Momentum in Jewish Education Today* (New York: 2006); see also Eric Levine, "Confronting the Tensions: Jewish Community Building in the 21st Century," *Journal of Jewish Communal Service* 83, nos. 2–3 (2008), 125–139.

113. Judit Bokser Liwerant, "Latin American Jewish Identities," 2.

114. For a good discussion of the many meanings of post-denominationalism, see Uriel Heilman, "Beyond Dogma," *Jerusalem Post International* (11 February 2005), 15.

115. Wertheimer, *All Quiet on the Religious Front?* 23–24.

116. Ibid., 25.

117. Lisa Grant, quoted in Ezra Kopelowitz and Shlomi Ravid, *Best Practices of Organizations that Build Jewish Peoplehood: A Policy-Oriented Analysis of a Field in Formation* (New York: 2010), 64–65.

118. Samuel C. Heilman, "American Jews and Community: A Spectrum of Possibilities," *Contemporary Jewry* 24, no. 1 (2003), 65.

119. In *Speaking of Jews: Rabbis, Intellectuals, and the Creation of an American Public Identity* (Berkeley: 2009), Lisa Berman suggests that consciousness of defining boundaries and concern with numbers may stem from the inordinate influence of social scientists on Jewish communal leaders in the United States.

120. Sergio Della Pergola, "Jews in Europe: Demographic Trends," in Schoeps and Glockner (eds.), *A Road to Nowhere?* 32.

121. Ruth Ellen Gruber, "Beyond Virtually Jewish."

122. Leonard Saxe, Benjamin Phillips, Theodore Sasson, Shahar Hecht, Michelle Shain, Graham Wright, and Charles Kadushin, "Intermarriage: The Impact and Lessons of Taglit-Birthright Israel," *Contemporary Jewry* 31, no. 2 (2011), 151–172. In their discussion of advocates of inreach, they cite, among others, Sylvia Barack Fishman (*Double or Nothing: Jewish Families and Mixed Marriage* [Hanover, N.H.: 2004]), Jack Wertheimer and Steven Bayme ("Intermarriage and Jewish Leadership in the United States," *Forward* [9 September 2005], 11); advocates of outreach include Kerry M. Olitzky and Elliot Dorff ("Like Abraham and Sarah, Jewish World Should Welcome All into a 'Big Tent,'" *Jewish Telegraphic Agency* [9 October 2007]), Egon Mayer ("American-Jewish Intermarriage in the 1990s and Beyond: The Coming Revolution in Jewish Demography and Communal Policy," in *The Imperatives of Jewish Outreach: Responding to Intermarriage in the 1990s and Beyond*, ed. Egon Mayer [New York: 1991], 37–62), and Keren McGinity (*Still Jewish: A History of Women and Intermarriage in America* [New York: 2009]).

123. Saxe et al. "Intermarriage."

124. *Mamzerut* pertains to the Jewish legal (halakhic) status of children born to a Jewish mother who remarried without first obtaining a *get*, a proper religious divorce.

125. Jack Wertheimer, *All Quiet on the Religious Front?* 1.

126. Samuel G. Freedman, *Jew vs. Jew: The Struggle for the Soul of American Jewry* (New York: 2000).

127. Wertheimer and Greenberg, "Denominations and the Jewish Future," 5.

128. Gershon Winkler, *The Way of the Boundary Crosser: An Introduction to Jewish Flexidoxy* (Lanham: 2005).

129. Rebhun, "Jewish Identity in America."

130. According to Woocher, Israel provided a central tenet of American Jews' "civil religion." See his *Sacred Survival: The Civil Religion of American Jews* (Bloomington: 1986).

131. Steven M. Cohen and Ari Y. Kelman, "Distancing is Closer than Ever," *Contemporary Jewry* 30, nos. 2–3 (2010), 145–148.

132. Peter Beinart, "The Failure of the American Jewish Establishment," *New York Review of Books* (10 June 2010), online at www.nybooks.com/articles/archives/2010/jun/10/failure-american-jewish-establishment/?pagination=false (accessed 3 July 2012). See also his *The Crisis of Zionism* (New York: 2012).

133. Sasson, Saxe, and Kadushin, "Trends in American Jewish Attachment to Israel"; see also *Contemporary Jewry* 30, nos. 2–3 (2010), which is devoted in its entirety to this issue.

134. Irving Louis Horowitz, "'Distancing' from Israel in Jewish American Life," *Contemporary Jewry* 30 (2010), 175–181; Morton Weinfeld, "The Distancing Debate," ibid., 279–328; Ronald W. Zweig, "Distancing or Transformation: Ties to Israel Come of Age," ibid., 283–285.

135. Reprinted in Steven Bayme, Arnold Eisen, Harold Shapiro, and David Ellenson (eds.), *Renewing the Jewish Social Contract: Bridging the Religious-Secular Divide* (New York: 2009), online at www.bjpa.org/Publications/details.cfm?PublicationID=315 (p. 5) (accessed 3 July 2012).

136. Arnold Eisen, "Judaism, Democracy, and the Israel-Diaspora Connection," ibid., 9–12.

137. Gal Beckerman, "Embattled Jewish Agency to Promote Identity over Aliyah," *Forward* (12 March 2010).

138. Kelner, *Tours that Bind.*

139. Eran Lerman, "A New Bird with Two Wings," in Bayme, Eisen, Shapiro, and Ellenson (eds.), *Renewing the Jewish Social Contract,* 31–33. See also Bethamie Horowitz, "Beyond Attachment: Widening the Analytic Focus about the American Jewish Relationship to Israel," *Contemporary Jewry* 30, nos. 2–3 (2010), 241–246.

140. Charles Liebman and Steven M. Cohen, *Two Worlds of Judaism* (New Haven: 1990); Calvin Goldscheider. "American and Israeli Jews: Oneness and Distancing," *Contemporary Jewry* 30, nos. 2–3 (2010), 205–212.

141. Boyarin and Boyarin, "Diaspora"; Aviv and Shneer, *New Jews.*

142. Jay Michaelson, "How I Am Losing My Love for Israel," *Forward* (25 September 2009); Jay Michaelson "Challenges to Jewish Peoplehood—Or, Why Israel May Now Present an Obstacle to Identification with the Jewish People," in *Interrogating Jewish Peoplehood: Concepts, Challenges, and Policies, Final Report* (1 March 2010), session 3.

143. Jack Wertheimer, "Go Out and See What the People Are Doing," *Contemporary Jewry* 30, nos. 2–3 (2010), 236.

144. Liwerant and Ben-Rafael, "Klal Yisrael Today."

145. Ibid., 329–331.

146. DellaPergola, "Jews in Europe," 188–189.

147. Marlene De Vries, "An Enduring Bond? Jews in the Netherlands and Their Ties with Judaism," *Journal of Ethnic & Migration Studies* 32, no. 1 (2006), 69–88.

148. Cohen, "Jewish Identity Research in the United States," 17. It is noteworthy that Cohen does not feel the need to mention antisemitism in any other context in his article.

149. Sartre, *Anti-Semite and Jew.*

150. The arguments by Trigano and Askénazi are cited in Cohen, "Jewish Identity Research: A State of the Art," 19.

151. Ira Sheskin and Arnold Dashefsky, *Jewish Population in the United States, 2011* (Storrs, Conn.: 2011), online at www.jewishdatabank.org/Reports/Jewish_Population_in_the_United_States_2011.pdf (accessed 3 July 2012).

152. Smith, *Jewish Distinctiveness in America.* Steven Cohen notes that the rise in intermarriage has also led to shifts in size among the various Jewish denominations. In the United

States, the intermarriage rate is about six times as high among the non-Orthodox as it is among the Orthodox. Coupled with higher fertility, this factor accounts for the fact that the Orthodox community is growing, especially in the younger age cohorts (Steven M. Cohen, "Demise of the 'Good Jew': Marshall Sklare Award Lecture," *Contemporary Jewry* 32, no. 1 [2012], 89).

153. Zygmunt Bauman, "Jews and Other Europeans, Old and New." Notwithstanding, it has been suggested that U.S. Jewry could benefit from a model in which Jews were recognized as a distinct group—this could be an aid, for instance, in cases involving hate crimes. See Eric L. Goldstein, *The Price of Whiteness: Jews, Race, and American Identity* (Princeton: 2006).

154. Pinto, "Asemitism or a Society without Antisemitism or Philosemitism."

155. Byers, "Post-Jewish?"

156. The reference here is to Yiorgos Anagnostou, "Model Americans, Quintessential Greeks: Ethnic Success and Assimilation in Diaspora," *Diaspora* 12:3 (2003), 279–328.

157. Liwerant and Ben-Rafael, "Klal Yisrael Today," 322–323.

158. Adam R. Gaynor, "Beyond the Melting Pot: Finding a Voice for Jewish Identity in Multicultural American Schools," *Journal of Jewish Communal Service* 86, nos. 1–2 (2011), 174–183.

159. Sarna, *American Judaism.*

160. Chaim I. Waxman, "What We Don't Know About the Judaism of America's Jews."

161. Cohen and Wertheimer, "Whatever Happened to the Jewish People?"

162. See more description at werepair.org.

163. Fern Chertok, Jim Gerstein, Joshua Tobias, Shirah Rosin, and Matthew Boxer, *Volunteering and Values: A Repair the World Report on Jewish Young Adults* (New York: 2011).

164. Uzi Rebhun, *The Wandering Jew.*

165. Harriet Hartman and Ira Sheskin, *The Influence of Community Context and Individual Characteristics on Jewish Identity: A 21-Community Study* (Storrs, Conn.: 2011) online at www.jewishdatabank.org/Reports/Report_Influence_of_Community_Context_Hartman_and_Sheskin.pdf (accessed 3 July 2012).

166. Erik H. Cohen and Rachel Werczberger, "Jewish Normativity: An Exploratory Study," in Elizur and Yaniv (eds.) *Theory Construction and Multivariate Analysis*, 35–48, online at www.bjpa.org/Publications/details.cfm?PublicationID=4809 (accessed 3 July 2012).

167. Charmé, Horowitz, Hyman, and Kress, "Jewish Identities in Action," 117.

168. Cohen and Werczberger, "Jewish Normativity."

169. Kelner, *Tours that Bind.*

170. Deborah Skolnick Einhorn, Sylvia Barack Fishman, Loraine Obler, and Shulamit Reinharz, *The New Jewish Family: Reproductive Choices and Opportunities in Contemporary U.S. Society* (Waltham: 2005).

171. Charmé, Horowitz, Hyman, and Kress, "Jewish Identities in Action."

172. Steven M. Cohen and Jack Wertheimer, "What is So Great About Post-Ethnic Judaism?" 5.

173. Tsvi Blanchard, "How to Think About Being Jewish in the Twenty-First Century: A New Model of Jewish Identity Construction," *Journal of Jewish Communal Service* 79, no. 1 (2002), 40.

174. De Vries, "An Enduring Bond?"

175. DellaPergola, "Jews in Europe," 33.

176. Cohen and Kelman "Thinking about Distancing from Israel," 294–295.

177. Blanchard, "How to Think about Being Jewish."

178. Cohen, "Demise of the 'Good Jew,'" 86.

179. Graham, *European Jewish Identity,* 51.

Defining and Measuring the Socioeconomic Status of Jews

Esther Isabelle Wilder

(LEHMAN COLLEGE, CUNY)

Social scientists and historians have examined the socioeconomic status (SES) of the Jews in many different contexts. Although pre-20th-century historical studies focused on European Jewry, most modern empirical studies have centered on the United States and Israel.[1] Given the distinctive socioeconomic profile of Jews in many modern industrial societies, much of this research has looked at the factors that have given rise to the Jews' extraordinary accomplishments as well as those responsible for variations in SES within Jewish populations.

In the United States, scholars have emphasized the evolving socioeconomic position of American Jews, along with the links between socioeconomic achievement and various forms of Jewish identification. In Israel, there has been a stronger focus on inter- and intra-ethnic differentials in SES. These different emphases reflect the unique socio-demographic characteristics of the two countries' Jewish populations, the concerns of the various Jewish communities (and the researchers who have studied them), and the kinds of statistical data available for each country. In the United States, the boundaries between Jews and non-Jews are more fluid than in Israel, and intermarriage rates are high (approximately 50 percent).[2] The American Jewish community is therefore especially concerned with the changing socio-demographic characteristics of the Jewish population and their implications for Jewish identification and continuity. Israel, in contrast, is comprised primarily of immigrants and the first-generation descendants of immigrants. (According to the Israel Central Bureau of Statistics, 29 percent of Israeli Jews are foreign-born.)[3] As a result, the Jewish community in Israel is concerned about the well-being and assimilation of Jews coming from widely varying countries of origin.

The methods used to investigate the socioeconomic position of the Jews have run the gamut from simple descriptive statistics to complex multivariate techniques. The more advanced methodological approaches are especially important for discerning trends in the Jews' socioeconomic position over time, since changes in SES may reflect shifts in the socio-demographic profile of the Jews as well as changes in the reference group to which the Jews are being compared. Given the wide range of data sources and the variety of ways in which Jews have been identified, sampled, and studied, it is important to consider how variations in definition and measurement can influence research findings.

In the discussion that follows, I describe the data sources that researchers have used to investigate the socioeconomic position of the Jews in the United States, in Israel, and in a variety of other countries, both historically and today. I discuss the strengths and weaknesses of the various data sources along with the challenges that researchers have faced in undertaking socioeconomic research in this area. I also examine some of the ways in which researchers have explained the Jews' socioeconomic distinctiveness and the implications of that distinctiveness for Jewish continuity. I conclude by offering recommendations for future research on Jewish SES, particularly insofar as data collection and research methods are concerned.

Sources of Data

Censuses and surveys are the data sources that social scientists have used most frequently when investigating SES. National censuses are an excellent source of information, since they are nationally representative and often contain information on a large number of socioeconomic variables such as education, occupation, and income. Census data do not always include information on religion, however, and most censuses provide limited opportunities for the investigation of SES within the Jewish population. For instance, they lack information on religious denomination, Jewish identification, observance of Jewish rituals, and/or involvement in Jewish organizations and communal networks, even though all these indicators have been linked to SES.[4]

Although the United States does not ask about religion in its national census, more than 70 countries do.[5] In recent years, national censuses have collected information about Jewish populations in such diverse countries as Australia (2011), Austria (2001), Azerbaijan (2009), Belarus (2009), Brazil (2010), Bulgaria (2011), Canada (2001), the Czech Republic (2011), Estonia (2011), Hungary (2011), India (2011), Ireland (2011), Kazakhstan (2009), Kyrgyzstan (2009), Latvia (2011), Lithuania (2011), Macedonia (2002), Mexico (2010), and South Africa (2001). Among those censuses that ask about religion, the response rates vary considerably. For instance, England and Wales introduced a question on religion in 2001. While the question was optional, only 7 percent of respondents declined to answer.[6]

The ways in which Jews are identified in any given census can have important ramifications for estimates of socioeconomic well-being. Jews can be identified as an ethnic group, a religious group, or both (as in Canada).[7] Thus, for example, the 1971 Canadian census found that 7 percent more people identified as Jewish by ethnicity than by religion. Since Jews comprise only a small percentage of the population, many census samples are too small for complex statistical analyses. In some countries where Jews are a small minority, they are subsumed within the category "other" on census forms.[8]

Surveys, both national and regional, are another resource for investigating the socioeconomic status of the Jews. Some surveys target the general population and collect information on religion along with other socio-demographic indicators, while others focus on particular subpopulations (Jewish households, for example). The former type allow for direct comparisons between Jews and other groups, although they tend to include only a small number of Jews; the merging of multiple datasets therefore becomes necessary for any kind of rigorous statistical analysis. Those of the latter type allow for analyses based on variables unique to the Jewish population (observance of specific religious rituals, for example).

Socio-demographic studies that include information on Jews have been conducted over the past few decades in a variety of countries, among them Argentina (2003, 2004, 2005), Brazil (2007), Italy (1994), Mexico (1991, 2000), South Africa (1991, 1998, 2008), Lithuania (1993), the United Kingdom (1995), Israel (1999, 2009), the Netherlands (1999, 2009), and Venezuela (1998–1999), as well as in broader geographical areas (for instance, the 2010–2011 European Social Survey).[9] In the United States, relevant information can be found in national surveys that target the general population (such as the General Social Survey) as well as those that are particular to the Jewish population—for instance, the National Jewish Population Surveys of 1970–1971, 1989–1990, and 2000–2001, and the American Jewish Identity Survey (AJIS) of 2001. In Israel, the Central Bureau of Statistics regularly carries out a number of national surveys dealing with such topics as labor force participation, income and savings, immigration, and aging. In addition, local community surveys (in the United States) and targeted surveys (for instance, of Jewish elites) provide useful information.

Socioeconomic research on the Jews has also made use of in-depth interviews, literary sources, and historical documents (for instance, memoirs, newspapers, and correspondence) as well as theological writings and analyses of Jewish texts. For example, Rodney Wilson has surveyed Jewish scholarly writing and thinking on economic theory and policy,[10] whereas others have examined Jewish views on specific economic issues such as usury.[11]

Socioeconomic Research on the Jewish Population of the United States

Many scholars have lamented the fact that there are "very limited data for the systemic study over time of the occupational attainment and earnings of the Jews of the United States."[12] The key challenges relate to data availability, data quality, and questions of definition and measurement.

Defining the American Jewish Population

One issue that permeates (and sometimes complicates) socioeconomic research on Jews in the United States is the fundamental question, "Who is a Jew?"[13] Historically, when intermarriage was rare and Jewish identity was strongly characterized by religious rituals, there were fewer questions concerning the boundaries between Jews and non-Jews. As Barry Kosmin and colleagues point out,

Studies done during the immigrant period [1880 to 1920] had relatively little to worry about.... There were few "patrilineal" Jews, few Jews who would not be buried as Jews, few intermarriages, few Jews who would not keep their children out of school on Yom Kippur, few Jews for whom Jewish identity was not of primary salience. As acculturation took its course, the question of Jewish identity arose, not just as a religious or communal concern but as a practical research matter.[14]

Indeed, ethnic and social forms of Jewish identification have increased in importance among many Jews, and the religious ties that once bound together Jews have gradually weakened. The boundaries between Jewish and non-Jewish identity have become more fluid, and there is less agreement concerning the characteristics that should be used to distinguish between Jews and non-Jews. Over time, definitions have shifted to encompass the notions of "core" and "enlarged" Jewish populations:

> The core Jewish population concept includes all those who, when asked, identify themselves as Jews or, if the respondent is a different person in the same household, are identified by him/her as Jews, and those of Jewish parentage who are identificationally indifferent or agnostic but do not formally identify with another religious group. The enlarged Jewish population concept also includes all other persons of Jewish parentage who are not Jews currently (or at the time of investigation) and all the additional non-Jewish members (spouses, children, etc.) in mixed religious households....It should be noted that an enlarged Jewish population may be growing while the respective core Jewish population is declining.[15]

While contemporary scholars continue to disagree about what defines Jewish identity in America,[16] Frank Mott and Diane Patel contend that "the definitional issues are too profound ever to expect that there can be a resolution. Arguably, presenting one definition that purports to be 'the' definition is perhaps counterproductive."[17] For empirical research, they suggest, it is appropriate to cast the net as wide as possible, acknowledging that there will never be a consensus. Indeed, in the words of Sidney Goldstein, "any survey that restricts its identification of the Jewish population only to those reporting being Jewish by religion runs the risk of excluding a substantial part of the total population of Jewish religio-ethnic identity."[18] In a similar vein, Sergio DellaPergola argues that, to "appropriately appraise Jewish population trends, one needs to address the broadest possible definition of the collective."[19]

The definition that one chooses is not merely a question of ideology; it also has important ramifications for the assessment of SES. Comparing results across studies and discerning trends over time is especially problematic in light of research showing that different techniques for identifying Jews yield different results. In one study, Sidney Goldstein documented how the educational and occupational distribution of Jews varied according to different Jewish identifiers—with regard to education, for example, he noted that "the differences among the various subcategories of core Jews [Jews by religion, secular Jews, or Jews by choice] suggests that the intensity of Jewish identity is related to levels of education; the stronger the intensity, the higher the level of achievement."[20]

The question of identifying Jews is complicated further by the use of different sampling methods:

> Crucial decisions are made at the sample stage that affect who will eventually be included or excluded from the study....The literature is replete with examples of reliance upon federation lists, distinctive Jewish names, language spoken, residential clustering, and

even friendship networks as mechanisms for identifying and/or screening Jewish households and Jewish individuals.... Serious questions remain about the representativeness of
samples that result from reliance upon one or another such mechanism for identifying
Jews.[21]

As a result, the Jewish populations identified in many studies are, in fact, Jewish
subpopulations comprised only of those with Jewish names, for instance, or those
who are members of local Jewish organizations.

U.S. Government Data Sources

The U.S. Census Bureau has asked for workers' occupations in every census since
1850 and has requested information on earnings or income since 1940. As noted,
however, the U.S. census has never included a question on religion, since that
would violate the traditional separation of church and state.[22] Notwithstanding,
there was a perceived need for more data on the Jewish population during the
period of Jewish mass immigration to the United States in the 1880s. At that time,
the U.S. Census Office conducted a survey of approximately 10,000 American
Jewish families, identified through congregation lists, who had been living in the
United States for five or more years. Published in 1890, the Billings Report provided information on occupation (though not earnings) that could be compared
directly with the findings of the 1890 census.[23] Although biased in favor of respondents of German Jewish origin (who were more likely than others to be living in the
United States for five or more years), the report is a valuable source of information—all the more so, as it marks the only time a federal survey has been devoted
exclusively to the U.S. Jewish population.[24]

A second significant data source is the 41-volume report issued by the Dillingham
Immigration Commission in 1911. This enormous report includes a survey of employers in selected immigrant-intensive manufacturing and mining industries. In the
survey, the weekly wages of workers in various industries are classified by "race" and
by immigrant/native-born status; Jews are identified either as "Hebrew-Russian" or
as "Hebrew-others." Barry Chiswick has conducted a systematic analysis of these
data.[25] Using survey data from the same period (1899–1914), Arcadius Kahan has
investigated the employment characteristics of Jewish immigrants prior to their arrival in the United States, as reported to the U.S. immigration authorities. Of course,
the data surveyed by Kahan are selective for immigrants and are likely to be biased
by immigrants' anticipation of the priorities of the immigration authorities.[26]

The Current Population Survey (CPS), a monthly survey conducted by the U.S.
Census Bureau for the Bureau of Labor Statistics (BLS), traces its roots back to
1940.[27] In March 1957, the CPS included a question pertaining to respondents'
current religion. Although the relevant microdata files have been destroyed, some of
the available data have been published.[28] Researchers have used the 1957 CPS data
to examine the education, occupational distribution, labor-force participation rates,
and income of Jews as compared with non-Jews.[29]

Researchers studying Jewish SES with U.S. census data from 1900 to 1970 have
also made use of two key "indirect Jewish identifiers" to identify individuals who are

likely to be Jewish. The "Russian-origin technique" is based on the working assumption that individuals are Jewish if they (or at least one parent) were born in Russia or Russia/Poland (as distinct from the "other Poland" designation). Likewise, the "traditional Jewish language technique" identifies those who speak Yiddish, Hebrew, or Ladino.[30] Since 1970, the census has included questions on ancestry, although the coding system does not allow for the determination of a person's religion. In any event, each of these approaches has significant limitations. As Chiswick has noted, the "Russian-origin technique" excludes Jews from Germany, Central Europe, and other areas, as well as Jews of Russian origin whose grandparents (rather than parents) immigrated to the United States—and, of course, it also incorrectly identifies some people as Jewish based on their (or their parents') place of birth.[31] While the "traditional Jewish language technique" is unlikely to designate non-Jews as Jewish, it excludes the many Jews who report a mother tongue other than Yiddish, Hebrew, or Ladino.[32]

These limitations notwithstanding, data from the early- and mid-20th century censuses have been used to study Jewish occupational attainment and distribution,[33] literacy,[34] and earnings.[35] Moreover, 1970 census data have been analyzed with regard to earnings,[36] education,[37] occupational distribution/labor market status,[38] and labor supply and investment in children.[39]

Joel Perlmann has looked at ethnic differences in schooling and social structure among the Irish, Italians, Russian Jews, and blacks in the city of Providence, Rhode Island, between 1880 and 1935, using census and school records as well as city directories containing information on occupation.[40] More recently, Yinon Cohen has made use of the 1980 census to examine the economic assimilation of Jewish and Arab immigrants from Israel and the territories occupied by Israel since the Six-Day War of 1967, using place of birth ("Israel" or "Palestine") as well as ancestry and language information to distinguish Jews from Arabs.[41] Although many of these later studies focus on particular subsets of the Jewish population (sometimes owing to data availability), they enrich our general understanding of the socioeconomic experience of Jews in the United States.

The National Jewish Population Survey and Other Surveys of American Jews

Many studies of SES have drawn on data sources that target the Jewish population. These include both national and local studies. Some of the earliest survey data on Jewish SES date back to the latter part of the 19th century. In 1890, for instance, the Baron Hirsch Foundation collected data from East European immigrants living in the 7th, 10th, and 13th wards on the Lower East Side of Manhattan. The data, which include employment information for heads of households, were based on a sample of 111,690 individuals—nearly 83 percent of the estimated 135,000 East European Jewish immigrants then residing in New York City.[42]

In the modern era, large-scale national surveys of the Jewish population have been central to socioeconomic research on American Jewry. In particular, the National Jewish Population Survey (NJPS) includes a variety of socioeconomic indicators for a nationally representative sample of the American Jewish population. Three NJPS surveys have been carried out in the United States, in 1970–1971, 1989–1990, and 2000–2001 (henceforth, 1970 NJPS, 1990 NJPS, and 2000 NJPS). However, differences in methodology, screening, and questionnaire design limit our ability to compare NJPS data over time. For example, the 1970 and 2000 NJPS surveys sampled an especially high proportion of households in metropolitan areas with high-density Jewish populations, whereas the 1990 NJPS did not. For the 1970 NJPS, the Jewish population was identified using a combination of Jewish federation lists and random area sampling; face-to-face interviews were conducted in respondents' households. In contrast, the 1990 and 2000 NJPS surveys relied on random digit dialing (RDD) and telephone interviews.[43] Moreover, the total survey response rate has varied considerably across surveys. It was 79 percent for the 1970 NJPS, 24 percent for the 1990 NJPS, and 28 percent for the 2000 NJPS.[44]

Unfortunately, the different methods used for the three National Jewish Population Surveys may systematically bias SES estimates in ways that are not necessarily consistent from one survey to the next. For example, higher socioeconomic status is generally associated with lower survey response rates, although this general relationship may not apply to particular surveys.[45] While there is no infallible way to test how the low response rates of the more recent surveys have affected the results, there is some evidence pointing to a possible overcount of better-educated individuals in the 2000 NJPS.[46] The 1990 NJPS probably better represented the total Jewish population, whereas the 1970 and the 2000 surveys are likely to have provided better coverage of individuals who had the strongest Jewish identity.[47] Moreover, the 1970 NJPS may have overrepresented Jews in the North Central region (the upper Midwest) while underrepresenting those in New England.[48] To the extent that NJPS non-responders have distinctive socioeconomic characteristics, any estimate of the socioeconomic status of the Jews will be biased to some degree. While the application of sampling weights may help to correct these problems, considerable controversy surrounded the sampling design of the 2000 NJPS, and the survey's sample weights remain the subject of considerable debate.[49]

As noted, the screening methods used to identify Jews have differed from one NJPS survey to the next. For the 1970 NJPS, respondents were identified as Jewish if they provided affirmative replies, for themselves and/or any household members, to one or more of the following questions: (1) Was the person born Jewish? (2) Is the person Jewish now? (3) Was the person's father born Jewish? and (4) Was the person's mother born Jewish? For the 1990 NJPS, respondents were screened for inclusion using four questions: (1) What is your religion? (2) Do you or anyone else in the household consider him/herself Jewish? (3) Were you or anyone else in the household raised Jewish? and (4) Do or did you or anyone else in this household have a Jewish parent? For the 2000 NJPS, the four questions were slightly different: (1) What is your or other adult's religion, if any? (2) Do you or other adult have a Jewish mother or a Jewish father? (3) Were you or other adult raised Jewish? and (4) Do you or other adult consider your/him/herself Jewish for any reasons?[50] As DellaPergola has noted, these definitions "have tended to evolve from the straightforward question 'What is his religion?' and its 'Jew' modality, through the several multivariate ideal constructs devised for the 1990 NJPS, reaching increasingly more nuanced solutions in the NJPS 2001."[51]

These different screening methods limit our ability to make direct comparisons, especially when researchers take the additional step of excluding certain individuals from their samples, as is often the case. Indeed, researchers have the "flexibility to define their own Jewish sample, which may differ from the sample produced by the survey's screening questions."[52] Laurence Kotler-Berkowitz shows how scholars have defined the Jewish population in a variety of ways even when using the same survey data from the 2000 NJPS.[53]

Beyond these considerations of sampling methods and screening, socioeconomic research that makes use of the NJPS is also constrained by each survey's distinctive questionnaire design and question-specific response rates. Several of the questions pertaining to SES are not directly comparable. While the 2000 NJPS collected information about individual earnings, the 1990 NJPS collected information on household income and the 1970 NJPS asked about family income. Question non-response is also a potential problem, since questions on income and other measures of SES tend to have especially low response rates. Research on Jewish income using the 1970 and 1990 NJPS surveys revealed that just over half the respondents answered the income questions, and responders tended to have higher levels of education than their non-responding counterparts as well as different occupational patterns. (For instance, they were more likely to work full-time and more likely to hold professional or technical jobs.)[54] Meanwhile, analysis of the 2000 NJPS income question revealed "little systematic pattern" when male responders were compared to non-responding males, although some differences were evident. (For instance, sales and clerical workers were more likely to report their earnings.)[55] Evidence from the 2000 NJPS also suggests that those who reported their incomes had higher earnings than those who did not.[56] These findings suggest a bias towards higher SES among NJPS responders to the income question.

These limitations notwithstanding, a number of researchers have used the NJPS to undertake socioeconomic research on the American Jewish population. The resulting descriptive reports and multivariate analyses have covered a wide variety of topics, including education,[57] labor force participation and occupational attainment,[58] earnings and wealth,[59] Jewish poverty,[60] the Jewish elderly population,[61] gender differences in SES,[62] and the relationships between Jewishness (or various forms of Jewish identification) and socioeconomic achievement.[63] Although Chiswick has noted the difficulty of comparing Jewish surveys to other data sources,[64] a number of studies have linked NJPS socioeconomic data to census or CPS data[65] or to other national surveys such as the National Survey of Religion and Ethnicity[66] and the Survey of Income and Program Participation.[67]

Socioeconomic data on the American Jewish population can also be found in the American Jewish Identity Survey (AJIS), which was conducted in 2001 by the Center for Jewish Studies at the City University of New York (CUNY).[68] The survey methods used for the AJIS were based on those of the 1990 NJPS, although the AJIS had an overall response rate of just 18 percent. While the AJIS was somewhat overshadowed by the 2000 NJPS, Egon Mayer and associates drew on AJIS data to illustrate how various forms of Jewish identity are linked to socioeconomic indicators such as education, employment, and income.[69] Moreover, Ariela Keysar used the AJIS and the American Religion Identification Survey of 2001, also undertaken under the auspices of CUNY, to compare the socio-demographic profiles of Americans of Jewish heritage who profess no religion with those of the general population of Americans who indicate no religious affiliation.[70]

Local community surveys have also been important to researchers studying Jewish SES. Most are small-scale surveys undertaken to meet specific local needs. As Sidney Goldstein has noted, "the surveys have varied considerably in scope and quality: they have relied on different questionnaires, varying sampling designs and coverage of the Jewish population, and diverse tabulation plans. The absence of standardized methods and definitions (including who was to be counted as a Jew) make it difficult and sometimes impossible to compare findings across communities."[71]

Ira Sheskin provides a detailed discussion of the various community surveys, how they have differed, and how the differences are likely to affect cross-study comparisons.[72] For example, some local studies have used random-digit-dialing to identify Jews; others have relied on samples drawn from local federation mailing lists, and still others have used distinctive Jewish name (DJN) samples drawn from telephone directories.[73] These different approaches have implications for the study of Jews' SES. For example, on average, Jews with DJNs tend to have more education than those without DJNs.[74]

Some of the more sophisticated local community surveys have been studied intensively by social scientists, often with an eye toward the Jews' socioeconomic achievements and the implications of those achievements for various forms of Jewish identity and continuity. Steven Cohen explored the socioeconomic status of Jews using two community surveys (1965 and 1975) from Boston,[75] while Sidney Goldstein and Calvin Goldscheider examined the changing social-class profile of Jews by means of a 1963 survey conducted in Providence, Rhode Island.[76] Many reports based on local studies have dealt with the socioeconomic profiles of local communities,[77] and a few have addressed specific socioeconomic topics such as Jewish representation among the economic and social elites of New Orleans.[78] Sheskin, together with Pnina Zadka and Henry Green, used community surveys from the United States and census data from Israel to compare the characteristics of older Jews in South Florida and Israel.[79]

Other research on Jewish SES in the United States has been more narrowly focused. For example, Stephen Steinberg's research on intergenerational mobility among Jews was based on interviews with 20 Jewish men who had immigrated to the United States early in the 21st century.[80] In spite of their methodological limitations, these kinds of analyses enrich our understanding of the Jews' socioeconomic position by rounding out the quantitative analyses with a much-needed qualitative perspective.

Privately Sponsored Surveys of the General Population

Several national surveys of the general population include variables that can be used to identify Jews and to compare the SES of American Jews with that of other religious or ethnic groups. While some of these surveys focus specifically on religion, others address a variety of social issues. Unfortunately, large-scale surveys seldom gather information specific to the Jewish population (observance of Jewish rituals, for instance), and some data sets have too few cases for sophisticated statistical analyses.

Most general surveys that collect information about religion include basic questions with just a few response categories, such as "What is your religious preference? Is it Protestant, Catholic, Jewish, some other religion, or no religion?"[81] This technique for identifying Jews fails to capture the complexities and multiple dimensions of Jewish identification in America. At the same time, many of the general population surveys use nationally representative sampling procedures, and the inclusion of non-Jews allows for relatively easy comparisons between the Jewish population (however defined) and other population groups.

Among the richest data sources for investigating SES are the surveys conducted by the National Opinion Research Center (NORC) at the University of Chicago.[82] One of these surveys, the General Social Survey (GSS), gathers information on the attitudes and demographic characteristics of U.S. residents, including current religion and religion at age 16. The survey dates back to 1972 and is currently conducted every other year. (Prior to 1994, it was conducted every year, with a few exceptions.) GSS data have been used to study socioeconomic achievement among many religious groups, including Jews, in investigations that have examined variables such as labor force participation and occupation/occupational prestige,[83] education,[84] earnings/income,[85] job status inequality,[86] and overall SES.[87]

Some of the earliest NORC survey data have been used to explore the relationships between religion and career plans among college graduates[88] as well as the impact of religion on the ideological orientations of young American scientists and engineers.[89] Several authors have used NORC data to examine the links between religion and SES.[90] Researchers have also combined NORC data with other nationally representative data sources in order to investigate differences in SES among religious groups. For instance, Reuven Brenner and Nicholas Kiefer used NORC survey data along with national surveys conducted by the University of Michigan to assess the educational and occupational characteristics of American Jews.[91] Likewise, Norval Glenn and Ruth Hyland used data from 18 national surveys (including Gallup polls and a NORC survey) to examine religious differences in socioeconomic well-being.[92]

Several other national surveys have also proven useful. Drawing on three surveys conducted by the Survey Research Center of the University of Michigan, Bernard Lazerwitz documented the relationships between religion, SES, and related variables.[93] Seymour Martin Lipset and Everett C. Ladd, Jr., examined the Jews' contributions to American higher education by means of several national surveys sponsored by the Carnegie Commission.[94] The Princeton Fertility Study has been used to investigate the socioeconomic status of white religio-ethnic groups,[95] and the 1987–88 National Survey of Families and Households (sponsored by the Center for Demography and Ecology at the University of Wisconsin) has been used to study the relationship between religious upbringing and educational attainment.[96] More recently, Lisa Keister has used the Bureau of Labor Statistics National Longitudinal Study of Youth to investigate the impact of religious affiliation and participation on early adult asset accumulation.[97]

Several researchers have relied on more narrowly focused data sources. For example, Robin Stryker has studied high school students to examine the effects of religion and ethnicity on early career attainment.[98] Two studies have estimated the prevalence of Jews among eminent Americans by evaluating the presence of distinctive Jewish surnames in *Who's Who in America*.[99] Of course, these data sources have their limitations. For example, *Who's Who* has somewhat arbitrary criteria for selection, and DJNs are becoming less reliable indicators of Jewish identification as rates of intermarriage rise.[100] At the same time, these studies add a unique dimension to research on the relationships between religion, ethnicity, and socioeconomic achievement.

Analyses of Published Evidence

A number of researchers have examined Jewish SES by drawing on previously published evidence (earlier studies and reports) rather than conducting new analyses of data. Typically, these studies synthesize earlier research in an attempt to document, explain, or interpret the Jews' socioeconomic accomplishments and their implications for Jewish continuity.[101] Paul Burstein summarizes numerous studies of Jewish socioeconomic achievement and discusses the various economic and sociological explanations that have been put forth.[102] Both Stephen Steinberg and Robert Cherry argue that structural rather than cultural factors have been central to the socioeconomic success of the Jewish population—that the success of Jews is not inherently "Jewish," but rather a result of the educational and occupational advantages that many Jewish immigrants brought with them to the United States.[103] In contrast, Thomas Sowell adopts a cultural perspective and argues that the "internal values and traditions of the Jews" have helped them succeed.[104] Others draw on secondary data sources but focus on narrower issues such as Jewish poverty[105] and the SES of Jewish immigrants.[106]

Several authors have discussed the relationships between socioeconomic achievement and the cultural and religious continuity of the American Jewish population. Carmel Chiswick argues that a fundamental problem for American Jews is how to find forms of Jewish expression that can be integrated into the lives of men and women who have heavy economic and time demands as well as shared household responsibilities.[107] She asserts that "despite many indications of increased vitality within the American Jewish community, the attachment of many (if not most) of its members is so loose as to call into question their ability to transmit the fundamentals of Judaism from one generation to the next."[108] The link between socioeconomic modernization and assimilation (that is, the erosion of various forms of Jewish identification) has been a concern of many social scientists.[109] At the same time, some scholars point to evidence of shared structural ties (such as high levels of education) that bind Jews together and promote Jewish continuity.[110]

Socioeconomic Research on the Jewish Population of Israel

With regard to data quality and measurement, research on the Jewish population of Israel is comparatively less complicated than research on the U.S. Jewish population. Whereas modernization has led to a radical transformation of Jewish identity in America, the boundaries between Jews and non-Jews in Israel remain more rigid, even as secularization has progressed. This can be explained by the demographics of

Israeli society, where Jews comprise the majority of the population[111] and intermarriage between Jews and non-Jews continues to be very rare. The many government data sources that include religious identifiers provide fertile ground for analyses of the Jews' socioeconomic position in Israel.[112]

As previously mentioned, the Israeli census collects information on religion.[113] The question typically asks, "What is your religion?" with "Jewish" being an option alongside "Moslem," "Christian," "Druze," and "other." Data from the Israeli census have been used to study many aspects of Jewish socioeconomic status: immigrant and ethnic differentials in SES within the Jewish population,[114] the status of Jews relative to that of non-Jews,[115] variations in SES over time and generation,[116] gender inequalities in earnings[117] and employment,[118] and the status of particular groups such as the elderly population.[119] The Israeli census does not, however, allow for the analysis of variations in SES by uniquely Jewish variables such as religiosity and ritual observance. Thus, for example, there is no direct way to identify ultra-Orthodox Jews. To investigate the sources of income among that group, Eli Berman defined ultra-Orthodox families as those in which at least one male reported that the last school he attended was a yeshiva.[120]

The Central Bureau of Statistics in Israel is responsible not just for the census, but for a number of regular surveys that focus on particular topics such as labor force characteristics, income and savings, immigrants, and geographic mobility. Like the census, these data have been used to investigate a variety of topics such as ethnic differences among Jews,[121] variations in SES between Jews and others,[122] social mobility and generational shifts,[123] and gender differences.[124] Fanny Ginor draws upon several of these surveys to provide a comprehensive account of social and economic disparities in Israel across multiple dimensions (gender, ethnicity, and the like).[125] Ethnic differences in SES have also been studied using special reports from the Central Bureau of Statistics,[126] the Statistical Abstract of Israel,[127] and numerous other government sources and official documents such as the Israel Government Yearbook.[128]

Researchers investigating the SES of Jews in Israel have also drawn upon independent surveys, some of which are nationally representative. For example, the 1994–1995 Survey of Families, sponsored by Tel Aviv University, has been used to investigate the influence of parental wealth on early living standards in Israel.[129] Yossi Shavit used two nationally representative life-history studies, one of Jews and one of Arabs, to explore the effects of segregation and tracking on the educational attainment of minorities (Arabs and Oriental Jews).[130]

Other researchers have used targeted data sources that focus on ethnic inequality. Israel Adler and Robert W. Hodge used a probability sample of first- and second-generation immigrants residing in Israel's largest cities to look at the role of ethnicity in status attainment,[131] and Oren Yiftachel used a survey of firms in three industrial zones of the Galilee region to examine Arab-Jewish economic differentials.[132] Eliezer Ben-Rafael studied social mobility among Oriental immigrant groups in Israel, drawing on interviews conducted with nearly 300 upwardly mobile Yemenites and Moroccans.[133] While these authors make no claim that their data are representative of the Israeli population, studies such as these enrich our understanding of socioeconomic inequality in Israel.

Historical and Comparative Analyses

A number of researchers, most notably historians, have drawn upon secondary sources as well as government statistics, journalistic documents, historical records, memoirs, and genealogical information to document and analyze the Jews' socioeconomic position, particularly as it emerged in Europe prior to the period of mass immigration to America. As Benjamin W. de Vries notes, "among the various aspects of Jewish history, the economic ones are of interest not only to economists and historians, but also to students of other fields, because the earliest and most intensive contacts the Jews had with the surrounding society often were in the economic field."[134]

Jews have long been recognized as a socioeconomically distinctive group, and scholars have considered both internal factors (for instance, specific aspects of ethnic culture, Jewish religiosity, and tradition) and external factors (for instance, political and social discrimination combined with economic opportunity) when explaining the unique socioeconomic characteristics of the Jewish population. Toward this end, Jerry Muller has examined the Jews' "special relationship" with capitalism and how it has shaped the fate of Jews in the modern world.[135] Likewise, Jonathan Karp has analyzed the debates surrounding the position of the Jews in the economy of Europe from 1650 to 1850.[136] Derek Penslar's book on economics and Jewish identity in modern Europe is not an economic analysis in the traditional sense, but rather a study that draws on many literary sources, among them the Jewish German magazine *Allgemeine Zeitung des Judentums*.[137] In a similar vein, Nobel prize-winning economist Simon Kuznets presents a rich history of the economic life of European Jews during the late 19th and early 20th centuries that is based on a variety of sources (which he describes as "woefully inadequate").[138]

Other studies have examined the Jews' socioeconomic experiences in particular countries such as England,[139] Hungary,[140] the Netherlands,[141] and Poland.[142] Werner Mosse's work on German Jewish economic elites relied primarily on archival and literary sources such as memoirs and correspondence.[143] Unfortunately, many of the same methodological problems found in quantitative research crop up in historical analyses. For example, Mosse begins his study with a discussion of methodological challenges, including sampling issues related to the definitions of "Jewishness" and "élites."[144]

Historical census data have been central to a number of studies, some covering eras as early as the 19th century. Arcadius Kahan's social and economic history of European and American Jews draws on a wide range of historical census data, including data for tsarist Russia and Prussia.[145] Louis Rosenberg presents a social and economic account of the Jews in Canada in the 1930s,[146] while Cormac Ó Gráda describes the socioeconomic characteristics of Irish Jewry during the early 20th century.[147] Using a special census administered in Budapest in 1935, Yehuda Don reports on the employment structure of the Jewish population and the effects of anti-semitic legislation in Hungary.[148]

Other studies that have used census data to look at the socioeconomic position of the Jews include René Decol's demographic profile of the Jews in Brazil from 1940 to 2000[149] and Moshe Syrquin's study of the Jews in Argentina and Mexico from

1940 to 1970.[150] Using census data from Iraq and Israel along with other secondary sources, Tikva Darvish examined the economic characteristics of the Jewish minority in Iraq in the mid-20th century.[151] With Yehuda Don, she also investigated the socio-economic development of the Jewish community in Ecuador by means of data obtained from a survey administered to every Jewish household in Quito in 1985.[152]

Conclusions

Socioeconomic research on the Jewish population has spanned a number of disciplines and topics. Research in this area runs the gamut from empirical studies that document and explain the Jews' socioeconomic position to theoretical models that account for why the Jews have achieved the success they have had. Popular accounts have even urged others to replicate these accomplishments. For example, *The Jewish Phenomenon: Seven Keys to the Enduring Wealth of a People* draws on a variety of anecdotal and statistical evidence and concludes by offering strategies to "set the stage for success."[153]

Most recent socioeconomic research on this topic has relied on empirical data sources such as government censuses and surveys, Jewish population surveys, and independent surveys such as the GSS. While this research provides incontrovertible evidence of the Jews' socioeconomic advantages, detailed comparisons across data sources are complicated by differences in definitions (for instance, "who is a Jew?"), sampling methods, response rates, questionnaire design, and statistical methods. In a paper utilizing data from the 1957 CPS, the GSS, and the 1970 U.S. census, Barry Chiswick noted that, "the data are not strictly comparable, as there are subtle and perhaps not-so-subtle differences in methodologies, definitions, and the manner in which the data were made available by the survey agency."[154]

These problems are especially salient in the United States, owing in part to the lack of government-sponsored surveys that collect information on the Jewish population. Writing in 1985, Sidney Goldstein stated: "We must continuously enhance and sub-stantially modify our thinking about the design, conduct, and utilization of Jewish population studies."[155] He has argued for the development of a gold standard against which to judge the representativeness or even the reasonableness of the results obtained in any given study. In the absence of such a standard, it is advisable to make use of a variety of data sources in analyzing the interrelationships among variables rather than presenting estimates for the Jewish population as a whole.[156] For example, we may be able to ascertain the relationships between SES and various measures of Jewish identity using data from the Jewish population surveys, but the same data cannot be so readily used to estimate exact levels of income, education, and occupa-tional prestige for the population of American Jews.

Empirical studies of Jewish SES are sensitive to both data quality and research methods. Nationally representative studies that allow for Jewish/non-Jewish comparisons are critical, as are data sets that include a wide range of variables for measuring SES (such as education, occupation, income, and wealth) alongside the Jewish identity variables that have been most often linked to socioeconomic well-being (for instance, religiosity, denomination, and ethnic background). One of the greatest challenges for research in this area is connected to the increasing diversity of Jewish identification in modern society; it is necessary to understand how the various interrelated aspects of Jewish identity influence socioeconomic status, and vice versa. Surveys of the Jewish population should cast their nets as wide as possible, leaving it to social scientists to define their populations of interest based on the goals of each study. This means that scholars must critically examine how particular Jewish identifiers are linked to SES, and how the various definitions of the Jewish population shape their research results.

Most social scientific studies of Jewish SES have relied on multivariate statistical models. These techniques are important both for ascertaining the independent effects of a variety of covariates and for evaluating how issues of measurement and definition affect research findings. At the same time, there is also a need for fuller investigation (and open acknowledgment) of the ways in which data sources and research methods influence our understanding of the links between Jewish identity and socioeconomic status. In particular, ethnographic methods are an important complement to the statistical studies that have become the hallmark of social scientific research on Jewish SES. Future studies will need to critically examine the approaches that have been used in earlier research—in terms of both data and methods—in order to ascertain trends in Jewish SES over time.

In addition to examining the nature and extent of Jewish socioeconomic distinctiveness, it is also important to take into account the historical forces that have given rise to this phenomenon as well as the factors that sustain it in the contemporary world. For this reason, both historical and comparative analyses are necessary. Further research will need to critically evaluate the ramifications of the Jews' socioeconomic distinctiveness as well as the implications of variations in SES within the Jewish population.

Notes

1. Taken together, Israel and the United States account for 81.8 percent of the world's Jewish population. (Israel has 42.5 percent and the United States has 39.3 percent.) See Sergio DellaPergola, "World Jewish Population, 2010," in *Current Jewish Population Reports* (Storrs: 2010), 1–77.

2. For Jews who married from 1996 to 2000, the intermarriage rate is 47 percent. Those who intermarry tend to be less involved in Jewish life and less likely to raise their children as Jewish. See United Jewish Communities, *The National Jewish Population Survey 2000–01: Strength, Challenge, and Diversity in the American Jewish Population* (New York: 2003), 16–19.

3. Israel Central Bureau of Statistics, *Statistical Abstract of Israel* 61 (Jerusalem: 2010), subject 2.

4. See, for instance, Barry Chiswick, "The Economic Status of American Jews," in *American Jewry: Portrait and Prognosis*, ed. David Gordis and Dorit Gary (West Orange: 1997), 247–260; Carmel Chiswick, "First Approach: The Economics of American Judaism," in *Economics of American Judaism*, ed. Carmel U. Chiswick (New York: 2008 [2005]), 12–25; idem, "The Economics of Jewish Continuity," *Contemporary Jewry* 20, no. 1 (1999), 30–56; Steven Cohen, *American Modernity and Jewish Identity* (New York: 1983); Harriet Hartman and Moshe Hartman, "More Jewish, Less Jewish: Implications for Education and Labor Force Characteristics," *Sociology of Religion* 57, no. 2 (1996), 175–193; idem, *Gender and American*

Jews: Patterns in Work, Education and Family in Contemporary Life (Waltham: 2009); Bernard Lazerwitz, "Denominations and Synagogue Membership: 1971 and 1990," in Gordis and Gary (eds.), *American Jewry*, 199–220; Bruce A. Phillips, "Los Angeles Jewry: A Demographic Portrait," *American Jewish Yearbook* 86 (New York: 1986), 126–195; Esther I. Wilder, "Socioeconomic Attainment and Expressions of Jewish Identification: 1970 and 1990," *Journal for the Scientific Study of Religion* 35, no. 2 (1996), 109–127; idem and William H. Walters, "Ethnic and Religious Components of the Jewish Income Advantage, 1969 and 1989," *Sociological Inquiry* 68, no. 3 (1998), 426–436.

5. Carl Bialik, "Elusive Numbers: U.S. Population by Religion," *WSJ Blog*, 13 August 2010, online at blogs.wsj.com/numbersguy/elusive-numbers-us-population-by-religion-978/ (accessed 4 June 2012).

6. Ibid.

7. Barry A. Kosmin, Paul Ritterband, and Jeffrey Scheckner, "Counting Jewish Populations: Methods and Problems," *American Jewish Year Book* 88 (1988), 207.

8. The available response options differ considerably by country. In England, respondents have several options, including none, Christian, Buddhist, Hindu, Jewish, Muslim, Sikh, and "any other religion." In Northern Ireland, the response options include Roman Catholic, Presbyterian Church of Ireland, Church of Ireland, Methodist Church of Ireland, or "other" (write in). Canadian census respondents were asked, "What is your religion?" and instructed to "indicate a specific denomination or religion even if you are not a currently practicing member of that group." They also had the option of selecting "no religion." In the 2007 census of Ethiopia, Jews did not have the opportunity to specifically register their religion; the response options included Catholic, Protestant, Muslim/Islam, Traditionalist, and Other. For samples of the questions used in several countries, see http://unstats.un.org/unsd/demographic/sources/census/censusquest.htm (accessed 4 June 2012).

9. DellaPergola, "World Jewish Population, 2010."

10. Rodney Wilson, *Economics, Ethics and Religion: Jewish, Christian and Muslim Economic Thought* (New York: 1997), 22–67.

11. Susan L. Buckley, *Teachings on Usury in Judaism, Christianity and Islam* (New York: 2000). Buckley argues that "a Judaic understanding of usury must be viewed in the light of its sources in the Hebrew Bible. . . . The religious teachings with regard to the Deuteronomic exemption which allowed Jews to accept interest on a loan from a foreigner, was paramount in establishing a specific model of 'Judaic economic man'" (ibid., 82, 84).

12. Barry Chiswick, "The Occupational Attainment and Earnings of American Jewry, 1890 to 1990," *Contemporary Jewry* 20, no. 1 (1999), 69. Chiswick further notes that while important insights can be gained from applying economic methods to the study of American Jews, economists have been largely absent from the social science field of Jewish studies. See idem, "American Jewry: An Economic Perspective and Research Agenda," *Contemporary Jewry* 23, no. 1 (2002), 156–182.

13. See, for instance, Sidney Goldstein, "American Jewish Demography: Inconsistencies that Challenge," in *Papers in Jewish Demography, 1985*, ed. U.O. Schmelz and Sergio DellaPergola (Jerusalem: 1989), 23–42.

14. Kosmin, Ritterband, and Scheckner, "Counting Jewish Populations," 217–218.

15. Sergio DellaPergola, "Was it the Demography? A Reassessment of U.S. Jewish Population Estimates, 1945–2001," *Contemporary Jewry* 25, no. 1 (2005), 89.

16. See, for instance, Laurence Kotler-Berkowitz, "An Introduction to the National Jewish Population Survey 2000–01," *Sociology of Religion* 67, no. 4 (2006), 387–390.

17. Frank L. Mott and Diane B. Patel, "The Implications of Potential Boundaries and Definitions for Understanding American Jewry: Can One Size Fit All?" *Contemporary Jewry* 28, no. 1 (2008), 52.

18. Sidney Goldstein, "Profile of American Jewry: Insights from the 1990 National Jewish Population Survey," *American Jewish Year Book* 92 (1992), 85.

19. DellaPergola, "Was it the Demography?" 88.

20. Goldstein, "Profile of American Jewry," 112.

21. Goldstein, "American Jewish Demography," 26.

22. Sidney Goldstein, "Socioeconomic Differentials among Religious Groups in the United States," *American Journal of Sociology* 74, no. 6 (1969), 612–631; idem, "Profile of American Jewry." A proposal to include a question on religion in the 1960 census failed on constitutional grounds, largely because of opposition from the American Jewish community. See discussions in DellaPergola, "Was it the Demography?" 85–131, and Charles Kadushin, Benjamin T. Phillips, and Leonard Saxe, "National Jewish Population Survey 2000–01: A Guide for the Perplexed," *Contemporary Jewry* 25, no. 1 (2005), 1–32. The United States Census Bureau website states: "Public Law 94–521 prohibits us from asking a question on religious affiliation on a mandatory basis" (www.census.gov/prod/www/religion.htm [accessed 4 June 2012]).

23. The report is named after John Shaw Billings, who played a leading role in the development and use of vital statistics and other data during his extended career in government service. See Barry Chiswick, "The Billings Report and the Occupational Attainment of American Jewry, 1890," *Shofar: An Interdisciplinary Journal of Jewish Studies* 19, no. 2 (2001), 53–75; idem, "The Occupational Attainment of American Jewry: 1990 to 2000," *Contemporary Jewry* 27, no. 1 (2007), 80–111; idem and Jidong Huang, "The Earnings of American Jewish Men: Human Capital, Denomination, and Religiosity," *Journal for the Scientific Study of Religion* 47, no. 4 (2008), 694–709.

24. Chiswick, "The Billings Report and the Occupational Attainment of American Jewry, 1890."

25. Barry R. Chiswick, "Jewish Immigrant Wages in America in 1909: An Analysis of the Dillingham Commission Data," *Explorations in Economic History* 30 (July 1993), 274–289; idem, "Occupational Attainment and Earnings of American Jewry, 1890 to 1990."

26. Arcadius Kahan, "Economic Opportunities and Some Pilgrims' Progress: Jewish Immigrants from Eastern Europe in the U.S., 1890–1914," *Journal of Economic History* 38, no. 1 (March 1978), 235–251.

27. John Bregger, "The Current Population Survey: A Historical Perspective and the BLS' Role," *Monthly Labor Review Online* 107, no. 6 (June 1984), 6, http://www.bls.gov/opub/mlr/1984/06/art2full.pdf (accessed 4 June 2012).

28. For details, see Samuel A. Mueller and Angela V. Lane, "Tabulations from the 1957 Current Population Survey on Religion: A Contribution to the Demography of American Religion," *Journal for the Scientific Study of Religion* 11, no. 1 (1972), 76–98.

29. See, for instance, Reuven Brenner and Nicholas M. Kiefer, "The Economics of Diaspora: Discrimination and Occupational Structure," *Economic Development and Cultural Change* 29, no. 3 (1981), 517–534; Barry Chiswick, "The Labor Market Status of American Jews: Patterns and Determinants," *American Jewish Yearbook* 85 (New York: 1985), 131–153; idem, "The Postwar Economy of American Jews," *Studies in Contemporary Jewry*, vol. 8, *A New Jewry? America since the Second World* War, ed. Peter Y. Medding (New York: 1992), 85–101; idem, "Economic Status of American Jews"; Goldstein, "Socioeconomic Differentials among Religious Groups in the United States"; Arcadius Kahan, *Essays in Jewish Social and Economic History*, ed. Roger Weiss (Chicago: 1986).

30. Chiswick, "Occupational Attainment and Earnings of American Jewry, 1890 to 1990." Chiswick further notes that some variant of a language question has been included in most censuses since 1890. In the 1980 and 1990 censuses, the question on mother tongue was replaced by a question on languages other than English spoken in the home. The 1950 census did not include a language question. In the censuses of 1910 and 1970, the question was sometimes asked only of the foreign-born, sometimes of all respondents, and sometimes of the respondent and his or her parents.

31. Chiswick, "Occupational Attainment and Earnings of American Jewry, 1890 to 1990," 70.

32. There is some evidence that Yiddish speakers are not representative of the Jewish population in general. In a comparative analysis of American Jews using the 1970 NJPS and the Yiddish mother tongue subpopulation of the 1970 census, Frances Kobrin reported that "Yiddish speakers are disproportionately older, of the first and second generations, with somewhat lower socioeconomic background and with origins more highly concentrated among Russia and eastern Europe." See Frances E. Kobrin, "National Data on American Jewry,

1970–71: A Comparative Evaluation of the Census Yiddish Mother Tongue Subpopulation and the National Jewish Population Survey," in *Papers in Jewish Demography, 1981,* ed. U.O. Schmelz, P. Glikson, and Sergio DellaPergola (Jerusalem: 1983), 136–137. At the same time, studies of the adult Jewish male population suggest that there are no systematic differences in earnings among Yiddish, Hebrew, and Ladino speakers. Although the proportion of non-identified Jews can be expected to vary by country of origin (that is, higher for Britain, Canada, and Western Europe; lower for Poland and Russia), there are no variations in men's earnings by country of origin. See Barry Chiswick, "The Earnings and Human Capital of American Jews," *Journal of Human Resources* 18, no. 3 (1983), 313–336.

33. Chiswick, "Occupational Attainment and Earnings of American Jewry, 1890 to 1990"; Calvin Goldscheider, "Stratification and the Transformation of American Jews, 1910–90: Have the Changes Resulted in Assimilation?" *Papers in Jewish Demography 1993 in Memory of U.O. Schmelz* (Jerusalem: 1997), 259–275.

34. Goldscheider, "Stratification and the Transformation of American Jews, 1910–90."

35. Chiswick, "Occupational Attainment and Earnings of American Jewry, 1890 to 1990."

36. Chiswick, "Earnings and Human Capital of American Jews"; idem, "Postwar Economy of American Jews"; idem, "Economic Status of American Jews." For the 1970 census, Chiswick uses the "mother tongue" variable to identify second-generation Jews. He estimates that this method captures approximately 60 percent of the second generation.

37. Chiswick, "Postwar Economy of American Jews"; idem, "Economic Status of American Jews."

38. Chiswick, "Labor Market Status of American Jews"; idem, "Postwar Economy of American Jews"; idem, "Economic Status of American Jews."

39. Barry Chiswick, "Labor Supply and Investment in Child Quality: A Study of Jewish and Non-Jewish Women," *Contemporary Jewry* 9 (1988), 2, 35–61.

40. Joel Perlmann, *Ethnic Differences: Schooling and Social Structure among the Irish, Italians, Jews, and Blacks in an American City, 1880–1935* (New York: 1988).

41. Yinon Cohen, "Economic Assimilation in the United States of Arab and Jewish Immigrants from Israel and the Territories," *Israel Studies* 1, no. 2 (1996), 75–97.

42. Kahan, "Economic Opportunities and Some Pilgrims' Progress," 250.

43. DellaPergola, "Was it the Demography?" 98.

44. DellaPergola warns that the trend of decreasing response rates for surveys sampling Jews (for instance, the 1957 Current Population Survey, the NJPS, and the American Jewish Identity Survey) "does not augur well for the future of survey research" (ibid., 103).

45. Robert M. Groves and Mick P. Couper, *Nonresponse in Household Interview Surveys* (New York: 1998).

46. Vivian Klaff and Frank L. Mott, "NJPS 2000/01: A Vehicle for Exploring Social Structure and Social Dynamics in the Jewish Population," *Contemporary Jewry* 25, no. 1 (2005), 226–256.

47. DellaPergola, "Was it the Demography?"

48. Kobrin, "National Data on American Jewry, 1970–71."

49. See, for instance, DellaPergola, "Was it the Demography?"; Kadushin, Phillips, and Saxe, "National Jewish Population Survey 2000–01."

50. DellaPergola, "Was it the Demography?"

51. Ibid., 89.

52. Laurence Kotler-Berkowitz, "Poor Jews: An Analysis of Low Income in the American Jewish Population," *Contemporary Jewry* 29, no. 3 (2009), 243. Kotler-Berkowitz embraces this flexibility and adopts a variety of definitions of Jewish identity in his own research. One of his studies ("Economic Vulnerability in the American Jewish Population," *Social Work Forum* 38 [2005], 27–47) includes analyses of all NJPS respondents as well as analyses restricted to the more strongly connected part of the Jewish population.

53. Kotler-Berkowitz, "An Introduction to the National Jewish Population Survey 2000–01."

54. William H. Walters and Esther I. Wilder, "American Jewish Household Income, 1969 and 1989," *Journal of Economic and Social Measurement* 23, no. 3 (1997), 197–212.

55. Chiswick and Huang, "Earnings of American Jewish Men," 704.

56. Ibid., 698.

57. Chiswick, "First Approach"; Goldscheider, "Stratification and the Transformation of American Jews, 1910–90"; Goldstein, "Profile of American Jewry"; Seymour Martin Lipset, "The Educational Background of American Jews," in Gordis and Gary (eds.), *American Jewry*, 134–198; Fred Massarik and Alvin Chenkin, "United States National Jewish Population Study: A First Report," *American Jewish Yearbook* 74 (New York: 1973), 284–285; United Jewish Communities, *The National Jewish Population Survey 2000–01*.

58. See, for instance, Chiswick, "First Approach"; Chiswick, "Economic Status of American Jews"; idem, "Occupational Attainment and Earnings of American Jewry, 1890 to 1990"; idem, "The Billings Report and the Occupational Attainment of American Jewry, 1890"; Goldstein, "Profile of American Jewry"; Massarik and Chenkin, "United States National Jewish Population Study"; United Jewish Communities, *The National Jewish Population Survey 2000–01*.

59. See, for instance, Chiswick and Huang, "Earnings of American Jewish Men"; Allen Glicksman and Tanya Koropeckyj-Cox, "Aging among Jewish Americans: Implications for Understanding Religion, Ethnicity, and Service Needs," *Gerontologist* 49, no. 6 (2009), 816–827; Massarik and Chenkin, "United States National Jewish Population Study"; United Jewish Communities, *The National Jewish Population Survey 2000–01*; Walters and Wilder, "American Jewish Household Income"; Wilder and Walters, "Ethnic and Religious Components of the Jewish Income Advantage, 1969 and 1989."

60. See, for instance, Kotler-Berkowitz, "Economic Vulnerability in the American Jewish Population"; idem, "Poor Jews."

61. See, for instance, Glicksman and Koropeckyj-Cox, "Aging among Jewish Americans."

62. See, for instance, Chiswick, "First Approach"; Hartman and Hartman, *Gender and American Jews*; Massarik and Chenkin, "United States National Jewish Population Study."

63. See, for instance, Goldstein, "Profile of American Jewry"; Hartman and Hartman, "More Jewish, Less Jewish"; Wilder, "Socioeconomic Attainment and Expressions of Jewish Identification"; idem and Walters, "Ethnic and Religious Components of the Jewish Income Advantage, 1969 and 1989."

64. Chiswick, "Labor Market Status of American Jews."

65. See, for instance, Chiswick, "Economic Status of American Jews"; idem, "Occupational Attainment and Earnings of American Jewry, 1890 to 1990"; idem, "Occupational Attainment of American Jewry"; Goldscheider, "Stratification and the Transformation of American Jews, 1910–90"; Hartman and Hartman, *Gender and American Jews*; Kahan, *Essays in Jewish Social and Economic History*; Walters and Wilder, "American Jewish Household Income"; Wilder and Walters, "Ethnic and Religious Components of the Jewish Income Advantage, 1969 and 1989."

66. United Jewish Communities, *National Jewish Population Survey 2000–2001*.

67. Hartman and Hartman, *Gender and American Jews*.

68. Egon Mayer, Barry Kosmin, and Ariela Keysar, *American Jewish Identity Survey 2001: An Exploration in the Demography and Outlook of a People* (New York: 2002).

69. Ibid.

70. Ariela Keysar, "Secular Americans and Secular Jewish Americans: Similarities and Differences," *Contemporary Jewry* 30, no. 1 (2010), 29–44.

71. Goldstein, "Profile of American Jewry," 80. See also DellaPergola, "Was it the Demography?" for discussion of the problems associated with community surveys.

72. Ira Sheskin, "Comparisons between Local Jewish Community Studies and the 2000–01 National Jewish Population Survey," *Contemporary Jewry* 25, no. 1 (2005), 158–192. On community surveys of U.S. Jews, see the essay by David Dutwin, Eran Ben-Porath and Ron Miller, "U.S. Jewish Population Surveys: Opportunities and Challenges," in this volume, 55–73.

73. Goldstein, "American Jewish Demography."

74. Bernard Lazerwitz, "Some Comments on the Use of Distinctive Jewish Names in Surveys," *Contemporary Jewry* 7 (1986), 83–91.

75. Cohen, *American Modernity and Jewish Identity*.

76. Sidney Goldstein and Calvin Goldscheider, *Jewish Americans: Three Generations in a Jewish Community* (Englewood Cliffs: 1968).

77. See, for instance, Bruce A. Phillips, "Los Angeles Jewry"; Jacob B. Ukeles and Ron Miller, *The 1999 Jewish Population Survey of Howard County* (Baltimore: 2001).

78. Wanda Katz Fishman and Richard L. Zweigenhaft, "Jews and the New Orleans Economic and Social Elites," *Jewish Social Studies* 44, nos. 3–4 (1982), 291–298.

79. Ira M. Sheskin, Pnina Zadka, and Henry Green, "A Comparative Profile of Jewish Elderly in South Florida and Israel," *Contemporary Jewry* 11, no. 2 (1990), 119.

80. Stephen Steinberg, "The Rise of the Jewish Professional: Case Studies of Intergenerational Mobility," *Ethnic and Racial Studies* 9, no. 4 (1986), 502–513.

81. Kadushin, Phillips, and Saxe, "National Jewish Population Survey 2000–01," 12.

82. See Andrew Greeley, *Ethnicity, Denomination, and Inequality* (Beverly Hills: 1976). Greeley provides a detailed discussion of the NORC surveys that include ethnic identification questions and of the limitations associated with using NORC data to assess socioeconomic trends over time.

83. Chiswick, "Postwar Economy of American Jews"; idem, "Economic Status of American Jews"; idem, "The Skills and Economic Status of American Jewry: Trends over the Last Half Century," *Journal of Labor Economics* 11, no. 1 (1993), 229–242; Greeley, *Ethnicity, Denomination, and Inequality*; Ralph E. Pyle, "Trends in Religious Stratification: Have Religious Group Socioeconomic Distinctions Declined in Recent Years?" *Sociology of Religion* 67, no. 1 (2006), 61–79; Wade Clark Roof, "Socioeconomic Differentials among White Socioreligious Groups in the United States," *Social Forces* 58, no. 1 (1979), 280–289.

84. Chiswick, "Postwar Economy of American Jews"; idem, "Economic Status of American Jews"; idem, "Skills and Economic Status of American Jewry"; idem, "Occupational Attainment and Earnings of American Jewry, 1890 to 1990"; Greeley, *Ethnicity, Denomination, and Inequality*; Pyle, "Trends in Religious Stratification"; Roof, "Socioeconomic Differentials among White Socioreligious Groups in the United States"; Christian Smith and Robert Faris, "Socioeconomic Inequality in the American Religious System," *Journal for the Scientific Study of Religion* 44, no. 1 (2005), 95–104.

85. Chiswick, "Skills and Economic Status"; Smith and Faris, "Socioeconomic Inequality in the American Religious System"; Greeley, *Ethnicity, Denomination, and Inequality*; Nigel Tomes, "The Effects of Religion and Denomination on Earnings and the Returns to Human Capital," *Journal of Human Resources* 19, no. 4 (1984), 472–488.

86. Smith and Faris, "Socioeconomic Inequality in the American Religious System."

87. Pyle, "Trends in Religious Stratification."

88. Andrew M. Greeley, "Influence of the 'Religious Factor' on Career Plans and Occupational Values of College Graduates," *American Journal of Sociology* 68, no. 6 (1963), 658–672.

89. Andrew M. Greeley, "The Ethnic and Religious Origins of Young American Scientists and Engineers: A Research Note," *International Migration Review* 6, no. 3 (1972), 282–288.

90. See, for instance, Galen L. Gockel, "Income and Religious Affiliation," *American Journal of Sociology* 74, no. 6 (1969), 632–647; and Michael Homola, Dean Knudsen, and Harvey Marshall, "Religion and Socio-economic Achievement," *Journal for the Scientific Study of Religion* 26, no. 2 (1987), 201–217. It is noteworthy that both Gockel and Goldstein (in "Socioeconomic Differentials among Religious Groups in the United States") reached much the same conclusions regarding socioeconomic stratification among religious groups using two different data sets and two different methodological approaches. As a result, the editor of the *American Journal of Sociology* (vol. 74, no. 6) invited them to comment on each other's papers, which they did.

91. Brenner and Kiefer, "The Economics of Diaspora."

92. Norval D. Glenn and Ruth Hyland, "Religious Preference and Worldly Success: Some Evidence from National Surveys," *American Sociological Review* 32, no. 1 (1967), 73–85.

93. Bernard Lazerwitz, "A Comparison of Major United States Religious Groups," *Journal of the American Statistical Association* 56 (1961), 295, 568–579.

94. Seymour Martin Lipset and Everett C. Ladd, Jr, "Jewish Academics in the United States: Their Achievements, Culture and Politics," *American Jewish Yearbook* 72 (New York: 1971), 89–128.

95. David L. Featherman, "The Socio-economic Achievement of White Religio-Ethnic Subgroups: Social and Psychological Explanations," *American Sociological Review* 36, no. 2 (1971), 207–222.

96. Evelyn L. Lehrer, "Religion as a Determinant of Educational Achievement: An Economic Perspective," *Social Science Research* 28, no. 4 (1999), 358–379.

97. Lisa A. Keister, "Religion and Wealth: The Role of Religious Affiliation and Participation in Early Adult Asset Accumulation," *Social Forces* 82, no. 1 (2003), 175–207.

98. Robin Stryker, "Religio-Ethnic Effects on Attainments in the Early Career," *American Sociological Review* 46, no. 2 (1981), 212–231.

99. See Stanley Lieberson and Donna Carter, "Making it in America: Differences between Eminent Blacks and White Ethnic Groups," *American Sociological Review* 44 (1979), 347–366; Monica McDermott, "Trends in the Race and Ethnicity of Eminent Americans," *Sociological Forum* 17, no. 1 (2002), 137–160.

100. Goldstein, "Profile of American Jewry," 79.

101. See, for instance, Paul Burstein, "Jewish Educational and Economic Success in the United States: A Search for Explanations," *Sociological Perspectives* 50, no. 2 (2007), 209–228; Carmel Chiswick, "Israel and American Jewry in the Year 2020," in *Economics of American Judaism*, ed. Carmel U. Chiswick (New York: 2008 [1995]), 149–169; Carmel Chiswick (with Barry Chiswick), "Economic Transformation of American Jewry" in idem, *Economics of American Judaism* (New York: 2008 [2007]), 53–58; Calvin Goldscheider, *Studying the Jewish Future* (Seattle: 2004); Calvin Goldscheider and Alan Zuckerman, *The Transformation of the Jews* (Chicago: 1984).

102. Burstein, "Jewish Educational and Economic Success in the United States."

103. Stephen Steinberg, *The Ethnic Myth* (Boston: 1981); Robert Cherry, *Discrimination: Its Economic Impact on Blacks, Women and Jews* (Lexington, Mass.: 1989).

104. Thomas Sowell, *Ethnic America: A History* (New York: 1981), 93.

105. Helen Ginsburg, "Holes in the Safety Net: Rise of Poverty and Economic Deprivation among Jews," *Jewish Currents* 38, no. 10 (1984), 12–17, 29; Ann G. Wolfe, "The Invisible Jewish Poor," *Journal of Jewish Communal Service* 48, no. 1 (1972), 260–265.

106. Carmel Chiswick, "The Economics of Jewish Immigrants and Judaism in the United States," *Papers in Jewish Demography 1997* (Jerusalem: 2001), 331–344.

107. Chiswick, "First Approach."

108. Ibid., 12.

109. See, for instance, Charles Liebman, *The Ambivalent American Jew: Politics, Religion and Family in American Jewish Life* (Philadelphia: 1973); idem, *Deceptive Images: Toward a Redefinition of American Judaism* (New Brunswick: 1988); Marshall Sklare, *America's Jews* (New York: 1971).

110. See, for instance, Goldscheider, *Studying the Jewish Future*; idem, "Stratification and the Transformation of American Jews, 1910–90"; Goldscheider and Zuckerman, *Transformation of the Jews*; Hartman and Hartman, *Gender and American Jews*.

111. According to the 2010 Israel Central Bureau of Statistics, Jews made up 76 percent of the population in Israel in 2009. This compares to 86 percent in 1949, the year after Israel declared independence.

112. Most studies of Jewish SES in Israel focus on education or occupation. "Not much work has been done on individual income in Israel. One of the reasons for this.... is the common assumption among Israeli social researchers that income data are so contaminated with errors that the analysis of income is meaningless." Vered Kraus and Robert W. Hodge, *Promises in the Promised Land: Mobility and Inequality in Israel* (Westport: 1990), 18.

113. The methods of the Israel census have changed over time. The most recent census, undertaken in 2008, was not a conventional census but rather an integrated census in which there was no effort to enumerate everyone in the population. Complete enumeration was felt to be unnecessary, since the Israeli Population Registry could be used to count the population.

Israel's 2008 integrated census included a sample survey, administered to 20 percent of the population, that collected demographic, social, and economic information that could be used to prepare estimates for the entire population. The earlier censuses also included 20-percent samples with detailed labor force characteristics and socioeconomic characteristics for the adults in each household. For a discussion of the Israeli census, see Charles S. Kamen, *The 2008 Israel Integrated Census of Population and Housing: Basic Conception and Procedure* (Jerusalem: 2005).

114. Within the Israeli context, ethnic differences among Jews are understood to refer to differences in ancestry (region or country of origin). Jewish intermarriage is typically defined as marriage between Jews of different ethnic backgrounds or different countries of origin. See Deborah Bernstein and Shlomo Swirski, "The Rapid Economic Development of Israel and the Emergence of Ethnic Division of Labor," *British Journal of Sociology* 33, no. 1 (1982), 64–85; Dov Friedlander, Barbara S. Okun, Zvi Eisenbach, and Lilach Lion Elmakias, "Immigration, Social Change and Assimilation: Educational Attainment among Birth Cohorts of Jewish Ethnic Groups in Israel, 1925–1929 to 1965–69," *Population Studies* 56, no. 2 (2002), 135–150; Yitchak Haberfeld, "Immigration and Ethnic Origin: The Effect of Demographic Attributes on Earnings of Israeli Men and Women," *International Migration Review* 27, no. 2 (1993), 286–305; Nabil Khattab, "Ethnicity, Class, and the Earning Inequality in Israel, 1983–1995," *Sociological Research Online* 10, no. 3 (2005); Vivian Z. Klaff, "Residence and Integration in Israel: A Mosiac [sic] of Segregated Peoples," in *Studies of Israeli Society*, ed. Ernest Krausz (New Brunswick: 1980), 53–71; Rebeca Raijman and Moshe Semyonov, "Gender, Ethnicity, and Immigration: Double Disadvantage and Triple Disadvantage among Recent Immigrant Women in the Israeli Labor Market," *Gender and Society* 11, no. 1 (1997), 108–125; Uzi Rebhun, "Immigration, Gender and Earnings in Israel," *European Journal of Population* 26, no. 1 (2010), 73–97; U.O. Schmelz, Sergio DellaPergola, and Uri Avner, "Ethnic Differences among Israeli Jews: A New Look," *American Jewish Yearbook* 90 (New York: 1990), 3–204; Moshe Semyonov and Tamar Lerenthal, "Country of Origin, Gender, and the Attainment of Socioeconomic Status: A Study of Stratification in the Jewish Population in Israel," *Research in Social Stratification and Mobility* 10 (1991), 325–343; Sammy Smooha, *Israel: Pluralism and Conflict* (Berkeley: 1978); Sammy Smooha and Yochanan Peres, "The Dynamics of Ethnic Inequalities: The Case of Israel," in *Studies of Israeli Society*, ed. Ernest Krausz (New Brunswick: 1980), 165–181.

115. See, for instance, Irit Adler, Noah Lewin-Epstein, and Yossi Shavit, "Ethnic Stratification and Place of Residence in Israel: A Truism Revisited," *Research in Social Stratification and Mobility* 23 (2005), 155–190; Khattab, "Ethnicity, Class, and the Earning Inequality in Israel, 1983–1995"; Noah Lewin-Epstein and Moshe Semyonov, "Local Labor Markets, Ethnic Segregation, and Income Inequality," *Social Forces* 70, no. 4 (1992), 1101–1119; Barbara Okun and Dov Friedlander, "Educational Stratification among Arabs and Jews in Israel: Historical Disadvantage, Discrimination, and Opportunity," *Population Studies* 59, no. 2 (2005), 163–180; Moshe Semyonov, "Bi-Ethnic Labor Markets, Mono-Ethnic Labor Markets, and Socioeconomic Inequality," *American Sociological Review* 53, no. 2 (1988), 256–266; idem and Yinon Cohen, "Ethnic Discrimination and the Income of Majority Group Workers," *American Sociological Review* 55, no. 1 (1990), 107–114. There is also a rich body of literature that evaluates the social and economic position of Arabs in Israel, often in relation to that of the Jewish population. See, for instance, Majid Al-Haj, *Education, Empowerment, and Control: The Case of the Arabs in Israel* (New York: 1995); Noah Lewin-Epstein and Moshe Semyonov, *The Arab Minority in Israel's Economy: Patterns of Ethnic Inequality* (Boulder: 1993); Ian Lustick, *Arabs in the Jewish State: Israel's Control of a National Minority* (Austin: 1980).

116. Friedlander, Okun, Eisenbach, and Elmakias, "Immigration, Social Change and Assimilation"; Haberfeld, "Immigration and Ethnic Origin."

117. Rebhun, "Immigration, Gender and Earnings in Israel"; Shosh Shahrabani, "Family Gap in Pay and Gender Wage Gap in Israel," *Studies in Culture, Polity and Identities* 7, no. 2 (2007), 105–128.

118. Raijman and Semyonov, "Gender, Ethnicity and Immigration."

119. Sheskin, Zadka, and Green, "A Comparative Profile of Jewish Elderly in South Florida and Israel."

120. Eli Berman, "Sect, Subsidy, and Sacrifice: An Economist's View of Ultra-Orthodox Jews," *The Quarterly Journal of Economics* 115, no. 3 (2000), 930.

121. Kraus and Hodge, *Promises in the Promised Land*; Nili Mark, "The Contribution of Education to Income Differentials among Ethnic Groups in Israel," *Israel Social Science Research* 11, no. 1 (1996), 47–86; Judah Matras, "Intergenerational Social Mobility and Ethnic Organization in the Jewish Population in Israel," in *Studies in Israeli Ethnicity: After the Ingathering*, ed. Alex Weingrad (New York: 1985), 1–23; Roslyn Arlin Mickelson, Mokubung Nkomo, and Stephen Samuel Smith, "Education, Ethnicity, Gender, and Social Transformation in Israel and South Africa," *Comparative Education Review* 45, no. 1 (2001), 1–35; Pnina O. Plaut and Steven E. Plaut, "Income Inequality in Israel," *Israel Affairs* 8, no. 3 (2002), 47–68; Moshe Semyonov and Vered Kraus, "Gender, Ethnicity, and Income Inequality: The Israeli Experience," *International Journal of Comparative Sociology*, 24, nos. 3–4 (1983), 258–272; Smooha, *Israel: Pluralism and Conflict*; Sammy Smooha and Vered Kraus, "Ethnicity as a Factor in Status Attainment in Israel," *Research in Social Stratification and Mobility* 4 (1985), 151–175; Smooha and Peres, "The Dynamics of Ethnic Inequalities"; Meir Yaish, "Class Structure in a Deeply Divided Society: Class and Ethnic Inequality in Israel, 1974–1991," *British Journal of Sociology* 52, no. 3 (2001), 401–439.

122. Jack Habib, Meir Kohn, and Robert Lerman, "The Effect on Poverty Status in Israel of Considering Wealth and Variability of Income," *Review of Income and Wealth* 23, no. 1 (1977), 17–38; Plaut and Plaut, "Income Inequality in Israel," Haya Stier and Varda Levanon, "Finding an Adequate Job: Employment and Income of Recent Immigrants to Israel," *International Migration* 41, no. 2 (2003), 81–107.

123. Yinon Cohen and Yitchak Haberfeld, "Second Generation Jewish Immigrants in Israel: Have the Ethnic Gaps in School and Earnings Declined?" *Ethnic and Racial Studies* 21 (1998), 507–528; Meir Yaish, "Old Debate, New Evidence: Class Mobility Trends in Israeli Society, 1974–1991," *European Sociological Review* 16 (2000), 159–183.

124. Yitchak Haberfeld and Yinon Cohen, "Earnings Gaps Between Israel's Native-born Men and Women: 1982–1993," *Sex Roles* 39, nos. 11–12 (1998), 844–872; Mickelson, Nkomo, and Smith, "Education, Ethnicity, Gender, and Social Transformation in Israel and South Africa"; Stier and Levanon, "Finding an Adequate Job."

125. Fanny Ginor, *Socio-economic Disparities in Israel* (Tel Aviv: 1979).

126. Yochanan Peres, "Ethnic Relations in Israel," *American Journal of Sociology* 76, no. 6 (1971), 1021–1047; idem, "Horizontal Integration and Vertical Differentiation among Jewish Ethnicities in Israel" in Weingrad (ed.), *Studies in Israeli Ethnicity*, 39–56; Smooha and Peres, "Dynamics of Ethnic Inequalities."

127. Judith Bernstein and Aaron Antonovsky, "The Integration of Ethnic Groups in Israel," *Jewish Journal of Sociology* 23 (1981), 5–23; Smooha, *Israel: Pluralism and Conflict*; Smooha and Peres, "Dynamics of Ethnic Inequalities."

128. Smooha, *Israel: Pluralism and Conflict*.

129. Seymour Spilerman, "The Impact of Parental Wealth on Early Living Standards in Israel," *American Journal of Sociology* 110, no. 1 (2004), 92–122.

130. Yossi Shavit, "Segregation, Tracking, and the Educational Attainment of Minorities: Arabs and Oriental Jews in Israel," *American Sociological Review* 55, no. 1 (1990), 115–126.

131. Israel Adler and Robert W. Hodge, "Ethnicity and the Process of Status Attainment in Israel," *Israel Social Science Research* 1, no. 1 (1983), 5–23.

132. Oren Yiftachel, "Industrial Development and Arab-Jewish Economic Gaps in the Galilee Region, Israel," *Professional Geographer* 43, no. 2 (1991), 163–179.

133. Eliezer Ben-Rafael, "Social Mobility and Ethnic Awareness: The Israeli Case," in Weingrad (ed.), *Studies in Israeli Ethnicity*, 57–79.

134. Benjamin W. DeVries, *From Pedlars to Textile Barons: Economic Development of a Jewish Minority Group in the Netherlands* (New York: 1989), 11.

135. Jerry Z. Muller, *Capitalism and the Jews* (Princeton: 2010).

132   Esther Isabelle Wilder

136. Jonathan Karp, *The Politics of Jewish Commerce: Economic Thought and Emancipation in Europe, 1638–1848* (New York: 2008).

137. Derek J. Penslar, *Shylock's Children: Economics and Jewish Identity in Modern Europe* (Berkeley: 2001).

138. Simon Kuznets, "Economic Structure and Life of the Jews," in *The Jews: Their History, Culture, and Religion*, ed. Louis Finkelstein (New York: 1960), 1597–1666. In discussing the implications of his findings, Kuznets writes: "For a clear picture of the economic structure of the Jews, the data are woefully inadequate. In many countries, the basic country-wide statistics do not distinguish Jews. In others, the data are limited to the kind associated with population censuses. This type of information covers the occupation and industrial attachment, but it tells us little about other important aspects of economic structure and life—size and distribution of wealth, size and distribution of income, earnings and savings patterns of minorities and majorities, and the like. No such information is available, barring some exceptional cases" (ibid., 1619).

139. Joseph Buckman, *Immigrants and the Class Struggle: The Jewish Immigrant in Leeds, 1880–1914* (Dover, N.H.: 1983); Harold Pollins, *Economic History of the Jews in England* (Rutherford: 1982). Buckman draws on a wide range of sources such as the 1888 minutes of the Sanitary Committee of Leeds Town Council.

140. Michael K. Silber (ed.), *Jews in the Hungarian Economy: 1760–1945* (Jerusalem: 1992). This book is a collection of essays with varying methodological approaches (among them, biography and statistical analysis), some of which examine the socioeconomic position of Jews in Vienna.

141. DeVries, *From Pedlars to Textile Barons*.

142. Bernard D. Weinryb, *The Jews of Poland: A Social and Economic History of the Jewish Community in Poland from 1100–1800* (Philadelphia: 1972).

143. Werner E. Mosse, *Jews in the German-Jewish Economy: The German-Jewish Economic Élite 1820–1935* (New York: 1987); idem, *The German-Jewish Economic Élite 1820–1935: A Socio-cultural Profile* (New York: 1989).

144. In *Jews in the German-Jewish Economy*, Mosse argues: "Perhaps the most acceptable definition of 'Jewishness,' whatever its imprecision, is that of membership of the Jewish 'ethnic group,' as the term is understood in the United States" (p. 2).

145. Kahan, *Essays in Jewish Social and Economic History*.

146. Louis Rosenberg, *Canada's Jews: A Social and Economic Study of Jews in Canada in the 1930s* (Montreal: 1993).

147. Cormac Ó Gráda, *Jewish Ireland in the Age of Joyce: A Socioeconomic History* (Princeton: 2006).

148. Yehuda Don, "The Economic Effect of Antisemitic Discrimination: Hungarian Anti-Jewish Legislation, 1938–1944," *Jewish Social Studies*, 48, no. 1 (1986), 63–82.

149. René Daniel Decol, "A Demographic Profile of Brazilian Jewry," *Contemporary Jewry* 29, no. 2 (2009), 99–113.

150. Moshe Syrquin, "The Economic Structure of Jews in Argentina and Other Latin American Countries," *Jewish Social Studies* 47, no. 2 (1985), 115–134.

151. Tikva Darvish, "The Jewish Minority in Iraq: A Comparative Study of Economic Structure," *Jewish Social Studies* 49, no. 2 (1987), 175–180; idem, "The Economic Structure of the Jewish Minority in Iraq vis-à-vis the Kuznets Model," *Jewish Social Studies* 47, nos. 3–4 (1985), 255–266.

152. Tikva Darvish-Lecker and Yehuda Don, "A Jewish Community in 'Isolation': The Socio-economic Development of the Jewish Community in Quito, Ecuador," *Contemporary Jewry* 11, no. 1 (1990), 29–48.

153. Steven Silbiger, *The Jewish Phenomenon: Seven Keys to the Enduring Wealth of a People* (Atlanta: 2000).

154. Chiswick, "The Postwar Economy of American Jews."

155. Goldstein, "American Jewish Demography," 38.

156. See Kadushin, Phillips, and Saxe, "National Jewish Population Survey 2000–01."

The Professional Dilemma of Jewish Social Scientists: The Case of the ASSJ

Chaim I. Waxman
(RUTGERS UNIVERSITY)

Scientific disciplines anchor their scholarly activities in professional associations that organize conferences, publish journals and other academic literature, and assist in initiating research projects. Each of the social science disciplines has its own associations; in addition, there are more general organizations that are concerned with a specific topic—for instance, migration, family, or religion—that can be tackled from varied perspectives. In similar fashion, certain professional associations are interested in a particular group of people. This essay deals with an organization falling into this last category, the Association for the Social Scientific Study of Jewry (ASSJ),[1] examining its history and underlying goals both in the context of American social science as a whole and the Jewish "guild" of social scientists in particular.

Founded in 1971, the ASSJ is one of a number of special-interest associations within the field of social science; others include the Association for the Sociology of Religion, the Society of Catholic Social Scientists, and the Association of Black Sociologists. All of these organizations were founded to fill a perceived gap in the discipline. As recalled by Harold Himmelfarb, a former president, the ASSJ was meant to provide a forum for "scholars interested in the social scientific...study of Jewry," and in particular to "encourage and support scholars who were interested in doing work in the area, because it was not a mainstream sub-discipline in either the social sciences or in Jewish studies." Another former president, Allen Glicksman, cited the importance of "getting members of ASSJ to participate in the wider world of social scientific research," while at the same time "engaging our colleagues outside of Jewish Studies in the discussion about the social scientific study of Jewry."[2]

The ASSJ and several other special-interest social science associations belong to a larger and broader-based organization, the American Sociological Association (ASA). This veteran society began as part of the American Social Science Association-American Association for the Promotion of Social Science, founded in 1886 with the aim of promoting social reform. This can be seen, for instance, in Article II of the association's constitution, which stated that the association's objectives were:

> to aid the development of Social Science, and to guide the public mind to the best practical means of promoting the Amendment of Laws, the Advancement of Education, the

Prevention and Repression of Crime, the Reformation of Criminals, and the progress of Public Morality, the adoption of Sanitary Regulations, and the diffusion of sound principles on questions of Economy, Trade, and Finance. It will give attention to Pauperism, and the topics related thereto; including the responsibility of the well-endowed and successful, the wise and educated, the honest and respectable, for the failures of others. It will aim to bring together the various societies and individuals now interested in these objects, for the purpose of obtaining by discussion the real elements of Truth; by which doubts are removed, conflicting opinions harmonized, and a common ground afforded for treating wisely the great social problems of the day.[3]

The ASA's mission statement, in contrast, proclaims that the organization, "founded in 1905, is a non-profit membership association dedicated to advancing sociology as a scientific discipline and profession serving the public good....As the national organization for sociologists, [the ASA] is well positioned to provide a unique set of services to its members and to promote the vitality, visibility, and diversity of the discipline."[4] As Robert Merton points out, such statements, with their "strong affirmation that they are designed, in the first instance, to work through their specialized competences for the welfare of the community in general and of their respective clienteles in particular," are fairly typical of professional associations.[5]

The idea of forming an organization of sociologists specifically interested in the study of Jewry first surfaced at an annual conference sponsored by the ASA in 1966. One of the sessions at that conference, titled "Sociology and History," was attended by Werner J. Cahnman, a German-born historical sociologist who was later affiliated with the Chicago school of sociology.[6] Cahnman introduced himself to Norman L. Friedman, who had just delivered a paper, and when they subsequently learned of their mutual interest in the study of Jewry, a strong collegial friendship ensued. Several years later, meeting in Boston at the annual meeting of the Eastern Sociological Society (so called because most of its members are based on the East Coast), they discussed the formation of a group focusing on the sociology of Jewry, which could present sessions at ASA annual conferences. Prior to this time, although various sociologists had occasionally written about Jews, few if any of them (apart from Marshall Sklare and Charles Liebman)[7] specialized in the sociology of Jewry.

According to Friedman, the ASSJ had its unofficial launching at a special-interest group meeting that was organized and co-chaired by him and Bernard Lazerwitz, a quantitative sociologist and survey researcher who specialized in ethnicity and religious involvement.[8] This meeting, billed as a special session on "The Sociological Study of Jewry," took place in September 1970 at the ASA annual conference and was attended by 35 individuals, among them Solomon Poll, Mervin Verbit, and Arnold Dashefsky. These three individuals submitted a motion to establish a formal group, which was voted upon and accepted; a year later, the first official meeting of the association took place.

A number of factors, some connected to U.S. society at large and others specifically Jewish, led to the establishment of the ASSJ at this particular juncture. For one thing, the preceding decade had been characterized by broad social activism. Toward the end of the 1960s, a growing number of committed Jews had become involved in the ongoing protest campaign on behalf of Soviet Jews wishing to emigrate, as well as in efforts to alleviate the situation of poor Jews in U.S. cities. Meanwhile, on the academic front, there was widespread rejection of the rigid, "values-free" approach within sociology in favor of more intensive engagement in matters of race and ethnicity. Indeed, American society as a whole was characterized at this time by heightened ethnic consciousness (for Jews, the watershed event was the Six-Day War of June 1967). The late 1960s was also marked by a heightened religious consciousness, which seemed to spell an end to previous discussions concerning "the death of God" or America as a secular society.[9]

Among college and university students, in particular, there seemed to be emerging a new breed of Jews—some of them survivors of the Holocaust or the children of survivors, many of them Orthodox or traditional Conservative in religious orientation—who were proud to be "Jewish Jews." Notable among these were individuals who had gone to Jewish summer camps, who belonged to Zionist or synagogue youth movements, and/or were members of Jewish student organizations such as Hillel or Yavneh. One of the main outcomes of this heightened Jewish identification was the establishment and rapid proliferation of Jewish studies courses and programs. Reflecting this new trend was the establishment of another specifically Jewish academic association, the Association for Jewish Studies (AJS). Founded in 1969, the AJS had about 1,400 members by 2000 and 1,881 members by 2011.[10]

Another factor contributing to the founding of the ASSJ were the strengthened links between Jewish communal agencies and scholars engaged in Jewish social research projects. Prominent among such projects was the National Jewish Population Survey (NJPS), which was first conducted in 1970–1971 under the auspices of the Council of Jewish Federations and Welfare Funds (CJF). Clearly, the existence of an organization such as the ASSJ could be expected to provide a reservoir of social scientists to help analyze and disseminate the data, which would then serve as an important planning tool for CJF and other communal agencies.[11] The hope was that such data would also further social science research. As it turned out, no full-scale analysis of the first NJPS ever appeared. However, several important reports were issued in the wake of the survey, and from the mid-1970s until the 1990s, these reports were the major source of empirical data for the growing social scientific literature on American Jews.

From the outset, the ASSJ had a limited number of members. In 1974, the first year for which membership figures are available, there were 154 individual (as opposed to institutional) members, a number that remained the same a dozen years later. In 2010, the association showed a slight drop in individual membership, down to 149.[12] On the face of it, this lack of growth may seem puzzling, especially given the impressive expansion of Jewish studies courses and programs since the late 1960s. On closer analysis, however, this seeming stagnation may reflect an inherent conflict felt by many Jewish social scientists with respect to their professional versus their personal lives.

In his classic work *Assimilation in American Life*, Milton Gordon suggested that there is a subsociety and subculture of intellectuals in the United States. As he put it, "intellectuals in the United States interact in such patterned ways as to form at least the elementary structure of a subsociety of their own." Moreover, the intellectual subsociety "is the only one in American life in which people of different ethnic backgrounds interact in primary group relations with considerable frequency and with relative comfort and ease."[13] A subsequent empirical test of Protestant and Jewish college and university professors conducted by Charles Anderson largely substantiated Gordon's hypothesis.[14] Similarly, research by Allan Mazur led to the conclusion that

> Jewish academicians—at least those in the social sciences—are relatively uncommitted to the Jewish religion, compared to the general Jewish population. However, their lack of religious commitment does not justify the stereotype of the Jewish intellectual as being totally detached from ethnic group concerns. Rather, the ethnicity of this group is an eclectic one, conforming to the general values of the academic community. For example, most academics disdain restricted, parochial behavior, and so the Jewish academic disdains, and dissociates himself from, Jewish clannishness. On the other hand, most academics value intellectuality, and so the Jewish academic is proud of the Jewish intellectual tradition. Ethnicity, viewed in this eclectic manner, is a very strong characteristic of many of the present subjects.[15]

In contrast, in a later cross-racial test of Gordon's hypothesis, William Banks and Joseph Jewell concluded that, "for African American intellectuals, the salience of racial group membership appears to counter and neutralize the hypothesized socialization away from ethnic attachments."[16] In other words, intellectual status did not prevent or weaken ethnic affiliations among blacks, in contrast to the tendency of Jewish social scientists (in particular, those just starting on their academic careers) to refrain from behavior and affiliations, especially but not exclusively in their scholarly work, that could be perceived as containing even a modicum of "Jewish clannishness."[17]

Back in 1963, Seymour Martin Lipset had essentially made the same claim, noting that, with few exceptions, American Jewish social scientists generally abstained from writing about their fellow Jews. "The failure of Jewish social scientists to engage in research on the Jews," he argued, "reflects their desire to be perceived as American rather than Jewish intellectuals. To write in depth about the Jewish community would seemingly expose them to being identified as 'Jewish Jews.'"[18] Today, notwithstanding the rise of "Jewish Jews" in the decades since the 1960s, there still seems to be a certain reluctance among American Jewish social scientists to engage in research focused specifically (or exclusively) on Jews.

In the past, a class factor may have been involved in Jewish social scientists' self-distancing from matters related to their own personal background. During the first half of the 20th century, many American Jews were immigrants or the children of immigrants, a significant segment of American Jewry still belonged to the working class, and the vast majority of those who had attained middle-class status had done so only recently. It was not uncommon for those who had "made it" into middle-class American society to draw apart from their working-class brethren. Interestingly, in this matter, American blacks manifested similar behavior. An extreme version of this pattern was delineated by E. Franklin Frazier, who in 1948 became the first black president of what was then known as the American Sociological Society.[19] Frazier castigated what he called the "black bourgeoisie":

> The emphasis upon "social" life or "society" is one of the main props of the world of make believe into which the black bourgeoisie has sought to escape from its inferiority and frustrations in American society. This world of make believe, to be sure, is a reflection

of the values of American society, but it lacks the economic basis that would give it roots in the world of reality. In escaping into a world of make believe, middle class Negroes have rejected both identification with the Negro and his traditional culture. Through delusions of wealth and power they have sought identification with white America, which continues to reject them. But these delusions leave them frustrated because they are unable to escape from the emptiness and futility of their existence.[20]

Very few middle-class American Jews adopted patterns similar to those of the black bourgeoisie. Middle-class Jews of German origin, for instance, rather than totally dissociating themselves from working-class East European Jewish immigrants, undertook major efforts to Americanize them as rapidly as possible, both through philanthropic organizations and through the establishment of educational and training courses.[21] Similarly, some Jewish social scientists joined forces with the Jewish welfare establishment to help improve the condition of needy Jews. Indeed, as Paul Ritterband and Harold Wechsler point out, during the first half of the 20th century, "communal agencies and specialized institutions dominated the social scientific study of contemporary Jewry."[22] At the same time, however, many social scientists, especially those influenced by Robert Park and the Chicago school of sociology, called for the sociologist's complete detachment from the subject matter being studied.

The debate, which to some extent continues to this day, revolved around the question of who was better qualified to study a given group, the "insider" or the "outsider." The "insider" position held that only insiders, having lived in and become sensitized to all of the experiences and meanings of the group, could truly understand its nature. Advocates of the outsider position argued that insiders were likely to be blinded (or at least blinkered) by issues of group loyalty. A more nuanced version of the outsider argument was expressed by Robert Park, who suggested that sociologist-researchers should approach their subject *as if* they were outsiders. For example, he told students who were interested in improving race relations that the "calm, detached scientist...investigates race relations with the same objectivity and detachment with which the zoologist dissects the potato bug."[23] Similarly, Eric Hobsbawm averred that historians must examine the evidence regardless of their own personal convictions. As he put it:

> To be Irish and proudly attached to Ireland—even to be proudly Catholic-Irish or Ulster-Protestant Irish—is not in itself incompatible with the serious study of Irish history. To be a Fenian or an Orangeman, I would judge, is not so compatible, any more than being a Zionist is compatible with writing a genuinely serious history of the Jews; unless the historian leaves his or her convictions behind when entering the library or the study.[24]

This is essentially the position taken by Robert Merton as well, who pointed out that both Georg Simmel and Max Weber clearly rejected the extreme insider doctrine in their assertion that "one need not be Caesar in order to understand Caesar."[25] Merton himself argued for recognition and appreciation of the strengths and weaknesses of each perspective while at the same time striving for theoretical and technical competence (which transcends both). The ideal, he suggested, was for the insider to study his or her subject as an outsider.[26]

In contrast, Marshall Sklare was a staunch advocate of the insider perspective. Moreover, he felt that the aim of Jewish studies should be the strengthening of the Jewish identities of those who study it. As he put it:

Above all we must remember that if Jewish studies in the American university are to have a vital future it will be because they fulfill a need which the young Jew experiences. Thus *the push to the study of Judaica must originate in the desire to explore personal identity.* It follows then that the future of Jewish studies in the American university will be abortive if they move too far in the direction of becoming a pure and impersonal science.[27]

It is perhaps this objective of exploring personal identity that Seymour Leventman had in mind when he asserted: "There is, after all, a difference between 'Jewish sociology' and the 'sociology of Jews'"[28]—namely, the latter is part of the broader field of sociology and has no goal of influencing identity, whereas the former does.[29]

It appears that, despite the cultural changes in American society and the American scholarly world over the past half-century, from an ideology promoting the melting-pot model to those in favor of cultural pluralism and, more recently, multiculturalism, the social scientific study of Jewry is still widely seen as parochial. In a series of exchanges on the ASSJ internet listserv that took place in late November 2011, a number of participants offered reasons for this widespread perception. For example, one recent president of the ASSJ suggested that "Jews are not seen as a disadvantaged minority, so their lessons are of less interest in terms of racial/ethnic intersectionality with other social forces." Another wrote:

> What was true for the veterans of the ASSJ remains true, I believe. A decade ago, as a graduate student at Brandeis, I was cautioned that focusing on a Jewish subject would severely limit my job prospects and that focusing on Jewish women would ghettoize me even further.... With the economic situation, coupled with the state of the fields of both Jewish and women's/gender studies, that advice is certainly relevant today.

Several participants argued that the social scientific study of Jewry continued to be perceived as parochial only for those who did not explicitly demonstrate how their research was important for the field of sociology as a whole, while others took the opposite tack, deploring the fact that they constantly needed to couple their interests in Jewish topics with involvement in the broader field, lest they be considered parochial. As one put it: "In my experience it is prudent to downplay one's Jewish research accomplishments in applying for a sociology position.... Emphasis must be put into 'de-parochializing' the scholarship... to clearly demonstrate how this is merely a case-study that wishes to illuminate broader sociological themes."

In the highly competitive academic world, the dilemma faced by social scientists seeking to specialize in "Jewish" subjects is very real. The camaraderie provided by membership in a professional organization such as the ASSJ is no substitute for a tenured position. Notwithstanding, the ASSJ remains a vibrant force in the realm of Jewish social science.

In large part this is due to the association's highly regarded publication, *Contemporary Jewry*. In the beginning, the journal had the character of an in-house publication, consisting mainly of organizational reports, accounts of members' professional accomplishments, and various other items of professional interest.[30] Eventually, the journal expanded and took on a more scholarly tone. In keeping with the ASSJ's stated mandate to be a broad social science association—notwithstanding its inclusion in the ASA—*Contemporary Jewry* publishes articles and reviews from the entire spectrum of social science, as well as from the realm of history. Special issues have been devoted to such topics as the National Jewish Population Survey (NJPS), Jewish community surveys, ultra-Orthodox Jews, women in the Holocaust, economic frameworks for understanding Jewry, and Israeli Jewry; individual articles have ranged from an analysis of rabbis' salaries to a historical study of Jewish women physicians in Central Europe.[31] Most of the contributors are from North America, with the second-largest group (many of them native English-speakers) based in Israel.

To the extent that Jewish social scientists form a "guild," the ASSJ provides a kind of professional home—a venue in which academic and personal/ethnic interests are allowed and even encouraged to comingle. Thus, the challenge for the ASSJ and other special-interest associations is to successfully accommodate particularistic interests within the broader disciplinary framework.

Notes

1. At the time of its founding, the association was known as the Association for the Sociological Study of Jewry. The name was changed during the 1980s in order to attract other social scientists of Judaism.

2. Personal communications from Harold Himmelfarb and Allen Glicksman (September 2011).

3. *Constitution, Address, and List of Members of the American Association for the Promotion of Social Science* (Boston: 1866), 3.

4. See the mission statement of the American Sociological Association, online at asanet.org/about/mission.cfm (accessed 4 September 2012).

5. Robert K. Merton, "The Functions of the Professional Association," *American Journal of Nursing* 58, no. 1 (January 1958), 50.

6. On Cahnman, see the editors' introduction to Werner J. Cahnman, *Jews and Gentiles: A Historical Sociology of Their Relations*, ed. Judith T. Marcus and Zoltan Tarr (New Brunswick: 2004); on the Chicago school of sociology, see Martin Bulmer, *The Chicago School of Sociology: Institutionalization, Diversity, and the Rise of Sociological Research* (Chicago: 1984).

7. Liebman began specializing in the social scientific study of Jewry in the 1960s, though his work in the field was not widely recognized until the following decade, with the publication of *The Ambivalent American Jew* (Philadelphia: 1973).

8. Norman L. Friedman, "Conception and Birth of the Association for the Sociological Study of Jewry: A Case Study in Associational Formation," *Ethnic Forum* 6 (1986), 98–111.

9. Michael E. Staub (ed.), *The Jewish 1960s: An American Sourcebook* (Hanover: 2004).

10. Personal communication from Rona Sheramy (28 July 2011). In contrast, as will be seen, the ASSJ has remained fairly constant in its membership.

11. Fred Massarik and Bernard Lazerwitz, who were responsible for the 1971 NJPS sample design and initial computations, were also founding members of the ASSJ.

12. These are the total individual memberships worldwide, the overwhelming majority coming from North America, with a handful from Israel and elsewhere.

13. Milton M. Gordon, *Assimilation in American Life: The Role of Race, Religion, and National Origins* (New York: 1964), 224.

14. Charles H. Anderson, "The Intellectual Subcommunity Hypothesis: An Empirical Test," *Sociological Quarterly* 9, no. 2 (Spring 1968), 210–227; reprinted in Charles H. Anderson and John D. Murray (eds.), *The Professors: Work and Life Styles Among Academicians* (Cambridge, Mass.: 1971), 229–245.

15. Allan Mazur, "The Socialization of Jews into the Academic Subculture," in ibid., 284.

16. William M. Banks and Joseph Jewell, "Intellectuals and the Persisting Significance of Race," *Journal of Negro Education* 64, no. 1 (Winter 1995), 82.

17. When I was a graduate student and began thinking about a topic for my doctoral thesis, my advisor, who was a committed Jew, advised me to choose a topic that was not specifically Jewish. This advice, which was given to me in the mid-1960s—when cultural pluralism and ethnic pride were part of the national cultural ideology—is perhaps as appropriate today as it was then (see later discussion in this essay). The fact is, however, that once someone acquires a reputation in a broader area of sociology, it is much less likely that he or she will choose to focus on the sociology of Jews, certainly not as a major specialization.

18. Seymour Martin Lipset, "The American Jewish Community in Comparative Perspective," in idem, *Revolution and Counterrevolution: Change and Persistence in Social Structures*, 3rd ed. (New Brunswick: 1988), 149.

19. The name was changed from Society to Association in 1959.

20. E. Franklin Frazier, *Black Bourgeoisie: The Rise of a New Middle Class* (New York: 1957), 237.

21. Chaim I. Waxman, *America's Jews in Transition* (Philadelphia: 1983), 42–46.

22. Paul Ritterband and Harold S. Wechsler, *Jewish Learning in American Universities: The First Century* (Bloomington: 1994), 202.

23. Robert E. Park, *On Social Control and Collective Behavior*, edited with an introduction by Ralph H. Turner (Chicago: 1967), xvi.

24. Eric J. Hobsbawm, *Nations and Nationalism since 1780: Programme, Myth, Reality*, 2nd ed. (Cambridge: 1992), 13.

25. Robert K. Merton, "The Perspectives of Insiders and Outsiders," in idem (ed.), *The Sociology of Science: Theoretical and Empirical Investigations* (Chicago: 1973), 123.

26. Ibid., 129 ff.

27. Marshall Sklare, "The Problem of Contemporary Jewish Studies," *Midstream* 16, no. 4 (April 1970), 35 (emphasis added).

28. Seymour Leventman, review of Marshall Sklare's *Observing America's Jews, Contemporary Sociology* 23, no. 5 (September 1994), 655. He further asserted that, "one need not be one to study them," which is certainly true. However, it is also the fact that, to a very large extent, research and writing on America's Jews has been (and continues to be) done by Jews.

29. See, for instance, the views expressed by Samuel Z. Klausner, then president of the ASSJ, in *ASSJ Newsletter* 2, no. 1 (1975), 1; ibid., no. 2 (1975), 27–28; idem, "What Is Conceptually Special about a Sociology of Jewry," *Contemporary Jewry* 8, no. 1 (1987), 73–89. Calvin Goldscheider and Alan Zuckerman were even more explicit, noting that "the study of contemporary Jews is no different from the study of contemporary Americans, Englishmen, Frenchmen, or whomever. The only difference is that to study Jews one must focus on cross-national analyses, since large Jewish subcommunities are located in many countries." See Calvin Goldscheider and Alan S. Zuckerman, "Contemporary Jewish Studies in the Social Sciences: Analytic Themes and Doctoral Studies," in *New Humanities and Academic Disciplines: The Case of Jewish Studies*, ed. Jacob Neusner (Madison: 1984), 75.

30. After the 1970s, the newsletter ceased publication. It was revived in 2009, when Ira Sheskin undertook to edit and produce the online semi-annual "ASSJ Newsletter."

31. More information about the journal can be found on the ASSJ website at www.assj.org.

Contradictory Constructions of "Jewish" in Britain's Political and Legal Systems

David J. Graham
(INSTITUTE FOR JEWISH POLICY RESEARCH, LONDON)
(UNIVERSITY OF SYDNEY)

Britain's political and legal systems have each independently defined the category "Jewish" and have reached two, contradictory outcomes. The political system constructs "Jewish" exclusively in *religious* terms, placing the label alongside "Christian," whereas the legal system constructs it exclusively in *ethnic* terms, placing "Jewish" alongside "Asian." This only serves to demonstrate what we already knew: an answer to "who is a Jew?"—the central question in Jewish demography—remains as incoherent, perplexing, and elusive as ever.[1]

But such a conclusion need not render the discipline unfeasible. It is argued here that such contradictory constructions should be both expected and embraced by demographers, as they represent a more practical interpretation of social reality. Two state-level case studies are presented to demonstrate why this conclusion is the only way forward if Jewish demographic research is to make progress in the future. The first example focuses on the British census and its political approach to the categories "religion" and "ethnicity," while the second concentrates on the way the law categorizes "Jewish" by examining a recent legal dispute between a Jewish day school and a pupil who was denied a place because the school did not regard him as authentically Jewish.

To explain why the labeling of identity is always likely to produce contradictory outcomes, this essay begins by exploring the critical literature on identity, which highlights the reality that "Jewish" is no different from other socially constructed categories. It is a fundamentally fluid concept, and any attempt to bound it or fix it in place merely synthesizes a false reality, from which problematic and contradictory outcomes will inevitably transpire. At the same time, in Britain, as elsewhere, the state relies upon the labeling and categorization of its citizens in order to function effectively. Therefore, in order to deepen our understanding of Jewish demographic data, analysts must go beyond the presentation of numbers, explaining the contradictions that ensue by such taxonomic practices and the implications these have both for the communities being encapsulated and for wider society.

Critical Approaches to Identity

There is a long and rich tradition in the sociological literature of addressing questions of the "who is a Jew?" nature. For example, in the 1960s, Peter Berger and Thomas Luckmann tackled the thorny issue of how we come to know the social world and what we construe as "reality" within it. Their conclusions were implicit in the title of their classic work, *The Social Construction of Reality*. They argued that what we know to be "true" about society only has merit in the social context in which it is established. There cannot be a *single* reality, since sociologists were fully aware that "men in the street take quite different 'realities' for granted as between one society and another."[2] Thus they contended that,

> the sociology of knowledge must concern itself with whatever passes for "knowledge" in a society, regardless of the ultimate validity or invalidity (by whatever criteria) of such "knowledge." And in so far as all human "knowledge" is developed, transmitted and maintained in social situations, the sociology of knowledge must seek to understand the processes by which this is done in such a way that a taken-for-granted "reality" congeals for the man in the street. In other words, we contend that *the sociology of knowledge is concerned with the analysis of the social construction of reality.*[3]

This kind of critical thinking led other scholars to argue that communities are ultimately "imagined" entities. For example, Benedict Anderson has argued that, at best, nations are

> imagined as *limited* because even the largest of them, encompassing perhaps a billion living human beings, has finite, if elastic, boundaries, beyond which lie other nations. No nation imagines itself coterminous with mankind.... [I]t is imagined as a *community*, because, regardless of the actual inequality and exploitation that may prevail in each, the nation is always conceived as a deep, horizontal comradeship.[4]

Stuart Hall articulates a view of identity as an unending creative process, noting that "cultural identity is a matter of 'becoming' as well as 'being': human existence precedes any alleged essence."[5] In other words, Hall argues that there is no essential being with respect to culture, that it is not something one can be born with; it must be created in order to have any meaning at all. Regarding "black" identity for example, Hall suggests:

> What is at issue here is the recognition of the extraordinary diversity of subjective positions, social experiences and cultural identities which compose the category "black"; that is, the recognition that "black" is essentially a politically and culturally *constructed* category, which cannot be grounded in a set of fixed trans-cultural or transcendental racial categories and which therefore has no guarantees in nature.[6]

Ultimately, what we choose to accept as legitimate or "authentic" representations depends on what we construe as being legitimate criteria. But as Stuart Charmé asks, which representations are authentic and which are inauthentic, and how ought we to choose between *competing claims to authenticity*?[7] Who are the "inquisitors" with the authority to claim that one position is authentic whereas another is not? From where, he asks, is the authority derived for inquisitors to label others phony; perhaps they themselves are inauthentic? Who authenticates *their* authenticity? For Charmé, the answers lie in accepting the "dynamic instability of identity"; in his view, "authenticity is not about finding one's 'true self' or the 'real tradition' but about maintaining an honest view of the process by which we construct the identities and traditions we need to survive. It requires lucidity about the lack of essence or permanent foundation of all identities, and vigilance against the idea that it can be realized."[8]

In other words, identity has no essential qualities, but is rather the outcome of an ongoing negotiation about what does and does not count as legitimate and authentic. Identity is therefore fluid, undergoing constant transformation and reconstruction; as a result, the boundaries between different identity groups are "fuzzy"[9] and "blurred."[10] This is a far more sophisticated understanding of social boundaries than traditional essentialist approaches have achieved, and it presents quantitative researchers with a considerable dilemma. If the "who is?" of identity will *always* have multiple answers, how can groups be uniquely identified and quantified? If progress is to be made, it seems that a fine line must be drawn by analysts between society's need for quantitative categorization, on the one hand, and the complex multifaceted "reality" of identity, on the other.

Getting that balance right is challenging, and many commentators have warned us not to go too far down the "postmodern" path. Paul Weller, for example, suggests that "the postmodern penchant for deconstruction can be taken too far when used to deny the utility of any form of self-identification that goes beyond the isolated self."[11] And Ceri Peach pointedly argues that "[a]bolishing the categories...does not abolish the issues; the issues simply become more difficult to quantify."[12] Intuitively, identity does exist, at least in the minds of people and state officials. As Keith Halfacree points out, the classification, categorization, and codification of the world around us is "integral to everyday life."[13] Ultimately, any attempt to represent social reality quantitatively will be limited, but as David Livingstone notes, "some representations, like some maps, are more or less adequate, more or less authentic, than others"; there are no "perfect" representations, just *more or less adequate ones*.[14]

Critiquing the "Jewish" Case

The Jewish context provides fertile ground for understanding the nature of the issues exposed by this brief discussion. Julius Gould has asked: "What, after all, is 'Jewishness?' What are the attributes that Jews share with each other but not with those who are not Jews—those who, in Jewish circles, are referred to, somewhat opaquely and residually, as *non-Jews*?"[15] The Orthodox halakhic definition of Jewish, is grounded in essentialist notions of ancestral inheritance—primarily matrilineal descent—yet it retains currency.[16] This is because, as Charmé articulates, "[i]t is easier to see oneself as an expression of a group identity that pre-exists one's birth and continues after one's death."[17] In this way, Jewish existence precedes Jewish essence, belonging to the future as much as to the past, a "fragile thread" that already exists, transcending place, time, history, and culture.[18]

However it is derived, Jewishness will form, for some, a central and salient part of his or her identity, while for others it will be merely incidental. Indeed, it may be even less than that. For example, in Jean-Paul Sartre's *Anti-Semite and Jew* (1965), being "Jewish" becomes an "inescapable fact" determined by antisemites from without, regardless as to whether or not the subject defines himself as such. Jewishness is "the crucial degree of difference that separates him from the non-Jews around him."[19] Increasingly, however, that "inescapable fact" is less and less malignant, and more and more escapable. For some years now, Jewishness has been a matter of free choice, not only about whether or not to *be* Jewish but also *how* to be Jewish. In many ways, Jewishness has become commodified: Jews "prefer to look at bits and pieces they can try on for a while, taste, enjoy, and then throw away."[20] "Pick'n'mix" Judaism is symptomatic of postindustrial society, where identities, like other commodities, are mass-produced.[21] Further, to *be* Jewish in the active sense requires more than a passive acceptance of having been born that way. It is therefore "impossible to 'be Jewish' in a simple way."[22] There are multiple authentic *Judaisms* that have constructed multiple understandings of the Jewish situation. Being Jewish in a postmodern world "is authentic—truthful about its own nature—only when it assumes the instability of all identities."[23]

In addition to the awkward "who is a Jew?" dilemma, the quantitative analyst must address another related question: What *kind* of category is "Jewish"? That is, what is the nature of the group it specifies? In his classic 1928 work, *The Ghetto*, Louis Wirth pondered a similar question:

> Who are the Jews? [...] There is probably no people that has furnished the basis for more *contradictory conclusions* than the Jews. The traits with which they have been credited by their friends, their enemies and themselves fairly exhaust the vocabulary. Still, the elementary question as to whether the Jews are a race, a nationality, or a religious or cultural group remains unsettled.[24]

Anthony Smith has suggested that Jewish historical myths such as Abrahamic ancestry, exodus from Egypt, and the "golden age" of the Davidic and Solomonic kingdom, retain a potency that is not just religious. Rather, even for secular Jews, such myths are "charters of their ethnic identity...as with the Greeks and Armenians, the Irish and Ethiopians, there is a *felt* filiation, as well as a cultural affinity, with a remote past in which a community was formed, a community that despite all the changes it has undergone, is still in some sense recognised as the 'same' community."[25] "Ethnic," of course, need not necessarily mean "secular," although Smith argues that there does not appear to be any a priori requirement for a religious component of Jewish identity.[26] Indeed, a wealth of scholarship demonstrates how the category "Jewish" exhibits dimensions well beyond the narrow confines of "religion." For example, Milton Gordon's classic 1964 treatise, *Assimilation in American Life*, characterized Jews as an "ethnic group" or a "religio-ethnic group" and referred repeatedly to the significance of Jewish "peoplehood."[27] Other examples include Benedict Anderson's imagining the Jewish people as a "nation" with respect to Jewish affiliation to political Zionism[28] and Frantz Fanon's racial construction of "Jewish" when contrasting the racist's valorization of "blackness" with the antisemite's valorization of "Jewishness," juxtaposing the "Negro" with the "Jew."[29]

Much of the literature concerning what is "Jewish" refers to mental states, cultural habits, and lifestyle. In Denmark, Andrew Buckser describes not only Jews whose identity is primarily religious, but also those for whom Judaism is "a culture, a tradition of rituals, foodways and patterns of thought and behaviour that had been handed down," whereas others conceive of "Jewishness ... primarily in social terms, as a set of family, personal, and business relationships within which they happened to live."[30] Finally, in the words of Bethamie Horowitz, "being Jewish has become a *state of mind* and is not simply a matter of inherited membership in a religious or ethnic group."[31]

That "Jewish" does not fit neatly into a religious, ethnic, or cultural social categorization is neither unique nor unexpected.[32] The reality is that the mental notion constituting "Jewish" is, like all identities, complex, contextual, and fluid—this in and of itself explains the contradictions and inconsistencies surrounding the way in which "Jewish" is constructed, both from within and without.

The Political Construction of "Jewish" in Britain: The National Census

Since 1991, Britain's decennial national census[33] has included a question on ethnic group; in 2001 and 2011 it also included a voluntary question on religion. The religion question conveniently sidesteps the "who is a Jew?" dilemma by simply asking "What is your religion?" and offering an array of possible answers, one of which is Jewish. The ethnicity question, in contrast, has no category for Jewishness.

Like all surveys, the census is a blunt and imperfect instrument, and there are several points that should be borne in mind when assessing the ensuing data. First, a majority of questions in most censuses are designed to count things. Generally these questions present largely unproblematic, objective categories such as the number of rooms in a house and the number of children in a family. Questions on identity are the exception, taking the census into completely different, and largely subjective, analytical territory. In so doing, it becomes the ultimate tool of myth creation in the modern age. As Anderson has noted: "The fiction of the census is that everyone is in it, and that everyone has one—and only one—extremely clear place. No fractions."[34] By presenting a fixed set of ethnic, ancestral, national, or religious labels, censuses implicitly draw a line between identities that are regarded as authentic and those that are not. That is, the census does much more than arbitrarily fix reality: it *constructs* reality by delineating boundaries and divisions that must then be battled over in subsequent struggles for recognition and resource allocation.[35] For example, census data on "race" and "ethnicity" are constructed out of a predesigned, fixed list of categories for respondents to choose from, although, as Ludi Simpson notes, "this is not a declaration of self-identity because the categories have already been set."[36] They are fixed despite identity being fluid, and worse, they are constructed for reasons of public policy, that is, to support government legislation against inequality and on behalf of equal opportunity.[37] Thus the taxonomies used in censuses serve to construct difference—or at least reinforce and reify it—presenting apparently clear-cut categories that may be alien to those being asked to "fit" into them.[38] In this way the census oversimplifies an inherently chaotic and dynamic reality, its "purifying" classifications misrepresenting highly complex and heterogeneous realities.

It is also an unavoidably political instrument, an "institution of power" shaping the way states imagine their dominion.[39] Even the decision to conduct a census is ultimately political, as are decisions to add or remove questions or amend the wording of existing ones, with politically powerful categories tending to lead the way.[40] But the census creates and imposes its "imagined" reality in an even more profound way than by simply defining which categories are authentic and which are not. It also defines what *kind* of response is expected. Thus, Britain's 2001 census clearly differentiated between "religion," on the one hand (with a note to "tick one box only"), and "ethnic group," on the other, presenting these as two separate and independent categories,[41] despite the fact that the boundary between them is decidedly blurred, especially for Jews but also for many Muslims and Sikhs.[42]

In the eyes of many, census data are devalued by such criticism, and data-users are accused of being "positivist" and "modernist," out of step with postmodern understandings of the "reality" of identity.[43] Given the enormous costs of running censuses, such arguments have sparked calls from around the world to abandon the instrument altogether. In Canada it has been proposed to replace the long-form census questionnaire with a new, voluntary "National Household Survey,"[44] and in Britain, arguing that the census is "expensive," "inaccurate," and "out of date almost before it has been done," the coalition government consisting of David Cameron's Conservatives and Nick Clegg's Liberal Democrats proposed abandoning it altogether in favor of existing public and private databases.[45] Indeed, the Office for National Statistics (ONS) has, since 2011, been undertaking a review process called "Beyond 2011" for assessing alternative solutions to the "costly" and "challenging" census instrument.[46]

Such threats are troubling because, despite the census' evident limitations, it can be confidently argued that the benefits of census-taking far outweigh the drawbacks. Stephen Fienberg and Kenneth Prewitt have recently suggested that "[g]overnment statistics are no less vital to a nation's scientific infrastructure than is an observatory or a particle accelerator, and [therefore] need stable funding and protection."[47] Similarly, David Kertzer and Dominique Arel argue that the census, "although only one of many government information-gathering devices, is arguably the most important."[48] It offers the only way a global picture of a population can be obtained, which in turn can be used to create baseline indicators for the purpose of calibrating sample survey data.[49] It also enables "rare" groups such as Jews to be sampled where this might be impossible or financially prohibitive to achieve by other means. And in response to anthropological criticisms that identity is constructed out of the categories of the census, it is also the case that "while identities have no reality independent of people's perceptions, the belief by social actors that their identities are real is itself a social fact."[50]

In Britain, the introduction of a question on religion in the 2001 census, and its subsequent inclusion in 2011, elicited a data bonanza for those interested in the detailed demographic analysis of the Jewish population—from local government authorities to large Jewish charities.[51] However, the data were ultimately limited to a definition of "Jewish" as a category of *religion only* even though the census also presented a question on ethnic group. As noted, the ethnicity question was constructed in such a way as to proscribe "Jewish" being entered as an authentic "ethnic" category. It is instructive to examine how the categories of religion and ethnicity were constructed in the 2001 census, as this sheds light on a far broader issue with direct relevance for Jews: the way in which concepts of race, ethnicity, and religion are politically constructed in Britain.

The 2001 census presented a question asking "What is your religion?" and one of the seven labeled categories it presented was "Jewish."[52] But the apparent objectivity of this question was ultimately illusory. For example, who decided that "Jewish" should be included as a category and why? Why seven categories? Why these ones in particular? Why this specific question wording and structure? Indeed, why a religion question at all? Any answer to each of these questions is, ultimately, political.

Although the question wording makes no reference to normative understandings of religion such as belief, affiliation, or practice, some inevitably interpret it to mean any or all of these facets of religion and answer accordingly. Allan Brimicombe has described it as a question on "religious affiliation" (despite there being no indication that it was asking about official membership of a religious body).[53] David Voas has argued that the "so-called religion question" is in practice quasi-ethnic because it immediately follows the question on ethnic identity, and the responses offered seem to refer to cultural heritage rather than organizational membership (for example, "Christian" is collapsed into a single category).[54]

Further, the question structure prevents any sort of syncretism since only one tick is allowed, despite the fact that many people live "mixed faith" lives.[55] David Voas and Steve Bruce also comment that the wording has a "positive presumption," suggesting that people are expected to have a religion[56] (although, it should be noted, the first category in the list of seven was "None" in 2001). They contrast this with the wording used in the annual British Social Attitudes survey,[57] which asked: "Do you regard yourself as belonging to any particular religion?" which, they suggest, does less to encourage an affirmative response; indeed, they have shown that the two questions elicit pointedly different results.[58]

The 2001 census question on "ethnicity" was, if anything, even more problematic. The question "What is your ethnic group?" was accompanied by an instruction to "tick the appropriate box to indicate your *cultural background*."[59] These boxes presented a set of five main categories ("White," "Mixed," "Asian or Asian British," "Black or Black British," "Chinese or other ethnic group"), plus 11 sub-categories, and five write-in options that liberally conflated skin color (for instance, "Black," "White"), race (for instance, "Asian," "African"), and nationality (for instance, "Indian," "Chinese") and had little, if anything, to do with culture or ethnicity. So many different facets of identity were included in this question that its purpose was ambiguous and confusing.[60] (The 2011 census arguably exacerbated the problems by including three additional sub-categories to the question.) "Jewish," as was the case for every other ethnic group lacking a distinctive skin color (with the peculiar exception of "Irish"), was not included. Sikhs were also left out of the ethnicity listing; in consequence, the UK Sikh Federation threatened legal action if "Sikh" was not included as a category in the 2011 census.[61] In the end, "Sikh," like "Jewish," remained absent in 2011, although "Arab" was added.

The pigeonholing of "Jewish" into a religious instead of an ethnic category in the 2001 census is no coincidence. Rather, it is a reflection of the way in which identity politics is played out in Britain. The multicultural discourse of the 1980s and 1990s was firmly anchored in the realm of *race*, not culture—quite literally colored by

Britain's recent colonial past and the subsequent waves of immigration that followed in the post-colonial period.[62] Recognizing this historical context is crucial to understanding the political complexity and exclusions in the census' ethnic question.[63] But the unfortunate result of this racial approach to ethnicity in Britain was that many ethnic groups who arguably ought to have been enumerated, among them Jews, were instead subsumed within a homogenous and largely meaningless catch-all category of "White." This was particularly problematic, as Dhooleka Raj has pointed out, because in Britain "White" is not simply a euphemism for "not coloured," but is also equated with "Anglo-Saxon," whereas Jews (like Hindus) do not see themselves as being (ancestrally) Anglo-Saxon.[64] At the same time, the term "religion" is constructed in Britain in the context of a national church—the Church of England (and the Church of Scotland). "Religion" is therefore rigidly viewed in terms of *faith* in Britain, with the faith of Judaism juxtaposed with the faith of Christianity.

Thus, insofar as political discourse is concerned, and as demonstrated by the construction of the census categories, "Jewish" is regarded as a *religious* category with no meaningful space for an ethnic dimension. Or is it? As will become clear, this political, religious construction of "Jewish" directly contradicts the way in which the judiciary has approached this fluid category.

The Legal Construction of "Jewish" in Britain: The JFS Case

To illustrate the very different approach toward the category "Jewish" in Britain's legal system, we turn to a recent (and now infamous) legal dispute between JFS,[65] a Jewish day school, and a boy known as "M" who had been denied a place at the school because he did not meet the school's eligibility criteria.

First, a few words of background. In Britain, Jewish day schools may choose to be publicly funded—in contrast with other western countries, such as the United States, where state funding to schools operated by religious groups is unavailable. This relatively unusual situation is a result of Britain's Education Act of 1944, which laid down the principle that state funding was available for schools in which "pupils are to be educated in accordance with the wishes of their parents."[66] It was not until Tony Blair's New Labour government came to power in 1997 that the full implications of this principle began to sink in. This period saw considerable political enthusiasm for schools to specialize in particular fields (through "academies"), not least because specialization appeared to lead to better educational outcomes as judged by national examination results.

To encourage parents and their communities to build their own schools, the government pledged to provide 90 percent of the capital costs involved in setting up the schools and all of the costs of running them. The sole exception was that the religious education component of such schools would be paid for by a voluntary contribution from parents. School governors were given control of staff recruitment and were allowed to define their own entry criteria in order to ensure the "religious character" of such schools.[67] As a result, Jewish parents in Britain found themselves in the enviable position of being able to access considerable state funds to contribute toward the cost of educating their children in Jewish state-funded day schools.[68] It should be clear that this outcome is very much a product of the political state machinery in Britain. As was demonstrated by the discussion about the census, this machinery firmly anchors "Jewish" in the *religious* context—that is, state-funded Jewish day schools in Britain are described tellingly as "faith schools," differing from Catholic and Church of England schools only in terms of denomination.

JFS is the oldest and largest state-funded Jewish day school in Britain. Currently located in North London, its pupils achieve excellent exam results; historically, the school has been consistently oversubscribed. The school's religious character is based on its current alignment with the nominally Orthodox United Synagogue movement, which itself looks to the Office of the Chief Rabbi (OCR) for guidance on Jewish law (halakhah). Thus, JFS's entry criteria, as set out by the school's governors, have been based on an Orthodox interpretation of halakhah with regard to determining who is authentically Jewish. To be eligible for a place at JFS, a student must either have been born to a Jewish woman (by birth or via conversion) or have been converted to Judaism. In either case, the woman/conversion must have been recognized as authentic by the OCR.

In April 2007, the governing body of JFS refused to offer a place to an 11-year-old boy on the grounds that he was not, in the eyes of the OCR, authentically Jewish.[69] Although his father was recognized as Jewish, his mother had converted to Judaism through non-Orthodox auspices, and this conversion was not recognized by the OCR. Following a failed appeal in response to his son's rejection, the father sought legal action in the form of a judicial review. The legal dispute escalated through the English civil court hierarchy and concluded in December 2009 in the Supreme Court of the United Kingdom. In an extraordinary turn of events, some of Britain's greatest legal minds were asked to test the "who is a Jew?" question to its logical limits.

The case, in which the JFS governors and the OCR were ultimately defeated, centered on a simple question: Had JFS contravened the Race Relations Act (1976) when it rejected the boy on the grounds that he was not Jewish because his mother was not deemed to be Jewish? That is to say, was he discriminated against on *racial* grounds? If "yes," then JFS's rejection of "M" was in contravention of the 1976 Act, of which Section 3 states:

3.—Meaning of "racial grounds," "racial group" etc.

(1) In this Act, unless the context otherwise requires—

"racial grounds" means any of the following grounds, namely colour, race, nationality or ethnic or national origins;

"racial group" means a group of persons defined by reference to colour, race, nationality or ethnic or national origins, and references to a person's racial group refer to any racial group into which he falls.[70]

As Kertzer and Arel note, in order to ensure full coverage of vulnerable groups, this anti-discrimination legislation mixed together, "in one fell swoop...race, ethnicity/cultural nationality, and citizenship."[71] Although Jews are not specifically mentioned in the Act, they are deemed to be protected by it based on the outcome of a separate (case law) ruling in the House of Lords known as *Mandla v Dowell Lee* (1983). This ruling laid out in great detail what the law considers to be an "ethnic group":

For a group to constitute an "ethnic group" for the purposes of the 1976 [Race Relations] Act it had to regard itself, and be regarded by others, as a distinct community by virtue of certain characteristics, two of which were essential. *First it had to have a long shared history, of which the group was conscious as distinguishing it from other groups, and the memory of which it kept alive, and second it had to have a cultural tradition of its own, including family and social customs and manners, often but not necessarily associated with religious observance.* In addition, the following characteristics could also be relevant, namely (a) either a common geographical origin or descent from a small number of common ancestors, (b) a common language, which did not necessarily have to be peculiar to the group, (c) a common literature peculiar to the group, (d) a common religion different from that of neighbouring groups or from the general community surrounding it, and (e) the characteristic of being a minority or being an oppressed or a dominant group within a larger community.[72]

Referring to the highlighted section in the above ruling, Lord Justice Phillips, the president of the supreme court, argued in his JFS judgment that Jews "evidently" fall within the "ethnic" criteria:

It is possible today to identify two different [Jewish] cohorts, one by the *Mandla* criteria and one by the Orthodox criteria. The cohort identified by the *Mandla* criteria forms the Jewish ethnic group.... The man in the street would recognise a member of this group as a Jew, and discrimination on the ground of membership of the group as racial discrimination. The *Mandla* group will include many who are in the cohort identified by the Orthodox criteria, for many of them will satisfy the matrilineal test. But there will be some who do not.[73]

Therefore the court agreed that discrimination against Jews, legally viewed as members of an "ethnic group," constitutes *racial* discrimination under the 1976 Race Relations Act.

The next issue for the court to deliberate was whether or not the test of Jewishness applied by the OCR/JFS Governors was *ethnic* rather than *religious* in nature. Lord Phillips, on behalf of the majority, noted that JFS argued "that the matrilineal test is a religious test and that discrimination on the basis of that test is religious, not racial. This argument falls into two parts: (i) the matrilineal test is a test laid down by Jewish religious law; (ii) the matrilineal test is not a test of ethnic origin or ethnic status but a test of religious origin and religious status."[74] He continued:

The first part of this argument focuses ... on the reason why the matrilineal test is applied. The reason is that the JFS and the OCR apply the test for determining who is a Jew laid down by Orthodox Jewish religious law. What subjectively motivates them is compliance with religious law, not the ethnicity of the candidates who wish to enter the school. My reaction to this argument will already be clear. It is invalid because it focuses on a matter that is irrelevant—the motive of the discriminator for applying the discriminatory criteria. *A person who discriminates on the ground of race, as defined by the Act, cannot pray in aid [invoke] the fact that the ground of discrimination is one mandated by his religion.*[75]

And the court further argued:

whatever their racial, national and ethnic background, conversion unquestionably brings the convert within the *Mandla* [court case] definition of Jewish ethnicity. She becomes a member of the Jewish people.... [Matrilineal descent] is a test which focuses on the race or ethnicity of the woman from whom the individual is descended. Where a Jew is descended by the maternal line from a woman who has converted to Judaism, the matrilineal link is with an ethnic Jew [in the *Mandla* sense].[76]

To be precise, the court considered the "matrilineal test" to be "a test of ethnic origin" and conversion to Judaism as the creation of an *ethnically* Jewish person. Since the law constructs ethnicity and race to be essentially the same thing, discrimination based on an ethnic test is discrimination on racial grounds under the Race Relations Act. Hence the court concluded that the boy "M" had been the victim of racial discrimination.[77] Although the judges were at pains to stress that they did not consider the policies of JFS or the OCR to be "'racist' as that word is generally understood,"[78] they nevertheless ruled in favor of "M."

The direct consequence of this and earlier rulings in the case was that Jewish day schools could no longer rely solely on the Orthodox halakhic test of Jewish status in their eligibility criteria. Instead, preference had to be made "by reference only to outward manifestations of religious practice."[79] This was in stark contrast to the existing policy; indeed, at no point in the original application procedure had it been necessary for "M" or his parents to demonstrate any level of Jewish observance or belief at all, as would have been required for acceptance to a church-affiliated day school. And this was despite the fact that both the boy and his parents belonged to a (Masorti) synagogue and that "M" was being brought up as a Jew in a Jewish household. As a result of the ruling, a points-based system was devised by schools in which a "priority applicant" was required to obtain a "certificate of religious practice" that "provided information on synagogue attendance (though not membership), previous Jewish education, and other previous communal activity ..."[80] Significantly, the certificate was non-denominational in that it made no distinction between, say, an Orthodox as opposed to a Masorti or Reform synagogue.

The JFS case provoked strong reaction from a variety of observers and community commentators. Journalist Joshua Rozenberg argued that the Supreme Court had effectively used a non-Jewish or Christian definition of who is a Jew;[81] Chief Rabbi Jonathan Sacks claimed that the courts had branded Judaism "racist."[82] Even Reform rabbis were aghast at what had transpired. For example, Tony Bayfield, then head of the Reform Movement for Great Britain, "condemned the ruling on the grounds that while the Reform Movement deplored JFS's entry policies, it was for the Jewish community to decide the grounds on which pupils were admitted into Jewish schools."[83] Others were highly critical of those who had allowed the case to go ahead in the first place rather than quietly admitting "M" to the school on the understanding that such acceptance was not a de facto recognition of his Jewish status: this move would have averted a situation that had provoked "far-reaching changes to schooling throughout the community ... creating a situation in which 'who is a Jew' judgements can be made outside the community."[84] Indeed, Kahn-Harris and Gidley argued that "[t]he case revealed JFS, the United Synagogue and the Chief Rabbi to be simultaneously stubborn, principled and hopelessly naïve."[85]

JFS and the OCR ultimately fell foul of the contradictory ways in which the category "Jewish" is constructed by different state institutions in Britain. The defense relied on the *political* construction of "Jewish" that related to the term in a narrow religious sense, and which had served them well with respect to the state funding of Jewish day schools. But the judiciary, whose responsibility is to protect Jews from discrimination, saw fit to construct the category in strictly ethnic terms. When these conflicting constructions of "Jewish" were brought together in the JFS case, the scene was set for an inevitably frustrating outcome.

Implications of Contradictory Constructions of "Jewish"

This essay has highlighted an inherent contradiction in the way the category "Jewish" has been institutionally constructed in Britain. The political system constructs "Jewish" firmly within *religious* parameters, simultaneously excluding it from ethnic constructions of identity, as was demonstrated in the discussion regarding the use (and lack of use) of the ethnic category in the 2001 and 2011 national censuses. The legal system, in contrast, constructs "Jewish" using primarily *ethnic* parameters in a deliberate attempt to ensure that Jews are protected by legislation relating to racial discrimination, as was demonstrated by the example of the JFS case. As this essay has repeatedly emphasized, such contradictory outcomes are inevitable given the nature of the task of fixing identity despite its inherently fluid and contextual nature. Like other socially constructed categories, "Jewish" is not a term that can be simplistically bounded by traditional, independent identity groupings. Jews see themselves multidimensionally,[86] a position that is not easily accommodated in the black-and-white world of the state and its myriad institutional tentacles.

This situation presents Jewish demography with a serious challenge, since it radically reshapes the traditional boundaries of the discipline. If there is no group of people which can be definitely labeled Jewish (if not by itself, then by outsiders), how then can demographers hope to enumerate and analyze them? Furthermore, what is identified as an authentic "Jewish population" by one institution (such as the state) may not coincide with the "Jewish population" identified by another institution (such as the legal system). Here is a "reality" in which multiple Jewish populations can exist in any one place, each based on assorted, authentic constructions of "Jewish." Such a reality has far-reaching implications for demographers, especially given that the bounding and categorization of society is unlikely to disappear simply because it has been shown to be illusory. The desire to demarcate boundaries is strong and, arguably, integral to everyday life; without them, all levels of society and state would struggle to function. Thus, demographers should engage with the reality of multiple and simultaneously valid definitions of "who is a Jew?" With no single answer, we are left with multiple answers, some being more or less adequate than others. The demographer becomes the inquisitor of authenticity, choosing between various definitions by drawing on the political, social, legal, and historical contexts in which they were constructed.

We might therefore ask how this translates empirically. Unfortunately, the British census and available survey data offer only a very limited insight into the likely impact of different definitions on the enumerated size of Britain's Jewish population. In England and Wales, the 2001 census[87] recorded 260,000 Jews by means of the question on religion. But it also recorded 13,500 people who chose to write "Jewish" in the ethnicity question. Although most of these also recorded "Jewish" in the religion question, a small number (2,600 people) were enumerated as Jewish by ethnicity *only*.[88] Given the difficulties related to the way in which the census dealt with the ethnicity question—and specifically its racially loaded approach—these figures fail to provide anything like a reliable assessment of the relative sizes of the Jewish populations based on ethnic and/or religious criteria.

An alternative approach is to use 2001 census data from Scotland, where religion of upbringing was asked in addition to current religion. Here 6,500 people were recorded as being currently Jewish in 2001, and a further 1,800 were recorded as being Jewish by upbringing while currently practicing another (stated) religion or else, by far the majority, responding "none" to the religion question.[89] Using this information it is theoretically possible to produce a very rough estimate of the "broader" national Jewish-by-upbringing population in Britain. Nationally, the unadjusted 2001 census population for people who described their current religion as Jewish was 267,000. Simple arithmetic based on the Scottish data suggests that a broader Jewish population existed in Britain of 340,000 Jews-by-upbringing (whether or not currently identifying as Jews [in 2001]). This of course assumes that Scottish Jews (who represent less than 3 percent of the national Jewish population) provide an accurate proxy for the rest of the British Jewish population. It also makes no attempt to adjust for underenumeration as a result of the voluntary nature of the religion question. UK survey data cannot be used to shed further light on this enumeration problem, because none of the large-scale studies that have been carried out in recent years has asked questions that would enable demographers to quantify the size of the different Jewish population groups.[90] This is a task for future studies to consider.

But in addition to identifying and enumerating the various populations that arise from different approaches to defining "Jewish," demographers have another responsibility—to assess the wider social implications, both positive and negative, of these definitions. It is only with this richer understanding of the numbers that we can be in a position to judge between them. For example, whichever way the British machinery of state chooses to classify its citizens, it will inevitably have implications for those being encapsulated. Britain's Jewish community is fortunate in that it benefits both from a publicly funded education system willing to educate children "according to the wishes of their parents" and laws that protect minorities by defining "race" in the broadest possible terms. Despite the drawbacks of the census' construction of "Jewish," especially in terms of the poor quality of ethnicity data, the community still benefits considerably from the vast quantities of religious data obtained about itself from this instrument; it is a tremendous resource that should not be underestimated.

At the same time, these benefits are grounded in a set of definitions that contradict each other and also deliver some important negative outcomes. In particular, the rigid, racial construction of ethnicity in Britain leads to most Jews being subsumed into an all-encompassing and meaningless "white" ethnic group. As a result, they are rendered *invisible* in the public and academic discourse on multiculturalism, segregation, community cohesion, and diversity in Britain. Examples in the academic literature abound,[91] as they do in the public arena.[92] This is to the detriment not only of Jews but to society itself. As Kahn-Harris and Gidley point out: "The Jewish community, despite the lessons its diasporic story might have for a multicultural nation, failed to get a place at the table of multiculturalism."[93] Consequently, and in the face of difficult debates about the integration of "ethnic minorities," British society has missed opportunities to learn from its Jewish brethren—how, for example, they rose from impoverished, immigrant beginnings to become a highly successful, well-integrated group within British society. Alternatively, Jews can be examined as a case study of the drawbacks of integration, since the Jewish community has, in recent decades, witnessed a gradual erosion of its cultural and demographic vitality through intermarriage and assimilation.[94]

Conclusion

Demographers of Jewish populations are now faced with multiple, authentic definitions of "Jewish," a situation that makes the task of enumeration considerably more complex. As demographers, we must not only identify what those definitions are (however contradictory they appear to be), but also describe them in the social contexts in which they were constructed. In Britain the political realm defines "Jewish" in religious terms and this arguably produces a smaller population size than the legal realm's ethnic approach to the term. But neither representation, nor the enumerated population each implies, is more "accurate" than the other; each is appropriate in its own context. It is clearly important that as many people as possible are protected by anti-racism legislation, however tangentially they might associate themselves with the Jewish community. But equally, the political system, which uses the public purse to fund "faith" schools (the vast majority of are Christian), relies on a definition of religion that is faith-based. Understanding such contexts is fundamental if, as demographers, we are to make sense of the numbers that ensue from these contradictory constructions of "Jewish."

Notes

1. Stanley Waterman and Barry A. Kosmin, "Residential Change in a Middle-class Suburban Ethnic Population: A Comment," *Transactions of the Institute of British Geographers* (n.s.) 12, no. 1 (1987), 107–112 (esp. 108); Sergio DellaPergola, "Was It the Demography? A Reassessment of U.S. Jewish Population Estimates, 1945–2001," *Contemporary Jewry* 25 (2005), 85–130, esp. 88.

2. Peter Berger and Thomas Luckmann, *The Social Construction of Reality: A Treatise in the Sociology of Knowledge* (London: 1996 [1966]), 14.

3. Ibid., 15.

4. Benedict Anderson, *Imagined Communities: Reflections on the Origins and Spread of Nationalism* (London: 1991), 6–7.

5. Stuart Hall, "Cultural Identity and Diaspora," in *Identity: Community, Culture, Difference*, ed. Jonathan Rutherford (London: 1990), cited in Stuart Z. Charmé, "Varieties of Authenticity in Contemporary Jewish Identity," *Jewish Social Studies* 6, no. 2 (Winter 2000), 144.

6. Stuart Hall, "New Ethnicities," in *Identities: Race, Class, Gender and Nationality*, ed. Linda Martín Alcoff and Eduardo Mendieta (Oxford: 2003), 91.

7. Charmé, "Varieties of Authenticity in Contemporary Jewish Identity," 147–148, 150.

8. Ibid., 150.

9. Robin Cohen, "Fuzzy Frontiers of Identity: The British Case," *Social Identities* 1, no. 1 (1995), 35–62.

10. Richard D. Alba, "On the Sociological Significance of the American Jewish Experience: Boundary Blurring, Assimilation, and Pluralism," *Sociology of Religion* 67, no. 4 (2006), 347–358.

11. Paul Weller, "Identity, Politics and the Future(s) of Religion in the UK: The Case of Religion Questions in the 2001 Decennial Census," *Journal of Contemporary Religion* 19, no. 1 (2004), 16.

12. Ceri Peach, "Social Geography: New Religions and Ethnoburbs—Contrasts with Cultural Geography," *Progress in Human Geography* 26, no. 2 (2002), 253.

13. Keith Halfacree, "Constructing the Object: Taxonomic Practices, 'Counterurbanisation' and Positioning Marginal Rural Settlement," *International Journal of Population Geography* 7 (January 2002), 395–411.

14. David N. Livingstone, "Reproduction, Representation and Authenticity: A Rereading," *Transactions of the Institute of British Geographers* (n.s.) 23, no. 1 (April 1998), 18.

15. Julius S. Gould, *Jewish Commitment: A Study in London* (London: 1984), 4.

16. The halakhic position is articulated by David Newman, "Data Collection Problems and the Identification of Jewish Ethnic Community Patterns: A Reply," *Transactions of the Institute of British Geographers* (n.s.) 12, no. 1 (1987), 113; and by Stanley Waterman and Barry S. Kosmin, "Ethnic Identity, Residential Concentration and Social Welfare: The Jews in London," in *Race & Racism: Essays in Social Geography*, ed. Peter Jackson (London: 1987), 254–271.

17. Charmé, "Varieties of Authenticity in Contemporary Jewish Identity," 136–137.

18. Ibid., 144.

19. Jean-Paul Sartre, *Being and Nothingness: An Essay on Phenomenological Ontology* (New York: 1956 [1943]) cited in ibid., 140, 145.

20. Alain Finkielkraut, *The Defeat of the Mind* (New York: 1995), 112, cited in Charmé, "Varieties of Authenticity in Contemporary Jewish Identity," 149.

21. Charmé, "Varieties of Authenticity in Contemporary Jewish Identity," 146.

22. Ibid., 148.

23. Ibid., 149.

24. Louis Wirth, *The Ghetto* (Chicago: 1956 [1928]), 63, emphasis added.

25. Anthony D. Smith, *National Identity* (London: 1991), 33.

26. Numerous scholars have addressed this point. See, for example, Jonathan Webber, "Jews and Judaism in Contemporary Europe: Religion or Ethnic Group?" *Ethnic and Racial Studies* 20, no. 2 (1997), 257–279, esp. 267; Herbert Gans, "Symbolic Ethnicity and Symbolic Religiosity: Towards a Comparison of Ethnic and Religious Acculturation," *Ethnic and Racial Studies* 2, no. 1 (1994), 1–20; Andrew Buckser, "Jewish Identity and the Meaning of Community in Contemporary Denmark," *Ethnic and Racial Studies* 23, no. 4 (July 2000), 712–734; Sergio DellaPergola, "Was it the Demography?"; Lynne Scholefield, "Bagels, Schnitzel and McDonald's—'Fuzzy Frontiers' of Jewish Identity in an English Jewish Secondary School," *British Journal of Religious Education* 26, no. 3 (2004), 237–248.

27. Milton M. Gordon, *Assimilation in American Life: The Role of Race, Religion, and National Origins* (Oxford: 1964).

28. Anderson, *Imagined Communities*, 149 (n. 16).

29. Frantz Fanon, "The Fact of Blackness," in Alcoff and Mendieta (eds.), *Identities*, 64.

30. Buckser, "Jewish Identity and the Meaning of Community in Contemporary Denmark," 718.

31. Bethamie Horowitz, *Connections and Journeys: Assessing Critical Opportunities for Enhancing Jewish Identity* (New York: 2003), 2. See also Marlena Schmool and Stephen Miller, *Women in the Jewish Community: Survey Report* (London: 1994), 350, who suggest that being Jewish is a matter of "lifestyle"; cf. Aryeh Lazar, Shlomo Kravetz, and Peri Frederich-Kedem, "The Multidimensionality of Motivation for Jewish Religious Behavior: Content, Structure, and Relationship to Religious Identity," *Journal for the Scientific Study of Religion* 41, no. 3 (2002), 509–519.

32. Jessica Jacobson, "Religion and Ethnicity: Dual and Alternative Sources of Identity among Young British Pakistanis," *Ethnic and Racial Studies* 20, no. 2 (April 1997), 238–256; Dhooleka Sarhadi Raj, "'Who the Hell Do You Think You Are?' Promoting Religious Identity among Young Hindus in Britain," *Ethnic and Racial Studies* 23, no. 3 (May 2000), 535–558.

33. In reality, Britain's census is carried out by three agencies working in parallel: the Office for National Statistics (England and Wales), the General Register Office for Scotland, and the Northern Ireland Statistics and Research Agency.

34. Anderson, *Imagined Communities*, 164, 169.

35. David I. Kertzer and Dominique Arel, "Censuses, Identity Formation, and the Struggle for Political Power," in *Census and Identity: The Politics of Race, Ethnicity and Languages in National Censuses*, ed. David I. Kertzer and Dominique Arel (Cambridge: 2002), 1–42.

36. Ludi Simpson, "Statistics of Racial Segregation: Measures, Evidence and Policy," *Urban Studies* 41, no. 3 (March 2004), 662–663.

37. Ibid., 662.

38. Kertzer and Arel, "Censuses, Identity Formation, and the Struggle for Political Power," 31–34; see also Peter J. Aspinall, "Collective Terminology to Describe the Minority Ethnic Population: The Persistence of Confusion and Ambiguity in Usage," *Sociology* 36, no. 4 (November 2002), 803–816; Calvin Goldscheider, "Ethnic Categorisations in Censuses: Comparative Observations from Israel, Canada and the United States," in Kertzer and Arel (eds.), *Census and Identity*, 71–91.

39. Anderson, *Imagined Communities*, 163–164.

40. Peter J. Aspinall, "The New 2001 Census Question Set on Cultural Characteristics: Is It Useful for the Monitoring of the Health Status of People from Ethnic Groups in Britain?" *Ethnicity and Health* 5, no. 1 (2000), 33–40; Weller, "Identity, Politics and the Future(s) of Religion in the UK," 11.

41. ONS (Office for National Statistics), Census 2001 England Individual Form I1 http://www.statistics.gov.uk/census2001/census_form.asp (accessed 5 January 2011).

42. On the same dilemma with regard to Muslims and Sikhs in Britain, see Jacobson, "Religion and Ethnicity"; Raj, "'Who the Hell Do You Think You Are?'"

43. Elspeth Graham and Paul Boyle, "Editorial Introduction: (Re)theorising Population Geography: Mapping the Unfamiliar," *International Journal of Population Geography* 7, no. 6 (November–December 2001), 390; Halfacree, "Constructing the Object," 367.

44. "Flawed Arguments for Census Changes," *The Globe and Mail* (18 July 2010), online at www.theglobeandmail.com/news/opinions/editorials/flawed-arguments-for-census-changes/article1643217/(accessed 7 January 2013).

45. Christopher Hope, "National Census to be Axed after 200 Years," *Daily Telegraph I* (9 July 2010), online at www.telegraph.co.uk/news/newstopics/politics/7882774/National-census-to-be-axed-after-200-years.html (accessed 7 January 2013).

46. ONS, "Background to Beyond 2011," online at www.ons.gov.uk/ons/about-ons/what-we-do/programmes—projects/beyond-2011/background-to-beyond-2011/index.html (accessed 6 March 2013).

47. Stephen E. Fienberg and Kenneth Prewitt, "Save Your Census," *Nature* 466 (26 August 2010), 1043.

48. Kertzer and Arel, "Censuses, Identity Formation, and the Struggle for Political Power," 35.

49. See for example, David J. Graham, *Surveying Hard-to-Reach Groups Online: Lessons from Surveying Britain's Jews about Israel* (London: 2011).

50. Kertzer and Arel, "Censuses, Identity Formation, and the Struggle for Political Power," 19–20; Peter J. Aspinall, "The Future of Ethnicity Classifications," *Ethnic and Migration Studies* 35, no. 9 (2009), 1417–1435. Paul Boyle and Danny Dorling offer a vigorous defense of the census, arguing that its utility "cannot be underestimated"; it has a "unique" status to which no other administrative data are comparable. "On balance,... the decennial census is a vital resource for a remarkable amount of demographic, economic, health and social research, which would not be possible using alternative sources of information." ("Guest editorial: The 2001 UK Census: Remarkable Resource or Bygone Legacy of the 'Pencil and Paper Era'?" *Area* 36, no. 2 [2004], 102, 109).

51. See, for example, David J. Graham, Marlena Schmool, and Stanley Waterman, *Jews in Britain: A Snapshot from the 2001 Census* (London: 2007).

52. The seven categories were as follows: "None," "Christian (including Church of England, Catholic, Protestant and all other Christian denominations)," "Buddhist," "Hindu," "Jewish," "Muslim," "Sikh," and "any other religion." This is in contrast to the religion question asked in Scotland in 2001, which was split into two parts. The first part asked about current religion and the second part about religion of upbringing. The wording of the Scottish version also clearly emphasized the phrase "belong to" in the question (see www.gro-scotland.gov.uk/files/hseform.pdf (accessed 7 January 2013).

53. Allan J. Brimicombe, "Ethnicity, Religion, and Residential Segregation in London: Evidence from a Computational Typology of Minority Communities," *Environment and Planning B: Planning and Design* 34, no. 5 (2007), 889.

54. David Voas, "Estimating the Jewish Undercount in the 2001 Census: A Comment on Graham and Waterman (2005) 'Underenumeration of the Jewish Population in the UK 2001 Census,' *Population, Space and Place* 11: 89–102," *Population, Space and Place* 13, no. 5 (September–October 2007), 401–407; see also David Voas and Steve Bruce, "The 2001 Census and Christian Identification in Britain," *Journal of Contemporary Religion* 19, no. 1 (2004), 26; Ceri Peach, "Social Geography," 255.

55. Weller, "Identity, Politics and the Future(s) of Religion in the UK."

56. Voas and Bruce, "The 2001 Census and Christian Identification in Britain."

57. See the NatCen social research site at www.natcen.ac.uk/series/british-social-attitudes.

58. Voas and Bruce, "The 2001 Census and Christian Identification in Britain."

59. 2001 Census form (p. 2), online at www.ons.gov.uk/ons/guide-method/census/census-2001/about-census-2001/census-2001-forms/england-individual-form-i1.pdf (accessed 6 March 2013).

60. Brimicombe, "Ethnicity, Religion, and Residential Segregation in London," 889; see also David J. Graham and Stanley Waterman, "Locating Jews by Ethnicity: A Reply to D. Voas (2007), 'Estimating the Jewish Undercount in the 2001 Census: A Comment on Graham and Waterman (2005) 'Underenumeration of the Jewish Population in the UK 2001 Census,'" *Population, Space and Place* 13, no. 5 (September–October 2007), 409–414; Simpson, "Statistics of Racial Segregation: Measures, Evidence and Policy," 662–663.

61. Dil Neiyyar, "Sikh Campaigners Threaten Legal Fight over 2011 Census," BBC (25 February 2010), online at news.bbc.co.uk/2/hi/uk_news/8535141.stm (accessed 7 January 2013).

62. See for example, Paul Gilroy, *There Ain't No Black in the Union Jack: The Cultural Politics of Race and Nation* (London: 2002), 187.

63. K. Sillitoe and P.H. White, "Ethnic Group and the British Census: The Search for a Question," *Journal of the Royal Statistical Society, Series A: Statistics in Society* 155, no. 1 (1992), 141–163.

64. Raj, "'Who the Hell Do You Think You Are?'" 551.

65. JFS, as it is universally known, began as a school for poor East European Jewish immigrants in 18th- and 19th-century London. It was then known as Jews Free School; these days, however, the school is always referred to by its abbreviated name.

66. UK Legislation, *Education Act 1944* Part IV s76, online at www.legislation.gov.uk/ukpga/1944/31/pdfs/ukpga_19440031_en.pdf (accessed 7 January 2013).

67. Guidelines are taken from the "Blue Book," online at www.education.gov.uk/schools/adminandfinance/schoolscapital/funding/voluntary-aidedschools/a0010939/blue-book-guidance-on-capital-funding-for-voluntary-aided-va-schools (accessed 7 January 2013); and the *School Admissions Code 2010*, Department for Children, Schools and Families, online at www.manchester.anglican.org/upload/userfiles/file/pdf/Resources%20for%20schools/The%20Admissions%20Code%202010.pdf (accessed 8 April 2013); see also Oliver Valins, Barry A. Kosmin, and Jacqueline Goldberg, *The Future of Jewish Schooling in the United Kingdom: A Strategic Assessment of a Faith-based Provision of Primary and Secondary School Education* (London: 2001), 6–10; Derek Gillard, "Never Mind the Evidence:

Blair's Obsession with Faith Schools" (2007), online at www.educationengland.org.uk/articles/26blairfaith.html (accessed 7 January 2013).

68. Not all Jewish day schools in Britain are publicly funded. The more religious schools, in particular, prefer greater independence in terms of setting their curriculum.

69. Faith schools are legally allowed to discriminate between children by faith, where demand from the relevant "faith" group outstrips the supply of places available.

70. UK Legislation, *Race Relations Act 1976*, online at www.equalityhumanrights.com/uploaded_files/race_relations_act_1976.pdf (accessed 7 January 2013).

71. Kertzer and Arel, "Censuses, Identity Formation, and the Struggle for Political Power," 13.

72. Lord Fraser, *Mandla and Another v Dowell Lee and Another*, House of Lords, 1983 2 AC 548, online at www.hrcr.org/safrica/equality/Mandla_DowellLee.htm (accessed 7 January 2013); emphasis added.

73. *Judgement: R (on the application of E) (Respondent) v Governing Body of JFS and the Admissions Appeal Panel of JFS (Appellants) and others R (on the application of E) (Respondent) v Governing Body of JFS and the Admissions Appeal Panel of JFS and others (United Synagogue) (Appellants)* UK Supreme Court, Michaelmas Term, (2009) 15 (par. 30), emphasis added.

74. Ibid., par. 34.

75. Ibid., par. 35, emphasis added.

76. Ibid., par. 41.

77. Ibid., par. 45.

78. Ibid., par. 9.

79. Ibid., par. 248.

80. Keith Kahn-Harris and Ben Gidley, *Turbulent Times: The British Jewish Community Today* (London: 2010), 107.

81. Joshua Rozenberg, "This Ruling Creates More Problems than It Resolves," *The Jewish Chronicle* (17 December 2009), online at www.thejc.com/comment/comment/25176/this-ruling-creates-more-problems-it-resolves (accessed 7 January 2013).

82. Simon Rocker, "JFS: What Next?" *The Jewish Chronicle* (3 July 2009).

83. Kahn-Harris and Gidley, *Turbulent Times*, 106.

84. Ibid., 108.

85. Ibid.

86. Lazar, Kravetz, and Frederich-Kedem, "The Multidimensionality of Motivation for Jewish Religious Behavior"; Stephen M. Miller, "The Structure and Determinants of Jewish Identity in the United Kingdom," in *Jewish Survival: The Identity Problem at the Close of the Twentieth Century*, ed. Ernest Krausz and Gitta Tulea (Piscataway: 1998), ch. 14; Steven M. Cohen and Arnold M. Eisen, *The Jew Within: Self, Family, and Community in America* (Bloomington: 2000).

87. The 2011 census was being carried out at the time of writing. The first results on religion were released on December 11, 2012 with a subsequent release on January 30, 2013; both included population counts only. Further releases including cross-tabulations and data for Scotland are expected during 2013 and 2014. For the sake of completeness, this essay presents data from the 2001 census.

88. Graham, Schmool, and Waterman, *Jews in Britain*.

89. Ibid.

90. For example, in a national study of Jews in Britain conducted in 1995 by the Institute for Jewish Policy Research (JPR), 44 percent of the respondents described themselves as "non-practising [that is, secular] Jew" or "just Jewish." In a JPR national survey of Jewish attitudes toward Israel conducted in 2010, 51 percent of the respondents described themselves as "secular" or "somewhat secular." However, these figures neither relate to ethnicity directly nor do they provide a basis from which relative population totals can be estimated.

91. For example, Jews are largely or entirely missing in the following studies: Chris Hamnett, *Unequal City: London in the Global Arena* (London: 2003); Ron J. Johnston, James Forrest, and Michael Poulsen, "Are There Ethnic Enclaves/Ghettos in English Cities?" *Urban Studies* 39, no. 4 (April 2002), 591–618; Phil Rees and Faisal Butt, "Ethnic Change and

Diversity in England 1981–2001," *Area* 36, no. 2 (June 2004), 174–186; Ludi Simpson and Nissa Finney, "Spatial Patterns of Internal Migration: Evidence for Ethnic Groups in Britain," *Population, Space and Place* 15, no. 1 (January–February 2009), 37–56.

92. Trevor Phillips, then head of the Commission for Racial Equality, argued that British society was "sleepwalking to segregation" (see "After 7/7: Sleepwalking to Segregation 22nd September 2005," online at www.humanities.manchester.ac.uk/socialchange/research/social-change/summer-workshops/documents/sleepwalking.pdf (accessed 6 March 2013). Similarly, Ted Cantle in "2001 Community Cohesion: A Report of the Independent Review Team," Home Office (London: 2001) claimed there was clear evidence of deep physical "segregation" and "separation" in Britain, and suggested that "many communities operate on the basis of a series of parallel lives." Neither Phillips nor Cantle refer to Jews as providing a positive example of a longer-term outcome. See also Deborah Phillips, "Parallel Lives? Challenging Discourses of British Muslim Self-segregation," *Environment and Planning D: Society and Space* 24 (2006), 25–40.

93. Kahn-Harris and Gidley, *Turbulent Times*, 7, 171.

94. For example, see Jonathan Sacks, *Will We Have Jewish Grandchildren: Jewish Continuity and How to Achieve It* (London: 1995) and Bernard Wasserstein, *Vanishing Diaspora: The Jews in Europe Since 1945* (Cambridge, Mass.: 1996). For a different view, see Daniel Vulkan and David J. Graham, *Population Trends among Britain's Strictly Orthodox Jews* (London: 2008), which presents strong evidence of a demographic revival, at least among religious Jews in Britain.

Sources for the Demographic Study of the Jews in the Former Soviet Union

Mark Tolts
(THE HEBREW UNIVERSITY)

> *The indication of ethnicity in a Soviet internal passport was a curse for the Jews but a blessing for statisticians.*[1]

Demographic study of the Jews in the former Soviet Union (FSU), based on a wealth of statistical data, has a long and well-established tradition. This essay first presents an overview of tsarist and Soviet demographic data regarding Jews. Because most of the Soviet data were kept hidden until the end of the Soviet period, the focus here is on findings of the last quarter century. Particular attention will then be given to the role of the Soviet internal passport (which, because it listed ethnicity, was the basis for Jewish statistics) and to the consequences of the elimination of compulsory ethnic identification in the post-Soviet Slavic countries.

Tsarist and Soviet Demographic Data

Vital statistics data were routinely collected and processed for European Russia starting in 1867, with Jews considered one of the empire's religious groups. In the first census of the tsarist empire in 1897, Jews were categorized on the basis of religion and/or language for the country as a whole and for each of its regions. At the beginning of the 20th century, data on Jewish marriages, births, and deaths over a 40-year period were complied and analyzed by Sergei Novoselsky and Veniamin Binshtok.[2] Another early 20th-century study, dealing with Jews recorded in the 1897 census, was carried out by Boris Brutskus.[3] In the 1970s, Bronislaw Bloch approached the data with much more sophisticated demographic techniques and established baselines (that is, total fertility rate and life expectancy) for the study of subsequent developments.[4] Several years later, Shaul Stampfer analyzed marriage patterns of Jews in the tsarist empire.[5]

During the years of revolution and civil war, statistical data collection was suspended in most parts of the country. In the 1920s, there was a resumption of coverage of Jewish vital events and the size and structure of the Jewish population. Whereas the tsarist statistics had covered religious groups, the Jews were now presented only as an ethnic group among many others.[6] Detailed statistics, including the results of the Soviet census of 1926, were published during the course of the decade, although some regions (in particular, Ukraine) were more comprehensively covered by vital statistics data than others. In the 1930s, especially in the first half, the quality of Soviet statistics dramatically declined. The statistical administration ceased its systematic publication of demographic statistics, and most of its results for the 1930s were kept secret until the last years of the Soviet regime.[7] Only in the 1990s, owing to the efforts of Mordechai Altshuler, were the Jewish demographic data for the 1930s assembled from archival sources and published.[8] To date, however, Altshuler's publications have not been accorded the attention they merit. As a result, obsolete and inaccurate data regarding the pre-Second World War Jewish population continue to appear even in serious scholarly publications.[9]

Combined with tsarist-era demographic data and the statistical data compiled during the 1920s, the previously unknown Soviet data for the 1930s provide a good basis for the study of Jewish demographic development for a period covering more than a century.[10] With the outbreak of the Second World War, there was another break in demographic data collection by ethnicity that lasted until the late 1950s.

Almost all data for the postwar period that were published in the Soviet Union before glasnost are presented and analyzed in Altshuler's first book, which is the best collection of knowledge concerning Soviet Jewish demography from the period preceding the revelation of hidden Soviet statistics.[11] We shall present here mostly data that was not available when Altshuler was writing his book.

Beginning in 1958, annual data on the total number of Jewish births and deaths were collected in the various republics of the Soviet Union. The total numbers of births to Jewish mothers were recorded, as were the numbers of births to Jewish mothers with fathers of other ethnicities. It is therefore possible to calculate residually the annual numbers of births of children with two Jewish parents. Among Jewish deaths, the numbers of deaths of children under one year old born to Jewish mothers were also counted. All of this data remained mostly unpublished until the end of the Soviet period.

Much of the postwar data regarding Jews were collected by a team headed by Leonid Darsky of the Institute of the Soviet Central Statistical Administration.[12] Together with Evgeny Andreev, Darsky pioneered in the publication of the total fertility rate and life expectancy of Soviet Jews.[13] The respective indicators were also computed and published separately for the Jewish populations of the Russian Federation and Ukraine.[14] Only after the dissolution of the Soviet Union were the annual numbers of Jewish births and deaths for the period starting from 1958 published for the Jewish populations of the three Slavic republics: Belorussia, Ukraine, and Russia.[15] To date, there has not been systematic publication of the annual data for other parts of the FSU. However, birth and death rates have been published for most of the republics for the years surrounding the Soviet censuses of 1959 and 1989.[16] In addition, data on mixed marriage by age and sex in 1988, coupled with the respective 1978 data, were promptly published for the three Slavic republics when glasnost was proclaimed.[17] In the post-Soviet period, the percentage of children of mixed origin among all children born to Jewish mothers was calculated by republic for the years surrounding the Soviet censuses.[18]

Four censuses were undertaken in the Soviet Union in the postwar period: in 1959, 1970, 1979, and 1989. In all of these censuses, ethnicity was recorded and data on Jews were collected, including statistics relating to geographical distribution, age-sex composition, and marital structure. Most of these data were not published before the dissolution of the Soviet Union. Even the total number of Jews in many large Soviet cities in the postwar period was not publicly known until Mark Kupovetsky presented findings based on previously inaccessible archival sources.[19] For most of the former Soviet republics, material relating to age composition of the Jewish population has been published only for large age groups.[20] Details regarding age-sex composition have been published for the Jewish populations of the three Slavic republics (from all postwar Soviet censuses), for Uzbekistan (from the 1959 and 1989 Soviet censuses), and for Dagestan (from the 1989 Soviet census).[21] To this should be added existing data on the number of children ever born to Jewish women from the 1979 and 1989 Soviet censuses, and information on the family structure of the Jewish population that was detailed in the results of the same censuses. Based on the special processing of the 1979 Soviet census data for different ethnicities, the incidence of mixed marriage among Jews and ethnic affiliation of children of mixed couples was also measured.[22]

In sum, Soviet censuses and vital statistics have resulted in a long and detailed series of data on ethnicity. Some of the previously suppressed data for the Jewish population were published in the post-Soviet period. Much other information remains to be studied. There is, however, a strong basis for future research on the Jewish population of the FSU.

The Soviet Internal Passport and Counting of Jews

Soviet internal passports that indicated ethnicity (*natsionalnost*) were introduced in 1932—though in fact such passports had long been part of the tsarist regime's tradition of population surveillance.[23] Under the tsarist regime, Jews had been categorized by religion rather than ethnicity and were subject as a group to official discrimination and persecution. In contrast, the early Soviet regime targeted segments of the population on the basis of social (class) status and origin. Thus, Jews as such did not fear unfavorable consequences when their ethnic origins were made known to the Soviet authorities.

Overall, the Jewish population constituted one of the most loyal components of the new Soviet society. Many Jews benefited from opportunities for rapid upward social mobility, in particular those who moved to cities and joined the Soviet elite.[24] Many others remained in the *shtetlach* of the former tsarist Pale of Settlement. Having endured pogroms both before and during the civil war, they feared anarchy and accepted the Soviet regime as the lesser evil among the various possibilities.[25] In consequence, the great majority of Soviet Jews voluntarily chose to be registered as Jews in their passports.

By the end of the 1930s, this ethnic identification had become permanent and could not be officially changed.[26] The ethnicity of every Soviet citizen aged 16 and above was written in his or her internal passport, and anyone with two Jewish parents had no choice but to be registered as Jewish. Soviet authorities, contrary to their proclaimed goal of assimilation, actually preserved Soviet Jewry by the compulsory labeling of individuals as Jews.[27] Only the offspring of mixed marriages had the option to choose the ethnicity of one or the other parent: most of them preferred to be listed under the ethnic label of the non-Jewish parent.[28]

The listing of ethnicity in Soviet internal passports formed a good basis for ethnic statistics.[29] Soviet vital statistics listed the ethnicity of the parents of a newborn child or that of a deceased adult on the basis of what was recorded in the internal passports.[30] For deceased children under the age of 16 (who did not have such passports), ethnicity was established on the basis of the parents' ethnicity. In the case of the death of a child whose parents belonged to different ethnicities, the child was recorded as having the ethnicity stated by the person who reported the death. Only if the deceased child was less than one year old was he or she automatically recorded as being of the mother's ethnicity.

Significantly, data from the Soviet censuses were based entirely on the self-declaration of respondents. There was no requirement to provide documentary evidence for any answer given, and with regard to ethnicity, census takers were given explicit instructions that ethnic identity was to be determined solely by the person polled—without any corroboration.[31] For children, ethnicity in censuses was determined by parents. In the first three postwar censuses (1959, 1970, and 1979), whenever there was difficulty in determining the ethnicity of a child whose parents belonged to different ethnicities, preference was to be given to that of the mother. In the last Soviet census (in 1989), some of the recommendations in this regard were removed from the instructions to the census takers.

Some scholars have claimed that a sizable number of Jews in the Soviet censuses were recorded under another ethnicity. Benjamin Pinkus, for instance, argued that 11 percent of Jews polled in the 1926 Soviet census, 8 to 10 percent in the 1939 Soviet census, and as many as 15 percent in the 1959 Soviet census were counted as members of another ethnic group.[32] Most scholars today, however, are in agreement that the Soviet census figures on Jewish ethnicity (adults only) are in fact very much in accord with the "legal" ethnicity recorded in internal Soviet passports.[33]

Uziel O. Schmelz was the first who properly studied the published data of the 1959 and 1970 Soviet censuses for Jews; based on their results (that is, in the absence of published birth and death data), he recognized that there was a negative balance of births and deaths among the Jewish population.[34] In this manner, the question regarding trends of demographic development for the Soviet core Jewish population was answered. As noted, data from the Soviet censuses was based entirely on the self-declaration of respondents, and therefore they are regarded as "a good example of a large and empirically measured core Jewish population in the Diaspora."[35]

According to the 1989 census, in all age groups under the age of 55 in the Soviet Union, there were more males than females among Jews. This finding was questioned by some scholars. For instance, Yoel Florsheim and Dorith Tal attempted to correct age-sex ratios for the Jewish population of the Soviet Union based on the respective ratios recorded for Soviet immigrants to Israel from 1989 to 1994.[36] However, their calculations ignored the fact that (as will later be discussed in more detail) many of the immigrants had not been listed in their internal passports as Jews, and were thus not listed as Jewish in the 1989 Soviet census. Moreover, this migration was highly selective. For all destinations, the emigration rates among Jews from the Russian Federation were generally higher for females than for males.[37] Therefore, using age-sex ratios of the immigrants is not a reasonable approach. It is important to note that, at my request, Evgeny Andreev computed a stable population model[38] that took into account mortality rates among the Jews in the Soviet Union in 1988–1989. According to this model, the male-female ratio for Jews in all groups up to (and including) that of individuals aged 50–54 was similar to that reported in the 1989 Soviet census.[39]

To be sure, some of the results of the Soviet censuses with regard to Jews were unintentionally distorted in the course of the concealment of certain groups—for instance, prisoners and military personnel—in the general results. The most striking example of unintentional distortion is the biased geographical distribution of some parts of the Jewish population in the official results of the 1939 Soviet census. Data in this census were falsified to some extent in order to mask the great population losses caused by the forced collectivization and famine of 1932–1933. The procedures used to falsify data were rather complicated, and resulted in a certain amount of distorted data with regard to all ethnic groups, among them the Jews.[40]

For instance, according to the 1939 census for the Kazakh SSR, an unusually high percentage of Jews—47.5 percent—lived in rural areas. In some provinces of Kazakhstan the reported percentage was even higher: 83.0 percent in Kustanai, 82.8 percent in Akmolin, 76.0 percent in Pavlodar. Moreover, these proportions correlate with an unusually high percentage of males among the Jewish population. These deviations were caused in the main by the redistribution of many census forms of gulag prisoners (held in the Russian Federation) to Kazakhstan, the most famine-ravaged republic, in order to conceal the concentration of huge numbers of prisoners in the northern and eastern parts of Russia. According to my calculations, some 5,600 Jewish prisoners were "reassigned" to the Kazakh SSR; in consequence, the Jewish population of Kazakhstan was inflated by more than 40 percent for this reason alone. Moreover, in the 1939 Soviet census in Kazakhstan, the general inflation ratio seems to be as high as about 3.0 for rural Jews (that is, showing three times as many Jews as were actually present) and more than 1.5 for total Jews.[41]

According to analogous calculations, it appears that the official results of the 1939 census reassigned 5,800 Jews imprisoned in the Russian Federation to Ukraine, the second most terribly famine-ravaged republic. However, given the large Jewish population of Ukraine (according to the official data, more than one and a half million), the same phenomenon had a much smaller impact on the total reported number of Jews in this republic.

From the above, we may conclude that the significant distortions estimated for the official 1939 census results of the Jews in Kazakhstan were the exception rather than the rule even in this census. In all, redistribution of prisoners' census forms from the northern and eastern parts of the Russian Federation did not seriously change the geographic distribution of the Jewish population as a whole.[42] Moreover, one should stress that both these parts of the Soviet Union—Kazakhstan and those places of the Russian Federation from which the filled-in census forms were taken—were not occupied by the Nazis during the Second World War; in the case of Ukraine, which *was* occupied, the inflation ratio is rather small. Consequently, these census falsifications are of marginal importance in terms of estimates of Jewish losses during the Second World War.

Similarly, there is a certain distortion of data in all postwar Soviet censuses, resulting from the fact that the census forms of many conscripts were not sent back to the regions from which they were drafted.[43] Since military draftees are almost exclusively males in a very narrow age range, the consequence can be a serious distortion of general census results, especially in the case of small ethnic groups. For example, according to the data of the 1989 census, the age-sex ratios for the Central Asian (Bukharan) Jews in Uzbekistan were most unusual. At age 18 there were only 55 males per 100 females, and at the age of 19 this ratio was as low as 39. Conversely, for the pre-draft age of 17, the ratio was 111 males per 100 females.

Even after Schmelz's analysis of the decline in core Jewish population was published, there continued to be a widespread perception that the total number of people of Jewish parentage (and their spouses) was on the increase. How was this broader category of the Soviet Jewish population to be measured? The solution was to employ an additional definition of Jewish population based on household data from Soviet censuses. This approach empirically measured the enlarged Jewish population, which includes core Jews as well as all their household members.[44] Based on the 1989 census results, the enlarged Jewish population was estimated for the Soviet Union as a whole and for its three Slavic republics.[45] These estimates showed that the spread of mixed marriage, concurrent with a low level of Jewish ethnic affiliation of the children of such marriages, brought about a situation whereby the enlarged Jewish population in the Soviet Union on the eve of its dissolution was much larger than the core Jewish population: in the late 1980s, the ratio of core to enlarged Jewish population was roughly 1 to 1.5.[46]

At the same time, estimates showed that this category of Jewish population was itself shrinking. For example, in the Russian Federation, the estimated size of the enlarged Jewish population decreased from about 1,100,000 in 1979 to 910,000 in 1989, despite an increase in the ratio of core to enlarged Jewish population from 1.5 in 1979 to 1.6 in 1989. This corresponds with the negative balance of total number of children born to Jewish parents and Jewish deaths beginning in the 1960s. By the end of the 1980s, the Jewish demographic balance was decidedly unfavorable in all the republics of the European part of the Soviet Union.[47] Thus, the demographic collapse of Soviet Jewry was discovered with the help of different indicators, all of which show that the trend began before the start of the great emigration of the 1990s.

Changes in Vital and Migration Statistics in the Post-Soviet Era

Following the dissolution of the Soviet Union in 1991, demographic statistics of the 15 newly independent states started to diverge. However, the old Soviet system of collecting and processing demographic information by ethnicity continued to operate in most of these countries. As a result, for 1993, it was possible to obtain and publish the number of births to Jewish mothers and the number of Jewish deaths for 13 of the post-Soviet countries (all except Georgia and Lithuania).[48] Moreover, Jewish mortality in Moscow in 1993–1995 was detailed and compared with that of the other ethnic groups.[49]

A microcensus conducted in 1994 in the Russian Federation has become an additional important source of post-Soviet Jewish demographic research.[50] This survey, encompassing a 5 percent representative sample of the total population, provided a new basis for estimating the core Jewish population along with its geographical distribution and structure.[51] Based on the data of this microcensus, geographical distribution and age-sex structure of the enlarged Jewish population were also estimated. The enlarged population was estimated for the country as a whole, as well as separately for the Jews in Moscow, St. Petersburg, and the provinces outside these two cities.[52] These estimates did not cover some non-Ashkenazi Jews, mostly Mountain Jews (with their non-Jewish household members). To include them, I accordingly adjusted the total number of the enlarged Jewish population in the Russian Federation.[53]

In the mid-1990s, authorities of the three post-Soviet Slavic countries made a decision to cancel the listing of ethnicity in their internal passports. In general, Jews and other ethnic groups (for instance, Germans) who had suffered from discrimination in the Soviet Union were pleased with this reform.[54] However, for the demographic study of the Jews in these countries, the consequences of such a change were disastrous. Over the next decade, vital and migration statistics by ethnicity ceased to exist for the great majority of FSU Jews.

In the Russian Federation, 1998 was the last year in which comprehensive information regarding births and deaths by ethnicity was collected. In 1999, a new form of birth certificate was introduced, for which ethnicity became an optional listing "to be filled out according to the wishes (*po zhelaniiu*) of the person making the statement."[55] The following year, the registered number of births to Jewish mothers decreased significantly (by 29 percent) despite the fact that the number of births for the total population of Russia saw no dramatic change.[56] Previously, from 1995 to 1998, the registered number of births to Jewish mothers had decreased more moderately (by 19 percent) over the entire period. Thus, the significant reduction in 1999 can probably be attributed to the new form of birth certificate. Interestingly, among the recorded births to Jewish mothers in 1999, the share born with Jewish fathers remained stable (26 percent). We may conclude that, in Russia today, many individuals who were once "officially recognized" Jews (those listed as Jews in Soviet passports) prefer not to declare their Jewish ethnicity, regardless of whether they are married to Jews or non-Jews.[57]

Among the total urban population of the Russian Federation, the share of newborns for whom ethnicity of mother was unknown increased from less than 2 percent in 1998 to 31 percent in 2002, and to 51 percent in 2008; the share of unknown among deaths increased from about 2 percent in 1998 to 17 percent in 2002, and to 65 percent in 2008. Consequently, in 2009, the Russian Federal State Statistics Service (Rosstat) cancelled the processing of data on births and deaths by ethnicity.

The preceding year, Rosstat had ceased the processing of data on migration by ethnicity.[58] Fortunately, however, enough data had previously been collected to allow for the investigation of an important phenomenon in the contemporary numerical dynamics of world Jewry—the massive shift in ethnic/religious status of immigrants from the FSU upon their arrival in Israel.

In the Russian Federation, the internal passport was revised in 1997. As noted, the new passports did not contain a listing for ethnicity. When these new passports were introduced, the Goskomstat of Russia (as the statistical agency was then called) recommended that ethnicity be specified in personal forms of the statistical registration of migration "as reported by the citizen himself (*so slov*)."[59] Children under 14 would not have their own passports, and in migration statistics their ethnicity would be determined, as previously, on the basis of that of their parents. If the father and mother belonged to different ethnic groups, "one registers the ethnic identity [of the child] as that of one of the parents, preference being given to the mother's ethnicity."[60]

Israeli statistics are based on the Ministry of Interior population register file, which defines "who is a Jew" in accordance with Jewish religious law (halakhah): either a person born to a Jewish mother (female lineage is decisive and the number of generations backwards is not determined) or one who has converted to Judaism. As in the Israeli Law of Return, only conversion to another religion can abrogate Jewish lineage. Logically, in the official Israeli data, the share of Jews among all immigrants from the FSU countries is much higher than what appears in FSU migration statistics, as is seen, for example, in the data regarding people who arrived from the Russian Federation (Table 8.1).

Obviously, the converse can also be true. Some of the immigrants who were considered Jews according to their former Soviet internal passports (as well as in population censuses)—that is, the offspring of a Jewish male and non-Jewish female—fall under the category of non-Jews in Israeli statistical data. However, the opposite situation is in fact more prevalent: there are many more immigrants who are counted as Jews in Israel than were registered as such in the FSU. These individuals, who had previously neither identified themselves nor had been regarded by FSU authorities as Jews, represent a significant recent addition to the core Jewish population in Israel and to world Jewry as a whole.

Lack of understanding with regard to provisions of the Israeli Law of Return has led to claims such as that, in 2006, "three-quarters of emigrants to Israel [from Russia] were [ethnic] Russians."[61] According to the Israeli data for that year, the share of Jews among immigrants from Russia was 46 percent—whereas in the comparable Rosstat count, it was only 20 percent. Moreover, according to the Israeli data, when only non-Jewish spouses and children of Jews are included in the reckoning in addition to Jews (that is, leaving out more distant relatives such as spouses of non-Jewish children, and non-Jewish grandchildren and their spouses), the figure rises to more than 70 percent of all immigrants from the FSU in 2006.

It is difficult to obtain current, detailed vital statistics for Jews (and other ethnic groups) in the post-Soviet countries: such studies that exist cover only small groups. The practice does continue in Latvia and Moldova. However, in general, the old tradition of collecting data on vital events by ethnicity, on which many demographic studies of the Jews in the FSU were based, has all but ended.

Post-Soviet Censuses and the Jews

Between 1995 and 2004, the first post-Soviet censuses were conducted in all the newly independent states, except Uzbekistan. A question on ethnicity, which counted Jews among many other ethnic groups, was included in each of these censuses.

Table 8.1. Percentage of Jews among Migrants to Israel from the Russian Federation and the Entire FSU, 1990–2009

Year	Russian Federation		Entire FSU
	Rosstat data[a]	Israel CBS data[b]	Israel CBS data[b]
1990		94	96
1991		87	91
1992	64[c]	82	84
1993	60	82	82
1994	58	77	77
1995	53	73	72
1996	49	67	67
1997	36	59	59
1998	31	54	53
1999	31	49	49
2000	27	47	45
2001	25	44	43
2002	24	43	41
2003	(24)	45	43
2004	(22)	45	41
2005	(21)	46	43
2006	(20)	46	45
2007	(22)	48	46
2008		44	45
2009		43	41

[a] Of the emigrants whose ethnicity was known; for 1990–1991 and 2008–2009, the data on ethnicity of the migrants were not processed by Rosstat. Between 2003 and 2007, the registered number of Jews among the migrants was lower than that of people of unknown ethnicity.
[b] Refers to immigrants whose ethnicity/religion was known by mid-2011.
[c] Data relate to the second half of 1992.
Sources: Rosstat; Israel Central Bureau of Statistics (CBS).

Data on Jews were presented very differently in each country's census. The most detailed information was offered by publications of the Russian Federation and Belarus, with much less material provided for the second-largest Jewish community of the FSU, that of Ukraine. Overall, results of these censuses empirically confirmed earlier predictions with regard to the dramatic demographic decline of the Jewish population in the former Soviet republics. For instance, in the Russian Federation, the October 2002 census numbered 233,596 Jews (including those recorded as Central Asian [Bukharan], Georgian, Mountain Jews, and Krymchaks), as against my own estimate of a core Jewish population of 254,000 for the census date (derived from the February 1994 Russian microcensus estimate of 401,000 Jews and subsequent vital and migration dynamics). As with previous Soviet censuses, the 2002 Russian census was based entirely on the self-declaration of respondents; in the post-Soviet Russian Constitution (Article 26.1), the collection of information on an individual's ethnicity against his or her will is expressly forbidden. For this reason, in the 2002 Russian census there appeared for the first time a rather large group (about 1.5 million) whose ethnicity was not recorded. Clearly, there were some Jews among them, a fact I took into account when making my own calculations.[62]

The gap of some 20,000 people between my estimate and that of the official census demonstrates the accelerated process of Jewish assimilation in contemporary Russia. As noted, since the introduction of the new internal passport in 1997, a significant portion of Jews in the Russian Federation have opted not to be recorded as Jewish.[63] This fits in with the findings regarding birth statistics, whereby many former "officially recognized" Jews prefer not to declare their ethnicity even when they are not part of a mixed marriage.

My correction is almost three times higher than that of Nikita Mkrtchian in the framework of general corrections by ethnicity in the results of the 2002 Russian census. He based his adjustment for Jews on 0.5 percent of the total number of people whose ethnicity was not recorded in this census (as noted above, these numbered about 1.5 million).[64] At the same time, my correction is much more conservative than that of Aleksandr Sinelnikov.[65] Like Yoel Florsheim and Dorith Tal in the above-noted paper devoted to the Soviet Jewish population as a whole, Sinelnikov based the necessity of his correction on the peculiarities of the recorded Jewish age-sex structure in the Russian Federation. According to the 1989 Soviet census, the number Jewish men in the Russian Federation was greater than that of Jewish women in all ages up to 60. In part, this dearth of Jewish women in Russia stems from the earlier migration to this republic of predominantly male Jews from Ukraine.[66] According to the 2002 Russian census, this shortage extended to all ages up to 70.

There must be a reason for this development. It cannot be explained by the difference in mortality rates between sexes, as male mortality rates are always higher than those of females in modern developed countries. A more plausible explanation is that in this period of mass emigration, Jewish females, as noted, were more prone to leave the country than were Jewish males.[67] Alternative interpretations such as higher rates of ethnic assimilation of Jewish women in mixed marriages and/or higher rates of ethnic reaffiliation with the Jewish people for men of mixed parentage seem less relevant, especially for the older age groups, in which the Jewish sex imbalance grew as well.

Sinelnikov, however, assumed that many Jewish women in the census count were simply "missed," that is, they were recorded as being of another ethnicity when census takers filled in census forms in their absence. He used the age-sex structure of the Israeli Jewish population in his correction. Yet the Israeli Jewish population, as rightly noted by Florsheim and Tal, is unusual in the extent to which it is affected by migration.[68] Sinelikov also relied on an arbitrary supposition that, in the 2002 Russian census count, half as many Jewish men as Jewish women were "missed." All in all, he inflated the census figure for Jews in the Russian Federation by 23 percent.[69]

The census results of two Baltic countries, Latvia and Estonia, were exceptional with regard to their findings on the Jews, as they showed a net increase in the Jewish population. In Latvia, the number of Jews recorded in the first post-Soviet census of 2000 (10,385) is substantially higher than the estimate based on the 1989 Soviet census and subsequent vital and migration balances by the local statistical agency (7,976).[70] It is known, however, that ethnicity in the 2000 Latvian census was drawn from the national population register rather than being based on answers to a census question.[71] In the first 10 years following the dissolution of the Soviet Union, only 12 Jews officially changed their identities to Latvian, whereas many more—122 Latvians—changed their identities to Jewish in the population register.[72] Moreover, Latvian Jews are mostly Russophones, and we may surmise that the number of persons of mixed Jewish-Russian origin who officially changed their identities from Russian to Jewish—for which there is no known information—was much greater: this may have produced most of the jump in the Latvian census results for the number of Jews. A corresponding shift for Estonia was also found.[73] Currently, the population registers of the three Baltic states of Latvia, Estonia, and Lithuania have become a source of annually updated information on the number of Jews.

Since 2009, a new round of censuses has begun in the FSU countries, and there is once again a question on ethnicity in each of these censuses. Uzbekistan is not planning a census count; for this country, the last census data are those from the 1989 Soviet census.

The October 2010 Russian census confirms a continuation of the accelerated process of Jewish assimilation; it recorded 157,763 Jews (including those recorded as Central Asian [Bukharan], Georgian, Mountain Jews, and Krymchaks) as against my own core Jewish population estimate of 200,000 for the census date (based on the same approach as for the previous census). Thus, at the 2010 census count there were many more Jews (approximately 42,000) among people whose ethnicity was unknown/unstated.

A novel feature of census questionnaires of several FSU countries is their inclusion of a question on religion. The data of the Lithuanian 2001 census show many fewer people counted as adhering to the Jewish religion (1,272) than as identifying as ethnic Jews (4,007).[74] The analogous results of the 2004 census of Moldova were 902 Jews by religion versus 3,608 ethnic Jews (with the territory east of the Dniester River not being covered).[75] Only the 2002 census of Georgia reported similar numbers for Jews by religion (3,600) and Jews by ethnicity (3,800) (this census did not include Abkhazia and South Ossetia).[76] Far more dubious were the results reported for Jews in the second census conducted in independent Kazakhstan (in 2009), which introduced a question on religion. According to the census, there were 5,281 Jews by religion and 3,578 Jews by ethnicity, with the latter figure including Central Asian [Bukharan], Georgian, Mountain Jews, and Krymchaks.[77] Yet of those recorded as Jews by religion, fully 37 percent were recorded by ethnicity as Kazakhs, and 27 percent as Russian. Another inexplicable finding concerned the age of Jews by religion: less than 11 percent were aged 65 and above. From all this, it is clear that the number of Jews by religion in this census was seriously overstated and that some people, in the main traditionally Muslim Kazakhs, were mistakenly counted as adherents to the Jewish religion.

The most comprehensive data for religious affiliation with regard to Jews were recorded in the results of the 2000 Estonian census.[78] This is the first census for which enough statistical data is available concerning apostasy. According to the 2000 Estonian census data, only 19.8 percent of Jews aged 15 and older (whose numbers totaled 1,989) were recorded as "followers of a particular faith"; of these, 11 percent stated Judaism as their religion, whereas more than 7.5 percent declared themselves to be followers of one of the branches of Christianity. More specifically, more than two-thirds of those professing Christianity belonged to the Orthodox [Christian] church (*pravoslavnye*). This is noteworthy, given that most Estonian Christians are Lutherans. One possible explanation for this anomaly is that, according to the census, more than 80 percent of Estonian Jews spoke Russian as their mother tongue. The closeness to Russian culture may explain the appeal of Russian Orthodoxy to those opting out of Judaism.

According to the 2000 Estonian census, only 38 non-Jews by ethnicity declared Judaism to be their religion, whereas 151 ethnic Jews were recorded as belonging to different branches of Christianity. Thus, the balance is clearly negative for Judaism. To be sure, none of the above-cited data can be utilized for any corrections of the core Jewish population, since approximately one-third of the Jews and one-sixth of the non-Jews either refused to answer the question regarding religious affiliation or (for technical reasons) their religious affiliation could not be determined. At the same time, data from the 2000 Estonian census clearly demonstrate erosion of the core Jewish population through apostasy.[79]

In post-Soviet Russia and Ukraine, a sampling of the Jewish population found that "over 10 percent see Christianity as most attractive."[80] Moreover, according to Elena Nosenko-Stein, many of the Jews attracted to Christianity—in particular, baptized Jews in Russia—identified themselves as being "Russian Orthodox Christian Jewish."[81] Another significant finding emerged in a study undertaken in St. Petersburg, which showed that all of the Jews (with two Jewish parents) who had converted to Christianity continued to identify themselves ethnically as Jews.[82] Given that our estimates of the core Jewish population (which, according to general definition, excludes persons of Jewish parentage who adopt another religion) are based on census data, FSU numbers with regard to core Jews are obviously somewhat overstated.

The 2002 Russian census data provided a new opportunity to update estimates of the enlarged Jewish population.[83] There is no analogous estimate based on the post-Soviet census published for any other FSU country. However, Mark Kupovetsky undertook the ambitious project of evaluating "the potential of Jewish emigration" based on an even broader definition than that defined by the Israeli Law of Return (which comprises Jews, their children and grandchildren, and all their respective spouses). Kupovetsky's category included Jews who had converted to another religion, who would be ineligible to immigrate to Israel under the provisions of the Law of Return. He produced the figures based on this definition for each FSU country for 1989 and 2003.[84] However, given the lack of much appropriate data for his computations, Kupovetsky inevitably made use of guesstimates. In addition, he did not outline the stages of his computations, which makes it difficult to judge their validity. At the same time, it is clear that the attempt to estimate the size and structure of broader categories of the Jewish population should be continued.

Conclusion

In the face of ample data pointing to a demographic collapse of Jewish population in the countries comprising the former Soviet Union, wishful thinking persists. With regard to the Russian Federation, for instance, highly inflated figures purporting to be the "real" number of Jews—ranging from 1,000,000–2,000,000 to the more fantastical figure of 10 million[85]—continue to circulate online and in the popular press, even as the number of pupils in Jewish schools and the roster of those receiving aid from Jewish charities continue to decline.[86] The problem is exacerbated when erroneous figures find their way into scholarly publications. Thus, for example, a 2002 Russian census figure of 259,000 has been presented for the total Jewish population of Russia, and it has been reported that the two largest cities, Moscow and St. Petersburg, have a Jewish population of, respectively, 148,000 and 55,200.[87] In fact, according to the officially published data of the 2002 Russian census, there are 233,596 Jews in the Russian Federation as a whole, 80,421 Jews in Moscow, and 36,650 Jews in St. Petersburg (including those recorded as Central Asian [Bukharan], Georgian, Mountain Jews, and Krymchaks).[88] The official census figures show that Moscow and St. Petersburg account for about half the total Russian Jewish population, whereas the erroneous figures show that 78 percent of Russian Jews live in these two cities. In terms of Jewish communal funding, a reliance on inaccurate data may lead to serious underfunding of provincial Jewish communities outside of Moscow and St. Petersburg.

The post-Soviet shift in data collection, in particular, the elimination of the categories of vital and migration statistics by ethnicity, has dealt a blow to Jewish demography. An especially serious consequence is the inability to obtain new information on Jewish mortality. At the same time, post-Soviet censuses have continued to collect data by ethnicity, and these provide scholars with much important information regarding Jewish age-sex structure, fertility, and nuptuality, including mixed marriage. In addition, migration statistics of receiving countries, especially those of Israel, remain of real importance. There is also a good deal of previously collected data; alongside new information, such data provide a solid basis for the continuing demographic study of Jews in the post-Soviet countries.

Notes

I am grateful to the late Leonid Darsky (of blessed memory) for stimulating interest in these problems from the start of my scholarly career, and to Uzi Rebhun for encouraging me to revisit them. I would also like to express my appreciation to Sergio DellaPergola for his advice and to Evgeny Andreev, Michael Beizer, Dmitry Bogoyavlensky, Rafi Pizov, Marina Sheps, Brian D. Silver, Shaul Stampfer, Emma Trahtenberg, Arkadi Zeltser, and Peteris Zvidrins for providing materials, information, and suggestions. Thank you to Judith Even for reading and editing an earlier draft.

1. Leonid Darsky, in conversation with the author. On Darsky, see n. 12.
2. Veniamin I. Binshtok and Sergei A. Novoselsky, *Materialy po estestvennomu dvizheniiu evreiskogo naseleniia v Evropeiskoi Rossii za 40 let (1867–1906 gg.)* (Petrograd: 1915).

3. Boris D. Brutskus, *Statistika evreiskogo naseleniia: raspredelenie po territorii, demograficheskie i kulturnye priznaki evreiskogo naseleniia po dannym perepisi 1897 g.* (St. Petersburg: 1909); see also idem, *Professionalnyi sostav evreiskogo naseleniia Rossii: po materialam pervoi vseobshchei perepisi naseleniia, proizvedennoi 28 ianvaria 1897 goda* (St. Petersburg: 1908).

4. Bronislaw Bloch, "Vital Events among the Jews in European Russia towards the End of the XIX Century," in *Papers in Jewish Demography 1977*, ed. Uziel O. Schmelz, Paul Glikson, and Sergio DellaPergola (Jerusalem: 1980), 69–81.

5. Shaul Stampfer, "Remarriage among Jews and Christians in Nineteenth-Century Eastern Europe," *Jewish History* 3, no. 2 (1988), 85–114.

6. The only exception was the 1937 Soviet census, in which a question on religion was asked. For data on religion for the Jews from this census, see Mordechai Altshuler, "Religion in the Soviet Union in the Late 1930s in the Light of Statistics," *Jews and Jewish Topics in the Soviet Union and Eastern Europe* 14, no. 1 (1991), 23–26.

7. See Mark Tolts, "The Failure of Demographic Statistics: A Soviet Response to Population Troubles," paper presented at the IUSSP XXIVth general population conference, Salvador-Bahia (Brazil), 18–24 August 2001; online at http://www.archive-iussp.org/Brazil2001/s00/S07_02_tolts.pdf (accessed 9 January 2013).

8. Mordechai Altshuler, *Soviet Jewry on the Eve of the Holocaust: A Social and Demographic Profile* (Jerusalem: 1998); see also idem (ed.), *Distribution of the Jewish Population of the USSR 1939* (Jerusalem: 1993).

9. See, for instance, Joshua Rubenstein and Ilya Altman (eds.), *The Unknown Black Book: The Holocaust in the German-Occupied Soviet Territories* (Bloomington: 2008), 383; cf. Altshuler (ed.), *Distribution of the Jewish Population of the USSR 1939*, 28, 30.

10. Mark Tolts, "Ethnicity, Religion and Demographic Change in Russia: Russians, Tatars and Jews," in *Evolution or Revolution in European Population/European Population Conference, Milano 1995*, vol. 2 (Milan: 1996), 165–179; idem, "Jews in Russia: A Century of Demographic Dynamics," *Diaspory/Diasporas* 1, no. 1 (1999), 180–198.

11. Mordechai Altshuler, *Soviet Jewry since the Second World War: Population and Social Structure* (New York: 1987); cf. the compilation of demographic data based on post-Soviet findings authored by Viacheslav Konstantinov, *Evreiskoe naselenie byvshego SSSR v XX veke* (Jerusalem: 2007), chs. 1–2.

12. See, for instance, *Skolko budet detei v sovetskoi sem'e (rezultaty obsledovaniia)*, under the direction of Leonid E. Darsky (Moscow: 1977), 23, 26–27, 76. Darsky, the chief adviser on problems of vital statistics analysis, used his influence at the Soviet Central Statistical Administration to assure that vital statistics on the Jews would continue to be collected (this evaluation is based on communications with Darsky and a number of his colleagues).

13. Leonid E. Darsky and Evgeny M. Andreev, "Vosproizvodstvo naseleniia otdelnykh natsionalnostei," *Vestnik statistiki*, no. 6 (1991), 3–10.

14. For a compilation of these indicators, which also include life expectancy for the Jews in Soviet Central Asia, see Mark Tolts, "Post-Soviet Aliyah and Jewish Demographic Transformation," paper presented at the 15th World Congress of Jewish Studies, Jerusalem, 2–6 August 2009, 17, 20; online at www.bjpa.org/Publications/details.cfm?PublicationID=11924 (accessed 4 December 2012).

15. Mark Tolts, "Demographic Trends among the Jews in the Three Slavic Republics of the Former USSR: A Comparative Analysis," in *Papers in Jewish Demography 1993*, ed. Sergio DellaPergola and Judith Even (Jerusalem: 1997), 174–175. It should be noted that no data were discovered for 1981 for any of the republics, and for 1969–1975 for Russia and Belorussia; such data may or may not exist.

16. Mark Tolts, "The Balance of Births and Deaths among Soviet Jewry," *Jews and Jewish Topics in the Soviet Union and Eastern Europe* 16, no. 2 (1992), 13–26; see also Mark Kupovetsky, "Liudskie poteri evreiskogo naseleniia v poslevoennykh granitsakh SSSR v gody Velikoi Otechestvennoi voiny," *Vestnik Evreiskogo Universiteta v Moskve* 9, no. 2 (1995), 148.

17. Goskomstat of the USSR, *Naselenie SSSR, 1988: statisticheskii ezhegodnik* (Moscow: 1989), 212–213, 222–223, 235.

18. Mark Tolts, "Mixed Marriage and Post-Soviet Aliyah," in *Jewish Intermarriage around the World*, ed. Shulamit Reinharz and Sergio DellaPergola (New Brunswick: 2009), 94, 96.

19. [Mark Kupovetsky], "Etnicheskaia demografiia sovetskogo evreistva," in *Kratkaia evreiskaia entsiklopediia*, vol. 8 (Jerusalem: 1996), cols. 300–301.

20. See, for instance, Mark Tolts, "Trends in Soviet Jewish Demography since the Second World War," in *Jews and Jewish Life in Russia and the Soviet Union*, ed. Yaacov Ro'i (London: 1995); 370–371; idem, "Demography of the Jews in the Former Soviet Union: Yesterday and Today," in *Jewish Life after the USSR*, ed. Zvi Gitelman, with Musya Glants and Marshall I. Goldman (Bloomington: 2003), 196.

21. Mark Tolts, "Demographic Trends among the Jews in the Three Slavic Republics of the Former USSR," 171–173; idem, "The Demographic Profile of the Bukharan Jews in the Late Soviet Period," in *Bukharan Jews in the 20th Century: History, Experience and Narration*, ed. Ingeborg Baldauf, Moshe Gammer, and Thomas Loy (Wiesbaden: 2008), 89–90; idem, "Demography of North Caucasian Jewry: A Note on Population Dynamics and Shifting Identity," in *Ethno-Nationalism, Islam and the State in the Caucasus: Post-Soviet Disorder*, ed. Moshe Gammer (London: 2008), 222.

22. Aleksandr A. Susokolov, *Natsionalno-smeshannye braki i sem'i v SSSR*, part 1 (Moscow: 1990), 97–99; Andrei Volkov, "Etnicheski smeshannye sem'i v SSSR: dinamika i sostav," *Vestnik statistiki* 8 (1989), 8–24. For Jewish-related data derived from this unique processing, see Tolts, "The Balance of Births and Deaths among Soviet Jewry," 22.

23. On prerevolutionary internal passports and the Jews, see Eugene M. Avrutin, *Jews and the Imperial State: Identification Politics in Tsarist Russia* (Ithaca: 2010).

24. See, for instance, Zvi Gitelman, *A Century of Ambivalence: The Jews of Russia and the Soviet Union, 1881 to the Present*, 2nd ed. (Bloomington: 2001), ch. 3.

25. Arkadii Zeltser, *Evrei sovetskoi provintsii: Vitebsk i mestechki 1917–1941* (Moscow: 2006), 182, 188.

26. See, for instance, Dominique Arel, "Fixing Ethnicity in Identity Documents: The Rise and Fall of Passport Nationality in Russia," *Canadian Review of Studies in Nationalism* 30, nos. 1–2 (2003), 130; see also David Shearer, "Elements Near and Alien: Passportization, Policing, and Identity in the Stalinist State, 1932–1952," *The Journal of Modern History* 76, no. 4 (2004), 835–881.

27. Zvi Gitelman, "Recent Demographic and Migratory Trends among Soviet Jews: Implications for Policy," *Post-Soviet Geography* 33, no. 3 (1992), 140.

28. For example, according to the 1979 census data, in the case of couples (in the Russian Federation) consisting of a Jewish husband and a Russian wife, only 6.1 percent of children under 18 were declared to be Jewish. The number was even lower (4.5 percent) in the case of children of couples consisting of a Russian husband and a Jewish wife (Tolts, "The Balance of Births and Deaths among Soviet Jewry," 22).

29. On Soviet ethnic statistics in general, see Iurii V. Arutiunian, Leokadiia M. Drobizheva, Valerii S. Kondrat'ev, and Aleksandr A. Susokolov, *Etnosotsiologiia* (Moscow: 1984), ch. 2; Galina A. Bondarskaya, "Nationality in Population Statistics in the U.S.S.R.," in *Challenges of Measuring an Ethnic World: Proceedings of the Joint Canada-United States Conference on the Measurement of Ethnicity* (Ottawa: 1993), 333–361; Brian D. Silver, "The Ethnic and Language Dimensions in Russian and Soviet Censuses," in *Research Guide to the Russian and Soviet Censuses*, ed. Ralph S. Clem (Ithaca: 1986), 70–97.

30. Some unwed Jewish mothers may have reported the ethnicity of the child's father as non-Jewish even if this was not the case. Such instances would obviously have been a rather marginal phenomenon.

31. Ward W. Kingkade, "Content, Organization, and Methodology in Recent Soviet Population Censuses," *Population and Development Review* 15, no. 1 (1989), 123–138.

32. See Benjamin Pinkus, *The Jews of the Soviet Union: The History of a National Minority* (New York: 1988), 89, 261.

33. See, for instance, Altshuler, *Soviet Jewry since the Second World War*, 21–24; Zvi Gitelman, "The Reconstruction of Community and Jewish Identity in Russia," *East European Jewish Affairs* 24, no. 2 (1994), 40; Mark Kupovetsky, "K otsenke chislennosti evreev i

demograficheskogo potentsiala evreiskoi obshchiny v SSSR i postsovetskikh gosudarstvakh v 1989–2003 gg.," *Evroaziatskii evreiskii ezhegodnik 5765 (2004/2005 god)* (Kiev: 2005), 82.

34. Uziel O. Schmelz, "New Evidence on Basic Issues in the Demography of Soviet Jews," *Jewish Journal of Sociology* 16, no. 2 (1974), 209–223.

35. Uziel O. Schmelz and Sergio DellaPergola, "World Jewish Population, 1993," *American Jewish Year Book* 95 (1995), 481.

36. Yoel Florsheim and Dorith Tal, "A Correction to the Jewish Population Data in the 1989 Soviet Census," *Jews in Eastern Europe* 30, no. 2 (1996), 18–23.

37. Mark Tolts, "Recent Jewish Emigration and Population Decline in Russia," *Jews in Eastern Europe* 35, no. 1 (1998), 12.

38. On this model, see for instance, Colin Newell, *Methods and Models in Demography* (New York: 1988), 120–126.

39. Cited in Mark Tolts, "Jewish Marriages in the USSR: A Demographic Analysis," *East European Jewish Affairs* 22, no. 2 (1992), 5.

40. Tolts, "The Failure of Demographic Statistics," 9–10.

41. Mark Tolts, "Ethnic Composition of Kazakhstan on the Eve of the Second World War: Re-Evaluation of the 1939 Soviet Census Results," *Central Asian Survey* 25, nos. 1–2 (2006), 143–148.

42. At the same time, such manipulation lowered the number of Jews in those places from which the filled-in census forms were taken. For instance, one may assume that 1,500 Jews were subtracted from the results for Komi autonomous republic. The official results of the census for this autonomous republic included data on only 570 Jews, that is, 2.6 times less than the estimated number of Jewish prisoners whose census forms were redistributed from there (Mark Tolts, "Figures that Came in from the Cold," *Jews in Eastern Europe* 25, no. 3 [1994], 82).

43. See Oleg N. Nikiforov, "Istochniki dannykh o naselenii," in *Demografiia i statistika naseleniia*, ed. Irina I. Yeliseeva (Moscow: 2006), 57–113.

44. See Sergio DellaPergola, "Jewish Demography," in *The Modern Jewish Experience: A Reader's Guide*, ed. Jack Wertheimer (New York: 1993), 277.

45. Mark Tolts, "Jewish Demography of the Former Soviet Union," in *Papers in Jewish Demography 1997*, ed. Sergio DellaPergola and Judith Even (Jerusalem: 2001), 112.

46. Ibid.; for an alternative estimate that attempts to cover all persons with Jewish parentage, see Aleksandr Sinelnikov, "Nekotorye demograficheskie posledstviia assimiliatsii evreev v SSSR," *Vestnik Evreiskogo Universiteta v Moskve* 5, no. 1 (1994), 95.

47. Tolts, "Jewish Demography of the Former Soviet Union," 123.

48. Ibid., 138.

49. Vladimir M. Shkolnikov, Evgueni M. Andreev, Jon Anson, and France Meslé, "The Peculiar Pattern of Mortality of Jews in Moscow, 1993–95," *Population Studies* 58, no. 3 (2004), 311–329.

50. On the microcensus, see Andrei G. Volkov, *Methodology and Organization of the 1994 Microcensus in Russia* (Groningen: 1999).

51. Mark Tolts, "The Interrelationship between Emigration and the Socio-Demographic Profile of Russian Jewry," in *Russian Jews on Three Continents*, ed. Noah Lewin-Epstein, Yaacov Ro'i, and Paul Ritterband (London: 1997), 151–155, 176.

52. Evgeny Andreev, "Jews in Russia's Households (Based on the 1994 Microcensus)," in DellaPergola and Even (eds.), *Papers in Jewish Demography 1997*, 141–159; Evgeny Soroko, "Jewish Households in Russia according to the 1994 Microcensus," in ibid., 161–179.

53. Mark Tolts, "Jews in the Russian Federation: A Decade of Demographic Decline," *Jews in Eastern Europe* 40, no. 3 (1999), 13. For an alternative estimate, see Aleksandr Sinelnikov, "Pochemu ischezaet rossiiskoe evreistvo?" *Vestnik Evreiskogo Universiteta v Moskve* 12, no. 2 (1996), 51–67.

54. Sener Akturk, "Passport Identification and Nation-Building in Post-Soviet Russia," *Post-Soviet Affairs* 26, no. 4 (2010), 319, 325.

55. Sobranie zakonodatelstva Rossiiskoi Federatsii 28 (13 June 1998), 6296–6297.

56. See, for instance, Goskomstat of Russia, *The Demographic Yearbook of Russia, 2000* (Moscow: 2000), 55.

57. Just before the loss of coverage by ethnicity in the Russian birth statistics became decisive (in the framework of a special processing of the birth certificates of 2002), data regarding premarital conceptions and out-of-wedlock births among children born to Jewish women in the Russian Federation were computed. See Mark Tolts, "Contemporary Trends in Family Formation among the Jews in Russia," *Jews in Russia and Eastern Europe* 57, no. 2 (2006), 10.

58. These data were analyzed in detail in Mark Tolts, "Statistical Analysis of Aliyah and Jewish Emigration from Russia," in *The World in the Mirror of International Migration*, ed. Vladimir A. Iontsev (Moscow: 2002), 171–185.

59. Goskomstat of Russia, *Rekomendatsii po zapolneniiu pervichnykh dokumentov statisticheskogo ucheta migrantov* (Moscow: 1997), 5.

60. Ibid.

61. Anatoly G. Vishnevsky (ed.), *Naselenie Rossii, 2006* (Moscow: 2008), 245.

62. For detailed analysis of the 2002 Russian census results for the Jewish population, see Mark Tolts, "The Post-Soviet Jewish Population in Russia and the World," *Jews in Russia and Eastern Europe* 52, no. 1 (2004), 37–47.

63. Ibid., 45–46.

64. Nikita Mkrtchian, "Vliianie migratsii na izmenenie etnicheskogo sostava naseleniia Rossii i ee regionov: predvaritelnaiia otsenka itogov Perepisi-2002," in *Etnicheskaia situatsia i konflikty v gosudarstvakh SNG i Baltii. Ezhegodnyi doklad 2004*, ed. Valery Tishkov and Enena Filippova (Moscow: 2005), 53.

65. Aleksandr Sinelnikov, "Vozmozhna li korrektsiia dannykh perepisi 2002 goda o chislennosti evreev v Rossii?" *Evroaziatskii evreiskii ezhegodnik 5766 (2005/2006 god)* (Kiev: 2005), 218–231; his adjusted estimate appears on p. 227.

66. Mark Tolts, "Demographic Trends among the Jews in the Three Slavic Republics of the Former USSR," 149.

67. Mark Tolts, "Recent Jewish Emigration and Population Decline in Russia," 10–13.

68. Florsheim and Tal, "A Correction to the Jewish Population Data in the 1989 Soviet Census," 21–22. Sinelikov does not mention this article, perhaps because he was unaware of it.

69. Sinelnikov, "Vozmozhna li korrektsiia dannykh perepisi 2002 goda o chislennosti evreev v Rossii?" 227.

70. Central Statistical Bureau of Latvia, *Demography 2000* (Riga: 2000), 38.

71. Brian D. Silver, *Nationality and Language in the New Censuses of the Baltic States* (East Lansing: 2002), 21–25; online at www.msu.edu/~bsilver/BalticCensus2000.pdf (accessed 4 December 2012).

72. Daniel A. Kronenfeld, "The Effects of Interethnic Contact on Ethnic Identity: Evidence from Latvia," *Post-Soviet Affairs* 21, no. 3 (2005), 267.

73. Kupovetsky, "K otsenke chislennosti evreev i demograficheskogo potentsiala evreiskoi obshchiny v SSSR i postsovetskikh gosudarstvakh v 1989–2003 gg.," 86.

74. United Nations Statistics Division, *Demographic Yearbook Special Census Topics 2000 Round*, Volume 2b—*Ethnocultural Characteristics*, Tables 4 and 6; online at http://unstats. un.org/unsd/demographic/products/dyb/dybcens.htm (accessed 4 December 2012).

75. National Bureau of Statistics of the Republic of Moldova, *Population Census, 2004*, vol. 1 (Chisinau: 2006), 301, 476.

76. Interstate Statistical Committee of the CIS, *Results of Population Censuses in the Countries of the Commonwealth of Independent States (2000 Round): Statistical Abstract* (Moscow: 2006), 268, 271.

77. Our analysis of these data is based on the (fortunately comprehensive) publication of the 2009 Kazakhstan census results on ethnicity and religion: The Agency of Statistics of the Republic of Kazakhstan, *Natsionalnyi sostav, veroispovedanie i vladenie iazykami v Respublike Kazakhstan: Itogi Natsionalnoi perepisi naseleniia 2009 goda v Respublike Kazakhstan* (Astana: 2010).

78. For a detailed presentation of data, see Mark Tolts, "Post-Soviet Jewish Demography, 1989–2004," in *Revolution, Repression and Revival: The Soviet Jewish Experience*, ed. Zvi Gitelman and Yaacov Ro'i (Lanham: 2007), 288–290.

79. On apostasy among Jews in the late Soviet period, see Judith Deutsch Kornblatt, *Doubly Chosen: Jewish Identity, the Soviet Intelligentsia, and the Russian Orthodox Church* (Madison: 2004).

80. Zvi Gitelman, "Thinking about Being Jewish in Russia and Ukraine," in Gitelman (ed.), *Jewish Life after the USSR*, 51.

81. Elena Nosenko-Stein, "Aliens in an Alien World: Paradoxes of Jewish–Christian Identity in Contemporary Russia," *East European Jewish Affairs* 40, no. 1 (2010), 19–41; see also Anna Shternshis, "Kaddish in a Church: Perceptions of Orthodox Christianity among Moscow Elderly Jews in the Early Twenty-First Century," *Russian Review* 66, no. 2 (2007), 273–294.

82. Boris Wiener, "Konstruirovanie sovremennoi ethnokonfessionalnoi identichnosti: ot bezveriia k vere chuzhogo naroda," *Diaspory/Diasporas* 6, no. 1 (2004), 196.

83. Tolts, "Contemporary Trends in Family Formation among the Jews in Russia," 16.

84. Kupovetsky, "K otsenke chislennosti evreev i demograficheskogo potentsiala evreiskoi obshchiny v SSSR i postsovetskikh gosudarstvakh v 1989–2003 gg.," 78–91.

85. See, for instance, [Anonymous], "Evrei 'vozvrashchaiutsia v Rossiiu," published on BBC Russian Service website (25 October 2004); online at http://news.bbc.co.uk/hi/russian/russia/newsid_3952000/3952609.stm (accessed 5 December 2012). See also Anna Rudnitskaya, "Fishing for Jews in Russia's Muddy Waters," *JTA* (23 February 2010), online at www.jta.org/news/article/2010/02/23/1010779/fishing-for-jews-in-russias-muddy-waters (accessed 5 Dec. 2012).

86. See, for instance, Zvi Gitelman, "Do Jewish Schools Make a Difference in the Former Soviet Union?" *East European Jewish Affairs* 37, no. 3 (2007), 377–398; Betsy Gidwitz, "Post-Soviet Jewry on the Cusp of Its Third Decade—Part 2," *Changing Jewish Communities* 68 (15 June 2011), online at www.bjpa.org/Publications/details.cfm?PublicationID=11906 (accessed 5 December 2012). See also Michael Beizer, "Simon Dubnov's Theory of Autonomism and Its Practicability in the CIS," in *Writer and Warrior. Simon Dubnov: Historian and Public Figure*, ed. Avraham Greenbaum, Israel Bartal and Dan Haruv (Jerusalem: 2010), 87*–102*.

87. See, for instance, *Istoriia evreev v Rossii: Uchebnik* (Moscow: 2007), 712; Gershon David Hundert (ed.), *The YIVO Encyclopedia of Jews in Eastern Europe*, vol. 2 (New Haven: 2008), 1205.

88. Rosstat, *Itogi Vserossiiskoi perepisi naseleniia 2002 goda*, vol. 4, part 1 (Moscow: 2004; CD-ROM Edition), Tables 1 and 2.

Latin American Jewish Social Studies: The Evolution of a Cross-disciplinary Field

Judit Bokser Liwerant
(UNIVERSIDAD NACIONAL AUTONÓMA DE MEXICO)

Latin American Jewish social studies has evolved along a highly diversified conceptual and methodological spectrum, with new challenges arising from developments
in the convergent disciplines as well as from transformations in Jewish life and in
Latin American society. Following the prevailing pattern of social sciences, it has
attained a high level of specialization and makes use of increasingly sophisticated
investigatory tools and techniques. At the same time, growing cross-disciplinary
interaction in the field—for instance, between history and sociology, political science and anthropology, psychology and economics, diaspora, ethnic and regional
studies, international relations, linguistics and literature, sociology of religions,
Jewish studies and contemporary Jewry, demography and semiotics—gives rise to a
good deal of complexity, as does the far from uniform path of regional development
in Latin America and an awareness of the global and transnational nature of Jewish
existence.

Jewish social studies and research were initially driven and defined by developments from abroad, which gradually were adjusted, contested, and refined. Resting
on the dual foundations of Jewish studies (centered on the social and cultural collective experience) and regional studies (focusing on Latin America), Latin American
Jewish studies has faced numerous obstacles in gaining a firm foothold in the academic and organized Jewish world. Until recently, Latin American culture stressed
"universal" concerns and homogeneous national identity rather than promoting the
study of particular and collective belonging, with liberals and nationalists alike seeking to downplay minority cultures and legacies; this attitude permeated the academic
milieu as well. Today, however, as part of the process of globalization, political and
cultural transformations in the region favor pluralism, and there is increased interest
in identity politics. Thus, while the transnational character of Jewish life acted as an
initial stimulus to the field, the growing visibility and legitimacy of Jewish life in
Latin America provides an additional incentive for research.

Notwithstanding its current growth, the field evidences strong disciplinary imbal-
ances, in part reflecting shifting theoretical conceptions and in part structural and
institutional constraints. As has been the general tendency of social sciences in Latin

America, Jewish social studies has developed within the framework of changing and often conflicting external expectations and demands.[1] The field's importance for communal life has been underestimated, and it is only recently that Jewish leaders have voiced a (belated) awareness of its relevance and importance for developing strategies and programs aimed at Latin American Jewish communities.

A Non-Linear Path of Development

Pioneering efforts in Latin American Jewish studies took the form of comparative studies of contemporary Jewry. The leading assumption was that local Jewish realities needed to be explained and understood through a systematic contrast with parallel processes elsewhere in the Jewish world. Such research sought to underscore the global and civilizational character of the Jewish world. In this larger context, Latin America presented a particular case or modality. During the late 1950s and the 1960s, the Institute of Contemporary Jewry at the Hebrew University of Jerusalem established the basis for such comparative research, the goal being to "outline, by means of comparison, some disparate and common elements in the three main Jewish centers in the Western Hemisphere [United States, Canada and Argentina]," emphasizing broad organizational issues as well as the study of representative institutions.[2] These first steps, led by Moshe Davis at the Institute of Contemporary Jewry, were followed by a second phase that featured frontier society as a basic analytical tool.

In 1983, political scientists Daniel J. Elazar and Peter Medding published *Jewish Communities in Frontier Societies*, a systematic study of Argentine, Australian, and South African Jewry.[3] "Frontier society" referred both to general societies and to their Jewish communities. The latter were frontiers in the sense of their being located far from the "motherland" in Europe or in the Middle East; this distance accounted for the persistence of cultural codes and patterns that were sometimes no longer present in the countries of provenance. The political-organizational approach that was developed by Elazar and Medding nourished fruitful comparative research with a strong typological character. Emphasis was placed on the development of Jewish institutions and on factors influencing community-building. A central theme was the process of institutional adaptation to the surrounding society, as influenced by key conditions such as the societies' level of development and the rhythm and profile of Jewish migratory trends.

In asserting that the Latin American experience differed from that of North America, these analyses stressed an incomplete process of integration that hindered the construction of strong and publicly recognized Jewish communities. The main obstacle, so it was argued, was the Catholic ethno-religious character of Latin American countries and the concomitant search for a homogeneous national identity, which marginalized from its national narrative those groups that were alien to its Hispanic/Catholic core. Other factors accounting for Latin American Jews' limited integration in the surrounding society were the socioeconomic profile of the Jewish communities, their high institutional density, and their intense internal socio-political dynamics. The autonomous character of Latin American Jewish communities was also explained by the significant role played by Israeli and Zionist organizations—far more central than in North America or Europe.[4] The comparative approach was largely based on a prevailing paradigm of middle-range theories of modernization, which posited that modernity, as it developed first in Europe and thereafter in the United States, would ultimately become the path for all other societies. Models that would apply to the particular characteristics of Latin America and its Jewish communities were lacking, and Shmuel Noah Eisenstadt's concept of "multiple modernities," which questioned the premise that cultural programs and institutional constellations of western modernity would necessarily dominate all modern societies, was not yet known.[5] Notwithstanding the shared characteristics and global trends of the Jewish world, Eisenstadt's pluralistic approach is a useful tool in analyzing the diverse trajectories of Latin American societies and their Jewish communities.

Although the comparative approach enabled significant data collection, the knowledge it generated was mainly descriptive. The lack of further theoretical elaborations limited its breadth and heuristic potential. However, the initial research on Jewish communities represented the first systematic and academic efforts to study Latin American Jewish life from a world perspective. Over time, there evolved a new orientation toward the study of both regional and national cases, combined with a global Jewish perspective.

The search for interconnections between societies and their Jewish communities served as the organizing principle of the new historical studies led by Haim Avni in the 1970s. His studies pivoted on an analysis of integration patterns that regulated the visibility and legitimacy of Jewish life in Latin America.[6] Avni drew a distinction between countries comprising "Euro-America" and those of "Indo-America," according to the impact of immigration on each country's population profile and ethnic composition, thereby enabling the analysis of the social role of minorities, in particular the Jews. Such categorization of the societies' ethnic and cultural composition provided a starting point for studying a diversity of political, economic, and historical trajectories. Thus, in "Euro-American" societies such as Argentina and Uruguay, massive immigration changed the socio-ethnic profile and gave rise to multiethnic societies that granted civil equality and constitutional rights to members of minorities—though this did not translate into the legitimization of minority cultures within the dominant culture. In "Indo-American" societies experiencing limited immigration, such as Mexico, Peru, or Ecuador, the original and *mestizo* ethnic composition of the population worked even more against the acceptance of diversity. Avni's comparative perspective focused on what was defined as the main shared dilemmas of Jewish life in Latin America: a lack of public legitimacy; limits on the right to be different; and dependency on international Jewish organizations. In addition, the central role played by the state of Israel in organized Jewish life was stressed.[7]

Communal diversity emerged as a major theme in the dominant historical approach focusing on the structure of Latin American Jewish communities. A variety of studies offered detailed descriptions of specific communities while at the same time examining their links with the international organized Jewish world and its institutions. This research model was applied globally as well as in connection with specific locales within the region, taking into account both migratory processes and sub-ethnic patterns of organization—for instance, the diverse Sephardi and Ashkenazi communities. Research dealing with each community's relationship with Israel was extensively developed, analyzing and also challenging the dominant assumption concerning unidirectional ties between a periphery diaspora and Israel.[8]

Simultaneously, the perspective advanced by Daniel Elazar combined political science with Jewish traditional thought, emphasizing the importance of organizational relationships, power distribution, and patterns of action within the Jewish collective. Highlighting federalism as the dominant model, it defined community as a multidimensional matrix with an extensive network of communication, in which interacting institutions share cultural patterns and work under a common leadership.[9] In this framework, political links of Jewish communities with their surrounding societies are analyzed in terms of how a given local, regional, or national Jewish leadership promotes group interests. This perspective is especially suited to research on Latin American Jewish life, which is structured around the communal rather than the congregational model. It also accommodates sub-ethnicities and, more significantly (at least in the Ashkenazi sector) varying political ideologies, parties, and organizations. In fact, the region provides a test case for approaches that privilege the *kehilah* as the main analytical focus.

Another advance in Latin American Jewish studies came about in the early 1980s, with Judith Elkin's research and establishment of the Latin American Jewish Studies Association (LAJSA) at the University of Michigan. Her book, *Jews of the Latin American Republics*, along with a collection of essays she co-edited with Gilbert Merkx, provided a systematic comparison between United States Jewry ("the North") and Latin American Jewry ("the South").[10] Elkin also analyzed exogenous factors influencing these different Jewries, such as the (Latin American) Hispanic legacy with its Catholic and medieval elements. Converging with previous approaches, her analysis pointed to the limited and partial integration of Jewish immigrants in Latin America, with greater integration in the cultural domain than in the political arena. In her view, Jewish loyalty was continually being questioned and Jews were invariably regarded as foreigners; consequently, Latin American Jews lacked "civic assimilation." Moreover, according to Elkin, they were essentially "history's orphans," with the vision of the South continually compared with an ideal-typical understanding of western processes. Whether due to "history by analogy," or the uncritical adoption of prevailing theories, the hierarchical conception of the world that represented the North as its model limited the understanding of the singularity of Jewish life in Latin America.[11]

Although the 1980s and 1990s witnessed several regional efforts to develop social research, mainly in the framework of communal structures such as the Center for Social Studies at the Asociación Mutual Israelita Argentina (AMIA), local communities did not follow suit. In line with a general tendency in Latin America, the Jewish leadership did not value empirical knowledge as a tool for policy-making. Paradoxically, even though the Jewish educational system was well developed, Jewish studies and research at the university level did not achieve a significant presence and started to emerge only at a handful of universities.

Expanding Disciplines and Approaches

As noted, Latin American Jewish studies received its first impetus through research carried out by the Institute of Contemporary Jewry in Jerusalem. Socio-demographic studies sponsored by the Institute gradually evolved from efforts to describe the main trends and characteristics of the Jews toward a more complex appraisal of the inter-action between Jewish communities and the surrounding societies. For example, in his analysis of socio-demography in the Latin American region, Sergio DellaPergola notes the relevance of a global perspective in identifying factors influencing the main (and changing) characteristics of the Jewish population.[12] Roberto Bachi was the first to address the need for tested data on Jewish demography, social structures, and iden-tity, both in order to conduct research and to formulate communal policies.[13] Through the Institute's division of Jewish demography and statistics, he actively promoted the collection of systematic data on Latin American Jewry. Another member of the Institute, Uziel Oscar Schmelz, began a critical revision of Jewish population esti-mates, which until then had been based on the assumption of continuing annual growth.[14]

By the 1970s, demographic research on Latin American Jewry was well estab-lished, thanks to the availability of a number of national censuses as well as data provided by Jewish community sources. An important technical and analytic turn-ing point was marked by Schmelz and DellaPergola's detailed and rigorous analy-sis of the 1960 census of Argentina. In looking at the country's main demographic trends, Schmelz and DellaPergola noted differentiation of its population's behavior at the detailed level of local geographical divisions, social and economic stratifica-tion, and changes in migratory patterns.[15] Trends such as low fertility rates, popu-lation aging, and the possible reversion of international migration patterns were also investigated and brought into the public realm of knowledge.[16] The interaction between relevant knowledge, advanced research methods, and empirical investiga-tion enabled a radical shift in socio-demographic research. The growing realization that information obtained through national censuses was often incomplete or seri-ously distorted led communal bodies to initiate their own studies of local Jewish populations.

The increasingly sophisticated level of methodological research also prompted theoretical and practical debates that reflected more general processes in the Jewish world—as illustrated in the demographic debate in the United States—as well as local realities and concerns.[17] Adding complexity to Jewish population studies was the fact that notions of identity and belonging were shifting, as shown in a number of more recent studies. In Argentina, research has focused on the Jewish population both in the Buenos Aires metropolitan area and in major provincial regions.[18] Some of these studies have shed light on the critical issue of changing parameters of Jewish identity and the mobile borders of belonging, especially in communities marked by decreasing rates of affiliation and high levels of exogamy. Ascription and self-ascrip-tion, identity and normative criteria, subjectivity, and institutional definitions have become part of the ongoing discussion. The contested nature of the subject is ex-pressed, for instance, in proposals to approach the issue of exogamy by moving the focus of analysis from individuals' family origins to families' self-ascription.

In Brazil, demographic research on organized Jewish life, social interaction, pat-terns of exogamy, and communal affiliation has revealed changing components of ethnicity in this multiethnic society.[19] In Mexico, a formative socio-demographic study was carried out in 1991 under the guidance of DellaPergola and Susana Lerner. Later updating of the data was handled directly by Jewish institutions, without academic involvement.[20] Other communities in countries such as Chile, Uruguay, and Venezuela have also sponsored socio-demographic studies in order to assess their changing profiles—reflecting local, regional, and global processes as well as longer-term historical constraints and opportunities presented by new and significant migratory processes.[21]

Historically, the growth of Latin American Jewry resulted from large-scale immigration waves. In recent decades, there has been a reversal, with about 150,000 Jews from Latin America migrating to places such as North America and Israel. Research has been undertaken on the rates of emigration and exogamy and the impact of both on organized Jewish life in Latin American communities. Uruguay and Colombia, for instance, experienced a sustained population decline; Brazil, Mexico, and (especially) Venezuela had varying degrees of growth followed by decline.[22] Panama remains the only country in Latin America that has significantly increased its Jewish population since 1970. The demographic profile of Jewish populations in Mexico and Venezuela has been more stable relative to other countries both because of more traditional socio-demographic patterns and because of an influx of Jews migrating from other parts of Latin America. In Mexico, the average level of affiliation remains at about 80 percent, in contrast with Argentina, where the average affiliation rate has declined to around 50 percent.[23]

Demography is probably the area that reflects in most visible and acute terms the relations and tensions between meta-theoretical assumptions, scientific knowledge and data, and public communal interests. For many years, Latin American Jewish communal leaders were interested in promoting a public image of continual growth, not only because this enhanced the status of the Jewish community vis-à-vis the society at large but also because their capability to provide services depended on international Jewish institutions such as the Jewish Agency that allocated resources based on population.

The dialectical relationship between demographic findings and public narratives persisted in the communal discourse and in interactions between Jews and non-Jews. The general perception of a numerically larger Jewish presence was due in part to the vibrancy of Latin American Jewish life. Eventually, as noted, socio-demographic findings regarding the drop in Jewish population were acknowledged not only by scholars but also by Jewish communal organizations, with the latter reorienting their priorities.

The changing character of Jewish communities and identities has also acquired a prominent place in the new research agenda. Part of this agenda is directed toward what is perceived as a twofold process of individualization and transformation of the organized Jewish communities. The growing number of non-affiliated Jews, especially in the Southern Cone (comprising Argentina, Brazil, Chile, Paraguay, and Uruguay), gives rise to questions connected with definitions of Jewishness and criteria of belonging. Debate is taking place both among scholars and within the Latin American Jewish community regarding the interaction between culture and ethnicity, religion and secularity, religious currents and conversion, and institutional affiliation versus non-affiliated options. In this regard, one should underscore the need for historical perspective on the transformations that are taking place. For instance, the argument claiming that research has concentrated exclusively on the formally constituted community while ignoring non-affiliated Jews does not take into account the methodology that initially built representative samples, nor the historical processes that modified the size and growth of the organized and affiliated Jewish world, nor the fact that percentages of affiliated versus non-affiliated Jews have changed over time.[24]

Growing social interactions have also led to an expansion of comparative studies that cover non-Jewish groups. Such research, variously characterized by valuable insights and reductive analyses, often highlights the singularity of historical connections between ethnicity and dispersion, as expressed, for instance, in the concept of "archetypal diasporas" (generally referring to that of Jews but also to that of the Armenians) or the functional formulation shared by various ethnic collectives falling into the category of "middle ground" groups.[25] Cultural attributes, internal cohesion, and organizational patterns, as well as objective visibility, have played a crucial role in the differential impact of external conditions on minorities, and specifically on Jews.

In the field of Jewish identity research, comparative approaches have fluctuated between those that stress structural factors and those that focus on instrumental, cultural, or symbolic dimensions. Although there are evident advantages in broadening the topics and referents of the research on Jews, the ideational motives and methodological weakness of some of these approaches come to the fore when they exclude parallel and systematic comparisons with Jewish life in other national, regional, and world experiences. It is precisely the interaction between the national, diaspora, and transnational dimensions of the Jewish condition that makes it a unique and universal case study.[26]

Certain scholarly work, while incorporating the diaspora-transnational analytical perspective, nonetheless privileges the ethnic category within the national framework. Raanan Rein illustrates this school of thought, which is centered on processes of integration by ethnic groups—Jews, Arabs, and others—into the nation. Although he characterizes Jewish communities as diasporas, his main focus is on defining local/national borders of Jews' collective identity; that is, as Argentine-Jewish, Mexican-Jewish, Brazilian-Jewish, or Jewish Latin American, rejecting the identity categorization of Latin American Jews. His critique of the historiography on Latin American Judaism largely questions the global character of the Jewish condition and thereby emphasizes the category of "ethnic group" over "ethno-national diaspora." Even though Rein rightfully characterizes Latin American Jews through hyphenated identities, the tensions between national and transnational identities are downplayed; instead, Rein's work highlights the fluidity of interactions between these two spheres.

Such arguments, which underscore the national realm as the main identity referent, seem to replicate the traditional theoretical assumptions of liberalism, namely, its expectation that all attributes of citizenship are to be subsumed in a national identity, with the public sphere (the universal) prevailing over the private (the particular) or the communal. This stance misses the point that collective membership, specifically with regard to the Jews—which includes ethnic, civic, and national layers of belongingness—has been informed by a shared and unique tension between being equal/being different.

The complex tensions and negotiations between ethnicity and the nation require a conceptual lens wider than Rein's. Rather than questioning the exceptionalism of the Jewish diaspora, Rein assumes that "transnational ethnicity is not necessarily an identity component with a heavier weight than the national identity."[27] Further, his analysis gives rise to questioning the relevance of ancestors' place of birth or the significance (or symbolic centrality) of an imaginary homeland. In our case, it challenges the prevailing Zionist identity of Latin American Jews and their links with Israel; the commitments of the latter toward its diasporas; and the recognition that there may be more than one "center" for ethnic communities outside the borders of their national state of residence.

The Institutionalization of Latin American Jewish Studies

As has been seen, Latin American Jewish social studies and research underwent a slow process of institutionalization in the academic world. Two professional associations contributed to the field's expansion: the Israeli Association of Latin American Researchers (AMILAT), established in 1975 at the Institute of Contemporary Jewry,[28] and the aforementioned U.S.-based Latin American Jewish Studies Association (LAJSA). Whereas AMILAT has emphasized the relevance of Judaic studies to advance regional knowledge, LAJSA has given priority to Latin American studies as the theoretical/regional framework.[29] Differences between the research developed by AMILAT and LAJSA are not only or even mainly theoretical and conceptual, but also result from diverse patterns and degrees of institutionalization.[30]

In the 1990s, following an increasingly dominant path of cultural studies dealing with the literature of minorities, Latin American Jewish studies in the United States expanded mainly in the literary area. This trend was accelerated by courses offered in university departments of Spanish and Portuguese literature. As has been correctly underscored, the main underlying premises of literary studies reflect a North American mode of academic discourse, as expressed by concepts such as diaspora, exile, immigration, antisemitism, assimilation and *mestizaje*—"living in the hyphen."[31] In this fashion, ethnic and cultural studies overshadow other theoretical and methodological approaches while projecting the dominance of imagined "Latino" and "Jewish" worlds in literary narratives. Radicalized constructivist approaches to ethnicity and identity are expressed in the questioning of concepts such as Jew, Jews, and Jewishness in order to "denaturalize" their meaning and to challenge alleged essentialist assumptions.[32] Attention has also been paid to multicultural motifs in literary works by Latin American Jews and in the function of Jews as a litmus test for cultural difference and multiculturalism—areas that partially parallel the cultural production of North American Jews and their place in general society. Literary studies have become an important point of entry to the research of Jewish life and identities. New generations of scholars have entered the field, a situation that both reflects and defines the growing influence of Latin American culture in the United States.

Various recent studies have focused on interactions between national and transnational aspects of identity among Latin American Jews in the United States. The complexities of identity are manifold: alongside a sense of continued "belongingness" to the Latino (Hispanic) world, there are clearly felt differences. The essential interplay between difference vis-à-vis the Latino/Hispanic migratory world and vis-à-vis the American Jewish community—and other groups of immigrants—marks a new reality. Additional disciplinary approaches are required in order to reconsider the transformation of the concept of Hispanic/Latino categorization and the place of Hispanic culture in the construction of a new transnational identity of Latin American Jews in the United States.[33]

Meanwhile, the number of academic courses in Latin American universities has been increasing apace, and research has also gradually been expanded. This is exemplified by institutions such as the Center for Judaic Studies at the universities of Sao Paolo and Rio de Janeiro, in Brazil; the Judaic Studies Center at the University of Chile; the Judaic studies program at Iberoamericana University and Universidad Hebraica, in Mexico; and in Argentina, among others, the Tres de Febrero University and more recently the Núcleo de Estudios Judaicos at the Instituto de Estudios Económicos y Sociales (IDES). In Israel, too, Latin American Jewish studies have expanded and diversified, expressing bifurcation, oscillation, and attempts to build convergences between Judaic studies and Latin American studies.

Traditionally, Latin American Jewish studies have been marked by an emphasis on history. Some of the research has been comparative in nature—for instance, that focusing on Latin American immigration policies and the role of rescue during the Holocaust. In contrast, the proliferation of research on antisemitism has focused less on comparisons within and/or outside the continent. Thus, historical and sociopolitical studies of European fascism and its impact on nationalist and populist Latin American regimes (1930s–1950s) have centered on specific national settings in their examination of ideology and social history. Attention has also been channeled to the creation of quantitative indexes that enable comparative historical research, based on the periodic reports published by the Stephen Roth Institute for the Study of Contemporary Antisemitism and Racism at Tel Aviv University and the Vidal Sassoon International Center for the Study of Antisemitism (SICSA) at the Hebrew University. However, additional in-depth conceptualization and theoretical formulations are required to address the issue of antisemitism in the region. Both the Centro de Estudios Sociales (CES-DAIA) in Argentina and Tribuna Israelita in Mexico have published periodic reports on antisemitic incidents that also include socio-political analyses.

Studies on antisemitism have become part of a broader spectrum of investigation dealing with societal parameters of inclusion and exclusion. This perspective considers the interfacing between national, social, and political antisemitism. Diffuse and latent prejudice in Latin America, which is present both on the structural level and in the (officially frowned upon) rhetoric of individuals and collective sectors, is yet to be identified by serious studies. The historical course of this prejudice, which does not necessarily translate into discriminatory practices, needs to be contextualized within each country's political culture.

At the same time, concern has been voiced with regard to an excessive focus on antisemitism as a primary characteristic of the continent—against a simplistic and reductionist identification of Latin America with intolerance and anti-Jewish displays.[34] This critique calls for more balanced and nuanced distinctions between different times, places, and modalities of antisemitism. As noted, we still face the challenge of linking standardized criteria (such as those provided by the aforementioned periodic reports) with comprehensive theoretical approaches that account for changing meanings of antisemitism.

Political regimes have posed diverse challenges to scholars focusing their studies on collective action and the political practices of community leaders and individual members. Authoritarian and military regimes in the Southern Cone have been analyzed from different perspectives—communal and civil demands, the role of actors, the behavior of individuals and communities, and the alliances and place of the organized Jewish world—emphasizing the wide political and ideological spectrum of local, provincial, and national political action.[35] This research has been bolstered by newly available archival material.[36]

As a younger generation of scholars enters the field, the debate has widened to include postmodern discourse. The traditional hard-core components of Jewish identity and ethnicity have been challenged, while the validity of the concept of Jewish peoplehood has been questioned. Although such debate is not exclusive to the Latin American context, it acquires a more acute and singular relevance in this region, given the fact that in Latin America, the modern and the post-modern coexist with pre-modern conditions.

A Conceptual Shift: The Transnational Paradigm

Whereas a comparative perspective of the Jewish world guided the first studies in the field, transnationalism provides a more current conceptual framework to explore theoretical and methodological venues related to the changing profiles and borders of Latin American Jewish communities. A transnational approach, partly enhanced by globalization theories, interacts with and challenges the scope of the concept of diaspora and its underlying assumptions. It underscores bordered and bounded social and communal units as transnational constituted spaces interacting with one another. Thus, a dual condition that involves both dispersion and national belonging is highlighted, influencing the ways in which identities and communal membership might be modified. The transnational framework is particularly relevant for Latin America, both past and present, in which migration processes, narratives, and parameters of Jewish identities are built in a shifting context of revival, transformation, and negotiation.[37]

During the past 40 years, as noted, more than 150,000 Jews emigrated from Latin American countries: in consequence, the Jewish population dropped from 514,000 in 1970 to 390,000 in 2010.[38] Contradictory trends that have characterized the region—democratization and de-democratization; liberalization and economic crisis; emerging civil societies and political instability; high levels of public violence alongside the search for new personal opportunities—have increasingly led to migration waves and to multiple experiences of leaving and joining. These processes have given rise to the contrasting realities of shrinking Jewish communities in some areas and revitalized Jewish life in others, both within Latin America and abroad. Accordingly, the focus of research now extends to four regions: Latin America, North America, Western Europe, and the Middle East as represented by Israel. Although migration, dispersion, and regrouping is a worldwide historical phenomenon affected by macro-level political and economic forces,[39] it assumes particular forms in Latin America and has had a differential impact on Jewish communities. Waves of migration were of different nature and scope. One type encompassed forced migration and exile of individuals under high risk, such as politically involved activists and intellectuals in the Southern Cone. Another was characterized by voluntary household decisions to emigrate, taking into consideration safety, security, and economic factors. Still others added to the previous determinants a number of ideational considerations, such as proximity to Jewish religious and communal institutions, the availability of Jewish educational frameworks, and prospects for Jewish continuity. Further research is needed in order to explore beyond the collective push-pull drivers of migration, focusing on the more particular Jewish collective dimension as well as on individual factors underlying forced and free-choice migration.[40] The transnational paradigm may be particularly relevant in developing pluralistic approaches toward migration that simultaneously take into account agency and structure, individuals, and the high institutional density of the local and global Jewish world.[41] Socio-demographic research on communities and identities may also benefit from this paradigm in confronting shifting (and increasingly porous) ethno-religious-cultural territorial population borders and the challenges derived from boundary maintenance, renewed dispersion, and connections to one or more (real or symbolic) homeland(s).

As with other social sciences, Latin American Jewish studies needs to overcome the burden of "methodological nationalism."[42] The concepts of diaspora and transnationalism cannot really be separated; moreover, their meaning can be inferred only from the ways in which these terms are used. Thus, while older notions of diaspora implied a return to a real or imagined homeland, the newer terminology replaces "return" with dense and continuous "linkages" across borders.[43] Similarly, the binomial terminology of "origin-destination" has been widened to comprise countries of onward migration, which also takes into account multilateral or lateral diasporic axes. Clearly, issues of multiple boundary expansion and redefinition are central to the Jewish experience as well as to the research concerns of the social sciences. In diaspora studies, the Jewish case has been attenuated, whereas transnational studies tend to lose sight of boundary maintenance related to the diasporic density present in contemporary migratory movements, with the latter subsumed under the rubric of the "ethnic lens."[44] In contrast, social science research in the realm of contemporary Jewry tends to leave out the global dimension of Jewish life, focusing on national cases and thereby underscoring exceptionalism.

Research agendas must therefore include mapping the relocation of Latin American Jews moving inside Latin America—for instance, migration from Argentina to Mexico or from Uruguay to Venezuela—and outside Latin America, mainly to the United States and Israel. There is also a need to address the reconstruction of the main transnational social networks following relocation, and the nature of persisting links with the countries of origin and, consequently, the need to differentiate and relate chain migrations, migrant regrouping, and processes of re-diasporization or de-diasporization. These new topics claim social and demographic perspectives and analytical tools that respond to the redefinition of spaces and territories.

The state of Israel and the Jewish/Zionist ethos have a singular, catalyzing role in both the traditional and newer conceptual frameworks of transnationalism.

Numerous scholars have analyzed the ways in which political concepts, values, aspirations, and organizational entities that were imported from previous Jewish locales were instrumental in the process of cultural and institutional formation of Jewish communities in Latin America—perhaps even more so than in other regions of Jewish immigration such as Western Europe or North America.[45] In this sense, the perception of a dialectical relationship between a perceived "center" in Palestine/Israel—with Latin America as an ideal "periphery"—was probably more widespread and acute in this region than elsewhere. Today, however, the social, cultural, and political transformations related to diffused patterns of international migration call for a serious and critical reconsideration of the earlier bipolar model, in light of a Jewish collective reality that has increasingly become multi-centered.

Final Remarks

As noted, Latin American Jewish social research reflects a nonlineal trajectory and faces challenges prompted by the trans-disciplinary nature of the field. One exemplary challenge illustrating the convergence of general and particular trends is that of analyzing the role of religion, and particularly the religious transformations of Jewish life in Latin America and worldwide. Historically, religion played a minor role in Latin American Jewish communities. However, more recent developments, both across the region and throughout the Jewish world, point to the increasing weight of religious claims and affirmation in the public domain, a situation that has led to the "de-privatization" of religion.[46]

During the 1960s, it was the Conservative movement that mobilized thousands of otherwise non-affiliated Jews into Jewish life. In recent years, however, in tandem with changing trends in world Jewry, Orthodox groups have taken the lead in forming new religious congregations. Today, for instance, the expansion of Chabad (Lubavitch) institutions, both in large and well-established communities and also in smaller ones, modifies the Latin American Jewish landscape. In Argentina, competing religious forces came to the forefront in the 2011 elections to AMIA, the central communal organization of Argentine Jewry. Brazilian Jewry, too, is displaying increased interest in Orthodoxy and in Orthodox outreach.[47] In Mexico, meanwhile, socio-demographic data indicate a marked trend toward greater religious observance. Categories such as "very observant" and "observant" increased, respectively, from 4.3 percent and 6.7 percent in 2000 to 7 percent and 17 percent in 2006, representing an overall growth of almost 300 percent. In contrast, "traditionalists," who still represent the majority of the Mexican Jewish population, experienced a reduction from 76.8 percent to 62 percent. When analyzing the population below 40 years of age, these trends appear even more acute: for "very observant" there was an increase from 7 to 12 percent, the "observant" category grew from 17 to 20 percent, and "traditionalists" decreased from 62 to 59 percent.[48] Across Latin America, ultra-Orthodox factions and self-segregated communities are still marginal; their presence, however, is growing. These trends are the subject of ongoing debate both in academic and public communal circles.

Throughout this essay, we have emphasized the need to guarantee a serious comparative approach that takes into consideration the specificity and distinctiveness of the object of study. Yet it is equally important to affirm the need to widen the study range of groups and referents as well as other experiences of the Jewish world. For instance, given the significant influence of past and present migratory movements of the Jewish collective, it is necessary to conduct rigorous comparisons of assimilation patterns, hybridity, reconfiguration processes, and changing ethnic profiles. There is also a need to compare and contrast recent Jewish emigration flows from the region with general migration waves of Latin Americans and with Jews worldwide. Concurrently, one has to bear in mind the paradigmatic transnational nature of the Latin American Jewish ethno-diaspora of the 21st century. In parallel, research needs to further focus on sub-ethnicity and its impact on the changing composition of Jewish communities.[49]

Latin American Jewish studies and research aspire to have a greater scientific and communal impact, a twofold goal that requires establishing procedures that link the new findings with appropriate institutions.

In the framework of a diversified Jewish world, new trends of theoretical knowledge and applied research need to address internal diversity. Researchers have to be aware that their work deals with categories and measures of inclusion and exclusion that delineate the contours of Jewish peoplehood: successfully meeting all of these challenges is the best guarantee of the field's continued growth, its scientific pertinence, and communal relevance.

Notes

1. Judit Bokser Liwerant (ed.), *Las Ciencias Sociales: Universidad y Sociedad* (Mexico City: 2003).

2. Moshe Davis, "Centers of Jewry in the Western Hemisphere: A Comparative Approach," *Jewish Journal of Sociology* 5, no. 1 (June 1963), 4–26.

3. Daniel Elazar and Peter Medding, *Jewish Communities in Frontier Societies: Argentina, Australia and South Africa* (New York: 1983). See also Leo Spitzer, *Lives in Between: Assimilation and Marginality in Austria, Brazil and West Africa* (Cambridge: 1989).

4. Daniel J. Elazar, *People and Polity: The Organizational Dynamics of World Jewry* (Detroit: 1989).

5. Shmuel N. Eisenstadt, "Multiple Modernities," *Dedalus* 129, no. 1 (Winter 2000), 1–30; Laurence Whitehead, "Latin America as a Mausoleum of Modernities," in *Globality and Multiple Modernities*, ed. Luis Roniger and Carlos Horacio Waisman (Brighton: 2002), 29–65.

6. Haim Avni and Yoram Shapira, "Teaching and Research on Latin America in Israel," *Latin American Research Review* 9, no. 3 (1974), 39–51; Haim Avni, "Argentine Jewry: Its Socio-Political Status and Organizational Patterns," *Dispersion and Unity* 12 (1971), 128–162; ibid., 13–14 (1972), 161–208; ibid., 15–16 (1972), 158–215; idem, *Argentina y las migraciones judías: de la Inquisición al Holocausto y después* (Buenos Aires: 2005); idem, *Judíos en América* (Madrid: 1992); idem, "*Impuros*": *prostitutas y esclavas blancas en Argentina y en Israel* (Tel Aviv: 2009).

7. Haim Avni, "Cuarenta años: El contexto histórico y desafíos a la investigación," in *Pertenencia y Alteridad: Judíos en/de América Latina: Cuarenta años de cambios*, ed. Haim Avni, Judit Bokser Liwerant, Sergio DellaPergola, Margalit Bejarano, and Leonardo Senkman (Madrid: 2011), 85–115.

8. Silvia Shenkolewsky; "La conquista de las comunidades, el Movimiento Sionista y la Comunidad Ashkenazi de Argentina (19239–1945)," in *Judaica Latinoamericana II,* ed. AMILAT *(*Jerusalem: 1992), 191–201; Haim Avni, "The Origins of Zionism in Latin America," in *The Jewish Presence in Latin America,* ed. Judith Laikin Elkin and Gilbert W. Merkx (Boston: 1987), 135–155; Judit Bokser Liwerant, "El lugar cambiante de Israel en la comunidad judía de México: centralidad y proceso de globalización," in *Judaica Latino-americana V,* ed. AMILAT (Jerusalem: 2005), 185–208, idem, "Globalization and Latin American Jewish Identities: The Mexican Case in Comparative Perspective," in *Jewish Identities in an Era of Globalization and Multiculturalism: Latin America in the Jewish World,* ed. Judit Bokser Liwerant, Eliezer Ben-Rafael, Yossi Gorny, and Raanan Rein (Leiden: 2008), 81–105.

9. Elazar, *People and Polity.*

10. Judith Laikin Elkin, *Jews of the Latin American Republics* (Chapel Hill: 1980); idem, "The Evolution of the Latin American Jewish Communities: Retrospect and Prospect," in Elkin and Merkx (eds.), *The Jewish Presence in Latin America,* 309–323. The Latin American Jewish Studies Association is currently based at the University of Texas at Austin.

11. Judith Laikin Elkin, *Jews of the Latin American Republics* (Chapel Hill: 1980).

12. Sergio DellaPergola, "¿Cuántos somos hoy? Investigación y narrativa sobre población judía en America Latina," in Avni et al. (eds.), *Presencia y Alteridad,* 305–341.

13. Ibid, 309.

14. Uziel O. Schmelz, "Evaluación crítica acerca de las estimaciones de población judía en Argentina," in *Comunidades Judías en Latinoamérica 1973–1975* (Buenos Aires: 1977), 198–223.

15. Uziel O. Schmelz and Sergio DellaPergola, *Hademografiyah shel hayehudim beargentina ubearatzot aḥerot shel amerika halatinit* (Tel Aviv: 1974).

16. See, for instance, Sergio DellaPergola and Uziel O. Schmelz, *The Jews of Greater Mexico City according to the 1970 Population Census: First Data and Critical Evaluation* (Jerusalem: 1978); Sergio DellaPergola, "Demographic Trends of Latin American Jewry," in Elkin and Merkx (eds.), *The Jewish Presence in Latin America,* 85–133; idem, "Autonomy and Dependency: Latin American Jewry in Global Perspective," in Liwerant et al. (eds.), *Jewish Identities in an Era of Globalization and Multiculturalism,* 47–80.

17. Cf. Sergio DellaPergola, "¿Cuántos somos hoy?"

18. Shmuel Adler, *Emigration among Immigrants from Argentina. Arrived during the Period 1.1.89–31.12.02* (Jerusalem: 2004); Adrian Jmelnizky and Ezequiel Erdei, *Estudio de población judía en ciudad de Buenos Aires y Gran Buenos Aires (AMBA)* (Buenos Aires: 2005); Yaacov Rubel, *La población judía de la ciudad de Buenos Aires, perfil socio-demográfico* (Buenos Aires: 2005).

19. See online reports at www.ibge.gov.br/english; René D. Decol, "Brazilian Jews: a Demographic Profile," paper delivered at the Jewish Agency Initiative on Jewish Demography conference, Jerusalem (2002); Federação Israelita do Estado dee São Paulo (FISESP), *Recadastramento comunitário 2000–01* (Sao Paulo: 2002); Instituto Brasilero de Geografia e Estatistica IBGE, *Population Census* (Rio de Janeiro: various years); René Decol, "Imigraçoes urbanas para o Brasil: o caso dos Judeus" (Ph.D. diss., Universidade Estadual, 1999); idem, "A Demographic Profile of Brazilian Jewry," *Contemporary Jewry* 29, no. 2 (2009), 99–113; Simon Schwartzman, "Fora de foco: diversidade e identidades étnicas no Brasil," *Novos Estudos* (November 1999), 83–96.

20. See Instituto Nacional de Estadística, Geografía e Informática, *XII Censo general de población y vivienda 2000* (Mexico City: 2002); Comité Central Israelita de México, *Estudio sobre tendencias de la educación judía en México: censo socio-demográfico de la comunidad judía de México* (Mexico City: 2000); Sergio DellaPergola and Susana Lerner, *La población judía de México: perfil demográfico, social y cultural* (Mexico City: 1995); Comité Central Israelita dee México, *Estudio poblacional de la comunidad judía de México* (Mexico City: 2006).

21. Gabriel Berger, Mauricio Tchimino, Susana Korinfeld, and Vicente Zuñiga, *Estudio socio-demográfico de la comunidad judìa de Chile* (Santiago: 1995); Nicole Berenstein and

Rafael Porzecanski, *Perfil de los egresados de la red formal de educación judía Uruguaya* (Montevideo: 2001); Sergio DellaPergola, Salomon Benzaquen, and Tony Beker de Weinraub, *Perfil sociodemográfico y cultural de la comunidad judía de Caracas* (Caracas: 2000). The survey was sponsored by the Asociación Israelita de Venezuela, the Unión Israelita de Caracas, and the Asociación de Amigos de la Universidad Hebrea de Jerusalén.

22. DellaPergola, Benzaquen, and Weintraub, *Perfil sociodemográfico y cultural de la comunidad judía de Caracas.*

23. Ezequiel Erdei, "Demografía e identidad: a propósito del estudio de población judía en Buenos Aires," in Avni et al. (eds.), *Pertenencia y Alteridad,* 341–364.

24. Raanan Rein, *Argentine Jews or Jewish Argentines? Essays on Ethnicity, Identity, and Diaspora* (Leiden: 2010); idem, "Waning Essentialism: Latin American Jewish Studies in Israel," in Liwerant et al. (eds.), *Jewish Identities in an Era of Globalization and Multiculturalism,* 109–124.

25. John Armstrong, *Nations before Nationalism* (Chapel Hill: 1982); Walter Zenner, *Minorities in the Middle* (Albany: 1991).

26. Jeff Lesser and Raanan Rein (eds.), *Rethinking Jewish-Latin Americans* (Albuquerque: 2008); Avni et al., *Pertenencia y Alteridad,* 85–114.

27. Rein, *Argentine Jews or Jewish Argentines?* 38–39.

28. AMILAT leads the Latin American Division of the World Congress of Jewish Studies. It has organized the corresponding congresses and has published seven volumes of the series *Judaica Latinoamericana* (Jerusalem: 1988, 1993, 1997, 2001, 2005, 2009, 2010).

29. Haim Avni, "Postwar Latin American Jewry: An Agenda for the Study of the Last Five Decades," in *The Jewish Diaspora in Latin America: New Studies on History and Literature,* ed. David Sheinin and Lois Baer Barr (New York: 1996), 3–19.

30. *Reflexiones sobre enseñanza e investigación académica del judaísmo latinoamericano,* report presented to the XIII Congress of LAJSA, Institute of Contemporary Jewry, Division of Latin America, Spain and Portugal (2007).

31. Edna Aisenberg, "Cuarenta años de la División América Latina, España y Portugal, o cómo bailar el hora-tango-swing," in ibid., 6–10; Saúl Sosnowski, "Fronteras en las letras judías latinoamericanas," *Revista Iberoamericana* 191 (April–June 2000), 270; "El tiempo y las palabras: literatura y cultura judía latinoamericana contemporánea," appearing in *Hostos Review* 4 (2006), ed. Stephen A. Sadow (CUNY-Hostos Community College).

32. See, for example, Erin Graff Zivin, *The Wandering Signifier: The Rhetoric of Jewishness in the Latin American Imaginary* (Durham: 2008); also see Judah M. Cohen, "The Ethnic Dilemmas of Latin American Jewry," in Lesser and Rein (eds.), *Rethinking Jewish-Latin Americans,* 231–266.

33. In 1970, seeking to provide a common language by which to "promote uniformity and comparability for data on race and ethnicity" for various population groups, the Office of Management and Budget (OMB) created a broad definition of Hispanic as "a person of Mexican, Puerto Rican, Cuban, South or Central American, or other Spanish culture or origin, regardless of race." In 1997, a revision was made to the definition to equate Hispanic with "Latino." See "Revisions to the Standards for the Classification of Federal Data on Race and Ethnicity," online at www.whitehouse.gov/omb/fedreg_1997standards (accessed 18 November 2012). The U.S. Census has a broader definition of what constitutes Hispanic; in theory, anyone who considers him/herself to be Hispanic or Latino is indeed defined as Hispanic or Latino, which therefore can also include persons of Portuguese and/or Brazilian descent. For a table showing comparisons in terminology, see Agency for Healthcare Research and Quality (AHRQ), "Race, Ethnicity, and Language Data: Standardization for Health Care Quality Improvement," online at www.ahrq.gov/research/iomracereport/reldata1tab1-1.htm (accessed 18 November 2012).

34. Luis Roniger, "Antisemitism: Real or Imagined? Chávez, Iran, Israel and the Jews," *ACTA—Analysis of Current Trends in Antisemitism* 33 (2009), 1–36; Leonardo Senkman, "El antisemitismo bajo dos experiencias democráticas: Argentina 1945–1966 y 1973–1976," in *El antisemitismo en la Argentina,* ed. Leonardo Senkman (Buenos Aires: 1989) 11–194; Maria Luiza Tucci Carneiro, (ed.), *O anti-semitismo nas Américas* (Sao Paulo: 2007).

35. Leonardo Senkman, Mario Sznajder, and Edy Kaufman (eds.), *El legado del autoritarismo: derechos humanos y antisemitismo en la Argentina contemporánea* (Jerusalem: 1995); Leonardo Senkman, "The Restoration of Democracy in Argentina and the Impunity of Anti-Semitism," *Patterns of Prejudice* 24 (Winter 1990), 34–60; Mario Sznajder and Luis Roniger, "From Argentina to Israel: Escape, Evacuation and Exile," *Journal of Latin American Studies* 37 (2005), 351–377.

36. Emmanuel Kahan, *Unos pocos peligros sensatos* (Buenos Aires: 2008); Emmanuel Kahan, Laura Schenquer, Damián Setton, and Alejandro Dujovne (eds.), *Marginados y consagrado: nuevos estudios sobre la vida judía en Argentina* (Buenos Aires: 2011).

37. Judit Bokser Liwerant, Sergio DellaPergola, and Leonardo Senkman, "Latin American Jews in a Transnational World: Redefining Experiences and Identities in Four Continents" (Jerusalem: 2010), online at www.givathaviva.org.il/hebrew/mifgashim/huji/Transnational%20 AmLat%20Proposal.pdf (accessed 30 April 2013); Judit Bokser Liwerant, "Latin American Jews: A Transnational Diaspora," in *Transnationalism: Diasporas and the Advent of a New (Dis)Order*, ed. Eliezer Ben-Rafael and Yitzhak Sternberg (Boston: 2009), 351–374; Leonardo Senkman, "Klal Yisrael at the Frontiers: The Transnational Jewish Experience in Argentina," in Liwerant et al. (eds.), *Jewish Identities in an Era of Globalization and Multiculturalism*, 125–150.

38. Sergio DellaPergola, "¿Cuántos somos hoy?"

39. Nicolas Van Hear, *New Diasporas: The Mass Exodus, Dispersal and Regrouping of Migrant Communities* (London: 1998).

40. Liwerant, DellaPergola, and Senkman, "Latin American Jews in a Transnational World."

41. Hein de Haas, "Migration and Development: A Theoretical Perspective," *International Migration Review* 44, no. 1 (Spring 2010), 227–264.

42. Andreas Wimmer and Nina Glick Schiller, "Methodological Nationalism, the Social Sciences, and the Study of Migration: An Essay in Historical Epistemology," *International Migration Review* 37, no. 3 (2003), 576–610.

43. William Safran, "Diasporas in Modern Societies: Myths of Homeland and Returns," *Diaspora* 1 (1991), 83–99; Rainer Baubock and Thomas Faist (eds.), *Diaspora and Transnationalism: Concepts, Theories and Methods* (Amsterdam: 2010).

44. Robin Cohen, *Global Diasporas: An Introduction* (Seattle: 1997); Linda Basch, Nina Glick Schiller, and Cristina Szanton Blanc, *Nations Unbound: Transnational Projects, Postcolonial Predicaments and Deterritorialized Nation-States* (New York: 1994).

45. Liwerant, DellaPergola, and Senkman, *Latin American Jews in a Transnational World*.

46. Jose Casanova, *Public Religion in the Modern World* (Chicago: 1994).

47. Marta F. Topel, *Jerusalem and Sao Paulo: The New Jewish Orthodoxy in Focus* (Lanham: 2008).

48. Comité Central Israelita de México, *Socio-demographic Study of the Mexican Jewish Community, 2006* (Mexico City: 2006).

49. Margalit Bejarano, "Sephardic Communities in Latin America—Past and Present," in AMILAT (ed.), *Judaica Latinoamericana V*, 9–26; idem, "A Mosaic of Fragmented Identities: The Sephardim in Latin America," in Liwerant et al. (eds.), *Jewish Identities in an Era of Globalization*, 268–279; Susana Brauner, *Los judíos de Alepo en Argentina: identidad y organización comunitaria (1900–2000)* (Buenos Aires: 2005); Liz Hamui Halabe, *Identidad colectiva: rasgos culturales de los inmigrantes judeoalepinos en México* (Mexico City: 1997).

Jews in Israel: Effects of Categorization Practice on Research Findings and Research Frameworks

Aziza Khazzoom
(INDIANA UNIVERSITY)

Racial!??

In research on Israeli ethnic inequality, the choice of categorization scheme carries great significance.[1] Early research on Jewish ethnicity dealt with Israel's two main aggregates—Mizrahim, who come from Muslim countries; and Ashkenazim, who come from Christian countries—but rarely attended to country differences within these aggregates. As a result, much of the complexity of Israeli ethnicity was hidden, including changing motivations for ethnic discrimination, the extent of ethnic discrimination, shifts over time in ethnic identity and in the distribution of government resources, and connections between ethnic inequality and other cleavages. A newer reading of Israeli ethnicity pays attention to country of origin as well as to the two main aggregates and seeks to chart a process of panethnic formation by which the categories of Mizrahi and Ashkenazi were created in the first years following Israel's establishment.[2] A more recent framework known as Orientalism (referring to the dichotomy between East and West) has the effect of making discrimination appear more prominent, but also implies that we should be moving beyond the discrimination framework in order to assess ways in which the global Muslim/Christian divide has affected a variety of Israeli cleavages.

In this essay, I describe the shift from old frameworks of modernization[3] in favor of the panethnic and Orientalist frameworks for research dealing with the 1950s immigrants. I then discuss three questions: What categorization issues exist with regard to other racial/ethnic groups in Israel? Do those categorization issues imply changes in theoretical frameworks, as did the issues associated with the 1950s immigrants? And, regardless of the answers to the first two questions, do the panethnic and Orientalist frameworks remain relevant for research on other groups? I find that, although some insights from research on the 1950s immigrants continue to be useful, other categorization issues are gaining in importance over time, especially with regard to groups such as third-generation Israelis, foreign workers, and recent immigrants from Ethiopia and the former Soviet Union (FSU).

A Brief History of Categories in Research on the First Post-state Immigrants

Early in the 1950s and 1960s, an article on ethnicity in Israel would open with a fairly succinct background section. This would note that Israeli Jews are divided into two groups; that "Orientals" arrived with lower human capital (for instance, in terms of professional or educational attainments) than "westerners"; and that in Israel there has been a corresponding ethnic gap in socially valued resources such as higher educational attainments, higher occupational attainments, or political power. With ethnic boundaries and inequality explained, the article would go on to its main topic, which was often a discussion of how inequality might be eliminated. This use of binary ethnic aggregates ("Orientals" versus "westerners") appeared, at the time, to be defensible and even obvious. Researchers noted broad similarities in culture and language within panethnic groups—all Jews from Muslim countries, for example, spoke Arabic, whereas most Jews from Christian countries spoke Yiddish—and quantitative evidence showed that Mizrahim (as Orientals are now more commonly termed) had significantly lower human capital than Ashkenazim. These observations of the salience of the binary categories gave researchers no reason to examine characteristics of specific country groups.

This is not to say that researchers were unaware that the binary Mizrahi/ Ashkenazi distinction represented new categories of identity for Jewish Israelis. Some research did track panethnic formation (or, in Israel, dichotomization, since Mizrahim/Ashkenazim were two different groups). Early studies of marital patterns, for example, suggested that an "Ashkenazi" identity was forming faster than a "Mizrahi" one, as European Jews began marrying across country lines (though within binary lines) earlier and more frequently than Middle Eastern Jews.[4] However, while this work used dichotomization as an overarching theme, it did not politicize it. Researchers did not yet know the extent to which the Mizrahi/ Ashkenazi gap in resources was an Israeli creation, and they believed that identity was simply following language and material circumstances among the immigrants. In this sense, they took the aggregate categories as an expected outcome, even as they examined their development.

Over the years, scholars began to focus more on ethnic discrimination as one component of the formation of ethnic inequality, and this shift came hand in hand with increasing attention to country differences within the Mizrahi group. Deborah Bernstein, for instance, argued that pre-state Ashkenazi veterans pauperized immigrants from Arab countries in order to use them as a reserve labor force. According to Bernstein, in using the lower educational attainment levels of Mizrahim to explain ethnic inequality, gatekeepers[5] ignored the large group of westernized, educated, and bourgeois Baghdadis who theoretically should have done well in Israel's modern economy.[6] As such, she implicitly connected use of the binary categories with the imposition of inequality. Similarly, Tom Segev asserted that treatment of Mizrahim as a single group was inconsistent with the stark differences between immigrants from different Middle Eastern countries.[7] Shlomo Swirski challenged arguments that Ashkenazi dominance was an expected outcome based on their uniformly western and educated origins, pointing out that large numbers of Ashkenazim came from areas of Russia and Poland that were in very early stages of modernization, whereas smaller groups, such as those from Germany or the United States, came from significantly more advanced societies.[8] These scholarly observations portrayed "Mizrahi" and "Ashkenazi" as a social construction—that is, as only one of several possible ways to categorize Jews—and read that social construction as part of a story of discrimination. Notwithstanding, shifts in ethnic boundaries were not their main focus.

It was not until Yaacov Nahon examined educational attainment by country of origin, rather than by Mizrahi/Ashkenazi aggregates, that dichotomization in its contemporary sense gained currency.[9] Using the 1983 census, Nahon examined educational attainments for two groups: older men who had immigrated to Israel, and younger men who were Israeli-born. He then used a statistical procedure that maps groups on a plane according to their closeness to one another in order to identify clusters of country groups characterized by similar levels of educational attainment. He found that, among older immigrant men, educational attainments varied widely among ten major country groupings—Egypt, Yemen, Iran, Morocco, Iraq, Bulgaria and Greece, Romania, Poland, the Soviet Union, and other countries of Eastern Europe—with no obvious clustering of Middle Eastern and European countries. Among younger Israeli-born men, however, educational attainments of the ten groupings clustered into the binary Mizrahi/Ashkenazi categorization scheme. Some years later, Karin Amit replicated Nahon's results with regard to income and occupation.[10] Similar arguments about initial diversity among the immigrants can be made regarding access to West European cultures prior to immigration.[11]

Fig. 10.1 uses census data from 1961 and 1995 to demonstrate this intergenerational dynamic.[12] The bars represent the proportion of men who attained at least 12 years of an academic education, by country of origin, for the six countries (Yemen,

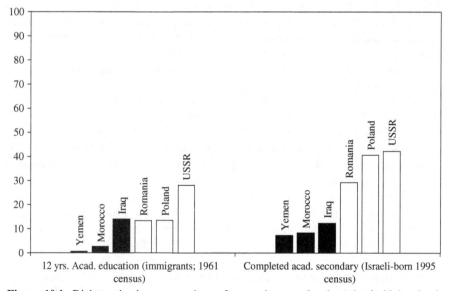

Figure 10.1. Dichotomization: proportions of men who completed academic high school, comparing immigrant men from the 1961 census and Israeli-born men from the 1995 census

Morocco, Iraq, Romania, Poland, and the Soviet Union) that produced the most immigrants in the decade following Israeli independence. Bars on the left side of the graph represent immigrants who arrived between the ages of 20 and 60 (that is, their educational attainments preceded their arrival in Israel), whereas those on the right side depict men who were born in Israel and are about the ages of the sons of the 1950s immigrants. Bars representing Middle Eastern countries are black; European countries are indicated in white. The panethnic dynamic can be demonstrated in the following way: if one were to see the left-hand graph without country labels or colors, and asked to draw a line between two groups that are represented on the graph, one would be unlikely to draw the line between the Iraqis and the Romanians. One would in fact be surprised at the request to demarcate two groups, since there appear to be three. If one were given the same task for the Israeli-born, however, it would be easy to find the two groups. This is because among the Israeli-born, educational attainments line up according to the binary, Mizrahi/Ashkenazi distinction.

The implication of Nahon's research is that Israel did not *receive* Mizrahim and Ashkenazim, but rather *created* them out of a diverse set of country groups. According to Nahon's research and follow-up research by others, educational attainment for all groups increased over the generation. In order to arrive at two groups that are so internally similar from groups that initially were so heterogeneous, the educational averages of different country groups had to grow at different rates. Among the initially similar Iraqis, Egyptians, Poles, and Romanians, Iraqi and Egyptian attainments increased to a lesser extent, while those of Poles and Romanians increased to the level attained by the children of German immigrants. In the meantime, the attainments of Yemenites, Moroccans, and other Mizrahi groups increased to the extent of approaching Iraqi and Egyptian levels.[13]

Implications

Discrimination

The differential growth rate in country groups' educational attainments is a good illustration of the ways in which panethnic formation enhances the plausibility of arguments about discrimination. In the case of Iraq, in particular, there are a variety of reasons why very limited growth in educational attainment would appear to be the result of discrimination. For one thing, the Iraqi Jewish community experienced a high rate of increase in educational attainment in the decades prior to immigration to Israel.[14] Second, Iraqi Jews came to Israel en masse, with their community leadership intact. Third, a relatively large segment of educated Jews successfully imported physical capital (that is, money) to Israel. And finally, most Iraqi Jews settled in Israel's geographical center, where there were greater employment and educational opportunities. Because all these indicators lead to an expectation that Iraqi educational attainment would grow in Israel, and because Polish and Romanian attainment did grow, Nahon's data would tend to strengthen prior arguments (such as that of Deborah Bernstein) that Ashkenazi gatekeepers placed a ceiling on Middle Eastern Jewish attainment in order to create a Mizrahi lower class. Thus, altering the research

categories—by attending to specific country of origin—affected how ethnic inequality was perceived.

Orientalism

In addition to reinforcing arguments about discrimination that were already circu-
lating in academia, Nahon's work could be used to support that of the emerging
"new Mizrahim" who were focused on the importance of the Orientalist discourse
in shaping group boundaries in Israeli society. Orientalism is a system of ideas that
posits a number of truths, among them, that easterners and westerners are different,
even opposite, cultural groups (in addition, it provides a list of central differences
between East and West—for instance, easterners are more emotional than westerners), and that the West is more advanced than the East. Nahon's research connects to
Orientalism because it shows that, in the second generation, resources came to be
distributed by the Middle East/Europe divide rather than by the initial attainments
of the immigrant "fathers." In other words, the East/West divide is what directed
gatekeepers to put a ceiling on Iraqi and not Romanian or Polish attainments; this,
according to the Orientalist argument, speaks to the strength of Orientalism in shaping Israeli society.

With the work of the new Mizrahim, categorization itself became the subject of
study, in the sense that researchers were concerned with understanding how the new
binary categories came to be salient in Israel, and what was the role of Orientalism in
creating those categories. The new Mizrahim have collectively told a story in which
gatekeepers, who were veteran immigrants and overwhelmingly European in origin,
imposed the binary categories on the new immigrants from Eastern Europe and the
Middle East. To follow this argument, it is useful to divide dichotomization into two
types: resource and representational. The dynamics charted by Nahon and Amit constitute resource dichotomization, in which social "goodies," such as high-status occupations, education, political power, or residential locations, come to be distributed
according to the binary categorization scheme. Representational dichotomization, in
contrast, refers to the *portrayal* of Israeli Jews as divided into two groups. Many new
Mizrahim argued that representational and resource dichotomization reinforced each
other in Israel. As Ella Shohat put it:

> According to that discourse, European Zionism...took [Mizrahim] out of "primitive
> conditions" of poverty and superstition and ushered them gently into a modern Western
> society characterized by tolerance, democracy and "humane values," values with which
> they were but vaguely and erratically familiar due to the "levantine environments" from
> which they came. Within Israel, of course, they have suffered from the problem of "the
> gap"... handicapped as they have been by their Oriental, illiterate, despotic, sexist, and
> generally pre-modern formation in their lands of origin.[15]

According to this approach, representational dichotomization makes resource dichotomization ("the gap") seem inevitable. Similarly, once inequality in resources is
established, representational dichotomization also looks more obvious, even to those
on whom it has been imposed. Eventually, this leads to institutionalization of the
binary lines as bases for the identity and political activity of all parties, in addition to
resource distribution.[16] Central to Shohat's arguments is the observation that Israel's

European Jews—who, after all, came from Eastern Europe—were considered in Europe to be not western but rather "Ostjuden," literally Eastern Jews.[17] Referencing the Oriental natures of Middle Eastern Jewish immigrants is therefore a case of the pot calling the kettle black; and, again, the story of Jewish ethnicity in Israel appears to be best told as a story of categorization, or of shifts in group boundaries (that is, panethnic formation).

Follow-up research examined East/West categorization practices in the diaspora and made links between them and dynamics in Israel. My own work built on earlier work to tell an encompassing story, in which a "chain of orientalizations" shaped Jewish identity and group relations across the Middle East and Europe.[18] I argue that, beginning with the era of Enlightenment, Jews in Germany and France came to read Jewish tradition as Oriental and, moreover, backward (because it was Oriental).[19] They became intent on "westernizing" themselves, and once they had succeeded, they began westernizing Jews in Eastern Europe and the Middle East. This project of westernization was then imported to Israel through Zionist ideology; the desire to produce a "western" Israel, in turn, determined who was included and who was excluded from the cultural center of the emerging state.[20] I also link westernization with both the strengthening and the amelioration of other Israeli social cleavages. On the one hand, since "western" is perceived as secular, Israel's founders preferred that the Orthodox not integrate into the center; on the other hand, Israel's promotion of gender equality and (later) gay rights is often attributed to the desire to uphold a western image.[21] Other work demonstrates the salience of country and aggregate boundaries to gatekeepers at various times in Israeli history.[22]

The research on westernization and the development of ethnic categories in Israel includes Yehouda Shenhav's *Arab Jews* (2006), which examines the processes of "de-Arabization" of Middle Eastern Jewish immigrants to the new state, with the aim of bringing them in line with Israel's western ethos.[23] Shenhav notes that Middle Eastern Jews who arrived in Israel were expected to change their names, stop speaking Arabic or listening to Arabic music, and adopt western entertainment forms such as classical music or theater. Shenhav and other new Mizrahim read this process as important because it created a disconnect between Jews and their Middle Eastern Muslim neighbors, reducing the chances for peace.

Further Quantitative Research on Ethnic Inequality

Nahon's work implied that future research on the formation of ethnic inequality in Israel should use two sets of categories—country of origin and binary ethnic category—in order to track the process by which resources such as education, which were originally distributed according to a country divide, came to be distributed according to the binary divide. When later research incorporated country of origin, more surprises emerged, and these, in turn, suggested further shifts in the theoretical frameworks used to understand ethnic inequality among Jews in Israel. The literature that described discrimination—in particular that by Deborah Bernstein and Shlomo Swirski—suggested that veterans (pre-state arrivals, who were overwhelmingly Ashkenazi) had discriminated against Middle Eastern groups in such a way as to make them a single Middle Eastern underclass.[24] One empirical implication was that among the largest groups of immigrants, those from Iraq, Yemen, and Morocco could be expected to obtain low-status jobs no matter what their educational attainments, while immigrants from Poland, Romania, and the Soviet Union would be the only ones to obtain high-status occupations. However, this turned out not to be the case. When occupational attainment was examined by country of origin, researchers found that labor market outcomes of Iraqis were nearly identical to those of Ashkenazim, and that only Moroccans and Yemenites experienced discrimination,[25] a finding that would appear to contradict the outcome of dichotomization. This is in fact a puzzle. One possible answer is that the finding of nondiscrimination against Iraqis is limited to the labor market, where job candidates generally met directly with prospective employers rather than dealing with a faceless bureaucracy. Another is that it was the children of Iraqi immigrants who experienced discrimination in the schools—thus it was their attainment, and not that of their fathers, that was lowered in Israel.[26]

In any event, this finding challenged many long-accepted beliefs about ethnicity in Israel and raised questions as to whether veterans identified along lines of country, continent, or language. This point is especially important to clarify, since nearly all prior explanations for inequality had relied on such arguments about veteran identification, and yet all these explanations are undermined by the finding that veterans did not discriminate against Iraqis in the 1950s labor market. For example, some have argued that Ashkenazim discriminated against Mizrahim because they wanted to restrict valued resources to a group that included themselves.[27] Iraqis were the only large group of Middle Eastern immigrants who had any chance of challenging the Ashkenazi monopolization of resources: it therefore would have made sense to discriminate against them as well as against Moroccans or Yemenites. Similarly, the claim that veteran Israelis gave Ashkenazim preference because they consciously or unconsciously bonded with individuals who shared their histories, manners, customs, cultures, political practices, or general knowledge implies that Ashkenazim would discriminate against Iraqis. Still others have argued that veterans were more likely to hire new Ashkenazi immigrants simply because they could communicate with them, since nearly all Ashkenazim at least understood Yiddish. Iraqis, though they often spoke several languages, did not speak Yiddish—yet they were treated similarly to those who did speak Yiddish.

As noted, I use quantitative data to argue that the goal of discrimination was not resource monopolization but rather preservation of Israel's western ethos. My claim is that Iraqi individuals were more likely to be able to prove westernization (for instance, by speaking western European languages, or by having attended a "modern" school rather than a heder),[28] and thus not be classified as a threat to Israel's westernization project.

Palestinians and Israel's Location in the Middle East

Any argument that the East/West "clash of civilizations" shaped Jewish identity and Israeli cleavages is by definition an argument for how Israeli Jews relate to Muslims, including those living in Israel and the occupied territories, and those in the surrounding

Muslim-dominated countries.[29] Thus the new focus on categorization, and therefore the East/West line, also shaped research on Palestinians. Although most new Mizrahim are empirically focused on internal ethnic cleavages in Israel, nearly all perceive their work as having implications for understanding the place of Palestinians in Israeli society. The most radical is Shohat, who refers to Mizrahi Jews as Zionism's "other" victims, thereby locating those of Arab background (both Jews and non-Jews) on one side of a conflict of interests, with Ashkenazim on the other side.[30]

Shenhav, along with many others, is focused on the complexity of identification and disidentification on the part of Arab Jews, particularly in the first generation after statehood. According to Shenhav, many immigrants from Arab countries earned their "entry ticket" into Israeli society by spying on the Arab enemy. The complexity here is that these Jews built on their Arab background to become *not* Arab, that is, to become full members of a Jewish society that perceived itself as distinctly not Arab. As noted, my own research looks at the ways in which Enlightenment-era categorizations of Jews as Oriental generated discomfort among Jews. One implication is that Israelis will be more comfortable with Israeli-Palestinian peace initiatives that relate to Israelis and Palestinians as separate populations, rather than those that build on commonalities between Middle Eastern Jews and Middle Eastern non-Jews. Gil Eyal, in contrast (along with many others who examine how Jews in Germany responded to being categorized as Oriental after the Enlightenment), emphasizes the ebbs and flows in the extent to which Jews identified with the Orient, and shows that there have been historical periods in which Jews have experimented with more "eastern" identities. (One example is a group known as Haroeh, whose members lived with Bedouins and sought to imitate their dress and shepherding activity. Eyal quotes a eulogy that described how these individuals "'were attracted to the free life of the Bedouin.'")[31] The suggestion is that, given the right conditions, Israelis may again consider identities that relate both to Arabs and to others perceived as eastern. In this case, too, categorization—in the sense of how Israelis draw or erase lines between Jews and Arabs—is the issue.

Current Directions

Using dichotomization as the overarching framework to describe Israeli society focuses research on the role of discrimination in creating ethnic inequality and on the role of Orientalism in shaping Israeli society. However, like all categorization schemes, it conceals some things even as it reveals others. Dichotomization is a framework that is based on dynamics among the new state's first immigrants, all of whom were Jews and the vast majority of whom came from the Middle East and Eastern Europe. For a variety of other groups, the most critical elements of inequality are not highlighted if one uses a dichotomization or East/West framework. Among these groups are Ethiopians; new immigrants from the former Soviet Union; Arab Israeli citizens; foreign workers; third-generation Israelis; and children of mixed (Mizrahi/Ashkenazi) marriages. Above, I argued that although the panethnic framework is not particularly relevant for research on the position of Palestinians, the Orientalism framework does provide a useful set of arguments regarding some dynamics that would determine the position of Muslims in Israeli society, as well as the relationship between Israel and its Arab neighbors. In what follows, I turn to the other groups mentioned here.

Categorization Issues in Research on Ethiopians

Paul Starr sees four stages to categorization.[32] The first is to pick a domain, or underlying principle of classification, such as occupation, employment status, religion, or, in this case, race/ethnicity/nation. The next step is to identify groups in a domain. This is what the panethnic issue is about: the argument is that identifying only two Jewish groups—Mizrahim and Ashkenazim—hides panethnic formation. This question of identifying groups does not appear to be relevant to the study of Ethiopian Jews, as there are no arguments that the group should be redefined, combined, or disaggregated. Issues of Ethiopian categorization center instead on Starr's third step in classification: naming. A name can be quite important—calling immigrants to Israel 'olim or mehagrim (migrants), for example, carries with it assumptions and definitional arguments that affect analysis. Moreover, names tend to signify identity in a larger sense; someone who calls herself an 'olah is likely to have a more Zionist identity than someone who calls himself a mehager. For Ethiopians, there are two naming issues: the extent to which Ethiopians are labeled Jews, and the extent to which they are labeled black. Starr's fourth stage—organizing the named groups relative to each other in a relational tree—articulates further implications of naming. The more Ethiopians are perceived to be black, the more one is likely to draw connections between them and other (non-Jewish) Ethiopians, as well as with other Africans worldwide. In contrast, the more they are perceived to be Jewish, the more Israel will be regarded as their natural home, and any form of exclusion in the Jewish state would appear to be all the more illegitimate.[33]

Several important works of research, as a group, tell a coherent story of naming and its consequences for research and identity. In a 1984 study of approximately 200 Ethiopian immigrants, Jan Abbink distinguished between those who had been in Israel for eight to ten years by the time of the interview, versus those who had arrived only six to eight months before. When asked how they would like "the people from Ethiopia" to be called by other Israelis, only about 10 to 20 percent of veterans and new immigrants preferred the names "Falasha," "Beta Israel/ Israelotch" or "Ethiopian," despite the currency of the first two in Ethiopia. The majority of both new and older arrivals preferred to be called "Ethiopian Jews" (61 percent of new arrivals versus 89 percent of later arrivals).[34] New arrivals were also more likely to prefer "Israeli" (18 percent versus 3 percent of the veterans). Abbink did not ask about the names "black," "black Jew," or "kushi" (a term used in Israel, presumably drawn from the label "Cushite"), but his numbers can be read as consistent with other arguments that the term black became more popular over time in Israel,[35] whereas preference for the term Israeli appears to be replaced over time by preference for something that references Ethiopia. There is also some evidence that Ethiopians found their Jewishness to be challenged in Israel; veterans were less likely than the newer immigrants to believe that Israelis regarded them as Jewish (13 percent versus 32 percent) and more likely to believe that other Israelis saw them as Ethiopian (56 percent versus 43 percent).

Why does it matter if Ethiopians are labeled black, Jewish, Ethiopian, Ethiopian Jewish, or something else? The first point is that most Israeli research takes it as self-evident that this group constitutes Israel's first black Jews, and the lack of attention to alternatives can cause it to miss important dynamics. One Israeli study, for example, replicated a U.S. study of African American internalized stigma, and showed that Israelis of Ethiopian origin considered white dolls to be prettier than black dolls. However, as Steven Kaplan points out, "the significance of this finding is greatly diminished owing to the authors' lack of awareness that the Ethiopians, while negatively evaluating blackness, did not assign themselves to that category."[36] Thus, just as it was posited earlier that the binary ethnic categories hid subtleties in the development of ethnic inequality among Jews in Israel, so it is argued that unexamined assumptions about how Ethiopians are to be named hide nuances of race and self-concept. In addition, to the extent that Kaplan is correct in asserting that the term "black" is associated in Israel with lower economic status and that its use by researchers makes some outcomes seem self-evident, labeling Ethiopian Jews "black" may blind researchers to internal variation among Ethiopians and to the effect of that variation on attainment in Israel. It may be noted, for instance, that a number of schools were established in Ethiopia by Jewish communities abroad; in consequence, some Ethiopians who arrived in Israel were Europeanized and educated.[37] Their fate may shed light on how economics and perceived race interacted to shape Ethiopian Jewish experience in Israel.

In contrast to the case of the 1950s immigrants (where attention to categorization led to the adoption of new theoretical frameworks for the analysis of Israeli society), the most interesting work on Ethiopians has focused on the history of categorization itself, and what different naming practices say about the changing identities of both namers and the named. Abbink argues that the reason Ethiopian Jews rejected the terms "Falasha" and "Beta Israel"—even though they had used them in Ethiopia—was their desire to integrate with other Israeli Jews. Similarly, although the immigrant generation strongly resisted the name "black," associating it with slavery in Ethiopia, there appears to be a trend among the Israeli-born of adopting the term.[38] Scholars generally agree that this trend is a reaction to the Israeli context and, in particular, perceived discrimination—with "black" referencing the black Atlantic or pan-African black diaspora in an attempt to redefine the position of Ethiopian Jews in Israeli society. As Kaplan put it, "young Ethiopians are able to tap into a resource with far greater prestige than the Ethiopian heritage of their parents … by claiming as their own a powerful, globalized, sophisticated, militant trans-national Black identity."[39]

Furthermore, as Kaplan notes, naming Ethiopians *the* black Jews renders other Israelis white by contrast. There is a long history of Jews "becoming" not just western (as previously described) but also white—alongside other groups, such as Irish and Italians, who were not initially read as white by the colonial West. Kaplan argues that the practice of naming Ethiopians black has a tendency to keep these histories of the naming of *European* Jews invisible, thus cementing the process of making other Israelis white. In this sense, naming Ethiopians black positions them—and other Israelis—in very specific places in Israeli and global society.[40]

The story told by Kaplan, Uri Ben-Eliezer, and others is focused on events in Israel; as such, they reference Ethiopian history only to the extent that it can shed light on transitions in naming practice in Israel. Bruce Haynes, Daniel Friedman, and Ulysses Santamaria, however, tell more elaborate stories of shifts in the perceived Jewishness and blackness of this group that hinge on religious and racial dynamics in the West and in Ethiopia.[41] Friedman and Santamaria's research is particularly interesting for the questions it raises about Jewish/Christian distinctions, an issue that is also important to research on immigrants from the former Soviet Union.[42] They make a convincing argument that Jews existed in Ethiopia prior to the advent of Christianity, and that one can assume that the current Ethiopian Jews are their descendants. They then detail a long history of conflict and alliance between Jews and various Christian groups, in which some Christian groups defected to the Jewish community. This absorbing of Ethiopian Christians, along with other dynamics, led to mutual effects on religious practice. The argument that Ethiopians blended aspects of the Christian and the Jewish has relevance with regard to immigrants from the former Soviet Union. Assimilation of Jews while in the Soviet Union, and the immigration of many non-Jews along with Jews to Israel, has the potential to generate hybrid Jewish-non-Jewish identities within the Jewish state.[43]

Whereas Friedman and Santamaria's history focuses on the Jewishness of Ethiopians across time, Haynes focuses on their perceived blackness. He argues that since "Jewish" and "black" have often been perceived as mutually exclusive, the Jewishness of Ethiopians has been used to read them as less black; similarly, their perceived blackness has been used to read them as less Jewish. He then locates this history within a larger history of the development of white supremacy and supremacists' evolving distinctions between "Caucasian" Africans of the north (for instance, Egyptians) and the true blacks of the south. Thus, for Haynes, the stances regarding the blackness of Ethiopian Jewish immigrants to Israel are not merely the result of blacks having been slaves, as other work suggests, but of global redefinitional moves regarding the categorization of Africa as a whole.[44] His article firmly locates Ethiopian Jewish categorization—naming and consequent identity—within a history of Africa, and in this way serves as a nice contrast to Friedman and Santamaria's firm location of Ethiopian categorization in a history of global Jewish dynamics.

Is research on the 1950s immigrants, with its use of the Orientalism framework, at all useful to conceptualize the experience of Ethiopian Jews in Israel? From one perspective, not only is the answer no, but the East/West framework actually obfuscates matters. This is because Orientalism does not have much to say about people who are perceived as non-white (white supremacy does that); and just as Palestinian non-Jews arguably disappear when Israelis are considered along black/white lines, so Ethiopians disappear when East/West lines are the framework. From other perspectives, however, there may be useful parallels between the 1950s immigrants and Ethiopian Jewish immigrants. For example, in both cases the more powerful groups in Israel are presented as using new immigrants to advance the construction of Israeli Jews, as a whole, as being closer to Western Europe than to areas outside of it. In the earlier case, presenting Palestinians as the ultimate easterners advanced the construction of Israeli Jews as a western group; in the later case, presenting Israeli Ethiopians as black underscores the whiteness (and westernness)[45] of the rest of the Israeli Jewish population.

Finally, although white supremacy and Orientalism are distinct discourses, they are also linked, and as Kaplan points out, portraying (most) Israelis as white also helps construct them as western.[46] In support of this argument, Kaplan references two colleagues: Shalva Weil talking about Israel as a primarily white, modern society, and Fred Lazin speaking of Israel as "a white, modern, educated, western country absorbing black Africans."[47] Along similar lines, work on Orientalism has deconstructed the modern/non-modern distinction that is often used to track Ethiopian Jewish integration into Israeli society, portraying the concepts as social constructions oriented more toward justifying European domination than describing reality. Such arguments are obviously relevant in producing new frameworks for understanding the Ethiopian experience in Israel.

"Russian" Immigrants

In contrast to the Ethiopian case, research on immigrants from the former Soviet Union is making good use of the panethnic and East/West frameworks used in research on the 1950s. The East/West distinction is highly salient to arriving FSU immigrants, who read themselves as eastern in relation to West Europeans but western in relation to Israeli society. How they construct that shift is the subject of current research.[48] The East/West line has also affected the variables used to categorize FSU immigrants in quantitative research. Although most research does not distinguish between "Asian" and "European" FSU immigrants, work that does use this distinction has found significantly more complex dynamics of integration than research that does not.[49] Regarding panethnic formation, Russian Jews should technically be integrated into the Ashkenazi group, which is itself dominated by the descendants of earlier arrivals from Russia. Yet in many respects (such as identity and language preservation), they do not seem to be integrating. On the one hand, this may suggest that the panethnic framework is not applicable to FSU experiences; on the other, examining the question of why FSU immigrants are not "becoming" Ashkenazi may be quite useful in understanding Israeli panethnic formation as a complex and historically changing force in Israeli society, which may simultaneously strengthen and weaken over time.

Jewishness is also an issue for FSU immigrants. As noted, frameworks that were developed to understand the 1950s immigrants assume the Jewishness of the immigrants and therefore do not take variation in Jewishness into account.[50] In the Ethiopian case, Jewishness is a discursive theme—that is, those questions that do arise concern the extent to which perceived blackness subconsciously undermines perceived Jewishness, or the extent to which Ethiopian Jewish practice was influenced by Christianity and should be brought in line with rabbinic practice.[51] The consensus is that the group is Jewish, since this position accords not only with the subjective identity of the immigrants, but also with Israeli law and with the way in which Ethiopian Jews are perceived by other Israelis. In contrast, many FSU immigrants identify—to differing degrees—as non-Jewish, and many are also registered by the state as non-Jewish. My own informal conversations with scholars who do research on FSU immigrants suggest that, just as Middle Eastern immigrants from the 1950s had to demonstrate westernization in order to avoid discrimination, FSU immigrants have to prove Jewishness. There is a discursive component to this point, since the often hidden nature of the non-Jewishness of so many Israeli citizens can undermine conceptions of the Israeli population as Jewish. In addition, "Jewishness" has found its way into recent quantitative research that shows how Russian immigrants who are not Jewish integrate less well into Israeli society.[52] An issue that remains to be resolved is how to classify an FSU immigrant and his/her descendants as Jewish (or not), since subjective identity, state classification, and perception by others may all differ.

Third-generation Israelis

Arguments that developed about the effect of Orientalism on Israeli society imply that these theories would remain relevant to research on the children and grandchildren of the 1950s immigrants, including those who are products of intermarriage between Ashkenazim and Mizrahim. In part this is because the treatment of individuals can be analytically separated from the impact of Orientalism on Israeli identity and social goals. Thus, it is possible for individual Israelis to become East/West hybrids or to move beyond ethnic differentiation, even as it continues to be the case that Israelis as a whole prefer that Israel become a western entity, with continuing effects on society and lifestyle. Geographical location may matter here, in that even as large groups of Mizrahim move beyond their Middle Eastern classification, others who were settled in development towns and other remote areas populated largely by Middle Eastern immigrants may continue to be classified as eastern. Finally, recent interview-based research has argued that the concepts of East and West, and often essentialist beliefs that ethnic background affects behavior, continue to play significant conscious and unconscious roles in intermarriages, the identity of the children of intermarriages, and the daily experience of handling stigma, even among third-generation Mizrahim.[53]

Countering all this are arguments that the panethnic and East/West frameworks are less relevant for hybrids and children of the third generation, as are the categorization practices and sociological dynamics articulated around dichotomization. For one thing, de-Arabization may not be a significant issue for third-generation Mizrahim who have grown up with little exposure or attachment to the cultures of Egypt, Iraq, or other Middle Eastern countries. This situation came about in part because the immigrations from Middle Eastern countries were nearly total, emptying those countries of their indigenous Jewish populations. In consequence, there are no new immigrants to "refresh" the Arabness of Mizrahim in the way that continuing Mexican immigration provides constant contact with Mexican culture even to third-generation Mexican Americans. De-Arabization in the first generation would obviously enhance such a process of disconnect between third-generation Israelis and their grandparents' putatively Arabic cultures. In addition, the first generation complained not only of de-Arabization but also of the imposition of East European Jewish culture (such as classical music) on their behavior. This may not be a salient issue for third-generation Mizrahim who have grown up attached to the "Israeli" culture taught in the schools. In sum, a variety of issues associated with panethnic formation and the East/West line may not be relevant for the third generation.

At the same time, although the Mizrahi/Ashkenazi dichotomous gap developed some time ago, and has remained stable through the third generation, there are so many mixed-ethnicity third-generation Israelis that it has become almost impossible to use a country-of-origin model to measure attainment.[54] As a result, the focus has now shifted from the formation of Mizrahim and Ashkenazim to the attainments of the increasing large group of children of intermarriage. This research consistently finds that among the second generation, educational attainments of the progeny of intermarriage fall between those who are from "pure" Mizrahi or Ashkenazi families.[55] However, not enough work has been done to determine what characterizes the third generation. Has this group comes to resemble Ashkenazim, thus preserving the dichotomous ethnic structure?[56] Or has it remained a separate group, which translates into creating a new structure? In one study, Barbara Okun examined how Ashkenazi-Mizrahi intermarriage affected ethnic inequality in the realm of educational attainment by examining levels of educational inequality under a variety of identity assumptions for the mixed group. Given that mixed marriages tend to involve the less educated of the Ashkenazi group and the more educated of the Mizrahi group, such ethnic intermarriage has the tendency to exacerbate the disadvantage of Mizrahim.[57]

Although there may well be technical categorization issues regarding how to define the mixed group in Israeli research, these cannot be addressed with the data that is currently available. Because the Israeli census records only fathers' country of origin, it is not possible to determine the complete ethnic heritage of third-generation Israelis. Most of the research uses a data set that connects the 1995 census to that of 1983, with researchers using the 1983 census to measure the first generation's country of origin. In this setup, information about the third generation is read from their individual 1995 file, and information about their second-generation parents is read from their parents' records in the 1983 file. Among the information recorded about these second-generation parents is their first-generation fathers' countries of origin. There are two problems with this procedure: first, because one can get parents' data only for those who lived at home in 1983, a large number of third-generation Israelis cannot be assigned an ethnic origin. In addition, because only fathers' country of origin is measured in the 1983 census, only the grandfathers' countries of origin can be measured for the third generation. The solution adopted by researchers has been to code people as Mizrahi only if all known immigrants in their family were from Middle Eastern countries and as Ashkenazi only if all known immigrants were from Europe. All others are considered to be of mixed origin, but clearly with information only about fathers, some mixed children are being coded as Mizrahi or Ashkenazi. Without appropriate data, it is impossible to know if this categorization issue is affecting empirical research.

Conclusion

A society's prevailing categories come to appear self-evident, and scholars in addition to laypeople tend to use them without question. This essay has shown how category choice in ethnic research in Israel affects social analysis. The shift from binary ethnic categories for Jews to specific country of origin had particularly dramatic effects on the ethnic picture drawn by scholars. While the large educational gaps among arriving Mizrahim and Ashkenazim suggested that a modernization framework was the best way to make sense of the experience of groups in Israel, attention to country of origin suggested that the frameworks of panethnic formation and Orientalism were more appropriate. In turn, the use of Orientalism to study Jewish Israeli society brought Palestinians into the framework in new ways. The effect of naming for Ethiopians is equally dramatic, in that thinking of Ethiopians as black and/or Jewish implies different research questions, different expectations for integration, and the expression of different identities. Similarly, asking why scholars treat Ethiopians as black puts the analytical spotlight on non-Ethiopian Israeli society, as much as on Ethiopians themselves. Finally, while the Jewish/non-Jewish distinction is generally not used in studies of Russian immigrants, evidence suggests that we can learn much more about their experiences if we do attend to this distinction.

Notes

1. Categorization scheme refers to the rules one uses to classify and describe groups. The idea is that no categorization scheme is neutral; rather, each draws from a set of beliefs regarding how individuals are related to each other.

2. Panethnic formation is a process in which aggregate identities become more salient, over time, than specific identities. In the United States, one such aggregate is "Asian," which contains the more "specific" groups of Korean, Japanese, Malaysian, Vietnamese, and Chinese, among others. Among immigrants, "Korean" means more than "Asian," but among the U.S.-born, Asian is more salient. In Israel, the parallel process is one in which "Mizrahi" became more salient than "Iraqi" or "Moroccan," and "Ashkenazi" became more salient than "Polish" or "German" (though in all cases, again, the specific identities never disappeared).

3. The modernization framework, which was popular in the 1950s, asserts that societies worldwide undergo a similar developmental trajectory. As a society modernizes, bureaucracies rationalize; rules become clear and are consistently applied by agents who set aside their own preferences and act as representatives of the organization (for instance, pro-life judges uphold pro-choice laws regardless of personal anathema); industries use large-scale and efficient methods of production such as assembly lines; occupational and educational success are dependent on individual attainment rather than tribal and familial affiliations; education increases; families shrink; and states take on more social tasks such as providing education, garbage collection, and regulation of banks and food impurities. Societies in the West appeared to have moved ahead faster than other societies, an observation that was central to later critiques of modernization theory (later critiques suggested that modernization theory was influenced by something between ethnocentrism and justification for western global dominance).

4. Roberto Bachi, *Studies in Economic and Social Sciences* (Jerusalem: 1956); Yossi Shavit, "Ethnicity and Education in Israel's Changing Marriage Market" (paper presented at the 1994 World Congress of the International Sociological Association, Bielefeld, Germany).

5. "Gatekeepers" in this context refers to those who have the power to distribute resources, among them teachers (who "distribute" educational degrees), and employers.

6. Deborah Bernstein, "Immigrant Transit Camps: The Formation of Dependent Relations in Israeli Society," *Ethnic and Racial Studies* 4, no. 1 (1981), 26–43.

7. Tom Segev, *1949: The First Israelis* (New York: 1986).

8. Shlomo Swirski, *Israel: The Oriental Majority* (London: 1989).

9. Yaacov Nahon, *Patterns of Educational Expansion and the Structure of Occupational Opportunities: The Ethnic Dimension* (Jerusalem: 1987).

10. Karin Amit, "Mizraḥim leumat ashkenazim: haḥalukah haetnit hadikhotomit vehatzla-ḥatam shel benei hador harishon vehasheni beshuk ha'avodah hayisreelit" (Ph.D. diss., Tel Aviv University, 2001); see also Tikva Darwish, "Changes in the Employment Structure of Iraqi Jewish Immigrants to Israel," *International Migration* 23, no. 4 (1985), 461–472; idem, "The Economic Structure of the Jewish Minority in Iraq vis-à-vis the Kuznets Model," *Jewish Social Studies* 47, nos. 3–4 (Summer-Fall 1985), 255–266; idem, "The Jewish Minority in Iraq: A Comparative Study of Economic Structure," *Jewish Social Studies* 49, no. 2 (Spring 1987), 175–180; Aziza Khazzoom, "The Formation of Ethnic Inequality among Jews in Israel" (Ph.D. diss., University of California at Berkeley, 1999).

11. See Harvey E. Goldberg (ed.), *Sephardi and Middle Eastern Jewries: History and Culture in the Modern Era* (Bloomington: 1996), in particular the article by Zvi Yehuda, "Iraqi Jewry and Cultural Change in the Educational Activity of the Alliance Israélite Universelle" (pp. 134–145); also see Daniel J. Schroeter, *Merchants of Essaouira: Urban Society and Imperialism in Southwestern Morocco, 1844–1886* (New York: 1988); Esther Meir, *Hatenu'ah hatziyonit vihudei irak, 1941–1950* (Tel Aviv: 1993); Yosef Meir, *Hitpatḥut ḥevratit tarbutit shel yehudei irak* (Naharaim: 1989); Nissim Rejwan, *The Jews of Iraq: 3000 Years of History and Culture* (Boulder: 1985); Heskel Haddad, *Jews of Arab and Islamic Countries: History, Problems, and Solutions* (New York: 1984); Michael M. Laskier, *The Alliance Israélite Universelle and the Jewish Communities of Morocco: 1862–1962* (Albany: 1983); Aron Rodrigue, *Images of Sephardi and Eastern Jewries in Transition: The Teachers of the Alliance Israélite Universelle, 1860–1939* (Seattle: 1993).

12. Amit, "Mizraḥim leumat Ashkenazim"; Aziza Khazzoom, *Shifting Ethnic Boundaries and Inequality in Israel, or: How the Polish Peddler Became a German Intellectual* (Stanford: 2008).

13. Fig. 10.1 shows similar but not identical findings, as it measures the proportion of men who attained 12 years of academic education. As shown in Fig. 10.1, Iraqi attainment slightly decreased.

14. Khazzoom, *Shifting Ethnic Boundaries and Inequality in Israel*.

15. Ella Shohat, *Israeli Cinema: East/West and the Politics of Representation* (Austin: 1989), 3.

16. Sami Shalom Chetrit, *Intra-Jewish Conflict in Israel: White Jews, Black Jews* (London: 2009); for a parallel in the United States, see Yen Le Espiritu, *Asian American Panethnicity* (Philadelphia: 1992).

17. See also Amnon Raz Krakotzkin, "Orientalizm, mada'ei hayahadut vehaḥevrah hayisreelit: mispar he'arot," *Jama'a* 3 (1998), 34–62; Steven E. Aschheim, *Brothers and Strangers: The East European Jew in German and German Jewish Consciousness, 1800–1923* (Madison: 1982); Aziza Khazzoom, "The Great Chain of Orientalism: Jewish Identity, Stigma Management, and Ethnic Exclusion in Israel," *American Sociological Review* 68 (2003), 481–510.

18. Khazzoom, "The Great Chain of Orientalism."

19. For other work that considers this East/West facet of Jewish identity in Europe, see Krakotzkin, "Orientalizm, mada'ei hayahadut vehaḥevrah hayisreelit"; Susannah Heschel, "Revolt of the Colonized: Abraham Geiger's *Wissenschaft des Judentums* as a Challenge to Christian Hegemony in the Academy," *New German Critique* (1999), 61–85; Aschheim, *Brothers and Strangers*.

20. For quantitative evidence, see Khazzoom, *Shifting Ethnic Boundaries and Inequality in Israel*, esp. ch. 7.

21. Khazzoom, "The Formation of Ethnic Inequality among Jews in Israel"; see also Amir Sumakai-Fink and Jacob Press, *Independence Park: The Lives of Gay Men in Israel* (Berkeley: 2000).

22. Yaron Tsur, "Haskala in a Sectional Colonial Society: Madia (Tunisia) 1884," in Goldberg (ed.), *Sephardi and Middle Eastern Jewries*, 146–167; Gabriel Piterberg, "Domestic Orientalism: The Representation of 'Oriental' Jews in Zionist/Israeli Historiography," *British Journal of Middle Eastern Studies* 23 (1996), 125–145; Daphna Hirsch, "'Interpreters of Occident to the Awakening Orient': The Jewish Public Health Nurse in

Mandate Palestine," *Comparative Studies in Society and History* 50, no. 1 (January 2008), 227–255.

23. Yehouda Shenhav, *The Arab Jews: A Postcolonial Reading of Nationalism, Religion, and Ethnicity* (Palo Alto: 2006).

24. Deborah Bernstein and Shlomo Swirsky, "The Rapid Economic Development of Israel and the Emergence of the Ethnic Division of Labour," *British Journal of Sociology* 33, no. 1 (1982), 64–85; Bernstein, "Immigrant Transit Camps."

25. Amit, "Mizraḥim leumat Ashkenazim"; Khazzoom, "The Formation of Ethnic Inequality among Jews in Israel"; idem, *Shifting Ethnic Boundaries and Inequality in Israel.*

26. Khazzoom, *Shifting Ethnic Boundaries and Inequality in Israel.*

27. Bernstein and Swirsky, "The Rapid Economic Development of Israel and the Emergence of the Ethnic Division of Labour."

28. In one specific example, an Iraqi immigrant in the Carmel market wrote his prices neatly on square pieces of cardboard, never shouted, and never altered his prices. He was noticed by an Ashkenazi accountant and in that way obtained a job that was more similar to the bookkeeping he did in Iraq.

29. Ironically, according to the accepted history, Jews did not create the clash. Rather, it was created by the Muslim and Christian societies in which Jews lived. Jews began using Orientalist thinking when their Christian hosts began to read them query their fitness for integration into Western European society. See Khazzoom, "The Great Chain of Orientalism."

30. Ella Shohat, "Sephardim in Israel: Zionism from the Point of View of Its Jewish Victims," *Social Text* 7 (1988), 1–36.

31. Gil Eyal, *The Disenchantment of the Orient* (Palo Alto: 2006), 44 (n. 22).

32. Paul Starr, "Social Categories and Claims in the Liberal State," *Social Research* 59, no. 2 (1992), 263–295.

33. Jan Abbink, "The Changing Identity of Ethiopian Immigrants (Falashas) in Israel," *Anthropological Quarterly* 57, no. 4 (1984), 139–153.

34. Ibid; see also Shalva Weil, "Collective Designations and Collective Identity among Ethiopian Jews," *Israel Social Science Research* 10, no. 2 (1995), 25–40.

35. Steven Kaplan, "Black and White, Blue and White and Beyond the Pale: Ethiopian Jews and the Discourse of Color in Israel," *Jewish Culture and History* 5, no. 1 (2002), 51–68; Uri Ben-Eliezer, "Multicultural Society and Everyday Cultural Racism: Second Generation of Ethiopian Jews in Israel's 'Crisis of Modernization,'" *Ethnic and Racial Studies* 31, no. 5 (2008), 935–961; Lisa Anteby-Yemeni, "From Ethiopian Villager to Global Villager: Ethiopian Jews in Israel," in *Homelands and Diasporas: Holy Lands and Other Places*, ed. André Levy and Alex Weingrod (Stanford: 2005), 220–244.

36. Kaplan, "Black and White, Blue and White and Beyond the Pale," 53.

37. Daniel Friedman and Ulysses Santamaria, "Identity and Change: The Example of the Falashas, between Assimilation in Ethiopia and Integration in Israel," *Dialectical Anthropology* 15 (1990), 56–73.

38. Kaplan, "Black and White, Blue and White and Beyond the Pale"; Ben-Eliezer, "Multicultural Society and Everyday Cultural Racism."

39. Kaplan, "Black and White, Blue and White and Beyond the Pale," 56.

40. Ibid.

41. Friedman and Santamaria, "Identity and Change"; Bruce Haynes, "People of God, Children of Ham," *Journal of Modern Jewish Studies* 8, no. 2 (2009), 237–254.

42. On Jewish/Christian distinctions among FSU immigrants, see Nelly Elias and Adrianna Kemp, "The New Second Generation: Non-Jewish Olim, Black Jews and Children of Migrant Workers in Israel," *Israel Studies* 15, no. 1 (2010), 73–94.

43. Julia Resnik, "Alternative Identities in Multicultural Schools in Israel: Emancipatory Identity, Mixed Identity, and Transnational Identity," *British Journal of Sociology of Education* 27, no. 5 (2006), 585–601.

44. Haynes, "People of God, Children of Ham."

45. Kaplan, "Black and White, Blue and White and Beyond the Pale," 59.

46. Ibid.

47. Quoted in ibid., 59.

48. Edna Lomsky-Feder and Tali Leibovitz, "Inter-Ethnic Encounters Within the Family: Competing Cultural Models and Social Exchange," *Journal of Ethnic & Migration Studies* 36, no. 1 (2010), 107–124.

49. Yitchak Haberfeld, Moshe Semyonov, and Yinon Cohen, "Ethnicity and Labour Market Performance among Recent Immigrants from the Former Soviet Union to Israel," *European Sociological Review* 16, no. 3 (2000), 287–299.

50. Elias and Kemp, "The New Second Generation."

51. Haynes, "People of God, Children of Ham"; Friedman and Santamaria, "Identify and Change." A distinction can be noted here between Ethiopian Jews—that is, those whose ancestors were regarded (and identified themselves) as Jews—and the Falash Mura, whose ancestors converted to Christianity in the 19th century.

52. Elias and Kemp, "The New Second Generation."

53. On the ways in which ethnic background affects intermarriages, both consciously and subconsciously, see Lomsky-Feder and Tali Leibovitz, "Inter-ethnic Encounters within the Family"; Orly Benjamin, "'He Thought I Would Be Like My Mother': The Silencing of Mizrahi Women in Israeli Inter- and Intra-Marriages," *Ethnic and Racial Studies* 27, no. 2 (2004), 266–289. Insights on the identity of children of intermarriages were provided by Talia Sagiv of the Hebrew University. On stigma among third-generation Mizrahim, see Nissim Mizrahi and Hanna Herzog, "Participatory Destigmatization Strategies among Palestinian Citizens, Ethiopian Jews and Mizrahi Jews in Israel," *Ethnic and Racial Studies* 35, no. 3 (2012), 418–435.

54. Yinon Cohen, Yitchak Haberfeld, and Tali Kristal, "Ethnicity and Mixed Ethnicity: Educational Gaps among Israeli-born Jews," *Ethnic and Racial Studies* 30, no. 5 (2007), 896–917.

55. Ibid.; Barbara Okun and Orna Khait-Marelly, "The Impact of Ethnic Intermarriage on Ethnic Stratification: Jews in Israel," *Research in Social Stratification and Mobility* 28 (2010), 375–394; Momi Dahan, Eyal Dvir, Natalie Mironichev, and Samuel Shye, "Have the Gaps in Education Narrowed?" *Israel Economic Review* 1, no. 2 (November 2003), 37–69; for qualitative research making a similar argument, see Uri Cohen and Nissim Leon, "The New Mizrahi Middle Class: Ethnic Mobility and Class Integration in Israel," *Journal of Israeli History: Politics, Society, Culture* 27, no. 1 (2008), 51–64.

56. Cohen, Haberfeld, and Kristal, "Ethnicity and Mixed Ethnicity."

57. Okun and Khait-Marelly, "The Impact of Ethnic Intermarriage on Ethnic Stratification."

Jewish Majority and Jewish Minority in Israel: The Demographic Debate

Arnon Soffer
(UNIVERSITY OF HAIFA)

Over the years, and with increasing vehemence, public discourse on demographic issues in Israel has dealt with two matters connected with the numerical balance between Jews and non-Jews.[1] The first, with significant ramifications for the Jewish-Arab conflict, concerns the possible annexation of territory located in what is often referred to as "greater Israel"—the West Bank (or, as it is officially termed, Judea and Samaria). The second issue, which to date has received less attention outside of Israel, relates to areas in Israel's periphery, specifically, portions of the Galilee and the Negev regions, in which Arabs constitute a majority of the local population.

Relationships between majority and minority populations have often been characterized by tension and conflict; as will be seen, various strategies have been adopted both by minority populations seeking greater autonomy and by majority populations anxious to retain control of territory and/or political rule. In Israel, demographic questions are especially fraught, as they engender not only political but also practical and moral debate.[2] For instance, in the context of the Israeli-Palestinian peace process, negotiations regarding the setting of permanent borders inevitably must deal with the fact that there are significant Jewish population clusters within Judea and Samaria. At the same time, proponents of annexing these territories to Israel are challenged by those who argue that annexation would produce a country in which Jews were outnumbered by non-Jews—thus threatening either the Jewish or the democratic character of the state. Such arguments, in turn, are countered by assertions regarding the (un)reliability of demographic data concerning Palestinians. Similarly, demographic issues played a key role in the fierce debates with regard to the unilateral Israeli disengagement from the Gaza Strip in 2005 and the decision to construct a separation barrier between "greenline" (pre-June 1967) Israel and Judea/Samaria, as well as those concerning proposals to encourage (or compel) a transfer of Arab populations living in Israel.[3]

Although dealing with demographic issues, this essay is written from the perspective of a geographer, and as such focuses on the spatial aspects of majority-minority relations in Israel. In contrast with demographers, who describe and analyze human populations with the aid of statistical data relating to such matters as childbirth, mortality, aging, and migration, geographers are concerned with the spatial spread of various phenomena, whether physical in nature (for instance, the rates of precipitation in different parts of a given country) or related to people (for instance, the spread of cities or areas of conflicts in different regions of the world). In accordance with the specific issue being investigated, geographers make use of tools employed by other professionals, among them geologists, biologists, sociologists, economists, demographers, and political scientists. Their main tool, however, is the *map*.

In this essay, demographic data are the basis for a geo-political analysis of specific spaces within Israel and the areas adjacent to it; in addition to statistics, the analysis relies on geopolitical models deriving from other areas of geography, political science, international relations, and history. Following a brief comparative and historical overview, we consider the two majority-minority issues outlined at the outset of this essay in light of geographic considerations. Though often overlooked, such considerations are especially salient in the analysis of the Israeli case.

Coexistence versus Separation

In both democratic and non-democratic countries, the proximity of two or more groups that are ethnically, culturally, or linguistically different from one another has often led to tension that at times escalates into violence, sometimes with dramatic geopolitical consequences.[4] Most often, mutual fears lead each side to take steps to protect its interests. Actions taken by minority groups seeking to defend their language or identity run the gamut from verbal violence to sporadic acts of terrorism to guerrilla war (consider, for instance, the "language wars" of Quebec and ongoing parliamentary disputes in Belgium, as opposed to acts of terrorism by Basque separatists or the decades-long "troubles" in Northern Ireland). In response, ruling governments or populations may resort to measures such as "flooding" a minority-populated region with members of the majority or ruling group (a practice followed by the Romans, the Ottomans, and in more recent times, the Serbs in Kosovo and Bosnia-Herzegovina) or encouraging (or forcing) minorities to migrate from the periphery to the more heavily populated interior, as was the case with Kurds in Turkey.[5] In more extreme cases, governments may employ violent measures such as mass expulsion or physical destruction.[6] Alternatively, the majority may seek to pacify the minority by granting them special privileges such as proportional representation in government or full or partial cultural, religious, or territorial autonomy.[7] When such measures fail, the two populations typically separate, either peacefully or violently.[8]

History teaches us that there are a number of necessary conditions for separatist procedures. One of these is a sufficiently large demographic mass in a specific territory. Second, the minority group needs some form of leadership and organization in order to rally the people to the cause (and later, to forestall the danger of post-separation chaos). It also helps if the minority group has an economic base with which to maintain itself as an independent entity—the new republic of South Sudan, for instance, benefits from recently discovered oil deposits. Events going on outside the country also have important consequences for any separation procedure. For instance, a group demanding partition or independence may receive financial, military, or political assistance (or some combination of the three) from compatriots living abroad or from a neighboring or more distant country seeking to advance its own interests. On the national level, the relative strength or weakness of the central government will either hinder or hasten the separation process. Finally, a history of discord between the majority and minority populations often underlies instances of secession, and in many instances affects the direction (non-violent or violent) in which the process leads.[9] The 20th century alone provides abundant examples of places in which bloodbaths preceded or accompanied partition (or attempted partition), among them India and Pakistan following the Second World War, Nigeria and Biafra in the late 1960s and, in more recent decades, Ruanda, Burundi, and Sudan.[10]

In the case of partition, a nation is divided and its borders are redrawn, as in Cyprus, where the de facto partition of the island following the Turkish invasion in 1974 is marked by a U.N. buffer zone.[11] In more localized disputes, the borders are often harder to define and the very concept of minority and majority may be subject to change—consider, for instance, an urban neighborhood populated almost exclusively by members of a "minority" group. In Israel, it is easy to identify the Arab versus Jewish neighborhoods in the city of Lod. It is much harder to identify Bedouin space in the Negev region, or Arab space in the central lower Galilee region or in Judea and Samaria, since these areas also contain regional Jewish councils whose very establishment represents an attempt to dilute or deterritorialize the "minority" population (see, for instance, Map 11.4, showing the Misgav municipal council).[12] Moreover, the very borders of Israel have never been formally ratified: the "green line," with minor modifications, represents the ceasefire lines drawn in 1949.

The Israeli Case

As of 2009, Jews constituted a clear majority of 77 percent of the population within the state of Israel (Table 11.1).[13] Approximately 58 percent of Israeli Jews reside in an area that I term the "state of Tel Aviv" (see Table 11.1[h] and Maps 11.1–11.3). If we add the Ashkelon, Acre, and Nahariya natural regions[14] and the Haifa district, excluding the Umm al-Fahm natural region, we find that 71 percent of all Israeli Jews live on the coastal plain, from Acre in the north to the Gaza Strip boundary in the south (Map 11.2).

By contrast, some 82 percent of the Arab population inhabits portions of Israel's periphery—the northern Negev; the Triangle (Wadi Ara) region, located east of Netanya and Hadera; East Jerusalem; and the lower central Galilee (Maps 11.1, 11.3).[15] The geographical distribution of the Jews throughout Israel is very different from that of the Arabs; there is hardly any mix between the two populations.[16]

Compiled by Israel's Central Bureau of Statistics, the demographic data on Israeli population are almost universally regarded as reliable—the only real dispute concerns the number of illegal residents, among them foreign workers and tourists whose visas have expired and illegal migrants entering Israel mainly via the Egyptian border.[17] The situation is different, however, with regard to estimates of the Arab population in Judea and Samaria and the Gaza Strip. Varying figures computed by three different sources—an Israeli governmental body (the Civil Administration, part of the Defense

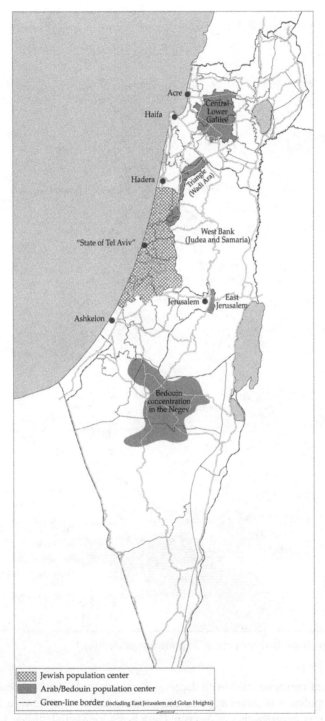

Map 11.1. Jewish vs. Arab/Bedouin population centers in green-line Israel

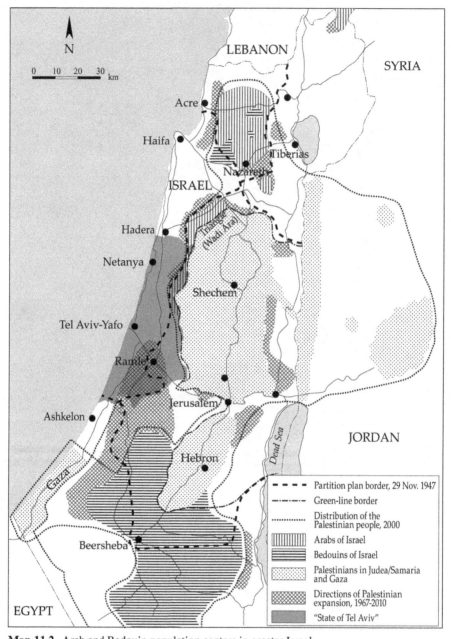

Map 11.2. Arab and Bedouin population centers in greater Israel

Ministry) and two academics with decades of experience in the field—indicate that
the Arab population in Judea and Samaria numbers somewhere between 2.2 million
and 2.5 million, whereas that of Arabs in Gaza lies somewhere between 1.47 million
and 1.58 million (Table 11.2). Contesting this range of figures is a right-wing group
known as the American-Israel Demographic Research Group (AIDRG), which claims

Table 11.1. Majority/Minority Status of Jews and Arabs in Various Regions in the Land of Israel and Its Environs, 1980, 2009 (in thousands)

Region	No. of Jews	%	No. of Arabs and others	%	Total Population
Middle East,[a] 2009	6,050	1.5	410,000	98.5	416,050
Greater Israel[b]					
1980	3,300	65	1,800	35	5,100
2009	6,017	52	5,622	48	11,639
"Green-line" Israel[c]					
1980	3,250	84	640	16	3,890
2009	5,742	77	1,758	23	7,500
Central lower Galilee[d]					
1980	100	28	260	72	360
2009	173	23	566	77	739
Palestinian Galilee (according to November 1947 partition plan)[e]	279	31	623	69	902
Wadi Ara,[f] 2009	5	4	120	96	125
City of Jerusalem (East and West)					
1980	292	72	115	28	407
2009	488	63	286	37	774
East Jerusalem,[g] 2009	189	40	286	60	475
"State of Tel Aviv,"[h] 2009	3,319	91	332	9	3,651
Beersheba district, 2009	386	67	193	33	579
Beersheba natural region, 2009	214	53	190	47	404
Northern Negev Bedouin space,[i] 2009	Few	–	200	100	200

Sources: 2009 World Population Data Sheet, online at www.prb.org/Publications/Datasheets/2009/2009wpds.aspx (for Middle East); Sergio DellaPergola, "Israel's Existential Predicament: Population, Territory, Identity," *Current History* (December 2010), (for Greater Israel); Israel Bureau of Statistics, *Statistical Abstract of Israel.*

[a] Israel, Jordan, Egypt, Syria, the Arabian Peninsula, Turkey, and Iran; also includes residents (Jewish and others) of Judea/Samaria and Gaza. See Arnon Soffer and Dalit Lan, *The Geography of the Middle East* (Tel Aviv: 2008).
[b] Differing figures for the Arab population in Judea/Samaria and Gaza are shown on Table 2. Not included are an estimated 650,000 foreign workers (with or without valid visas) and illegal tourists; see Evgenia Bystrov and Arnon Soffer, *Israel: Demography 2012–2030, On the Way to a Religious State* (Haifa: 2012), 17.
[c] Includes East Jerusalem and the Golan Heights.
[d] Lower Galilee mountains, including natural regions of Karmiel, Shefar'am, and Nazareth.
[e] Natural areas of Acre, Nahariya, Yehiam, Eilon, Karmiel, Shefar'am, and Nazareth.
[f] Includes settlements on both sides of the Wadi Ara highway from the Barkai junction to the Megido junction; among these are two Jewish settlements, Katzir and Mei Ami.
[g] Territory annexed by Israel in 1967.
[h] Includes the natural region of Hadera, the central district, and Tel Aviv district, plus the natural regions of Ashdod, Malakhi, and western Samaria (see Map 11.3).
[i] Not including Bedouin population in the Mitzpe Rimon-Ovdat region or Bedouin encampments between Rahat and Rishon LeZion (see Map 11.6).

Table 11.2. Estimated Arab Population in Judea/Samaria and Gaza (in millions)

	Judea/Samaria	Gaza
Civil Adminstration (2011)[a]	2.5	1.5
Sergio DellaPergola (2010) [b]	2.2	1.47
Arnon Soffer (2010)[c]	2.4	1.58

[a] Figures compiled by the Civil Administration supplied to Arnon Soffer, 17 February 2011.
[b] Sergio DellaPergola, "Israel's Existential Predicament: Population, Territory, Identity," *Current History* (December 2010), 385.
[c] Evgenia Bystrov and Arnon Soffer, *Israel: Demography 2012–2030, On the Way to a Religious State* (Haifa: 2012), 17.

that only 1.6–1.8 million Arabs live in Judea and Samaria, with another one million in Gaza. Despite its name, none of the members of this group are professional demographers.[18] Nonetheless, they have been prolific in publishing articles attacking the data produced by what they call the "demographic establishment"—referring, in particular, to Sergio DellaPergola and to me—and their counterclaims have been taken up by a number of Israeli politicians eager to promote the annexation of territories, among them former Minister of Information Yuri Edelstein.

A key argument made both by the AIDRG and by one of its members, Yoram Ettinger, who writes a blog known as the Ettinger Report, is that the Palestinian census data of 1997 and 2007 are unreliable (both censuses, it should be noted, were conducted under the auspices of the Norwegian government). Additional claims are that Arab migration from the occupied territories is increasing, whereas the birthrate among Palestinian Arabs is falling. According to the AIDRG, Jews currently constitute the decided majority in greater Israel, and (with increased Jewish immigration) this majority will increase, thereby ensuring that Israel will continue to be a Jewish state even if it annexes territory and grants citizenship to all those living there.[19]

In his accompanying essay in this symposium, Sergio DellaPergola points to the serious methodological and factual flaws in these arguments. I would add that the publications and blogs put out by Ettinger and the AIDRG exhibit at best a lack of professionalism and at worst a manipulation—or even fabrication—of data. For instance, in an article written by Yakov Feitelson for the Institute for Zionist Strategies, the claim is made that 10,000–50,000 Arabs annually exit the area of Greater Israel, and do not return. Feitelson cites Ettinger with regard to the figures concerning Judea and Samaria; a journalist, Amit Cohen (of *Maariv*), with regard to Gaza; and in other places presents hearsay ("according to rumor") or otherwise vague sources.[20] I checked the matter with Israeli border officials, who were in agreement that there is no mass exit of Palestinian Arabs from Judea and Samaria: those who leave do so temporarily. In the same article, Feitelson writes: "The demographic laws, which are known to all who work in the area, speak of three main stages in population development: population explosion, stability, and afterwards a subsiding of natural increase."[21] After vastly oversimplifying the demographic transition theory in this manner, he goes on to assert confidently that the Palestinian birthrate is falling.[22]

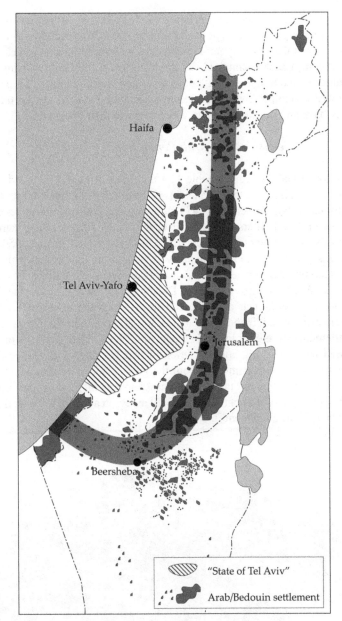

Map 11.3. Arab/Bedouin population continuum

As noted, claims made by the AIDRG, the Institute for Zionist Strategies, and blog-
gers such as Ettinger have been promoted by a number of Israeli politicians. Political
agendas, rather than a sober appraisal of the data at hand, underlie the adoption of
unsubstantiated data regarding a continuing Jewish majority in greater Israel. Yet just
as serious is the fact that, amid all the rhetorical flourishes, arguments, and counterargu-

ments, an issue of equal importance is being overlooked: that of the vanishing Jewish majority in Israel's peripheral regions. As will be seen, Jews are already a minority population in several areas of green-line Israel as well as in the annexed eastern portion of Jerusalem, Israel's capital. Given the historical realities of recurring tensions between minority and majority populations that often lead to demands for partition or to outright war, it is imperative to devote serious attention to this issue, so that policymakers may have an informed basis on which to make their decisions.

Jewish versus Arab Populations in Israel

The central lower Galilee region (Table 11.1 and Map 11.5) was included as part of the area originally allocated to the Palestinians in the partition plan approved by the United Nations on November 29, 1947; following the War of Independence, it fell within the green-line borders of Israel. Over the succeeding decades, there were a number of efforts to promote Jewish settlement in the region. In the 1950s, for instance, dozens of agricultural settlements were built along the borders with Lebanon and Syria. The mountainous terrain was not conducive to agriculture, however, and many of the settlements were abandoned. During the following decade, the "At Last" (Sof sof) project was launched, in the course of which the towns of Karmiel and Ma'alot were established. In the 1970s and 1980s, about 50 additional rural and community settlements were established in the heart of the Galilee. Yet none of these efforts resulted in a mass migration of Jews, in part because of a relative dearth of employment opportunities combined with the lack of adequate state support in the form of housing subsidies and tax exemptions. Consequently, the proportion of Jews in the total population of the central lower Galilee region actually fell over time, from 28 percent in 1980 to 23 percent in 2009.

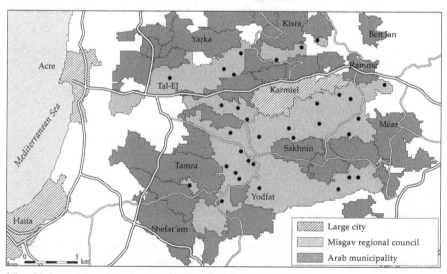

Map 11.4. Jewish and Arab municipalities in central lower Galilee

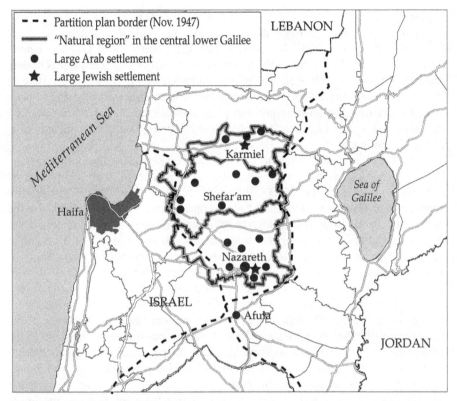

Map 11.5. Central lower Galilee

A second trend in this region is that of weakening Israeli sovereignty, as evidenced by increasing non-compliance with the law (the incidence of non-payment of taxes, for instance, is on the rise)[23] and growing political militancy. In October 2000, following a visit by Israeli prime minister Ariel Sharon to the Temple Mount in Jerusalem and in the wake of incitement on the part of radical political and religious Muslim leaders, violent clashes broke out between Arab protesters and police, resulting in numerous injuries and the deaths of 13 Arabs (a Jewish Israeli was also killed). A commission of inquiry investigating the events concluded as follows:

> The intensity of the violence and aggression expressed in the events was extremely powerful. Against security forces, and even against civilians, use was made of a variety of means of attack, including a small number of live fire incidents, Molotov cocktails, ball bearings in slingshots, various methods of stone throwing and the rolling of burning tires.[24]

Another area of Arab concentration is located in the Triangle (Wadi Ara) region. As shown on Table 11.1, Wadi Ara is populated almost exclusively by (Muslim) Arabs—some 96 percent of a total population of 125,000. The area includes the cities of Umm al-Fahm and Baqa al-Garbiya as well as approximately 15 towns and smaller villages. In contrast, the Jewish population is limited to two small settlements. Here, too, there are signs of growing anti-Israel militancy, manifested in part by a rise in support for radical Islamic political parties and by a number of incidents in which individuals have been convicted of collaborating with Palestinian terrorist groups. In contrast with the lower central Galilee region, Wadi Ara is located adjacent to the green-line border. For this reason, this region presents a good candidate for territorial exchange in the event of an Israeli-Palestinian peace agreement: in exchange for it becoming part of a Palestinian state, Israel could gain sovereignty over parts of Judea and Samaria (for instance, the Gush Etzion bloc between Bethlehem and Hebron) that have a concentration of Jewish settlements.

A third area of Arab concentration is East Jerusalem, annexed to Israel in 1967, which contains more than 300,000 legally registered Arab inhabitants in addition to approximately 100,000 illegal inhabitants (Table 11.1).[25] The Jewish population of East Jerusalem, numbering approximately 190,000, lives mostly in neighborhoods constructed after 1967. Here as elsewhere in Israel, there are few mixed Jewish-Arab areas; in neighborhoods containing a small number of Jews living among or in close proximity to larger number of Arabs, there is relatively greater tension between the two groups. Moreover, Jerusalem over the years has experienced numerous violent incidents in addition to acts of terrorism. Although Jews still constitute a majority of the total population of Jerusalem, the relative Jewish share of the population has been declining, from 72 percent in 1980 to 63 percent in 2009. If this trend continues, the Arab share of population will increase to approximately 50 percent by the year 2035.[26] Among the factors contributing to the loss of Jewish population are high housing prices (fueled in part by the massive purchase of luxury apartments by wealthy Jews abroad) and ongoing tension between haredi and secular Jews. The Arab population, in contrast, has benefited from accelerated in-migration, especially since the erection of the separation barrier.

Finally, there is the concentration of Bedouin population in the northern Negev, totaling approximately 200,000 inhabitants (Maps 11.1, 11.6). This territory, which spreads over some 10 percent of green-line Israel, forms a barrier between the "state of Tel Aviv" and strategic Israeli facilities located further to the south, including army bases, military fire zones, and the nuclear plant in Dimona. In the northeast, the Bedouin region touches the green line at the Hebron hills; in the south it is near Bedouin areas located in Jordan; in the southwest, it draws close to the Israeli-Egyptian border. In addition, as shown on Map 11.6, there are extensive ties between Israeli Bedouins and Bedouin populations outside of Israel (mainly in Sinai and south Jordan).

The spread of the Bedouin region goes hand in hand with a continuous rise in population. The annual growth rate among Bedouins in the south is 5.5 percent, which translates to a doubling of the population every 12–13 years.[27] The inevitable result is a spreading of population across a much wider area: there are now hundreds of small, illegal Bedouin settlements lacking roads, electricity, or water mains, many of them abutting Jewish towns and cities.[28] Just as inevitably, friction between the groups is growing. Bedouin demands that their settlements be officially recognized are countered by arguments relating to the enormous cost of providing the necessary infrastructure for numerous, scattered settlements.

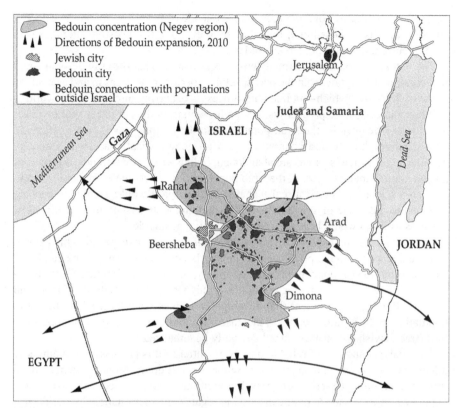

Map 11.6. The Bedouin concentration in the Negev

Demography and Israeli Public Policy

Is it legitimate to introduce demography as an element in the debate concerning the possible annexation of territories in Judea and Samaria or that regarding strategic planning in Israel's periphery?

With respect to Judea and Samaria, there are weighty geographic, historical, and security reasons on behalf of annexation. Yet countering all of these is the real fear that, in such a scenario, the Jewish population would wind up constituting a minority of the total population of "greater Israel." If the entire area of Judea and Samaria was to be annexed and if democratic elections were subsequently held, an Arab majority could take power and effectively put an end to the Jewish-Zionist entity in the Middle East. Alternatively, some kind of power-sharing framework between the two groups might be created. Historically, however, such frameworks have proven to be fragile, particularly in the case of groups sharing a longstanding history of conflict: one needs to look no farther than Lebanon to see the possible consequences.

For most Israelis, it is clear that annexation of the territories would pose a strategic threat to Israel. Indeed, the only people in favor of annexation are those belonging to the far Left (who support a bi-national state) or to the far Right (who believe that demographic problems can be solved in "other ways," namely, by encouraging or compelling the transfer of Arab populations outside of Israel). Assuming that annexation is not a likely possibility, I would like to examine two possible alternatives in light of current demographic trends in Israel.

The first scenario may be termed "business as usual." That is to say, Jews in Israel will continue to migrate from the less developed periphery to areas in and around the "state of Tel Aviv," which—in line with processes occurring throughout the world—will become ever more prosperous. Jews who remain in the periphery will be fewer and poorer. Meanwhile, the Arab population in the periphery will gain in strength, both demographically and economically. Arab geographical space will gradually become larger as Jewish areas are abandoned; in line with current trends, it is reasonable to assume that, as a result, the Arab population will become even more militant. In such a scenario, there is a real fear that Jewish space would eventually become confined to the "state of Tel Aviv"—a city-state unable to sustain itself. Ultimately, business as usual would become a recipe for national suicide.

The second alternative is an intensive policy of population dispersal, which would provide a response to the population surplus in Israel's center, on the one hand, and a boost to the Jewish population in the periphery, on the other. Increased Jewish settlement in Israel's peripheral areas would not only strengthen Israeli sovereignty and security. Rather, to the extent that development projects are targeted to the entire population in the region, leading to increased economic and employment opportunities, Arab-Jewish co-existence would actually be enhanced.

The analysis and use of reliable data is essential in this process, as the aim is to direct Jewish settlement to areas that pose the greatest demographic or geographical threat to continuing Israeli sovereignty. It is legitimate and even necessary to raise the majority/minority issue in public discussion regarding Israel's national security. Just as important, the aim of this settlement policy must not be to expel Arabs, expropriate Arab land, or neglect Arab sector development at the expense of Jewish development.

Events taking place beyond Israel's borders must also be kept in mind. If there are processes of population concentration taking place along the Palestinian-controlled areas at the edge of Judea and Samaria or along the Syrian, Lebanese, Jordanian, or Egyptian borders, Jewish settlement should be directed toward these areas. It is necessary, for example, to augment population in the Ta'anakh region near Jenin, and along the western line of the Sharon area near Kalkilya and Tul Karem. Similarly, it is important to expand Jewish settlement adjacent to Gaza and also in the Arava and the Eilat environs along the northern border with Egypt.[29]

Conclusion

The issue of tensions between minority and majority population groups is not new—as has been seen, minorities who reside in a national periphery have repeatedly come into conflict with a majority population living mainly in the territorial core. In some instances, friction between groups may simmer over a lengthy period before erupting into confrontation or violence. In the case of Israel, majority-minority tension may be exacerbated by a number of additional factors. Apart from containing a large Arab minority within its borders, Israel is involved in a decades-long conflict not only with the Palestinian population in Judea/Samaria and Gaza but also with Arab countries both along its borders and within the greater Middle Eastern region. Moreover, the Arab minority within Israel increasingly defines itself as part of the Palestinian "nation" and maintains close ties with Palestinians in Judea and Samaria, while Bedouins (especially in the south) have frequent contact with neighboring tribes across the border. It is natural, therefore, that formulating a security strategy to protect the country necessitates a long and varied series of means, including a settlement strategy that will respond to demographic-territorial challenges.

From here, it is but a short road to the introduction of the demographic dimension in macro-level strategy-planning. This is especially the case concerning the possible annexation of areas of greater Israel, where a situation of Jewish minority would give rise either to apartheid rule—and severe international repercussions—or the continuation of western democratic rule, which would inevitably lead to the end of the Jewish Zionist state. With regard to this and other key issues in Israeli society, demography cannot be dismissed as an academic exercise whose data can be manipulated at will. Instead, it is a reality with existential security implications.

Notes

1. Arnon Soffer, "The Changing Status of Majority and Minority and Its Spatial Expression: The Case of the Arab Minority in Israel," in *Pluralism and Political Geography*, ed. Nurit Kliot and Stanely Waterman (London: 1983), 80–100.

2. Arnon Soffer, "Ma karah la'iton Haaretz?" *Nativ* 5 (September 2004), 51–56; Yaniv Gambash, *Gevul etni: mikreh gader habitaḥon bagadah* (Haifa: 2010).

3. Gambish, *Gevul etni*; Arnon Soffer and Evgenia Bystrov, *Israel: Demography 2004–2020, in Light of the Process of Disengagement* (Haifa: 2004), 10–11; Arnon Soffer, *'Al hamatzav hademografi vehageografi beeretz yisrael—haomnam sof haḥazon hatziyoni?* (Haifa: 1988), 33–52.

4. Many articles and books detail ethnic tensions around the world. See, for instance, the volume by Alexis Heraclides, *The Self-determination of Minorities in International Politics* (London: 1991), which deals with seven cases, among them Bangladesh, Biafra, and Katanga. See also Soffer, "The Changing States of Majority and Minority and Its Spatial Expression"; and John Wood, "Secession: A Comparative Analytical Framework," *Canadian Journal of Political Science* (1981), 107–134.

5. Similarly, Rasem Khamaisi and Amiram Gonen proposed the creation of new Arab towns close to Tel Aviv. See their policy paper, *Towards a Policy of Urbanization Poles for the Arab Population in Israel* (Jerusalem: 1993).

6. James M. Rubenstein, *The Cultural Landscape: An Introduction to Human Geography* (Upper Saddle River, N.J.: 1994), 100–129.

7. Heraclides, *The Self-determination of Minorities in International Politics*; Sammy Smooha, "Mediniyut kayemet vealternativot kelapei ha'aravim beyisrael," *Megamot* 1 (1980), 6–37; Will Kymlicka, *Multicultural Citizenship: A Liberal Theory of Minority Rights* (Oxford: 1995).

8. Heraclides, *The Self-determination of Minorities in International Politics*; Wood, "Secession"; Arnon Soffer, "'Arviyei yisrael likrat otonomiyah: mikreh tat-hama'arekhet hahavlit shel hagalil," *Meḥkarim begeografiyah shel eretz yisrael* 13 (1992), 198–209.

9. Wood, "Secession," 107–134; Soffer, "'Arviyei yisrael likrat otonomiyah."

10. Heraclides, *The Self-Determination of Minorities in International Politics*, 58–196.

11. The drawing up of new borders is often a drawn-out and violent affair, especially in instances in which there are no well-defined divisions between groups. During the break-up of Yugoslavia in the 1990s, when it proved to be exceedingly difficult to demarcate the area of Bosnia-Herzegovina, the result was a period of terrible bloodshed. See John B. Allcock, *Explaining Yugoslavia* (New York: 2000); Noel Malcolm, *Bosnia: A Short History* (London: 2002).

12. Arnon Soffer, "Hityashvut yehudit bagalil 1948–1980," *Teva' vaaretz* 7, no. 1 (1981), 10–16. Although the Bedouins (and, according to some, the Druze) are sub-groups within the Arab population, they are perceived as culturally distinct. Bedouins are traditionally nomads whereas other Arabs live in towns or villages; they are more tightly linked to tribal groupings; and their men are more likely to make polygamous marriages. In addition, although they are formally exempted from serving in the Israel Defense Forces, many Bedouin do opt to serve. This has important implications, as veterans of the army enjoy enhanced social status in Israeli society as well as being entitled to various financial benefits.

13. "State of Israel" (or elsewhere, "Israel") refers to the area located within the green-line demarcations, plus East Jerusalem and the Golan Heights. Although the latter two areas are not recognized by the international community as part of the state of Israel, they are governed by Israeli civil law.

14. Israel is divided into six districts (meḥozot): Jerusalem (both the city and surrounding areas, including Beit Shemesh); the northern district (including the cities of Nazareth, Afula, Karmiel, Safed, Acre, Shefar'am, and Tiberias); Haifa (including Hadera); Tel Aviv; the central district (including Netanya, Petah Tikva, Ramle, and Rehovot); and the southern district (including Beersheba, Ashkelon, Ashdod, Arad, Dimona, and Eilat). Each district is further divided into subdistricts, and each subdistrict contains what are known as "natural regions" (*eizorim tiv'iyim*), which include urban and rural settlements.

15. *Statistical Abstract of Israel* 61 (Jerusalem: 2010), 106–107.

16. Ibid.

17. According to data compiled by the population and migration authority of the Ministry of the Interior, as of April 2012, there were 60,000 infiltrators from Africa residing in Israel, alongside 90,000 foreign workers (both legal and illegal) and about 100,000 tourists who had not returned to their homelands. My own data indicate that there are a further 300,000 Palestinians who entered Israel between 1967 and 2012, resulting in a total of some 550,000 non-citizens currently residing in Israel (according to an informal police source, the actual figure is 750,000, or 10 percent of the total population of citizens). See Evgenia Bystrov and Arnon Soffer, *Israel: Demography 2012–2030, On the Way to a Religious State* (Haifa: 2012), 17; Arnon Soffer and Gil Shalev, *Mimushah befo'al shel "tevi'at hashiva'" hapalestinit* (Haifa: 2004).

18. Among the leading members of the group are Yoram Ettinger, Bennett Zimmerman, Roberta Seid, Michael L. Wise, and Yaacov Feitelson.

19. See the paper published by Yaacov Feitelson for the Institute for Zionist Strategies, *Hamegamot hademografiyot beeretz yisrael (1800–2007)* (Jerusalem: 2008); blogs by Yoram Ettinger online at www.theettingerreport.com.

20. Feitelson, *Hamegamot hademografiyot beeretz yisrael*, 31, 36, 44, 47, 53, 60.

21. Ibid., 11.

22. On the Palestinian birthrate, see Segio DellaPergola, "Jewish Demography: Fundamentals of the Research Field," in this volume, 26. For a more detailed rebuttal of the manipulated data presented by Ettinger and others, see Yaniv Gambash and Arnon Soffer, *Ta'atu'ei pa'ar hamilyon* (Haifa: 2007); Arnon Soffer, *Bemalkodet haradikaliyut* (Haifa: 2011), ch. 8. See also the website of the chair in geo-strategy at the University of Haifa, online at http://web.hevra. haifa.ac.il/~ch-strategy/index.

23. According to Rafiq Haj of the Dirasat Arab Center for Law and Policy (Nazareth), the tax compliance rate of Arabs ranges between 16–47 percent, whereas that of Jews ranges between 79–95 percent. The report (in Arabic) is available online at www.dirasat-aclp.org/arabic/isda-rat/2/79-90.pdf (accessed 9 September 2012).

24. *Official Summary of the Or Commission Report* (par. 1), online at www.sikkuy.org.il/ english/2004/OfficialSummary.pdf.

25. See Soffer and Shalev, *Mimushah befo'al shel "tevi'at hashivah" hap alestinit*, 25; Yisrael Kimchi, *Arba'im shanah leiḥud ha'ir* (publication of the Jerusalem Institute for Israel Studies) (Jerusalem: 2007); updated estimates were provided by the civil administration of Judea and Samaria on January 12, 2012 and again on July 9, 2012; Table 11.1 reflects official figures for the year 2009.

26. Kimchi, *Arba'im shanah leiḥud ha'ir* (slide presentation).

27. The population growth rate is lower for Bedouins living in the north because there is less polygamy and a longer history of living in permanent settlements.

28. By 2011, about 130,000 Bedouins were living in approximately 20 permanent Bedouin towns (the largest settlement, Rahat, was designated a city in 1994). About 70,000 Bedouins still live in small, scattered settlements.

29. Pnina Gazit and Arnon Soffer, *Merḥav hatefer bein sharon leshomron* (Haifa: 2005), 79–86; Arnon Soffer, *Haḥaklaut: even yesod bevitaḥon shel yisrael* (Haifa: 2010), 24.

Essay

Funding Aliyah: American Jewry and North African Jews, 1952–1956

Avi Picard
(BAR-ILAN UNIVERSITY)

In matters regarding the fulfillment of the Zionist dream, the relationship between the state of Israel and American Jewry has been characterized by a division of labor: American Jews have provided political and financial backing while their Israeli counterparts have gone about the business of building the land.[1] One of the prominent expressions of this relationship can be discerned in the area of aliyah and the absorption of new immigrants in Israel. This essay focuses on one specific episode, the attempt to raise funds from American Jewry to finance the aliyah from North Africa in the mid-1950s. The "From Ship to Village" project was aimed at bringing immigrants directly to agricultural settlements and to development towns in the periphery, thereby bypassing the need to provide temporary housing. In theory, this project should have been enthusiastically supported by the American Jewish community, as it conformed with a number of lofty goals—among them, the rescue of Jews from a politically instable area and the transformation of poor, "backward" immigrants into modern, westernized workers. As will be seen, however, the fundraising campaign met with a number of obstacles and failed to produce the desired level of funding.

Mass Aliyah Absorption and Population Dispersion

The absorption of a massive number of immigrants was the heaviest civil burden faced by the state of Israel in its first years of existence. Some 680,000 immigrants arrived between 1948 and 1951; preeminent among the social and financial challenges was the need to find some form of housing for them. At first (from 1948 to 1949), immigrants were sent to live in abandoned Arab houses. When the flow of aliyah increased, the immigrants were assigned to special camps, the majority of which had been used previously by the British Army. In May 1950, temporary neighborhoods (also known as transit camps, or *ma'abarot*), comprising tents and makeshift structures, were established for the new immigrants. Plagued by overcrowding and problems with hygiene, both the camps and the *ma'abarot* were regarded with disfavor by the veteran Israeli public. Moreover, difficult absorption conditions were held responsible for a wave of emigration that began in 1952, in the aftermath of the mass aliyah.

The *ma'abarot* served as a constant reminder of the great burdens of mass absorption and also marked the creation of a social and geographic divide. Whereas the main division had previously been between new immigrants and longtime residents, the major fault line was now between Mizrahim and Ashkenazim.[2] The concentration of immigrants in *ma'abarot* also damaged the Zionist mission of acquiring land and establishing agricultural settlements in Israel. In the pre-state period there had always been pioneers who volunteered to settle new sites. Indeed, groups who wanted to establish a new settlement sometimes had to wait many years until a plot of land was made available for them. The issue of accessible land was influenced by political considerations (restrictions imposed by the British Mandate) and security issues (from 1936 onwards). Among the "pioneers," youth movement graduates imbued with ideological fervor, only a select few were to be sent to the periphery to settle the land, and there was keen competition to be granted the honor.[3]

With the establishment of the state, a shift transpired in the relationship between settlement needs and the availability of suitable candidates. The task of settlement continued to be a military, political, and economic necessity, and agricultural settlement was still perceived as the ultimate goal of the Zionist revolution.[4] In the meantime, however, veteran Israelis had grown weary after years of struggle and war; most were now unwilling to leave established communities for the periphery. Even among youth movement graduates, fewer and fewer were willing to answer the call.[5] In the absence of volunteers, it was necessary to find others who would provide the manpower for agricultural settlement and activity on the frontier. The mass aliyah was regarded as answering this need.

Although the willingness of new immigrants to fulfill pioneering tasks was no greater than that of veteran Israelis, many of them had no resources of their own and were thus dependent on the state and on the Jewish Agency. In theory, this situation allowed for their transfer to the periphery.[6] During the state's early years (1948–1951), practical considerations worked against carrying out a policy of population dispersal. A great majority (76 percent) of the *ma'abarot* were sited in close proximity to existing settlements that were able to supply basic services and places to work; only a few transit camps were set up in uninhabited areas of the country.[7] Moreover, despite their dependence on state assistance, immigrants generally refused to be sent to the distant *ma'abarot* and to the remote settlements, and those who did go tended to leave soon thereafter.[8]

Instability in North Africa and the Increase in Aliyah

Toward the end of 1951, mass aliyah began to diminish and the overcrowded *ma'abarot* slowly emptied out. For two and a half years, aliyah remained at a low level. During this period, almost half a million Jews lived in French North Africa (Tunisia, Algeria, and Morocco)—the majority, totaling approximately 250,000, residing in Morocco, the largest Jewish diaspora in the Muslim countries. Until 1954, most Moroccan Jews felt reasonably secure in their country. Although there had been a number of physical attacks against Moroccan Jews over the years, the French colonial government (established in 1912), was largely successful in safeguarding the Jewish population. Even when the Moroccan independence movement began in the 1940s, Moroccan Jews put their faith in continued French rule. Apart from a serious outbreak of violence in the town of Oujda during the Israeli War of Independence in June of 1948, in which 47 Jews were killed, Moroccan Jews did not experience casualties during this period.

A dramatic change occurred in August 1954, when seven Jews were killed in the town of Petitjean. This event served as a catalyst for the increase of aliyah from Morocco. Exacerbating the Jews' sense of threat was the escalating Moroccan nationalists' struggle and the French defeat at Dien Bien Phu in Vietnam (then Indo-China), which damaged France's reputation as a powerful colonial power. Throughout the year following the Petitjean incident, violent attacks increased, culminating in August 1955. The prevailing feeling among Moroccan Jewry was that of increasing precariousness. This concern was shared by Israeli and foreign officials, among them representatives of the American Jewish Joint Distribution Committee (known as the JDC).[9]

As opposed to Algeria (where all the Jews had been granted French citizenship in 1870), and Tunisia (where 25 percent of the Jews held French citizenship), only 6 percent of Moroccan Jews were French citizens. The vast majority of Moroccan Jews, as Moroccan nationals, were not able to immigrate freely to France. Nonetheless, due to the widespread influence of French culture, numerous Moroccan Jews did have a good command of the French language, in particular those who were graduates of French-language educational institutions such as the Alliance Israélite Universelle (AIU). The connection to French culture facilitated integration into a wide variety of occupations and white-collar professions. Yet many Moroccan Jews, mainly those who lived in villages in the Atlas Mountains and those of the older generation who lived in Jewish urban neighborhoods known as *mellahs*, had little or no exposure to European culture (though their children often did, especially if they attended an Alliance school). The majority of these Jews lived in great poverty.[10]

Prior to 1954, difficult absorption conditions in Israel and economic development in Morocco discouraged Moroccan Jews from making aliyah; only Jews from the poorest parts of society were prone to leave the country.[11] However, following the pogrom in Petitjean and a growing sense of insecurity, a considerable number of Jews—including those who were more established and more involved in French culture—applied for aliyah. Overall, aliyah applications among Moroccan (and Tunisian) Jews increased from 250 a month to between 5,000 and 6,000.[12]

In the face of an emerging second wave of mass immigration, Israeli officials faced the need to implement a change in absorption policy. The new policy was designed both to prevent the establishment of slums and to facilitate the growth of Israel's peripheral regions. Previously, as noted, new immigrants (as well as veteran Israelis) had been reluctant to settle in the periphery, preferring to stay near established settlements and cities where there were more opportunities for employment. This situation had not only impeded population dispersion but had also prevented the government from disbanding the *ma'abarot*, since even when housing solutions were found for residents, their places were often taken by others who had abandoned the periphery.[13]

In addition, new immigrants who arrived in the *ma'abarot* were apt to be advised by more veteran residents to stay put rather than agree to be sent to a distant village.[14]

With all this in mind, policymakers came to the conclusion that it was a mistake to send new immigrants to temporary absorption camps. Instead, they would be sent directly to settlements located in the periphery. This new policy, termed "From Ship to Village," began to be implemented in the summer of 1954. In accordance with the plan, prospective immigrants signed documents in their country of origin that committed them to take up residence wherever the Jewish Agency sent them. Immigrants were to be sent to agricultural settlements in the north or in the south, and also to "development towns" (among them, Kiryat Shmona, Netivot, Beit Shean, and Sederot) located in the midst of agricultural settlement regions. The decision where to send them was made in advance of their arrival; upon reaching Israel, the immigrants were sent directly to their destination. Most were given some form of permanent housing, and they were also provided with food and other provisions for the first few days.

The first immigrants sent directly from "ship to village" arrived from Morocco and were assigned to a sparsely populated moshav (farming village) in the Beit Shean valley. Previous immigrants who had come to the moshav had not remained, and most of the houses were unoccupied. In contrast, almost all of the newer immigrants stayed in the moshav. Encouraged by the initial success of the "From Ship to Village" project, officials sent additional groups of North African immigrants to moshavim that had available housing. Soon, all the empty houses were filled.[15]

With the demand for aliyah still high, a need arose to build more houses and establish more villages. The problem was that neither the state nor the Jewish Agency had adequate resources to embark on massive construction or settlement projects. Not wishing to revert to the *ma'abarot* model of temporary housing, government officials reluctantly decided to slow the rate of aliyah. In consequence, for the first time since Israel's establishment, aliyah was regulated in accordance with the country's capacity for absorption. With the quota set at approximately 2,000 a month, long lines began to form at Jewish Agency offices in Morocco, where many prospective immigrants had their applications delayed or even rejected. According to a study conducted by the aliyah department in Morocco, during the last half of 1954, only about 20 percent of those registered for aliyah actually left for Israel.[16] As time went on, the lines for aliyah continued to grow. At the start of 1955, about 68,000 Moroccan Jews were candidates for aliyah; by the end of the year, only 25,000 of them had been approved. By the beginning of the following year, the waiting period between submission of an application and aliyah had increased to more than a year.[17]

Increasing the Budget for Immigrant Absorption

In the summer of 1955, despite the increasingly serious situation in Morocco, executives of the Jewish Agency and the government reaffirmed the policy of controlling the rate of aliyah and restricting absorption to preexisting sites in the periphery.[18] This was a hard matter to accept, as it went against the Zionist ethos regarding the ingathering of the Jewish people. Yet the only way to respond to the increased demand of aliyah was to create more absorption venues in the periphery, which involved not only constructing new housing but also providing for livestock and agricultural tools for people sent to moshavim. Such expenditures could not be implemented without an increase in the absorption budget, whether by the government or by external sources.

In terms of financing, there was a division of responsibility between the Jewish Agency and the Israeli government. The Jewish Agency was responsible for bringing immigrants to Israel and providing for their needs during their first year (the absorption department in Israel was a branch of the Jewish Agency). In addition, the Jewish Agency undertook the construction of new settlements, with the government sharing part of the costs. The government was also responsible for the planning of the settlements and for providing financial assistance to new settlers in the period following their first year in Israel. Overall, the Israeli government financed approximately 60 percent of the absorption process.

For more than a year, the Jewish Agency executive tried without success to get Israeli government officials to expand the level of funding. However, there was no way for the government to raise the necessary money without imposing additional taxes, and this option was not to be considered: 1955 was an election year, and new taxes had a great political price.[19] Thus, the Jewish Agency was forced to rely on its own resources, which stemmed from contributions obtained from world Jewry. American Jews provided more than 80 percent of the donations,[20] almost all of which came via the United Jewish Appeal (UJA), which collected money both for Israel (at first through the United Palestine Appeal and, starting in 1951, through the United Israeli Appeal [UIA]) and for the JDC.[21] Following the War of Independence, there was a gradual decrease in funds brought in from the UJA campaigns, as the sense of emergency diminished. At this point, the focus of fundraising shifted from wartime financing to that of facilitating immigrant absorption.

The renewal of large-scale aliyah from North Africa in 1954 brought with it a revived feeling of urgency. Herbert Friedman, who became the executive head of the UJA in May 1955, regarded the aliyah from North Africa as an opportunity to dramatize the situation in Israel, engendering a feeling of crisis that would enhance fundraising efforts. In fairness, he was also convinced that the crisis was real: following a visit to Morocco, he wrote a letter urging that 150,000 Moroccan Jews be brought to Israel as soon as possible. At the current pace of aliyah, he calculated, it would take a full six years to bring the Moroccan Jewish community to Israel, but wondered, "Do we honestly have more than three years in which to do the job?"[22]

During 1954 and 1955, a number of U.S. organizations, among them the UJA, the American Jewish Committee (AJC), and Hadassah sent delegations to North Africa. In December 1954, the Jewish Agency organized a large-scale gathering in New York to increase fundraising efforts. At a national conference of UJA donors around that time, Levi Eshkol, finance minister and head of the Jewish Agency's settlement department, made the aliyah of North African Jews and their subsequent settlement in the periphery the focus of his speech. "As minister of finance," he noted, "I am bound to tell you that our sources of foreign currency income are inadequate. We need increased funds if we are to carry out all the obligations facing us today with respect to immigration and development."[23] In 1955 and 1956, English-speaking films focusing on the Jews of North Africa were shown to Jews across the United States. These films portrayed the great need for financial support as well as the potential for change that donations to the UJA could make.[24]

However, despite these considerable efforts, fundraising efforts resulted in an amount that barely covered the Jewish Agency's portion of the cost of absorption and did not allow for the required increase in aliyah. Indeed, after the first fundraising attempts in the summer of 1954, it became clear to Giora Yoseftal, the Jewish Agency treasurer (who was also head of the absorption department), that "there is no reason to hope for another penny before the beginning of October."[25] The disappointing level of fundraising reflected a more general trend of decline in revenues of the UJA, which dropped from $150 million in 1948 to $60 million in 1955.[26] A number of factors accounted for this decline, ranging from inadequate fundraising abilities on the part of UJA leaders prior to Herbert Friedman[27] to a turn inward on the part of American Jewry. Following the tumultuous period preceding and immediately after the establishment of the state of Israel and the settlement of displaced survivors from Europe, American Jewry turned to more domestic concerns. During the 1950s, the U.S. Jewish community put its energies into the local physical infrastructure and built synagogues, hospitals, community centers, and schools. Between 1948 and 1955, some $225 million was allocated to communal buildings. These investments took a considerable bite out of the income of the UJA, whether for funds destined for Israel (UIA) or those sent for the welfare of Jews in distressed countries such as Morocco or Poland (via the JDC). Whereas 74 percent of the funds collected by the Jewish federations throughout the United States in 1948 were sent to the UJA, only 46 percent of the money went to the appeal in 1954.[28]

Other fundraising obstacles related to the specific nature of the project on behalf of aliyah from North Africa. There was justified concern that such a campaign could have serious diplomatic repercussions, since portraying North African Jewry as a community in imminent danger was tantamount to declaring that French rule in North Africa was unstable. In fact, reports of plans for the mass evacuation of Jews from North Africa led to a number of diplomatic incidents. One such occurrence took place at a Hadassah conference held in August 1954, when the head of the Youth Aliyah department, Moshe Kol, announced that, in light of the security situation, Israel planned on bringing in 450,000 Jews from North Africa (a number representing the combined Jewish population of Morocco, Algeria, and Tunisia).[29] This declaration was publicized by the American press and later, according to Alex Easterman, the political secretary of the World Jewish Congress, "was widely publicized in the Moroccan press...and caused the greatest disquiet in French and Arab-Moroccan circles."[30] The issue was also raised at meetings of the Israeli cabinet and the Jewish Agency executive. Yaakov Tzur, the Israeli ambassador to France, reported to the government that Kol's words had spread to the French settlers in North Africa, who became convinced that France's (Jewish) prime minister, Pierre Mendes-France, was planning a French withdrawal from Tunisia. Rumor had it that Mendes-France had wanted the Jews to know of his intentions in advance so that they would be able to make escape plans.[31]

Although, as noted, Jewish delegations went on fact-finding missions to North Africa at this time, plans to send a delegation of North African Jews to the United

States were cancelled in light of the sensitive diplomatic situation.[32] Nonetheless, a certain amount of damage had already been done: starting in the second quarter of 1955, the French government restricted emigration from Morocco. In conversations with Israeli diplomats, French officials cited publicity regarding mass aliyah as one of the reasons behind the new policy.[33] Accordingly, they demanded that the aliyah process be conducted discreetly as a condition for removing the restrictions. In light of the need to consider French interests during the fundraising campaign in the United States, Ambassador Tzur asked fundraisers "to shout quietly"—that is, to strike a balance between dramatizing the situation in North Africa and acting with discretion so as to avoid further antagonizing the French government.[34] Only after August 1955, when the end of French rule in Morocco and Tunisia was clearly in sight (Morocco and Tunisia became independent in March 1956), was it possible to launch large-scale public fundraising efforts.

Yet even then, many U.S. Jews remained unconvinced that North African Jews were in imminent danger. American Jews were familiar with the Zionist argument that Jews had no place in the diaspora and that the only true refuge was the state of Israel. However, given that they themselves lived in the diaspora, they did not necessarily accept this argument. They were naturally inclined to view calls for an emergency fundraising campaign with a certain amount of skepticism, regarding them as an attempt to arouse an artificial sense of panic. Moreover, notwithstanding their support for Israel, both Zionist and non-Zionist organizations stressed the importance of Jews being integrated in the surrounding society. One example of this mindset could be discerned in the activities conducted by the (non-Zionist) American Jewish Committee, which had maintained a presence in North Africa since 1949. Believing that Jews should join the national struggles of the countries in which they lived, the AJC supported a small group of North African Jews who identified with the nationalist movement and encouraged Jews to remain in Morocco and Tunisia.[35] Its main concern was to ensure equal civil rights of the Jewish minority, believing that, in a democratic society, it was incumbent on Jews to be loyal citizens of the state.

In early 1955, a delegation of the AJC visited Morocco and reported that the "Zionists are attempting to stir up a frenzy for aliyah."[36] The AJC opposed this, believing that a mass emigration of North African Jews after the removal of the French would "represent a victory for Hitlerian concepts" by serving to deprive Jews of the opportunity to integrate into the surrounding society.[37] According to the AJC, it was "best to avoid sowing panic among the Jews of North Africa and triggering a mass exodus before the time was right."[38] This approach remained steadfast even as nationalist violence escalated. According to Nachum Goldmann, founder of the World Jewish Congress (and a member of the Jewish Agency executive): "In speeches by the AJC people all over the U.S., they were saying that emigration to Israel from Morocco is not so urgent and that the Zionists create an artificial panic. This position was very harmful to the UJA fundraising."[39]

Even American Zionists had voiced some criticism of plans to promote the mass aliyah of North African Jewry. Back in 1950, for instance, an unsigned memorandum of the Bonds argued that proposed aliyah efforts that would involve the mass aliyah of North African Jewry living under French rule (as part of an emergency rescue program) would not win support among Jewish community circles in the United

States.[40] In 1954, Hadassah president Rose Halperin claimed that, as opposed to the aliyah from Yemen, an increase in aliyah from other Arab countries would not resonate among American Jews:

> The Yemenite aliyah... appealed to all of us and for them as really Messianic. But after Yemen I don't think one can expect the same reaction on the American scene—except if it was a question of real danger. For example when it came to the question of Iraq, many people felt that excitement was stimulated and many people felt that this caused a lot of damage.

In her opinion, only in the case of serious danger would American Jews mobilize in order to garner support for aliyah fundraising efforts.[41]

In the summer of 1955, a delegation of the UJA visited North Africa. The delegation's description of the circumstances in North Africa implied that the situation there did not require urgent action.[42] Not surprisingly, this description had a negative impact on fundraising. It also sparked tension between members of the delegation and JDC activists and Jewish Agency workers based in Morocco. Samuel Haber, the director of the JDC in Morocco, argued that there was no foreseeable future for Jews in Morocco and that aliyah efforts should be escalated. In addition, he said, it was the responsibility of the UJA to supply the JDC with additional funding to cover educational and medical costs to prepare Jews for aliyah. His words were backed by Jacques Dahan, head of the Jewish community council in Morocco and a French loyalist, who told the UJA delegation (off the record, out of fear that whatever he said would be passed on to the French authorities) that it was necessary for 50,000 Jews to leave Morocco immediately, out of a total of 150,000 that would eventually emigrate, most of them to Israel.[43] Berl Locker, the head of the Jewish Agency, accused the UJA delegation of acting maliciously and presenting the situation as better than it was. "I must say that quite frankly the delegation that went to North Africa have done a great deal of mischief," he noted. "They have painted a very rosy picture of the situation of the Jews in North Africa, which is very wrong, and I would ask the members of that delegation whether they would agree to stay in the United States under similar conditions."[44]

In response to such criticism, Joseph Schwartz, who had served as executive head of the UJA and now headed the Bonds, explained that the delegation had not been "convinced about the advisability of evacuation" because acts of violence that had taken place "were [not] directed against the North African Jews as such"; rather, a number of Jews had been injured in the course of riots directed against pro-French activists. Schwartz went on to note that "the North African situation was used very effectively in this year's campaign—some people say too much. It was used, and did have a response." At the same time, he acknowledged, statements made by the UJA delegation had been "very misleading and very dangerous."[45]

Even the new director of the UJA, Herbert Friedman, who put aliyah from North Africa at the center of fundraising efforts, commented that "Jews in America are not yet convinced that immigration of Jews from North Africa is absolutely necessary."[46] For his part, Dr. Israel Goldstein, a member of the Jewish Agency executive in New York, argued that "if it is a question of Hatzala [rescue], it would be possible to raise the money in the U.S., but I have the feeling that there is no feeling in the States of this. I also have no feeling that this is a question of Hatzala. . . . it is not a precarious emergency." For this reason, he concluded, fundraising efforts did not result in massive contributions.[47]

In retrospect, it is clear that the allegation that Zionists were "attempting to stir up a frenzy for aliyah" had no real basis. The increase in applications for aliyah on the part of Moroccan Jewry came at a time when the country was not ready to deal with another wave of new immigrants; rather than encouraging aliyah, the Israeli government was taking steps to slow it down. Quite obviously, North African Jews were signing up for aliyah without any Zionist "coercion."[48] As to the charge that the Zionist establishment had exaggerated its assessment of the danger posed to North African Jewry, at least one Zionist concern—that restrictions would be placed on emigration—turned out to be well-founded. Soon after Morocco became independent in the summer of 1956, emigration to Israel was banned: 80,000 Moroccan Jews who were already registered for aliyah remained stuck in Morocco.[49] Some of them managed to leave in an illegal manner. Other waited until 1961, when Jewish emigration was (clandestinely) authorized by Moroccan authorities.[50]

A Question of Image

To some extent, the relative lack of American Jewish support for fundraising on behalf of the aliyah of North African Jews was linked to political matters such as the complex situation regarding French colonialism or the basic attitude of modern and well-integrated Jews that one should be loyal to the country in which one resides. Beyond this, however, there were other factors at play—among them, cultural stereotyping of North African Jews. In Israel, there was a generally negative attitude toward Jews from the Muslim world, and in particular those from Morocco.[51] Among other things, Moroccan Jews were perceived as primitive, lazy, drunken, and hot-blooded.[52] American Jews who followed events in Israel were undoubtedly aware of these views and may have been influenced by them.

Moshe Kol was among those who explicitly commented on the stereotypes. "We [in Israel] circulated legends about them being Jewish thugs," he noted at a Jewish Agency executive meeting, adding that such individuals accounted for only an insignificant minority of the Moroccan Jewish community. However, he warned, this negative stereotype could well work against fundraising efforts, American Jews being likely to respond that "you're about to bring over new Jews from there while we still regret bringing the previous ones."[53] Similarly, Golda Meir, then serving as minister of labor, interpreted the Israeli lack of willingness to fund the North African aliyah as being responsible for the decline in UJA revenues: "New York Jews are not obliged to worry more about developing Israel than [our own] government ministers."[54]

To some extent, American Jews also lacked a sense of identification with North African Jewry. According to Giora Yoseftal, "the North African issue does not speak to their hearts; what they care about is security and settlement."[55] Despite the fact that the aliyah from Yemen had sparked an impressive mobilization of American efforts,[56] the aliyah from other Islamic countries, especially Morocco, did not have the same effect.[57] In the eyes of many Americans, Jews from Muslim countries were uneducated, primitive, poor, sick, and unhygienic.[58] For instance, Myrtle Karp, the vice president of Hadassah, visited Morocco in 1953 and was appalled by the poor hygiene of the Moroccan Jews:

I don't think I'll ever get the stench of that Mellah out of my nostrils…to see the children with the shaved heads and their eyes all infected with trachoma…and to realize that this is the way those human beings live[,]…to see the little girls of ten years old, selling their bodies for a piece of candy.…[W]e visited a community in the hills where the women were sitting on the ground. I remember it so vividly—one woman plucking a chicken, with her baby feeding at her breast and feathers flying all over. And we wouldn't think of going near a new-born child without a mask on our faces.[59]

In many cases, the Jews of Morocco were presented as idlers who needed to be taught how to work. One of the movies dealing with absorption of the Moroccan immigrants contains a scene filmed in a village in the Lachish region of Israel, in which men and women are shown to be leaping and playing on the ground. According to the narrator:

They are relaxed and happy. They will be looked after—God or someone will provide. That is the Oriental philosophy, and work, consistent work, is a brand-new idea.

[Scene of old men in ghalabias playing backgammon]

To amuse themselves, to wait for the next meal, the next day, this they had done all their lives.…Now, before anything else, we have to make the men understand that the burden of supporting their families rests on their own shoulders. No work—no pay. No pay—no food.…

[T]hey heard that the Israelis were crazy. Now they're sure of it. Working? When one can sit in the sun and do nothing? It's very tough at first, and it will take some time before their aches and pains disappear. But their reward will be a land once barren made rich and prosperous by their own labor. The first payday is a big event. It's the first tangible proof of a promise made to them—that Israel will be a land of opportunity. They will have to work, to be sure, but that work will be rewarded in spirit and in economic advance.

[Scene of immigrants marking documents with their thumbs as a sign that they received money]

Not many of them can write. Only a few had received even an elementary education.[60]

A JDC report on the organization's activities in Morocco noted that the Jews' life-style was similar to that of several centuries in the past.[61] Or as Moses Beckelman, director general of JDC's overseas operations put it: "When one moves from Europe to North Africa, one moves from the twentieth century to the twelfth, from the present to the past."[62] Samuel Haber, director of the JDC in Morocco, described why the Moroccan Jews were interested in immigrating to Israel: "There was no place for them to go, for literally no doors were open to receive this mass of destitute, sick, hungry and backward people."[63] In an oral history interview conducted years later, he recalled the differing attitudes of American Jews:

A Jew from Dallas, Texas, might very well have said, "What are we doing with these blacks?" But very few were like that.…[Most] identified [to] some extent with the million "forgotten Jews" of the Moslem Arab world, who had never been thought about.… [T]he attitude on the part of the American Jew, largely speaking, was no different than it was for any other program.

Nonetheless,

> More questions were asked because it was a strange world to them; the Jew identified
> with the Eastern European Jew. It was easier to identify with the Ashkenazi Jew from
> where his father or grandmother or grandfather stemmed than it was to identify with this
> fellow who lived in the "drek" or the dirt of Morocco....[64]

Paula Borenstein, a JDC worker who dealt with North African Jews in Marseilles
on their way to Israel, admitted that she had never seen Jews from Arab countries. In
the beginning, "they looked exactly like Arabs." She continued:

> Many of them didn't speak a word of French, only Arabic. They looked to me exactly like
> Arabs and certainly to the other people....[T]hey came with their *pecklach*, very poor
> and very ill—they had trachoma and other diseases....I said to myself, "what do I have
> in common with these people? I don't have any common language, no common culture,
> we don't look alike."[65]

One of the major concerns of various American activists when they first met the
Jews of North Africa was the potential damage to Israel's image in the event that a
mass aliyah took place. Israel was perceived as an island of western civilization in the
heart of the Middle East—and yet relatively few immigrants to Israel came from
western countries.[66] What would happen to Israel's image if "primitive" immigrants
were to arrive en masse? Karp put it this way: "[A]ll we could think of was that they
would make a Mellah of any place they lived in Israel. It was a terrible thought."[67]
Clearly, American Jews—almost all of whom were of European descent—felt
greater empathy for the plight of European Jews than for those from North Africa.[68]
Various memos written by Jewish Agency officials made this clear. Yoseftal quoted
UJA officials as saying that the aliyah of North African Jewry did not make an impression on the philanthropic community in the United States: "This is not the aliyah
from Eastern Europe which American Jews associate with, but of North African
Jews....[W]ith a plan like this no impression will be made and we will not receive
additional donations."[69] Moshe Kol quoted American Jews as saying, "let them sit
there with all their troubles."[70] During the summer of 1955, as violence in Morocco
worsened, Shazar remarked: "There are no Casablanca *landsmanshaftn* there [in the
United States]. Therefore, a catastrophe in Casablanca does not arouse the sympathy
of American Jewry in the way that catastrophe in Hungary or Kishinev would."
Shazar went on to note that the disturbances in North Africa were a serious matter,
and added: "I ask, to what extent is this felt among Jews in America?"[71] Eliyahu
Dobkin believed that among American Jews it was no longer possible to tug at the
heartstrings with regard to the aliyah of North African Jews. According to him, UJA
leaders characterized the matter in this way: "[T]hey are Moroccan, blacks. If Russia
or one of its neighbors opened its gates...the response would have been different."[72]
Kol added that if the current situation of escalating violence had been occurring in a
European country, American Jews would have a different attitude: "There's some
truth that the feelings toward these Jews are different."[73]
In many ways, Moroccan Jews *were* different from American and East European
Jews. At the same time, as has been seen, Moroccan Jewry comprised people from a
wide social and economic spectrum, from French-speaking professionals to poor,

illiterate Atlas Mountain villagers. Notwithstanding, representatives of the UJA—and the programming material they and others produced—focused exclusively on that sector of the population that was most foreign to western culture. The objective was to dramatize the distress in Morocco in order to increase donations. However, this strategy failed because of the negative image it projected. Instead of identifying with the prospective immigrants, American Jews mostly felt alienated from them.

In 1956, the last year legal aliyah was allowed from Morocco, the UJA failed to significantly increase fundraising. Despite a special appeal and the energy evinced by UJA director Herbert Friedman (who set a goal of $105 million for the regular appeal and another $25 million in an emergency appeal for the Jews of North Africa), only $75 million came in, including funds earmarked for the JDC.[74] It is noteworthy that this drop in U.S. funding did not characterize the entirety of the diaspora. To be sure, the main portion of funds for Israel and for aliyah and absorption efforts did come from American Jewry, and the Jewish Agency would not have been able to maintain its budget merely from contributions originating in countries outside the United States. However, an examination of the funding provided by other Jewish communities during that time reveals that a majority of contributions to Israel from outside the United States either remained stable (as in Britain) or even increased (Canada, South Africa, and Latin America).[75]

The aliyah from Morocco and Tunisia between 1954 and 1956 prompted an ambitious absorption plan: transferring immigrants upon arrival to pre-prepared homes in Israel's periphery. From the perspective of absorption officials, this program proved to be a big success. However, making aliyah dependent on the country's ability to absorb immigrants led to a situation in which, for the first time since the establishment of the state, many of those who wanted to come to Israel were forced to wait. Hopes that the deep pockets of American Jewry would enable the state and the Jewish Agency to bridge the gap between needs and available resources were dashed. U.S.-based contributions barely enabled Israel to keep up with the initially prescribed pace of aliyah and did not allow for an increase or a response to the demand in Morocco. The lack of funds prevented Israeli authorities from increasing the pace of aliyah even as the level of violence escalated. In the summer of 1956, activities of the Jewish Agency were outlawed by the new, independent Moroccan government—a move that essentially brought to an end the wave of aliyah from North Africa. At the time, 80,000 Jews were still registered for aliyah; the majority were not able to come to Israel.

Among the factors underlying the reluctant response of American Jewry to contribute to aliyah fundraising efforts on behalf of North African Jewry was the complex relationship between Jews of European origin (both in the United States and in Israel) and Jewish communities in Islamic countries. Influenced by colonialist thinking that deemed European culture superior to that of African and Asian "natives," the mostly Ashkenazi U.S. Jewish community (and its Israeli counterpart) looked down upon Jews from North Africa and to some extent found it difficult to identify with their plight. Yet alongside the colonialist worldview, American Jews—especially the Zionists among them—were affected by a national ethos that served as a unifying force. The best illustration of this sense of Jewish solidarity can be found in the words of Shlomo Zalman Shragai before a plenum of the Zionist General Council in the summer of 1955:

I would like members here... to feel this great tragedy: more than 100,000 Jews in North Africa—fine and healthy Jews who are willing to go and settle our country's desolate regions, ready to strengthen Israel's army and security, and there is nothing preventing them from leaving North Africa.... And yet we cannot open our arms... and say to them: come to us, we are your brothers and sisters, we are the children of one mother and father, come to us, help us and help yourselves.[76]

It is difficult to assess the weight of solidarity relative to other issues. What is clear is that the lean years of the UJA proved to be a difficult test of the unwritten contract between American Jews and Israel, according to which the former provided funding in return for the latter not pressuring them to make aliyah. In the critical years for Moroccan Jewry, American Jews did not come through in helping Israel provide a refuge for those who sought it. During periods of war (both in 1948 and in 1967, and to a certain extent in 1956), American Jewry demonstrated a capacity for both political and financial mobilization.[77] However, the project of financing aliyah absorption of North African Jewry did not elicit a similar response.

Notes

1. Marianne R. Sanua, *Let Us Prove Strong: The American Jewish Committee, 1945–2006* (Waltham: 2007), 58–63.
2. Moshe Lissak, "The Demographic-Social Revolution in Israel in the 1950s: The Absorption of the Great Aliyah," *Journal of Israeli History* 22, vol. 2 (2003), 1–31.
3. Gabriel Lipshitz, *Country on the Move: Migration to and within Israel, 1948–1955* (Dordrecht: 1998), 39.
4. Jacob Metzer, "Economic Structure and National Goals—The Jewish National Home in Interwar Palestine," *The Journal of Economic History* 38, no. 1 (1978), 101–119.
5. On the change in orientation, see Dan Horowitz and Moshe Lissak, *Trouble in Utopia: The Overburdened Polity of Israel* (Albany: 1989), 112–113.
6. Lipshitz, *Country on the Move*, 44.
7. Ibid., 46–47.
8. Devorah Hacohen, *Immigrants in Turmoil: Mass Immigration to Israel and Its Repercussions in the 1950s and After* (Syracuse: 2003), 156.
9. Report by Zvi Bar Zakai (of the Israeli embassy in Paris) on the meeting of JDC representatives in Europe, 8 November 1954, Israel State Archives (hereafter: ISA), RG 43/G/5558/4. On the situation in Morocco, see Avi Picard, *'Olim bimshurah: mediniyut yisrael kelapei 'aliyatam shel yehudei tzefon afrikah, 1951–1956* (Sde Boker: 2012), 178–183.
10. On the social structure of Moroccan Jewry at that time, see Yaron Tsur, *Kehilah keru'ah: yehudei maroko vehaleumiyut, 1943–1954* (Tel Aviv: 2001), 33–36. Since there was no formal legal distinction between those who were influenced by European culture and those who were not, it is difficult to assess accurately the exact proportions of each group. One estimate is that those completely engrossed in western culture accounted for about 20 percent of the Moroccan Jewish population, with approximately 50 percent of the Jewish children in Morocco receiving modern education (ibid., 37; see also the report by Knesset member Eliyahu Elisar on his visit to Morocco [1952], ISA/LG 71/ME/1085/2).
11. Picard, *'Olim bimshurah,* 188.
12. Ibid., 178, 187; see also Michael M. Laskier, *North African Jewry in the Twentieth Century* (New York: 1994), 123–127. In Algeria, the situation was different. The state was defined as a part of France, and therefore it did not seem likely that France would withdraw (in fact, the end of French rule came in 1962). In addition, Algerian Jews had French citizenship

and were able to move to France, a privilege not shared by a considerable portion of Jews from Morocco and Tunisia. During the years 1954–1956, about 86,000 North African Jews immigrated to Israel, of whom approximately 80 percent came from Morocco, 18 percent from Tunisia, and 2 percent from Algeria.

13. Giora Yoseftal, minutes of the Jewish Agency Executive (hereafter: JAE), 13 July 1954, Central Zionist Archives (hereafter: CZA), S100/94; report (marked "secret") by Chaim Bar-Ilan of the Jewish Agency settlement department, titled "Regarding the Situation in Immigrant Settlements," 30 July 1951, CZA S15/9604.

14. See quotes in Avi Picard, "The Reluctant Soldiers of Israel's Settlement Project: The Ship to Village Plan in the Mid-1950s," *Middle Eastern Studies* 49, no. 1 (January 2013), 40.

15. Ibid., 34.

16. Arieh Avrahami to Shlomo Zalman Shragai, 1 April 1955, CZA S6/7282.

17. *Mikan* 10 (bulletin of the immigrant selection committee in Morocco), 20 January 1956, CZA S6/6002.

18. Cabinet meeting, 28 August 1955, ISA, sixth government, vol. B; meeting of the JAE, 19 August 1955, CZA S100/100; meeting of coordinating committee (consisting of members of the Jewish Agency and the Israeli government), 18 August 1955, CZA S100/511.

19. Remarks by Moshe Kol at meetings of the JAE, 25 April and 6 June 1955, CZA S100/98; see also remarks by Kol at the coordinating committee meeting, 8 June 1955, ISA/RG43/G/5383/17.

20. JAE, *Report Submitted to the 24th Zionist Congress* (Jerusalem: 1956), 444.

21. Ibid., 436. The UJA had almost complete exclusivity when it came to fundraising for Israel in the United States. Zionist and Israeli bodies that wished to carry out separate fundraising projects needed to obtain special approval from the committee of control and authorization of campaigns; such approvals were given sparingly (JAE, *Report Submitted to the 25th Zionist Congress* [New York: 1960], 69–71). On the UJA, see Ernest Stock, *Partners & Pursestrings: A History of the United Jewish Appeal* (Lanham: 1987). See also idem, "HaMagbit vehaJoint," in *Hatziyonut umitnagdehah ba'am hayehudi*, ed. Haim Avni and Gideon Shimoni (Jerusalem: 1990), 401. Money that was raised was divided between the Jewish Agency and the JDC, and later was also allocated to Holocaust survivors, in accordance with an agreement that was renewed annually. Following the establishment of the state of Israel, the portion allocated to the UIA (which collected for the Jewish Agency) increased to more than 60 percent of the total UJA funds (JAE, *Report Submitted to the 25th Zionist Congress*, 20; Marc Lee Raphael, *A History of the United Jewish Appeal 1939–1982* [Providence: 1982], 136–137). It is important to note, however, that since the JDC spent a sizable portion of its budget on projects in Israel, approximately 90 percent of the UJA funds were transferred to Israel (JAE, *Report Submitted to the 24th Zionist Congress*, 20).

22. Herbert Friedman to Reuven (Dobek) and others, 1 August 1955, ISA/RG 43/G/5558/4. See also Raphael, *A History of the United Jewish Appeal 1939–1982*, 71.

23. "Levi Eshkol Extends Israel Thanks for Success of Consolidation Loan," report to members of the UJA national campaign council, vol. 9 (pp. 7–8), 28 December 1954, CZA S42/163.

24. See, for example, the following films, all of them found in the Steven Spielberg Jewish Film Archive in Jerusalem (hereafter: SSJFA): *Nobody Runs Away*, VT DA 153; *New Roots*, VT DA 146; *The Lachish Story*, VT DA 038; *None Shall Make Them Afraid*, VT DA 090.

25. Yoseftal's telegram as quoted by Shragai at a meeting of the coordinating committee, 20 September 1954, ISA/RG43/G/5383/16.

26. Raphael, *A History of the United Jewish Appeal*, 136 (table 4:1) and 141 (table 7:3).

27. Menahem Kaufman, "Hashpa'at milḥemet sheshet hayamim 'al haMagbit," *Yahadut zemanenu* 9 (1994), 207.

28. Menahem Kaufman, "Envisaging Israel: The Case of the United Jewish Appeal," in *Envisioning Israel: The Changing Ideals and Images of North American Jews*, ed. Allon Gal (Detroit: 1996), 224–225; Lloyd [Aryeh] Gartner, "Maavak vehashlamah bein tziyonim lelo tziyonim beartzot habrit meaz 1946," in Avni and Shimoni (eds.) *Hatziyonut umitnagdehah ba'am hayehudi*, 397; Abraham J. Karp, *To Give Life: The UJA in the Shaping of the American*

Jewish Community (New York: 1981), 120; *Session of the Zionist General Council, Sixth Session after the 23rd Congress, Jerusalem, August 23–31, 1955: Addresses, Debates, Resolutions,* (Jerusalem: 1955), 37–38.

29. "Rescue of Jews in Africa Urged; Hadassah Hears Plea and is Expected to Help Shifting of Children to Israel," *New York Times* (25 August 1954).

30. Alex Easterman to Prime Minister Moshe Sharett, 3 September 1954, ISA/RG 130/mfa/2398/4. Sharett promised that he would deal with the situation (see Zeev Shek [Sharett's political secretary] to Easterman, 12 September 1954, ibid.).

31. Yaakov Tzur at cabinet meeting, 19 September 1954, ISA, fifth government, vol. 11; Tzur at JAE meeting, 6 September 1954, CZA S100/95.

32. JAE, 14 July 1954, CZA S100/94; coordinating committee, 20 July 1954, ISA/RG43/G/5383/16.

33. Yaakov Karoz (from Israeli embassy in France) to office of the prime minister, 20 May 1955, ISA/RG43/G/5558/4.

34. Meeting of the coordinating committee, 18 August 1955, ISA/RG43/G/5383/17.

35. Yaron Tsur, "Ḥevrah yehudit batar-masortit: yehudei kazablankah beshalhei hashilton hatzorfati," in idem and Hagar Hillel, *Yehudei kazablankah: 'iyunim bemodernizatiyah shel hanhagah yehudit betefutzah kolonialit* (Tel Aviv: 1995), 63. See also Laskier, *North African Jewry in the Twentieth Century,* 172–176.

36. Quoted by Yoseftal at meeting of the coordinating committee, 7 February 1955, ISA/RG43/G/5383/17. The visit and subsequent report by the AJC delegation created much bitterness among Jewish Agency officials, who often made reference to it. See, for instance, Shragai and Yehuda Braginsky at meeting of the JAE, 18 January 1955, CZA S100/97; Kol at meeting of the JAE, 15 February 1955, CZA S100/98; Eliyahu Dobkin at meeting of the JAE, 19 August 1955, CZA S100/98; Israel Goldstein, member of the New York Jewish Agency executive, cited in *Session of the Zionist General Council, Sixth Session after the 23rd Congress, Jerusalem, August 23–31, 1955,* 107; Rabbi Mordechai Kirshblum, president of the American Mizrachi organization, cited in ibid., 150.

37. Irving Engle, president of the AJC, quoted in Sanua, *Let Us Prove Strong,* 71.

38. Report by Tzur to the ministry of foreign affairs, 10 February 1955, ISA/RG 43/g/5558/4.

39. Nachum Goldmann to Tzur, 6 October 1955, ISA/RG 130/mfa/2398/1. There was a deep rivalry between Goldmann and the AJC. Thus, this quote, though accurately reflecting the AJC's basic position, should be regarded with caution.

40. Memorandum written on stationary of the law office of Ginzburg and Leventhal, 14 August 1950, Ben-Gurion Archives (Robert Nathan archive).

41. Rose Halperin at meeting of the JAE, 14 July 1954, morning session, CZA S100/94.

42. The UJA delegation's trip was discussed at a meeting of the JAE, 1 August 1955, CZA S100/99 and in other sources (for example in a report from Baruch Duvdevani to Shragai, 10 August 1955, CZA S6/6211). I was unable to find a copy of the UJA delegation's original report.

43. Report on the meeting between representatives of the delegation and activists in Morocco on 5 August 1955; Baruch Duvdevani to Shragai, 10 August 1955, CZA S6/6211.

44. Berl Locker at meeting of the JAE, 1 August 1955, CZA S100/99.

45. Joseph Schwartz at meeting of the JAE, ibid.

46. Friedman at meeting of the JAE, 19 August 1955, CZA S100/100.

47. Israel Goldstein at meeting of the JEA, 20 August 1955, CZA S100/100.

Levi Eshkol's impression was that American Jews did not sense the urgency of bringing North African Jews to Israel, in part because they were aware of Moshe Sharett's position regarding the importance of maintaining good relations with France. According to Eshkol, American Jews felt that "this issue is important but not urgent" (Levi Eshkol at cabinet meeting [19 September 1955], sixth government, vol. 3, 20).

48. See, for instance, a letter in which a Moroccan Jew writes that if there were to be ships at the Casablanca port headed for Israel, they would be filled instantaneously (E. Ohayon to M. Rechef, 14 June 1955, ISA/RG 43/g/5558/9).

49. Picard, *'Olim bimshurah,* 291.

50. Ibid., 344, 365–367.

51. On this attitude, see Yaron Tsur, "Carnival Fears: Moroccan Immigrants and the Ethnic Problem in the Young State of Israel," *Journal of Israeli History* 18, no. 1 (1997), 73–103.

52. Lissak, "The Demographic-Social Revolution," 3–6.

53. Kol at meeting of the JAE, 14 July 1955, CZA S100/94. Kol suggested spreading information about Israeli settlements that had been established by the North African Jews, in order to show how much they had contributed to the country.

54. Cabinet meeting, 5 January 1955, fifth government, vol. 5. Golda was not the only one who made this connection. After it was decided (in September 1955) to levy taxes in order to finance the aliyah, Ben-Zion Dinur, the minister of education, predicted that the outcome could be an increase of funds for the UJA: "There would be more revenue from the diaspora if people there knew that we are levying taxes on ourselves" (Dinur at cabinet meeting, 1 September 1955, sixth government, vol. 3).

55. Letter from Yoseftal (who remained in the United States during the fundraising campaign), read by Shragai at a meeting of the coordinating committee, 20 September 1955, ISA/RG43/G/5383/16.

56. Karp, *To Give Life*, 120; see also Rose Halperin at meeting of the JAE, 14 July 1955, morning session, CZA S100/94. The Yemenites were perceived in a positive light for two reasons. First was the fact that they were cut off from western culture, which gave them an air of authenticity and romanticism that sat well with western Jews. Second, Yemenites were a relatively small group that numbered less than 50,000; when they made aliyah in 1949, a majority of the Jews in Israel (and also among the new immigrants) were of European origin. In contrast, there were some 500,000 North African Jewish candidates for aliyah at a time when 300,000 Jews from Islamic countries were already living in Israel, and this made for a vastly different demographic situation.

57. Kaufman, "Hashpa'at milḥemet sheshet hayamim 'al haMagbit," 207.

58. See, for example, *The Lachish Story*; Dalia Ofer, "Vatikim ve'olim be'enei hairgunim hayehudiyim beeiropah uvaamerikah," in *Bein 'olim levatikim: yisrael ba'aliyah hagedolah 1948–1951*, ed. Dalia Ofer (Jerusalem: 1996), 43.

59. Interview with Myrtle Karp, 15 March 1976, Avraham Harman Institute of Contemporary Jewry, Oral History Division (hereafter: OHD) (Jerusalem), file no. 128–26 (pp. 28–29).

60. *New Roots*. It is important to note that many aspects of this portrayal had no basis in reality. In Morocco, a majority of the Jews worked to support themselves. In addition, as noted, about 50 percent of Jewish children attended modern schools; of the remainder, a majority received a religious Jewish education in *talmudei torah*. The claim that only some children knew how to read and write is contradicted by the data (see n. 10).

61. *A Guide to Overseas Operations 1955* (undated publication of the JDC).

62. "Moses W. Beckelman Urges Action Now on Behalf of Jews in North Africa," report to members of the national campaign council, vol. 9 (p. 8), 28 December 1955, CZA S42/163.

63. Report of Samuel Haber, director of the JDC in Morocco, given at the conference of JDC country directors, September 1956 (Paris), CZA, S42/576.

64. Interview with Samuel Haber, 7 November 1975, OHD, file no. 128–18 (pp. 18–19).

65. Borenstein also said, however, that the stories she heard about the persecution of North African Jewry made her feel a sense of solidarity with them (interview with Paula Borenstein, 23 February 1979, OHD, file no. 128–103 [p. 6]).

66. See also Alon Gal, "Overview: Envisioning Israel—The American Jewish Tradition," in Gal (ed.), *Envisioning Israel*, 31; and other articles in the volume.

67. Interview with Myrtle Karp, 29.

68. Karp, *To Give Life*, 111.

69. Meeting of the JAE, 14 July 1954, CZA S100/94.

70. Meeting of the JAE, 27 June 1955, CZA S100/99.

71. Meeting of the JAE, 1 August 1955, CZA S100/99.

72. Meeting of the JAE, 19 August 1955, CZA S100/100.

73. Ibid.

74. Raphael, *A History of the United Jewish Appeal,* 141. This represented an increase from the amount collected in 1955 ($60 million), but it did not come close to covering the needs.

75. JAE, *Report Submitted to the 24th Zionist Congress,* 442; idem, *Report Submitted to the 25th Zionist Congress,* 449.

76. Shragai at the Zionist General Council, cited in *Session of the Zionist General Council, Sixth Session after the 23rd Congress, Jerusalem, August 23–31, 1955,* 80.

77. Kaufman, "Hashpa'at milḥemet sheshet hayamim 'al haMagbit," 206.

Review Essays

Toward a Broader View of Jewish Rebuilding after the Holocaust

Margarete Myers Feinstein, *Holocaust Survivors in Postwar Germany, 1945–1957*. New York: Cambridge University Press, 2010. viii + 330 pp.

Atina Grossmann, *Jews, Germans, and Allies: Close Encounters in Occupied Germany*. Princeton: Princeton University Press, 2007. xv + 393 pp.

Laura Jockusch, *Collect and Record! Jewish Holocaust Documentation in Early Postwar Europe*. New York: Oxford University Press, 2012. xv + 320 pp.

Tamar Lewinsky, *Displaced Poets: Jiddische Schriftsteller im Nachkriegsdeutschland, 1945–1951*. Göttingen: Vandenhoeck & Ruprecht, 2008. 288 pp.

Dalia Ofer, Françoise S. Ouzan, and Judy Tydor Baumel-Schwartz (eds.), *Holocaust Survivors: Resettlement, Memories, Identities*. New York: Berghahn Books, 2012. xi + 345 pp.

Avinoam J. Patt and Michael Berkowitz (eds.), *"We Are Here": New Approaches to Jewish Displaced Persons in Germany*. Detroit: Wayne State University Press, 2010. x + 357 pp.

Alan Rosen, *The Wonder of Their Voices: The 1946 Holocaust Interviews of David Broder*. New York: Oxford University Press, 2010. xvii + 310 pp.

In the immediate aftermath of Germany's defeat, several million civilians displaced during the Second World War crisscrossed Central and Eastern Europe. The four major victorious nations, the United States, Great Britain, France, and the Soviet Union, assumed responsibility for these displaced persons (DPs) in their respective zones of occupation in Germany and Austria. According to Allied military directives and the guidelines of the United Nations Relief and Rehabilitation Administration (UNRRA), DPs included foreign workers, slave laborers, prisoners of war, and liberated concentration camp inmates—that is, refugees deemed worthy of assistance, as distinguished from those who did not deserve assistance. Of course, many refugees who had served in pro-German military units or had assisted the Germans in other capacities melted into DP communities.

The four powers favored the rapid return of all DPs to their home countries. Between the spring and fall of 1945, military and UNRRA officials succeeded in returning six to seven million DPs to their countries of origin. Citizens of West European countries willingly and quickly returned home, and the Soviets insisted on the forcible repatriation of their nationals to the USSR. Even so, after the completion of these mass return operations, approximately 1.2 million DPs remained homeless and unrepatriable in makeshift assembly facilities in the American, British, and French zones in Germany; in addition, there were an estimated 210,000 people in DP camps in Austria and Italy. They could be divided into two distinct groups: non-Jewish anti-Communist refugees, and Jewish survivors of the Holocaust. About half of the non-Jews, some 400,000–500,000 individuals, were Poles and Ukrainians—these formed the largest national group following the forced repatriation of Soviet nationals. Approximately 175,000–200,000 were Balts from Estonia, Latvia, and Lithuania, and there were also smaller groups of Hungarians, Czechs, and Slovaks who refused to return to countries under Soviet control. The rest, between 10 and 20 percent, were mostly Jewish survivors of the Holocaust, including those who had spent the war years in forced exile in the Soviet Union. Although UNRRA helped re-patriate approximately 742,000 DPs from Germany and about 202,000 from Austria between the fall of 1945 and the summer of 1947, a large influx of "post-hostilities refugees" from Eastern Europe reinforced the DP population.[1] When the International Refugee Organization (IRO) assumed responsibility for DPs from UNRRA in July 1947, they still numbered 712,000.[2]

Fewer than 60,000 survivors of the Holocaust from several European countries, alongside approximately 28,000 German Jews, were liberated on German soil. However, during the next two years, their numbers were augmented by tens of thousands of Jews who fled Eastern Europe, especially Poland and the Balkans. Between April 1946 and October 1946, the Jewish population in the American zone of Germany alone increased almost 200 percent, to 141,000. In the spring of 1947, the number of Jewish DPs in the western zones was approximately 250,000. The majority of Jewish DPs, who referred to themselves as *sheerit hapeleitah* (the saving remnant), lived in DP camps in the American zone in Germany (182,000); smaller numbers resided in DP camps in occupied Austria (44,000) and Italy (19,000). Although they formed only a small proportion of the DP population immediately after the war, by the end of 1947 they were about 25 percent of the total DP population. In other words, Jews formed a significant percentage of DPs, though they were outnumbered by Poles and even Ukrainians.

Non-Jewish DPs refused to be repatriated because they did not want to live under repressive Communist regimes or because they feared repercussions in instances in which they had cooperated with the German occupiers or homegrown fascist regimes. For their part, Jews were both unwilling and unable to return to their former homes because, in addition to their distrust of Communism, there was no one left from their families and communities to return to, and antisemitic sentiments and periodic violent attacks made them feel unwelcome and unsafe. Indeed, a majority of Jewish DPs arrived in 1946 in the wake of widespread antisemitism and anti-Jewish violence, particularly in Poland. Most of them were Jews who had spent the war years in Soviet Central Asia.

Although Jews were similar to other DPs in their resistance to repatriation, their insistence from the beginning of the postwar period on living in separate, homogeneous camps and their assertion of a national identity (under the mantle of Zionism) in justification of their argument for permission to leave Europe for Palestine distinguished them from other groups of DPs. Indeed, they took pains to emphasize this distinction. The initial British and American attitude, however, was that Jews, like all other DPs, ought to return to their countries of origin as soon as possible. British policy remained unbending, since Britain had decided to limit immigration to Palestine and to separate the issue of Jewish DPs from the Palestine question. In contrast, the American approach changed in light of the Harrison Report of August 1945, which criticized the treatment of Jewish DPs and recommended American intervention with the British government to allow the transfer of 100,000 Jewish DPs to Palestine. Taking into account the friction between Jewish and non-Jewish DPs, the report further encouraged the American administration to consider the Jewish DPs a distinct national group, entitled to separate DP camps and preferential treatment. For political reasons, the British refused to follow the American example and grant the 20,000 Jews in their zone separate national status, but they did place the Jewish DPs and non-Jewish DPs in two separate sections of the Bergen-Belsen DP camp, where the majority of the Jewish DPs lived.

By 1950, two years after the creation of the state of Israel and the dismantlement of all but a handful of DP facilities, about 170,000 Jewish DPs, between 60 and 70 percent of the total, had emigrated to Israel. By 1951, the United States had accepted some 312,000 DPs, including 96,000 Jews. Canada accepted 8,000 Jewish DPs. Australia had accepted 50,000 DPs by September 1949—among whom only about 150 were Jews. However, by 1954, about 17,000 Holocaust survivors had migrated to Australia. The British Labour government, for its part, blocked the migration of Holocaust survivors, while admitting about 300,000 European immigrants between 1946 and 1948. Several thousand Jewish DPs remained in Germany and Austria after the closure of the DP camps.[3]

Beginning with the publication in 1994 of Angelika Königseder and Juliane Wetzel's *Lebensmut im Wartesaal: Die jüdischen DPs (Displaced Persons) im Nachkriegsdeutschland*, myriad studies have examined the DPs' remarkable accomplishments, using documentary sources generated by the DPs themselves.[4] Among the most important initial accounts of the DPs' achievements in the years 1945–1950 are books authored by Michael Brenner, Zeev Mankowitz, Ruth Gay, and Hagit Lavsky.[5] Highlighting the DPs' self-governing bodies, their social and cultural institutions, and their lively (often contentious) political organizations, with an emphasis on Zionist parties and youth movements, these books performed an invaluable service in reinscribing DPs into postwar Jewish and European history. In so doing, they transformed the image of a demoralized, dispirited, and feckless flotsam of Jewish humanity into agents both in their own postwar rehabilitation and in that of the Jewish people. Like their immediate predecessors, the current books under review, all published in the last few years, are primarily social and cultural histories. Released from the obligation to return Jewish DPs to the historical stage, these more recent works argue for new and more complex interpretations of Jewish DPs' personal and collective rehabilitation.[6]

Before reviewing these works, it is important to note one major caveat: the vast majority of Holocaust survivors did *not* live in DP camps. One million Soviet Jewish survivors remained in the USSR; thousands of Jews in Eastern Europe either made their peace with Soviet-installed regimes or else were unable to leave; and West European Jews returned home, either rebuilding their lives in their countries of origin or emigrating to Israel or to North America, England, or Australia.

Understandably, their postwar experiences largely differed from those of the DPs. To their credit, several of the current books under review incorporate both categories of Jewish survivors.

"We Are Here": New Approaches to Jewish Displaced Persons in Germany sets the agenda for the further study of DPs. As noted by its editors, Avinoam J. Patt and Michael Berkowitz, a number of essays "challenge prior assumptions about the DPs and Holocaust survivors...including the supposedly unified background of the DP population, the notion of a general reluctance to confront the past, the idea of Zionism as an inevitable success after the war, and the suggestion that Jews, despite their presence in Germany, strenuously avoided contact with Germans" (p. 4). This is a yeomanly and useful collection of first-rate scholarship, almost all of whose essays are abbreviated versions of book-length studies—among them, some of the other books reviewed in this essay.

Several common themes, treated in novel ways, emerge from the books under review. The first is the role of Zionism among the DPs. Without a doubt, Zionism set the tone in the DP camps. Most DPs desired a connection with Zionism and with the land of Israel, and the vast majority supported Zionist political parties and the creation of the state of Israel, even if 35 percent ultimately rebuilt their lives in the Jewish diaspora. What drove the DPs to embrace Zionism? In *Life between Memory and Hope: The Survivors of the Holocaust in Occupied Germany* (2002), Zeev Mankowitz, representing a traditional view, underlined the DPs' "intuitive Zionism," infused by a strong ideological legacy and an unerring common goal to participate in the creation of a Jewish state in the land of Israel.[7] Hagit Lavsky has refined this view in her study of Jewish DPs in the Bergen-Belsen DP camp in the British zone. In her essay in the *"We Are Here"* collection, titled "The Displaced Persons in Bergen-Belsen: Unique or Typical Case?" Lavsky attributes the centrality of Zionism in DPs' lives to its "functional advantages." "Zionism," she writes, "was the only political agent that could supply an operational, ready-made organizational and ideological paradigm, some hope for the future, and a cause worth fighting for" (p. 247).

As Lavsky shows, the situation of DPs in the British zone of western Germany —10,000–12,000 of them residing in Bergen-Belsen, 5,000–6,000 in cities, and 1,000–2,000 in smaller camps or assembly centers—was generally more severe than that of DPs in the American zone in western Germany, Austria, and Italy. Britain's resistance to Jewish independence in Palestine, combined with the relatively harsh living conditions for Jews in the British zone, prompted defiance and reinforced the Jewish national struggle. Apart from its political agenda, the Zionist cause was important in "elevating the morale of the DPs and preparing them for the future" (p. 248). Notwithstanding, many of the refugees viewed their future as being in the diaspora. An example was the chairman of the Central Committee of Jews in the British zone, Yossel Rosensaft (a staunch advocate for the Zionist cause), who eventually settled in the United States. Indeed, one lesson to be learned from a number of the books under review is that there was often a discrepancy between one's support for Zionism and one's final destination. As Patt puts it in his essay in *"We Are Here"* (titled "Living in Landsberg, Dreaming of Deganiah: Jewish Displaced Youths and Zionism after the Holocaust"): "For the wider DP population, Zionism filled a symbolic need that had arisen for the Jewish people in the wake of tragedy, even if not all would make the Zionist dream their personal reality" (p. 123).

In "Living in Landsberg," as well as in *Finding Home and Homeland*, his book-length study of the lives of some 3,000 young DPs on training farms (kibbutzim) in occupied Germany, Patt builds on Lavsky's argument by supplying a psychological slant.[8] For young Jewish survivors attracted to the kibbutzim (who accounted for a disproportionate percentage of the surviving Jewish population), the appeal of Zionism was as much practical and psychological as it was ideological. According to Patt, in addition to "providing a secure environment for vocational training, education, and rehabilitation," Zionism offered "a surrogate family that could ultimately restore their faith in humanity" (ibid.).

Like Lavsky and Patt, Hannah Yablonka, in an essay titled "Holocaust Survivors in Israel: Time for an Initial Taking Stock" (her contribution to *Holocaust Survivors: Resettlement, Memories, Identities*, edited by Dalia Ofer, Françoise S. Ouzan, and Judy Tydor Baumel-Schwartz), downplays the ideological component of the mass aliyah from Europe in the immediate postwar years. The survivors' Zionism, she argues, "was not the ideological Zionism that we know from the pre-war era, but rather...an instinctive 'gut' Zionism rooted in a loss of faith in the European emancipation and the profound sense of humiliation that they felt during the years of destruction. Many felt that the main problem in their being Jews was the lack of a homeland, and they wished to rebuild their lives among their brethren" (p. 187). Even Mankowitz, who placed a premium on the role of Zionist ideology, perceived the functional and psychological role of Zionism in the DPs' disrupted lives. "Their Zionism," noted Mankowitz parenthetically, "was an attempt to reconstruct their chaotic lives, a bid for meaning and dignity."[9] In other words, there is a growing scholarly consensus that, although its central political role in the lives of DPs is indisputable, the grassroots appeal of Zionism was less ideological than practical ("functional"), psychological, and emotional.[10]

Another important theme to emerge from several of the books reviewed here is that, contrary to conventional wisdom, Jewish DPs did not lead isolated or insular lives. Although their leaders enjoined DPs in the American zone to avoid contacts with Germans (since they were all presumed to have Jewish blood on their hands unless proven otherwise), contacts between the Jewish survivors and Germans were plentiful. Atina Grossmann makes this abundantly clear in her innovative and adroit book, *Jews, Germans, and Allies: Close Encounters in Occupied Germany*, from which her essay in *"We Are Here"* derives. She recounts how Jews and Germans confronted each other on the black market; how Jewish DPs who lived in cities encountered German neighbors; how Germans insulted (and here and there even assaulted) Jews on the streets of German towns; and how Jews often clashed with local German officials—one common source of disagreement was the designation of land for the dignified burial of Jewish victims whose remains were often discovered in mass graves scattered over the German countryside. In addition, there were frequently more intimate relations between Jewish survivors and Germans. A significant number of Jewish men had sexual relations with German women; German doctors and nurses delivered the babies of pregnant Jewish women; after their children were born, Jewish mothers hired Germans to help them care for the infants.

Apart from Germans, DPs regularly encountered westerners from Allied forces, both military personnel and staff of outside organizations whose mission was to extend assistance to the survivors, and they also came into contact with Jewish representatives from Palestine. Grossmann's intricate description of these engendered close encounters breaks new historiographical ground.

Jewish babies play a central role in Grossmann's account. She depicts how survivors discovered their sexuality after several years spent in camps or in hiding. These mostly young and lonely men and women, undernourished, exploited, their nerves strained to the breaking point—many of them the only surviving members of their families—were eager to marry and start families. Not every couple was a match made in heaven, and many a young man and woman would not have been attracted to one another under normal circumstances. Here, however, they were thrown together by a common fate, and giving birth to children was charged with symbolism. For many parents, children were a tribute to the memory of murdered grandparents, parents, and siblings. They were also living proof that the Nazi extermination plan had not totally succeeded. In the immediate postwar years, Jewish DPs had the highest birthrate in Europe, while Germans had the lowest—sweet revenge, however modest and symbolic, for the DPs. The baby boom also carried a contemporary national symbolism. Images such as mothers pushing baby carriages, fathers celebrating the circumcisions of their sons, and toddlers playing represented a political argument for Zionism. As Grossmann puts it: "Jewish women survivors, living in a kind of extraterritoriality on both German and Allied soil, were prefiguring in their pregnant bodies a kind of imaginary nation that they hoped—at least this was the public message—to realize in Palestine/*Eretz Yisroel*" (p. 200).

Grossmann extends her focus to the survivor community in Berlin, which numbered 6,000–7,000 in the summer of 1945. Most of the German Jews who resurfaced in Berlin in 1945 were married to non-Jews or were the children of intermarried couples. Grossmann chronicles the tentative revival of the official Jewish community (Gemeinde) in Berlin and varied struggles on the part of the Gemeinde and individual Jewish survivors to reclaim bank accounts and confiscated property and to receive restitution. Ironically, in order to be eligible for aid, many of those who had adopted false Christian identities during the war or who had severed their ties with the Gemeinde before the war (especially if they had non-Jewish spouses) now had to provide proof of their Jewish identity.

Returning German Jews pondered whether they had a future in Germany, especially given the persistence of antisemitism and apparent lack of remorse among Germans. (In this they differed from some 8,000 non-German Jews, mostly from Poland, who lived in DP camps scattered on the outskirts of Berlin and were overwhelmingly determined to leave Germany as soon as possible.) In a nice personal touch, Grossmann refracts the trajectory of German Jewry through the lens of her grandfather, Heinrich Busse. After evading Gestapo agents when they came for him at his "Jews' house" in Berlin—his wife had already been deported to Auschwitz—he lived an underground existence until liberation. By war's end, he had lost everything. With time he received ever-important identity cards from the Gemeinde (attesting to the fact that he was a full-fledged Jew), from the municipal authorities (affirming that he was both a Jew and a victim of fascism), and from the police (acknowledging that he was a German citizen). All of these enabled him to cope with the struggles of life in Berlin. Nonetheless, in ascribing his survival to willpower, determination, and plain "dumb luck," Busse was also aware that mourning would always be part of his lot. This quintessential assimilated German Jew—by his own admission more German than Jew—eventually left Berlin forever in 1947, profoundly disappointed by the persistence of antisemitism even among "decent Germans."

Grossmann also calls attention to various acts of symbolic revenge on the part of Jewish survivors, occasionally abetted by American Jewish soldiers and recruits from Palestine serving in the British Army's Jewish Brigade. Jewish women brandishing their babies, Zionist banners flying from former official German buildings, Jews conducting parades or processions in German towns or strolling in the streets of German spa towns whose hotels and personnel had been commandeered for the treatment and rehabilitation of survivors—all of these were forms of revenge. As one DP quoted by Grossmann bluntly put it:

> Revenge did not mean only killing Germans. We had revenge when we saw the Germans acting as hewers of wood and drawers of water...when we saw them cleaning Jewish houses, the Jewish school I attended, buying cigarettes and paying for them in gold—gold that had undoubtedly been taken from Jews. We sold them bread and coffee and they gave everything they had....Revenge also meant sleeping with German women (Grossmann, 226–227).

With the exception of a couple of abortive schemes to assassinate SS men and Gestapo prisoners in American custody, there were few real efforts at large-scale revenge. The reason, Grossmann suggests, is that "the survivors were painfully aware that in the face of genocide there could be no adequate retribution" (ibid., 231). Jewish DPs did, however, have a number of violent confrontations with Germans and non-Jewish DPs, as described by another scholar, Margarete Myers Feinstein, in a monograph titled *Holocaust Survivors in Postwar Germany, 1945–1957*, from which her essay "Jewish Ritual Observance in Amalek's Shadow: Mourning, Marriage, and Birth Rituals among Displaced Persons in Germany" in *"We Are Here"* derives. Feinstein details a string of violent encounters between German police and Jewish survivors in various DP camps in the first half of 1946, in which a handful of survivors were killed and others injured. Strained nerves also led to a few violent altercations between American soldiers and Jewish DPs.

Like Grossmann, Feinstein emphasizes the role of gender and shows that sex, marriage, and birth were not just stations in the life cycle but symbolic forms of vengeance. She also takes a close look at the role of religion in survivors' lives and, in so doing, revises the conventional wisdom that a large number of survivors lost their faith in the camps. Feinstein shows that the percentage of DPs who abandoned their belief in God as a result of the Holocaust was less than one might expect, and further argues that Orthodox Judaism was a potent force in DP camps. Regardless of belief, a large number of DPs continued to perform Jewish rituals. They said kaddish because it made them feel connected to their murdered relatives. They were wed by rabbis in Jewish ceremonies and had their sons circumcised according to Jewish ritual because these and other customs helped them feel the presence of their parents.

Memory, a theme common to several of the books under review, plays a key role in Feinstein's narrative. She documents DP mourners' processions through German towns, DPs' attention to the proper burial of Jews who died both before and after the war from disease, the establishment of special days of remembrance, and the popularity of a new form of commemoration known as "mourning academies" (*troyer akademyen*), specifically gatherings of survivors to commemorate the liquidation of a certain ghetto or the slaughter of Jews in an area. Aside from their commemorative function, "DP mourning academies helped to establish common ground among DPs of different socio-economic backgrounds and wartime experiences," writes Feinstein. "Mourning academies provided a forum in which nonobservant Jews and observant Jews could meet in shared grief and remembrance" (p. 77).

However, mourning academies inadvertently accentuated differences between the commemoration of victims of ghettos and concentration camps, on the one hand, and resistance fighters, on the other. This occurred, for instance, when DPs held mourning academies in honor of resistance fighters in the Warsaw ghetto. While the Warsaw ghetto uprising became a symbol that all survivors could embrace, it drew attention to the fact that not all Jews had supported Jewish resistance for fear of German retaliation against the community, and it highlighted the contrast between those who chose a heroic death and those who perished without putting up armed resistance. Feinstein shows that DPs resolved this apparent tension by asserting the commonalities among the survivors. DP newspapers took the lead in this reconciliation process by presenting all Jewish communities as having supported Jewish resistance and by reminding DPs that ghetto fighters and partisans had emerged from the same communities as had concentration camp victims, had shared in the loss of family and friends, and had also faced the terror tactics of Germans and antisemites.

Feinstein is not afraid to tackle tough issues. Although she doesn't present any numbers, she hypothesizes that a large number of survivors committed suicide in the DP camps. "To proceed in a strange and hostile world without family left some survivors feeling that the sorrow was too difficult to bear," she notes (p. 66). There were also numerous instances in which survivors who had been able to locate relatives abroad committed suicide when American or British immigration officials refused to provide a visa. One has to give Feinstein credit for broaching this topic, since it runs counter to the standard upbeat narrative that all survivors exhibited remarkable resilience and restorative powers.

The importance of memory also animates the books by Alan Rosen and Laura Jockusch. In *The Wonder of Their Voices*, Rosen follows David Broder, the famed American psychologist (himself born in Lithuania and educated in Russia and Germany), who traveled to Europe armed with a wire-spool tape recorder in order to interview survivors. Over the course of just two months in 1946, visiting DP camps and also shelters in France, Italy, and even Switzerland, Broder recorded 120 interviews in nine different languages. These interviews are significant because they were among the first, affording survivors an opportunity to give expression to their "fresh wounds." (Broder, Rosen notes, was concerned that he had arrived too late to collect the spontaneous memories and impressions of survivors.) In addition to survivor testimony, Broder also collected songs and poetry. Only eight of the edited and condensed interviews were published in his 1949 study, *I Did Not Interview the Dead*. Seventy additional interviews appeared in their entirety in a sixteen-volume self-published series, *Topical Autobiographies of Displaced People Recorded Verbatim in the Displaced Persons Camps with a Psychological and Anthropological Analysis*, which appeared between 1950 and 1957. Broder could not find a publisher for the series, in part because of its size and his reluctance to abridge the interviews, and in part because, during the decade immediately after the war, the subject matter did not appeal to most publishing houses.

Given his interest in the impact of catastrophe on personality, Broder encouraged his interviewees to relate not only what happened but also why, in their view, it had happened. Thus one finds commentary by survivors in many of the interviews. Broder was also inclined to experiment with narration. In this spirit, instead of having his subjects give an account of their lives from the eve of the war to its end, he asked several of those who happened to witness events from a particular vantage point to recount, in his formulation, a "special episode" during the war years. In one case it was the Warsaw ghetto uprising, it another it was the administrative apparatus at Auschwitz.

Broder was not a passive listener, however. Indeed, he frequently interrupted his interviewees with questions, occasionally voiced skepticism, and even argued with survivors when their tales were beyond his ken. To their credit, the survivors rarely ceded ground. One telling example is the exchange between Broder and a concentration camp survivor named Abraham Kimmelmann (whose name Broder changed to Abe Mohnblum in *I Did Not Interview the Dead*). Kimmelmann has just told Broder that he saw a boy eat ten liters of soup. Broder questions Kimmelmann's account because he couldn't fathom that anyone could eat such a huge quantity. Kimmelmann assures him that he saw it and that, moreover, on more than one occasion he himself downed almost that amount. Broder remains skeptical, prompting Kimmelmann to question the limits of psychologists' grasp of human nature—putting Broder on the defensive. From the end of the interview we read:

> *Mohnblum* [Kimmelmann]: The psychologists, well, they have said that they have ascertained something. But after this war it became apparent that they were wrong.
> *Question* [Broder]: Oh, no.
> *Mohnblum*: They said that they had found out. But after this war it became apparent that they were mistaken.
> *Question:* No—
> *Mohnblum*:—that they are absolutely incapable of appraising what really can happen. And although this war has revealed *such* things we still cannot be sure that it may not come to much worse situations.
> *Question:* Excuse me, Abe. You are a fine young man, but you should never argue about things you don't really know. The psychologists never claim that they have ascertained everything. The psychologists never said that. Scientifically trained psychologists have always been the first to admit that they know very little. How could a psychologist know what would happen under Hitler when such a situation never occurred before? Isn't that so....
> *Mohnblum*: Well, we may still have an opportunity to discuss this when I shall talk about the time I was in Buchenwald (quoted in *The Wonder of Their Voices*, p. 135).

As Rosen sums up the interview:

> Clearly nothing is resolved. Broder believes his professional authority should be respected, whatever its limitations. Some things are known about "what is man"; the war does not overturn everything. Kimmelmann's experience has taught him otherwise; knowledge has to be tested against what he himself has witnessed and, when it is, it is found wanting. Neither man gives ground (ibid.).

Rosen refuses to take sides, but from what we know now, Kimmelmann had the upper hand in this argument. Moreover, while Rosen tends to place Broder on a pedestal, his interview methods would certainly meet with disapprobation today, and one wonders to what extent Broder's numerous interventions affected the survivors' narrations of events.

In *Collect and Record!*, an amplification of her contribution to *"We Are Here,"* Laura Jockusch also examines memory, but she broadens the geographical scope of research on DPs to include those Jews who were not DPs, comparing the DPs' postwar Jewish historical commission with those in Poland, France, and Austria. Staffed by Holocaust survivors whose paths had followed similar trajectories (even if in different regions), the historical commissions' self-delegated task was to document Jewish life under Nazi occupation and Nazi crimes against the Jewish people. The various commissions collaborated in undertaking *khurbn-forshung* (Holocaust research), and certain individuals took part in two of the historical commissions—Philip Friedman, for one, led the Jewish historical commission in Poland until he departed for occupied Germany, where he played a leading role in the DP historical commission. Even outside Poland, Holocaust survivors of East European background were predominant in the various postwar Jewish historical commissions, partly because of their familiarity with Jewish documentation projects that emerged in response to anti-Jewish violence in Eastern Europe in the period preceding the Second World War. In addition, the historical commissions took their cue from efforts in a number of ghettos to document Jewish life under Nazi oppression, in particular the Oyneg Shabes project in the Warsaw ghetto that had been spearheaded by historian Emanuel Ringelblum. Thus, the postwar historical commissions collected diverse materials generated by Jews as well as by the German perpetrators.

At the same time, the postwar commissions sought to extend the work of ghetto documentation projects. They published a large number of historical publications, including document collections, monographs on various aspects of Jewish life under Nazism based on meticulous research, anthologies of poems and songs composed in camps and forests, and memoirs. For example, the Central Jewish Historical Commission in Poland, based in Lodz (with affiliates in several cities), released more than forty publications between 1945 and 1948, and the DP historical commission, headquartered in Munich, published ten volumes of the journal *Fun letstn khurbn* (From the last catastrophe), which featured eyewitness testimonies and reports on specific geographic areas, places, towns, ghettos, and camps, as well as essays on folklore and popular culture. The historical commissions organized grass-roots campaigns to recruit and train interviewers and to solicit testimony from survivors, resulting in thousands of testimonies, including those of children, on all aspects of Jewish life under Nazi occupation. The historical commissions also rendered assistance to prosecutors in pursuit of Nazi criminals. They gathered evidence, provided documentation of Nazi crimes, and identified Jewish witnesses to testify for the prosecution, while professional historians from the historical commissions testified as expert witnesses at trials for the prosecution.

As Jockusch writes: "Many survivors of Nazi rule saw documenting the recent catastrophe as a moral imperative for the sake of the dead and the generations to come: survival had bequeathed on them an obligation to publicize the truth of DP German genocide and to write the history of the Holocaust from the perspective of its victims" (*Collect and Record!*, p. 36). In this spirit, Jockusch quotes Dr. Ada Eber, a native of Lvov who became active in the work of the Jewish historical commission in Poland. Years later, Eber recalled her commitment to documentation in immediate postwar Poland:

> What really mattered for us survivors was the power of our recent terrible past that we shared and remembered. . . . Eyewitness reports, fresh records of inhumanity—this is what we, the survivors of the Holocaust, had in common. Our moral obligation was to put on paper what we remembered, for the sake of *documentation*, for bringing the culprits to justice, for preventing the evil to happen again, not only for the Jewish people but [also] for the good of all mankind (ibid.).

Notwithstanding, as early as two or three years after war's end, members of historical commissions found it increasingly difficult to persuade fellow survivors to provide testimony or to fill out questionnaires. Some survivors wanted to forget; more commonly, the survivors—especially the younger among them—were increasingly preoccupied with efforts to establish normal lives.

Alongside numerous commonalities among the various historical commissions, there were also important differences, as Jockusch points out. In Paris, the Center of Contemporary Jewish Documentation (CDJC) had to deal not only with the French propensity to commemorate political "deportees," which tended to ignore Jewish victims of racial legislation, but also with the fact that many among the French population had aided the German effort to deport Jews to their deaths. Moreover, after the war, the overwhelming tendency was to obfuscate this dark side of the French reaction to Nazi occupation. "Thus," writes Jockusch, "the CDJC workers saw their main goal as breaking the French public's 'blockade of silence' regarding the Jewish tragedy" (p. 57). In addition, they had to rewrite French Jews into the fate of the French body politic, simultaneously equating them with and differentiating them from all other French citizens. In Poland, in contrast, members of the Central Jewish Historical Commission were operating under a Soviet-installed regime that was intent on incorporating Jewish victims of the Nazis into the overall toll of victims classified by country of origin. In common with the historical commission in Paris, they sought to emphasize the specificity of Jewish suffering, in particular the murder of three million Polish Jews under Nazi occupation. Their method of doing this was to stress the fact that, whereas the Jews were first to be slated for annihilation, Poles were next in line.

The DP historical commission, for its part, faced competing claims from within the DP community. A prime example of such claims were the memorial books (*yizker-bikher*) published by various associations of survivors from the same town or region (*lands-manshaftn*). Israel Kaplan, the editor of *Fun letstn khurbn* and the head of the historical commission, dismissed such efforts on the grounds that they were both nonfactual and sentimental, blurring the line between fact and fiction and therefore of minimal historical value. His efforts, however, were to no avail. As Jockusch observes, he

> sought to secure a monopoly on history writing and publication for the historical commission. This proved to be a losing battle. In addition to fierce competition from periodicals published by landsmanshaftn, professional organizations, and political parties, *Fun Letstn Khurbn*'s comprehensive treatment of the past did not resonate with a reader affiliated with Zionist parties and youth movements and eager for laudatory works on ghetto uprisings and resistance movements (p. 140).

Despite the remarkable achievements of the various Jewish historical commissions, they never established their rightful place in the foundation of research and writing on the Holocaust. As Jockusch explains, there are two overriding reasons for their failure to make an impact on Holocaust studies. In the first place, the leading members of the historical commissions had no students. With few exceptions (one being Philip Friedman, who received an appointment at Columbia University thanks to the intervention of the famed Jewish historian Salo Baron), they were unable to land teaching or research positions after the immediate postwar period, especially in Israel and the United States. Even Friedman left no disciples behind. Second, the victim-centered approach to Holocaust documentation and research, which drew heavily on documents generated by Jews, did not square with the perpetrator-driven methodology that long dominated research and writing on the Holocaust, from the publication of Raul Hilberg's monumental *The Destruction of the European Jews* (1961) until relatively recently. Indeed, it was conventional wisdom (accepted even by Friedman) that research and writing by survivors could not possibly be "objective." It is to be hoped that burgeoning scholarly engagement with Jewish responses to the Holocaust, which are reflected in a large variety of sources generated by Jews, will spark interest in the research produced by the early postwar Jewish historical commissions. Leading the charge in this direction are Jan T. Gross' recent landmark books, *Neighbors: The Destruction of the Jewish Community in Jedwabne, Poland* (2001) and *Fear: Antisemitism in Poland after Auschwitz* (2006), in which testimony collected by the Central Jewish Historical Commission in Poland plays a central role.

Taken together, *The Wonder of Their Voices* and *Collect and Record!* are significant for their categorical dismantling of the so-called myth of silence, according to which all survivors were reluctant to tell their stories in the first years after liberation.

In *Displaced Poets: Jiddishe Schriftstellter im Nachkriegsdeutschland, 1945–1951* (Yiddish writers in postwar Germany, 1945–1951), Tamar Lewinsky examines the remarkable revival of Yiddish culture among the DPs. She counts some seventy Yiddish-language newspapers and journals that appeared regularly, including those published by youth movements, political parties, and religious groups, and almost 300 books published by DPs, including novels and collections of short stories, poetry, memoirs, reprints of classic Yiddish literature, religious tracts, political writings, and schoolbooks. The roughly fifty Yiddish writers whom Lewinsky salvages from obscurity saw it as their duty to provide Yiddish reading material to survivors hungry for a written Yiddish word; to make a modest dent in replenishing the innumerable, valuable Yiddish books and periodicals that had been destroyed during the war; and to introduce Yiddish culture to the unschooled younger generation of survivors whose youth had been spent in ghettos and camps.

It should come as no surprise that the publications of DP writers reflected a deeply felt need to process Jewish pain and suffering during the Holocaust. As Lewinsky writes: "In general, the gaze from the past was directed toward the present....The transition between both narratives was fluid. For those DPs stranded in Germany, the Holocaust did not simply come to an end with the collapse of the Third Reich. The past formed, moreover, a component of their present" (p. 110).

Despite the apparent promise of a postwar efflorescence of Yiddish belles-lettres, conditions militated against it. Lewinsky quotes from a letter written in November 1946 by the American-born Lucy Schildkret (later, the distinguished historian Lucy Dawidowicz), who was employed by the American Joint Distribution Committee to assist the DPs. After attending a literary gathering, a dispirited Schildkret wrote:

> This afternoon I was invited to attend a literary meeting....It was the first public meeting of the Jewish Writers Union, recently organized in Munich, and was devoted to a reading from the work of S. Berlinski, a young writer who had won some measure of recognition in pre-war Poland. The meeting was held in one of the rooms of Kultur Amt, unheated because today is Saturday, with a total of about 18 people, including Berlinski, the chairman, and the author's wife....Berlinski read some excerpts from a novel and a couple of stories, one of which was a gem, except for a few very minor flaws....[But] since the place was freezing, I left. Berlinski, I am told, is the only writer here who has pre-war recognition and the only one of undisputed ability. Certainly it would seem so. The bad lighting, the cold, the small audience, the general depressing character of the meeting made me very sad. Especially when I make comparisons with what I know used to be in Warsaw and Vilna (p. 82).

In fact, DPs' literary efforts were practically ignored by Yiddish writers and readers in the United States and Israel. One DP writer called it a "spiritual blockade." According to Lewinsky, the reason (as Schildkret intimated) was that the quality of DP writers' work did not meet the standards expected by the arbiters of Yiddish culture abroad. Moreover, the alienation most DPs felt from their German surroundings propelled them to attempt to recreate literary types and situations borrowed from the Yiddish classics. In this vein, Lewinsky describes the strategy of DP writers:

> In their literary attempt to distance themselves from actual post-war Germany, they freed Jewish topography from the German and depicted a parallel topography with Munich as the capital...and the surrounding DP camps as shtetls. Then only in this way could the internal problems of the *sheerit hapeleitah* be discussed without having to consider them within the larger context of German–Jewish relations (pp. 130–131).

This orientation may have suited the needs of DP writers, but it may also have contributed to their lack of popularity abroad, since it was out of sync with the evolving tastes and interests of the few remaining Yiddish readers in the United States and Israel. The latter were preoccupied with different issues: in the United States, by the tension between the pressure of assimilation and the preservation of Jewish identity; in Israel, by existential danger and the promise of a new future that negated Jewish existence in the diaspora. It is not surprising that most DP writers never felt at home regardless of where they settled after departing from the DP camps, be it North America or Israel. In the end, the Yiddish writers who are the protagonists of Lewinsky's study fought a losing battle. Apart from the case of diehard Yiddishists, who were (and continue to be) devoted to the retrieval of Yiddish, their work had no lasting impact.

In their introduction to *Holocaust Survivors*, Ofer, Ouzan, and Baumel-Schwartz, all Israeli historians, call attention to the transformation of "Jews who were still alive after the war—'DP's'—into 'survivors,'" and ultimately of "'survivorship' into a larger definition of their complete postwar identity" (p. 4). In his essay (titled "Jewish Shoah Survivors: Neediness Assessment and Resource Allocation"), Israeli demographer Sergio DellaPergola goes so far as to suggest that a definition of Holocaust survivors should include

> those who were in concentration camps or ghettos, or who were otherwise submitted to slave labor...[or] were involved in flight and illegality, or whose life was disrupted in similar ways [or] were submitted in their locations to a regime of duress and/or limitation of their full civil rights in relation to their Jewish background—whether by a Nazi foreign occupying power or by a local authority associated with the Nazi endeavor—or who had to flee elsewhere in order to avoid falling under the aforementioned situations (p. 299).

In accordance with this definition, DellaPergola would count among the survivors not only Jews from the European continent but also those from German-occupied North African countries and even Middle Eastern countries—Syria, Lebanon, Libya—who were subjected to discriminatory measures under the colonial or mandatory rule of Germany's allies, Vichy France and Italy.

The transformation of DPs into survivors is reflected especially in those chapters that deal with Jews who settled in the diaspora. Essays by Joanna Michlic, David Weinberg, Jean-Marc Dreyfus, Françoise Ouzan, Leo Senkman, and Sharon Kangisser-Cohen deal, respectively, with survivors' efforts to rebuild their lives in Poland, the Netherlands, Belgium, France, the United States, Argentina, and Australia. (The *"We Are Here"* collection also features a contribution on the theme, an essay by Beth Cohen on the rehabilitation of survivors who found asylum in the United States.)

Finally, several of the books under review begin to probe topics that should be taken up by subsequent books. Two in particular stand out. The first, touched upon by Grossmann and Lewinsky in their respective works, is the significant proportion of Polish Jews in DP camps who had spent the war in forced exile in the Soviet Union. These Jews survived either by fleeing or by being deported by the Soviets to the Soviet interior, thus remaining out of the reach of the Germans. The German invasion in June 1941 prompted the release of those in forced labor camps and a rush south to the central Asian republics. Some 200,000 were repatriated to Poland from the Soviet Union after the war, and the vast majority of them quickly fled Poland and continued farther west into Germany. These Polish Jews differed from those who had survived in Poland or in camps on German soil. Their lives had been harsh but could not be compared with the ordeals of Polish Jewish survivors of ghettos and camps. Many arrived in family units; most of those who survived in Poland or Germany were alone in the world. Moreover, life in the Russian interior had prepared them for the privations of DP camps. Several of the writers showcased by Lewinsky spent the war years in the Soviet Union. In a recent article published in *Holocaust and Genocide Studies*, Lewinsky and Jockusch show that the wartime ordeals of DPs who survived in Russia were practically ignored by the DP historical commission and the DP press.[11] How did they interact with other survivors? Were they active politically in the DP camps? What was their contribution to commemorations in the DP camps? Were they more likely to establish relations with Germans because they had been spared their wrath during the war? These and many other questions remain to be answered.

The other issue that deserves much more attention is the interaction between Jewish and non-Jewish DPs. Feinstein refers to an attack by Polish DPs on the synagogue in the DP camp of Bergen-Belsen during Hanukkah in 1945 and another incident in which armed Poles terrorized Jewish DPs at the Neu-Freimann (Munich) Siedlung camp after Jewish survivors denounced a Polish kapo to American authorities in February 1946. American soldiers briefly provided protection to the camp, but after their removal in March, Polish DPs fired on Jews on two separate occasions. The second shooting, in March 1946, led to a riot in which one American soldier and one Jewish DP were wounded. Feinstein also points out that the Jewish DP police force in Belsen searched for non-Jewish kapos and collaborators both in Belsen (which became exclusively a Jewish DP camp in June 1946) and in the neighboring camp populated solely by non-Jewish Hungarian DPs. The best comparative study of DPs from various countries is Anna Holian's *Between National Socialism and Soviet Communism: Displaced Persons in Postwar Germany* (2011). Holian makes several references to relations between Jewish and non-Jewish DPs. She notes that Jews generally saw Polish, Ukrainian, and Russian DPs as persecutors rather than as fellow victims of persecution, whereas Polish, Ukrainian, and Russian DPs regarded Jews as competitors for scarce resources. Overall, as Holian observes, "persecution per se was not a source of solidarity."[12] Holian's book far from exhausts the topic of relations between Jews and non-Jews in DP camps, but does set an example for future research. It is to be hoped, in the spirit of Holian's book, that both the edited volumes under review and Jockusch's book signal a trend to wrest Jewish DPs from their splendid, scholarly isolation.

GABRIEL N. FINDER
University of Virginia

Notes

1. In the meantime, in the wake of the escalation of the Cold War during 1947, Washington and London opposed the forced repatriation of DPs to Communist-dominated countries.

2. See Arieh J. Kochavi, *Post-Holocaust Politics: Britain, the United States, and Jewish Refugees, 1945–1948* (Chapel Hill: 2001), ch. 1; idem, "Liberation and Dispersal," in *The Oxford Handbook of Holocaust Studies*, ed. Peter Hayes and John K. Roth (New York: 2010), 509–510; Anna Holian, *Between National Socialism and Soviet Communism: Displaced Persons in*

Postwar Germany (Ann Arbor: 2011), ch. 1; Gerard Daniel Cohen, *In War's Wake: Europe's Displaced Persons in the Postwar Order* (New York: 2012), introduction.

3. Kochavi, "Liberation and Dispersal," 510–522; Hanna Yablonka, "Holocaust Survivors in Israel: Time for an Initial Taking of Stock," in *Holocaust Survivors: Resettlement, Memories, Identities*, ed. Dalia Ofer, Françoise S. Ouzan and Judy Tydor Baumel-Schwartz (New York: 2012), 186–187.

4. Angelika Königseder and Juliane Wetzel, *Lebensmut im Wartesaal: Die jüdischen DPs (Displaced Persons) im Nachkriegsdeutschland* (Frankfurt: 1994); in English: *Waiting for Hope: Jewish Displaced Persons in Post-World War II Germany*, trans. John A. Broadwin (Evanston: 2001). This book represented a departure from earlier works on the DPs that tended to focus on the roles of groups assisting Jewish DPs and the role of the DPs in the creation of the state of Israel.

5. Michael Brenner, *After the Holocaust: Rebuilding Jewish Lives in Postwar Germany*, trans. Barbara Harshav (Princeton: 1997); Zeev W. Mankowitz, *Life between Memory and Hope: The Survivors of the Holocaust in Occupied Germany* (New York: 2002); Ruth Gay, *Safe among the Germans: Liberated Jews after World War II* (New Haven: 2002); Hagit Lavsky, *New Beginnings: Holocaust Survivors in Bergen-Belsen and the British Zone in Germany, 1945–1950* (Detroit: 2002).

6. There has also been a recent spate of excellent books on DPs in general, all of which consider the fate of Jewish DPs together with non-Jewish DPs. See Ben Shephard, *The Long Road Home: The Aftermath of the Second World War* (London: 2010); Holian, *Between National Socialism and Soviet Communism*; Mark Mazower, Jessica Reinisch, and David Feldman (eds.), *Post-War Reconstruction of Europe: International Perspectives, 1945–1949* (Oxford: 2011); Cohen, *In War's Wake*; Jessica Reinisch and Elizabeth White (eds.), *The Disentanglement of Populations: Migration, Expulsion and Displacement in Post-War Europe, 1944–9* (New York: 2011).

7. Mankowitz, *Life between Memory and Hope*, 69.

8. Avinoam Patt, *Finding Home and Homeland: Jewish Youth and Zionism in the Aftermath of the Holocaust* (Detroit: 2009).

9. Mankowitz, *Life between Memory and Hope*, 69.

10. On the role of Zionism, see also Grossmann, *Jews, Germans, and Allies*, 178–182.

11. Laura Jockusch and Tamar Lewinsky, "Paradise Lost? Postwar Memory of Polish Jewish Survival in the Soviet Union," *Holocaust and Genocide Studies* 24 (2010), 373–399.

12. Holian, *Between National Socialism and Soviet Communism*, 268.

The Holocaust and Its Aftermath in the Yishuv and the State of Israel

Shlomo Bar-Gil and Ada Schein, *Viyshavtem betaḥ: nitzolei hashoah bahityashvut ha'ovedet* 1945–1955 (Dwell in safety: Holocaust survivors in the rural cooperative settlement). Jerusalem: Yad Vashem, 2010. 357 pp.

Dina Porat, *Israeli Society, the Holocaust and Its Survivors*. London: Vallentine Mitchell, 2010. 459 pp.

As is often the case in popular and scholarly publishing, Holocaust-related publications tend to appear in waves. One example is the plethora of survivor memoirs appearing from the late 1970s onward, which can be attributed at least in part to Gerald Green's four-part television mini-series, *Holocaust*. First aired in 1978, this critically acclaimed drama about two families under Hitler (it later won eight Emmy awards) heralded an awakening of public interest in the topic; it was even credited with persuading the West German government to repeal the statute of limitations on Nazi war crimes. Growing interest in the Holocaust was also manifested in the cultural, academic, and artistic spheres. Holocaust memorials were erected in dozens (and later hundreds) of cities, often funded by money donated by survivors. Similarly, Holocaust chairs and research institutes began to be established in universities worldwide.

As public interest in the Holocaust swelled, publishing houses began seeking out popular histories, along with survivor memoirs, fiction, and academic studies. Meanwhile, Holocaust-related films moved from art houses to wide-screen cinemas. Claude Landsmann's 9-hour-and-36-minute opus, *Shoah* (1985), drew vast audiences throughout the world, as did *Sophie's Choice* (1982), based on William Styron's novel about a Polish Catholic Auschwitz survivor who had been forced to choose which of her two children would be saved.

In the academic world, a shift in Holocaust-related research became apparent at about this time. In the first two decades following the war, only "mainstream topics" such as Jewish leadership, Jewish resistance, rescue, the "Final Solution" and (at a later stage) issues relating to life in the ghettos and camps were deemed worthy of academic attention. Beginning in the late 1970s and early 1980s, however, academic interest in the Holocaust turned to broader matters, focusing, among other things, on the actions of free-world governments during the wartime years. The impetus for much of this research was the opening of British and American government archival collections that dealt with the prewar and wartime period. Researchers, historians, and publicists began studying these collections and analyzing the data that came to light. The result was a number of studies, most of which blasted the wartime British

and American administrations for their reluctance to rescue European Jews both
before and during the Second World War. The American journalist Arthur Morse laid
the groundwork for future books on this topic with his path-breaking study, *While Six
Million Died*; this was soon followed by works written by David Wyman, Saul
Friedman, and Henry Feingold, in the United States, and by Alan Joshua Sherman
and Bernard Wasserstein in Britain.[1] In Israel, where much of the archival material
from the war years had long been available, a wave of studies centering on the Yishuv
and its leadership during the Second World War was authored by a new generation of
Holocaust scholars—no longer former refugees or survivors, but rather those born at
the end of the war or soon thereafter. The earliest book on this topic actually appeared in 1963, when Yehuda Bauer (who had been born in prewar Europe, but who
came to Palestine at the age of 13) published a reworking of his Ph.D. dissertation
that dealt with the Zionist leadership between 1939 and 1945.[2] For close to a decade
there was little follow-up on the topic, but beginning in the early 1980s, Yoav Gelber,
Dalia Ofer, Yechiam Weitz, Hava Eshkoli, Tuvia Friling, and Dina Porat authored
works that examined various aspects of the Yishuv during the Holocaust era.[3]

Another wave of Holocaust research focused on the war's aftermath. Historical
work on *sheerit hapeleitah*, the surviving remnant of European Jewry, began more
than 30 years ago, though the bulk of historical studies on this topic were published
during the past two decades.[4] Growing out of those studies, as will be seen, were a
number of works that dealt with the resettlement of survivors in areas far from the
sites of incarceration and liberation.

All of this serves as background to a review of two recently published books on the
Holocaust and its aftermath from the more specific vantage point of the Jewish community in Palestine (the Yishuv) and later, the state of Israel. The first is a collection
of essays authored by Dina Porat, a professor at Tel Aviv University and the recently
appointed chief historian of Yad Vashem. For close to three decades, Porat has
studied various aspects of what Yehuda Bauer succinctly describes in his foreword to
her book as "the relationships between the Jewish Diaspora in Europe and the emerging Jewish community in Palestine and later the Israeli Jewish society in the shadow
of the Holocaust." Many of Porat's best and most innovative articles have been collected in *Israeli Society, the Holocaust and Its Survivors,* which offers an integrative
portrait of her research.

The first section, titled "Between Personalities and Comprehension," considers the
ways in which Yishuv intellectuals and leaders, among them David Ben-Gurion and
Martin Buber, processed and internalized the information they received (both during
and immediately after the war) about the situation in Nazi-occupied Europe. This
section includes two stand-out essays that immediately came to mind even before
I had opened the book. The first, originally published in English in 1984, tells the
story of Al-domi (literally, "do not remain silent"), a group of Palestinian Jewish intellectuals who banded together in an attempt to rouse the Yishuv and the rest of the
free world to take action to save European Jewry. While Al-domi's efforts were not
immediately successful, their existence was a catalyst for additional scrutiny of the
problem. In contrast, the central figure of the second essay, Ruzka Korczak, was
based in Vilna; at the end of 1944, she became the first partisan who managed to
make her way to Palestine, where she reported on events in wartime Europe. In both

these essays, as with others in this section, Porat deals with the juxtaposition of those from "there" with those from "here" in a manner that is both historically accurate and emotionally sensitive, making use of printed source material as well as interviews with some of the surviving historical figures.

In the second section, "Between the Yishuv and Jewish Communities," Porat examines Yishuv leaders' response to three Holocaust-related events: the Transnistria affair, in which the Romanian government put forth a proposal to permit Jews to leave Romania in exchange for money; the annihilation of Hungarian Jewry; and the encounter, at war's end, between Italian Jews, Yishuv representatives, and Holocaust survivors. In each instance, she shows, most of the Yishuv leaders were willing to commit scarce resources in an attempt to rescue European Jews even when the chances of success were minimal—a finding that runs counter to the argument put forth by others that these leaders, focusing on what might be called "bottom-line politics," neglected rescue opportunities because they were so involved in building the Yishuv's political future.

Involvement is also a key theme of the third section, "Between the Yishuv and Youth Movements in Europe," in which the attitude of the Yishuv toward European Jewish youth movements during the Holocaust is examined alongside the attitude of those movements toward Eretz Yisrael during that same period. Zionist youth movements were considered the future of the Jewish state-in-the-making, and as Porat demonstrates, this sense of mission accounts for the resilience and spirit of mutual responsibility displayed by Zionist group members both during and after the war.

Porat deals with both practical and ideological matters in the fourth section, "Decisions Taken between Hope and Reality." Among the essays appearing in this section are an account of the attempts undertaken by the Yishuv to rescue 29,000 Jewish children from Transnistria in 1942; various forms of public response to the Holocaust (ranging from newspaper reports to public gatherings and protests); and the question of whether the ideological concept of "negation of the diaspora" influenced the Yishuv leadership's activities in the sphere of rescue. Time and again, Porat's discussions point to an inescapable conclusion: the Holocaust created a reality completely different from the one in which various ideological precepts of Zionism had flourished. As a result, the Yishuv leadership's wartime discussions, including those of an ideological nature, were inevitably colored by what was happening in Europe.

Finally, "Between the Public and the Holocaust and Its Survivors" takes up the issue of varying attitudes toward the Holocaust over time and among different population groups in Israel. This section features one of Porat's most famous and controversial essays, " 'Amalek's Accomplices,' " which analyzes how and why anti-Zionist and ultra-Orthodox (haredi) circles in Israel of the 1980s blamed Zionism for the Holocaust. Porat's brief essay, first published in 1992, was one of the first to deal with the topic of how the haredi world responded to the Holocaust, both in real time and afterwards; as noted, it provoked spirited scholarly debate.[5]

Although Porat is hardly the only scholar to deal with the Yishuv and the state of Israel vis-à-vis the Holocaust and its aftermath, she is undoubtedly one of the most highly regarded authorities in the field. In part, this is due to her wide range of scholarly interests. Unlike others who have chosen to concentrate primarily on one or two major political figures or Yishuv institutions, Porat embraces an entire spectrum of Yishuv (and later, Israeli) society, her articles and books populated by a large cast of intellectuals, kibbutzniks, survivors, the Orthodox and ultra-Orthodox, demographers, academics, and students.[6] In addition, as is abundantly evident in this collection, her writing is characterized both by wry humor and a down-to-earth warmth and humanity.

In contrast to Porat's multifaceted collection of essays, *Viyshavtem betaḥ* (Dwell in safety) presents a single topic, the absorption of Holocaust survivors in the rural sector, in the framework of two scholarly studies authored, respectively, by Shlomo Bar-Gil (on the kibbutz movement) and Ada Schein (on the moshav movement). This volume is one of the latest in a growing field of Holocaust-related research dealing with the rehabilitation, resettlement, and absorption of displaced persons (DPs).

Yehuda Bauer's classic study of the *beriḥah*, the illegal immigration of Holocaust survivors from Europe to Palestine, was first published in 1970. It was not until the late 1980s that research on the "surviving remnant" in Allied-occupied Germany began to appear, starting with Zeev Mankowitz's doctoral dissertation on DPs living in the American zone.[7] Since then, the number of articles and books has multiplied. Among them are my study of Kibbutz Buchenwald, the first *hakhsharah* (pioneering) kibbutz, founded in liberated Germany after the war; Irit Keinan's analysis of the work of Palestinian emissaries in the DP camps;[8] Haim Genizi's examination of the special advisors to the American occupying forces in liberated Germany on the DP problem; Hagit Lavsky's exploration of the surviving remnant and, later, the Bergen Belsen DP camp; and a number of works on specific groups of DPs such as women and the Orthodox.[9] Two of the pioneers in the realm of research on former DPs in their countries of resettlement are William B. Helmreich, who studied survivors who moved to the United States, and Hanna Yablonka, who investigated survivors in Israel during the early years of the state.[10] More recent works have narrowed their historical sights from entire countries to sectors—for instance, my ongoing examination of young female Holocaust survivors who were later killed in the course of service in the Israel Defense Forces during the 1950s.[11] *Viyshavtem betaḥ*, focusing on the first decade after the war and the ways in which survivors were absorbed by rural cooperative settlements, fits into this last category.

Bar-Gil's story of the kibbutz movement's campaign to attract and absorb Holocaust survivors begins in the DP camps of Europe and the detention camps of Cyprus. There the Zionist cause was promoted by emissaries dispatched by the various kibbutz movements. Former Zionist youth group members were a prime target of their attention, as were children later brought to Palestine under the auspices of Youth Aliyah. Between 1944 and 1948, the kibbutz movement absorbed more than a third of the DPs who reached Palestine either legally or via the clandestine Aliyah Bet movement. As shown by Bar-Gil by means of four representative examples, the absorption process varied greatly. In Yagur, the survivors became part of a large and flourishing kibbutz; in Nir David, they were confronted by a community in the throes of economic and social crisis. In Ramot Menashe, Holocaust survivors became the founders of a new collective, whereas in Netzer Sereni (originally known as Kibbutz Buchenwald), survivors founded a new settlement that later absorbed a group of veteran kibbutz members.

Ada Schein's parallel account of the moshav movement's absorption of Holocaust survivors appears at first to have fewer success-story elements. In the immediate aftermath of the war, the moshav movement, like the kibbutz movement, sent emissaries to the DP camps, but these were too few and arrived too late, resulting in a failed recruitment campaign. A few years later, however, as large numbers of survivors began to reach the newly founded state of Israel, the moshav movement once again took up the challenge, this time with more success. Eventually, the number of survivors who joined moshavim far surpassed that of survivors who went to the kibbutzim. Many of the newer moshavim were in fact founded by new immigrants, often a combination of European Holocaust survivors and Jews from the Middle East and North Africa.

Schein charts the process whereby a moshav populated by new immigrants (*moshav 'olim*) was gradually transformed into a workers' moshav (*moshav 'ovdim*), with the "culture of the land" becoming an integral part of the survivors' lives. Ultimately, however, attempts to integrate Holocaust survivors and "Oriental" immigrants were largely unsuccessful. Schein, herself a moshav resident, notes that there is still a chance that such integration may become the norm among the next generation of moshav dwellers. In this spirit, she devotes her final chapters to a description of school-based activities among the younger generation of survivors who were absorbed on the moshavim, and the hope that they would ultimately be part of the greater "melting pot" that was to characterize Israeli society.

In a sense, Bar-Gil and Schein's book complements that of Porat by filling in some of the chronological gaps. Most of Porat's essays are set in the war years, whereas Bar-Gil and Schein begin their narrative in the war's immediate aftermath. The two works also deal with more recent decades—apart from her essay on anti-Zionist attitudes among the haredim, Porat also discusses how the Holocaust was taught to Israeli students during the 1970s and 1980s, and how Israeli attitudes toward Holocaust survivors and victims had changed by the 1990s. Despite obvious differences in scope and emphasis, both these books provide scholars with fascinating, in-depth analysis of some of the ways in which the Yishuv (and later, the state of Israel), dealt with the Holocaust and those who survived it.

JUDITH TYDOR BAUMEL-SCHWARTZ
Bar-Ilan University

Notes

1. Arthur Morse, *While Six Million Died: A Chronicle of American Apathy* (New York: 1968); David Wyman, *Paper Walls: America and the Refugee Crisis 1938–1941* (Amherst: 1968); Henry L. Feingold, *The Politics of Rescue: The Roosevelt Administration and the Holocaust 1938–1945* (New Brunswick: 1970); Saul S. Friedman, *No Haven for the Oppressed: United States Policy towards Refugees 1938–1945* (Detroit: 1973); Alan Joshua Sherman, *Island Refuge: Britain and Refugees from the Third Reich* (Berkeley: 1973); Bernard Wasserstein, *Britain and the Jews of Europe 1939–1945* (London: 1979).

2. Yehuda Bauer, *Diplomatiyah umaḥteret bamediniyut hatziyonit 1939–1945* (Merhavia: 1963); in English: *From Diplomacy to Resistance: A History of Jewish Palestine 1930–1945*, trans. Alton M. Winters (Philadelphia: 1970).

3. Yoav Gelber, "Ha'itonut ha'ivrit beeretz yisrael 'al hashmadat yehudei eiropah," *Dapim leḥeker tekufat hashoah vehamered* (n.s.) 1 (1970), 30–58; idem, "Zionist Policy and the Fate

of European Jewry 1939–1942," *Yad Vashem Studies* 13 (1981), 129–157; idem, "Problems in the Historiography of the Response of the Yishuv and Free World Jewry to the Holocaust," in *Historiography of the Holocaust*, ed. Yisrael Gutman and Gideon Greif (Jerusalem: 1987), 571–584; Dalia Ofer, "Pe'ulot 'ezrah vehatzalah shel hamishlahat haeretzyisreelit beKushta 1943," *Yalkut moreshet* 15 (Nov. 1972), 35–58; Yehiam Weitz, "Sheerit hapeleitah bediyunei-hem uveshikuleihem shel hevrei hanhalat hasokhnut miyemei 1945 'ad november 1945," *Yalkut moreshet* 29 (May 1980), 53–80; idem, *Muda'ut vehoser onim: Mapai lenokhah hashoah 1943–1945* (Jerusalem: 1994); Hava Eshkoli (Wagman), *Elem: Mapai vehashoa 1939–1942* (Jerusalem: 1994); Tuvia Friling, *Hetz ba'arafel: David Ben-Gurion, hanhalat hayishuv venisyonot hatzalah bashoah* (Sde Boker: 1998)—in English, *Arrows in the Dark: David Ben-Gurion, the Yishuv Leadership and Rescue Attempts during the Holocaust*, trans. Ora Cummings (Madison: 2005); Dina Porat, *Hanhagah bemilkud: hayishuv nokhah hashoah, 1942–1945* (Tel-Aviv: 1986)—in English, *The Blue and Yellow Stars of David*, trans. Ora Cummings (Cambridge, Mass.: 1990).

4. See, for instance, Judith Tydor Baumel, *Kibbutz Buchenwald: Survivors and Pioneers* (New Brunswick: 1997); Irit Keinan, *Lo nirga' hara'av: nitzolei hashoah ushlihei eretz yisrael, germaniyah 1945–1948* (Tel Aviv: 1996); Haim Genizi, *Yo'etz umeikim: hayo'etz latzavah haamerikani ulesheerit hapeleitah 1945–1949* (Tel Aviv: 1987); Hagit Lavsky, "Sheerit hapeleitah meobyekt lesubyekt: megamot mehkar," *Yahadut zemaneinu* 6 (1989–1990), 25–43; idem, *New Beginnings: Holocaust Survivors in Bergen-Belsen and the British Zone in Germany 1945–1950* (Detroit: 2002); Yehuda Bauer, *Flight and Rescue: Bricha: The Organized Escape of the Jewish Survivors of Eastern Europe 1944–1948* (New York: 1970); Zeev W. Mankowitz, *Life between Memory and Hope: The Survivors of the Holocaust in Occupied Germany* (Cambridge: 2002); Leo Schwartz, *The Redeemers: A Saga of the Years 1945–1952* (New York: 1953); Leonard Dinnerstein, *America and the Survivors of the Holocaust* (New York: 1982).

5. See, for example, Kimmy Caplan, "The Holocaust in Contemporary Israeli Haredi Popular Religion," *Modern Judaism* 22, no. 2 (2002), 142–168; Ruth Ebenstein, "Remembered Thru Rejection: 'Yom Hashoa' in the Ashkenazi Haredi Daily Press 1950–2000," *Israel Studies* 8, no. 3 (2003), 141–167.

6. This broadness of scope can be perceived as well in Porat's additional areas of interest, which include manifestations of modern antisemitism; the Holocaust in Lithuania, particularly Kovno and Vilna; and underground movements in Nazi-occupied Europe. See, for instance, the following articles: "The 'New Anti-Semitism' and the Middle East," *Palestine-Israel Journal of Politics, Economics and Culture* 12, nos. 2–3 (2005), online at www.pij.org/details. php?id=343 (accessed 18 March 2012); "Defining Antisemitism," *Anti-Semitism Worldwide* 2003–2004 (2005) 5–17; "Zionists and Communists in the Underground during the Holocaust: Three Examples—Cracow, Kovno and Minsk," *Journal of Israeli History* 18, no. 1 (1997), 57–72; "The Justice System and Courts of Law in the Ghettos of Lithuania," *Holocaust and Genocide Studies* 12, no. 1 (1998), 49–65; "The Legend of the Struggle of Jews from the Third Reich in the Ninth Fort near Kovno, 1941–1942," *Tel Aviver Jahrbuch für Deutsche Geschichte* 20 (1991), 363–392; "The Vilna Proclamation of January 1, 1942, in Historical Perspective," *Yad Vashem Studies* 25 (1996), 99–136.

7. The updated and expanded dissertation later appeared as a book: see Mankowitz, *Life between Memory and Hope.*

8. Keinan, *Lo nirg'a hara'av.*

9. On women, see, for instance, Judith Tydor Baumel, "DPs, Mothers and Pioneers: Women in the She'erit Hapletah," *Jewish History* 11, no. 2 (Fall 1997), 99–110; Atina Grossmann, "Trauma, Memory and Motherhood: Germans and Jewish Displaced Persons in Nazi Germany 1945–1949," *Archiv fuer Socialgeschichte* 38 (1998), 215–239; idem, "Victims, Villains and Survivors: Gendered Perceptions and Self-Perceptions of Jewish Displaced Persons in Occupied Germany," *Journal of the History of Sexuality* 11 (2002), 291–318; Margarete L. Meyers, "Jewish Displaced Persons: Reconstructing Individual and Community in the US Zone of Occupied Germany," *Leo Baeck Institute Year Book* 42 (1997), 303–324; Margarete Meyers Feinstein, "Jewish Women Survivors in the Displaced Persons Camps of Occupied

Germany: Transmitters of the Past, Caretakers of the Present and Builders of the Future," *Shofar* 24, no. 4 (2006), 67–89. On the Orthodox, see, for instance, Judith Tydor Baumel, "The Politics of Religious Rehabilitation in the DP Camps," *The Simon Wiesenthal Center Annual* 6 (1990) 57–79; idem, "Sidurei tefilah umigba'ot: ḥayei hadat shel sheerit hapeleitah," *Yalkut Moreshet* 48 (April 1990), 55–68.

10. William B. Helmreich, *Against All Odds: Holocaust Survivors and the Successful Lives They Made in America* (New York: 1992); Hanna Yablonka, *Survivors of the Holocaust: Israel After the War* (New York: 1999).

11. Judith Tydor Baumel-Schwartz, *Nitzolot, 'Olot, Ḥayalot, Noflot: The Story of the Women Survivors Who Lost Their Lives in the IDF during the 1950s* (forthcoming).

Beyond Nuremberg: New Scholarship on Nazi War Crimes Trials in Germany

David Bankier and Dan Michman (eds.), *Holocaust and Justice: Representation and Historiography of the Holocaust in Post-war Trials*. Jerusalem: Yad Vashem, 2010. 342 pp.

John Cramer, *Belsen Trial 1945: Der Lüneburger Prozess gegen Wachpersonal der Konzentrationslager Auschwitz und Bergen-Belsen*. Göttingen: Wallstein, 2011. 426 pp.

Patricia Heberer and Jürgen Matthäus (eds.), *Atrocities on Trial: Historical Perspectives on the Politics of Prosecuting War Crimes*. Lincoln: University of Nebraska Press, 2008. 327 pp.

Tomaz Jardim, *The Mauthausen Trial: American Military Justice in Germany*. Cambridge, Mass.: Harvard University Press, 2012. 276 pp.

Kim C. Priemel and Alexa Stiller (eds.), *Reassessing the Nuremberg Military Tribunals: Transitional Justice, Trial Narratives, and Historiography*. New York: Berghahn Books, 2012. 321 pp.

Almost seventy years after Nazi Germany's surrender, the war crimes trials instituted by the victorious Allies in occupied Germany continue to attract the interest of historians and legal scholars alike. The trial of 22 "major war criminals" at the four-power International Military Tribunal (IMT) at Nuremberg, which met between late November 1945 and early October 1946 and handed down 12 death sentences, has received greatest attention. No doubt this is due to the prominence of its defendants (among them, Hermann Göring, Albert Speer, Ernst Kaltenbrunner, Rudolf Hess, Hans Frank, and Baldur von Schirach), who represented the surviving Nazi leadership. In addition, the IMT is widely regarded as having provided the basis for international criminal law. It instituted a legal precedent in determining that state leaders could be held individually accountable for mass atrocities against enemy civilians and combatants, and it made use of the neologism "genocide" alongside such relatively new legal concepts as "crimes against peace" and "crimes against humanity." Not least, by establishing the scope and death toll of the mass murder of European Jews, the IMT trial played a crucial role in bringing the crimes of the Holocaust to public consciousness.

To be sure, historians often note the IMT's failure to account for the historical complexity of the atrocities it adjudicated and its inaccurate accounts of historical events. Legal scholars, for their part, have critiqued the historical, political, and pedagogic agendas underlying the trial and have faulted historians for overlooking the IMT's unprecedented legal concepts and procedural challenges. In any event, the scholarly focus on the IMT trial has overshadowed hundreds of other trials conducted by the victorious Allies in occupied Germany before, during, and after the tribunal, as well as trials held by German courts under Allied proxy.[1]

Each of the five works under review aims to shift historiographic attention from the trial of the top surviving Nazi leaders to proceedings against representatives of a broader range of institutions and agencies of the Nazi state (the SS, the army, industry, the police, and the diplomatic corps) and against individuals representing the lower echelons of Nazi perpetrators—that is, the "ordinary" men and women who served in the regime's concentration camp system. By paying particular attention to the grass-roots processes involved in the preparation and functioning of Nazi war crimes trials, these works highlight the roles of investigators, translators and, in particular, the victims of Nazi aggression who shared their intimate knowledge of the crimes, thereby emphasizing the agency of victims in bringing historical wrong to justice.

The volumes under review also pay considerable attention to the legal treatment of crimes now known as "the Holocaust," namely, the systematic mass murder of European Jews. At the same time, they demonstrate a commitment to unearthing the legal responses to the more broadly defined crimes of "genocide." Thus, they consider the legal treatment of millions of other victims of the Third Reich in relation to the Nazi "Final Solution to the Jewish Question." Both the effectiveness and limitations of legal concepts underpinning the trials, and their lasting significance and impact on later prosecution of mass atrocities, are examined.

As with previous research on the IMT, the current works place an emphasis on the German public's reaction to war trials. In addition, they provide a broad analysis of the media coverage of the trials, especially that of radio and film, and examine the reception of the trials beyond Germany and the Allied countries by considering both media coverage and public opinion in former German-occupied countries—in particular, among groups of victims (especially Jews). Finally, these newer works take seriously what Jeffrey Herf has called "the brief Nuremberg interregnum between the end of the war and the crystallization of the Cold War,"[2] paying close attention to the East-West divide that developed in the wake of the Second World War and the ways in which political choices and preferences of the western Allies affected their war crimes trial program.

John Cramer's *Belsen Trial 1945: Der Lüneburger Prozess gegen Wachpersonal der Konzentrationslager Auschwitz und Bergen-Belsen*, is one of two recent monographs that shed light on two major concentration camp trials that preceded and immediately followed the IMT proceedings. Cramer gives a thorough and well-researched account of the first war crimes trial against German defendants, conducted by a British military tribunal in the German town of Lüneburg, which convened in mid-September 1945 and ended two months later. Although the trial startled the world and received widespread attention at the time, it was largely forgotten after the Nuremberg trial. Cramer meticulously reconstructs the manner in which former SS-Hauptsturmführer Josef Kramer, the last commandant of the Bergen-Belsen concentration camp, and 43 other camp personnel (16 SS men, 16 female camp guards, and 11 prisoner functionaries) were accused and tried for war crimes committed against

"Allied nationals." Although it soon became known as the "Belsen trial," it was also the first Auschwitz trial, since Kramer and almost all the other defendants had earlier committed crimes at Auschwitz-Birkenau before their deployment to Bergen-Belsen in late 1944 and early 1945. The fact that the trial focused on events at two different camps was problematic, not least because the British showed a lack of awareness regarding the different functions of the two camps: at the Bergen-Belsen concentration camp, as many as 50,000 inmates died of violence, exposure, and disease, whereas some 1.1 million individuals met their death at Auschwitz-Birkenau, which operated a concentration labor and death camp.

Cramer begins his chronological account by exploring the trial's pre-history, focusing in particular on the genesis of the British program to prosecute war crimes and on the legal prerogatives of the Lüneburg court. The court's conservative focus on violations of "laws and custom of war" (as defined in the 1899 and 1907 Hague conventions) resulted from British reluctance to apply ex-post-facto law and also from the fact that the Royal Warrant of June 14, 1945, which authorized British military courts to try and punish violations of the "laws and usages of war," predated the London Charter. (Signed on August 8, 1945 by the United States, Great Britain, the Soviet Union, and France, the London Charter codified the novel charges of "crimes against peace" and "crimes against humanity" that would shape the IMT proceedings.) What all this meant was that the British military court could adjudicate only crimes committed against British and Allied nationals after the beginning of the war. However, the indictment also applied a novel concept of "concerted action," which—similar to the conspiracy charge later used at Nuremberg—enabled prosecutors to hold defendants responsible for crimes by way of their membership in the camp personnel community, without the need to prove individual criminal acts. Cramer concludes this part with an account of the camp's liberation on April 15, 1945. British soldiers witnessed an unprecedented scale of human suffering and mass death, with 14,000 people dying after the liberation as a consequence of their incarceration. Investigations for the trial began amid these chaotic conditions, even as the liberating army personnel frantically buried the dead and cared for those still living. Cramer highlights the indispensable help that the War Crimes Investigation Team No. 1 received from the liberated inmates, who, despite their desperately weakened condition, labored to make available their intimate knowledge of the camp and its personnel, to amass evidence, and to serve as translators.

The monograph's second part discusses the two-month trial and its major protagonists. The prosecution, led by Colonel Thomas M. Backhouse, was committed to adjudicating an unprecedented crime—namely, the "quite deliberate and cold-blooded extermination of millions of people"[3]—yet demonstrated little understanding of the functional and conceptual differences between concentration and death camps, and moreover seemed unaware that Jews had not merely been disfranchised, deported, and killed en masse along with other nationalities in those camps, but also subjected to a systematic campaign of murder. Since the Germans had destroyed camp archives, Backhouse had to resort to witness testimony and other unorthodox evidence such as film footage shot by the liberating British troops and some 200 written affidavits. Thirty-four survivor witnesses took the stand. Of these, 21 were Jews; although the prosecution related to them as Allied nationals, they called the court's attention to the fact that they had been persecuted as Jews.

Cramer sensitively explores the diverging needs of the prosecution and the survivor witnesses. The latter sought to relate the unspeakable crimes they had witnessed, whereas the former was interested in forensic evidence, not harrowing stories of human suffering. As a result, survivor witnesses were often treated in a cold and matter-of-fact manner, and their testimony was frequently cut short. Meanwhile, the defense team, consisting of one Polish and eleven British army officers, each representing up to six defendants, rejected the concept of "concerted action" and, with the help of 34 mostly German defense witnesses, sought to minimize the nature of the crimes. Its strategy of attacking prosecution witnesses and questioning their reliability by exploiting the slightest inconsistencies in their accounts culminated when Kramer's defense counsel, Major T.C.M. Winwood, referred to them as "dregs of the ghettos of Europe"—a characterization that drew protests from international Jewish organizations.

Cramer dedicates considerable attention to the self-images and defense strategies of the heterogeneous group of the accused, who either denied knowledge of the crimes or else blamed superiors, peers, or subordinate prisoner functionaries in the course of presenting themselves as victims of the Nazi regime. The six-member court, although it rejected the "common action" concept in favor of individual accountability, sentenced 11 defendants to death and 14 to prison terms of varying lengths (14 were acquitted). By the time the first group of convicted defendants was hanged in mid-December 1945 in Hameln, none of the defendants had shown any regret. Instead, they bemoaned the fact that they had fallen victim to the Allied victor's justice after having served the German people.

The third part of Cramer's study is devoted to the trial's later history and consequences. His comparative analysis of public discourse on the trial is particularly valuable, covering Germany (not just Germans, but also former Jewish camp inmates) as well as Great Britain, Poland, France, the United States, and the Soviet Union. He also includes a brief discussion of the two Belsen "successor trials" against nine SS personal and camp guards, held in May 1946 in Celle and in April 1948 in Hamburg. Cramer concludes that the Belsen trial, despite its many flaws, was "a positive achievement of the British" (p. 390). He rightly maintains that Lüneburg was not Nuremberg, since its task was not to punish the regime as such, but rather perpetrators at the bottom of the Nazi hierarchy; rather than seeking to create a new kind of international criminal law, it aimed to mete out justice and thereby bring about a change in German public opinion about the Nazi past. Leaving open the question whether the British succeeded in this regard, Cramer argues for the importance of the Belsen trial in the context of other war crimes trials. Given the hastiness of its preparation so soon after the end of hostilities, the Belsen trial might in any event have presented the most difficult case of all the trials. Certainly it foreshadowed problems commonly ascribed to later trials: the dilemmas of prosecution teams in identifying perpetrators against whom there was sufficient evidence; prosecutors' need to rely on former camp inmates in their investigations, and the gap between prosecutors' interest in reliable evidence as against victims' urge to bear witness; the Allies' need to adhere to the rules of a fair trial; the challenge of conveying a pro-democracy message to an essentially reluctant German public; and the ultimate problem: the Allies' inadequate understanding of the unprecedented and essentially racialist nature of the mass atrocities and of the new type of perpetrator they were bringing to justice.

Tomaz Jardim examines another important but hitherto unexplored trial in his tightly argued and thoroughly researched monograph, *The Mauthausen Trial: American Military Justice in Germany*. Between 1938 and 1945, some 100,000 people—comprising political opponents, Soviet POWs, Jews, Sinti and Roma, among others—were worked or starved to death, or else died from disease, exposure, executions, or gassings at Mauthausen and its dozens of sub-camps in Austria. Nonetheless, the trial of 61 accused camp personnel "has remained an unexamined footnote" (p. 3), largely because archival material remained classified until the early 1990s. The trial, held from March to May 1946 at the American military tribunal in Dachau, was one of the most important of a series of U.S. Dachau trials (462 in all) that altogether prosecuted almost 1,700 war criminals from mid-1945 through the end of 1947. At only 36 days, the trial was remarkably brief, with an average of only four hours spent to hear the case of each defendant. Yet the Mauthausen trial stands out in its handing down the largest number of death sentences in the history of American jurisprudence, as well as in its controversial use of lax rules of evidence and questionable interrogation techniques—all of which indicate that prosecutors were less concerned with producing unimpeachable evidence and a fair trial than with the expedient sentencing of war criminals held in American custody.

Even more than Cramer, Jardim is committed to studying the role of the victims and survivors of Nazi terror in the preparation and implementation of the trial. Cooperation between former Mauthausen inmates and the American investigators and prosecutors proved vital, given the formers' intimate knowledge of the camp and the latters' inexperience and ignorance, and also resulted in the survivors having an unaccustomed degree of power in the proceedings. Jardim challenges the commonly held contention, particularly with regard to the IMT trial, that the Allied trials in postwar Germany failed to give voice to survivors and to act on their behalf. Indeed, he shows that the Mauthausen proceedings provided a stage where victims of Nazi persecution could tell their stories.

Jardim opens his analysis with an informative and concise summary of the origins of U.S. war crimes trials more generally and particularly the Dachau series, at which common-law military commissions, comprising one presiding judge and up to nine senior officers (only one with legal training) adjudicated Nazi crimes by applying preexisting international law in instances in which the laws and customs of war had been violated. In addition, the Dachau courts applied two new legal concepts. The first was a "common design" to commit crimes. Like the "concerted action" argument used in the Belsen trial, the "common design" concept relieved prosecutors of the need to prove the existence of a previously conceived plan or agreement to commit crimes (as was the case in the conspiracy charge at the IMT trial). Instead, they merely needed to prove that the accused had known about, participated in, or maintained a criminal enterprise that resulted in the deaths of inmates. Second, the Dachau court used "parent concentration camp cases," allowing it to hold an initial trial for each main camp and then use its findings for sub-camps, without having to reestablish the evidence.

In Chapter 2, Jardim traces the investigations for the trial, which began three weeks after Mauthausen's liberation on May 5, 1945. This chapter features an impressively detailed discussion of the work of Jewish investigators such as future Nuremberg prosecutor Benjamin B. Ferencz, and also recounts the determined efforts of liberated victims to procure information, witnesses, and documentary evidence—some of which they had retrieved in the weeks and days before the liberation, most notably the death books of Mauthausen and Gusen, which registered the deaths of almost 72,000 prisoners. Making use of this material a mere five weeks after the liberation, Major Eugene S. Cohen, the army official in charge of the investigation, wrote the 300-page report on crimes at Mauthausen that provided the basis for the indictment.

The third chapter details the indefatigable efforts of Chief Prosecutor Lieutenant Colonel William Denson and his assistant, Paul Guth, a 22-year-old intelligence officer with an Austrian Jewish émigré background, to synthesize the evidence into an indictment and to line up 61 defendants from among the 15,000 detainees in American custody. Since camp commandant Franz Ziereis was dead, the highest-ranking defendants were August Eigruber, the Gauleiter of Upper Austria, and two of Ziereis' adjutants, Adolf Zutter and Viktor Zoller, along with 19 guards from Mauthausen and 11 in sub-camps. While crediting the comprehensive American efforts to prepare the trial, Jardim correctly points to some crucial limitations. The absence of either a female defendant in the dock or a female witness on the stand meant that the fate of the 4,000 women prisoners registered at the camp received no attention in the courtroom. Further, since the American mandate only focused on crimes against non-German nationals that were committed after the joint first declaration by 26 "united nations" fighting the Axis Powers on January 1, 1942, all prewar crimes and crimes committed against Germans and Austrians—who made up some 10,000 of Mauthausen's dead—remained unacknowledged and unaccounted for.

Jardim devotes Chapter 4 to the trial itself, which opened at the end of March and closed in mid-May 1946. He explores the strategies of the prosecution, which showed little understanding of the centrality of racial ideology in the crimes it brought to trial, and the defense, which denied the defendants' roles and positions in the camp; justified and mitigated their acts by pointing to superiors' orders and duress; and sought to discredit the written confessions of the accused, claiming that they had been obtained by physical abuse, coercion, and deceit. As noted, he also devotes considerable attention to the former inmates who testified for the prosecution (more than 100 in number). A short sub-chapter on testimonies by Jews reveals that, as in the Belsen trial, Jewish witnesses faced antisemitic resentment and attacks from the defense, which sought to brand them as vengeful and unreliable.

Verdicts and sentences stand at the center of Chapter 5. While the prosecution's final plea portrayed Nazi crimes as a "deviation from Western civilization" (p. 175), the defense depicted the defendants as victims of the Nazi regime. After spending an average of 55 seconds to discuss each defendant's culpability, the Mauthausen court acquitted none, sentenced 58 to death and the remaining three to varying terms in prison. While nine death sentences were commuted to life, 49 defendants were hanged in late May 1947 at the Landsberg prison.

Conviction rates dropped radically in later trials of the Dachau series; moreover, all surviving Mauthausen convicts were awarded early release by the end of 1951, in consequence of the American desire to retain Germany as a viable ally in the Cold War. Jardim comes to the correct yet somewhat disturbing conclusion that, given the flaws of the Mauthausen trial, "the measure of justice won at Dachau was achieved by recourse to a legal system that denied the accused full and fair trial" (p. 215). More specifically, a compressed timetable, questionable interrogations, lax rules of evidence, and the active role of the former victims of the camp made it possible to bring to trial a large number of perpetrators who would otherwise have escaped justice. Jardim sees the Mauthausen trial as a formidable example of the ability of a legal process to empower victims of mass violence. Not least, the trial produced an important historical record of the everyday functioning of the camp and of the world-view and motivations of lower-level perpetrators.

Three edited volumes, equally concerned with shedding light on hitherto overlooked cases against lower-echelon perpetrators, cover a much broader geographic scope and time frame than the two monographs discussed above. *Atrocities on Trial: Historical Perspectives on the Politics of Prosecuting War Crimes*, edited by Patricia Heberer and Jürgen Matthäus, explores the juridical ways in which victors and vanquished have dealt with mass violence, and with the changes over time in the conceptualization of acts of atrocity and their application in judicial process. It examines the historicization of war crimes trials—historians sitting in judgment of prosecution, court, and defense—and explores the relationship between historical reality, judicial treatment, and public perception. The book focuses on the legal treatment of the murder of European Jews, but it goes beyond merely examining what historical knowledge can be gained from the courtroom; it also analyzes the legal and political contexts of Holocaust trials. Like Cramer and Jardim, Heberer and Matthäus seek to retrieve other Allied war crimes trials from the shadow of the IMT. The particular strength of their volume lies in its broad scope in terms of time span and location, as well as the range of victim groups it discusses.

The first of the book's four parts examines the precedents set in adjudicating German war crimes in the 20th century, both in the Weimar Republic and immediately after the Second World War. Matthäus begins by exploring the lessons of the "fiasco of the Leipzig trials" (p. 3), when the victorious Allies of the First World War failed to set up an international tribunal to adjudicate war crimes committed by Imperial Germany. Punishment of alleged war criminals thus fell to the German Supreme Court sitting in the city of Leipzig. Of 861 such cases heard between 1921 and 1927, only 13 ended in a verdict. As indicated by the closing of cases, rapid procedures, and light sentences, the German court failed to criminalize war crimes when national honor and political interests were at stake. The German public largely perceived these trials as a national disgrace, and as Matthäus concludes: "Elements of this distorted, yet unchallenged, perception survived the Second World War and clearly contributed as much to the prevailing German unwillingness to confront crimes committed during the Nazi era as did the continuity of German elites including officers and jurists" (p. 19). Likewise, the negative memory of the Leipzig trials provided a frame of reference when the victorious Allies of the Second World War prepared to hold trials in Germany.

Several articles examine early war crimes trials held in the vicinity of the trial against the "major war criminals" at Nuremberg. Of these, studies that focus on the victims of "euthanasia" killings and medical experiments are particularly instructive. Heberer's chapter explores the Hadamar trial of October 1945, the first mass atrocity trial held in the U.S. zone of occupied Germany. The defendants were seven German civilians, former employees of the state facility for the mentally ill at Hadamar, one of six killing sites in Nazi Germany's euthanasia program, in which an estimated 200,000 mentally ill and handicapped patients were murdered between 1939 and 1945. In many ways, this trial was a test case for the American occupying force's quest to prosecute civilians of foreign governments under international law. Although the American military tribunal at Wiesbaden had originally intended to try the Hadamar personnel for the murder of 15,000 individuals, the existing legal framework forced prosecutors to concentrate on the murder of Allied nationals, notwithstanding the fact that Germans and Austrians comprised the majority of Hadamar's victims. Ultimately, the American military court sentenced three defendants to death, one to life imprisonment, two to prison terms of 35 years, and one to 25 years for their murder of 476 Soviet and Polish forced laborers.

In a similar vein, Ulf Schmidt looks at the Ravensbrück trials—in particular, the first of a series of seven trials adjudicating crimes committed at this major women's concentration camp, which were held from December 1946 to February 1947 under the auspices of a British military tribunal. In total, the tribunal conducted 357 trials in Germany against a total of some 1,000 defendants. In the first Ravensbrück trial, the defendants included 16 doctors alongside medical staff and other camp personnel, who were all charged with war crimes and crimes against humanity through their criminal medical research. The trials resulted in 11 death sentences. Although the British deemed this trial essential to their reeducation campaign in Germany, the tribunal refrained from touching on the broader ethical issues of medical experiments. It is deplorable that Schmidt does not sufficiently address the fact that seven of the 16 defendants at the first Ravensbrück trial were women and that more than half of the total of those accused (21 out of 38) in the Ravensbrück cases were female doctors and camp personnel of various ranks. This is a missed opportunity to address issues of gender in the perpetration and prosecution of medical crimes.

Michael R. Marrus discusses this deficit in his analysis of the Nuremberg doctors' trial (December 1946–July 1947), the first of 12 American Nuremberg "successor trials," which considered the crimes of German medical personnel against the inmates of various concentration camps. Marrus sees the trial of 23 physicians and medical researchers as a missed opportunity to arrive at a "grand historic assessment of medicine in the Third Reich" (p. 105) that would encompass the perpetrators' "common ideological and institutional culture" (p. 106) as well as a deeper understanding of the role of medicine in genocide. Lacking adequate knowledge of such matters, the Americans allowed important perpetrators of the regime's medical crimes to escape justice. Thus insufficient evidence in these cases led to the acquittals of seven defendants, a relatively high number. And once again, the narrow focus on war crimes against Allied nationals ignored those crimes that German doctors had inflicted upon the bodies and minds of German victims as well as crimes committed before the outbreak of the war. Marrus suggests that the narrow definition of war crimes was not the only reason that sterilization and euthanasia crimes were over-looked; rather, he argues, the popularity of eugenics in the United States and in other Allied countries helps to explain the failure of prosecutors and judges to understand the racialist ideology behind Nazi euthanasia. Viewing euthanasia in utilitarian terms, they regarded medical experiments as an accessory to Germany's war of conquest. These shortcomings, Marrus concludes, "may even have facilitated the evasion of responsibility that has characterized much of postwar German medicine" (p. 119).

This section's predominant focus on American and British trials is counterbal-anced by Jonathan Friedman's chapter on the Sachsenhausen trial, held during October 1947 in the Soviet zone of occupation. Adjudicating the murder of approxi-mately 100,000 prisoners—half the inmates who passed through the camp between 1936 and 1945—the ten-day trial, which Friedman describes as "a curious mixture of rational jurisprudence and old-fashioned show trial" (p. 168), stands out in several respects: for one thing, all 16 defendants pleaded guilty but none received death sentences (instead, they were sentenced to varying terms in Soviet prisons, where five of them eventually died). Friedman, as with other contributors, does justice to the volume's aim to contextualize earlier and later trials by tracing several other Sachsenhausen cases tried before West German courts between 1948 and 1967.

The second part of the volume highlights the problems experienced by Germany and Austria, the societies most responsible for perpetrating the Holocaust, in dealing with their own criminal pasts—in particular, the challenges of adjudicating crimes while also undergoing a process of national rebuilding. In two case studies, Jürgen Matthäus and Patricia Heberer illustrate how individual Nazi perpetrators managed to escape justice and pursue respectable postwar careers. Matthäus examines the case of Georg Heuser, a Gestapo officer and SS-Hauptsturmführer involved in the depor-tation and killing of thousands of civilians, mainly Jews, in the Soviet Union and Slovakia. In postwar Germany, after rising to a prominent position in the criminal police in Rhineland-Palatinate in the 1950s, Heuser was tried in 1962–1963 and sen-tenced to 15 years' imprisonment. Given his responsibility in the murder of 11,000 Jewish men, women, and children, this punishment, Matthäus notes, amounted to "less than half a day per person murdered" (p. 200); moreover, after serving a mere six years, Heuser was released. In Heberer's case study, we learn of a gas van driver who was never punished for his crimes: although he confessed to the gassing of 340 Jews in Minsk-Mogilev, the driver was acquitted of murder in 1970 on the grounds of putative duress, that is, the fear of reprisal should he fail to carry out orders. Heberer argues that Austria's self-image as Nazi Germany's "first victim" translated into a denial of responsibility for crimes of the Final Solution, as reflected in the small number of postwar trials conducted on Austrian soil. Compared with nearly 700 West German war crimes trials between the mid-1950s and the late 1970s, Austria held only 28 such proceedings.

Rebecca Wittmann reviews a number of German mass atrocity cases tried in the Federal Republic between the 1960s and 1980s. In addition to highlighting the prob-lems of applying the German penal code of 1871 (which was designed for "ordinary" murder) to unprecedented instances of mass murder, she also detects a generational divide between a "young, committed, and probing prosecution" (p. 211) and an older generation of judges who served under the Nazi regime and whose support for a conservative interpretation of the law was tantamount to holding only top Nazi leaders such as Hitler, Himmler, and Heydrich responsible for murder. From this perspective, all other Nazi functionaries—even the trigger-pullers in mass executions—remained mere accessories, unless it could be proven that they had acted from a "base motive" such as antisemitism. Thus, many defendants were successful in their claims that they had not been aware of the illegality of their acts, that they had obeyed German law of the time, or that they had merely been following orders. Wittmann's comparison of the number of German legal proceedings conducted against perpetrators of Nazi crimes as against those dealing with members of left-wing terrorist groups is as instructive as it is shocking: members of the latter were judged more harshly than former Nazis precisely because they had not acted in the name of the state. Whereas a total of 100,000 Nazis were investigated and 6,000 were tried in the period between 1949, when the Federal Republic was established, and Germany's reunification in 1990, more than 125,000 left-wing extremists were investigated and 6,500 were tried in the same period, thus demonstrating the priorities of the West German state.

The volume's concluding section considers the legacy of the early war crimes trials with regard to current attempts to prosecute mass atrocities. Donald Bloxham examines the efficacy of the IMT in delivering justice and in serving as a deterrent against future war crimes. According to Bloxham, Nuremberg did not inspire social change in the societies of either the defendants or the prosecutors and judges. Rather, social and political changes such as the fall of Communism and greater awareness of the historical events of the Holocaust, as well as more recent cases of genocide, have led to a sea change in this area, including a belated appreciation of Nuremberg and its significance. In the following essay, John K. Roth explores the ethical aspects of punishment for mass atrocities and makes the claim that, although punishment of the perpetrators of the Holocaust was not equivalent to justice for its victims and survivors, it nevertheless is an essential ingredient of human civilization. This is so even if the punishment remains disproportionately mild in comparison with the actual crime, which seems inevitable in the case of the Holocaust.

Whereas Matthäus and Heberer's volume is noteworthy for its contextualizing of the legal treatment of crimes against Jews with that of other persecuted groups, *Holocaust and Justice: Representation and Historiography of the Holocaust in Post-War Trials*, edited by David Bankier and Dan Michman, focuses more narrowly on the destruction of European Jewry. The first of the book's three sections is devoted to the genesis, context, and wider significance of the Nuremberg trials, highlighting the role of organizations and individuals who pushed for inclusion of the "Jewish issue." Lawrence Douglas sets the stage with a brief but wide-ranging discussion of the relationship between history and memory in perpetrator trials, from the IMT trial of "major war criminals" to the trial of Serbian president Slobodan Milosevic at The Hague. In addition to meting out justice and "reimposing norms into spaces in which rule-based legality has been either radically evacuated or perverted" (p. 13), trials against the perpetrators of mass atrocity aim to be didactic and to deliver clear-cut morals about the historical event and the way it should be remembered. Their success is also a matter of location and spectatorship: geographically remote tribunals that lack an "organic connection" to the history of a region, as well as proceedings that are physically and emotionally disconnected from their audience, are less likely to have an impact. Moreover, the memory of trials is often disconnected from what actually happened in the courtroom. The IMT trial, for example, is falsely remembered as a "Holocaust trial," and while most Germans at the time rejected the Allied trials, the proceedings are widely respected in Germany today.

In a similar vein, Donald Bloxham sets the record straight on a number of myths concerning the success of the Allied war crimes trials in the first postwar decade by exploring the "other side" of the trials. Historians, he claims, have tended to ignore the sentence reviews, amnesties, and premature releases dictated by the changing political context and Germany's geopolitical significance in the Cold War era. A more positive perspective of the trials is presented by Michael J. Bazyler, who argues that, in the long run, the Allies' legal treatment of the Holocaust and other mass atrocities during the Second World War paved the way to the founding of the International Criminal Court (ICC) at The Hague. Most notably, the early postwar trials cemented the notion of individual criminal responsibility of heads of state, and also codified international legal concepts such as crimes against humanity. Observing that "'Nuremberg' has acquired a mythical meaning among international jurists" (p. 54), Bazyler highlights significant differences between the IMT and current ICC procedures, such as the right of appeal, the prohibition on trial in absentia, and the absence of a death penalty.

In a tightly written historical analysis, Arieh J. Kochavi discusses how the mass murder of European Jews was dealt with in preparations for the Nuremberg trials and the coining of the new concept of crimes against humanity. Focusing on Great Britain and the United States and highlighting in particular the roles played by a number of committed Jewish and non-Jewish individuals, Kochavi traces how the prosecution of war crimes, initially a low priority for both powers, gradually assumed greater importance. In the end, however, because of a variety of political, military, and geopolitical considerations, "the murder of the Jews of Europe never occupied an important place on the agendas of the British and Americans; consequently the punishment of those who had committed these crimes was not very important to them, either" (p. 80).

Boaz Cohen explores the agency of Jews in seeking active participation in the IMT trial. Focusing on the World Jewish Congress, he examines the multifaceted yet ultimately unsuccessful attempts of that international Jewish organization to attain official status at the Nuremberg tribunal in order to represent the victims and survivors of the Holocaust. In the absence of a Jewish state, the World Jewish Congress sought to speak in the name of the "Jewish people." Although Cohen's article would have profited from further problematizing of the concept and significance of the "Jewish people" in the postwar Jewish and Allied discourse, his text is valuable and innovative, demonstrating how the Jewish perspective on Allied trials needs to be researched in greater detail.

The volume's second section considers West German legal proceedings against Nazi perpetrators, paying close attention to the roles of jurists, journalists, and historians in the gradual rise of Holocaust awareness in Germany. Dieter Pohl considers the relationship between German Holocaust trials and German historiography on the mass murder of European Jews. He highlights the role of historians as witnesses in various trials, showing how they focused on the "high-level history" of the Nazi regime and, in so doing, supported the defense argument that most of those being tried were merely accessories to murder. Moreover, Pohl argues, the trials themselves had little impact on historical research, which for many years remained mainly concerned with foreign policy matters, military history, and German resistance, while devoting scant attention to the Holocaust.

Two articles focus on specific trials from different perspectives. Inge Marszolek analyzes radio coverage of the British Bergen-Belsen trial and of the 1963–1965 Auschwitz trial in Frankfurt, focusing on the prominent journalist Axel Eggebrecht and offering a glimpse into an underresearched aspect of media coverage of trials. Katrin Stoll, for her part, tells the history of the Bialystok trial in Bielefeld in the years 1965–1967, giving a comprehensive account of the legal basis and constraints of this case against four members of the security police of the SS's Security Service (SD), which was responsible for deporting the Jewish population of the Bialystok district to Auschwitz and Treblinka. Stoll argues that German prosecutors—rather than historians—undertook ground-breaking historical research on the chronology and scope of atrocities against the Jewish population of the district of Bialystok, the level of involvement of several German agencies, and the willingness of ordinary Germans to perpetrate genocide.

Similarly, Annette Weinke credits jurists and journalists, not historians, with the most crucial roles in informing the West German public of the crimes of the Holocaust in the period from the late 1940s to the late 1970s. Especially in the first postwar years, the German public displayed a strong aversion to the trials: still attending to their own wartime suffering, they could hardly evince empathy for the victims of German crimes. Moreover, in a judiciary system that, to a significant extent, was staffed with former Nazis, many jurists saw their proceedings less as a means to punish monstrous crimes than as a way to rehabilitate the German people as victims of war, while at the same time exonerating millions of fellow-travelers who had merely followed orders.

The third section of the volume broadens the perspective by looking at trials in various countries formerly occupied by Germany. Nico Wouters examines the genesis and history of Belgian military court trials against Germans and Austrians accused of war crimes committed on Belgian soil. Between 1947 and 1951, 37 such trials prosecuted 106 defendants, of whom 92 were convicted. Of the 19 defendants who received the death penalty, only two Germans eventually were executed in Belgium. Just how little the Belgian military court understood the distinct nature of the persecution of the Jews, both on Belgian soil and beyond, is exemplified by the fact that one of the two executed men was a German Jewish prisoner who had served as a guard at the Breendonk concentration camp. Most of the German defendants who received prison sentences were granted early release in 1951–1952.

Michael R. Marrus explores the attempt of a French Jewish family to sue the French railway company (SNCF) for the deportation of four relatives who, after being denounced and arrested by the Gestapo in the French Pyrenees in May 1944, were handed over to the French police and transported from Toulouse to Drancy, where they remained incarcerated until the liberation. The trial, held in a Toulouse court 60 years after the event, was unprecedented in its focus on the "independent liability of a specific government agency" (p. 247). The plaintiffs initially succeeded, but ultimately lost when the Administrative Appeal Court in Bordeaux ruled that the SNCF had acted under the authority of the Vichy regime and the German occupation.

In an essay centering on Poland, Edyta Gawron reconsiders the long-forgotten trial of 1946 in which the notorious Ammon Goeth, the Austrian commandant of the Plaszow labor and concentration camp near Cracow, was convicted and sentenced to death for his crimes of "genocide of Poles and Jews" (p. 287). One of seven trials of German war criminals held before the Supreme National Tribunal between 1946 and 1948, this trial is noteworthy for being the first to pronounce a death sentence for an act of genocide. Gawron highlights the roles of Jewish witnesses at the tribunal and considers the trial's wider reception among the survivor community in Poland. The volume concludes with Paolo Pezzio and Guri Schwarz's exploration of Italian court cases involving German and Italian perpetrators of mass atrocities during the Second World War, in which crimes against Jews were marginalized. They also show how, in the 1980s, a shift in Italian collective memory and an erosion of the myth that all Italians were anti-Fascists finally made possible a more nuanced perspective on the past.

Overall, *Holocaust and Justice* is a welcome addition to Holocaust scholarship. However, the volume would have benefited from a stronger editorial hand in bringing together individual contributions and in balancing their inequality in density and length. It also suffers from a lack of thorough and uniform copy-editing, as evidenced, for example, in the list of contributors at the end of the book, which includes the name of an individual whose work does not appear.

In contrast, *Reassessing the Nuremberg Military Tribunals: Transitional Justice, Trial Narratives, and Historiography*, edited by Kim C. Priemel and Alexa Stiller, is marked by meticulous editing. Central to this collection is the intention to consider American "successor trials" in their own right. Placing at center stage a number of trials that have long been regarded as a mere "coda" or "footnote" to the IMT, the essays in this collection seek to analyze the narratives that evolved from the later U.S. Nuremberg Military Tribunal (NMT) proceedings, and to fill in those narratives—particularly of the victims—that the trials themselves ignored. Priemel and Stiller point out that, whereas the IMT sought to punish the surviving leadership of the Third Reich, the NMT aimed to punish the entire Nazi state, in addition to analyzing its functioning and organization. Thus, "structures rather than individuals, and institutional representatives rather than easily identifiable villains were to be publicly prosecuted" (p. 2). Between December 1946 and April 1949, 185 defendants stood trial in a dozen separate (though partially simultaneous) proceedings, at which "the courtroom became the site of the (pre)scholarly dispute over the nature of the German dictatorship, its power structures and dynamics, and most important of all, the highly charged issue of who was answerable for the regime's crimes" (ibid.).

Two essays in the volume focus on the personal experience and professional expertise of trial protagonists. In the first essay, Dirk Pöppmann traces the role of Robert M.W. Kempner, a lawyer on the American team at the IMT and prosecutor of the Ministries trial, Case 11 (January 1948–April 1949) against officials in the German foreign office and other government agencies. Born in Germany, Kempner lost his job as a high-ranking official in the police department of the Prussian interior ministry as a result of anti-Jewish legislation. Subsequently expelled from Germany, he eventually reached the United States, where he worked for the Department of Justice, the Office of Strategic Services, and the FBI. After the war, he returned to Germany as Chief Justice Robert H. Jackson's assistant at Nuremberg and as Telford Taylor's deputy in the successor trials. Pöppmann observes that while German spectators at the IMT initially regarded the German expatriate Kempner as "our man in Nuremberg," his role as chief prosecutor in the case against former Secretary of State Ernst von Weizsäcker turned German opinion against him.

In the second essay, Hilary Earl offers a well-documented and compelling portrait of the three key figures in the Einsatzgruppen trial (Case 9 of the NMT proceedings), which lasted from September 1947 until April 1948. The defendants in this trial were 24 members of the SS who were essentially stand-ins for the entire Einsatzgruppen apparatus, which, comprising 80 officers and some 3,000 troops, were responsible for the murder of more than a million (mostly Jewish) civilians in the Soviet Union. Earl focuses on the interplay between the main defendant, SS-Gruppenführer Otto Ohlendorf, head of Einsatzgruppe D; Chief Prosecutor Benjamin B. Ferencz, a 27-year-old Harvard-educated lawyer of Jewish immigrant background (who also appears in Jardim's account of the Mauthausen trial); and Judge Michael A. Musmanno, the son of Italian immigrants who, in addition to his legal career, was a writer and actor. Lacking in this essay, and in the volume as a whole, is any reflection on the fact that this particular trial was the only Nuremberg proceeding that focused primarily on the mass murder of Jews. On the one hand, the Einsatzgruppen trial can hardly be called a "Holocaust trial," as it dealt solely with mass shootings of Jews on Soviet territory, which constituted only one aspect of Nazi Germany's Final Solution. On the other hand, the Einsatzgruppen's mass shootings of Jews no doubt precipitated the process of wholesale mass murder of European Jewry, in addition to accounting for approximately one sixth of the Holocaust's total number of victims. The trial, however, denied both survivors and witnesses to the killings any voice in the proceedings, as it relied exclusively on documentary evidence.

In focusing on the doctors' trial, and in particular on the active role played by witnesses, Paul Weindling revises some of the views offered in Michael Marrus' article on the subject (in the *Atrocities on Trial* collection). Looking beyond the official trial proceedings on which Marrus based his analysis, Weindling uncovers behind-the-scenes aspects of the trial, for example, the prosecutors' decision to abandon the documentary approach that dominated the IMT and many of the NMT proceedings in favor of letting victims testify, thus providing a human face to the crimes. At the same time, the prosecution carefully chose its witnesses with an eye to their relevance to the case and their potential ability to make the desired impression on the judges. Contrary to Marrus, Weindling argues that the trial succeeded in highlighting the central role of medical crimes in genocide and as an essential ingredient of Nazi criminality.

Alexa Stiller traces the use of the term "genocide" through all the Nuremberg trials as well as in some contemporaneous Polish court cases. She claims that, early on, the term was applied exclusively to the mass murder of European Jews. As a result, NMT jurists lost sight of the fate of many non-Jews killed by the Nazis, whose victimization the term was initially created to encompass. While one might agree that limiting use of the term to the mass murder of European Jews is inaccurate and deplorable, Allied prosecutors' vague understanding of the Nazis' systematic and Europe-wide mass murder of Jews *as* Jews raises questions as to the accuracy of Stiller's argument as it pertains to the late 1940s; it may be that the exclusive application of "genocide" was a later phenomenon.

Jan Erik Schulte examines the three "SS cases"—the Pohl trial (Case 4, April–November 1947), the RuSHA trial (Case 8, October 1947–March 1948), and the Einsatzgruppen trial—which together brought 54 SS officers to justice. He shows that, whereas it was imperative to put various branches of the SS on trial, this decision resulted in some negative consequences. In particular, by distancing the SS from German society, the trials allowed Germans to scapegoat the organization, providing an "alibi" for army, police, and civilian administrators who had worked hand-in-hand with the SS.

Kim C. Priemel's analysis of the Flick trial (Case 5, April–December, 1947), the Krupp trial (Case 10, December 1947–July 1948), the IG Farben trial (Case 6, August 1947–July 1948), and the Ministries case discusses legal actions against a number of German industrialists. The American prosecutors had a clear sense of the culpability of industrialists in the crimes of the Third Reich, and they viewed changes in the quasi-feudal structure of German industry as essential to the democratization process. However, because of the mandate to rebuild a strong capitalist economy to meet the looming challenges of the Cold War, they let industrialists get away with light sentences. Of 42 defendants, 13 were acquitted while the remainder received prison terms ranging from 18 months to eight years; most of those in prison were released before the end of their terms.

By looking at three NMT cases dealing with the Wehrmacht—the High Command trial (Case 12, November 1947–October 1948), the Milch trial (Case 2, January–April 1947), and the Hostages trial (Case 7, July 1947–February 1948)—Valerie Hébert addresses the myth of the German army's clean hands. Since some twenty million German men had served in the Wehrmacht, these cases, like no other, put on trial the actions of "ordinary Germans," hence sending a highly provocative message to the German public. The trials, which sentenced 20 defendants to varying terms of imprisonment (including life imprisonment), brought the issue of war crimes and crimes against humanity to public attention. However, post-trial clemency rulings and the lack of German-language publication of the trial's evidence of criminality and complicity fostered the myth of a blameless army. Indeed, the defense counsel's narratives of a preemptive strike against the Soviet Union and of soldiers who had merely done their duty would begin to be seriously questioned only in the 1990s.

Ulrike Weckel's chapter on the use of filmic evidence at all the Nuremberg trials adds a new dimension to the volume by tracing the role and impact of that medium on both perpetrators and German spectators. Weckel enriches her analysis by tracing the "career" of the film footage between its debut at the IMT and the NMT. She also gives a meticulous account of historical inaccuracies in the filmic representation of the trials themselves in post-trial popular culture.

Devin O. Pendas offers a pessimistic verdict on the NMT's overall significance in re-educating the German public, at least in the short and medium terms. The majority of Germans, he argues, rejected the trials as victors' justice; moreover, members of the German legal profession who served as defense counsel succeeded in promoting revisionist arguments in the German legal press. The greater impact on German democratization, Pendas believes, came about as a result of numerous trials conducted by German courts under Control Council Law No. 10, which brought to justice Germans who had committed crimes against other Germans or stateless individuals in the years from 1945 to 1950.

Lawrence Douglas ends the volume on a celebratory note in his discussion of how the NMT ameliorated some of the legal limitations of the IMT in ways that ultimately proved crucial in the international prosecution of mass atrocities. While the NMT trials are often treated as a "footnote" to the IMT, they in fact had much greater significance for international criminal law as currently practiced (this, despite the fact that the IMT had, in many ways, "invented" international criminal law). The NMT had less prestigious legal personnel, less notorious defendants, and less funding for its operations and the publication of its proceedings. At the same time, it avoided a number of the IMT's limitations. Less focused on aggressive war as the prerequisite for considering crimes against humanity, it could consider a broader range of Nazi crimes and perpetrators and allow a greater role for victims and witness testimony rather than focusing solely on documents. Thus it paved the way for more recent proceedings against the perpetrators of mass atrocities.

The five volumes reviewed here each make significant contributions to the fields of European history, Jewish history, Holocaust studies, and legal history by means of retrieving a number of trials from scholarly oblivion. They explicate the political contexts and compromises intrinsic in these trials as well as their origins, implementation, outcomes, and short- and long-term societal, legal, and cultural impacts. It is to be hoped that additional studies on individual trials will further enhance our knowledge of Allied postwar justice and enrich our understanding of the texture of justice after the perpetration of historical wrong.

LAURA JOCKUSCH
The Hebrew University

Notes

1. Among the classic works on the IMT trial are Donald Bloxham, *Genocide on Trial: War Crimes Trials and the Formation of Holocaust History and Memory* (New York: 2001); Lawrence Douglas, *The Memory of Justice: Making Law and History in the Trials of the Holocaust* (New Haven: 2001); Whitney R. Harris, *Tyranny on Trial: The Trials of the Major German War Criminals at the End of World War II at Nuremberg, Germany, 1945–1946* (Dallas: 1999 [1954]); Michael R. Marrus, *The Nuremberg War Crimes Trial 1945–46: A Documentary History* (Boston: 1997); Joseph E. Persico, *Nuremberg: Infamy on Trial* (New York: 1994); Bradley F. Smith, *The Road to Nuremberg* (New York: 1981); Ann Tusa and John Tusa, *The Nuremberg Trial* (New York: 2010).

2. Jeffrey Herf, *Divided Memory: The Nazi Past in the Two Germanies* (Cambridge, Mass: 1997), 69.

3. Raymond Phillips (ed.), *The Trial of Josef Kramer and 44 Others (The Belsen Trial): War Crimes Trial Series*, vol. 2 (London: 1947), 17.

The God of History

Yaakov (Jacob) Barnai, *Shmuel Ettinger: Historiyon, moreh veish tzibur* (Shmuel Ettinger: Historian, teacher, and public figure). Jerusalem: Zalman Shazar Center for Jewish History, 2011. 487 pp.

Albert I. Baumgarten, *Elias Bickerman as a Historian of the Jews* (Texts and Studies in Ancient Judaism 131). Tübingen: Mohr Siebeck, 2010. vi + 377 pp.

Michael Brenner, *Prophets of the Past: Interpreters of Jewish History*, trans. Steven Rendall. Princeton: Princeton University Press, 2010. xiii + 301 pp.

Readers of the Hebrew Bible often notice that, for what is supposed to be the foundational epic of the nation of Israel, the authors of the long narrative sections stretching from Genesis to Kings are remarkably stingy with praise of the people who represent not only their main object of concern but probably also their intended audience. On the contrary; they seem to go out of their way to show that, with a small number of conspicuous exceptions, the Israelites were obstinate, ungrateful, scheming, greedy, and susceptible to the worst kind of religious and political demagoguery. Even the patriarchs exhibit ordinary human flaws. For subsequent Jewish commentators, the tendency of their biblical predecessors to dwell with singular relish on ancestral faults presents something of an embarrassment. There is a long exegetical tradition of grappling with the dubious ethics of cheating one's brother out of his birthright, slaughtering an entire population in reprisal for the questionable behavior of one person, or orchestrating the death of a man in order to sleep with his wife. It is sometimes claimed that such an unsparing reading of the Israelite past is meant to highlight the transcendence of God, who chooses where He will, and to show His divine readiness to forgive. But not, apparently, to forget. For, if the Bible makes for an odd sort of national epic, it remains an outstanding example of Jewish history-writing, adapted to the point of view of a God who remembers everything.[1] Writing in the shadow of His omniscience, the authors who deserve to be called the first Jewish historians were prepared to be impartial.[2] They did not shrink from the knowledge that God's elected were neither ethically nor intellectually privileged. In their estimation, the Israelites were no better than the people among whom they lived. No better, and sometimes even a little worse.

Impartiality ought not to be confused with objectivity; the latter constitutes an insoluble problem of epistemology, while the former is a matter of judgment. To assert the possibility of objectivity is to make claims about the limited nature of our own cognitive capacity that are both presumptuous and unsustainable, a categorical error to which the authors of the Bible, all too painfully aware that only God knows the absolute truth, never succumb. Impartiality, in contrast, involves the exquisitely rare but entirely human ability to hold one's friends and relations accountable to the same kind of dispassionate scrutiny that informs the way one assesses the behavior of one's most cherished enemies. Impartiality rests on an understanding that all human actions are conditioned by social circumstances and the calculation of individual motives from which no one—not even the chosen people—are exempt. Alive to the responsibility exacted by the transcendent God of history, the biblical authors faced up to the realization that the past of one's own people is bound up with the generally deplorable moral record of the entire species in ways that are impossible to disentangle. Which is to say, they understood that the universal and the particular are not opposites, an insight that eludes most of the modern practitioners of the Jewish historian's craft.

In the works under review by Jacob Barnai, Albert Baumgarten, and Michael Brenner, the God of history has been scaled down to fit the dimensions of memory. In affirming the ideological prerogatives of Jewish history-writing in our own secular age, Barnai, Baumgarten, and Brenner offer proof for Yosef Hayim Yerushalmi's famous contention that "history is the faith of fallen Jews."[3] Exclusively concerned with the ways in which the study of the Jewish past ministers to the spiritual needs of modern Jews, all three authors show a conspicuous lack of interest in the development of Jewish history as a critical discipline. Baumgarten's biography of Elias Bickerman is perhaps the most extreme example of the tendency, anticipated by Yerushalmi and inaugurated by Hayden White, to blur the difference between historiography and hermeneutics.

Until fairly recently, it was easy to miss the paradox at the heart of Yerushalmi's fine dialectical point. As late as 1995, Shmuel Feiner could still proclaim that the "emergence of modern Jewish historical consciousness" among 19th-century Jewish intellectuals in the German-speaking lands contributed to the secularization of Jewish culture.[4] Ten years later, Yerushalmi's own students were no longer so sure. In 2005, Nils Roemer first suggested that the a prodigious investment of the German Jewish founders of Wissenschaft des Judentums in recovering the Jewish past from the rabbis was far from the dramatic break with collective memory that a one-sided reading of Yerushalmi's elegiac treatment of the *Wissenschaftlers* might have suggested. Roemer argued that history offered 19th-century German Jews a form of theological inoculation against both the punitive logic of rabbinic theodicy and the undeniable force of philosophical skepticism. Subtitled "between history and faith," his *Jewish Scholarship and Culture in Nineteenth-Century Germany* expressly ventured into the domain of myth from which Yerushalmi rather disingenuously exempted the modern Jewish practitioners of the historian's craft. Pursuing Yerushalmi's paradoxical formulation to its logical conclusion, Roemer's pioneering monograph advanced the idea that scholarly historical works served as a "means to strengthen a decisively religious Jewish identity, not a secular one."[5] His reception history of Wissenschaft demonstrated that the German Jewish public venerated Jewish historians as "religious leaders" and "canonized" their studies as a "source of consolation and pride."[6]

By the end of the 19th century, the celebrity of Heinrich Graetz exemplified the transformation of the historian into the guardian of Jewish conscience against the depredations of secularization. Graetz identified his own persona not with the first historians of the Jews but with the last of the biblical prophets, charged with the awe-some responsibility of religious renewal in the diaspora. Following Malachi, Graetz resolved to write the kind of history that would "reconcile [traditional] parents with the [secular] hearts of their children," and, as Roemer put it, helped to "set the stage for the arrival of the messianic age."[7] Roemer showed that Graetz operated with a providential sense of Jewish time, in which the dramatic evocation of a heroic past served up a vision for a perfected Jewish future. A similar idea about the modern ten-dency to collapse the difference between history and poetry echoes in the title of Michael Brenner's wide-ranging study of historical "master-narratives" (p. 15) that followed Graetz in his attempt to fortify the faith of fallen Jews.

Brenner, also a student of Yerushalmi, published his book in Germany just a year after Roemer's came out in the United States. Now available in English translation, *Prophets of the Past* reinstates Jewish history within the evolution of collective "foundational myths" (p. 12) that Yerushalmi had outlined in *Zakhor*. Aligned with the scholarship on Jewish memory, Brenner's study of historical "interpretation" does not really fall under the rubric of historiography. He does not tell us much about the ways in which Jewish historians sifted and evaluated evidence, uncovered new information, or tested their hypotheses. He is not concerned with research findings at all, except as symptoms of a pre-existing ideological condition. Even though Brenner insists that "literary analysis of texts cannot replace the search for historical facts" (p. 4), his own work is more concerned with the *Dichtung*—the Jewish poetics—than the *Wahrheit*—the truth values—of history. In a sense, Brenner's book is a missed opportunity to do for Jewish historical scholarship what Peter Novick did for its American counterpart in *That Noble Dream* (1988), a pioneering work whose influ-ence is detectable in other attempts to address the difficult "objectivity question" in modern Jewish scholarship. Less intellectually ambitious, Brenner's leisurely stroll through the familiar landmarks of the field lacks both the precision that Peter Schäfer brought to his early study of Gershom Scholem's Kabbalah project and the impres-sive range of new sources that characterizes David Engel's more recent articles on Salo Baron and "neo-Baronianism."[8] Reading Brenner, one is hard pressed to see Jewish history as a rich and complex body of knowledge about the past that, in recent generations, has had a galvanic effect on Jewish textual engagement, supplementing and often subverting more traditional forms of Jewish learning. Nowhere does Brenner indicate that an obsession with history is no longer confined to secular Jews but has had a discernible, if still uncertain and highly contested, effect on the faith of the most inveterate Jewish traditionalists.[9]

Like Roemer, Brenner identifies Graetz as the father figure of the modern Jewish search for a usable past. Taking the story beyond the late 19th century when Graetz's work was still popular, Brenner effectively shows that the influence of Graetz's mode of prophetic self-fashioning has infiltrated every subsequent attempt at a "detached" pursuit of Jewish history as a "secular, scientific endeavor."[10] In pointed contrast to the painstaking researches of the *Wissenschaftlers,* which Ludwig Philippson had, in 1879, dismissed as pedantic "Geschichtsmikroskopie," Graetz cast Jewish history in the form of a glorious "classical [...] tragedy which extends over fifteen centuries" (p. 63). In this story, "the Jew, driven over the whole earth but respected and free as a bird, took a sublime, noble pride in being the bearer and sufferer for a doctrine in which eternity is mirrored" (p. 62), while "all the peoples of Christian Europe outdid the savage Mongols in barbarism towards the Jews" (p. 68). In its own time, Graetz's unapologetically Jewish depiction of the Middle Ages was of a piece with the modern "medievalism" of his French, German, and English contemporaries, who were likewise less invested in critical inquiry than in recovering a shiny new national culture from the remnants of Arthurian romance.[11]

Graetz proved remarkably difficult to dislodge. In the second half of his book, Brenner considers a variety of alternative "perspectives" on Jewish history, including Simon Dubnow's "diaspora nationalism," the Anglo-American "whiggishness" of Salo Baron and Cecil Roth, the Zionist "Jerusalem school," and finally postmodern "subjectivism."[12] But, in fact, all these represent more or less unsuccessful attempts to supplant Graetz's Jewish *Trauerspiel*. Dubnow, for instance, actively sought to extricate his own "system" from the religious influence of Graetz; still, the imaginative scaffolding that Graetz had erected around the Jewish past proved impregnable. Like Graetz, the self-consciously secular Dubnow also saw himself as a prophet of the "national conception of Judaism" (p. 105). Although Brenner refers to "diaspora nationalism" as a political construct, it was really more akin to an article of faith or, perhaps, a powerful literary conceit. In the final analysis, there is very little substantive difference between Graetz's profoundly ahistorical "idea of Judaism" and Dubnow's insistence on the "eternity" of Jewish peoplehood, which apparently "existed beyond the boundaries of time and space" (p. 100).

Even Baron, who set out to liberate Jewish history from Graetz's famously "lachrymose theory of [pre-modern] woe" (p. 125), inclined to the imaginative immediacy of a historian in whose work he professed to "hear the beating of the heart that grieves over the sufferings of his people and rejoices in describing the few happy periods" (p. 126). Baron wrote this in 1918, when he was only 23. He would subsequently devote most of his career to writing an 18-volume "social and religious history of the Jews" that was destined to remain unfinished and that reads like a *roman fleuve*, absorbed in the "play of ideas and the richness of documentation" (p. 126). Baron deliberately suspended the possibility of total thematic unity—precisely the sort of reassurance that readers found in Graetz—and refused to reveal "what it might all mean" in the end. Not surprisingly, his long, inconclusive "view of Jewish history," Brenner writes, "did not become prevalent outside a narrow academic spectrum," where the project of getting through the second edition of the *Social and Religious History of the Jews* (1952–1993) in its entirety, footnotes included, still retains the mark of heroic idiosyncrasy.

Ironically, no one did more to keep Graetz alive in the 20th century than the European-born founders of the Jerusalem school of Zionist historiography, some of whom professed undisguised filial hatred of his work. Scholem's well-known diatribe against Wissenschaft in particular, and German Jewish scholarship in general, assailed Graetz and his followers as the "spokesmen of a certain polite self-satisfaction" and the purveyors of "morose sentimentality" (p. 166). Scholem avowed that the only place where it was possible to write Jewish history that was free from partisanship and apologetics, untainted by "any ideological coloring" (p. 170), was Jerusalem. His colleague, Yitzhak (Fritz) Baer, also born and educated in Germany, saw no inconsistency in the assertion that the "Zionist worldview which we adopt in our

historical research, may not twist events to fit well-known ends, as earlier generations did, but must see things as they are" (p. 172).

The emphatic purge from Zionist history of the pernicious "worm of apologetics"
obscured just how much it owed to Graetz's romantic historicism. To begin with, the
founders of the Jerusalem school resisted any attempt to dismantle the tragic "lachrymose" ideal that Graetz had located at the core of Jewish experience. In a 23-page
review of Baron's original three-volume *Social and Religious History of the Jews*
(published in 1937 in *Zion*, the house journal of the Jerusalem school that Baer himself co-founded), he proclaimed that "despite everything the irreversible fact remains
that Jewish history in the Middle Ages" constitutes "an uninterrupted series of persecutions" (p. 128). Moreover, like Graetz, both Baer and Scholem located the formative period of Jewish consciousness in the pre-modern period, "the original creative
epoch of the national genius" (p. 175). To be sure, they replaced Graetz's valorization
of Sephardi "rationalism" with Ashkenazi "mysticism" but, like Graetz, they characterized the encounter between Jews and non-Jews as a moral struggle waged by a
long-suffering and heroic minority against the political domination of an immovably
hostile and oppressive majority. Like Graetz, they saw history as a way of mobilizing
Jewish consciousness and preserving Jewish commitment in a secular society. It was
the Jerusalem school, Brenner concludes, that raised "the new statehood [...] to the
status of a religion" (p. 192). Finally, as David Myers has shown, like Graetz, Baer
and Scholem saw themselves as "prophets of the past," heralds of the much-vaunted
Zionist "return" to history.[13]

Brenner argues that the "post-modern" turn in Jewish studies has diminished the
general credibility of "all-inclusive master narratives" (p. 198), especially the overtly
political ones rooted in nationalism (which, as all intelligent people now know, is
dead) and Marxism (even deader). At the same time, postmodern "subjectivism" is
still remarkably welcoming to the likes of Graetz, who might well be considered the
first exponent of a Jewish "difference" from medieval Christian Europe, just as his
Breslau seminary classmate Abraham Geiger has recently been rediscovered as the
preeminent Jewish post-colonialist *avant la lettre*.[14] Formally abjuring any kind of
commitment to impartiality, "post-modern" histories celebrate Jewish self-assertion
and frankly dispense with the line that separates "scholarly work" from narrative
statements of identity that are more readily associated with the writing of novels and
autobiographies (p. 201). As Roemer and Brenner both attest, it was Graetz who first
appealed to the spirit of personal engagement that has now become almost a methodological requirement. And, of course, the accompanying proclamations in praise of
Jewish "difference" are drafted into the same pedagogical project (to "reconcile"
wayward Jewish hearts and to convince a potentially hostile gentile public that Jews
are just like everyone else, only better) that Graetz first conceived as the prophetic
métier of the modern Jewish historian.

This is a tall order. Surely some among Graetz's biblical predecessors—the original "prophets of the past" invoked in Brenner's well-calibrated title—tottered under
the strain of *their* appointment with history, not to mention the immediate pressure of
demographic dispersion, political dispossession, and the loss of the vital center that
had held their culture together. The conditions that inform the recent proliferation of
Jewish "master narratives" are just as fraught as those that shaped the search for

historical "coherence" in the first age of the Exile. But the modern ideological shifts, so neatly catalogued by Brenner, refuse to line up with the contingencies of personal experience that have shaped the production of Jewish historical knowledge in the 20th century. Like Brenner, Baumgarten and Barnai seem more comfortable with the sanitized, epic image of the Jewish historian as prophet than with the complex and troubled 20th-century figures whose lives they document. In one instance—Barnai on Ettinger—we have a case of biographical hyperinflation. In the case of Baumgarten on Bickerman, we are presented with its opposite: a reductive and unsatisfying attempt to sum up a lifetime of scholarly achievement with an editorial on the modern Jewish condition.

The most striking thing about Barnai's attempt to do justice to Ettinger's career as a "teacher, historian, and public figure," is that it is probably longer than the collected works of its subject. Taught and continuously mentored not only by Baer but by two other members of the Jerusalem school—Ben-Zion Dinur and Israel Halpern—Ettinger (1919–1987) was professionally well-placed to build on the achievements of his predecessors; yet the completion of an original monograph in his own field of research (early modern Eastern Europe), to say nothing of the grand synthetic narrative to which he aspired, continued to elude him. Despite having been virtually hand-picked to succeed Dinur (after the latter was appointed minister of education) as the historian of modern Jewry for the fledgling Jewish state, Ettinger's lifelong service to the Hebrew University and to the Israeli public was marked by anxiety about his conspicuous inability to complete a book and a mounting sense of failure about his meager publishing record.

When he was not in the classroom, Ettinger spent most of his time organizing and attending conferences, delivering lectures, running seminars, and developing the infrastructure of Jewish studies at the Hebrew University. Barnai convincingly argues that Ettinger's impassioned nationalist faith and his enthusiasm for institution-building actually left a deeper imprint on the study of modern Jewish history than anything he wrote. Like the hasidic *rebbeim* (with whom Ettinger apparently evinced not only a genealogical but also an emotional kinship), he cultivated affective connections with his prodigious community of disciples. Ettinger's *toyre* came down mostly in the form of the *shmues*, conducted not only in seminar rooms but in the informal and intimate setting of his own home, where he gathered friends, followers, and colleagues for regularly scheduled conversations. People still remember him as a tireless polemical talker—a talent that probably owed as much to his early days in the Communist party as to a familial tradition of hasidic piety. Ettinger, who arrived in Palestine from Soviet Russia in 1936, maintained his allegiance to the radical left until roughly 1949, by which point, as Barnai puts it, he had "abandoned not one but two religions—Orthodox Judaism and Stalinism—in favor of a third: Zionism" (p. 77).

Barnai does far better with Ettinger the "teacher" and "public figure" than with Ettinger the "historian." When it comes to evidence of original scholarly achievement, the sources are admittedly thin; but Barnai's own relationship to Ettinger—who was his teacher—obtrudes on his ability to assess clearly even such material as there is. In addition to several edited volumes, some review essays and a score of articles (many of them culled from lecture material), Ettinger produced only one piece of history-writing that even came close to being a book: the long synthesis of the "modern period" included in the *History of the Jews*, which he edited together with his close friend and departmental colleague, Haim Hillel Ben-Sasson (1914–1977), another figure closely associated with the second generation of the Jerusalem school. Published in 1969 and reissued widely thereafter for use in Israeli high schools and universities, the so-called "red book," long known by the original color of its cover, identified Ettinger with the consensus nationalist view of the Jewish past. Barnai treats this text as most characteristic of Ettinger's commitment to the "continuity, singularity and totality" of Jewish historical experience—the ethos of the Jerusalem school as articulated by Ben-Sasson in his general introduction to the volume (p. 336)—and his own near-exclusive focus on Western Europe in that work as the signifier of the "new age" in Jewish history. Ettinger's personality as a Zionist educator emerges most clearly in *History of the Jews*, from which Barnai, along with hundreds of other students who heard Ettinger's Hebrew University lectures between the late 1960s and the mid-1980s, received their dose of Zionist wisdom about the underlying "unity" of Jewish history.

Barnai identifies a number of problems with Ettinger's contribution to the "red book," primarily the scanting of America and the total dismissal of non-western Jewries. But the problem runs deeper than these sins of omission. In some sense, Ettinger's near-total focus on emancipated, liberal, secular West European Jewry as the signifier of Jewish modernity represents a radical disavowal of his own autobiography; in his own case, Jewish modernity had involved neither emancipation into a nation-state nor the adoption of a liberal worldview. In the act of disowning his own radical East European past, Ettinger was forced to rewrite the history of Zionism (necessarily the highlight of his account) as a response to the "failure of emancipation," and also to adopt a neo-Herzlian liberal vision of the modern Jewish state that did not exactly tally with the basic facts of Israeli history. Like Ettinger himself—and unlike Herzl—most of the founders of Israel were not secular Jewish liberals from Western Europe but rather East European Jewish populists, many of them graduates of the Russian socialist movement. A significant proportion were rabbis and religious activists. In any case, few were interested in transplanting Herzl's liberal, secular utopia to the Middle East. Most saw emancipation not as a solution to the Jewish question but as the preeminent problem of modern Jewry, the reason for the decline of Jewish culture for the sake of material advantages, and the underlying cause for the deterioration of Jewish collective discipline. Why Ettinger could not tell *this* story is hardly a mystery; more surprising is Barnai's failure to address it even in passing. By the late 1960s, the East European origins of the Jewish state and the close genealogical connection between Zionism and socialism had become geopolitical liabilities. Given the importance of new Cold War alignments between the United States and the only democracy in the Middle East, Ettinger understandably felt pressure to produce a popular account of Jewish modernization that privileged West European Jewish "emancipation" while downplaying East European Jewish illiberalism of both the left and the right variety.

Indeed, despite Ettinger's political convictions as a Labor Zionist and his prodigious contribution to the study of Hasidism as a modern phenomenon, the "red book" relegated both religion and socialism to the margins of modern Jewish history. As the author of a new consensus narrative, Ettinger effectively became complicit in erasing from the collective memory of the Israeli public his own guilty defection from the two Jewish orthodoxies of the 20th century. Trying to convince himself that his version of the "modern age" was true, Ettinger fixated on the "enigma" of West European antisemitism. Worse still, having emptied Zionism of Judaism and leveled modern Jewish culture to a pale version of European liberalism, Ettinger was reduced to ritual iterations of the idea that the persistence of Jewishness after emancipation could be explained only in metaphysical or even mystical terms.

It appears that, riven by doubts about the cogency of the historical narrative for which he felt institutionally responsible, Ettinger could never give himself over to the pleasures of investigating the past. His summary treatments of Hasidism, the Jewish economy on the Polish frontier, and the Emden-Eibeschütz controversy are marked by energy and imagination; any of these works, if expanded, might have made a serious contribution to scholarship. But Barnai never explains why someone who was capable of producing this kind of work never fulfilled his intellectual promise. It is almost as if the venerable "teacher and public figure," burdened by the duties of national stewardship, stymied the professional "historian" that Ettinger had set out to become. Unfortunately, Barnai underplays the political and cultural context of the acute tension between Ettinger's various personae, a narrative strategy that has the unintended effect of making his subject seem merely neurotic.

Although Ettinger's story is painfully familiar, Barnai's explanation for Ettinger's scattershot publication record as a historian does not justify the investment of the reader. Numerous scholars, after all, have brandished "obligations to the field" as an excuse for a conspicuous lack of ideas, courage, or self-discipline. In the absence of something other than feeble psychologizing, the significance of Barnai's interest in Ettinger's biography remains unclear. To fulfill the initial promise of its title, this book might have focused more on Ettinger's contribution to the formation of Jewish consensus culture in Israel, and less on university politics and the strain of overwork. A minimalist explanation of the gap between the reach and grasp of a "public figure" says little about the "role of the historian in the process of nation-building" (p. 12).

Barnai's biography of Ettinger presents a story of unexpected, and largely unexplained, failure. In contrast, Albert Baumgarten's biography of E.J. Bickerman (1897–1981) offers a portrayal of a man who was ostensibly distanced from the precincts of Jewish history (because he knew no Hebrew) and from classics (because he deliberately chose controversial Jewish topics), and yet was unaccountably successful in both fields. Whereas Ettinger, securely cast in the role of history teacher to the nation, was a deeply moral person, ruthlessly honest about himself and profoundly serious about his task, Bickerman (despite several close calls with the perils of the 20th century), did not try to take himself too seriously and had what can only be described as an imperfect conception of the truth—especially when it came to his own life. Baumgarten points to Bickerman's notorious evasiveness about his marital status and his outright misrepresentation of his military service record. Yet Bickerman's prodigious scholarly output not only testifies to a rigorous standard of scholarly achievement but has actually stood the test of time. While the "red book" now seems completely outdated, Bickerman's work is very much alive; to meet the needs of a new generation of readers, Brill has recently reissued a two-volume collection of Bickerman's "studies in Jewish and Christian history," some of which were written as far back as the 1930s.[15] For any student of early Jewish history, Bickerman is one of those figures who remains simply unavoidable.

My first encounter with Bickerman's work came quite early in my education and probably had a great deal to do with shaping my subsequent intellectual inclinations. I graduated from a religious Zionist high school where the curriculum mandated two years of Jewish history (ancient to modern), taught, naturally, in Hebrew. My teacher, Dr. Wyszkowski, an immigrant twice over—once from Poland and then from Israel— had far more in common with Ettinger's view of the world than with Bickerman's. Whenever Dr. Wyszkowski mentioned Bickerman's name, he would go through contortions of visible discomfort, accompanied by eloquent eye-rolling and shoulder-twitching, and followed by the quintessential epithet of resigned Jewish disgust "*that one.*" *But he always assigned him.* Thanks to Dr. Wyszkowski's biblical impartiality, I had read *God of the Maccabees* (1936) in the 11th grade. As a matter of fact, aside from the biblical historians—whose work I encountered in other classes—Bickerman was the first Jewish historian I ever read. And having now read Albert Baumgarten's sympathetic and sprightly account of Bickerman's lives and times, I understand why Dr. Wyszkowski was both exasperated and impressed by the man whose work challenges the distinction between Athens and Jerusalem and whose career as a "*Jewish historian*" (p. 11) is the subject of an altogether unlikely story.

To begin with, Bickerman displayed none of that moral earnestness that runs like a red thread through the discipline of Jewish history, from Graetz to Ettinger. Bickerman seems to have approached his academic interests with the same high spirits that attended his enthusiastic pursuit of women (in contrast, reading Barnai, one gets the distinct impression that, during the period covered by his book, all of the men at the Hebrew University were both humorless and dead from the waist down). Furthermore, Bickerman did not embrace Jewish history as a public cause. Ambitious and driven, he was set upon a career, not a vocation. Possessed of an astonishing capacity to bounce back from every potential and actual disaster, both personal and collective, he could carry on writing even when it became highly uncertain whether or not he would continue to carry on *living.* Bickerman seems to have sailed through not one but two of the major catastrophes of the 20th century—the Russian Revolution and the Second World War—completely unfazed. It is incredible that he produced *God of the Maccabees*, a lapidary masterpiece of historical writing that rivals anything written in any field, between 1933 and 1936, as a refugee from two countries (Soviet Russia and Nazi Germany), with neither a passport nor the prospect of permanent employment. Equally, it comes as a shock to realize that Bickerman did not settle into a secure academic position (at Columbia University) until he was 55 years old, at which point history finally stopped interfering with his work.

Baumgarten, a former student of Bickerman's who until recently taught Jewish history at Bar-Ilan University, seeks to return Bickerman, an orphan from Judaism, to his true intellectual home (p. 303) and to enlist Bickerman's notorious "Hellenism" in the modern search for a Jewish usable past (p. 10). Baumgarten positions Bickerman alongside Eugen Täubler, a German-trained classicist whose protégés included Baer and Dinur, and who was, in some sense, the grandfather of the Jerusalem school. Täubler "saw an almost total identification between his personal dilemmas as a Jew in the modern world and the issues faced by Jews in antiquity," just as Bickerman was (ostensibly) attentive to the "resonances between ancient Hellenistic Judaism and modern Europe" (pp. 188–189). According to Baumgarten, Bickerman not only explored the integration of Jews into ancient society with a view toward enriching the understanding of Hellenism, but also judged "which Jews conceived and executed their relationship with the larger culture correctly and which ones erred" (p. 222). In taking a position on this question, Baumgarten implies, Bickerman was, perforce, a Jewish historian. Even more striking, in Baumgarten's view, is that Bickerman's conception of who got it wrong in the ancient world (the "Hellenizing reformers") versus who got it right ("Pharisees, rabbis and diaspora Jews") anticipates the ideological victory of those who locate Jewish identity somewhere along the "continuum between counter-culture [and] sub-culture" (p. 290) over the 19th-century Jewish "reformers" whose ultimate goal was (allegedly) assimilation.

To be sure, Bickerman refers to Abraham Geiger in his introduction to *God of the Maccabees*. However, this glancing mention does not justify Baumgarten's rather strange suggestion that Bickerman's hidden agenda was to draw a comparison between Geiger (and other reformers) and Hellenists. Moreover, Baumgarten's claim that Bickerman's indictment of the "Hellenizers" in *God of the Maccabees* was really an indictment of modern Jewish "paganism which he wished to denounce" (p. 268) seems completely out of character and out of temper with the times. Given Bickerman's naturally pugnacious temperament, one wonders why he did not simply denounce whomever he wished to denounce. Why did he have to cover his tracks and wait for Baumgarten to discern a hidden distaste for "Reform Jews in Germany ... enlightened Jews in nineteenth-century Russia, Jewish communists and contemporary Russian-Jewish thinkers ..." (p. 268)? Nowhere else in his academic or personal life did Bickerman exhibit the kind of coyness that Baumgarten attributes to him, even when the stakes were higher and his position more likely to be unpopular or misunderstood. Moreover, in the 1930s, when the entire Jewish world was in the throes of a profound and very public cultural upheaval, the ostensibly radical anti-assimilationism that Baumgarten ascribes to Bickerman would have sounded perfectly reasonable not only in Palestine but also in Germany and even in Soviet Russia (where Marxists openly castigated deracinated Jewish "thinkers" and German Jewish "reformers" as lackeys of the Jewish bourgeoisie and as servile "assimilationists," for having betrayed the cause of the Jewish masses). Why Bickerman should have resorted to an Aesopian strategy only so that he could articulate a position that had, by the 1930s, become a virtual commonplace among Jewish intellectuals is difficult to fathom. Still harder to comprehend is Baumgarten's perverse claim that Bickerman defended the historical rectitude of the Maccabees in order to deliver a "positive message for Jewish readers of the Nazi era," namely, that the "heroic sacrifice of martyrdom made over and over by Jews in loyalty to [the] truth" of the "uniqueness of God," was "never in vain" (p. 269).

Let us look at this proposition a little more closely. First of all, the situation of the Maccabees—who had actually won their war against both the Hellenizing party and the Greek occupiers of the temple-state—is hardly comparable to the kind of threat that European Jews, both the Orthodox and the faithless, faced under the Nazis. Despite the Jewish penchant to collapse one instance of anti-Jewish persecution into another, in this case one really must beg to differ. Second, could Bickerman really have been so crass as to suggest that the Jews of Europe should in any way (or for any "truth") *embrace* Nazi persecution as an opportunity to martyr themselves? Finally, in the entirety of Baumgarten's account there is absolutely no evidence that Bickerman had an abiding concern with comforting anyone at any time. In fact, as Baumgarten himself relates, *God of the Maccabees* was greeted as a singularly discomfiting (and still controversial view) of the Jewish past, in that Bickerman dared to impugn Jewish solidarity and to suggest that Jewish individuals always operated from mixed motives. German Jews were perhaps more likely to be affronted rather than comforted by *God of the Maccabees*, since Bickerman's argument about the role of the Hellenizing party in instigating the Greek persecution could easily be regarded as a case study in blaming the victim.

All this being said, the reason that I do not find Baumgarten's tortuous reading of Bickerman's hidden Jewish transcript overly persuasive is not because his logic is flawed and his evidence thin, or even because his understanding of Russian Jewish culture is superficial and frequently descends to the level of cliché. My real problem with Baumgarten's attempt to rehabilitate Bickerman's Jewish credentials is that Bickerman was *manifestly* a Jewish historian. I do not see the need for an elaborate intervention in order to uncover what is in plain view. Can anyone really doubt that Bickerman, the self-described "Hellenist," was seriously interested and professionally invested in the study of the Jewish past? I suspect that what really bothers Baumgarten is not that Bickerman was not a historian of the Jews (not even Dr. Wyszkowski would have made such a claim) but rather that he was not a *Jewish* historian—that is, he did not confine his pursuit of Jewish history to the narrow precincts of political or religious advocacy. The possibility that Bickerman's engagement with the Jews of the Greek age was anything other than narrowly partisan seems not to have occurred to Baumgarten.

Bickerman had no trouble constructing and reconstructing a conveniently "usable" personal past. At the same time, he had an abiding respect for history as a universally impartial discipline, for Bickerman's God was the God of history. Like his biblical ancestors, Bickerman wrote about the Jews with the conviction that "only universal history can uncover the deepest meaning of the particular... and of God's role for His people" (p. 230). Impatient with the long view, the modern heirs of the biblical prophets were inclined, as Brenner shows, to construe the past as a fulfillment of contemporary needs, forcing the inexorably slow passage of time into compliance with their own assumptions about who got it right and who got it wrong. "O Lord!" raged Heine, in the accumulated frustration of two thousand years of Jewish waiting to find out what God ultimately intended, "I know You are Wisdom and Justice itself, and all You do is just and wise. But I pray You: whatever it is You mean to perform, do it a little more quickly! You are eternal and have time enough. You can afford to wait. But I am mortal and I shall die."[16] Heine, a renegade from Wissenschaft des Judentums, had abandoned the scholarly pursuit of "historical microscopy," for the more immediate imaginative gratification of German literature, which enabled him to dispense his own brand of poetic justice and to avenge himself on his enemies; so, in a way, had Graetz (whose ideological opponents were, like Heine's, legion). Bickerman, speaking with the monumental self-assurance of the first Jewish historians rather than the anxieties of belated Jewish prophets, had this to say: "As a Hellenist, the writer sees the men and events he describes not as a link between the Hebrew Scriptures and the rabbinic period, but as a part of universal history, the final meaning of which only He knows, before Whom a thousand years are like one day."[17]

OLGA LITVAK
Clark University

Notes

1. See Mark S. Smith, *The Memoirs of God: History, Memory and the Experience of the Divine in Ancient Israel* (Minneapolis: 2004).

2. See John Van Seters, *In Search of History: Historiography in the Ancient World and the Origins of Biblical History* (New Haven: 1983); Baruch Halpern, *The First Historians: The Hebrew Bible and History* (University Park: 1996).

3. Yosef Hayim Yerushalmi, *Zakhor: Jewish History and Jewish Memory* (Seattle: 1982), 86.

4. Shmuel Feiner, *Haskalah and History: The Emergence of a Modern Jewish Historical Consciousness*, trans. Chaya Naor and Sondra Silverston (Portland: 2004). The original, in Hebrew, was published by the Zalman Shazar Center in 1995.

5. Nils Roemer, *Jewish Scholarship and Culture in Nineteenth-Century Germany: Between History and Faith* (Madison: 2005), 10.

6. Ibid., 108.

7. Ibid., 103.

8. On Scholem, see Peter Schäfer, "'Die Philologie der Kabbala ist nur eine Projektion auf eine Fläche': Gershom Scholem über die wahren Absichten seines Kabbalastudiums," *Jewish Studies Quarterly* 5 (1998), 1–25. The article was recently republished in French as "'La philologie de la kabbale n'est qu'une projection sur un plan': Gershon Scholem sur les intentions véritables de ses recherches," in *Gershom Scholem*, ed. Maurice Kriegel (Paris: 2009), 302–315. On Baron, see David Engel, "Crisis and Lachrymosity: On Salo Baron, Neo-Baronianism and the Study of Modern European Jewish History," *Jewish History* 20 (2006), 243–264, as well as his *Historians of the Jews and the Holocaust* (Stanford: 2009). For a recent discussion of Engel's controversial thesis, see the review forum in *Jewish Quarterly Review* 102 (2012), 81–111.

9. On "orthodox historiography," see Ada Rapoport-Albert, "Hagiography with Footnotes: Edifying Tales and the Writing of History in Hasidism," in *Essays in Jewish Historiography; In Memoriam Arnaldo Dante Momigliano, 1908–1987*, ed. Ada Rapoport-Albert (Middletown, Conn.: 1988), 119–159; and Israel Bartal, "'True Knowledge and Wisdom': On Orthodox Historiography," in *Studies in Contemporary Jewry*, vol. 10, *Reshaping the Past: Jewish History and the Historians*, ed. Jonathan Frankel (New York: 1994), 178–192.

10. Roemer, *Jewish Scholarship and Culture in Nineteenth-Century Germany*, 102.

11. For examples of 19th-century medievalism, see Lorretta M. Holloway and Jennifer M. Palmgren (eds.), *Beyond Arthurian Romances: The Reach of Victorian Medievalism* (Houndmills: 2005); Elizabeth Emery and Laura Morowitz, *Consuming the Past: The Medieval Revival in Fin-de-Siècle France* (Aldershot: 2003); and Maike Oergel, *The Return of King Arthur and the Nibelungen: National Myth in Nineteenth-Century English and German Literature* (Berlin: 1988).

12. For the post-modern "subjectivist" turn in Jewish history, see David Biale's introduction to *Cultures of the Jews* (New York: 2002) and the selection of essays included therein.

13. See David N. Myers, *Re-Inventing the Jewish Past: European Jewish Intellectuals and the Zionist Return to History* (New York: 1995).

14. See Susannah Heschel, *Abraham Geiger and the Jewish Jesus* (Chicago: 1998).

15. E. J. Bickerman, *Studies in Jewish and Christian History*, ed. Amram Tropper, 2 vols. (Leiden: 2007). The paperback came out in 2011.

16. Cited in S.S. Prawer, *Heine's Jewish Comedy: A Study of His Portrait of Jews and Judaism* (Oxford: 1983), 274.

17. Bickerman, *The Jews in the Greek Age* (New York: 1988), ix, cited in Baumgarten, 228.

Book Reviews

Antisemitism, Holocaust, and Genocide

Yehuda Bauer, *The Death of the Shtetl*. New Haven: Yale University Press, 2009.
viii + 208 pp.

In his introduction to this concise and impressive study, Yehuda Bauer succinctly points out that no one to date has written an in-depth historical study of the shtetl during the Holocaust era, even though these small towns were the basis for so many stories of Jewish life written from the mid-19th century onward.

Bauer is probably one of the world's foremost Holocaust historians, and as anyone who has ever read his books or has heard him speak knows, he is a master storyteller. "To be a good historian you first have to know how to tell a good story," he has often stated in his lectures, an adage that I have often quoted to my students when explaining the role of the anecdote—its importance and limitations—in teaching history. But as Bauer reminds us, both in this book and elsewhere, one needs not only stories but also historical analysis in order to be a good, responsible historian. "To deal with only stories or only historical analysis is unsatisfactory in the extreme. Real history combines both" (p. vii).

Bauer begins here with the story of the shtetl—or rather that of the end of the shtetl, first under Soviet domination and then as it underwent Nazi destruction—focusing on those of the marshlands of eastern Galicia, known as the Kresy, today part of Belarus, Lithuania, and Ukraine. From Sholem Aleichem and Mendele Mokher Sforim to I.L. Peretz, the shtetl has played a major cultural role in creating the image of East European Jewry even for those who never stepped onto European soil. Between 30 to 40 percent of prewar Polish Jewry lived in small towns and communities; in eastern Poland, Bauer notes, the number was closer to 60 percent. Bauer defines a shtetl as "a township with between a thousand to 15,000 Jews who formed at least a third of the total population, [whose] life was regulated by the Jewish calendar and by customs derived from a traditional interpretation of the Jewish religion" (p. 3). These parameters were chosen deliberately. By excluding village Jews living in small towns, Bauer concentrates on communities that were blessed with a wealth of voluntary organizations; in leaving out larger towns, he is able to focus on those that offered the intimacy of social life as was possible only in smaller communities. These two parameters of size and Jewish influence were paramount in creating the special framework and flavor of life in the shtetl.

Bauer's narrative of the shtetls in the Kresy is divided into eight chapters, some chronological, others topical. After giving the background of the shtetl and its characteristics, he devotes a chapter to a lesser-known period of prewar history: the shtetl in the 1930s. Here we are introduced to various towns that will delineate the study's geography, various political parties that will play a role before suddenly disappearing during the war, and the communal framework that is soon to dissolve and never reappear. Chapter 3 focuses on the period of the Soviet occupation of eastern Poland, from September 1939 until the German invasion of the Soviet Union in June 1941. Emphasizing how the purpose of the Soviet leadership was to make these areas into integral parts of the U.S.S.R. as quickly as possible, Bauer discusses why the Jewish population apparently welcomed their Soviet conquerors; the dynamics behind the sudden disappearance of Jewish schools; and the Soviet attempts to quell Jewish religious worship by heavily taxing synagogues, forbidding the sale of religious books, and providing entertainment programs for Jewish children on religious holidays to prevent them from practicing traditional customs. Chapter 4, titled "The Holocaust in the Kresy," is the heart of the book and the last of the chronological chapters, describing the annihilation of the Jews in eastern Poland following the Nazi invasion in June 1941.

The next four chapters are topical, with Bauer turning his attention to the shtetl community and its leadership, asking pointed questions about who became leaders during the Soviet occupation, and why. Another chapter is devoted to "neighbors," that is, the relationship between the Jews of the Kresy and their surroundings, and what happened to that relationship both during the Soviet period and after the German occupation. The next chapter, "Rebels and Partisans," offers a tale of ostensible hope and courage: Jews fighting against the Nazis, where they fought, in what units, how they tried to survive. Bauer discusses underground groups in the shtetls, armed rebellions, flight into the forest, family camps, and partisan fighting. He reminds us that most underground groups were led by former members of prewar Zionist youth movements (of all political hues), and that in some places the presence of Soviet partisans meant a better chance of successful rebellion. Indeed, rebellion and armed resistance occurred in a number of shtetls, among them Tuczyn, Lachwa, Dereczin, Kleck, Nieswiez, Glebokie, Stolpce and other places in the north. Elsewhere, there was mass flight into the forests, but in most shtetls, survival was the result of pure chance. The bottom line, as Bauer quotes historian and former partisan Shalom Cholawsky, was that the Soviet partisan movement gave Jews their only real chance to survive. However, when the Jews of the shtetls needed the partisans, the partisans were not usually there, and by the time they arrived en masse, most of the shtetl Jews had already been murdered. The final chapter, the death of the shtetl, sums up a number of the book's salient points and leads us to the tragic end of the story, the destruction of the Jews of the Kresy.

Bauer's genius as a historian lies not only in his ability to tell a coherent, fascinating and, in this case, tragic story but also in his skill at homing in on the phenomena he describes, analyzing them in depth without drowning his audience in academic jargon. One example is his discussion of the Nazis' motivation both in their attempt to conquer the Soviet Union and its territories (including the Kresy) and in the policies they carried out in the areas they conquered, including their measures against the Jews. Bauer's answer, articulated as well in other works

written by him over the past two decades, is decisive: they were motivated by ideology. He does not, however, leave this as a declarative statement of fact, but
rather devotes a great deal of effort to engaging with other opinions, in particular
that of Christian Gerlach, whose book on German economic and annihilation policies in White Russia is characterized by Bauer as "a masterpiece of historical
writing" (p. 57).[1]

Gerlach's claim—namely, that the German invasion of Poland and the Soviet
Union was spurred by the need to gain access to the area's vast natural resources—is
backed by ample German documentation. Bauer, however, points out that the Nazis
systematically refrained from documenting their antisemitic policies; thus, the available documentation does not necessarily reveal their primary war goals. He then
takes the discussion one step further. What did the Germans plan to achieve in the
war, he asks, and why did they need these resources? After all, the Stalinist regime
was willing to supply Germany with all its needs; in that case, why turn against a
powerful ally?

Bauer's answer takes into account the official and possibly misleading German
documentation, but also applies logic and an analysis of events as they occurred. The
need for expansion, he writes, was purely ideological: Nazi ideologues viewed
Germany as the future power controlling Europe and, through Europe and with allies,
the world. Control of Europe necessitated control of the riches of the Soviet Union.
Further, the forces standing against Germany were orchestrated, so the Nazis believed, by the enemies of the Aryan race, the Jews. Thus, whereas economic factors
were extremely important once it came time to implement Nazi ideology, the core
impetus for the invasion was ideological.

Another example of Bauer's unique historical method are his questions regarding the Soviet occupation of the Kresy. How is it, he asks, that the rich ethnic
and religious tradition of the shtetl, developed into a distinct culture over a period
of centuries, collapsed like a house of cards within a few weeks of the establishment of totalitarian rule? Is it possible that all totalitarian regimes can eradicate
cultures that easily, or was the Soviet regime somehow unusual? After all, Bauer
notes, Jewish communal life continued to exist for quite a while in Nazi Germany
after the rise of Hitler, and even under the Nazi occupation of Poland during the
early 1940s.

Bauer explores a number of interesting hypotheses. For one thing, the Soviet
occupiers took action against overt antisemitism, effectively driving it underground.
In gratitude, many young Jews, in particular, drew closer to the Soviet regime and
were willing to abandon their traditions in exchange. Another hypothesis points in
the opposite direction, to Soviet terror and repression. A third possibility is that poor,
overwhelmed communities responded positively to a theoretically utopian system
that would help the poor and downtrodden. Bauer is not satisfied with any of these
answers. Could it be, he asks, that another contributing factor was the total collapse
of the Jewish middle class in the wake of the sudden change in the local economic
system? What about the radical social change that came about when women were
forced to enter the workforce in order to support their families? Or the fact that even
older Jews who had been peddlers and shopkeepers could hardly find work, as they
were branded capitalists and petite bourgeoisie? In Bauer's view, none of these

answers is conclusive. His final word on the matter is a warning: at a time of severe challenges and persecution, a traditional system must strengthen itself or else face possible eradication, even without the threat of physical annihilation.

Bauer's study does not remain within the narrow parameters of the Kresy. Following his discussion of the fate of Kresy Jews, he asks a number of comparative questions. Did the Jews of the Kresy respond differently to the Nazi destruction and annihilation policy than did other populations? Did the shtetl Jews behave differently from Jews elsewhere? Bauer's answer to both is negative: the Kresy Jews were marked by the same disorientation, despair, individual and group heroism, collaboration with the perpetrators in the hope of surviving, family cohesion (with occasional instances of abandonment of children or parents) and resistance (mainly armed resistance) as were other groups. The major difference between the Jewish and non-Jewish response was what Bauer terms "Amidah," loosely translated by him as a spiritual (though not necessarily religious) resistance to the Nazis.

To be sure, the Jews of the Kresy had alternatives that were not available to Jews of other areas. For one thing, the shtetls were located within a forested region, which afforded at least a slight opportunity for escape; this option did not exist in central and western Poland, where the land was only lightly forested. Second, there was a massive Soviet partisan movement in the northern Kresy, and this made it possible for a Jewish remnant to survive, whether as fighters or as family groups protected by the fighters. In this regard, the only other comparable place in Nazi-dominated Europe was the forests of Yugoslavia, where a proportionately large number of Jews survived as members of Tito's army.

Bauer's brilliant analysis of the lives and deaths of Kresy Jews ends with his summary of three elements that may explain differences in behavior under extreme duress: character, chance, and luck. Character came into play, for example, in the question of Jewish leadership—for instance, how Judenräte leaders acted under various circumstances. Chance determined which particular person was chosen to head a given Judenrat; whereas luck is defined by Bauer more broadly as an entire set of circumstances at a particular time. Bauer notes that he was trained to analyze both long- and short-term factors, concentrating primarily on economic, political, and social forces. This comment reminds us that a successful historical study is, above all, the product of a historian willing to go beyond usual methods and to consider alternatives that are not always part of the traditional historical discipline.

JUDITH TYDOR BAUMEL-SCHWARTZ
Bar-Ilan University

Note

1. Christian Gerlach, *Kalkulierte Morde: Die Deutsche Wirtschafts-und Vernichtungspolitik in Weissrussland, 1941 bis 1944* (Hamburg: 1999).

Jonathan C. Friedman (ed.), *The Routledge History of the Holocaust*. London: Routledge, 2011. 516 pp.

The burgeoning field of Holocaust studies necessitates "handbooks" (or "textbooks") to be used first and foremost for university teaching, but also as an aid for scholars in the field. Since the beginning of the 1950s, a series of attempts to write comprehensive studies have been undertaken, some more successful than others: the outstanding examples among them are Raul Hilberg's *The Destruction of the European Jews* (in its various editions), Leni Yahil's *The Holocaust: The Fate of European Jewry 1932–1945*, Saul Friedländer's two-volume *Nazi Germany and the Jews*, and Peter Longerich's *The Holocaust: The Nazi Persecution and Murder of the Jews*. These and other comprehensive studies are written by a single author who develops a cohesive, chronological narrative of the unfolding Holocaust "story" by integrating a broad variety of phenomena and issues. This, however, rules out a systematic analytical and multifaceted grappling with the diverse pieces of the larger picture—something much needed in university teaching and for researchers seeking concise overviews of various topics. Although several Holocaust encyclopedias offer short entries on a wide range of topics, personalities, and countries, they cannot serve as textbooks.[1] Similarly, while there are several historiographic overviews that deal with interpretational debates, schools of research, stages in the development of Holocaust research, and the impact of political, social, and cultural developments on the field,[2] such volumes generally cover a limited number of major topics. Recently, however, two collective volumes of a somewhat different nature than the types mentioned above were published: the volume reviewed here and *The Oxford Handbook of Holocaust Studies*.[3] Each volume is the product of efforts of a battery of Holocaust scholars who were recruited to write condensed overviews of a broad array of topics—42 in the volume reviewed here, 47 in *The Oxford Handbook*—the aim being a "comprehensiveness that reaches as wide an audience as possible" (p. 2).

In his words, the editor of *The Routledge History of the Holocaust*, Jonathan C. Friedman, "adopted a framework that is chronological and then thematic" (ibid.). Thus, the first section, titled "The Nazi Takeover and Persecution in Hitler's Reich to 1939," depicts the preconditions for the events of the 1940s. Included in this section are overviews of the Jewish world on the eve of the Second World War; European antisemitism; Germany and the Armenian genocide; eugenics and race hygiene; Weimar Germany; Hitler and the functioning of the Third Reich; anti-Jewish legislation; gender; and Austrian Jewry. In the following section, "Germany's Racial War in Poland and the Soviet Union, 1939–1941," readers are provided with the main factors underlying the escalation of extreme (including murderous) violence against the Jews, from the outbreak of the war in 1939 until the first stages of the Final Solution. Chapters in this section discuss the ghettos, Nazi racial policy in Poland, the "euthanasia" program, the *Einsatzgruppen* (the special killing units of the SS) and the ordinary killers, the conceptual and bureaucratic origins of the Final Solution, forced labor of Jews, and concentration and extermination camps (two chapters).

"The Final Solution in Europe" presents essays on the varying proportions of fatalities caused to Jewish communities in different countries of Nazi-occupied

Europe—*Reichskommissariat Ostland* (mainly the Baltic states, eastern Poland and Belorussia), Western Europe, Norway, Hungary, Southeastern Europe, Romania, and Croatia. Several countries are left out or else covered in very limited fashion (France, Belgium, and the Netherlands, for instance, are analyzed together in a 10-page essay), whereas others (for instance, Norway) are given a disproportionate amount of space. Following this is a section titled "The Responses from Victims, Bystanders, and Rescuers," which includes essays on Sweden and the rescue of Danish Jewry; portraits of a variety of rescuers; Jewish armed and spiritual resistance; "being Jewish and female"; and the DP experience (this last chapter should have been placed in the following section, together with that dealing with surviving children). In addition, this section covers church reactions (including theological responses) as well as the fate of non-Jewish victims of Nazism: Jehovah's Witnesses, Romanies ("gypsies"), and gay men and lesbians.

A concluding section gathers six post-Holocaust issues under the heading of "The Holocaust in Law, Culture, and Memory": the trials of war criminals in the two Germanys; Holocaust documentaries; sequential art narrative; the role of survivors in the remembrance of the Holocaust; the fate of children survivors in Poland in the immediate aftermath of the Holocaust; and "post-Holocaust theology in art." There is also an essay on music in the Nazi ghettos and camps, which should have been included in the previous section.

Overall, *The Routledge History of the Holocaust* contains many helpful and insightful contributions, although the volume's quality varies from chapter to chapter. It brings together the work of veteran and well-established scholars such as Marion Kaplan, Christopher Browning, Robert Jan van Pelt, Wolf Gruner, Michael Berenbaum, Ian Hancock, and the late Stephen Feinstein, alongside that of younger and upcoming scholars such as Kinga Frojimovics and Boaz Cohen. And although the editor is a historian and most of the contributions are historical in nature, one will also find scholars from other disciplines, such as the law professor Michael Bazyler and the sociologist Helen Fein. The Jewish aspect of the Holocaust, which in recent years has often been marginalized in studies dominated by the perspectives of perpetrators or of genocide studies, is relatively well-covered in this book.

To be sure, any volume of this nature cannot be all-inclusive—while undeniably tempting, it is not entirely fair for a reviewer to question the editor's judgment as to why one topic was included while another was not. This said, my feeling is that *The Routledge History of the Holocaust* lacks several "musts." There is no essay devoted to the multifaceted economic spoliation and persecution that took place throughout the Third Reich's existence, even though this topic is absolutely essential for an understanding of Nazi antisemitism and its escalation, as well as for its links with former types of antisemitism. Economic spoliation was no by-product of the Holocaust but rather an essential part of it—expressing, from the very first moments of the Third Reich, a comprehensive drive to destroy "the Jews." A second important issue is that of the Jewish councils, which is addressed only in passing in Helene Sinnreich's essay on the ghettos. In fact, it is entirely wrong to regard such councils as part of the ghetto system: the Jewish Council idea and system began evolving a year and a half before the Second World War, and Jewish councils (and "Jewish associations") were later installed in almost all of the Nazi-occupied countries as well as in several Nazi-allied states (including Nazi-occupied areas of North Africa). Ghettos, in contrast, existed only from 1939 and were an East European phenomenon.

Last but not least, the volume lacks any clear definition of "the Holocaust." In his introduction, Friedman explains that "World War II, history's deadliest military conflict, accounted for 72 million... deaths, 47 million civilians in total, 12 million of whom were murdered in the Holocaust." Yet he also brings the U.S. Holocaust Memorial Museum's definition of the Holocaust as "the systematic, bureaucratic, state-sponsored persecution and murder of approximately six million Jews by the Nazi regime and its allies during World War II," adding that "six million non-Jewish victims also suffered grievous oppression and destruction" (p. 1). The reader will ask: are the non-Jewish victims part of "the Holocaust," or does this term relate only to the fate of the Jews, while the fate of the other persecuted groups is in fact a separate story? This conceptual issue should have been elaborated much more fully, perhaps in a separate chapter devoted both to terminology ("Holocaust," "Shoah," "*Churbn*," etc.), and to historians' differing periodizations of the Holocaust era.

DAN MICHMAN
Bar-Ilan University
Yad Vashem

Notes

1. Examples of such encyclopedias are Israel Gutman (editor-in-chief), *Encyclopedia of the Holocaust* (New York: 1990); and Walter Laqueur (ed.), *The Holocaust Encyclopedia* (New Haven: 2001).

2. The most notable of these are Lucy S. Dawidowicz, *The Holocaust and the Historians* (Cambridge, Mass.: 1981); Israel Gutman and Gideon Greif (eds.), *The Historiography of the Holocaust* (Jerusalem: 1988); Michael R. Marrus, *The Holocaust in History* (London: 1989); Ulrich Herbert, "Vernichtungspolitik: Neue Antworten und Frage zur Geschichte des 'Holocaust'," in *Nationalsozialistische Vernichtungspolitik 1939–1945. Neue Forschungen und Kontroversen*, ed. Ulrich Herbert (Frankfurt: 1998), 9–66; Dan Michman, *Holocaust Historiography: A Jewish Perspective. Conceptualizations, Terminology, Approaches and Fundamental Issues* (London: 2003); Dan Stone (ed.), *The Historiography of the Holocaust* (Basingstoke: 2004); David Bankier and Dan Michman (eds.), *Holocaust Historiography in Context: Emergence, Challenges, Polemics and Achievements* (Jerusalem: 2008); and Tom Lawson, *Debates on the Holocaust* (Manchester: 2010).

3. Peter Hayes and John K. Roth (eds.), *The Oxford Handbook of Holocaust Studies* (Oxford: 2010); this work contains an essay that I wrote.

Ariel Hurwitz, *Jews without Power: American Jewry during the Holocaust*. New Rochelle: Multieducator, 2011. 331 pp.

In 1936, American Jewish pressure helped scuttle a British plan to shut down Palestine to Jewish immigrants, thus enabling 50,000 additional European Jews to reach the country before the White Paper was imposed. In 1939–1940, American

Jews partly financed the smuggling of thousands of Jews from Europe to Palestine. And in 1943–1944, protests by Jewish activists played a major role in bringing about the creation of a U.S. government agency that helped rescue more than 200,000 Jewish refugees. All of which suggests that Ariel Hurwitz has his work cut out for him in trying to argue, as he does in *Jews without Power*, that American Jews were politically too weak to facilitate the rescue of Jews from the Nazis.

Jews without Power begins with a survey of American and American Jewish responses to Nazi outrages in the 1930s. In Hurwitz's view, all Jewish protests were ineffective, the U.S. Congress and the public were hopelessly antisemitic, and there was nothing more that could have been done to aid Europe's Jews. American Jewry's boycott of German goods in the 1930s "was incapable of changing Nazi policies towards the Jews," he insists, although, curiously, he later concedes that the boycott "did succeed in moderating the Nazi attacks on the Jews" and even quotes Joseph Goebbels admitting as much (p. 34).

Hurwitz makes no mention of Rabbi Stephen S. Wise's successful pressure on President Franklin D. Roosevelt to block the planned British closure of Palestine in 1936. He also ignores the role of American Jews in helping to underwrite the smuggling of Jews from Europe to Palestine (coordinated by the underground Irgun Zvai Leumi) in the late 1930s. These two episodes sharply contradict the central thesis of *Jews without Power*.

The immigration issue reveals much about the strengths and weaknesses of Hurwitz's case. FDR was "an astute politician," Hurwitz stresses. Thus, in advancing his goal of "containing German aggression," Roosevelt could not "waste his political capital...on a confrontation with Congress on the question of opening up the U.S. to Jewish refugees" (p. 26). In any event, Hurwitz continues, since Congress and the public were both deeply antisemitic, such a confrontation would surely have failed.

Yet the fact is that no confrontation was necessary; thanks to the administration's policy of looking for any excuse to turn down applicants, immigration quotas to the United States were significantly under-filled between 1933 and 1945. Had the entire quota from Germany and Axis-occupied countries been accepted, more than 190,000 Jews would have been saved. All Roosevelt had to do was to quietly instruct the State Department to permit the existing quotas to be filled—there was no need for congressional approval. Although Hurwitz alludes to the matter of the unfilled quotas (p. 38), he never acknowledges how this contradicts his claims regarding Roosevelt's alleged need to avoid a clash with Congress. Interestingly, the one time Roosevelt did permit the quotas to be filled (in the wake of the *Anschluss* of 1938), he announced it publicly, with this move sparking only scattered criticism. Likewise, there were no protests of note over FDR's decision, following the Kristallnacht pogrom of November 1938, to allow 15,000 Germans to remain in the United States after their visitors' visas expired. It would seem, then, that Hurwitz goes too far in his sweeping portrayal of the American public as profoundly antisemitic. Many antisemitic groups were indeed active, and polls showed that certain anti-Jewish stereotypes were widespread, but there is evidence, too, of genuine sympathy for German Jewish refugees among many ordinary Americans.

Hurwitz's thesis does not fare much better as *Jews without Power* moves into the period of the Nazi genocide, between 1941 and 1945. After news of the mass murder was confirmed, the Roosevelt administration insisted that nothing could be done to rescue Europe's Jews apart from winning the war. Mainstream Jewish leaders rejected that claim but feared challenging the president, especially in wartime. This left a vacuum that was soon filled, in part, by the maverick group of Jewish activists known as the Bergson group.

Hurwitz acknowledges that the hundreds of newspaper advertisements sponsored by the Bergson group "did much to publicize the tragedy that had overtaken European Jewry and the need for the Allies and [American] Jews to act quickly if any Jews were to survive" (p. 163). He also concedes that Bergson's efforts helped create "a climate of protest in the American Jewish community and a cry for 'Rescue Now!' " (p. 164). Hurwitz acknowledges that a remarkable number of non-Jewish writers, artists, actors, intellectuals, and public officials signed the Bergson group's newspaper ads, participated in its rallies, or contributed financially to its rescue campaign. Yet he fails to grasp how this phenomenon contradicts his broad claims about the American public's antisemitism.

Hurwitz's assessment of the mood in Congress likewise seems skewed. In late 1943, Bergson's allies in Congress introduced a resolution urging FDR to create a refugee rescue agency. According to Hurwitz, since Congress was "totally opposed" to more immigration, there was no chance that "such a body would pass a resolution . . . whose intention was to impel the government to rescue" (p. 243). He somehow forgets to mention that the Senate Foreign Relations Committee unanimously adopted the resolution—a move rather at odds with Hurwitz's depiction of Congress as "indifferent to the fate of the Jews" (p. 263).

Against this backdrop of Bergson-generated congressional pressure, Treasury Secretary Henry Morgenthau, Jr., was able, shortly before the full Senate vote, to convince FDR to establish the War Refugee Board. Hurwitz insists that Bergson and Congress had nothing to do with Morgenthau's success. Yet Morgenthau's own words (not mentioned by Hurwitz) are revealing. In a March 16, 1944 meeting with his staff, the treasury secretary referred to "the Resolution in the House and the Senate by which we forced the President to appoint [the Board]."[1] During the final 15 months of the war, the War Refugee Board played a central role in the rescue of an estimated 200,000 Jews.

Jews without Power began as a Ph.D. thesis written 20 years ago. Although it is the least of Hurwitz's problems, it does not help that the published book is replete with grammatical errors and awkward abbreviations, that many of the endnotes are indecipherable, and that the names of significant individuals and organizations are repeatedly misstated. Much more troubling is the fact that Hurwitz has not chosen to take into account a large body of scholarship on American Jewry and the Holocaust that has been published during the past two decades. Among the works that go unmentioned are Bat-Ami Zucker's book on the role of U.S. consuls in Europe; Laurel Leff's work on the *New York Times* and the Holocaust; Stephen Norwood's account of the U.S. academic community and the Nazis; Efraim Zuroff on the response of American Orthodox Jews to the Holocaust; my volume on the struggle between the Treasury Department and the State Department; a book on Jewish student protests co-authored by David Golinkin and me; Judith Baumel's work on the Bergson group, and another volume on the Bergson group co-authored by David Wyman and me.[2] Much of the research presented in these works lends no support to Hurwitz's thesis but instead points to a different question that has yet to be fully answered, namely, why senior American Jewish leaders who possessed a measure of political influence sometimes chose to refrain from exercising it.

RAFAEL MEDOFF
David S. Wyman Institute for Holocaust Studies

Notes

1. Morgenthau Diaries, 710/94, Franklin D. Roosevelt Library, Hyde Park, N.Y.
2. Bat-Ami Zucker, *In Search of Refuge: Jews and U.S. Consuls in Nazi Germany, 1933–1941* (London: 2001); Laurel Leff, *Buried by the* Times: *The Holocaust and America's Most Important Newspaper* (New York: 2005); Stephen H. Norwood, *The Third Reich in the Ivory Tower: Complicity and Conflict on American Campuses* (New York: 2009); Efraim Zuroff, *The Response of Orthodox Jewry in the United States to the Holocaust: The Activities of the Vaad-ha-Hatzala Rescue Committee, 1939–1945* (New York: 2000); Rafael Medoff, *Blowing the Whistle on Genocide: Josiah E. DuBois, Jr. and the Struggle for a U.S. Response to the Holocaust* (West Lafayette, Ind.: 2009); idem and David Golinkin, *The Student Struggle against the Holocaust* (New York: 2010); Judith Tydor Baumel, *The "Bergson Boys" and the Origins of Contemporary Militancy* (Syracuse: 2005); David S. Wyman and Rafael Medoff, *A Race against Death: Peter Bergson, America, and the Holocaust* (New York: 2002).

Otto Dov Kulka and Eberhard Jäckel (eds.), *The Jews in the Secret Nazi Reports on Popular Opinion in Germany, 1933–1945*, trans. William Templer. New Haven: Yale University Press, 2010. civ + 959 pp.

An impressive undertaking, *Jews in the Secret Nazi Reports on Popular Opinion in Germany, 1933–1945* examines the attitudes and behaviors of the German population toward its Jewish neighbors and highlights the perceptions and reactions of Jews toward increasing ostracism and persecution. In addition, Otto Dov Kulka and Eberhard Jäckel tackle the question of how much Germans may have known about the extermination of the Jews and what they thought about it—again, as reflected in these secret reports. The collection illuminates facts and issues that were previously known only to specialists, making them accessible to a far broader reading public.

The collection is extraordinarily comprehensive. The editors and their research teams scoured the Federal German Archives and more than 30 archives in the German states and former German territories in Poland. In addition, they consulted 15 additional archives as well as the Moscow Special Archive, the Imperial War Museum in London, and the Center de Documentation Juive Contemporaine in Paris. In this volume of 959 pages, they present 752 documents winnowed from the 3,744 documents found in the original German edition. William Templer's translation excellently evokes dry bureaucratese as well as a spectrum of written prose ranging from that of an educated, university-trained intelligence officer to the colloquialisms of a village policeman. English-language readers also benefit from an extensive glossary of names, institutions, and Nazi terminology. Most unusual, but welcome, the book includes a CD that allows access to the German sources, including both the original 3,744 documents and many longer versions of the documents contained in the English volume. Moreover, the book has a concordance that lets readers turn easily to the CD, and the CD itself has a search and filter function in English and German.

Who was involved in the writing of these reports? Tens of thousands of intelligence officers and average citizens, from the local to the national level. The collection presents not only SD reports (the Security Service of the SS shaped and implemented regime policy on the Jews and the "Final Solution") but also reports from the secret police (Gestapo), district governors, local police, and Nazi organizations such as those for teachers. An especially helpful introduction sets forth the issues as seen through these reports: the daily public lives of Jews; how the German population's attitudes toward Jews became radicalized both before the Nuremberg laws of 1935 and the November pogrom of 1938; and what Germans thought about the fate of the Jews during the war.

What is new here? Historians of German Jewry know that persecutions increased and that the daily lives of Jews was marked by intensified humiliation and discrimination, depending on place and time. These documents, however, show the Nazis' own surprise at the vitality and variety of Jewish organizational life that continued or emerged in response to persecution. Jewish memoirs, both published and unpublished (some of the latter, available online), refer to many organizations for economic and social support, political representation, cultural enrichment, and Jewish education and retraining. These new documents—through the eyes of the perpetrators—show "the freedom of the outcasts" (p. xiv) and an even more vibrant, pluralistic society than Jewish memoirs indicate. For example, in the small district of Kassel, a report listed many Jewish organizations that "have become active once again" (p. 19) and ended with this statement: "The office of the state police is busy...putting together an exhaustive card catalogue of all Jewish associations...in order to make constant surveillance easier" (p. 20). Jewish businessmen, too, tried to help each other by publishing a small book listing Jewish shops so that Jews could patronize them (p. 197). In the early years, we see active Jews "mak[ing] their own history,...but...not under circumstances chosen by themselves."[1] More German historians need to take note of this, since they tend to focus on victimhood rather than addressing the (albeit limited) agency of these very same victims.

Similarly, previous scholarship has traced increasing antisemitism in 1935. Yet these documents—particularly the completely preserved ones from Prussia and Bavaria—are far more definitive. In addition, the editors subjected them to computer-aided quantitative analyses and then to deeper qualitative analyses. Well before the Nuremberg laws, we note that 58 percent of the reports between January and September 1935 (389 out of 667) highlight boycotts, rallies, and violence against Jews, and the demand, most vocally among the SA (the paramilitary wing of the Nazi party), to finally "solve" the Jewish Question. And yet, despite the increasing torment of Jews, contradictions appear as well. The editors emphasize how rioters in Berlin accused the police of becoming "Jewish lackeys" when they intervened to protect Jews and Jewish property. Why did the police do this? And what about the "Jew friends" who also appear in the reports? In January 1935, a local court initiated criminal proceedings against a leader of the National Socialist farmers' organization on the grounds of "attempted extortion of a Jew" (p. 79). Is the glass half empty or half full? Yes, Germans engaged in extortion, blackmail, and the like. But Jews still brought suit, and courts—more or less—responded to them. Moreover, in the spring of 1935, the district governor of Trier reminded his superiors that "the greater mass of the population...does not accept being prevented from shopping in Jewish stores, especially if there are low-cost, high-quality goods to be purchased" (p. 128). Contradictions are important, even if few and far between.

Well before the Nuremberg laws, crowds also attacked those whom they suspected of having sexual relations with Jews or those who had married Jews. The fact that families, neighbors, marriage registrars, employers, and the Nazi party frowned on intermarriages even before the Nuremberg laws has been previously documented. For example, as of June 1934, Berlin schools fired "Aryan" teachers who had married Jews after July 1933. And six months prior to Nuremberg, a Berlin Catholic priest faced three months' incarceration for marrying a mixed couple and hence abetting "racial defilement." These secret reports, however, demonstrate the extent to which thousands of Germans protested against such "race mixing." The editors use quantitative and textual analyses: between August 1 and September 10, 1935, forty of 158 documents reported on "race defilement"; textual analysis shows that these 40 sources reported 185 cases (p. lii).

Such data underline the editors' theme of agitation from below, not merely decrees initiated at the top. I would disagree, however, that Hitler, "in the end,...followed the pressure from below" (p. liii). Instead, I would argue that he used such pressure to support his radical inclinations, and even when those "outside the solid national Socialist-oriented population" reacted with "indifference" to or "very little appreciation and understanding" (p. 155) of the Nuremberg laws, Hitler did not change his mind.

Turning to the months before the November 1938 pogrom, the editors offer documents that report on the increasing scale of local riots and violence against Jews. They see the regime as escalating a grassroots "pre-history" of the pogrom. Again, the emphasis is on the German populace—a good corrective, perhaps, to previous scholars who focused only on Hitler. But the sources show a dialectical relationship between leadership (Hitler and his henchmen) and followers that ended in cumulative radicalization. Further, how can we be sure that these reports aren't themselves, in Ian Kershaw's terminology, "working towards the Führer?" Leaders and populace traveled a two-way street.

The documents clarify how Germans reacted when they first saw Jews wearing the yellow star in September 1941. Based on nationwide investigations, the reports indicated that many Germans seem to have known about the marking of Polish Jews almost immediately upon the invasion of Poland in 1939, and that they frequently demanded similar identification for German Jews. Once the decree to wear the star had taken effect, some Germans demanded that Jews married to "Aryans" also wear it, and that the apartments of Jews indicate their "race." No doubt Germans expressed such sentiments, commonly and ubiquitously. But how many of these reports, too, "worked towards the Führer?"

When one examines the memoirs of Jewish victims, a more nuanced picture emerges. Victor Klemperer called September 19, 1941 "the most difficult day in the twelve years of hell," and many Jews note occasional outbursts against the "star-wearers" (*Sternträger*), but most report indifference. And some also maintain that strangers stuck fruit, cigarettes, and other tokens of sympathy into their pockets. Moreover, the secret reports themselves bemoan those "Jew friends" who did not approve of the regime's excesses (pp. 352, 405). In consequence, the regime passed special laws against "persons of German blood" who engaged in "friendly relations with Jews" (p. 706). Thus, the reporters' and the editors' choices of sources can open new vistas, while closing off others.

As to the deportations, this volume—once and for all—documents what Germans knew and when they knew it. At first, they learned that the deportations to the east involved forced labor, but that elderly and weak Jews were to be shot. Detailed reports about mass shootings in Russia trickled in very early (July 1941). Soldiers on furlough provided details. In fact, Inge Deutschkron's memoirs report that she and her mother were warned by the mother of one such soldier to avoid deportation at all costs.[2] It has always been clear that non-Jewish Germans knew more than Jews, being closer to the soldiers, the bureaucrats, and the industries that went east. However, these secret documents indicate that far more Germans saw the deportations and knew what happened in the east than most historians have thought, and that a majority of Germans approved, with a minority expressing sympathy.

Otto Dov Kulka and Eberhard Jäckel are to be congratulated for this exhaustive study, the careful organization, the helpful footnotes (rendering each document an independent unit that teachers can use) and the CD. This project offers a wealth of data for modern German and modern Jewish historians. The latter will certainly use it. Hopefully, historians of modern Germany and of the Nazi era will take it into consideration in their debates about "victims, perpetrators, and bystanders," in Raul Hilberg's famous formulation.

MARION KAPLAN
New York University

Notes

1. Karl Marx, *The 18th Brumaire of Louis Bonaparte* (New York: 1852). "Men make their own history, but they do not make it just as they please; they do not make it under circumstances chosen by themselves ..." See online at books.google.com/books?id=G52CrJIClgAC& printsec=frontcover& source=gbs_ge_summary_r& cad=0#v=onepage& q& f=false (accessed 20 January 2013).

2. See Inge Deutschkron, *Ich trug den gelben Stern* (Munich: 1986); in English, *Outcast: A Jewish Girl in Wartime Berlin* (New York: 1990), trans. Jean Steinberg.

Anna Lipphardt, *Vilne: Die Juden aus Vilnius nach dem Holocaust. Eine transnationale Beziehungsgeschichte*. Paderborn: Schöningh, 2010. 545 pp.

The city of Vilna, now known as Vilnius (and known in Yiddish as Vilne), was completely transformed by genocide and large-scale forced migration during the Second World War and in its aftermath, as were other cities with significant Jewish populations in Eastern and Southeastern Europe such as Lemberg (Lvov) and Salonica (Thessaloniki). Once the Soviet authorities had established full control over Vilna (following the division of Poland by Hitler and Stalin), they deported more than 30,000 "enemies of the people" and "bourgeois elements" to the *gulag*, in many instances only days before the German invasion in June 1941. Among the Jewish deportees (numbering approximately 6,000) were leading members of the community. Shortly after the German army and the mobile killing units reached Vilna, mass executions of Jews began at the nearby Ponar forest. By December 1941, the Germans and their Lithuanian collaborators had murdered about 40,000 Jews at this killing site alone. Another 20,000 Jews were forced into a ghetto that was brutally eradicated in September 1943, with the survivors deported to camps in Estonia, Poland, and Germany. At the end of the war, no more than 5,000 Jews from Vilna and surrounding communities were still alive. They were scattered across Europe: most had managed to flee to the Soviet Union (or had been deported there). Small groups had gone into hiding or had fought against the Germans as partisans; others were liberated from concentration camps in Poland and Germany in 1944–1945. Few Jewish survivors stayed in, or returned to, Vilna after the war.

In *Vilne: Die Juden aus Vilnius nach dem Holocaust*, Anna Lipphardt, a German cultural anthropologist, attempts to uncover both the loosely linked diaspora of Jews from Vilna and Jewish sites of memory in the present-day city. Once a culturally diverse city belonging to a multiethnic empire, and a leading center of Jewish learning, Vilnius today is the capital of Lithuania, and most of its inhabitants define themselves as Lithuanians. Although the city center largely escaped destruction during the Second World War, the remarkable Jewish legacy of the "Jerusalem of Lithuania" is hardly visible. The famous Great Synagogue, badly damaged during the German occupation but still standing in 1945, was torn down in the mid-1950s. The two Jewish cemeteries were flattened in 1955 and 1959 to make way for an athletic complex and apartment buildings. After Lithuania became independent, the former KGB headquarters in the city center was turned into the "Museum of Genocide Victims"—commemorating Lithuanian victims of Soviet rule without mentioning the involvement of Lithuanian collaborators in the Holocaust, let alone their Jewish victims. After discussing the origins of the small Jewish Museum in Vilnius, the different memorials at the former Ponar killing site, and a few inconspicuous monuments across the city, Lipphardt takes the reader to more distant memorial "sites" of Jewish Vilna, such as a section of a giant cemetery in suburban Long Island, the YIVO Institute in New York, and meetings of associations comprising Jews from Vilna (and their descendants) in Israel and the United States.

More than six decades after the end of the Second World War, research about Holocaust victims is still an underdeveloped field. Surprisingly few Holocaust historians make use of Yiddish-language sources. Samuel Kassow's important study of Emanuel

Ringelblum and the Oyneg Shabes archive, and the edited and translated edition of Herman Kruk's Vilna ghetto diary by Benjamin and Barbara Harshav, provide insights into the victims' experiences and their assessment of the unfolding catastrophe. Recently published studies about Jewish DPs by Atina Grossmann, Laura Jockusch, Tamar Lewinsky, and others have opened a perspective on the immediate post-liberation phase and early reflections of Jewish survivors. Lipphardt adds a further dimension by tracing the evolution of a post-Holocaust Vilna diaspora, describing her book as "multi-locale mobile cultural history."

Her study presents innovative methodological approaches and is based on extensive research. The complex organization and length of the book, however, betrays its origins as a partly revised doctoral dissertation. Seventeen chapters are organized in six parts: "Origins"; "Transit Stations"; "The Vilne Diaspora in New York, Israel and Vilnius"; "Vilne Sites of Memory"; "Vilne Voices"; and a concluding section (unfortunately, there is no index). The book comprises several sub-studies, each worthy of a separate volume, such as the intriguing section on Jewish burial sites in Vilna and the New York metropolitan area, or the subchapters that deal with the gradual loss of the Yiddish language in the diaspora. Lipphardt went to great lengths to uncover Vilna Jewish life after the Holocaust: in addition to archival research, she conducted more than 30 interviews and collected a large number of Yiddish songs. The book contains almost fifty illustrations, with several photographs documenting Lipphardt's field research.

The lengthy historical overview at the beginning will be familiar to specialists of modern Jewish history. The story really begins nearly a hundred pages later, as Lipphardt describes how groups of survivors and returning refugees from Soviet exile came together in Lodz, an important stopover for surviving Jews from different places in East Central Europe. Most of the survivors remained in Lodz for only a short time; this interval was followed by a phase of dispersal, and often isolation and disconnectedness. Some Vilna Jews moved to Palestine, with the help of the Bricha organization, others to DP camps in the American zone of Germany. After settling in Israel and the United States, DPs formed several mutual aid organizations (*landsmanshaftn*). In Israel, these organizations initially focused on practical support; only in the 1960s did they begin to emphasize the cultural Yiddish legacy. Meanwhile, for Vilna Jews in the United States, the transplanted YIVO Institute in New York served as an important first port of call. Lipphardt also discusses Jewish life in Vilnius after 1945. The section describing the post-Holocaust diaspora is based on interviews and detailed accounts of the author's field research. Two other lengthy sections might have worked better as separate studies: a 150-page section on Vilna sites of memory (in and beyond the city), and a section on "Vilne Voices" that deals with the impact of Yiddish on the identity of Vilna Jews in the post-Holocaust diaspora.

Vilne: Die Juden aus Vilnius nach dem Holocaust is not a concise study with a succinct argument but rather a combination of reprinted sources, accounts of interviews and field trips, and different analytical sections examining various aspects of the post-Holocaust Vilna diaspora. With this book, Lipphardt has made an important contribution to the history of the Holocaust and to modern Jewish history.

TOBIAS BRINKMANN
Penn State University

Shimon Redlich, *Life in Transit: Jews in Postwar Lodz, 1945–1950*. Boston: Academic
Studies Press, 2010. xvi + 264 pp.

Shimon Redlich was born in 1935 in Lwow and spent his prewar childhood in
Brzezany, a town in eastern Galicia (then part of Poland, now located in Ukraine).
With the outbreak of the Second World War, Brzezany came under Soviet rule. After
the German invasion of the Soviet Union in June 1941, the Nazis established a ghetto
in Brzezany. When they initiated the deportation of Jews, Redlich and his family
secreted themselves in the attic of their home; later, he and his mother were hidden
by a courageous Ukrainian family. In 1945, Redlich and his mother settled with remnants of their family in Lodz. Five years later, they immigrated to Israel.

As a historian of 20th-century Poland and the Soviet Union, Redlich became
renowned for works dealing with the ill-fated Jewish Anti-Fascist Committee.
Beginning in the late 1990s, his scholarship took an additional, more personal turn.
In two published volumes—a third is still in the works—he has examined the history
of Jews in prewar, wartime, and immediate postwar Poland and in the fledgling state
of Israel during the years of his childhood and adolescence.[1] Redlich writes from the
vantage point of an eyewitness to history who is also a trained historian, combining
personal memories with documentary evidence and numerous oral interviews to produce historical writing of a distinctly different genre.

The first volume, *Together and Apart in Brezany*, provoked both admiration and
disparagement because of Redlich's relatively positive portrayal of the interaction
between his fellow Jews and their Polish and Ukrainian neighbors in prewar eastern
Galicia, as well as his sympathetic depiction of several heroic Ukrainians who risked
their lives to help him and his family during the period of Nazi occupation. This account ran afoul of the conventional wisdom that Polish-Jewish and Ukrainian-Jewish
relations before and especially during the Second World War were characterized by
immutable distance, friction, and outright hostility. In the view of Polish sociologist
Kaja Kaźmierska, Redlich's unorthodox approach, which she herself admires, has
condemned him to the margins of the academy.[2] Redlich, for his part, appropriates the
label of "marginal historian" with pride, since it permits him to be an "intermediary
among different and conflicting groups and societies"—no small matter, since "such
intermediary work is significant and important for a better future."[3]

In *Life in Transit: Jews in Postwar Lodz, 1945–1950*, Redlich amply demonstrates
the significance of Lodz to Jewish life in Poland in the immediate aftermath of the
Holocaust. Prewar Lodz had been home to a thriving Jewish community: in 1939,
Jews accounted for approximately a third of the city's population, numbering some
233,000. When the Red Army entered the city in January 1945, only 877 Jewish
survivors were present. Yet an estimated 20,000 Jews from Lodz had survived the
Holocaust, and in the weeks and months following the city's liberation, thousands of
Jews passed through the city, or else settled there for greater or shorter periods of
time. The Jewish population fluctuated greatly between 1945 and 1950, reaching a
zenith of 57,000 by June 1946. By comparison, some 70,000 Jews—mainly resettled
from the Soviet Union—resided in the newly acquired territories of Lower Silesia
and Pomerania by mid-1946, with most living in Wrocław and its environs.

Several factors accounted for Lodz's status as a postwar transit station for refugee Jews. The villages and towns from which many survivors hailed were unsafe because of rampant antisemitism, and Warsaw was devastated and largely uninhabitable. Lodz, in contrast, remained largely intact, and the city also proved to be hospitable to the establishment of prominent Jewish institutions. Thus, Jews went to Lodz to look for relatives, find shelter, secure employment, place their children in school, and renew Jewish communal and cultural life. Others, meanwhile, passed through Lodz without any intention of remaining in Poland. In the wake of the Kielce pogrom of July 1946, during which local Poles, on the grounds of a blood libel, killed 42 Jews, the majority of Jews in Poland departed from the country; the Jewish population in Lodz also dropped precipitously, to 15,000. The regime's dismantlement of Jewish institutions in 1948–1949 prompted more Jews to leave, and the legal emigration of Polish Jews to the newly established state of Israel in 1949–1951 reduced the city's Jewish population even further.[4] Other Lodz Jews settled in North America or Australia, while many who stayed in Poland moved to Warsaw.

Readers of Jan T. Gross's *Fear: Anti-Semitism in Poland after Auschwitz* (2006) and other books on Jews in postwar Poland may expect this volume to contain numerous accounts of friction and animosity between Jews and Poles, including eruptions of antisemitic violence in immediate postwar Lodz. *Life in Transit* does call attention to antisemitic sentiments, rumors, and violence. According to one rumor, the regional arm of the security establishment was permeated and run by Jews; according to another, Jews were kidnapping Polish children. Following the violence in Kielce, antisemitic graffiti in Lodz called for an anti-Jewish pogrom—in one incident, a hostile crowd surrounded a house inhabited by Jewish residents before the police arrrived and scattered the mob. Redlich calls attention to the killing of 55 Jews in Lodz and the wider area of Lodz province during the first year and a half after liberation. He counts bandits and members of the nationalist underground among the perpetrators, but other, "ordinary" antisemites also must have taken part in the killings. After the pogrom in Kielce, self-defense units known as "special commissions" were formed in several Jewish communties, including Lodz. Redlich notes, however, that the fact that more Jews were killed in areas with smaller Jewish populations (such as the Lublin province) than in the Lodz province indicates that "it was relatively safer for Jews to live in and around Lodz than in other areas" (p. 80). He adds that it seems that most of the killings took place in Lodz province rather than in Lodz proper.

But antisemitism is decidedly not the focus of this book. Indeed, what distinguished postwar Lodz, as Redich vividly demonstrates, was the city's vibrant Jewish organizational and cultural life. Lodz boasted a robust local Jewish committee that helped Jews secure apartments, employment, and other forms of material assistance. Twenty-eight Jewish cooperatives for tailors, shoemakers, carpenters, metal workers, and printers employed 1,600 Jewish workers in 1948. The highly respected Jewish Historical Commission, whose task was to document the Nazi genocide of Polish Jews, was headquartered in Lodz. The city was also a center of postwar Zionist and Bundist activities among both adults and youth. A large number of Jews were active in the socialist and communist parties. There were two Jewish schools (the Hebrew Ghetto Fighters School and the Yiddish Y.L. Peretz School) as well as a progressive Jewish children's home. *Dos naje lebn*, the Yiddish-language newspaper of the

Central Committee of Polish Jews, was printed in Lodz. Jewish audiences were re-
galed by the legendary Ida Kaminksa and others in the city's Yiddish theater. There
was also a Jewish film cooperative, Kinor (which, among other things, produced
Undzere kinder, the last Yiddish-language feature film made in Poland). Thanks to
abundant cultural opportunities, a large number of Jewish writers, artists, and actors
called Lodz home in the early postwar years, and Jewish life in the city exuded
vitality, hope, and optimism.

Life in Transit is populated by living, breathing people—rendered unfiltered by
Redlich—who, in the shadow of the Holocaust, evinced a tremedous will to live. My
own favorite among these memorable and colorful figures is Benyamin Majerczak
(1917–2005), who, after spending the war years first in the Soviet Union and then in
General Zygmunt Berling's Polish army, settled in Lodz in 1946 with the intention of
eventually emigrating to Palestine. Majerczak became active in the Zionist movement and was briefly involved in Bricha, the semi-clandestine organization responsible for bringing tens of thousands of Polish (and other) Jews to Palestine. But
there was an even more urgent need for his military expertise in setting up Jewish
self-defense units; consequently, he took part in the special commission for Jewish
self-defense in Lodz and also traveled thoughout Poland to train Jewish volunteers
for the Haganah. The indefatigable Majerczak was employed part-time by both the
Peretz School and the Ghetto Fighters School to teach gym and physics. He would
come to school dressed in his Polish army captain's uniform, which, as he recalls,
"made a big impression on the children." As he told Redlich: "The students kept
asking me about the war, and how many Germans I had killed. Until then they had
heard only about ghettos and camps, and here was a young Jewish officer who had
fought the Nazis. Whatever I did for those kids was done with great love" (p. 169).

Majerczak's memories and those of Redich's other interviewees, not to mention
Redlich's own, are the heart of the book. The interviews were mostly conducted six
decades after the war, and they are generally upbeat or even bouyant. Yet just below
the surface, it is possible to detect a more complicated relationship between Jewish
life in postwar Lodz and later memories of that life. For instance, in writing about
Heniek Napadow, a schoolmate at the Ghetto Fighters School, Redlich notes the
following:

> Heniek attended the Hebrew school, but did not remember any details. What he did recall
> very well were his fights with Polish youngsters. He even told me about an incident in
> which I was involved, which I didn't recall at all. "We walked together and two goyim
> started in with you. I told them to stop, and they asked me why I defend a Jew-boy."
> Heniek was blond and blue-eyed; I was dark, with a typical Jewish face. "Then they
> pushed you, and I started hitting them. When I started hitting I never knew how to stop.
> My first thought was always to avenge the Jews. I don't know how I got this idea, but it
> was always there. I was taking revenge for the Jews who were kicked around by the
> goyim. I hit one of those boys on his head with a lead toy gun, which I always carried
> around. He fell down. I think he fainted. And then we fled" (p. 175).

It is telling, I would suggest, that Redlich forgot this harrowing event from his adolescence in postwar Lodz. To be sure, the immediate postwar years were much brighter
than those of the war. Citing Polish sociologist Hanna Świda's study of Polish youth
in the immediate postwar years (based partly on the sociologist's memories of Lodz),

Redlich acknowledges that "young people, both Poles and Jews, tended to suppress wartime experiences and memories. They mostly lived in the present and for the future" (p. 52). Later, he notes that what was common to Jewish adolescents and young adults during this time "was a prevailing urgency to start a new life after years of war, exile, and loss" (p. 78). All this notwithstanding, at least some of the memories recounted in this book seem to contain a dose of wishful thinking.

Like the first book in Redlich's projected trilogy, *Life in Transit* is bound to elicit both praise and opprobrium, in part because of Redlich's generally positive approach to Jewish life in immediate postwar Poland, and also because it poses a direct challenge to Zionist-oriented historiography, showing persuasively that not all Jews at that time were single-minded Zionists.[5] Beyond this, the distinctive contribution of *Life in Transit* is its emphasis, as shown through the lens of the remarkable Lodz Jewish community, on the vitality of the remaining remnant. Far from being dispirited demoralized, or helpless, these Jews were protagonists both in their own survival during the Holocaust and in the rebirth of Jewry in its aftermath. In portraying this community—and, in so doing, revising the predominant historiographical reconstruction of postwar Polish Jewry—Redlich has produced a wondrous book.

GABRIEL N. FINDER
University of Virginia

Notes

1. This review deals with the second volume in Redlich's projected trilogy. The first volume, titled *Together and Apart in Brzezany: Poles, Jews and Ukrainians, 1919–1945*, appeared in 2002. In the third volume, the focus will be on adolescent Holocaust survivors in Israel's emerging society.

2. Kaja Kaźmierska, *Biografia i pamięć: Na przykładzie pokoleniowego doświadczenia ocalonych z Zagłady* (Cracow: 2008), ch. 6.

3. Shimon Redlich, "Some Remarks on the Holocaust by a Marginal Historian," in *The Holocaust: Voices of Scholars*, ed. Jolanta Ambrosewicz-Jacobs (Cracow: 2009), 109.

4. A wave of Jews who were repatriated from the Soviet Union in 1956 revived the community temporarily, but most of the arrivals soon emigrated. By the early 1960s, Lodz had fewer than 3,000 Jews. See Robert Moses Shapiro, "Łódź," in *The YIVO Encyclopedia of Jews in Eastern Europe*, ed. Gershon David Hundert (New Haven: 2008), 1086.

5. Although most Polish Jews eventually did leave for Israel, they did so because the Zionists were better organized and funded than their opponents, a point made as well by David Engel in his *Bein shiḥrur livriḥah: nitzolei hashoah bepolin vehama'avak 'al hanhagatam, 1944–1946* (Tel Aviv: 1996).

Cultural Studies, Literature, and Thought

Leora Batnitzky, *How Judaism Became a Religion: An Introduction to Modern Jewish Thought*. Princeton: Princeton University Press, 2011.

"Is Judaism a religion? Is Jewishness a matter of culture? Are the Jews a nation? These are modern questions, and this book tries to explain why this is the case" (p. 1). With these words, Leora Batnitzky opens *How Judaism Became a Religion*, which both examines the meaning of Judaism and Jewishness in the modern age and outlines the tensions that, from the end of the 18th century, accompanied the redefinition of Judaism as a religion. As Batnitzky demonstrates, the historical process of the change in thinking that led to a definition of Judaism in terms of religion (rather than in the broader sense of community, nationhood, culture, ethnicity, or the like) is intertwined with the development of modern western philosophy. Batnitzky takes account of the work of figures such as Benedict Spinoza, Immanuel Kant, Friedrich Schleiermacher, and Friedrich Wilhelm Hegel, in addition to examining Jewish religious thought and the ways in which it was influenced by transformations in the modern world.

How Judaism Became a Religion can be read in several ways. It surveys, in mostly chronological order, the evolution of Jewish thought in the modern era, from Moses Mendelssohn and Haskalah literature to developments taking place in the second half of the 20th century in Israel, France, and the United States. It can also be viewed through the lens of its fascinating central thesis, according to which Jewish thought in modern times is an extended grappling with modernity by Jewish culture. Batnitzky shows how three basic stances toward Judaism—regarding it as a religion, a culture, or as the manifestation of a specific nation—resulted in widely varying definitions of "Jewish identity," ranging from ultra-Orthodox to religiously innovative to secular. In addition to analyzing the thought and works of numerous Jewish and non-Jewish thinkers (albeit overlooking several prominent women, among them Margareta Susman, who was active as a poet and as a philosopher in the first half of the 20th century in Germany and Switzerland; and Judith Plaskow, with her influential writings on feminist theology), Batnitzky provides glimpses into their personal lives and their social and cultural experience, while at the same time sketching the influence of their thought within the Jewish world.

Batnitzky informs us that her search for an introductory book on contemporary Jewish thought was what prompted the writing of *How Judaism Became a Religion*. Considered in this light, her book is an undoubted success: in a manner both fascinating and potentially controversial, it broadens the scope of what is defined as "thought" by including literary and political figures, rabbis, and academic scholars in the conversation. Batnitzky's viewpoint can be better understood if we compare it to two of Eliezer Schweid's projects: his histories of Jewish thought and of the Jewish religion in the modern era. Batnitzky follows in Schweid's footsteps in her efforts to be widely inclusive, as evidenced, for instance, in her discussion of texts both philosophical and non-philosophical. However, in contrast to Schweid's historical reading of Jewish thought in the modern age, which finds expression in his Zionist conclusion (or, at least, in his examining Jewish thought in light of Zionism and its supporters and opponents), Batnitzky defines the Jewish religion as independent of nationalist elements, leading her to depart from Zionism as the guiding idea of Jewish thought in our epoch.

In Batnitzky's view, the "the making of Judaism into a religion" was an outcome of the displacement of religion from its previously all-encompassing role. In the era of secularization, religion was regarded as one (but not necessarily the most central) aspect of human experience. Thus, a clear distinction could be drawn between religion and nationality—its personal and communal dimension, on the one hand, and its political aspect, on the other. This opened up the possibility of limiting Judaism's national self-perception to the limited context of religious culture.

Batnitzky does not consider another possibility: regarding Judaism as a hybrid religion-nation. Among those who championed this view was Joseph Klausner, who, in *From Plato to Spinoza*, described the Jewish rejection of Neoplatonism from Philo through Ibn Gvirol to Judah Abravanel: "And so the matter is clear: as long as Judaism was sustained on religion alone, without land, without language, without a national foundation, it is possible that all those who wished to graft onto it a Platonic or Neoplatonic pantheism were in fact a danger." However, he continues, history taught the Jews to regard the aspiration to land and language as part of Judaism's desires as a religion-nation. Klausner quotes with approval Spinoza's amazing formulation that, "at the proper opportunity, since human affairs are subject to change, [the Jewish nation] will at some time reestablish its state and God will choose it once again"—adding that the first part of Spinoza's prophecy had already been realized and expressing his fervent hope that the second part would one day be realized as well.[1]

Batnitzky concludes her review of the research and literature with developments of the 1980s. As such, there is no discussion of postmodern trends, including the widening of boundaries characteristic of New Age discourse, deconstructionism, and the new mysticism. One may hope that Batnitzky will one day be able to write a sequel covering more recent developments. In the meantime, she deserves our thanks for undertaking this project—a comprehensive philosophical examination that is guided as well by historical and biographical thinking. A careful reading of *How Judaism Became a Religion* invites the reader into the world of Jewish thought in the modern world, in which the spirit of creativity and activism are manifestly evident.

HANOCH BEN-PAZI
Bar-Ilan University

Note

1. Yosef Klausner, *MiApleton 'ad Shpinoza: masot filosofiyot* (Jerusalem: 1955), 327–329.

David Biale, *Not in the Heavens: The Tradition of Jewish Secular Thought*. Princeton: Princeton University Press, 2011. xiii + 229 pp.

In this stimulating and original book, David Biale has undertaken to construct a "genealogy" linking the key components of Jewish secularism—ideas that, while fully crystallizing only at the beginning of the 20th century, can be traced back to the distant past.[1] Using this approach, Biale holds that *Jewish* secularism can be considered distinctively Jewish because it is "a revolt grounded in the tradition that it rejected" (p. 1)—a revolt that subverts Jewish religiosity in a very Jewish way.

Biale's erudite work (the notes are a scholar's delight) traces the articulation of the venerable Jewish trilogy of "God, Torah, and Israel," drawing on writers not often included in the mainstream of Jewish thought. Biale is catholic in his knowledge: prominent are such diverse writers as Solomon Maimon, Heinrich Heine, Moses Hess, Rebecca Lazarus, Bernard Lazare, Sigmund Freud, Albert Einstein, and Hannah Arendt—together with the more obvious Theodor Herzl, Ahad Ha'am, Hayim Nahman Bialik, Yosef Berdichevsky, Chaim Zhitlovsky, Gershom Scholem, Uri Zvi Brenner, Vladimir Jabotinsky, and David Ben-Gurion. The central personage in almost every chapter is Bento/Baruch/Benedict Spinoza. This extreme rationalist philosopher and critic of traditional religion, inspired by Descartes and the new sciences of his time, is portrayed by Biale not as a maverick, but rather as a paradigmatic figure embodying the traumas to be faced by those in later centuries who sought to modernize notions of Jewishness.

Biale's genealogical investigation uncovers a wealth of connections between ideas espoused by a varied group of Jewish scholars, thinkers, and artists. His chapter on Torah begins by noting that conceptions of God's direct involvement in human affairs were already challenged in the biblical books of Esther, Job, and Ecclesiastes. In the Middle Ages, Abraham ibn Ezra hinted that our Torah did not originate solely at the time of God's revelation to Moses at Sinai. The 10th-century Arabic work *The Nabatean Agriculture* prompted Maimonides to aver that sacrificial worship represented a temporary concession to the ancient Israelites' need to conform to the ritual systems of surrounding peoples, and that these ritual laws therefore had lost their religious validity. Later in the chapter, Biale even picks up Freud's idiosyncratic version of the biblical Moses as an Egyptian prince murdered by the Hebrews, and he ends by discussing secular Zionism's appropriation of biblical themes relating to the land of Israel as the historical Jewish homeland.

In the section on the political and cultural dimensions of modern conceptions of Jewish peoplehood, Biale calls attention to the contractual in contrast to the covenantal dimension of Jewish law, the difference being that the former "is not grounded in revelation" whereas the latter was seen as divine in origin. The contractual aspect is therefore "a distinctly secular theory of the power of the community" to exert its legal authority over its members in certain critical matters (p. 94). He recalls use of the fashionable term "race" by 19th-century figures such as Moses Hess and Israel Zangwill—for a while, until it was discredited by antisemitism, reference to a

"Jewish race" was a means of alluding to the family-like nature of the Jewish bond as "a community of descent," biological rather than theological in nature (p. 107).

Biale attempts, sometimes in a rather forced way, to create a genealogy of the secular view of the nonexistence of a transcendent God. He explains this as an unintended consequence of Maimonides' conception of negative attributes, as evidenced, for instance, in a ploy by Kant's disciple Solomon Maimon, whom Biale deems one of "Spinoza's children": "Using a classically Maimonidean argument, Maimon claimed that the statement 'God exists' is no more meaningful than the statement 'God does not exist'" (p. 32). Biale calls attention to Hayim Nahman Bialik's use of *ayn* (in the Ayn Sof of the Kabbalah) in the latter's essay "Revelation and Concealment in Language." The poet "argued that language cannot reveal the essence of things but, on the contrary, language itself stands as a barrier before them" and goes on to conclude that "the void takes the place of God; the void *is* God" (p. 49). (Biale improbably labels this a reincarnation of Gnosticism.) The Jewish revolt against the Jewish God is most blatant in Shaul Tchernichovsky's defiant extolling of the beauty represented by the pagan god Apollo. In these and other instances, the subversion of traditional Jewish concepts means that the past is used by turning it upside down.

All modern Jewish movements—especially Reform Judaism and cultural Zionism—have constructed genealogies to place themselves in the historic Jewish timeline. The ancient rabbis did so in Avot 1.1, which traces the (Oral) Torah from Moses at Sinai to the Prophets to the Men of the Great Assembly, bypassing the priests entirely. Moses de Leon, in the Zohar, presents his Kabbalah as the teaching of Shimon bar Yohai, who lived about a thousand years earlier. Why should secular humanistic Judaism not do the same?

Locating pre-modern Jewish roots of distinctively modern ideas enables Biale to show that certain nonobservant (or even anti-religious) Jews indirectly affirmed their Jewishness by a universalizing of Jewish particularism in order to render it compatible with contemporary modernity.[2] *Not in the Heavens* calls attention to a history of modernization different from the paths constructed by other religious traditions. With its lack of a dogmatic theology, Judaism might be said to have been more open to secular possibilities than Christianity, where faith is so central.

The limitation of Biale's method is that it relegates to an implied background the context in which the critical ideas came into focus—for example, Aristotelianism in the case of Maimonides; Cartesian philosophy in the case of Spinoza; Kantianism in the case of Solomon Maimon; modern science and the Enlightenment, without which the rise of militant secularism cannot be understood; and above all fin-de-siècle cultural nationalism. Thus, several generations of supposedly "assimilated" Jews can be fit into Jewish as well as general intellectual history, despite (or because of) their "heretical" opinions about the Jewish God, the canonized Torah, or the people of Israel. What remains an open—and troubling—question is whether Jewish secularism, in and of itself, can sustain Jewish culture and history, or whether it is merely a bow to the past by those on the way out.

ROBERT M. SELTZER
Hunter College of the City University of New York

Notes

1. Use of the term "genealogy" in this sense was popularized by Michel Foucault in *The Archeology of Knowledge* (1969), though it goes back to Nietzsche's *Genealogy of Morals* (1887).

2. In his epilogue, Biale acknowledges the attenuation of secularist ideologies in the wake of the Holocaust and the establishment of the state of Israel, and among recent acculturated generations of American Jews.

Leonid Livak, *The Jewish Persona in the European Imagination: A Case of Russian Literature*. Stanford: Stanford University Press, 2010. xi + 498 pp.

Recent years have seen a growing academic interest in Jewish-Russian cultural contacts, as expressed in a continuing series of conferences and publications. However, the bulk of research has mainly revolved around the affinity of Jewish literature, thought, and politics to Russian culture. In a nutshell, we can label this tendency as an attempt both to map Jewish-Russian cultural identity and to understand the integration of Jews in Russian society, politics, and economics. Discussion of the *Jewish* component in Jewish-Russian contacts has been based on the assumption that the hegemonic, imperial Russian culture exerted a one-directional influence on traditional-national Jewish culture. Thus, while the Jewish exposure to Russian culture has been widely discussed, there is a profound lack of research concerning the other side of the relationship, namely, the presence of Jewish components in Russian culture. This vacuum begs the question whether Jewish-Russian cultural contacts can be considered a dialogue at all, if a dialogue is taken, in the Bachtinian sense, as communication between two equal partners. This is the key question in Leonid Livak's book *The Jewish Persona in the European Imagination: A Case of Russian Literature*.

Livak opens his book with a detailed discussion of the perception of the Jew as the ultimate "Other" in European Christian culture, which dates back to the very beginning of European civilization. In light of the persistent Jewish refusal to accept the superiority of Christianity, the Jew remains fundamentally apart from the surrounding culture. Livak outlines the two contradicting roles of the Jew in the Christian narrative: Helper (heralding redemption) versus Opponent (delaying redemption). These two strands are also present in 19th- and 20th-century Russian literature.

As an example, Livak first cites Gogol's epoch of *Taras Bul'ba*, in which Yankel, a Jewish peddler, accompanies Taras, the Kozak chief, on his way to martyrdom in the war with the Poles. Taras' martyrdom marks a renewal of the Christian covenant with God and the victory of Orthodox Christianity, whereas Yankel personifies modern antisemitic stereotypes of the Jews as greedy and manipulative. Antisemitic stereotypes are also the starting point of Livak's discussion of the representation of Jews in two stories written by Ivan Turgenev, "Zhid" and "Neschastnaia" (Wretched one). To his mind, these two texts express Turgenev's empathy to Judeophilic tendencies among 19th-century European liberal intelligentsia. For example, in "Zhid" there is a negative depiction of Girshel the Jewish peddler, who is willing to spy for whoever pays him more money and who even pimps his daughter, Sara. However,

Sara's portrayal shows a total identification with Jewish suffering. The combination of Jewish misery and violated femininity is also found in "Neschastnaia," which describes the hardships of a talented pianist born of an affair between a Russian aristocrat and a Jewish woman. Here, Livak claims, Turgenev tries to answer Wagner's intellectual antisemitism and particularly his infamous monograph *Jews in Music*.

Livak offers fascinating interpretations of Anton Chekhov's stories "Tina" and "Skripka Rotshil'da" (Rothchild's violin), in which he finds evidence of antisemitic prejudice on the part of the author—Chekhov's liberal image notwithstanding. The protagonist of "Tina" is a young Jewish woman who is both a loan shark and a courtesan with a literary salon. According to Livak, this story should be seen as a blatant attack against Jews' increased presence in the European economy and culture. In contrast, "Skripka Rotshil'da," which portrays the sad history of a poor Russian coffin-maker who dies shortly after giving his violin to a Jewish musician, hints at a possible Russian-Jewish dialogue but is still contaminated by a Wagnerian discontent concerning the Jewish "invasion" of music and the arts.

The last part of *The Jewish Persona in the European Imagination* deals with the influence of Russian literary representations of Jews on the works of Russian Jewish writers such as Isaac Babel and Iurii Felzen. Livak claims that the allegory of the Jewish pogrom in "Moi pervyi gus'" (My first goose), let alone the satire on Jewish decadent bourgeoisie in "Guy de Maupassant," are a clear manifestation of Babel's intention to disguise his Jewish subjectivity, whereas three novellas written by Felzen (*Deceit, Happiness*, and *Letters about Lermontov*) indicate the marginality of Jewish themes in Russian émigré literature, whose foundations are (anti-Jewish) Christian thought. According to Livak, Babel's and Felzen's works point to the impossibility of a true Jewish-Russian intellectual merger, even in the wake of the internationalist revolution.

The first question that comes to mind after reading Livak's book concerns the choice of texts that can reflect the place of Jews in Russian literary imagination. All of the texts discussed by Livak do, in fact, respond to the growing presence of Jews in the Russian cultural and political discourse. Furthermore, most of these texts, as Livak justly notes, are clearly interrelated: Gogol's *Taras Bul'ba*, Turgenev's "Zhid," and Babel's "Moi pervyi gus'," on the one hand, (sympathetic to Jewish suffering) and Turgenev's "Neschastnaia," Chekov's two short stories and Babel's "Guy de Maupassant," on the other (with antisemitic tendencies). Detecting this inter-textuality, Livak is in a position to note variations in the Russian public discourse on the Jewish question, from Gogol's traditional theological approach to Turgenev's Judeophilic liberalism and Chekhov's partially hidden antisemitism. With regard to Babel, Livak comes to a rather controversial conclusion, namely, that the founding father of Russian Jewish literature internalized the suspicious attitude toward the Jews. The consequence was a feeling of Jewish self-hatred on Babel's part, a perception that, in order to be accepted as a "Russian" author, he had to rid himself of his Jewish identity. In Livak's view, this strategy undermines the very possibility of "Russian Jewish" authorship.

However, a reading of other stories by Babel, among them "Gedalya," "Rabbi," and "The Rabbi's Son," indicates that he sought to make plain his Jewish-Russian subjectivity and authorship. To Babel, the Jewish component is invaluable when

establishing an internationalist revolutionary culture. His Jewish characters—
Gedalya, the founder of the ideal International; or a rabbi's son, the last scion of a
famous Hasidic dynasty, who, not unlike Jesus, sacrifices himself for humanity—
represent the revolution's prophetic, biblical universality. Furthermore, if Jewish literature is defined as texts written by Jews for Jews, and which deals with Jewish
topics, then Babel's works belong to a quintessential Russian Jewish literary tradition. To be sure, the acculturation of Jews to Russian culture was accompanied by an
abandonment of writing on specifically Jewish themes. Notwithstanding, the difficulty of maintaining a Russian-Jewish dialogue stems mainly from the marginality of
the Jewish theme in Russian literature. The "Jewish question" was of course a central
issue in Russian journalistic writing. Yet the examples of Jewish themes in Russian
literature per se are quite scarce, and most of them have found their way into this
book.

RAFI TSIRKIN-SADAN
Columbia University

Shachar Pinsker, *Literary Passports: The Making of Modernist Hebrew Fiction in
    Europe*. Stanford: Stanford University Press, 2011. 487 pp.
Michael Weingrad, *American Hebrew Literature: Writing Jewish National Identity in
    the United States*. Syracuse: Syracuse University Press, 2010. 275 pp.

Academic studies of modern Jewish literature have for a number of years engaged
and problematized the idea of a literary "center." Both of the books under review—
Michael Weingrad's *American Hebrew Literature: Writing Jewish National Identity
in the United States* and Shachar Pinsker's *Literary Passports: The Making of
Modernist Hebrew Fiction in Europe*—speak to the shifting communities of Hebrew
authors whose lives and works intersect with the geographic centers and peripheries
in which they resided.

Michael Weingrad's study of American Hebrew literature explores the small community of American Hebraists, focusing primarily on the first half of the 20th century. This is an often overlooked group of writers involved in a larger intellectual and
cultural enterprise, that of seeding Hebrew language and letters in the United States,
to which its devotees applied singular amounts of energy and dedication. In its seven
essays, the book sketches out some of the primary literary figures, landmark texts,
and noteworthy common themes. Weingrad has read widely and enthusiastically in
these authors' often varied writing (belletristic, critical, and personal—the latter
including diaries and letters), and this enthusiasm may have led him to assume that
his readers would share his feelings. We are told that these texts are important; we are
shown exemplary samples; we are invited to sympathize with a committed group of
cultural activists struggling against what we know are rather insuperable odds. But at
the same time, we are not told why their work—and struggle—is important; we are
not given the stakes of the discussion; nor are we shown how this work fits into the
scholarly landscape. For example, the American Hebraists' work manifests a rather

conservative literary aesthetic of committed Zionists who regarded themselves as sojourners in America, surrounded by far more numerous Yiddish urban modernists to whom they were linked by shared European origins and mother tongue but with whom they often strongly disagreed in matters of literary taste and political affiliation. This fascinating dynamic is mentioned in numerous places, but left unexplored. Such lacunae leave the reader longing for something more.

The first chapter surveys the discontents of Hebraism in America, focusing on the tensions connected with the very idea of Jewish national commitment in a nation defined by a transcendence of such parochial allegiances. "Americanness" is something of an obsession with the American Hebraists: its freedoms were exhilarating, like its natural vistas, but also a source of what they saw as profound, indeed existential, dangers, including assimilation and an all-corrupting materialism. These dangers were most consistently symbolized in the city, New York. Weingrad pursues this love-hate relationship with urban Jewish America in presenting three poems by Shimon Ginzburg (1890–1944). While interesting on their own for readers unfamiliar with the kinds of content and style used by American Hebrew writers, the poems are given to us with relatively little context aside from some preliminary biographical comment. In the absence of further explanation, one is left wondering just how good these poems are; even if we are told that they achieve a certain effect or else are of uneven quality—statements that we have to take on faith—little indication is given of what is at stake in paying such close attention to them.

The next chapter, dealing with the relationship between American Hebrew literature and modernism, is the best argued section of the book. In it, the predominant reading of American Hebraism is as a transatlantic branch of the Haskalah, or Jewish Enlightenment. Modernism, especially the Yiddish-inflected, big-voiced metropolitan version of it encountered by the Hebrew writers in New York, is the natural antagonist to the conservative, classicizing (that is, biblicizing), and even neo-Romantic cultural tendencies of these writers. However, given the lived experiences of many of the Hebrew writers, their engagement with the urban poetics and thematics of their fellow Jews could not be ignored. One result is a kind of "literary schizophrenia" (p. 36), as Weingrad calls it: a reined-in poetry, on the one hand, and an often truly experimental prose, on the other.

Weingrad goes on to outline a series of essayistic exchanges involving two of the central figures of American Hebrew letters, Shlomo Grodzensky (1904–1972) and Hillel Bavli (1893–1961), which are themselves a kind of intellectual prelude to a larger debate in Jewish letters between Hebrew writers in America and their counterparts in Palestine—the so-called "Americanness debate" (which would involve writers such as Ginzburg and the young Shimon Halkin, perhaps the most famous of the American Hebraists). In large part a debate about modernism and its perceived role in nation-building, the back-and-forth about poetic "purity" or "ugliness," the legitimacy of poetic trends, and ideological freedom reveals something interesting about how communities of writers construct their own identities. One can sense in the debate an acute (if subtextual) resentment concerning the deflation of the potential for an American center as an outcome of the growth in importance of an actual Palestinian center for Hebrew literature—one whose aesthetic was in close conversation with those trends in European modernism that the American Hebraists found difficult to stomach.

The ideological tension of the second chapter dissipates in the essay that follows. Indeed, the third chapter, dealing with the image of Native Americans, points up many of the problems with the book as a whole. There is very little scholarly apparatus or critical engagement. The readings are presented without any explanation of their theoretical or methodological underpinnings. And most often these are not so much readings, in an analytic sense, as they are plot summaries. The chapter presents three works of poetry featuring central Native American characters—B. N. Silkiner's "Mul ohel Timurah" (Before the tent of Timurah), Y. Efros' "Vigvamim shotekim" (Silent wigwams), and E. Lisitzky's "Medurot doakhot"[1] (Dying campfires). The presentations lack balance, evidence little comparative engagement, and drape only a thin veil of analysis over the plot summaries. While we are told that the image of Native Americans is one of the most significant features of American Hebrew literature, we are not told why only works written in the style of epic poetry have been chosen, and only three (albeit significant) works, at that. There is clearly a tension between what these Hebrew writers sought to achieve in their poetry and in their prose, but there is little explanation of why authors chose their preferred genres. The image of Native Americans is offered as a touchstone for ideas about communal cohesion, national identity, ethnic distinctiveness, and the like, especially against threats both internal and external. But aside from discussion of Werner Sollors' justly important research, and reference to (but little engagement with) Alan Trachtenberg's *Shades of Hiawatha* (2005), there is almost no mention of the wealth of critical scholarly resources on this and related subjects. For example, what benefits are to be had from Rachel Rubinstein's most appositely titled *Members of the Tribe: Native America in the Jewish Imagination* (2010), or Maeera Shreiber's investigation of Jewish-American poetics, *Singing in a Strange Land* (2007), or Joan Shelley Rubin's *Songs of Ourselves* (2010), a detailed study of how poetry was read and used in America at precisely the same time as the American Hebraists' heyday? Unfortunately, these are paths not taken.

In the next chapter we find three interdependent images quickly touched upon: the Hebraists' use of the image of rural life; the small town; and Protestant literacy in the Bible in rural and small-town locales. Again, Weingrad takes us through a selection of works dwelling on these themes, most taking the form: "The plot of *X* runs as follows." Such imagery reflects these writers' rather vexed obsession with Americanness. However, Weingrad barely pursues the interesting question of how this relates to the authors' primary commitments to Jewishness and Zionism.

The fifth chapter considers the image of Mordecai Manuel Noah in American Hebrew literature. Noah is a curious and intriguing figure from Jacksonian America who served for a time as U.S. consul in Tunis and had the improbable idea of turning Grand Island, New York, into a temporary Jewish national way-station to Palestine. It takes little imagination to see why Noah fascinated American Hebrew writers. But almost from the start, the reader finds the chapter confusing. Early on we read, "It is not that the Hebraists devoted obsessive attention to Noah, certainly not compared with their attention to the figure of the American Indian, an even more central motif for American Hebraist self-understanding" (p. 145). In that case, why would a chapter devoted to Noah demand 43 pages when a chapter devoted to an even "more central motif" gets 29 (and covers only three poems)? It is an odd choice on its own terms. And it is made stranger still given that, outside of two primary works by American Hebraists on the subject (Harry Sackler's play *Mashiakh, nosakh ameri-kah* [Messiah, American-style], and Yochanan Twersky's novel *Eifo Ararat?* [Where is Ararat?]), Weingrad spends several pages outlining a story by Israel Zangwill (hardly an American writer!) before concluding the chapter with discussions of Ben Katchor's recent graphic novel *The Jew of New York*—a work in English—and the Israeli writer Nava Semel's 2005 novel *Iyisrael* (also known as *Isralsland*). These are interesting texts, and ones that certainly deal with Mordecai Noah, but they are not elements of the corpus of American Hebrew belles lettres. Although Weingrad does not define what are the necessary attributes of an "American Hebrew writer," surely these last three individuals do not qualify.

The sixth chapter poses another intriguing subject: a comparison of Shimon Halkin and Gabriel Preil. These are two of the most famous, and least representative, American Hebraists: one an experimental novelist and a committed and vocal Zionist, the other a modernist poet (in Yiddish as well) of retiring demeanor. While this unexpected pairing offers manifold opportunities to flesh out the numerous (topical, generic, ideological, aesthetic, biographical, and sociological, among others) tensions and complexities of American Hebrew, Weingrad again simply fails to follow through.

The final chapter is based on an essay the author wrote for *Commentary*, a presentation of the afterlife of Hebrew literature in America after the implosion of the American "center" in the 1940s. Weingrad gives the examples of Eisig Silberschlag, Arnold Band, Chana Kleiman, and Chana Farmelant. (The last two are additionally significant because, as Weingard rightly notes, they were some of the few women among the American Hebraists.) These writers are all intriguing late blossoms of a cultural movement that attempted to create a durable infrastructure of Hebrew-language-based cultural institutions, and whose far-reaching ambition was belied by the rhetoric of America as a sojourning "refuge." It is curious, then, that Weingrad chooses to designate a contemporary poet, Robert Whitehill (b. 1947), as a "last Mohican." As a teenager, Whitehill, the child of an assimilated family, taught himself Hebrew; he later began to write modern, Israeli-inflected Hebrew poetry. The interest and importance of his work notwithstanding, Whitehill is by no means a representative or even a literary descendant of the American Hebraist movement.

This book has its moments of insight and it does bring to the fore a number of texts that deserve more literary attention. It is simply unfortunate that Weingrad does not provide the depth of analysis his subject demands. This fact is put into sharper focus by the almost simultaneous appearance of Alan Mintz's *Sanctuary in the Wilderness: A Critical Introduction to American Hebrew Poetry* (2011), with its meticulous, nuanced, and detailed analyses of the major American Hebrew poets and the central ideas and trends they pursue and investigate.

By contrast, Shachar Pinsker's *Literary Passports: The Making of Modernist Hebrew Fiction in Europe* is a deft and dense analysis of one of the most important aspects of modern Hebrew literary history—the modernist Hebrew republic of letters in Europe in the first third of the 20th century as a distinctly and (almost by definition) multi-city and multinational experience. Pinsker pursues this topic in three parts: (1) a tour of some of the primary cities of modernist Hebrew fiction—those that feature prominently either as subjects in the literature itself or in the lives of its writers; (2) the role of innovations in the treatment of sexuality and gender; and (3) the treatment of religion and religious tradition. These are well-chosen rubrics for fleshing out both the complexities and innovations of these often challenging works because they coexist with equal importance in European modernism, a literary landscape in which Pinsker is quite rightly at pains to situate Hebrew modernism.

From the outset this book makes an astute choice: it displaces ideology, especially political ideology, from the first tier of essential analytical components. First and foremost it deals with works of literature *as* works of literature, not as political tracts, where, too often, literariness takes a back seat to the elaboration of political stakes. Moreover, this displacement is motivated by the two essential elements singled out by Pinsker. The first is the "restless mobility" of writers who, almost as a rule, moved from city to city and from country to country, often creating temporary "centers" of Hebrew literary creativity in places where a number of them happened to settle at any given time. The second is the so-called "inward turn" in the literature itself, which "involved a drastic change in what was represented in fiction and its modes of representation and expression" (p. 14), namely the psychological and emotional landscape of the Jewish intellectual. Itinerary is therefore related to both form and content, to both psychological self-exploration and linguistic and literary experimentation.

These explorations and experiments are part and parcel of a larger trend that forms the subtext of the volume, namely, the relationship between Hebrew modernism and wider European modernism. In reading this book, one realizes the degree to which modernist Hebrew fiction was a distinct inflection of European fin-de-siècle culture. As Pinsker very rightly notes, one needs to focus not on the model of "influence"—which presumes European innovators and Jewish copycats—but rather on "participation" (p. 20). The importance of such a participatory model, in which Jewish writers were neither "catching up" to European trends nor "influenced" by them but instead were participating in the modernist literary-cultural complex, lies in the fact that, as Pinsker astutely observes, it includes those moments in which Jewish writing was "anticipatory"—that is to say, instances in which modernist literary trends appear in Hebrew *before* their other European literary counterparts.

The first part of *Literary Passports* sketches out what Pinsker calls the "geography of modernist Hebrew fiction" (p. 36), with chapters on two urban pairs (Odessa and Warsaw, and Homel and Lvov [Lemberg]), as well as an exploration of London, Vienna, and Berlin. In this panoramic overview, Pinsker nicely highlights the diversity, creativity, and distinctiveness of the various "centers," outlining the shifting casts of characters and offering readings of some of the exemplary literary works produced in or about these places. What rather gets submerged or lost in these journalistic profiles and selected pieces is the shifting character of the communicative, periodic, and familial *network* that connects them—the overlay that brings the disparate projects into, if not perfect harmony, then consonance.

When Pinsker focuses his attention on the literary aspects of his subject he is on firm ground, describing how, in this modernist literature, "the city as physical space gave way to the city as a state of mind" (p. 31). Given that feelings of loneliness, estrangement, and dislocation predominate in the modern experience of urban space, Jews become ideal exemplars of modernist urban subjectivity. On the one hand, in the wake of these fine readings, one is left much better equipped to contextualize the more in-depth readings in the rest of the book. On the other hand, that literary format is better equipped to raise important questions than to provide definitive answers. For example, Pinsker offers a fascinating comparison of Odessa and Warsaw as literary centers. Odessa is described as having become rapidly outmoded as a literary home. Warsaw, by contrast, was "overly rooted," having in effect too much Jewish history—especially for the Hebrew modernists, for whom wandering was an essential experience. These intriguing observations, merely hinted at, deserve much more expansive treatment. If Pinsker is correct in his description of a representative attitude of local literati, noting of the writer and critic Ya'akov Fichman that his "heart was focused . . . on the city [Warsaw] itself" (p. 51), why indeed were there so few Hebrew literary representations of that city, a fact that Pinsker himself acknowledges?

The section on Vienna is perhaps the most successful of the portraits, especially its analysis of how, through the works of Gershon Shofman and David Fogel, "the cityscape itself becomes a mental space" (p. 100). Pinsker revels in the invigorating novelty of Fogel's novel *Married Life*, in which there are "a staggering multiplicity of forms and actions that we experience as a seemingly endless parade of urban scenes" (p. 100). For these writers, with their wandering sensibilities and biographies, it often seems that the literature *itself* functions as a substitute for a "real" home.

Pinsker reserves considerable energy for the last sketch, which is devoted to Berlin, one of the most important expatriate literary way-stations in the interwar period for Hebrew and Yiddish authors. His persistent focus on the image of the café and the importance of café culture, which he describes as a kind of literary-cultural "thirdspace," is a useful, if circumscribed, access point. Pinsker spends a good deal of time on Berlin's generic concentration on the modernist long poem (*poema*). (His perceptive analysis of the poetry, though, is a bit more of a teaser than a help in a book devoted to modernist fiction.) His perspective then abruptly shifts back to prose as he concentrates on the Yiddish novelist Dovid Bergelson and the Hebrew writer Sh.Y. Agnon. The choice of the Bergelson–Agnon pair is not explained (other than both being popularly associated with Berlin), nor are they really appreciably compared. One is left asking why, all of a sudden, a Yiddish writer is being offered as a counterpoint to a Hebrew writer—nowhere else in these urban case studies, nor indeed really in the book as a whole, are such Yiddish counterpoints pursued.

The second section of Pinsker's book, on sexuality and gender, offers a terrific opening gambit, making use of the importance of the work (and indeed the image) of Oscar Wilde for the development of Hebrew modernism. This choice places front and center precisely the role of sexuality and gender, and especially the "crisis in masculinity," as a crucial constituent in that modernism. Pinsker's thesis is that the "inward turn" in the fiction was accompanied by an equally deep and exploratory "sexual turn," which was not only internally motivated but also catalyzed by intimate literary contact with European texts, especially late 19th-century aestheticism, symbolism, and decadence (p. 158). To set his thesis up, Pinsker first presents the traditionally accepted scholarly framework for dealing with this "crisis of masculinity" in modern(ist) Hebrew literature—notably, its relationship to the ubiquitous figure of the *talush*, or physically and spiritually "uprooted" intellectual—and explains why this framework is inadequate and inapplicable to much of modernist Hebrew literature.

The following chapters pursue extended close readings of primary texts on the themes of companionship among men, the relationship of the erotic with the image of writing itself, and the presentation of the "new Jewish woman." All of this Pinsker does with theoretical precision and a sensitive ear for the language of the texts. At times, however, some of his points are just a bit overwrought. For example, much is made of the fetishization of, and eroticized gazing at, body parts as synecdoches for people. Pinsker sees this as an innovation in Hebrew modernism, though surely body-part catalogs have been an easily eroticized trope in Hebrew literature since the Song of Songs. More useful in such cases would be a strong ligature between this and the third section (on the uses of tradition and religiosity). Or take the important discussion of homosocial desire, in which Pinsker focuses on the image of the love triangle as representative of the homosocial. This makes sense in the larger sweep of the "participatory" model. However, investigation of the traditional study-house (*beit midrash*) culture as an equally important site of complex relationships between men would be most apposite both here and in connection with the third section.

The third section most consistently unpacks the book's thesis that modernist Hebrew fiction is a distinctive idiom of European fin-de-siècle culture. In fine, "what distinguished the modern Jewish 'search for a usable past' ready for reinvention [...] was the ever-present tension between a desire to break away from traditional religious Jewish identity altogether and the impulse to create a new Jewish culture that would serve as a kind of 'substitute' for it" (p. 277). In some form or another, this is the line of argument pursued in all of the chapters of this section. Pinsker begins by outlining the focus of the "transitional" figures—Hayim Nahman Bialik, Micha Berdichevsky, and Yehudah Leib Peretz—on rabbinic texts and sources, on the one hand, and Hasidic texts and sources, on the other, in a twin, if tense and ambivalent, process of secularization and nationalization of the material. The important contribution here is Pinsker's tracing of the significance of these transitional figures as canonical figures. It is precisely in the tension, ambiguity, and opacity of these imperfectly worked-out systems of thought that Jewish modernism found its most fertile ground. Pinsker goes on to discuss how the modernist prose rejected the approach of the transitional generation by reworking traditional materials and discourses from within.

Pinsker is largely successful in his argument and his analyses. Because of their depth and sensitivity, his readings deserve to be part of the necessary scholarly apparatus for understanding these texts. There is reason to have wished that Pinsker might have chosen to expand his choice of authors. His triumvirate of Brenner, Shofman, and Uri Nissan Gnessin—while understandable from the point of view of quality (though some of Brenner's work, especially, may be due for a reappraisal) and their place in Hebrew literary historiography—is overrepresented. There are voices in need of recovery that would doubtless bolster his argument. Furthermore, Pinsker sidelines Yiddish, again for obvious and to some extent understandable reasons; Hebrew, not Yiddish, is the subject of the book. Yet Yiddish is perhaps too much the silent partner here. Given that many of these Hebraists were also accomplished Yiddish authors, any appraisal of their work in Hebrew is incomplete without at least some consideration of the influence of Yiddish.[2] At the same time, Pinsker's book makes a real contribution on the Hebrew side, especially as a participant in a trend of reevaluation and close literary analysis of Jewish modernisms. Indeed, *Literary*

Passports offers a compelling case for what is lost when scholarship outside of Jewish studies ignores these literatures.

Hebrew literary studies have long been dominated by a narrative in which the peripheral diaspora and its cultural attainments could only be perfected after the longed-for return of Jews to Palestine. Placing Weingrad's and Pinsker's works side by side usefully highlights both the myth of such a single center and the deficiencies of this historiographic model of monolithic center versus disparaged periphery. The communities and networks of writers and cultural activists in Europe and America were too dynamic for that model's static overlay. But while Weingrad's account falls short of explaining the stakes of worrying about the American writers, Pinsker's book shows us why, if anything, European Hebrew modernism was one of the great productive, innovative, and sophisticated corpora of Jewish literature.

JORDAN FINKIN
University of Illinois, Urbana-Champaign

Notes

1. Although the transliteration here follows Weingrad, one might question his decision to use "Israeli" (Sephardi) transliteration, given the fact that the Hebraists made use of the Ashkenazi pronunciation of Hebrew, with all the attendant implications for prosody and scansion.

2. See, for example, Allison Schachter's recent *Diasporic Modernisms: Hebrew and Yiddish Literature in the Twentieth Century* (New York: 2011), which encompasses both languages masterfully.

Art Spiegelman, *The Complete Maus*, 25th anniversary edition. New York: Pantheon, 2011. 296 pp.
Art Spiegelman, *MetaMaus*. New York: Pantheon, 2011. 300 pp., plus DVD.

Art Spiegelman's *Maus: A Survivor's Tale*, initially published in a variety of formats between 1980 and 1991, is now widely recognized as a landmark work on several counts. *Maus* is hailed as an exemplar of the use of comics—or "comix," as Spiegelman prefers to term the medium, for its "co-mixing" of text and graphics—to create a work of complex sophistication in a medium hitherto largely derogated (at least in the West) as lowbrow, frivolous, and juvenile. Many scholars of art and literature regard *Maus* both as a major work in its own right and as a signpost of signal shifts in American Jewish culture or of Holocaust remembrance. *Maus* is also recognized as a key work in the creative engagement of contemporary artists and writers with issues of memory and of personal and family history. The broad acclaim for *Maus* has elevated Spiegelman's stature from an artist little known outside the milieu of avant-garde cartooning to a figure of international renown. In addition to having become the doyen of comics and graphic novels, Spiegelman is sought after for his views on Holocaust art, literature, and other forms of its remembrance.

Maus relates the prewar and wartime experiences of the artist's parents, Vladek and Anja Spiegelman, both of whom were Polish Jewish survivors of the Holocaust, imbricated with their son's account of his efforts to learn about this story from his father (the artist's mother had committed suicide in 1968 at the age of 56) and to render it as a book-length comic. This work had a long process of creation, beginning with short, preliminary pieces printed in collections of avant-garde comics ("Maus," in *Funny Animals #1*, in 1972; "Prisoner on Hell Planet," in *Short Order Comix #1*, in 1973). These efforts were followed by years of research, centered on many hours of Spiegelman's interviews with his father, which the artist recorded and transcribed. After beginning to draft the book in 1978, Spiegelman published the first installment of *Maus* in *RAW* (an avant-garde comics serial founded and co-edited by the artist and his wife, Françoise Mouly) in 1980; the final installment appeared a little more than a decade later, printed in the English-language Jewish weekly *The Forward*, which ran the entire second part of *Maus*. The first volume of *Maus: A Survivor's Tale* (*My Father Bleeds History*) was issued in book form in 1986; the second volume (*And Here My Troubles Began*) followed in 1991. The complete *Maus* was subsequently issued as a two-volume boxed set and then, in 1996, as a single volume. In addition to appearing serially in individual installments and in different book editions, *Maus* has been published in a score of translations and was issued as a CD-ROM in 1994.

The protracted process of creating *Maus* and its multiform presentation has, in turn, engendered unusually extensive interest in both the finished work and the course of its creation. In 1985, before the first volume of *Maus* was published, the critic Ken Tucker wrote an essay on Spiegelman's work-in-progress for the *New York Times Book Review*, a most unusual subject for this widely read weekly publication.[1] Shortly before the first volume of *Maus* appeared, some of Spiegelman's working drawings were displayed in an exhibition on contemporary Jewish art at the Jewish Museum in New York. A solo show, *Making Maus*, opened at the city's Museum of Modern Art in 1991, the first of several similar exhibitions presented by museums around the world. The creation of *Maus* was also the subject of a ZDF/BBC documentary in 1987; another documentary, *Art Spiegelman, Traits de Mémoire* (also released under the title *The Art of Spiegelman*), aired on European television in 2010. This special attention to the making of *Maus* responds not only to its subject matter or the artist's provocative decision to portray all the characters as animals (Jews are mice, Germans are cats, Poles are pigs, and so on), but also to its form. Spiegelman's creative process of uncovering and relating the story of his parents' past is integral to the narrative. Moreover, the initial publishing of *Maus* in serial installments underscored the processual nature of the work's creation for its first readers, whose encounter with *Maus* extended over many months.

The original reception of *Maus*, in the wake of the first volume's publication, was mixed. Some critics found the work offensive and denounced its use of the "vulgar" medium of cartooning to address the ontologically daunting subject of the Holocaust, or they inveighed against Spiegelman's depicting of Jews as mice, with all its disturbing resonances (including the association of Jews with vermin in Nazi antisemitic propaganda). Others found the genre of the work baffling, even as they admired its contents; indeed, *Maus* has variously received awards as an outstanding work of "biography/autobiography," "graphic album," "Jewish writing," and "fiction." The work soon attracted a wide readership and also drew attention from scholars and critics in a variety of fields. *Maus* continues to generate interest in the academy. A search of the RAMBI database of recent Jewish studies scholarship generates a list of some 70 essays on the work, written in French, German, Hebrew, Italian, Polish, and Spanish, in addition to a preponderance in English (including a collection of essays on *Maus* published in 2003),[2] by scholars of anthropology, art, history, literature, psychology, religion, and sociology, as well as Holocaust studies and Jewish studies.[3]

Part of the attraction that *Maus* holds for scholars is Spiegelman's self-consciousness as an artist, which is integral to his approach to creating comics. This self-consciousness is informed by an extensive knowledge of the medium's history and an ongoing attention to its theorization (as, for instance, in his analyzing how the interrelation of text and image structures the narrative within the modular unit of the page). Such self-reflection is foundational to the structure of *Maus*, which interrelates the making of the work with the work itself in a double helix of narratives: Vladek's and Anya's lives in the 1930s and 1940s; Art's pursuit of their stories in the 1970s and 1980s. In this respect, *Maus* has always been "meta."

Marking the 25th anniversary of the first publication of *Maus* in book form, *MetaMaus* provides scholars and devotees of Spiegelman's work with a trove of resources for contemplating the creation and reception of what the cover of this new publication vaunts as a "modern classic." In addition to 300 pages of interviews, transcripts, images, a family tree, and a timeline, *MetaMaus* comes with a DVD that hyperlinks each page of *Maus* with related sketches, audio recordings, video footage, and other documentary materials (much like the earlier CD-ROM version), and also provides a search mechanism for finding particular words in the text.

MetaMaus revisits the process of researching, planning, and executing *Maus* well after the fact, remediating elements of this process—working sketches, interview transcripts, research notes, documents, diverse sources of inspiration—in an artfully designed collage, correlated with Spiegelman's retrospection on the work's realization and reception. The artist is present as creator of both *Maus* and *MetaMaus* and, at the same time, as a subject of attention in his own right. Discussion of the work's creative process is integral to *Maus*, especially in Part II, which includes an extended discussion of the challenges Spiegelman encountered both in making the comic and in addressing public responses to it (*The Complete Maus*, pp. 201–207). In *MetaMaus*, however, Spiegelman's creativity is scrutinized not within the realization of a work centered on relating his parents' story. Rather, Spiegelman himself is now the center of attention, albeit refracted through an interviewer's questions and complicated by the artist's role as his own archivist, analyst, and editor.

This shift of attention is reflected in the contrasting formats of *Maus* and *MetaMaus*. Whereas the former is a tightly integrated comic with a distinct, consistent aesthetic, the latter offers a wide-ranging multimedia assemblage of graphic images (many in color, whereas *Maus* is in black and white, except for the cover art), photographs, video footage, sounds, and words. *Maus*, the "modern classic," is both central to *MetaMaus* and (in the pages of the book) at the same time absent; familiarity with the work is assumed. The DVD's digital reproduction of *Maus* places each of its pages at the center of linked source materials and comments, somewhat comparable to digital versions of the Talmud that reproduce the searchable text in the form of the *tzurat hadaf*, supplemented with additional commentaries and cross-references to other texts. (In fact, a small selection of critics' essays on *Maus* that is included on the DVD is termed the "Maus Midrash.")

MetaMaus culminates Spiegelman's ongoing self-scrutiny of his masterwork. In 1991, shortly after the second volume of *Maus* was published, I saw him give a public talk, illustrated with slides, about the work's creation and reception. Much of what *MetaMaus* addresses was already in place in that presentation: key questions (Why the Holocaust? Why mice? Why comics?), source materials (ranging from family documents to period antisemitica), the creative process (research, including taped interviews with Vladek and photographs of the artist's 1979 trip to Poland, as well as a wealth of preliminary drawings), and the work's place in Spiegelman's career as an avant-garde cartoonist.

Like *Maus*, *MetaMaus* is founded on interviews, but instead of being the interviewer, Art Spiegelman is now the interviewee (the questions are posed by literary scholar Hillary Chute). And like *Maus*, *MetaMaus* is a family (auto)biography, though centered not on Spiegelman's parents, but on Spiegelman himself. The father of grown children, the artist is now almost the same age that his father was when they recorded their first interviews in 1972. Thus, *MetaMaus* also profiles Art Spiegelman's wife as well as their daughter, Nadja, and son, Dashiell (who, having fallen under the penumbra of celebrity surrounding *Maus*, are all interviewed in *MetaMaus*). As manifest in the timeline that concludes the book, *MetaMaus* tracks a history extending over a century, from 1906 (the year of Vladek Spiegelman's birth) until 2010. In this chronology, 20th-century Jewish life, centered on the Holocaust, merges with its remembrance, as family history merges with the history of its documentation and reception, centered on the career of the artist (including when he received various awards and honorary degrees).

Spiegelman presents *MetaMaus* as "a project I kept resisting," noting that "it was hard to revisit...the book that both 'made' me and has haunted me ever since" (*MetaMaus*, p. 6). Yet the attention that *Maus* and its creator have received has clearly proved irresistible to Spiegelman, feeding the penchant for artistic introspection evinced by *Maus* itself. *MetaMaus* includes several short cartoons by the artist, in which he reflects on the impact that *Maus* has had on his life and work (*MetaMaus*, pp. 8–9, 12–13, 57, 81–82, 156–157). Revisiting the project's reception includes some expression of vindication as well—thus, *MetaMaus* includes a two-page spread reproducing a sheaf of rejection letters that *Maus* had received (*MetaMaus*, pp. 76–77).

More poignantly, *MetaMaus* returns to a primary motivation for the project: Spiegelman's effort to recover the story of his mother, who committed suicide when the artist was 20 years old. "Prisoner on Hell Planet," one of the short works that prefigures *Maus*, offers an expressionistic fantasy in response to his mother's suicide; this four-page comic is incorporated into Part I of *Maus* (*The Complete Maus*, pp. 102–105). Part I culminates with Art's outrage on discovering that Vladek, after his wife's suicide, destroyed the diaries she had kept (*The Complete Maus*, pp. 160–161). *MetaMaus* includes notes from interviews that Spiegelman conducted with women who had known his mother during and after the Second World War (*MetaMaus*,

"Searching for Memories of Anja," pp. 278–288). The DVD accompanying *MetaMaus* includes "Anja's Bookshelf," a selection of books and pamphlets about the Holocaust, published in Europe shortly after the war, that Spiegelman's mother had collected.

MetaMaus provides admirers and scholars of *Maus* with the opportunity to see not only how this rich, complex work was created but also how an artist revisits the act of creation as a(nother) creative act in itself. As an autobiographical project, *MetaMaus* tracks the impact of an internationally renowned work of art on its creator, transforming him from an avant-gardist into the patriarch of comics, as the stature of this medium has been greatly elevated, and into an arbiter not only of this medium but also of Holocaust remembrance and of contemporary Jewish culture. Seldom does a work receive such extensive documentation and analysis—but seldom does a work attract the broad popular and scholarly attention that *Maus* has, and seldom does such a work have behind it a creator so avidly engaged in its scrutiny.

JEFFREY SHANDLER
Rutgers University

Notes

1. Ken Tucker, "Cats, Mice, and History: The Avant-Garde of the Comic Strip," *New York Times Book Review*, 26 May 1985.
2. Deborah R. Geis (ed.), *Considering "Maus": Approaches to Art Spiegelman's "Survivor's Tale" of the Holocaust* (Tuscaloosa: 2003).
3. The database is found online at http://jnul.huji.ac.il/rambi/(searched 27 May 2012).

History, Social Sciences, and Biography

Rebecca T. Alpert, *Out of Left Field: Jews and Black Baseball.* New York: Oxford University Press, 2011. ix + 236 pp.

In this book, two themes of rising prominence in Jewish studies converge: the relations between Jews and other minorities (in this case, the American blacks) and the Jewish dimension in modern sports history. Rebecca T. Alpert's specific subject, to which she has devoted serious research, is the role of Jews in the bad old days of segregation, when black baseball players, rejected by the lily-white major leagues, were obliged to play on black teams, sometimes organized into the so-called "Negro leagues." Given the unique status of baseball as the "national pastime" back in the 1930s and 1940s, the campaign to desegregate it and the eventual addition of Jackie Robinson to the Brooklyn Dodgers' roster in 1947 are of considerable significance in the history of American sports in particular and American race relations in general. In fact, this book performs a useful service in recalling the significance of black baseball teams during the apartheid era in American sports, both amateur and professional.

In truth, the Jewish role in black baseball, as delineated in this study, was limited to the activities of a few prominent owners, investors, booking agents, and promoters, of whom the most famous by far was Abe Saperstein (better known for his activities in the world of black basketball as the boss of the Harlem Globetrotters, but also active on the black baseball scene). In the words of the author, her book tells the story of "how a small group of Jews of different class and national backgrounds negotiated the process of becoming American in the first half of the twentieth century through their involvement in the segregated world of black baseball" (p. 5). It would be nice to report that these men, anxiously climbing the greasy pole of americanization, were attracted to black baseball because of their sympathy with the plight of another despised minority, but this does not appear to be the case. For them, African American baseball was a business, not a cause, a way to make money (according to some hostile black critics) by means of exploiting the labor of black men. The author counters this critique by reminding her readers that they did, after all, employ black men during the depression and that many black athletes were grateful to them for having done so; there is even evidence that in the case of some black ballplayers, including the immortal pitcher Satchel Paige, friendly relations developed between themselves and their Jewish employers.

These Jewish entrepreneurs, along with their non-Jewish colleagues, were deeply involved in black baseball comedy, in promoting comic routines in order to liven up this rather staid game and thereby gain greater public interest. One black team, run by the Jewish promoter Syd Pollack, was called the "Ethiopian Clowns," a name that did not endear him to some in the African American community. Saperstein's Globetrotters, of course, also engaged in comic antics. Alpert, interestingly, locates the roots of this combination of sports and buffoonery in the traditions of white vaudeville, Tin Pan Alley, and black-faced minstrelsy: "In the world of independent baseball, the traditions of black comedy and aesthetics came together with Jewish vaudeville humor and entrepreneurship" (p. 96).

In general, Alpert is good at analyzing the complicated racial politics of black baseball, a field in which blacks and whites co-existed, usually with a degree of unease on the side of the blacks, who thought that this business should be under their control, just as they thought that stores on 125th St. in Harlem should be owned by blacks, not by whites (among the latter were many Jews). She also captures our attention when she claims that the campaign to desegregate baseball and other sports was not championed by the Jewish entrepreneurs, mainly because it threatened their monopoly on black talent. Indeed, as desegregation gathered force, the black leagues faded away. Saperstein was particularly against the idea of desegregating professional basketball, since he thought it would signal the end of his beloved Globetrotters (it didn't).

In the most interesting part of the book, Alpert shows how the campaign for integration in baseball was led by Jewish sportswriters working for the Communist-run *Daily Worker*. We are told, rather naively, that "Communism was compatible with the Jewish vision of social justice, including beliefs in human equality and dignity, and the rights of laborers to fair wages and decent working conditions" (p. 137). Whatever the reason for the large number of American Jews attracted to Communism, and whatever one makes of the paradox of American Communists championing the rights of blacks at a time when the Great Purges, supported by the *Daily Worker*, were underway in the Soviet Union (a paradox ignored by the author), it is a fact that the party adopted the movement for desegregating baseball as one of its great causes, beginning in 1936 and continuing on into the postwar years. Communist support for desegregation actually acted as a stumbling block for those anti-Communists who wanted blacks to play in the major leagues, among them the celebrated owner of the Dodgers, Branch Rickey, a fierce anti-Communist and religious Christian. Still, thanks to Rickey and others, integration did come to baseball some 20 years before it was enforced nationwide.

Today it is impossible to imagine American professional sports without the massive presence of black players. Ironically, these days baseball is far less "black" than are football and basketball, which are more or less dominated by African American athletes. If anything, major league baseball has undergone a process of "hispanization," while American blacks have been focusing on other sports.

Alpert is probably correct in her belief that Jews have been more liberal with regard to the "race question" than other white Americans, and that this is due both to their own status as a disliked (though officially white) minority and to their belief that Judaism (presumably in its Reform guise) advocates racial equality. She illustrates this point with an interesting chapter on the good relations between the great Jackie Robinson and various Jews—neighbors, fellow athletes, and the like. Her book, though rather thin (she did not consult the Yiddish-language press, which might have yielded some useful material), is a valuable addition to our knowledge both of black-Jewish relations and of the interest of Jews in the business side of sports in the United States.

EZRA MENDELSOHN
The Hebrew University

Gur Alroey, *Bread to Eat and Clothes to Wear: Letters from Jewish Migrants in the Early Twentieth Century*. Detroit: Wayne State University Press, 2011. xii + 228 pp.

When the history of migration emerged as a new field in the first half of the 20th century, Jewish history had a pioneering function in supplying subject matter and case studies. Over the following decades, however, the Jewish aspect of migration history became less pronounced, in part because the approach shifted from the history of migrating peoples to the history of individuals on the move. During the last few years, Gur Alroey has been one of those most active in transferring this approach back into Jewish history. As such, it seems only natural that his latest book is a finely introduced edition of 66 letters written by Jewish migrants.

The letters, found in different collections of the Central Zionist Archives and the archives of the International Refugee Organization (IRO), provide deep insights into the aspirations of would-be Russian Jewish emigrants and the problems they encountered when they attempted to leave the tsarist empire. Alroey has decided to let them speak for themselves and has added only a few annotations and explanations. Thus, *Bread to Eat and Clothes to Wear* is essentially a set of snapshots of various phases of the emigration process, with an emphasis on the initial stages of decision-making and information-gathering. In many instances, we do not even know whether the letter-writers actually emigrated.

Fully two thirds of the texts focus on the initial process of decision-making and seeking information from various relief organizations. In his introduction, Alroey argues that migrants displayed rational behavior as they evaluated the economic costs and benefits of overseas migration, propelled by pull rather than push factors. A second group of letters (eight in number) presents the problems Jews encountered during the process of migration. These highly interesting letters, written en route, depict the catastrophic circumstances at the border stations, where they felt exposed to vermin, harassment, thievery, and "dangers to their lives" (p. 99ff.). They also describe the immense logistical problems faced by Russian Jews when entering or passing through Germany in order to reach its northern harbors. Another group of eight letters were written by wives who had not only been left behind but who also had lost contact with their husbands. Many such wives were in fact deserted by men who had sought an entirely new life overseas; in addition to economic hardship, they were also in the tragic position of being unable to obtain a Jewish divorce.

Alroey's detailed introduction does a fine job of placing the letters into historical context. At the same time, it is marked by a certain ambiguity. Alroey frames his introduction by stating his theoretical position, namely, that "migration is an individual experience and not a collective one" (xii, 80f.). On the one hand, the letters would seem to support this position, as they rarely mention specifically "Jewish" factors, but rather emphasize individual expectations or problems. On the other hand, all of them were written by Jews from the Russian Empire, who were part of what Alroey calls a "worldwide network of communication" that linked the Jewish populations in Eastern Europe with the new communities overseas (p. 9). Moreover, these letters were all addressed exclusively to Jewish relief organizations. Thus, the absolute "individualization" of the migrant experience would seem to be a methodological reduction that is contradicted, at least in part, by the letters themselves.

The aforementioned letters written by abandoned wives, while detailing individual woes, point to a collective problem defined by Jewish law and as such have a larger cultural and religious context. Similarly, among the ostensibly heterogeneous group of writers who asked for information on possible destinations, there are a number of striking similarities. What unifies them—and the migrant experience in general—is the search for economic opportunities as a *collective* experience, bound to particular forms of education and expectations. In turning to the relief agencies, these prospective migrants knew very well that their economic opportunities were defined by ethnic or economic boundaries shared by many others. This point is made manifest by those letters that were written not by an individual but by a group of men (131f.).

Migration history has come a long way from Marcus Lee Hansen's focus on the "social atom" over "chain migration" to the contemporary emphasis on networks; in my view, this development should be applauded. It is striking that Alroey himself uses "individual migration" more as a conceptual frame than as a coherent argument. He acknowledges collective authorship; the collective experience of dealing with smugglers and swindlers; shared experiences of humiliation at the German border; the central role of family. In the end, it is not theoretical narrowing, but rather variety and ambiguity that turn this small but highly valuable book into a major stepping-stone in recent Jewish migration history. *Bread to Eat and Clothes to Wear* provides highly useable sources for teaching Jewish history as well as general migration history. But it is also to be hoped that this book will inspire further research on migrants' experiences that does not go too far in the direction of methodological individualism. The many expressions to be found in these letters demonstrate that in Jewish history, individual and collective factors as well as experience and agency are closely related. They deserve to be discussed as highly ambivalent parts of a single fascinating story.

FRANK WOLFF
Osnabrück University

David Cesarani, Tony Kushner, and Milton Shain (eds.), *Place and Displacement in Jewish History and Memory: Zakor V'makor.* London: Vallentine Mitchell, 2009. 189 pp.

This edited volume presents a reader with the collection of 12 essays that originated in a conference under the same title held in Cape Town in 2005. *Place and Displacement in Jewish History and Memory* pursues an interdisciplinary approach to what has been, since the publication in the 1980s of Pierre Nora's ground-breaking work on sites of memory and Yosef Hayim Yerushalmi's seminal study on Jewish memory, one of the central issues in humanities in general and in Jewish studies in particular. Building on historical, sociological, and cultural analyses of politically and geographically diverse Jewish life worlds and concentrating mostly on the 20th century, this collection traces multiple functions of place in the shaping of Jewish belonging. Addressing the various Jewish migrant communities of Trieste, New York, Cape Town, London and many other cities, it focuses not only on reconstructions of places through memory but also on the recollection of the experience (both cultural and everyday) of the urban spaces as it was transformed through political events and catastrophes.

The volume consists of three thematic parts that suggest a broader understanding of Jewish urban life through a series of juxtapositions of place with other key concepts such as race, migration, and memory. This methodological approach enables the editors to stress the crucial impact of ethnicity and cultural policies on the formation of various places inhabited by Jews.

The first section, "Place, Displacement and Belonging," addresses both collective and individual forms of Jewish belonging in four different countries: Fascist Italy, post-Second World War Australia, pre-apartheid and apartheid South Africa, and Scotland. Maura E. Hametz tracks the drastic change in self-perception of the Triestine Jewish community during the Fascist regime, describing the gradual process of political transformation as members of this once secure, cosmopolitan society became subjected to expulsion, deportation, and death. Michele Langfeld analyzes the childhood experience of Holocaust survivors who immigrated to Australia both before and after the war. According to Langfeld, the survivors' notion of home was reshaped after the Holocaust and underwent additional changes in the course of their lives through a continuous reflection on the past, a process that also affected the formation of their Jewish identities. Richard Mendelsohn and Milton Shain examine the construction of the historical past in three seminal studies on South African Jewry written between 1930 and 1955. In looking at the common meta-narrative of these books (all of which left unmentioned the political and ideological contradictions within the Jewish community), the authors explore the crucial role these histories played in the shaping of collective memory among South African Jewry in the apartheid era. Finally, William Kennefick reconstructs the Jewish life worlds of Scotland in the past century, as revealed in a collection of oral histories. In a comparative description of the Jewish and Irish communities, he outlines the social transformations within the communities as well as their different forms of co-existence, pointing, among other things, to the much stronger discrimination directed against Catholic Irish migrants.

The second section, "Race, Place and Periphery," turns to less-known histories of Jewish communities, stressing the influence of intercultural relationships between Jews and their neighbors on the formation of collective and individual identities. Wieke Vink addresses the process of cultural changes within the Surinamese Jewish community starting from the 17th century onward. In studying Surinamese Jewish cemeteries as sites of memory and, more importantly, as places that indicate cultural transformation, he uncovers practices both of exclusion and of inclusion of colored Jews within the Portuguese and Ashkenazi colonial community; these testify to the ongoing localizing or "creolising" of the Jewish diaspora in Suriname. Moshe

Terdiman concentrates on the contrasting socioeconomic conditions of Livorno Jewish and native Jewish communities in 17th- and 18th-century Algiers. This essay demonstrates how the strong economic and cultural ties of Livorno Jews with Europe not only enhanced their status among the majority Muslim population (far beyond any legal benefits they received) but also shaped their cosmopolitan identity—which in turn led to an ambivalent relationship between this group and the native Jewish community. Jonathan Goldstein's essay tells the story of two rarely studied multiethnic Jewish communities, in Rangoon and Surabaya. In both communities, the juxtaposition of memory with location was extremely significant in shaping Jewish identity, particularly after the establishment of the state of Israel, to which most of the members of the communities emigrated in the early 1950s. John Simon rounds out the section with a study of two influential Jewish communities in Cape Province, examining their socioeconomic life worlds through the prism of their relationship with their Afrikaans neighbors, with its myriad political and cultural ambiguities.

The final section of the volume, "Place, Migration and Memory Works" might have been better placed at the beginning, as it provides a conceptual frame for the entire collection. The articles in this section present methodological tools that assist in articulating the essential epistemic constellation of migration, location, and memory. Nancy Foner advances the comparative approach to a study of immigration experiences of East European Jews, which contextualizes the particular locations in which their new homes were established. David Cesarani provides an important theoretical insight on the mnemonic and ethno-cultural functions of place, focusing on an under-explored group of Jewish intellectuals in London. Tony Kushner demonstrates how assumptions of mobility and social success regarding the Jewish immigration to Britain, which are dominant in the current research, cease to be valid once they are applied to a group that is more marginalized in the collective memory: the Southampton Jewish community of the first half of the 20th century. Finally, Veronica Belling unfolds the history of the contesting relationship between Hebrew and Yiddish culture as manifested within the East European immigrant community in South Africa. In the course of analyzing the Yiddish theatre repertoire, she also explores the Zionist political and cultural mechanisms that led to the gradual disappearance of South African Yiddish theatre after the Second World War.

NATASHA GORDINSKY
Leipzig University

Jonathan Dekel-Chen, David Gaunt, Natan M. Meir, and Israel Bartal (eds.), *Anti-Jewish Violence: Rethinking the Pogrom in East European History.* Bloomington: Indiana University Press, 2011. xvi + 220 pp.

John Doyle Klier, *Russians, Jews and the Pogroms of 1881–1882.* Cambridge: Cambridge University Press, 2011. xxiv + 492 pp.

It is high time to reconsider the nature of pogroms in Russia/Poland. For a long time, scholarship was deeply influenced by Semyon Dubnov and others who argued that the tsarist government was involved in inciting the pogroms of 1881–1882, and also those that followed. In recent years, thanks to research by Hans Rogger and John Klier, the opposite view has become dominant: namely, that the tsarist government was an opponent of pogroms, viewing them as a destabilizing threat to its own rule. Now, in these two exemplary books, we have a more nuanced perspective.

According to evidence presented both in the edited collection *Anti-Jewish Violence* and in John Klier's posthumous volume, *Russians, Jews and the Pogroms of 1881–1882*, the government was neither entirely at fault nor can it be fully exonerated. At various times and in various places, government officials did instigate pogroms. Moreover, even if they did not directly orchestrate the violence, government officials tacitly promoted violence for political purposes. In a way, then, the latest scholarship has inched closer to Dubnov without accepting his conviction that the government conspired to beat, maim, rape, and kill Jews. A broader contextualization is apparent, with scholars looking more closely at such issues as the government's "management" of post-pogrom information, legal contexts, the attitudes of Jews and non-Jews regarding one another, and internal relations among the Jews.

Anti-Jewish Violence, edited by a team from three continents, is an excellent example of this new approach. After noting that "several researchers follow up recent observations that pogroms were closely related to the degree to which a locality was affected by modernization, urbanization, industrialization, and economic competition," the editors provide a general articulation of goals for their collection:

> In going beyond the geographic and even the chronological boundaries normally associated with pogroms in Eastern Europe, this volume seeks to describe them as a transitional form of ethnic violence. Pogroms can, therefore, be seen in a number of ways: as last emanations of ancient religious-based hatred; as early signs of officially sponsored racial warfare; and as precursors to full-scale genocide (pp. 1-2).

To my mind, the most interesting aspect of *Anti-Jewish Violence* is the way in which authors differentiate among pogroms. There seems to be a consensus that 1881–1882 needs to be distinguished from 1903, and that the pogroms of 1905 and 1914–1917 were not the same as those of 1918–1920. Moreover, anti-Jewish violence in Belorussia had different causes than in Ukraine or Lithuania, and for this reason the kinds of acts perpetrated there were different (the number of casualties was also lower). In short, examining anti-Jewish pogroms under the rubric of regional studies has the positive effect of undermining various generalizations that have long been regarded as proven fact.

Among the contributions to this volume are a study of the relations between Jews and non-Jews in Kiev by Nathan Meir; an examination of the pogroms in Eastern Siberia by Lilia Kalmina; an essay describing the four-sided situation (involving Jews, Russians, Poles, and Lithuanians) in Lithuania by Vladas Sirutavicius and Darius Staliūsas, and a pair of articles on Belorussia authored by Arkadi Zeltser and Claire Le Foll. In addition, Jonathan Dekel-Chen treats the issue of violence in the early Soviet period in the Crimea. Although one should not draw final conclusions, it is interesting to consider the possibility that anti-Jewish violence was less destructive in those areas in which Jews were poorer (as in Belorussia) and where capitalism had not made significant inroads. Another thesis explored by Dekel-Chen is that the generosity of foreign Jews (in this instance, from the Agro-Joint) in aiding not just Jewish farming collectives but also their non-Jewish neighbors, reduced animosity among different ethnic groups.

As in all collections, there is a diffuse focus. The two pieces on the First World War, by Eric Lohr and Peter Holquist, seem to stand apart from the others, as they focus on the perpetrators and Russian policy rather than on the victims. In an essay titled "The Role of Personality in the First (1914–15) Russian Occupation of Galicia and Bukovina," Holquist offers an unusual perspective, assigning the responsibility for much of the Russian army's maltreatment of Jews to specific individuals, notably General Nikolai Ianushkevich, chief of staff for the supreme commander in chief, and Valer'ian Nikolaevich Murav'ev, the foreign ministry's attaché on occupation issues in Bukovina. In a different essay, Vladimir Buldakov discusses a subgenre of violence that he calls the "revolutionary anti-Jewish pogrom." The genre is defined by motivation: opponents of the Bolsheviks fought the revolution by committing acts of violence against Jews during the Civil War period of 1917–1918.

I found Vladimir Levin's "Responses to Pogroms" to be especially enlightening. Levin underscores the energetic means by which Jewish community leaders sought to mitigate the threat against their people in the early years of the 20th century. As he sees it, the various methods of intercession, self-defense, and systematic struggle against antisemitism were all ultimately aimed at the government, which, in their view, had the power to come to the Jews' defense.

In my view, the most profound article in *Anti-Jewish Violence* is David Engel's "What's in a Pogrom? European Jews in the Age of Violence," which deals with the very definition of "pogrom." Engel notes that the term seems to lose its meaning if it is used to designate all the different kinds of violence perpetrated against Jews in 19th- and 20th-century Europe. Nonetheless, Engel cautiously argues that popular conceptions of pogroms have helped to create a single taxonomy of anti-Jewish violence. Perhaps more meaningfully, he puts forth the view that such violence is not random, but rather is initiated at times when the broad public perceives that the state cannot or refuses to establish justice. In such times, the people feel compelled to take up violence in order to attain justice (as they understand it). For example, he argues that the pogroms of 1881–1882 occurred two decades after the liberation of the serfs, when it had become clear that the state had not delivered on its promise of a better life for the peasantry. Engel also considers a (seeming) shift that occurred following the Second World War:

Indeed, it was ultimately the ability of European states in the second half of the twentieth century to persuade their populations that they could effect justice with regard to Jews that brought about the virtual disappearance since the middle of the twentieth century of the particular sort of anti-Jewish violence under discussion here. [...] That process is hardly complete, however. Nor is it irreversible. Groups that have traditionally enjoyed significant advantages in societies divided according to social rank have much to lose when assertion of rank's privileges comes to be seen as unjust. Such losses may not be of great consequence in times of plenty nor generate much anxiety when states appear to provide generally stable environments. Let plenty vanish, though, or stability be threatened, and both the claim of traditional subalterns to scarce resources and state protection of that claim in the name of abstract notions of justice are liable to be contested with vigor (p. 35).

In other words, the circumstances that brought about persecution in the past may one day be repeated, and Jews and other minorities could again become the brunt of popular anger. The pogrom, as this and the other essays make clear, is far from extinct.

Anti-Jewish Violence is dedicated to the well-known scholar of Russian Jewry, John Doyle Klier, who passed away in 2007. Among his unfinished works was a manuscript dealing with the pogroms of 1881–1882, which has now been published in monograph form through the efforts of Klier's wife, Helen, his colleague François Guesnet, and his editor at Cambridge University Press, Lars Fischer. *Russians, Jews and the Pogroms of 1881–1882* is essentially a study of this particular wave of pogroms in the broad context of Russia's social, political, economic, and intellectual life. The work has three main parts, the first devoted to a description of the pogroms, the second to the government's reaction, and the third to the Jewish reaction. Also included is a section dealing with depictions of these pogroms in literature and journalism, especially in the work of Dubnov. In certain ways, this monograph complements Michael Aronson's earlier work on the 1881–1882 pogroms.[1] Klier's work is superior, however, because of the author's extensive use of Russian history in explaining the pogrom phenomenon. As Klier notes, his aim was to "integrate the history of the Russian pogroms into the emergent study of ethnic and nationalist conflicts and collective violence" (p. xiv).

Despite the deep respect I have for Klier, I must note that the section dealing with Jewish reactions to the pogroms is less original than are other parts of the book. Klier himself acknowledges that this issue was previously explored by Jonathan Frankel.[2] What does stand out in this section is Klier's examination of the ways in which Baron Horace Gintsburg used his resources to oppose Count N.P. Ignat'ev, the minister of the interior, in attempting to lessen the impact of what became known as the "May Laws" (which imposed a number of onerous economic liabilities on Jews). As Klier notes:

> It was evident from the beginning that the May Laws gave wide scope for malevolent interpretation by the enemies of the Jews, and this has been the dominant motif in the historiography. Less well appreciated has been the ample ground they contained for evasion. They also supplied the basis for appeals to higher jurisdictions that, from pragmatic or ideological considerations, were less ill inclined toward the Jews. There are ample illustrations of these phenomena (p. 226).

What differentiates this book from others on the subject is Klier's close look at the Russian press of this period and his examination of the government's internal political struggles. Klier is convinced of the importance of the newspaper sources:

> The diversity of opinion on the pogroms, ranging from condemnation of the Jews themselves to open calls for complete Jewish emancipation, demonstrates the comprehensive nature of the coverage. It is obvious that the censorship had little effect in dampening debate, in part because the censors themselves were uncertain as to the correct line to follow. In the search for scapegoats, journalists took aim at journalistic rivals and specific local authorities, especially in newspapers that were outside the latter's reach (pp. 149-150).

Klier displays the views of right-wing, liberal, and centrist commentators, illuminating how the government and Russian society came to formulate and accept the discriminatory regulations against Jews. Similarly, Klier does a wonderful job in showing that the government did not have a predetermined response to pogroms, but rather formulated its position less with regard to Jews than to Russian society. Thus, it shifted its argument from blaming the violence on revolutionaries to seeking the cause in Jewish exploitation of the general population. For instance, government officials ignored statistics that showed that drinking habits or the level of poverty had nothing to do with the relative presence or absence of Jews in a given location. If Jewish tavern owners promoted drinking among the Russian peasants, it is clear that others, too, were promoting it.

Klier also identifies those responsible for the violence. In contrast to Aronson, who concentrates on railroad workers, Klier points out that a variety of people committed acts of violence, while acknowledging that the perpetrators tended to be young men with few economic prospects, helped by vagabonds, poor women, and railroad workers. Russia, he asserts, was an underpoliced state—although he shows, too, how Dmitry Tolstoy, the minister of interior after Ignat'ev, was able to stop pogroms by putting governor-generals on notice that they would be held responsible for preserving the peace, at the risk of demotion or dismissal.

Russians, Jews and the Pogroms of 1881–1882 is an important book and a fine companion to Klier's earlier *Imperial Russia's Jewish Question, 1855–1881* (1996). But what is really at stake in this tome? Certainly, the display of internal debates in the government and society points to a more diverse and dynamic Russia than that portrayed in previous studies. In addition, we learn that anti-Jewish legislation was meant to give support to a conservative (not the most conservative) wing of the government, which sought to restrain reform as a way of protecting the peasantry—at least in the western provinces—from the ills of run-away capitalism. At times, however, Klier seems a bit too sympathetic in his portrayal of how the government desired to restrain Jews and other subaltern groups from gaining wealth and power too quickly, seemingly at the expense of the native population. Political reaction is presented as a responsible step aimed at providing aid and defense to the less capable members of the Russian national family—a stance, I would argue, that is open to debate.

Notwithstanding, these two volumes offer much to scholars in terms of conceptual, empirical, and methodological material. They are accessible to readers across the spectrum, and I recommend them heartily.

BRIAN HOROWITZ
Tulane University

Notes

1. Michael Aronson, *Troubled Waters: Origins of the 1881 Anti-Jewish Pogroms in Russia* (Pittsburgh: 1990).
2. Jonathan Frankel, "The Crisis of 1881–82 as a Turning Point in Modern Jewish History," in *The Legacy of Jewish Migration: 1881 and Its Impact*, ed. David Berger (New York: 1983), 9–22.

Marion A. Kaplan and Deborah Dash Moore (eds.), *Gender and Jewish History*.
Bloomington: Indiana University Press, 2011. viii + 416 pp.

This volume, edited by Marion Kaplan and Deborah Dash Moore, is a tribute to the
late Paula Hyman, and especially her contribution to the study of women and gender
in Jewish history. As the editors acknowledge in the introduction, when Hyman
began her career at Columbia University in the early 1970s, the primary emphasis in
Jewish history was on intellectual and political history. Hyman, however, was deeply
influenced by the emerging field of social history. Together with a group of younger
scholars in modern Jewish history, including Todd Endelmann, Marion Kaplan, and
Steven Lowenstein, she began to focus on non-elite Jews, who generally did not
leave written records. As Deborah Lipstadt writes in her acknowledgement to Hyman:
"From the outset of her career, she has devoted herself to rescuing many people—
primarily, but not only, women—from historical oblivion. Whether it was women on
New York's Lower East Side who wanted to stop corruption in the pricing of kosher
meat or women organizational leaders whose contributions have been lost or simply
ignored, she made it her passion to place them where they well deserved to be: in the
historical record" (pp. 317–318).

   In order to capture the role of non-elites, Hyman turned to new sorts of sources—
among them, census and notarial records, tax records, and ceremonial objects—in
order to document aspects of the Jewish experience that had previously been ignored,
such as internal migration patterns, social mobility, aspects of family life (including
age of marriage and family size), and linguistic change. Moreover, together with
Marion Kaplan, Hyman argued that women experienced assimilation differently than
men in that they served as guardians of Jewish tradition. Hyman also drew attention
to the role of Jewish women, especially immigrant women, in political protest, and
she pointed out ways in which involvement in the labor movements in both the
United States and France served as important vehicles of assimilation.

   The essays in this volume represent a wide array of disciplines and focus exclusively
on gender, although Richard I. Cohen's concluding essay attempts to link Hyman's
work on gender to her equally pioneering work in modern French Jewish history. Since
it is unfortunately impossible to discuss all the essays here, I would like to use this
occasion to emphasize a few themes that run throughout a number of these essays.

   First, a number of contributions follow Hyman's example by making use of innovative sources such as private letters, diaries and memoirs, and public opinion surveys to provide insight into the private as well as public life of Jews. For example,
Ismar Schorsch, in his essay on the relationship of Leopold Zunz and his wife,
Adelheid, uses a collection of private letters to elucidate the nature of their relationship. Leopold Zunz, a member of the first generation of German Jewish university
graduates and one of the founding fathers of the Wissenschaft des Judentums movement, experienced great difficulty in securing a post that would enable him to pursue
his scholarship, since he was scorned by the Jewish Orthodox elite, on the one hand,
and shunned by the German academic establishment, on the other. Zunz has often
been depicted as arrogant and pompous. In 1821, for example, he wrote to his wife
that he had no hope for Jews "until the present sclerotic and cowardly generation dies

out" (p. 36); the following year, he was forced to resign as preacher at the Beer Temple in Berlin after he delivered a sermon in which he castigated the board of directors for its lack of religiosity and its excessive materialism. At the same time, Schorsch's portrait of Zunz's home life portrays him as a loving, and indeed, an adoring husband. Moreover, Adelheid, who was an intellectual in her own right, was by no means a guardian of Jewish tradition. Although they kept a kosher home, both of them occasionally ate non-kosher food, especially while travelling, and they corresponded with one another on the Sabbath if one of them was away from home. Indeed, Schorsch shows that they had a remarkably modern marriage, with Zunz regarding his wife as his intellectual soul mate. On the occasion of his 70th birthday celebration, Zunz admitted that his scholarly work would not have been possible without the "insight, nobility and contentedness," of his "dear wife, my beloved Adelheid" (p. 40).

Rebecca Kobrin, in her essay, "The Murdered Hebrew Maidservant of East New York," uses trial records from the 1870s to examine the case of a Jewish domestic servant, Sarah Alexander, who was murdered by her cousin and employer, Pesach Rubinstein, after she became pregnant with his child. Although this story gripped the New York City public when it broke, it has since slipped out of our collective memory. Kobrin, however, reminds us that prior to the advent of sweatshops in the garment industry in the 1880s and 1890s, many East European Jewish women served as domestic servants, frequently finding employment with their relatives. Kobrin furthermore challenges the romantic myth of the traditional Jewish family that always took care of its own. Indeed, even had Sarah Alexander not been murdered by her own cousin, she was clearly being exploited by her family—she was responsible for cleaning three different apartments, for daily food preparation, and for caring for ill family members, which is how her relationship with Pesach developed in the first place.

Marsha Rozenblit's fascinating essay on Jewish courtship in post-First World War Vienna also relies on an unpublished diary and private correspondence, in addition to marriage ads in the Jewish press. Rozenblit, too, demolishes longstanding stereotypes. She shows that after the First World War, there was a breakdown in traditional marriage practices, largely as a result of a general breakdown in social mores, and also because parents had become reluctant to force their children into arranged marriages. As a result, non-arranged marriages became more prevalent, although contrary to what one might expect, not all of these were love matches. Rozenblit shows that pragmatic motivations, especially the desire to find someone who was responsible and who would make a comfortable home, were at least as important, if not more so, than love.

One other essay noteworthy for its innovative use of sources is Lila Corwin Berman's "Gendered Journeys: Jewish Migrations and the City in Postwar America," which focuses on Jewish residential patterns in post-Second World War Detroit. Berman uses contemporaneous reports and surveys carried out by social researchers to assess Jewish attitudes toward the influx of African Americans who began to move into their neighborhoods. On the basis of these surveys, which were heavily based on interviews with women, since they were more likely to be at home when the pollsters came by, Berman shows that Jews were among the first to move out of a neighborhood when African Americans began to move in, in part because the Catholic church actively discouraged white flight, and in part because a lower proportion of Jews were homeowners. Yet during the 1960s, some Jewish women protested when the neighborhood association in Northwest Detroit decided to buy up properties to prevent them from being purchased by African Americans. When one Jewish woman compared this practice to what the Nazis had done to Jews in the 1930's, she was told by some of her neighbors to "go back to where she came from" (p. 344).

In addition to the use of unconventional sources, some of the topics discussed here tend to be relatively neglected in the field of Jewish studies. Lauren Strauss, in her essay on American Jewish women artists as political activists, shows how the New Deal opened up new opportunities for women artists in the 1930s. Despite their considerable success, these women artists did not achieve full equality with their male counterparts. Although men and women artists who worked for the Works Progress Administration (WPA) received equal pay, this practice extended only to single women, since it was assumed that married women would be taken care of by their spouses. Moreover, Strauss shows that women artists continued to be treated dismissively. As one male German expressionist artist exclaimed with regard to the work of Lee Krasner: "This is so good you would not know it was painted by a woman" (p. 274).

In her essay on American Jewish women photographers in the 1930s, Deborah Dash Moore shows how these women professionals experienced remarkable success. According to Moore, Jewish women, mostly from immigrant backgrounds, accounted for as many as 30 percent of those connected with the "New York School" of photography, which stressed the depiction of everyday life on the streets of the Lower East Side. Moore argues that these women brought a different gaze to their work. She suggests that their work was less political than that of their male colleagues, placing greater emphasis on interpersonal relationships. As Moore explains, the aim of these female artists was to depict the Lower East Side not only in its poverty but also as a place of dignity.

Finally, it should be mentioned that several of these essays offer excellent overviews of the scholarship on Jewish women in various fields. Dalia Offer's essay provides a comprehensive survey of recent scholarship on gender and the Holocaust. Todd Endelmann offers a comparative analysis based on data from five cities to assess the degree to which gender acted as a determinant of conversion in the 19th and early 20th centuries. He ultimately concludes that each of these cases was distinct, and that multiple socioeconomic and demographic factors, as opposed to gender alone, conditioned who was most likely to convert. Finally, Michael Meyer's essay on the Reform Movement in Europe presents an insightful comparative analysis that focuses not only on Germany but also on France and Great Britain. As he shows, despite the fact that members of the Reform movement paid far more attention to the role of women than did Orthodox Jews, they too were extraordinarily slow to deal with the issue. The matter was not formally raised until the Augsburg rabbinical synod of 1870, and specific reforms, such as mixed seating, emerged only in the 20th century. Indeed, it was the disparagement of women by all mainstream Jewish denominations that encouraged some women to support sectarian or countercultural Jewish movements, such as Sabbatianism in the 17th century or the Jewish renewal movement in the late 20th century, as is shown in Chava Weissler's essay on "vernacular kabbalah."

Gender and Jewish History will ultimately be valuable to both scholars and graduate students in a number of disciplines. Although these essays did not arise out of a conference, they nevertheless engage in dialogue with one another to a remarkable degree. They constitute a fitting tribute to Hyman in that they show the enormous impact of her work on gender across a wide array of disciplines, and they exemplify how looking at gender aids in breaking down stereotypes and challenging longstanding assumptions. By affording us a means of illuminating the private as well as the public lives of Jews, Hyman, along with the contributors to this volume, will continue to reshape our understanding of the modern Jewish experience well into the future.

Vicki Caron
Cornell University

Rebecca Kobrin, *Jewish Bialystok and Its Diaspora*. Bloomington: Indiana University Press, 2010. 361 pp.

The migration of more than two and a half million Jews from Eastern Europe between the years of 1881–1924 was one of the formative events in modern Jewish history. This mass migration changed the face of Jewish society in Eastern Europe, as centers of Jewish population slowly began to lose their importance and influence until their final disappearance during the course of the Second World War. Meanwhile, Jewish migrants who arrived in the various countries of destination became integrated in the surrounding society with relative rapidity, gradually ascending the socioeconomic ladder.

At first, research on this mass wave of Jewish migration fell within the purview of sociologists and demographers who made use of quantitative methods to study the social components and main characteristics of the movement. A dramatic shift occurred at the beginning of the 1960s when two historians, Lloyd Gartner and Moses Rischin, published their respective books on Jewish immigration to England and to New York.[1] Unlike earlier researchers, Gartner and Rischin focused on the *people* who had migrated. Their studies began with an examination of Old World society and the reasons Jews had for migrating and then followed the migrants to their place of destination, charting the birth pangs of their absorption in the new country. These two landmark studies had tremendous influence on those that followed. For each country of destination to which Jewish migrants had arrived, studies were written about their absorption in the surrounding society and its influence upon them. In most cases, scholars dealt with such issues as the patterns of absorption, working conditions, relations between veterans and newcomers, and similarities and distinctions between Jewish migrants and other ethnic groups that had migrated to the same country or city. In the main, they considered Eastern Europe as a single geographical unit, confining themselves to a general description of the social, political, and economic processes that occurred in Galicia, the Russian Empire, or in Romania.

Kobrin's exceptional and innovative book, in contrast, focuses on one Jewish community in Eastern Europe whose rate of migration was high in comparison with other cities in the Jewish Pale of Settlement. Updating a research typology first presented by Samuel Baily,[2] she tracks Bialystok Jews who migrated to five different cities on four continents, without losing sight of those who stayed behind.

Jewish Bialystok and Its Diaspora has five chapters (plus introduction and conclusion). Kobrin first traces the formation of the Bialystok community and how it became a city and a major Jewish center in Eastern Europe. Her second chapter, "Rebuilding a Homeland in Promised Lands," focuses on Jews of Bialystok who migrated to New York, Argentina, Palestine, and Melbourne. This comparative chapter shows how the Bialystok migrants (like those from other cities) set up *landsmanshaftn* in each destination country, published a newspaper, and maintained connections both with their city of origin and with Bialystok migrants in other countries. The third chapter deals with Bialystok philanthropy in diaspora communities, which was intended both for East European Jewry in general and Bialystok Jews in particular—here, Kobrin demonstrates that Jewish migration not only improved the economic status of the migrants but also benefited those who remained behind. The fourth chapter examines how the self-image of Bialystok Jewry took shape in their dispersed communities, especially via the landsmanshaftn and the migrants' newspapers. Finally, Kobrin discusses how Bialystok migrants who had already become established and integrated in the new society were able to cope with the outcome of the Holocaust, the annihilation of Bialystok Jewry, and the attempt to commemorate the destruction. Replete with painful testimony, this chapter movingly demonstrates the ways in which migration from Eastern Europe was one of the most dramatic and important events of modern Jewish history. By swelling the Jewish diaspora, the mass migration laid the groundwork for a lasting memorial to East European Jewry and a lifestyle that no longer exists.

In addition to original and illuminating research, *Jewish Bialystock and Its Diaspora* is to be commended for its lucid style of writing. Kobrin knows how to tell a story, arousing the reader's curiosity from the very first page. This is not a self-understood matter in books in general and in academic works in particular. Hopefully, this book will be translated into Hebrew—it is regrettable that, to date, Jewish American historians engaged in writing about modern Jewish history have rarely endeavored to translate their books into Hebrew, even though there is a large audience in Israel for studies of this kind. For now, readers of English can benefit from this highly important contribution to the historiography of East European Jewry, and of general and Jewish migration in particular.

Gur Alroey
University of Haifa

Notes

1. Lloyd P. Gartner, *The Jewish Immigrant in England, 1870–1914* (London: 1960); Moses Rischin, *The Promised City: New York's Jews, 1870–1914* (Cambridge: 1926).

2. See *Immigrants in the Lands of Promise: Italians in Buenos Aires and New York City, 1870–1914* (Ithaca: 1999), 16, where Baily outlines four types of comparative research: several immigrant groups in the same city; the same immigrants in different cities of the same country; the same immigrants in cities in different receiving countries; and the same group in its place of origin and destination. Kobrin's work makes use of the last two categories.

Zionism, Israel, and the Middle East

Shaul Kelner, *Tours that Bind: Diaspora, Pilgrimage, and Israeli Birthright Tourism.*
New York: New York University Press, 2010. xxv + 261 pp.
Leonard Saxe and Barry Chazan, *Ten Days of Birthright Israel: A Journey in Young
Adult Identity.* Waltham: Brandeis University Press, 2008. 223 pp.

Taglit-Birthright Israel is one of the most important programs linking diaspora Jews
and Israel to be initiated in recent decades. Since its inception in 1999, more than
300,000 diaspora Jewish students have traveled on free, ten-day trips to Israel. The
program targets a student population (aged 18–26) with weaker ties to Israel or to the
Jewish community. The massive promotion of short-term visits as a means of strengthening Jewish identity, combating weakened Jewish commitment, and increasing ties to
Israel is nearly unprecedented, and can be compared only with the state-sponsored
Israeli trips to Poland. Birthright participants visit significant historical and religious
sites, guided by a professional tour guide who also acts as a role model. Each Birthright
group, generally numbering about 40 participants, is also accompanied by local and
Israeli tour leaders (*madrikhim*) and by Israeli soldiers who are about the same age as
the students. The program includes encounters with Israeli public figures, discussion
groups, Sabbath experiences, and a concluding mega-event attended by all the groups.
This combination is designed to create a multi-sensory, hands-on experience lived out
entirely within the bubble of a Jewish and Israeli community. Rarely has tourism been
granted such a significant role in furthering Jewish identity or ties between diaspora
and homeland. Indeed, Birthright has served as a model for other diasporic communities seeking to strengthen ties to ancestral homelands. This phenomenon invites investigation into its effectiveness and its implications for contemporary Jewish belonging,
as well as for diasporic and religious identity and (trans-)nationalism in an age of multiple identity choices and increased mobility.

The two books reviewed here focus on North American visitors to Israel (by far the
largest group) and have been written by authors who were part of Birthright's evaluation process and who are familiar with Israel, American Jewish life, and issues in
contemporary sociology and education. Both are highly readable accounts, providing
a thorough description of the origins, structure, and dynamics of the program.

Shaul Kelner's work, *Tours that Bind,* provides an analysis of the tours that is
based on interviews, evaluations, personal reflections, and participant-observation of
at least three Birthright trips. As reported by Kelner, the carefully chosen site tours,
discussions, casual conversations, and follow-up responses provide a complex and
nuanced description of Birthright. The book frames the trip as a cultural practice of

political socialization, and asks: "What is the nature of socialization that occurs when tourism is used as a strategy for introducing diaspora ethnics to a national homeland?" (p. xvii). Kelner explores the negotiations and possible conflicts between the sometimes divergent visions of Israeli and diaspora organizers and staff, gaps between organizers' intentions and staff implementation, and the contradictions that inhere in tourism itself. In his discussion, he strikes a balance between the structure of the trips as reflected in planning meetings, position papers, publicity and itineraries, on the one hand, and agency—the actual performance by the participants *in situ*—on the other. In contrast with most other studies that rely heavily on evaluation surveys (which often reify the trip initiators' goals), Kelner places more emphasis on the students' agency. He also expands his analytic purview beyond the tours of Jews coming to Israel through descriptions of "homeland tours" designed for African Americans as well as Lebanese, Indians, and Taiwanese living in the United States. In order to examine diaspora tours as a means of shaping identity, Kelner has developed methodological tools and a broad conceptual and comparative frame that highlights what the tours do, what they don't do, and especially, what one can and cannot expect such tours to do.

Kelner repeatedly reminds us of the nature of tourism as a semiotic enterprise, a particular mode of experience and a set of knowledge practices that center on scanning the touristed landscape for signs that can be interpreted as the essence of the place. This is what John Urry refers to as the "tourist gaze": "When tourists see two people kissing in Paris, what they capture in the gaze is 'timeless, romantic Paris'.…Without the tourist gaze, a kiss is just a kiss, even in Paris" (quoted in Kelner, p. 9).

While the tours seek to increase personal identification with Israel and Jewish history, the semiotic stance of tourism, by its nature, opens a gap between toured sites and everyday life. The combination of nearness and distancing is inherent in tourism and is reflected in the variations and contradictions in the approach to Israel among the various groups sponsoring Birthright. Whereas Israeli leaders may preach aliyah, this is merely lip service to a project that seeks to foster connections to Israel, which in turn will invigorate a *diaspora* identity.

Few aspects of the tour escape Kelner's purview. Not only the guiding performances, but the self-understandings and the taken-for-granted social roles of Israeli tour guides, the perceptions of the Israeli soldiers accompanying the group, and the influence of group participants on each other (ranging from mutual affirmation to censorship to the dynamics of "hooking up"). Kelner also trains his eye on the integration of downtime into the text of the tour, and manages to elicit responses from the silent participants whose voices are rarely heard in group discussions. He has, moreover, a keen ear for language and an ability to draw rapid personality sketches (without caricature or kitsch) that contextualize the individual players within the group. We recognize the various participants: his Israelis speak "Israeli English," the speech of his non-committed participants expresses distance and ambivalence, and his New Yorkers sound like, well, New Yorkers. The same fine-tuned descriptions encapsulate the closed bubble of the bus, the open vistas of the outlook, and the fluid interactions of half-focused groups on tour—thirsty for knowledge, but worn out after a night of hard partying. The pertinent but not overly lengthy theoretical introduction on semiotics and social interactionism teases out the various strands of the dynamics without overwhelming us with jargon. Kelner's reflections on how trips to Israel shaped his Jewish scholarly interests and life choices lend his arguments credibility as well as color.

In his conclusion, Kelner eschews both the delegitimization of the diaspora still voiced by certain Zionist leaders and the glorification of diasporic existence proposed by scholars such as Daniel and Jonathan Boyarin. He argues that diasporic identity involves the formation of an *imagined community*, no less than in the case of nations and nationalisms. "Programs like Taglit," he says, "bring diaspora Jews to Israel as co-ethnics, yet …enforce tourists' awareness that they are engaging the country as foreign nationals" (p. 200). Diaspora tourism, he concludes, is suited for territorializing culture by inscribing meaning in places, enacting relationships with those places, and incorporating experiences of place into understandings of self. On the one hand, the attachment of emotional valence to places has the effect of marginalizing alternative self-definitions. At the same time, the evanescence of the tour environment renders fragile such constructions of self. Furthermore, the gaps between the ways of seeing and experiencing the world on tour and those of everyday life make the translation of such experiences into other (off-tour) behavior inconsistent. The sustained, broad reflection on the potential of tourism to create links between diasporic communities and homelands is a refreshing addition to a field often researched by "professional Jews" whose horizons of inquiry are bounded by the Jewish world. Such studies often implicitly confirm that Jewishness and the Jewish connection to Israel are *sui generis*.

Leonard Saxe and Barry Chazan's *Ten Days of Birthright Israel* provides a complementary and partially overlapping view. Birthright's goals, as proclaimed in the book, are: "to promote Jewish identity, create a sense of Jewish Peoplehood and …create love of Israel" (p. 185). The greatest strength of the book lies in its grounding of the program in an educational philosophy emphasizing multi-sensory experience, peer-group creation, and "doing things Jewish" as the means of internalizing educational messages and fostering community ties and individual growth. It then shows how these aims are translated into organizational and programmatic terms, and documents the struggles among a variety of stakeholders (individual philanthropists, Jewish Federations, Israeli politicians, educators, and travel agents) with regard to the translation of desired messages into a workable project of unprecedented magnitude. These behind-the scenes accounts of the structuring of the Birthright trip offer a broad and vividly rendered context of educational goals and Jewish communal politics.

Saxe and Chazan also offer a detailed, though less critical, description of trip events. Following an opening vignette of group members' ecstatic arrival at Ben-Gurion airport, they present highly flattering portraits of Michael Steinhardt and Charles Bronfman, going so far as to compare them with Theodor Herzl! Although *Ten Days of Birthright Israel* provides much in-depth ethnography, its self-declared goal is to "share what we view as the extraordinary story of Birthright Israel and to …explain how and why this has affected the lives of its participants" (p. 3). The understanding of "young adults' quest for meaning and the dynamics of identity formation" (ibid.) is mentioned as a second—and secondary—endeavor. The volume is primarily the detailed documentation of a success story, and only secondarily a sociological study seeking to raise theoretical questions.

Both books analyze Birthright events as they unfold, but have obvious differences in emphases and areas of strength. Kelner's description of the voyage is much finer. His character sketches display a wide variety of acceptance, negotiation, or rejection of program goals, whereas Saxe and Chazan's portraits are cooperative and sometimes hagiographic (as in the case of the philanthropists). It is not clear to the reader whether Saxe and Chazan were on the scene with their notebooks or whether they received reports from research assistants; Kelner, in contrast, was clearly *there*, as evidenced by his thick description of successes, misfires, and murmurings from the sidelines, as well as the characterization of his own position on the scene. Where *Ten Days* tends to generalize from an observed reaction, speaking of what a group "probably" or "undoubtedly" experienced, Kelner takes the opportunity offered by downtime to more deeply probe the reactions of various group participants. *Ten Days* often assumes basic familiarity with Judaism on the part of many participants, whereas Kelner graphically illustrates the tremendous distance to be covered between the students' life worlds and the text of the trip organizers. Where Saxe and Chazan speak of muffled whispers of jokes or protest at the military cemetery, Kelner gets the voices on tape; where *Ten Days* sometimes waxes ecstatic over the value of face-to-face encounters with Israeli peers that lead to lasting personal ties, romances, and a few marriages, *Tours that Bind* ponders how "hooking up" may preserve and perpetuate Orientalist stereotypes.

Occasionally, Saxe and Chazan allow the assumptions of establishment-identifying Jews to slip into their descriptions, as when Israeli speakers are contrasted with what might take place "in a synagogue where students have encountered their rabbis" (p. 57)—do most of these students *have* rabbis? Where Kelner sympathetically problematizes the political messages of the voyage and inquires as to how itinerary and voice make certain understandings of the Israeli-Palestinian conflict more salient than others, Saxe and Chazan raise the issue once, only to relegate it to the sidelines, conflating "Israelis," without caveat, with Israeli Jews (p. 71). Where Kelner critically examines the program's aims and structure, Saxe and Chazan are eager to present the project in a positive light—thus "beer flows that night, to quench thirst, not to create drunkenness" (p. 76). (Some of my Israeli students who have accompanied Taglit groups beg to differ.) When speculating about long-term effects, Saxe and Chazan extrapolate from short-term surveys to predict that, in the long term, the Birthright experience will result in increased "bonding social capital" with other Jews, greater involvement with Israel, and even broader concern for the welfare of others (pp. 180–185). Kelner is far more reserved: he insists that the translation of tourist practices into other types of behavior "back home" is uneven and inconsistent (p. 192). He also wonders if Israel-experience travel does not encourage the construction of diasporic Jewish identities as "consumer identities to be realized through consumption of commodified symbols, products and experiences" rather than long-term commitments to communities (pp. 106–107). For many of *Ten Days'* exclamation points, *Tours that Bind* substitutes question marks—reminding us of the limits of our knowledge and challenging us to extend them by posing new doubts and new theoretical and comparative reflections.

Saxe and Chazan have written a highly readable, if sometimes overly celebratory report evaluating what Birthright attempts to do and how it does it, and extolling its successes. Kelner describes and evaluates with a measure of skepticism, posing new and extremely important questions on the nature of tourism, diasporic identity, and transnationalism. Beyond the merits and weaknesses of each of the two books, their shared focus provides a unique opportunity for educators in Jewish studies, education, and sociology to show how different methodological orientations result in very different analyses of a common object of study close to students' life worlds. I hope that educators and college faculty will rise to the occasion and assign both books for reading and comparison.

JACKIE FELDMAN
Ben-Gurion University

Henry Near, *Where Community Happens: The Kibbutz and the Philosophy of Communalism*. Bern: Peter Lang, 2011. 238 pp.

Henry Near is no longer with us and this book is, to some extent, his spiritual testament on the topic to which he devoted his intellectual life. It is in this sense, I suggest, that we should regard his final work on the kibbutz, the institution that has always been at the center of his writings. Born in England, Near was a member of a kibbutz-oriented youth movement; as a young university graduate, he came to Israel and joined a kibbutz. He also continued his academic studies, training as a historian, and in this role became an expert on the ideological and spiritual tenets that animated the kibbutz movement. Indeed, it was his fidelity to the ideals of the kibbutz that led him to investigate the movement's sinuous historical path.

Where Community Happens consists in the main of previously published essays on the kibbutz—both in its concrete, physical sense and as an event in human history. Rounding out the essays are two new chapters and an afterword. The resulting volume is a clear and coherent presentation of Near's ideological-philosophical agenda, both confronting and answering issues regarding the nature, contribution, and impact of the kibbutz and, more generally, communalism.

The title of the book draws from Near's aspiration to set his work in a wide intellectual context in which communalism and the kibbutz experience are the focus of reference for any kind of reality in which "community happens." As a historian, he knew while preparing the volume that the older essays (written in the 1980s and 1990s) did not reflect the updated reality of the kibbutz sector. Some of the problematic issues outlined in those essays—among them, the ambitions and limitations of pioneering vis-à-vis engagement with the society at large—are hardly pertinent to kibbutzim whose members receive differential salaries; where many permanent inhabitants are non-members; where houses have become private property; and where major public functions are often operated by salaried outsiders. Consequently, *Where Community Happens* does not attempt to offer predictions or guidelines for the future of kibbutzim. Instead, Near focuses on what can be learned from the collectivistic kibbutz experience in general.

The book is divided into four sections. The first deals with theory and ideological perspectives: one of the basic questions Near ponders is whether there is any rational basis for communalism (that is, does communalism "make sense"?). Assessing the ties between communalism and utopianism, Near comes to the somewhat paradoxical conclusion that the dynamic processes of communalism are, in effect, a concretization of utopia that inevitably gives way to a more grounded, "post-utopian" reality. The second section picks up this theme and develops an approach toward utopia that distinguishes various sequences (up to post-utopianism). This approach is then applied to the case of the communal experience and thinking under the Soviets and during the first stage after the collapse of the Soviet system.

In the third section, Near turns to a broader national-historical perspective, analyzing the ways in which the notion of pioneering was actualized, first by kibbutz-oriented youth movements and later in the kibbutzim. Following this, the concluding section turns its gaze outward, examining the historical—and ongoing—interactions between the kibbutz and the larger Israeli society.

In his afterword, Near looks to the future, considering the relevance of the kibbutz to the realities of the 21st century. According to him, the communal experience represents a moral challenge for those moved by utopian aspirations for equality, sharing, and direct democracy. Thus, even if the vicissitudes of life and the pragmatics of collectivism result in something less than utopia, utopianism may remain one of the driving forces of the collective and a factor of social evolution. Despite the transformations that kibbutzim have undergone (and despite the limitations of other communal frameworks throughout the world), communalism continues to "keep the spark of human brotherhood, equality and mutual aid alive" (p. 222). Near's well-written volume will be welcomed by all those who believe that the collectivistic past is still relevant—both for its value-based assessment of reality and its insistent striving for a better world.

ELIEZER BEN-RAFAEL
Tel Aviv University

Noam Pianko, *Zionism and the Roads Not Taken: Rawidowicz, Kaplan, Kohn.* Bloomington: Indiana University Press, 2010. x + 277 pp.

In a book that constitutes both a contribution to our historical knowledge and an effort to influence contemporary Jewish politics, Noam Pianko aims "to rehabilitate and revive" several "dissenting streams of Zionist thought that offer models of Jewish nationality as distinct from, and even defined in opposition to, the nation-state model" (p. 23). Following an analysis of various aspects of the work of Simon Rawidowicz, Mordecai Kaplan, and Hans Kohn, he outlines the ways in which these men's neglected ideas can help the Jewish people cope with some of its current predicaments. Unfortunately, Pianko's advocacy has interfered to a considerable degree with his scholarship, and his overall project is essentially unrealistic.

What Pianko mainly wishes to highlight is the commitment of his three subjects to forms of Jewish nationalism that are neither Zion-centered nor unfriendly to Zionism. He succeeds in doing so with Rawidowicz and Kaplan, even if he fails to demonstrate that either of these men could be considered to have developed a well-founded ideology.

But in his eagerness to reclaim the one-time Zionist official Hans Kohn as a loyal member of the Zionist movement (despite the fact that Kohn abandoned the movement after the 1929 disturbances in Palestine), Pianko has presented a selective and highly dubious interpretation of Kohn's writings.

After acknowledging how much Kohn seems to deserve the reputation he acquired in the postwar United States "as the founder of a civic nationalism that stands in direct opposition to ethnic, or cultural varieties," Pianko struggles to identify a contrary tendency in Kohn's thought. He contends that Kohn's *American Nationalism* (1957), a virtual paean to the 19th- and 20th-century American melting pot, includes a chapter that contains "a subtle counternarrative that nuances an association of Kohn with a level of complete assimilation suggested by the melting-pot concept." One of his key pieces of evidence is Kohn's citation of the (Zionist) Sir Alfred Zimmern's account of how Americans, on the eve of the First World War, "awoke to the strange reality that in spite of all the visible and invisible agencies of 'assimilation,' their country was not one nation but a congeries of nations such as the world has never seen before within the limits of a self-governing state." The use of the word "congeries," Pianko tells us, would have brought to mind Zimmern's broader multicultural vision, at least to "anyone familiar with Zimmern's writings on nationalism" (p. 168). But so what? Could Kohn have expected to find more than a handful of such people in his mid-century American audience? And as Pianko himself admits, far from endorsing ideas anything like those of Zimmern, Kohn continues shortly afterwards with an explicit rejection of Horace Kallen's rather similar vision of America as a nation of nationalities.

Pianko's effort to keep Kohn in the Zionist camp is no more convincing than his attempt to identify him as a surreptitious critic of the idea of the melting pot. One of his main proofs for Kohn's enduring loyalty to cultural Zionism is an article published in *Commentary* in 1951, in which Kohn praised Ahad Ha'am as a man who "belongs in the age of nationalism to the small company of men of all tongues who in their unsparing search for truth and in the sobriety of their moral realism are the hope of the future." But these words come at the end of an essay in which Kohn depicts Ahad Ha'am as a man whose philosophy was defeated by history, whose worst fears of the Zionist movement's spiritual disintegration were realized after his death, and who "might have felt today even lonelier among the Zionists than he did during his lifetime" (p. 173). Kohn's *Commentary* essay was in essence an obituary for Ahad Ha'am's brand of Zionism.

Pianko's strained and unconvincing effort to rope Kohn back into the Zionist fold was not really necessary. Had he wished, he could have relied on Rawidowicz and Kaplan alone in his attempt to promote new theories of Jewish peoplehood that would be capable of replacing state-centered Zionism, serving "as an effective strategy for articulating the ties that bind the global Jewish community" (p. 201). I have my doubts, however, about whether the hunger for such theories is as great as Pianko thinks it is. It may be the case that the number of Jews interested in "rethinking the boundaries of groupness has grown dramatically," (p. 184), but their numbers are still quite small and they are most unrepresentative of the Jewish population at large, both in Israel and in the diaspora.

Pianko may be correct to say that diaspora Jews' reliance "on a symbolic homeland disempowers local initiatives to galvanize sustainable models of communal affiliation" and "drains creative energy and financial resources that could invigorate local, self-sustaining cultural centers" (p. 205). But this need, even if it is widely felt, can hardly supply the basis for a new national consciousness among the masses of already de-nationalized diaspora Jews. And if they do not already feel like members of one nation, it is hard to imagine why they would respond positively to the ideas of the nationalists Pianko wants to revive and bring back into circulation. Thus his call for a "program for global Jewish nationalism following the logic of Kaplan's and Rawidowicz's Zionism" (p. 207) seems rather quixotic to me. Pianko's well-meant proposals are a product of the academic world and are destined to remain there, and even in American colleges and universities they are likely to obtain very little purchase.

ALLAN M. ARKUSH
Binghamton University

Matthew Silver, *Our Exodus: Leon Uris and the Americanization of Israel's Founding Story*. Detroit: Wayne State University Press, 2010. 266 pp.

In the aftermath of the Second World War, the Zionist movement and the leadership of the Yishuv began preparing Holocaust survivors in Europe for immigration to Palestine. This illegal immigration, referred to as *ha'apalah,* was initiated in response to the policy adopted in the wake of the British White Paper of 1939, which led to a closing of Palestine's gateways. Between 1945 and 1948, a total of 64 ships sailed in the service of Mossad Le'aliyah Bet, an underground organization that facilitated the survivors' migration. Each of these ships had its own fascinating story with regard to the people on board and the various endeavors to break the British blockade and safely reach the shores of Palestine. Yet *Exodus* is undoubtedly the most famous of those vessels, considered by many to symbolize the entire enterprise.

In 1946, an old steamer ship, the *President Warfield*, was purchased in the United States. After it had been renovated and brought to Italy, the ship was loaded with 4,500 immigrants and set sail to Sete, in southern France, where it was renamed *Exodus*. Although French authorities prohibited *Exodus*' departure, the captain successfully slipped the ship out of the harbor. British destroyers followed. As *Exodus* approached its destination, the crew was warned by British soldiers not to attempt to touch shore; when the order was defied, the soldiers decided to take over the ship and forcefully prevent the passengers from disembarking. In the course of the ensuing battle on July 18, 1947, two of the passengers and one crew officer were killed, and many were wounded. In light of the damage caused to *Exodus*, British authorities allowed it to anchor at Haifa. There, the immigrants were transferred to three deportation ships that were instructed to send them back to Europe rather than to a detention camp at Cyprus, as had been done in previous cases. However, the immigrants refused to disembark at Port-de-Bouc (France), and they also started a hunger strike. In consequence, the British sent the ships to Germany, where the refugees were compelled to get off at Hamburg. From there they were taken to a displaced persons (DP) camp in the British occupation zone in northern Germany.

This historical incident was the basis of a novel written by Leon Uris, the son of an East European Jewish immigrant who arrived in the United States just after the First World War. Both in his personal life and in his works, Uris embodied the history of the American Jewish community and its integration into U.S. society. He joined the Marine Corps when he was 17 and fought in the Pacific Ocean theater during the Second World War; his first two books dealt with that war's battles. *Exodus*, published in 1958, was a tremendous success, remaining on the bestseller list for five months. More than 1,500,000 copies of the book were sold. It was translated into fifty languages, and it was adapted into a script for a movie of the same name that came out in 1960.

In *Our Exodus: Leon Uris and the Americanization of Israel's Founding Story*, Matthew Silver maintains that Uris' presentation of events in *Exodus* reflected postwar American Jewry's desire to shape the founding-of-the-Jewish-state-in-Palestine narrative. Silver indicates four spheres in which the book's influence is apparent. First, although Zionists (among them, many journalists and diplomats) had been promoting the cause of a Jewish state in Palestine for decades, it took the publication of *Exodus* to truly popularize the idea. Second, *Exodus* played an important role in restoring Jewish self-confidence: unlike other popular works of the post-Holocaust period, it offered an uplifting, positive message of Jewish renewal and potency rather than a tragic tale of ruin and devastation. Both the Jewish heroism depicted in *Exodus* and its scenes of cooperation between Americans and Jews in Palestine encouraged American Jews in the 1950s to overtly express their pride in the Jewish state. Finally, although the plot of *Exodus* takes place in Palestine and the book itself was the work of an American Jewish writer, its effect on modern, post-Holocaust Jewish identity extended well beyond Israel or the United States.

Although Uris' work took great liberties with the historical facts, *Exodus* enhanced the interest in the original ship and its passengers. The mythic aspects of the *Exodus* story began to emerge at the time the event was unfolding. The immigrants' endurance in the face of the British Empire's futile exercise in holding them back caused their struggle to be likened to David's triumph over Goliath. At about this time, a U.N. committee was deliberating on the future status of Palestine; several months later, on November 29, 1947, the U.N. approved a proposal to partition the area. This proximity of events became linked in Zionist consciousness and historiography.

On one level, the *Exodus* affair can be viewed as a set of political and operational decisions and their implementation. On the human level, it is a captivating and thoroughly moving story of a fearless act of bravery. Any clichés or superlatives added to the plot would detract from its power. Notwithstanding, writing first and foremost for an American audience, Uris set out to shape the Zionist ethos by means of a variety of non-canonical literary and cinematic models. Elements of a war novel, a western, a romance, and melodrama are all present in *Exodus*. As in many war novels, the military struggle is accorded a central place: *Exodus* expresses the notion that with courage, resourcefulness, and the conviction of fighting a just cause, one can overcome even a great and powerful enemy.

Taking liberties with Zionist history, Uris positioned his Haganah hero, Ari Ben-Canaan (a "simple farmer" who finds himself obligated to take up arms), at the head of the daring break into the Acre prison, even though this prison break was orchestrated by the rival Irgun movement. In a more significant shift from the historical account, he included children among the passengers of *Exodus* and added to the story a threat of collective mass suicide in the style of Masada. Moreover, Ari Ben-Canaan and other characters are portrayed in exaggerated fashion as representatives of the "New Jew" in the land of Israel—tough, courageous men who have shed the traits of their diaspora counterparts. The "New Jew" is tall, muscular, and strong, the descendant of the fearless ancient Hebrew in the land of Israel. This link between the biblical past and present was emphasized through the use of biblical quotes and references throughout the book and screenplay. Another myth offered by the novel concerns the relationship between Arabs and Jews. In Uris' version, Jewish settlement in Palestine is a blessing to the Arabs. Hence, the war between Jews and Arabs emanates from an inexplicable hatred, a continuation of the irrational hatred of Jews in the diaspora, with the Jews representing the sons of light and the Arabs the sons of darkness.

In *Exodus*, Uris managed to be staunchly admiring of the Zionist country-in-the-making while remaining a fervent American patriot. He avoided identifying with any specific faction within the Zionist movement; in his romantic descriptions of the kibbutzim, he refrained from any mention of socialism. Throughout the novel, Uris lionized American values and lifestyle. Further, wishing to please American Jews in particular, he not only stressed the importance of their assistance to the Zionist endeavor but also provided justification for their status as Jews who did not immigrate to Israel. In one scene, for instance, the American Jewish captain of an immigrants' ship to Palestine emphasizes his loyalty to America and his strong desire to remain an American citizen.

The story of *Exodus* has indisputable status as one of the foundational narratives of the Zionist ethos and the ultimate bravery that led to the establishment of the Jewish state. Silver's volume is not the first to deal with the illegal immigration in general and the *Exodus* affair in particular; in this regard, Aviva Halamish's landmark study from more than two decades ago should be mentioned.[1] Based on archival material and various secondary sources, *Our Exodus* provides an account of the affair from an American point of view, and in this manner adds to the body of historical research.

ARIEL FELDESTEIN
Ben-Gurion University

Note

1. Aviva Halamish, *Eksodus—hasipur haamiti: parashat oniyat hama'apilim "yetziat eiropah 1947"* (Tel Aviv: 1990).

Gadi Taub, *The Settlers and the Struggle over the Meaning of Zionism*. New Haven: Yale University Press, 2010. x + 217 pp.

During the 1970s and 1980s, there was a sense that the most crucial debate with regard to the fate of Israel and the future of Zionism was that between religious fundamentalist settlers and their left-wing opponents. Considering the issue today, it seems as though Israelis, especially the younger among them, no longer feel that way; from my experience in teaching about the settler movement in university classes, I can attest that today's students lack the intensity I felt toward the subject when I was their age. Gadi Taub, in his introduction to *The Settlers and the Struggle over the Meaning of Zionism*, offers testimony from the other side of the fence: that of a young woman who was shocked to learn that the political and legal status of her settlement was different from that of other places in Israel. In her worldview (at least until the traumatic disengagement from Gaza in 2005), the settlements were an integral part of the national territory.

In his thoughtful and well-written book, Taub attempts to restore the debate that dominated Israeli existential discourse for decades. With the hindsight of years of observation, Taub returns to the settlers and contends that the questions their movement has raised are far from being resolved. To the contrary, no other issue challenges the future of Zionism and the definition of Israel in such profound ways.

Taub does not occupy himself with a simple historical narrative of the West Bank settlement movement, claiming (with much justification) that the basic facts are well known. Instead, he concentrates on the crux of the matter, namely, just what the phenomenon of the ideological West Bank settlement is all about, and how it stands vis-à-vis modern Zionism. In his view, the ideological options of political Zionism are opposed to those of messianic religious Zionism. These two ideological currents are traveling on a clear collision path that may well become violent and that, in the worst-case scenario, could even escalate into civil war. Taub concentrates on several historical events that are especially important for his thesis, among them the Israeli supreme court decision of 1979 regarding Alon Moreh (the court, having determined that the settlement was located on private Palestinian land, ruled that it had to be moved), the assassination of Prime Minister Yitzhak Rabin in 1995, and the Gaza disengagement plan of 2005. To be sure, there are other dramatic occurrences in the turbulent history of the settlers that he does not mention, and even the events that are covered in this book have been interpreted by others in various and often opposing ways. Taub, however, is to be commended for zooming in on what he regards as the essence and for evading the background noises created by both the settlers and their opponents.

Political Zionism, according to Taub, remains viable and relevant, with more than a fighting chance of prevailing against the settlers' attempts to appropriate and restructure the future of Israel according to their worldview. In his view, the ideological settlers are a distinct group with a peculiar theology, and it is a grave mistake to claim that they in any way represent Zionism as a whole. In this fashion, Taub sets himself against critical scholars who assert that political Zionism has incorporated and secularized a messianic ethos (as expressed, among other things, in appropriating land through whatever available means) and that there is a harmonious continuity leading from the early pioneers to the West Bank settlers. Such ideas, Taub forcefully argues, are not all that different from those espoused by right-wing ideologues who claim that "greater Israel" is one integral unity. For his part, Taub makes a compelling and detailed argument that reinstates the differences between settler ideology and classic political Zionism. In so doing, he follows what political left-wing movements such as Peace Now and leaders of the Labor party have been claiming all along. In the last few decades, however, their voices have weakened considerably, while the settlers have attained political respectability.

Taub believes that the basic characteristic that makes the ideological West Bank settlers such a menacing presence in Israeli political history is their integration of politics and religion, a dangerous mix that disables any rational decision-making process and precludes any meaningful dialogue with the secular Zionists. Living in an enclave of believers, the settlers cultivate mistaken and condescending perceptions about the shallowness and blindness of modern Israelis. Given the settlers' limited numbers and resources, Taub has little doubt regarding who will emerge victorious from the historical clash between the two competing versions of Zionism; his book therefore returns to what was a debate in the past, but which has lost its passion in the present. According to him, the fact that secular Israelis and religious settlers are not always aware of the historical implications of the differences between them does not mean that the ideological (not to mention practical) challenge put forth by the settlers is over. Indeed, it is as important now as it was when it divided Israelis not so long ago.

MICHAEL FEIGE
Ben-Gurion University

Studies in Contemporary Jewry XXVIII

Edited by Anat Helman

Note on Editorial Policy

Studies in Contemporary Jewry is pleased to accept manuscripts on subjects generally within the contemporary Jewish sphere (from the turn of the 20th century to the present) for possible publication. Please address all inquiries to: **studiescj@savion.huji.ac.il.**

Essays that are submitted undergo a review process.